Em   o s

understanding the
employment relationship

PEARSON
Education

We work with leading authors to develop the strongest
educational materials in business, bringing cutting-edge
thinking and best learning practice to a global market.

Under a range of well-known imprints, including
Financial Times Prentice Hall, we craft high-quality print and
electronic publications which help readers to understand
and apply their content, whether studying or at work.

To find out more about the complete range of our
publishing, please visit us on the World Wide Web at:
www.pearsoned.co.uk

Employee Relations

understanding the employment relationship

Philip Lewis

Adrian Thornhill

Mark Saunders

FT Prentice Hall
FINANCIAL TIMES

An imprint of **Pearson Education**
Harlow, England · London · New York · Boston · San Francisco · Toronto · Sydney · Singapore · Hong Kong
Tokyo · Seoul · Taipei · New Delhi · Cape Town · Madrid · Mexico City · Amsterdam · Munich · Paris · Milan

Pearson Education Limited

Edinburgh Gate
Harlow
Essex CM20 2JE
England

and Associated Companies throughout the world

Visit us on the World Wide Web at:
www.pearsoneduc.com

First published 2003

© Pearson Education Limited 2003

ISBN 0 273 64625 7

British Library Cataloguing-in-Publication Data
A catalogue record for this book is available from the British Library

10 9 8 7 6 5 4 3 2
07 06 05 04

Typeset in 10/12.5 pt Sabon by 30
Printed by Ashford Colour Press Ltd, Gosport

Contents

Introduction

The origins of this book go back to the mid-1980s when two of us were teaching what was then called *industrial relations* to a variety of undergraduate and professional students. Most of those students approached the subject with trepidation. They thought that industrial relations was going to be the most 'difficult' of the subjects that were then grouped under the umbrella term *personnel management*. Since that time little has changed. Our students still have expectations about employee relations that cause them concern about its likely content. They think that it will be full of facts, of history, of law and, above all, trade unions, of which most of them have little or no knowledge. But we are delighted to say that evaluations at the end of modules have shown us consistently that these fears have not been realised. It would be nice to think that this was due to our magnetic personalities as teachers but this, sadly, is not the case. Employee relations is not simply facts, history or law, and it is certainly not just about trade unions. These are just some of the ingredients in the rich mix that goes to make up the subject. Far from being dry and factual, employee relations is about the everyday events that make up all of our working lives. It is fascinating and exciting, as many of our students' post-module evaluations tell us. Employee relations is a subject that lends itself to discussion, debate, argument and, sometimes, unshakeable prejudice. It is a subject in which one is forced to confront and question one's values.

It is often quite difficult to convey the fascination and excitement of employee relations in a textbook. But this is the challenge we have set ourselves in *Employee Relations: Understanding the Employment Relationship*. Our challenge has been to achieve the traditional academic rigour of industrial/employee relations that the subject deserves while adopting a contemporary approach that students will find chimes with their working lives. In short, we have tried hard to make the book accessible and enjoyable.

Employee Relations: Understanding the Employment Relationship is different from many of the employee relations textbooks currently available because it takes as its central theme the employment relationship between the employer and the employee. This concept is defined and discussed in Chapter 1. It is sufficient to say here that changes in employee relations over recent years mean that increasingly it is the individual relationship that each of us has with our employer (or, in some cases, employers) that is central in defining our working lives.

The book is divided into three parts that reflect key aspects of the employment relationship. The first part is concerned with understanding the employment relationship. This comprises two chapters. Chapter 1 sets the scene for the rest of the book by defining and explaining the multi-faceted nature of the employment relationship. Chapter 2 investigates how the employment relationship is changing as a result of changes in the wider environment.

The second part of the book is the most extensive of the three. In this part, we deal with regulation of the employment relationship. This starts with a chapter on some of the most important aspects of the employment relationship that relate to power and justice. Within Chapter 3, we also investigate the impact on the employment relationship of a concept that has grown in significance in recent years: culture. The next three chapters feature three key parties that have a role in regulating the employment relationship: managers (Chapter 4), trade unions (Chapter 5) and government (Chapter 6). The ways in which these parties regulate the employment relationship provide the focus of these three chapters. Chapters 7, 8, 9 and 10 change the emphasis and examine the processes and procedures that regulate the employment relationship. These are collective bargaining; employee involvement and employee participation; discipline and grievance; and reward. These chapters are concerned principally with the formal processes that regulate key aspects of the employment relationship. However, our intended emphasis in this text is to encourage readers to consider these aspects of the employment relationship by also thinking about them in relation to the content of other chapters in this book, notably Chapters 1–4.

The third part of the book concentrates on ending the employment relationship. In this part, Chapters 11 and 12 deal with dismissal and redundancy respectively. Chapter 11 on dismissal complements the earlier chapter on discipline. Chapter 12 on redundancy and organisational downsizing covers an important feature of any book on the employment relationship, given the importance of this topic in recent years.

■ Using the book

Each chapter in the book follows the same format. Chapters commence with a set of *learning outcomes*. Within each chapter, there are a number of *self-check questions*. These are designed to help readers check that they have understood sections of a chapter. Answers are provided to self-check questions towards the end of each chapter. Each chapter also contains a *summary* of its key points. *References* are included to the material used in each chapter, which may also be used to indicate further reading. At the end of each chapter a *case study* has also been included that relates the themes discussed in the chapter to an organisational context. These case studies are accompanied by a number of focus questions to allow readers to explore and discuss important issues. These case studies should therefore allow further reflection about the theoretical material introduced in the main body of the chapter with the intention of reinforcing learning. A *glossary* has also been included in the book that lists key terms used in its chapters.

We have designed this book to be of use to students on a range of programmes. Undergraduate and postgraduate programmes in business and management generally contain one or more modules related to employee relations, or to understanding the employment relationship. The coverage of this book is intended to offer students of such modules a useful and accessible reader around which to base their studies.

The book has also been designed to be of use on Chartered Institute of Personnel and Development (CIPD) programmes of study. In particular, the book is designed to provide a broad coverage of the CIPD's Professional Standards related to Employee Relations (CIPD, 2001). The following table indicates the relationship between the book's chapters and the indicative content of the CIPD Employee Relations module.

Content of CIPD Employee Relations	Related chapters*
Employee relations management in context	**2**, *3*, **5, 6, 7**, *11*
Parties in employee relations	**4, 5, 6**, *8*
Employee relations processes	*1, 2, 3*, **4, 5, 6, 7, 8, 9, 10**, *11, 12*
Employee relations outcomes	*1, 2, 3*, **4**, *5, 6*, **7**, *8, 9, 10, 11, 12*
Employee relations skills**	**7, 9**, *11*, **12**

* Principal chapters offering coverage are listed in bold; other chapters offering some related coverage are listed in italics.

**Employee relations skills also covers managing change. Many of the case studies in the book are related to the management of change and are therefore likely to be useful to explore the skills required to engage in this process.

Reference

Chartered Institute of Personnel and Development (2001) *CIPD Professional Standards*, London, CIPD.

■ Acknowledgements

We would like to thank those who helped to make the production of this book possible. We would particularly like to thank those who granted access and provided cooperation to allow us to generate the case studies that are featured in this book, and those who allowed us to reproduce extracts from the employee relations policies of their organisations.

The case studies in this book are based on events that relate to aspects of the employment relationship in real organisations. Some of these have been anonymised. However, others are based on organisations that we have been able to name. Some of these named case studies are based on published or publicly available information. However, in most cases they are based on data we collected from participants in these organisations. We would therefore like to thank the following people and organisations who provided access to data to generate these case studies and permission to use them.

- *Case 6*: Tony Stark, HR Practice Manager, Policy and Strategy at Vertex, for permission to use this case study and for his assistance and that of Janie Hazelwood (Head of Communications at Vertex) in its preparation.
- *Case 7*: Philip Parker, Industrial Relations Manager at Magnox Electric plc, for his assistance in the preparation of this case study and permission to use it.
- *Case 8*: Steve Colledge, Headteacher of The Grange Community School, and the South Gloucestershire Local Education Authority for permission to use this case study and for his assistance in its preparation.
- *Case 11*: Mandy Clarke, Director for Human Resources at Halcrow Group Ltd, for her assistance in the preparation of this case study and permission to use it.
- *Case 12*: Bob Green, BT Group Human Resources Policy Manager, for his assistance in the preparation of this case study and permission to use it.

We would also like to thank the following people and organisations for permission to reproduce organisational procedures or related extracts, or to cite from organisational documentation.

- Allan Blake, Director of Human Resources at Bristow Helicopters Ltd, and Amicus for permission to use the recognition and negotiation agreement between Bristow Helicopters and Amicus.
- Andrew Powles of Nationwide Building Society, for permission to use the Nationwide Building Society grievance and capabilities procedures.
- Russell Govan, Human Resources Director at RM plc, for permission to use the RM disciplinary procedure.
- The General President of the Graphical Paper and Media Union (GPMU) for permission to use its Rulebook, and Steve Sibbald of the GPMU for facilitating this permission.

We would also like to thank all of the staff at Pearson Education (both past and present) who supported us through the project of writing this book. Our thanks go in particular to Jacqueline Senior and Alison Kirk, our Commissioning Editors, and to Becky Taylor. We would also like to express our thanks to Mary Lince, as desk editor, and Lionel Browne, as copy editor.

Finally, our thanks go, once again, to Jenny, Jan, Jane, Andrew, Katie, Jemma and Ben for putting up with the long hours when we absented ourselves to think and write.

About the authors

Philip Lewis BA, PhD, MSc, MCIPD, PGDipM, Cert Ed, is a Principal Lecturer in Human Resource Management at the University of Gloucestershire Business School. He has taught employee relations, HRM and research methods to postgraduate, undergraduate and professional students and is involved in research degree supervision. Phil's research interests are principally related to reward management and performance management, on which he has published several articles. He is co-author with Adrian, Mark and Mike Millmore of *Managing Change: A Human Resource Strategy Approach*, published by Financial Times Prentice Hall, and with Mark and Adrian of *Research Methods for Business Students*, published as a third edition by Financial Times Prentice Hall. He has undertaken consultancy in both public and private sectors. Prior to his career in higher education, Phil was a training adviser with the Distributive Industry Training Board.

Adrian Thornhill BA, PhD, PGCE, FCIPD, is Head of the Department of Human Resource Management at the University of Gloucestershire Business School. He has taught employee relations, HRM and research methods to postgraduate, undergraduate and professional students and is involved in research degree supervision. Adrian has published a number of articles principally associated with employee and justice perspectives related to managing change and the management of organisational downsizing and redundancy. He is co-author with Phil, Mark and Mike Millmore of *Managing Change: A Human Resource Strategy Approach*, published by Financial Times Prentice Hall, and with Mark and Phil of *Research Methods for Business Students*, published as a third edition by Financial Times Prentice Hall. He has undertaken consultancy in both the public and private sectors.

Mark N.K. Saunders BA, MSc, PGCE, PhD, MCIPD is Reader in Research Methods at Oxford Brookes University Business School. Prior to this, he was head of the Human Resource Management Research Centre at Gloucestershire Business School. He has taught HRM and employee relations to a range of students and is involved in research degree supervision and the teaching of research methods. Mark has published a range of articles including those related to downsizing and organisational justice perspectives on the management of change. He is co-author with Adrian, Phil and Mike Millmore of *Managing Change: A Human Resource Strategy Approach*, published by Financial Times Prentice Hall, and with Phil and Adrian of *Research Methods for Business Students*, published as a third edition by Financial Times Prentice Hall. He has undertaken consultancy in the public, private and not-for-profit sectors, prior to which he had a variety of research jobs in local government.

■ Publisher's acknowledgements

We are grateful to the following for permission to reproduce copyright material:

Table 1.1 reprinted from *European Management Journal*, Vol. 13, No. 3, Hiltrop, J.M., The Changing Psychological Contract, page 290, September 1995, with permission from Elsevier Science; Table 1.2 developed from *Developments in the Management of Human Resources*, Blackwell Publishing, (Storey, 1992); Figure 2.6 developed from *Flexibility, uncertainty and manpower management*, Institute of Manpower Studies Report No. 89, Brighton, Institute of Manpower Studies, (Atkinson, 1984); Figures 3.1 and 12.2 from *Managing Change: A human resource strategy approach*, (Thornhill *et al*, 2000) with permission from Pearson Education Limited; Tables 4.2, 4.3, 7.1 and 7.2 from *Britain at Work*, Routledge, (Cully *et al*, 1999); Box 5.1 adapted from <http://www.certoffice.org> and Table 5.1 adapted from Certification Officer's Annual Reports, Certification Office for Trade Unions and Employers' Associations; Box 5.3 adapted from <http://www.tuc.org.uk/>, Box 5.4 adapted from <http://www.tuc.org.uk/the_tuc/tuc-5927-f0.cfm>, Table 5.5 adapted from *Focus on recognition*, (TUC, 2002a) and Box 5.5 adapted from <http://www.tuc.org.uk/pi/partnership.htm> and related material (TUC, 2002b), with permission from the TUC; Box 7.2 reproduced with the permission of Bristow Helicopters Ltd and Amicus; Tables 7.3 and 10.3 from 'Labour disputes in 2000',

Labour Market Trends, June, 302, HMSO (Davies, 2001), Tables 10.1 and 10.2 from 'Patterns of pay: results of the 2001 New Earnings Survey', *Labour Market Trends*, March, 129–39, HMSO (Jenkins, 2002), Box 7.5 adapted from <http://www. acas.org.uk> and Chapter 9 extracts from *Code of Practice; disciplinary and grievance procedures*, (ACAS, 2000a). Crown copyright material is reproduced with the permission of the Controller of HMSO and the Queen's Printer for Scotland.

In some instances we have been unable to trace the owners of copyright material, and we would appreciate any information that would enable us to do so.

■ Supplements

Accompanying supplementary material is available for lecturers to download at www.booksites.net/lewis_er

Part One

Understanding the employment relationship

Chapter 1

What is the employment relationship?

At the end of this chapter you should be able to:

- define the employment relationship;

- explain the concept of the employment relationship as the theoretical framework for this book;

- describe the contract of employment and its significance for the conduct of the employment relationship;

- define the psychological contract and identify its relationship to the employment relationship;

- explain the importance of adopting different perspectives on employee relations and their impact upon the conduct of the employment relationship.

1.1 Introduction

A skim through the titles of books covering this subject area over the past 20 years will give an idea of how the emphasis has changed. In the 1970s and 1980s impor tant authors such as Clegg (1979) and Bain (1983) used the term 'industrial relations' in their book titles. More recently the terms 'employee relations' (e.g. Gennard and Judge, 2002) and 'employment relations' (e.g. Rose, 2001) have been used. Undoubtedly there is an element of fashion at work here. However, 'industrial relations' is associated with the declining 'smokestack' industries and blue-collar workers and the accompanying emphasis upon collective bargaining between employers and trade unions. 'Employee relations' suggests that a wider employment canvas is being covered with equal importance being attached to non-union employ-ment arrangements and white-collar jobs. Nonetheless, the emphasis still tends to be on the structure of 'perspectives, participants, processes and practices' adopted by writers such as Salamon (2000).

We have used the term *employment relationship* in the title of this book. This is deliberate. As the preface indicates, this is because we wanted to examine the nature of the interaction between employers and employees in the employment relationship to a greater extent than has traditionally been the case in employee relations text-books. Thus particular attention is given to the expectations of the parties to the employment relationship (Chapter 1), the concepts of power and justice in the relationship (Chapter 3), the behaviour of managers and their employees (Chapters 4 and 9), the rewards that accrue to the relationship (Chapter 10), and the ways in which the employment relationship is brought to an end (Chapters 11 and 12).

■ Defining the employment relationship

Gospel and Palmer (1993: 3) define the employment relationship as 'an economic, social and political relationship in which employees provide manual and mental labour in exchange for rewards allotted by employers'. To this we would add that there is a psychological element to the employment relationship, as will become clear later in this chapter. Gospel and Palmer go on to note that there are certain characteristics of the employment relationship that mark it out as different from, say, the relationship that may exist between the customer and the supplier. The list of characteristics below makes clear that the circumstances of the employment relationship may vary considerably. Some of the variations are:

- the type of organisation in which the employment relationship is set;
- the wide range of purposes of the employment relationship and, consequently, the nature of the tasks performed by employees in the employment relationship;
- the location in which the tasks are performed;
- the amount of hours devoted to the employment relationship and the length of the relationship;
- the rewards that flow from the employment relationship;
- the way in which the main terms and conditions of the employment relationship are determined;
- the degree to which employees and employers possess and deploy power in the employment relationship;
- the effect that the degree of success of the employment relationship has on the employing organisation and the wider economy.

The employment relationship may, for example, be set in a public sector, not-for-profit or private sector organisation. Even this is not as simple a division as it once was, as much 'public sector work' is now done by private sector organisations in so-called public–private partnerships. An example of this is Capita, a company that collects TV licence fees, sends out council tax reminders, generates pension statements and runs the Criminal Records Bureau (*The Times*, 2002a). Within each sector the type of organisation varies considerably: so, for example, the employment relationship in cutting edge hi-tech companies may be very different from those in charities. In the hi-tech sector one would expect to find employees with a high commitment to technology and to their own training and career development; in charities employee commitment is likely to be to the mission of the particular organisation.

The range of jobs expressed in the employment relationship encompasses, for example, airline pilots to cleaning operators. Clearly the tasks performed by these different types of employee are so different that the main issues in the employment relationship, for example training and qualification periods, mean the relationships vary enormously. Another difference in this example is the location in which the tasks are performed. Like airline pilots, many professional employees are now working away from their main workplace. The 1998 Workplace Employee Relations Survey (Cully et al., 1999) notes that more than one-third of managers and one-fifth of professional employees were able to work from home. However, the same opportunity was given to only 3 per cent of employees in personal and protective services and only 1 per cent of workers in operative and assembly work. This raises issues of seeming loss of direct management control and the necessity for managers to exercise greater flexibility in managing the employment relationship.

The amount of hours devoted to the employment relationship and the length of relationships vary considerably. As Chapter 2 notes, the number of UK employees who now work less than full-time (nominally 35 hours) has increased in recent years – so much so that in 1999 some 36 per cent of UK employees worked 34 hours or less per week (European Commission Directorate-General for Economic and Financial Affairs, 2000b). The proportion of part-time jobs in UK manufacturing doubled between 1994 and 1999 (European Commission Directorate-General for Economic and Financial Affairs, 2000a). The 1998 Workplace Employee Relations Survey shows that part-time workers now account for a quarter of all jobs in workplaces of 25 or more employees. In addition, part-timers formed the majority of the workforce in 26 per cent of workplaces surveyed (Cully et al., 1999). These part-time workers are predominantly female. At the same time one-third of UK employees work more than 41 hours (European Commission Directorate-General for Economic and Financial Affairs, 2000b). Both extremes of part-time and 'more than full-time' working highlight differences in the employment relationship, not the least of which is the centrality of paid employment to the lives of workers. This raises the question about the length of the relationship. The growth in part-time working has been accompanied by a rise in the number of 'non-standard' employees with a looser attachment to the employing organisation than the traditional permanent employee. The 1998 Workplace Employee Relations Survey (Cully et al., 1999) reports that 44 per cent of all workplaces surveyed used fixed-term contract workers (72 per cent of all public sector workplaces) and 13 per cent of all workplaces used freelance workers.

The rewards that flow from the employment relationship, as detailed in Chapter 10, are both financial and non-financial. It is obvious that employment relationships vary by the amount of financial reward. However, it is equally important to consider the non-financial rewards (Armstrong and Murlis, 1998), which vary according to not only the nature of the employment relationship but also the personal characteristics of the employee. These may include feeling part of a community, a sense of personal achievement, social recognition and social and societal responsibility. In general, the 1998 Workplace Employee Relations Survey (Cully et al., 1999) reflects a positive attitude to their employment relationships among employees in workplaces with 25 or more employees. The majority of them seem to have been satisfied with their jobs and their treatment by managers. Across all employees surveyed well over one-half reported a high commitment to their workplace, 89 per cent of whom noted that they enjoyed their work.

Another variation in the employment relationship that is important to the content of this book is the way in which the main terms and conditions of the employment relationship are determined. The two main variants are individual 'negotiation' between the employer and the employee – albeit that in reality little negotiation may actually occur, terms and conditions being decided by the employer – and a rather more 'arm's length' arrangement where collective bargaining arrangements between the employees' representatives and the employer or the employer's representatives determine the main terms and conditions.

It is clear from this brief account of some of the differences in the employment relationship that there are great variations in the extent to which employees and employers possess and deploy power in the relationship. This will be affected particularly by the nature of the tasks performed and by the amount of hours devoted to the employment relationship together with its tenure. In turn this may be a reflection of the labour market power possessed by the employee. It is fanciful to assume that the cleaners and porters in hospitals have equal power with consultants. Not only are there obvious differences in the prestige that society attaches to these occupations, but also cleaners and porters are normally easier to replace when they leave. As Chapter 3 details, power is a fundamental ingredient of the employment relationship and has a marked effect on the way it is conducted and its outcomes.

Finally, it is apparent that a successful, or indeed unsuccessful, employment relationship will differ in the impact that this level of success has on the employment relationship both in the employing organisation and in the wider economy. This last point is frequently demonstrated in industrial disputes that affect the 'essential services'. These serve as an indication of a breakdown of the employment relationship. As we write (Autumn 2002), there is a pay dispute in the fire-fighting sector that may have significant effects upon the safety of the public. Its high public profile is evidence of its potential impact on the wider economy.

Two further points need to be made before we summarise this section by framing our own definition of the employment relationship. The first is that the employment relationship does not exist in a vacuum. It is a reflection of what goes on in the wider society. As Blyton and Turnbull (1998: 32) succinctly put it: 'to understand what goes on inside the workplace it is also necessary to look at what goes on outside it'. One simple illustration of this, noted in Chapter 9, is the growth in the amount of disciplinary offences at the workplace as a result of the increasing use of email and the Internet. Secondly, it is important to return to the reason why we make the employment relationship the central concept in this book rather than structure it around the more traditional 'participants, processes and practices'. This is because participants such as trade unions and governmental organisations, such as the Advisory, Conciliation and Arbitration Service (ACAS), and processes such as collective bargaining and employee participation together with procedures for discipline and grievance and equal opportunities evolve from the employment relationship, albeit that their existence and the part they play in the employment relationship influence its character.

From the preceding analysis we offer a definition that is similar to that of Gospel and Palmer (1993: 3), albeit modified in the light of that analysis:

> The employment relationship is an economic, legal, social, psychological and political relationship in which employees devote their time and expertise to the interests of their employer in return for a range of personal financial and non-financial rewards.

You will notice that the word 'legal' has been included in our definition. Clearly the employment relationship has a legal dimension as it is based on the individual contract of employment. We explain some of the key concepts in the employment contract in Section 1.2. The psychological dimension is covered in Section 1.3. In Section 1.4 we examine the differing perspectives from which the employment relationship may be viewed.

self-check question

1.1 Why do you think that there is now so much attention paid to the concept of the employment relationship in the study of the topic we refer to more generally as employee relations?

1.2 The contract of employment

It is not the intention of this section to give a detailed and definitive explanation of the contract of employment. There are many legal texts that do this. Our aim here is to give an overview of the main concepts of the employment contract in order that you may appreciate the importance of the legal dimension in the conduct of the employment relationship.

■ What is the contract of employment? *It is already more than ...*

A contract of employment is formed when an offer of employment is made and is accepted. An immediate distinction needs to be made between those workers who work under a contract of employment (a contract *of* service) and those who work under a contract *for* services. The former group are defined as 'employees' and the latter group are normally thought of as being self-employed. The distinction is difficult to define. In actual cases where the distinction is unclear it is left to a legal case hearing to make the decision. Among the questions that the legal hearing may address are:

- Did the person alleged to be the employer control the alleged employee in respect of the work done and the performance of the work?
- Is the work done by the alleged employee an integral part of the employer's business?
- Is the alleged employee in business on his or her own account?
- Does the alleged employee provide his or her own tools and equipment?
- Who is responsible for the alleged employee's tax and national insurance?
- To what degree is there 'mutuality of obligation'? (That is, the alleged employer is under no obligation to supply work and the alleged employee is free to refuse it.)

This raises the question of why the distinction between those workers who work under a contract of service (contract of employment) and those who work under a contract for services is so important. The answer is that employees who work under a contract of employment are legally entitled to a series of employment rights: rights that those who work under a contract for services do not enjoy. Among these employment rights are:

- the provision of a statement of terms and conditions of employment;
- the provision of an itemised pay statement;

- statutory sick pay;
- time off for public duties;
- maternity leave and pay;
- parental leave;
- minimum notice periods;
- trade union rights;
- protection against unfair dismissal;
- redundancy payments.

What form does the contract of employment take?

Although it is necessary, under the Employment Rights Act 1996, for an employer to provide a written statement of terms and conditions of employment, this is not the same as assuming that the contract of employment needs to be in writing. So the written statement does not, in itself, form the contract of employment. It is merely an indication that the contract exists and of its main content.

The content of the written statement is likely to include:

- names of employer and employee;
- date employment commenced;
- job title;
- pay details;
- hours of work;
- holiday arrangements;
- sickness arrangements;
- pension arrangements;
- length of notice;
- disciplinary rules;
- arrangements for dealing with grievances;
- arrangements for trade union membership (where appropriate).

However, the list above does not cover all the terms and conditions of the contract. An example illustrates this important point. It may be, for example, normal practice that restaurant employees clean and tidy the kitchen and dining areas before the restaurant closes. This is unlikely to be written down. It is part of the normal daily routine and as such forms a significant part of the contract of employment. It becomes an important issue only when there is a dispute over the way it operates. This may be when the employer decides to 'tighten up' and insists that the work is done after the restaurant closes, and the workers object that this is unfair. The dispute then, at law, becomes a contractual one. This raises another important point about the contract of employment. This is that the terms and conditions should not be altered without mutual agreement. Unless the contract contains a clause entitling the employer to make contractual changes, for example to the hours of work or the location of work, then doing so without the agreement of the employee may leave the employer open to a legal claim from the employee. An example of this occurred recently when a government agency was held to be in breach of contract for unilaterally altering the subsistence allowances of its employees (*Security and Facilities Division* v. *Hayes and others*, 2001).

Sources of contract terms

A greater understanding of the content of the contract of employment may be gained from a consideration of the origins of the terms and conditions. These may be considered under seven headings:

- minimum statutory standards;
- express statements of the parties to the contract;
- collective agreements;
- organisational rules;
- custom and practice;
- common law duties of employers;
- common law duties of employees.

Minimum statutory standards

The content of the written statement of terms and conditions listed above is an indication of some of the minimum statutory standards that are, in effect, part of the contract of employment. It is a general principle of employment law that those statutory rights and duties that apply to the employment relationship may be said to form part of every contract of employment. It is not possible for the parties to the contract of employment to 'contract out' of the statutory provisions. As the term 'minimum' suggests, the contract of employment may contain terms and conditions that are more generous than the statutory minimum. A good example of this is redundancy provision, where the redundant employee often enjoys much better terms than provided for as a statutory minimum (for more detail see Chapter 12). There are other notable statutory provisions in addition to the terms and conditions from the written statement listed above. An important example is that the employee has the right not to be discriminated against because of his or her gender, marital status, ethnic origin or disability.

Express statements of the parties to the contract

These may be contained in the written statement of terms and conditions or have been expressed either orally or in writing. An employer may agree, for example, by a confirmatory memo that the employee may have two weekdays off for every Saturday worked at the employer's request, or such an offer may be made without written confirmation. In either case the contract term becomes part of the contract of employment, which may not be subsequently altered without mutual agreement. Note, however, that in the event of the employer altering a term of the contract unilaterally – that is, without the prior agreement of the employee – then if the employee works under the new contract term without expressing disagreement the employee may be said to have accepted this new contract term.

Collective agreements

As will be noted elsewhere in this book (in particular in Chapter 7), approximately one-half of UK employees have their main terms and conditions of employment determined by the collective bargaining process. A collective agreement is the outcome of the collective bargaining process, and may be defined as an agreement between a trade union(s) and an employer(s) that determines, among other things, the terms and conditions of employment of the employees of the employer who is party to the agreement. Most contracts of employment of employees who enjoy terms and conditions that have been collectively determined will have a written clause in the contracts to the effect that the terms of the collective agreement are incorporated into their contracts. That is not to say that all terms and conditions are covered in this way, but such major issues as pay, hours and holidays will be. This topic is dealt with in more detail in Chapter 7.

Organisational rules

These are often contained in an employing organisation's personnel handbook or equivalent publication and given to employees upon commencement of their employment. A glance through a large organisation's personnel handbook, for example, includes rules on when holidays may be taken, sickness absence reporting, confidentiality, use of the organisation's computer equipment, and dress regulations. It may be that such rules form part of a separate policy, say, on the use of email and the Internet. This does not alter the fact that such rules would normally form part of the contract of employment, particularly if their existence has been made clear and the employee has acknowledged his or her awareness of their existence. Publication of organisation rules may not be only through the form of the personnel handbook. Posting the rules on a notice board or company intranet, or lodging them in the personnel department, may achieve the same contractual effect. What is important here is that the employee's attention is drawn to the existence of the rules and the contractual implications of their being observed.

Custom and practice

We noted earlier the example of restaurant employees cleaning and tidying the kitchen and dining areas before the restaurant closes. This is an example of custom and practice, and is the type of activity referred to by Lord Goddard in a famous case (*Marshall* v. *English Electric Co. Ltd*) in 1945:

> ... an established practice at a particular factory may be incorporated into a workman's contract of service and, whether he knew it or not, it must be presumed that he accepted employment as applied to other workers in that factory.

Such custom and practice arrangements relate to a particular workplace or a particular trade or profession. So the introduction of stringent 'clocking-in and clocking-out' arrangements for university lecturers may be seen to be in contravention of the customary terms of employment!

Implied duties of employees

Custom and practice introduces the principle that not all terms of the contract of employment need to be expressly stated. This principle is reflected in a set of implied, or common law, duties of both employees and employers that are part of the contract. These duties are derived from the principles developed by the courts over the last 100 years. The cases that have created these duties are ones where the points of law have been complex to interpret. In the event, the judgments made in these cases have led to decisions that clarify the law and act as precedents for later, and more junior, courts to follow. This is what is referred to as case, or common, law, and it has the same legal effect as statutory laws passed by Parliament. Like statute law, the common law duties are of great importance to the employment relationship. They have legal significance in that their breach by either the employee or the employer may lead to either party taking legal action. They also have practical importance because they inform many significant guidelines for the everyday conduct of the employment relationship. The main implied duties of employees are to:

- be ready and willing for work;
- take reasonable care and skill in performing the job;
- obey the employer's lawful orders;
- take care of the employer's property;
- act in good faith.

The duty of the employee to be ready and willing for work means that in the event of absence without reasonable justification the employee is breaching the contract of employment and may be dismissed. The duty to take reasonable care and skill in performing the job refers principally to negligence by the employee. The duty to obey the employer's lawful orders does not extend as far as orders that are either illegal (for example, an order for the employee to drive a company vehicle while that employee is disqualified) or outside the scope of the contract of employment: that is, performing duties that are outside the contract. The duty to take care of the employer's property is self-explanatory and therefore much more straightforward than the last: the duty of the employee to act in good faith. This can extend to the duty to be honest and not to act to the detriment of the employer. Breaching this obligation may involve disclosing confidential information, say, to a competitor organisation or to the news media. This final point raises the issue of what has become known as 'whistle-blowing'. In the event of the employee making public information regarding the employer's activities that he or she feels is in the public interest, protection may be offered by the Public Interest Disclosure Act 1998, which protects 'whistle-blowers' from dismissal or victimisation. This statutory legislation was passed 30 years after the case where the disclosure of a potentially unlawful price-fixing agreement to a national newspaper was not held by the Court of Appeal to be a breach of the employment contract (*Initial Services* v. *Putterill*, 1968).

Of course, breaches of the contract of employment by the employee due to failure to meet the duties implied by common law will not invariably give rise to dismissal, and any legal test of the legal validity of the employer's action will be by employment tribunals under unfair dismissal legislation. We go into greater detail on this in Chapter 11.

Implied duties of employers

Many of the duties that employers have to employees are minimum statutory standards that we have outlined above. However, there are also some that derive from common law. Among these are the duties to:

- treat employees with trust and confidence;
- indemnify employees;
- provide references.

In the case of *Woods* v. *WM Car Services (Peterborough) Ltd* (1981) Lord Denning aptly summed up the duty of the employer to treat employees with trust and confidence:

> ...It is the duty of the employer to be good and considerate to his servants. Sometimes it is formulated as an implied term not to do anything likely to destroy the relationship of confidence between them...

Chapter 4 notes the behaviour of some 'bad bosses' who indulge in workplace bullying. The example of the boss who made staff wait half an hour with their hands up before being given permission to go to the toilet (BBC Online, 1997) is hardly an example of good and considerate behaviour.

The duty to indemnify employees means that, in general, employers are liable for any wrongs committed by the employee in the pursuit of that employee's duties although, of course, this does not cover criminal wrongdoings. Finally, there is no duty, as such, to provide references, but when this is done they should be correct to the best of the employer's knowledge.

Breaches of the contract of employment by the employer now will often lead to the employee resigning and claiming constructive dismissal. In such cases the legal validity of the case will be judged by an employment tribunal under unfair dismissal legislation. We also go into greater detail on this in Chapter 11.

self-check question	**1.2** Why do you think that a knowledge of both statutory and common law provision is so important in understanding the concept of the contract of employment?

Whereas the contract of employment represents the traditional way of defining the employment relationship, in recent years there has been increasing interest in the non-legal aspects of the relationship. This is particularly because the very foundations of the relationship, in many cases built upon years of mutual understanding, have been threatened. This has given rise to the employment relationship being analysed in terms of the psychological contract that exists between employer and employee.

1.3   The psychological contract

The *psychological contract* was a term first used by Argyris (1960). It refers to the expectations of employer and employee that operate in addition to the formal contract of employment. It has been defined by Rousseau (1994, cited by Hiltrop, 1995: 287) as 'the understanding people have regarding the commitments made between themselves and their organisation'. It is therefore concerned with each party's perceptions of what the other party to the employment relationship owes them over and above that which may be specified in the contract of employment. As this contract is based upon perceptions it is clear that the 'content' of this contract is not written and often not explicitly stated. Mullins (1996) points out that there is a continual process of balancing and explicit and implicit bargaining over the contract's content and, moreover, that the individual and the organisation may not be aware consciously of the contract 'terms'. However, these 'terms' still affect relationships between them and have an effect upon behaviour.

The aspect of psychological contract that has been the major focus of attention in recent years is the traditional employee perception that the organisation promises a 'job for life' in return for employee loyalty and commitment. Such reciprocal expectations characterised (and to some extent still characterise) the employment relationship in many areas of employment. Typical examples of this are local government, the civil service and banking. In banking the contract has changed dramatically in the past 15 years. The traditional image of the bank manager as the 'community ambassador' has changed (Cressey and Scott, 1993; Lewis, 1999). The role has become that of a business manager or, as one branch manager in a research interview conducted by one of us (Lewis, 1997) less flatteringly portrayed it, a 'salesman'. With this, the job for life had disappeared. In addition, lending decisions by the bank manager about retail business have been de-skilled in that computers make the decision for the manager by using 'credit-scoring' software. All this points to the need for managers different from the 'pillar of the community' stereotype. Managers now needed to be less experienced, more commercially aware, more energetic; and they could be obtained, and retained, more cheaply than their predecessors.

Research reviewed by Sparrow (2000) highlights the changing nature of the organisation of work and its implications for the psychological contract. Experiences of redundancy, for example, are often viewed by older workers as a violation of the psychological contract, and are significantly related to their adoption of personal responsibility for their career development (Sparrow, 2000). In addition, research suggests that more traditional contracts implicitly depending upon trust, loyalty and a degree of job security are being replaced by contracts where, for example, employees provide commitment to a project in exchange for high pay and training. Such changes to the psychological contract have been summarised as a move from one that is *relational* – based on mutual trust and commitment – to one that is *transactional* – based upon mutual instrumentality of the work-effort–reward bargain (Herriot and Pemberton, 1995). The resultant employment relationship is more fragile and individual, as evidenced by the frequency with which employees are having to apply for their own jobs. It has also heightened employees' need to gain recognisable skills and qualifications to demonstrate their employability within the wider labour market. In short, a new type of psychological contract is emerging that assumes that each party is less dependent upon the other for survival and growth (Hiltrop, 1995). This is defined by Hiltrop (1995: 289) as one where

> There is no job security. The employee will be employed as long as he or she adds value to the organisation and is personally responsible for finding new ways to add value. In return the employee has the right to demand interesting and important work, has the freedom and resources to perform it well, receives extra pay that reflects his or her contribution, and gets the experience and training needed to be employable here or elsewhere.

Table 1.1 summarises the characteristics of the 'old' and 'new' psychological contracts.

Table 1.1 **Characteristics of the 'old' and 'new' psychological contracts**

Characteristic	Old	New
Focus of the employment relationship	Security and a long-term career in the company	Employability to cope with changes in this and future employment
Format	Structured and predictable	Flexible and unpredictable
Duration	Permanent	Variable
Underlying principle	Influenced by tradition	Driven by market forces
Intended output	Loyalty and commitment	Value added
Employer's key responsibility	Fair pay for a fair day's work	High pay for high job performance
Employee's key responsibility	Good performance in present job	Making a difference to the organisation
Employer's key input	Stable income and career	Opportunities for self-development
Employee's key input	Time and effort	Knowledge and skills

Source: Adapted from Hiltrop (1995:290)

self-check question

1.3 To what extent is the 'new' psychological contract a myth dreamed up by HR commentators to add a new dimension to discussion about HRM?

The psychological contract is based on exchange theory (Cox and Parkinson, 1999), where individuals make an investment in expectation that an appropriate reward will be forthcoming. This is succinctly summed up by one middle manager from British Telecom, who told Newell and Dopson (1996: 17) in their research 'I am quite happy to give myself to an organisation if I get something back in return'. More romantically it is based on the ancient Chinese concept of *mei mei* (buy/sell) on which, it is argued, all human relationships are based (Yen Mah, 2001):

> If the transaction is perceived by either party as lopsided or unfair, if one side has to 'eat losses' too many times, the buy/sell will fail and the relationship will eventually end. (Yen Mah, 2001: 137)

What are the implications for the conduct of the employment relationship when the psychological contract is broken? Like the contract of employment its major significance becomes apparent when it is breached. This occurs when one party perceives the other to have failed to fulfil the 'duties' or promises owed. Unlike the contract of employment there is no necessity for management to consult with the employee over the terms of the 'new' psychological contract, with the result that changes that the employee sees as a breach of that contract are unilaterally imposed by management. It is tempting to think that this situation may be easily rectified by either party walking away from the contract by employee resignation or, less likely, dismissal. But the reality in most situations is that partial breakdown of the relationship happens. Rather than one major breach promoting radical action there are a series of breaches that have a cumulative effect, ending in a litany of potential dysfunctional effects. These may see the employee deciding to 'get even' (Brooks, 1999) owing to feelings of betrayal and anger, and will lead to low levels of job satisfaction and poor job performance

(Newell, 2000). Indeed, Schein (1978) suggests that breaching the psychological contract is one of the main root causes of employee relations disputes, albeit that the causes more often cited tend to be the more predictable areas of pay and hours.

Guest and Conway (1999), in their research on the employment relationship for the Institute of Personnel and Development (now the Chartered Institute of Personnel and Development), surveyed over 1000 employees and drew an interesting conclusion that suggested the power of the psychological contract. They contrasted the existence of HRM policies (such as training opportunities, employee involvement, or internal recruitment) with trade union membership in order to establish which contributed to greater employee satisfaction. In the event they found that, even in their so-called 'black hole' organisations (typically small private-sector employers in textiles, hotels and catering, repair and maintenance, who are not noted for their 'good' treatment of employees), the most significant determinant of positive attitudes among employees was neither HRM policies nor trade union membership but the psychological contract between the employer and the individual. The 'terms' of the contract included 'fairness of treatment, delivery of promises on issues such as pay, promotion and workload and trust that these will be delivered in the future' (Guest and Conway, 1999: 382).

Guest and Conway (2002) also conducted research among over 1300 senior HR managers on the way in which they felt their organisations managed the psychological contract for their employees. Their major conclusion was that communication has a significant role to play in managing the psychological contract. Communication related to initial entry to the organisation (job descriptions, initial training, the recruitment process and staff handbook) and the practice of the job (objective setting, team targets, performance appraisal, informal day-to-day interaction, briefing by line management, training and development). Communication had a positive association with a number of factors. These were:

- the explicitness of the psychological contract;
- lower-level breaches of the contract;
- a fairer exchange;
- management perceptions of the impact of the psychological contract on such employee-related outcomes as employee performance, employee commitment, employee trust in the organisation, employee motivation, employee well-being and employment relations.

Top-down communication had a less positive effect. In addition, the report also notes that senior managers often were felt by the HR management respondents not to keep their promises, particularly in relation to fairness of rates of pay, attractiveness of benefits, fair treatment, job security and a pleasant and safe working environment.

Research on the psychological contract conducted by Coyle-Shapiro and Kessler (2000) in two large local authorities combined the views of managers and employees. Their findings were less positive than those of Guest and Conway (1999, 2002). They found that the majority of employees had experienced contract breaches, a view supported by the respondent managers who, in general, felt that the organisations had not fulfilled their obligations to their employees to they extent they could have done. The most interesting conclusion drawn by Coyle-Shapiro and Kessler (2000) is that employees who felt their psychological contracts were being breached were 'getting even' by reducing their commitment and their willingness to engage in 'organisational citizenship behaviour'. Organ (1988) defines organisational citizenship behaviour as 'readiness to contribute beyond literal contractual obligations'. As Organ (1988) notes, this is clearly discretionary behaviour that depends on the organisation's treatment of the individual.

Finally the overall conclusion of Guest and Conway (2002) is that the psychological contract is a very useful tool to help us understand and manage the employment relationship.

1.4 Differing perspectives on the employment relationship

We spent some time at the start of this chapter defining the employment relationship. It is implicit in that definition that a number of different parties are involved in the operation of that relationship, employees, employers, trade unions, employer's associations and state agencies being the principal parties. Each of these parties brings to the employment relationship a different perspective. The definition we have developed is one that may be thought of as that of the detached analyst. Whether this is so will be judged better by you, the reader, than by us. The point here is that none of us approaches social phenomena in an entirely detached way. We all have sets of beliefs and values that affect our judgements. This is particularly so when dealing with social phenomena that are contentious and likely to rouse strong opinions. Employee relations is just such a topic. Asking a handful of people each to define employee relations or, indeed, the employment relationship is likely to yield quite different definitions, and the differences are liable to reflect the different ways in which those definers view the world. Viewing the world in different ways may be thought of as similar to different-coloured lenses in spectacles: each tint will produce a slightly different view of the same visual image. So it is unrealistic to think that the employee scraping along on the National Minimum Wage (note the value-laden words 'scraping along') will have the same view of the employment relationship as the owner-manager desperately trying to maintain costs in a highly competitive product market. In such a case, the employee may define the employment relationship in terms of exploitation, whereas the owner-manager is likely to view it as a 'necessary evil'.

Two contrasting perspectives have dominated employee relations writing in the 40 years since they were conceptualised by Fox (1966): *unitarism* and *pluralism*. We now examine these, and other different perspectives on the employment relationship.

■ Unitarism

Fox (1966: 2) defined unitarism as a way of thinking about the organisation 'as a team unified by a common purpose', that common purpose being the success of the organisation. Among the principal characteristics of unitarism are the following:

■ the employees of the organisation are seen as a team, unified by a common purpose with all employees pursuing the same goal;

■ there is a single source of authority, that source being management;

- as all employees are pursuing the same goal, conflict is irrational: it must be the result of poor communication or 'troublemakers' at work who do not share the common purpose;
- the presence of third parties to the employment relationship is intrusive: therefore there is no place for trade unions.

It is not difficult to see that unitarism is principally a management ideology. It fits with the view that many managers would like to have of the employment relationship in their own organisation, even if they acknowledge that it may be somewhat idealistic in general. These are the managers who talk in their mission statements of 'people being the organisation's greatest asset'. To be charitable, it is probably often well meant. To be less charitable, the unitarist view may be seen as a device for ensuring that management is seen as the single source of authority in the organisation. This creates what is known as the *management prerogative* – the ability of management to make decisions without hindrance from those who may disagree with those decisions. In other words, adoption of the unitary perspective is consistent with the view that 'management knows best'. Moreover, as Rose (2001) notes, the unitarist ideology may be useful for projecting to the outside world that management's decisions are right and any challenge to them comes from those who are either misguided or subversive.

Fox (1966: 4) argued that unitarism 'has long been abandoned by most social scientists as incongruent with reality and useless for the purposes of analysis'. The first part of this critique may be valid. The analogy of the team, for example, invites comparison with the idea of a professional football team. At first glance it is reasonable to assume that the team is an organisation unified by a common purpose, with all team members pursuing the same goal – to win honours for the club. But this ignores the fact that individual team members have their own personal goals: one to stay in the team, another to obtain a new contract, and yet another to increase his attractiveness to a rival club, which is keen to secure his transfer. There may be an overall common purpose and a layer of separate individual purposes below this. What is important is the extent to which that aggregate of individual purposes hinders the pursuit and achievement of the common goal. If you accept the legitimacy of this argument it follows from this that conflict is perfectly rational and predictable. It would also be difficult to sustain the argument that management is the single source of authority in a professional football club. So-called 'player power' is thought to be a result of the massive salaries earned by the top players – salaries that are frequently higher than those of the team manager!

But the view that unitarism is 'useless for the purposes of analysis' is questionable. It is a way of thinking about the employment relationship that has gained great currency in recent years, as it chimes with one of the central tenets of the so-called human resource management movement. In his frequently quoted list of 27 dimensions that differentiate human resource management from personnel management, Storey (1992) notes that the nature of (employee) relations is 'unitarist'. This is expanded in Table 1.2.

Examination of Table 1.2 reflects Fox's (1966) definition of unitarism as a way of thinking about the organisation 'as a team unified by a common purpose' in several ways. The common thread that runs through many of the human resource

Table 1.2 Differences between personnel management and human resource management

Dimension	Personnel management	Human resource management
Nature of employee relations	Pluralist	Unitarist
Employment contract	Emphasis upon duties being consistent with written contract	Emphasis upon going 'beyond contract' and doing what needs to be done
Reference point for employee behaviour	Norms and 'custom and practice'	Values and mission of the organisation
Focus for employee commitment	Commitment to self, job, career, trade union	Commitment to organisation
Conflict	Mechanisms to cope with conflict built into organisational procedures. Handled by reaching temporary truces	De-emphasised by managing the climate and organisational culture such that conflict is kept to an absolute minimum
Key relations	Labour–management	Customer driven
Employee communication	Indirect, often through trade union shop stewards	Direct with employees
Determination of terms and conditions of employment	By collective bargaining with trade unions	Direct with employees by individual contracts
Job design	Division of labour by employee task specialisation	Teamwork
Organisation change	Achieved through changing procedures	Achieved through changes to organisational cultures and structures

Source: Developed from Storey (1992)

management characteristics is that of organisational culture. Developing a culture that is consistent with unitarist principles, in which the needs of the individual take second place to those of the organisation, dominates the thinking. There is a persuasive rationale for this in that it is argued that this is what the competitive product market dictates.

Unitarism dressed up as human resource management may be attractive to some, and there is little doubt that it is a way of thinking about the employment relationship that has been in the forefront of much management analysis in recent years. But we must counsel caution in assuming that UK managers have transformed employee relations at the workplace by pursuing human resource management based practices. After reviewing survey evidence over the 1990s Guest (2001) notes very low adoption of so-called high-commitment/'progressive' human resource management work practices based upon the principles in the right-hand column of Table 1.2. This leads Guest (2001: 112) to conclude that 'the popular cliché that "people are our greatest asset" is patently untrue'.

Even if there had been wholesale adoption of the unitarist perspective by UK managers it raises the question of whether this is consistent with the new psychological contract. On the face of it the two ideas are contradictory. Unitarism stresses the absorption of the individual into the organisation, shedding her own identity and interests. The new psychological contract, on the other hand, suggests that she is 'on her own' to a very much greater extent, responding to her own interests. This may mean that a fruitful employment relationship results as long as those interests chime with those of her employer. What the new psychological contract does is recognise that there is a plurality of different interests in the employment relationship rather than one common purpose: a view that has traditionally dominated employee relations thinking and practice.

■ Pluralism

An understanding of the central tenets of pluralism is vital to an understanding of employee relations because many of the principles, procedures, processes and practices that exist to manage the employment relationship are based on the principle of pluralism. Fox (1966: 2) defined pluralism as the organisation being a 'miniature democratic state composed of sectional groups with divergent interests over which government tries to maintain some kind of dynamic equilibrium'. These 'sectional groups with divergent interests' in democratic society are simple to identify. As we write (2002), one of these, the Countryside Alliance, has held a major march and rally in London to promote rural interests in general and fox-hunting in particular. There are, of course, many other groups representing every possible interest, from environmental protection to gay rights. In a democratic society the legitimacy of these groups is recognised and welcomed. They are an essential part of a democratic society and have a vital role to play in checking the power of government in order to ensure that it does not practise absolute authority over the way we live our lives.

In essence, employing organisations are a microcosm of society as a whole. The sectional groups with divergent interests in organisations are equally easy to identify. Employees and their managers represent obvious potentially divergent groups. They may differ not over the need to achieve certain goals, but over how these may be achieved. Again, the legitimacy of these differing interests is recognised. Managers are responsible for ensuring the overall effectiveness of the organisation and the achievement of organisation goals. Employees, on the other hand, are more likely to be concerned with personal goals, in particular the wish to obtain better terms and conditions of employment.

Within the community of employees there may be separate groups based on different functions or occupational categories. In universities, for example, academic and support or administrative staffs have separate interests stemming from the differing nature of the tasks performed and the terms and conditions each enjoy. Similarly, separate managerial groups may have differing interests depending upon their function. Clearly the objectives of the research and development function in a commercial organisation are quite different from those of production, if only because the time horizons vary radically. Research and development's success is evident at the end of a period measured in years, whereas production has much more immediate goals.

The existence of these sectional groups with divergent interests in the organisation signals the potential for conflict, as their interests may clash over, say, the distribution of scarce resources. Each group makes a case for it to have what it sees as its 'fair' share of those resources, just as each spending department in central government (e.g. education or health) makes a case to the Treasury for higher funding. The key point here is that there have to be mechanisms to avoid such conflicts spilling over into anarchy with the consequent effects upon organisational effectiveness. Indeed, such mechanisms designed to prevent harmful conflict have to achieve what Fox (1966: 2) called 'dynamic equilibrium': a state where the conflict is used in such a way that it leads to a sort of 'creative tension' where better-quality solutions to problems result from a discussion based upon original disagreement.

There is a good deal of material in this book that relates to these mechanisms designed to prevent harmful conflict. The very existence of trade unions (the subject of Chapter 5), for example, is rooted in the notion of pluralism. Without an acceptance of the inevitability of conflict and its legitimacy there is no legitimate role for trade unions. The point has been made by John Monks, General Secretary of the TUC, and others, that if trade unions did not exist they would have to be invented. As Fox (1966: 8) said, trade unions 'simply provide a highly organised and continuous form of expression for sectional interests which would exist anyway'. This is obviously in stark contrast to the unitarist perspective, which sees the presence of conflict as irrational and consequently sees no place for 'intrusive' trade unions. The principal ways in which trade unions and management seek to reconcile differences of interest are collective bargaining (Chapter 7) and joint consultation (Chapter 8). Particular attention is given in Chapter 7 to the collective dispute resolution procedures designed to ensure that it is rare for conflict to get out of control. Mechanisms designed to contain conflict also exist to prevent disputes between the individual employee and management. Study of formal procedures for grievance and discipline handling (Chapter 9) and the handling of redundancies (Chapter 12) illustrates that most organisations take great care to ensure that differing views of employees and managers are expressed and considered before action is taken. The point to emphasise here is that these procedures and processes, like the existence of trade unions, are tangible evidence of the adoption of a pluralist perspective in the organisations in which they operate.

The conflict-handling mechanisms outlined above depend for their effectiveness on a final point about pluralism that Fox (1966) stressed: that is, that the differences between the parties are not so 'fundamental or wide as to be unbridgeable' (Salamon, 2000: 8). The parties must have an interest in the survival of the organisation of which they are a part. Clearly, if the employees or the trade union were hell-bent on 'smashing' the organisation all the conflict-handling procedures imaginable would be ineffective. There must be some overall shared view about the legitimacy of the organisation and its goals that is the basis for common ground.

self-check question	**1.4** Fox asserted the validity of pluralism as a perspective on employee relations in 1966. How persuasive do you find the view that unitarism is a more appropriate way to think about the employment relationship in the early part of the twenty-first century?

■ Marxism

The overall shared view about the legitimacy of the organisation and its goals that are the basis for common ground between employees, trade unions and employers, which in turn is the basis for the 'dynamic equilibrium' inherent in the pluralist view of employee relations, is not one that is shared by those who take a Marxist view of the subject. Salamon (2000: 9) summarises this view in the following four principles:

1 'Class conflict is the source of societal change – without such conflict the society would stagnate.
2 Class conflict arises primarily from the disparity in the distribution of, and access to, economic power within the society – the principal disparity being between those who own capital and those who supply their labour.
3 The nature of society's social and political institutions is derived from this economic disparity and reinforces the position of the dominant establishment group, for example through differential access to education, the media, employment in government and other establishment bodies.
4 Social and political conflict in whatever form is merely an expression of the underlying economic conflict within the society.'

Those who hold this view would argue that employee relations processes, in particular collective bargaining, do little more than produce marginal changes to the distribution of wealth within society. An extra 3 per cent on the pay and 30 minutes less on the day are hardly the stuff of social and economic revolution. Indeed, the critics of collective bargaining would go further and assert that it reinforces the legitimacy of management by providing an accommodation of the interests of employees within a framework that management find acceptable. Moreover, it does little to threaten the status quo – which is the existence of overall management control.

It would be easy to dismiss the Marxist analysis of employee relations, particularly in the developed economies, as outdated and irrelevant. It is true that those who call for radical change in society leading to a fundamental redistribution of wealth and power do not play a major part in mainstream politics. However, the language of class struggle often permeates the declarations of union leaders. Indeed, the first years of this century have seen the rise of a cohort of trade union leaders who have their roots in Marxist thinking and have little time for the notion of partnership with employers. At the time of writing (Autumn, 2002) one of these leaders, Derek Simpson, the leader of the engineering and manufacturing union Amicus, has led the disbandment of the so-called no-strike deal at Honda, Swindon, with threats of similar action on other no-strike agreements at Nissan and Toyota signed in the 1980s (*The Times*, 2002b). The tearing up of a 'sweetheart' deal between an employer and a trade union is clearly a long way from root and branch societal reform, but the Marxist strand of employee relations analysis is one that can never be ignored.

■ Individualism and collectivism

Some of the changes that have occurred in society in general and employee relations in particular since the mid-1960s have given rise to two further perspectives on the employment relationship: *individualism* and *collectivism*. The thrust of this section is to point out that there has been a move towards individualism and away from collectivism in the past 20 years. We start by explaining what these terms mean and then identify the practical ways in which the change has manifested itself at organisation level. We then attempt to speculate on the reasons why this change has occurred. We do, however, sound a warning note that the movement is not quite as straightforward as it appears. Caution should be exercised in assuming that there has been a dramatic and irrevocable shift to individualism from collectivism.

From the perspective of the employee, individualism refers to the will of the individual to look after her own interests rather than relying on another person or body to do this for her. Kessler and Purcell (1995) evoke the example of the Victorian writer and sage Samuel Smiles, who promoted self-reliance and the moral virtue of work, and the idea that 'the spirit of self-help is the root of all genuine growth in the individual' (Kessler and Purcell, 1995: 337). In contrast, collectivism sees the spirit of self-reliance subordinated to the collective interests of the work group, whether that is at workplace, company or national level. Such subordination may be by individual choice, the employee deciding that his own interests are best served by banding together with individuals in a similar situation to him. Alternatively it may be that the individual has little choice as his employer is already part of an arrangement whereby the employees' interests are progressed through a collective arrangement.

From the employer's perspective he may prefer to pursue an individualist approach with his employees. In this way he is free to deal with his employees in the way he thinks best fits the interests of the organisation without what he sees as 'interference' from outside bodies such as trade unions and government. On the other hand he may prefer to deal collectively with employees, as dealing with one body on behalf of hundreds of employees is seen as more efficient than dealing with employees individually. This is not to imply, however, that such decisions, whether taken by the individual or by the employer, are value-free. Far from it. The decision whether to adopt an individualist or a collectivist approach is not only based upon personal beliefs about the way to progress in life but also about the way in which society should be organised. It is a decision of great importance for the organisation of the employment relationship.

Few would deny that there has been a shift towards individualism in recent years. Evidence of this is suggested by the growth of certain HR strategies that are usually associated with individualism. Perhaps the most self-evident of these is the growth of performance management (Bach, 2000), in which the individual employee is set targets and held accountable for their achievement. This approach forces the employee into a one-to-one relationship with that employee's manager. Therefore the treatment that the employee receives from the manager is individualised according to the extent to which success has been achieved in pursuit of the targets. Part of this treatment is pay. Individual performance-related pay (IPRP) is usually an intrinsic part of performance management. (We go into more detail on IPRP in Chapter 10.) IPRP is clearly quite different from the old collective maxim of a 'fair day's pay for a fair day's work' where the same level of reward is given to all irrespective of performance. Naturally this latter method of payment has often been preferred by trade unions, who see it as their aim to secure the same level of reward for all based on the principle of the 'rate for the job'. IPRP is the antithesis of this principle.

More evidence for the rise of individualism is the change in the way employees receive communication from management. The 1998 Workplace Employee Relations Survey (WERS; Cully *et al.*, 1999) notes the prevalence of such communication methods as team briefings, the 'cascading' of information via the management chain, regular newsletters distributed to all employees, and regular meetings with the workforce. All of these bypass the traditional method of communicating with employees in collectively organised workplaces: through the union representatives who sit on various committees and are charged with the responsibility of representing their members' views at those committees and disseminating the results of the committee meetings after they have met.

By communicating directly with employees management is trying to forge an affective link with employees. By involving them through giving them details about the progress of the organisation the intention is that it will engender a stronger link between the individual employee and the organisation. The evidence from WERS 1998 suggests that this effort is quite successful, as generally quite positive results were recorded for employee involvement and employee commitment. It is difficult to argue with the logic that an employee who is kept in the picture as to what is going on in his or her organisation is likely to have more positive attitudes than the employee who is kept ignorant of such developments.

The list of some of the characteristics of the new psychological contract in Table 1.1 shows that these characteristics have distinct echoes of individualism, particularly as they impose upon the employee a greater level of self-reliance. The essence of the new psychological contract is the lack of security and predictability, which demands greater flexibility on the part of the employee. Such flexibility means that the employee faced with a limited time in one organisation or one career must accept greater responsibility for equipping herself with the knowledge and skills to be able to make the transition. This is emphasised by Boxall and Purcell (2003). In the context of the widespread belief that there has been a move in recent years to the idea of 'employability' rather than employment security, they feel that

> ...the onus is placed on the individual to ensure accumulation of training and experience in order to remain attractive in the labour market, whether internal or external. The employer may provide opportunities for human capital development but it is up to the individual to take advantage of them. (Boxall and Purcell, 2003: 117–18)

The employer's preference to pursue an individualist approach to the management of the employment relationship is reflected in the decline in the number of organisations recognising trade unions, and the consequent drop in trade union membership. Both of these are charted in detail in Chapter 5. However, it would be too simplistic to assume that there is a direct cause–effect relationship between this employer preference and the decline in trade union influence. This situation is far more complex, as Chapter 5 explains.

There are a number of possible reasons that may explain why this general change from individualism to collectivism has occurred in recent years. At the root of these may have been the dramatic social and political changes wrought by Thatcherism in the 1980s. Mrs Thatcher's famous phrase 'There is no such thing as Society. There are individual men and women and there are families' (cited in Kessler and Purcell,

1995) set the tone for changes that saw people encouraged to buy their council houses, and buy shares in newly privatised public utilities such as gas and telecommunications and rail. Indeed, it may be argued that the decline in investment in public services for many years was an invitation for individuals to be more reliant on their own privately financed means and less on services to be provided for the community at large. The rise in home ownership and private medical provision are two examples of this.

The composition of the workforce and the jobs that workers do, as Chapter 2 notes in detail, have also contributed to the rise in individualism. Jobs in the old 'smokestack' industries often bred a sense of community, which grew from many workers doing the same jobs and often sharing in the difficulties imposed by the difficult and demanding nature of these jobs. The historian William Woodruff (1993) has presented one such account of life in the textile mills of Blackburn in the early twentieth century. A similar sense of community existed in coalmining, shipbuilding and dockwork. Such traditional work-based communities no longer exist, as Woodruff noted on his return to Blackburn after half a century:

> The Blackburn of my childhood had had a forest of red brick chimneys belching great twisted coils of smoke. Where were they? The few chimneys I could see were cold and smokeless. I looked at my watch. It was 5.30. The light was fading. Seventy years ago, at this hour, Blackburn's streets would have been filled with the clip-clap sound of clogs, as thousands of factory workers, the women in grey shawls, the men wearing dark caps, hastened home from work. Now there were few people about; they were better dressed – no shawls, few caps, no clogs – but there was no haste in their step. At this hour the Blackburn into which I was born would have been noisy, urgent, crowded, vibrant, alive. The Blackburn I saw was becalmed – like a demasted ship after a storm. (Woodruff, 1993: 5–6).

The opportunity for workers to work at a distance from their nominal place of work, facilitated by the advent of computer technology, has created the opportunity for a type of social organisation of work that is radically different from Woodruff's Blackburn. Although these two images may be thought of as extreme stereotypes, they do serve to illustrate the way in which changes in work have created the move to greater individualisation of the employment relationship.

However, it would be misleading to suggest that collectivism is a thing of the past and that there has been an irrevocable shift to individualism. Indeed, as Sisson and Storey (2000) point out, it is not a question of *either–or* but both: both individualism and collectivism may be appropriate in a given organisational context. Let us take two of the examples of individualism at work that we mention above: IPRP and direct communication with employees. In the case of IPRP, the introduction of this predominantly individual pay initiative is often negotiated with trade unions. The size of the annual pay budget increase may also be the subject of collective bargaining, and trade unions will be involved in the representation of employees at appeals in the event of a grievance existing over the implementation of the individual awards. Similarly, with direct employee communication, Kessler and Purcell (1995) argue that the presence of a union may be accompanied by an increase in the amount of strategic information given to the union and members of the joint consultative committee.

There is a great temptation with all changes in employee relations to say that the world has changed and that the 'old' has been replaced by the 'new'. The reality is never as simple as the previous paragraph suggests. The message from this is a useful one to take into the succeeding chapters of this book: be wary of making rash generalisations!

---

self-check question   **1.5** Given the debate on the move towards individualism and away from collectivism in the past 20 years, how would you account for the rise in interest in teamwork?

1.5   Summary

- The employment relationship is defined as 'an economic, legal, social, psychological and political relationship in which employees devote their time and expertise to the interests of their employer in return for a range of personal financial and non-financial rewards'.
- The circumstances in which the employment relationship is conducted vary considerably.
- Both the contract of employment and the psychological contract are important components of the employment relationship.
- The psychological contract has changed greatly in recent years, owing largely to changes in the context in which employment is enacted.
- Unitarism, pluralism and Marxism represent three differing ways in which the employment relationship may be viewed.
- There has been a general move away from collectivism towards individualism in recent years.

References

Argyris, C. (1960) *Understanding Organisational Behaviour*, Homewood, IL, Dorsey Press.

Armstrong, M. and Murlis, H. (1998) *Reward Management: A handbook of remuneration strategy and practice* (4th edn), London, Kogan Page.

Bach, S. (2000) 'From performance appraisal to performance management', *in* Bach, S. and Sisson, K. (eds) (2000), *Personnel Management: A comprehensive guide to theory and practice* (3rd edn), Oxford, Blackwell.

BBC Online (1997) 'Employees moan on the 'phone', [online] [cited 22 December] Available from <http://news.bbc.co.uk/hi/english/business/newsid%5F41000/41714.stm>

Bain, G. (1983) *Industrial Relations in Britain*, Oxford, Basil Blackwell.

Blyton, P. and Turnbull, P. (1998) *The Dynamics of Employee Relations* (2nd edn), Basingstoke, Macmillan.

Boxall, P. and Purcell, J. (2003) *Strategy and Human Resource Management*, Basingstoke, Palgrave Macmillan.

Brooks, I. (1999) *Organisational Behaviour: Individuals, groups and the organisation*, London, Financial Times Management.

Clegg, H. (1979) *The Changing System of Industrial Relations in Britain*, Oxford, Basil Blackwell.

Cox, P. and Parkinson, A. (1999) 'Values and their impact on the changing employment relationship', *in* Hollinshead, G., Nicholls, P. and Tailby, S. (eds), *Employee Relations*, London, Financial Times Pitman Publishing, pp. 535–66.

Coyle-Shapiro, J. and Kessler, I. (2000) 'Consequences of psychological contract for the employment relationship: a large scale survey', *Journal of Management Studies*, 37:7, 903–30.

Cressey, P. and Scott, P. (1993) 'Employment, technology and industrial relations in the UK clearing banks: is the honeymoon over?', *New Technology, Work and Employment*, 7:2, 83–96.

Cully, M., Woodland, S., O'Reilly, A. and Dix, G. (1999) *Britain at Work*, London, Routledge.

European Commission Directorate-General for Economic and Financial Affairs (2000a) *European Economy: Supplement B: Business and Consumer Survey Results*, No. 1, January.

European Commission Directorate-General for Economic and Financial Affairs (2000b) *European Economy: Supplement B: Business and Consumer Survey Results*, No. 3, March.

Fox, A. (1966) *Industrial sociology and industrial relations*, Royal Commission Research Paper No. 3, London, HMSO.

Gennard, J. and Judge, G. (2002) *Employee Relations* (3rd edn), Wimbledon, Chartered Institute of Personnel and Development.

Guest, D. (2001) 'Industrial relations and human resource management', *in* Storey, J. (ed.), *Human Resource Management: A critical text* (2nd edn), London, Thomson Learning, pp. 96–113.

Guest, D. and Conway, N. (1999) 'Peering into the black hole: the downside of the new employment relationship in the UK', *British Journal of Industrial Relations*, 37:3, 367–89.

Guest, D. and Conway, N. (2002) 'Communicating the psychological contract: an employer perspective', *Human Resource Management Journal*, 12:2, 22–38.

Gospel, H. and Palmer, G. (1993) *British Industrial Relations* (2nd edn), London, Routledge.

Herriot, P. and Pemberton, C. (1995) *New Deals: The Revolution in Managerial Careers*, Chichester, Wiley.

Hiltrop, J.-M. (1995) The changing psychological contract: the human resource challenge of the 1990s, *European Management Journal*, 13:3, 286–94.

Initial Services v. *Putterill* (1968) 3 All ER, 145.

Kessler, I. and Purcell, J. (1995) 'Individualism and collectivism in theory and practice: management style and the design of pay systems', *in* Edwards, P. (ed.), *Industrial Relations: Theory and practice in Britain*, Oxford, Blackwell, pp. 337–67.

Lewis, P. (1997) *Searching for the Holy Grail: developing an explanatory theory of the success of performance-related pay*, unpublished PhD thesis, University of Bath.

Lewis, P. (1999) 'Exploring Lawler's New Pay theory through the case of Finbank's reward strategy for managers', *Personnel Review*, 29:1/2, 10–32.

Lewis, R. (1986) *Labour Law in Britain*, Oxford, Blackwell.

Marshall v. *English Electric Co. Ltd* (1945) 1, All ER, 653.

Mullins, L. (1996) *Management and Organisational Behaviour* (4th edn), London, Pitman Publishing.

Newell, H. (2000) 'Managing careers', *in* Bach, S. and Sisson, K. (eds), *Personnel Management: A comprehensive guide to theory and practice* (3rd edn), Oxford, Blackwell, pp. 218–38.

Newell, H. and Dopson, S. (1996) 'Muddle in the middle: organisational restructuring and middle management careers', *Personnel Review*, 25:4, 4–20.

Organ, D. (1988) *Organisational Citizenship Behavior: The good soldier syndrome*, Lexington, MA, Lexington Books.

Rose, E. (2001) *Employment Relations*, Harlow, Pearson Education.

Rousseau, D. (1994) cited by Hiltrop, J.-M. (1995) 'The changing psychological contract: the human resource challenge of the 1990s', *European Management Journal*, 13:3, 286–94.

Salamon, M. (2000) *Industrial Relations: Theory and practice* (4th edn), Hemel Hempstead, Prentice Hall.

Schein, E. (1978) *Career Dynamics: Matching individual and organisation needs*, Reading, MA, Addison-Wesley.

Security and Facilities Division v. *Hayes and others* (2001) Industrial Relations Law Reports, 81.

Sisson, K. and Storey, J. (2000) *The Realities of Human Resource Management: Managing the employment relationship*, Buckingham, Open University Press.

Sparrow, P. (2000) New employee behaviours, work designs and forms of work organization: what is in store for the future of work? *Journal of Managerial Psychology*, 15:3, 202–18.

Storey, J. (1992) *Developments in the Management of Human Resources*, Oxford, Blackwell.

The Times (2002a) 'Boring is beautiful for faceless company', 2 September.

The Times (2002b) 'New militancy as union ends no-strike deal', 20 September.

Woodruff, W. (1993) *The Road to Nab End*, London, Abacus.

Woods v. *WM Car Services (Peterborough) Ltd* (1981) ICR 666.

Yen Mah, A. (2001) *Watching the Tree*, London, Harper Collins.

self-check Answers

1.1 *Why do you think that there is now so much attention paid to the concept of the employment relationship in the study of the topic we refer to more generally as employee relations?*

Perhaps the most telling reason for this is that, as this chapter points out, and Chapter 2 notes in much more detail, the nature of employment in the developed world has changed. The structural changes are well known and documented, but these have had the effect of making people think about the 'employee relations' dimension to their working lives in a different way. As the latter part of Chapter 1 notes, the perspective that most of us adopt is now a much more individualistic one. Rightly or wrongly, we tend to think about our individual relationship with our employer rather than the relationship that exists between our work colleagues and us as a collective and our employer. It is a short step from this to seeing why we are less likely to think in terms of our relationship with a trade union. It is this different way of thinking about the experience of work that we think makes the concept of the employment relationship a more appropriate focus for the early part of the twenty first century.

1.2 *Why do you think that a knowledge of both statutory and common law provision is so important in understanding the concept of the contract of employment?*

In effect statutory and common law operate in tandem in the contract of employment. For example, as Lewis (1986) argues, there can be no proper understanding of what amounts to a dismissal for the purposes of the statute of unfair dismissal without a grasp of the common law rules regarding breach of contract due to contravention of common law duties.

1.3 *To what extent is the 'new' psychological contract a myth dreamed up by HR commentators to add a new dimension to discussion about HRM?*

Like many other similar ideas, for example 'the flexible firm' (see Chapter 2), there may be an element of overstatement here in that the idea may be running somewhat ahead of the reality. However, nobody can deny the enormous number of redundancies that have occurred in the developed countries in recent years, or the development of more flexible working patterns (again, see Chapter 2). We find it a very persuasive proposition that the 'new' psychological contract is an inevitable consequence of two principal trends. The first is the need that all organisations have to be mindful of the operating costs. In such a climate a 'promise' of a job and career for life is an expensive one. Look, for example, at the companies (such as BT and Iceland) that have offered their new employees pension schemes linked to stock market performance rather than the more expensive final salary schemes. The second trend is the desire that many employees have to take greater control of their lives. This means that the idea of tying themselves to one company and one career for 40 years no longer has the appeal it once had.

1.4 *Fox asserted the validity of pluralism as a perspective on employee relations in 1966. How persuasive do you find the view that unitarism is a more appropriate way to think about the employment relationship in the early part of the twenty-first century?*

You could characterise pluralism as reflecting adversarial relationships between employers and employees and trade unions; highly formalised procedures based on collective bargaining and joint consultation; contests over virtually everything (in particular, anything involving change); and, of course, frequent disruption of work processes. You could say that such a model referred to the sort of smokestack industries (e.g. steel production, ship building, coal mining) that have been in decline in recent years.

This may be contrasted with 'new style' employee relations in which, at least the HRM rhetoric would lead us to believe, we are all unitarists and the UK economy is populated with employers who have highly committed employees as a consequence of employee involvement and family-friendly policies. This would lead you to describing unitarism as 'new' and pluralism as 'old'.

But, of course, the reality is that it's not quite so simple as that (nothing in the social sciences ever is). There are, in the UK, continental Europe and North America, plenty of organisations that are recognisably 'pluralist' in the way in which they manage their employee relations. Indeed, much of the public sector in the UK, at the least on the face of it, falls into this category. Even many employers who do not have formalised employee relations can be characterised as promoting employee relations that are far from the HRM rhetoric. The world is not full of software engineers and actuaries; there are also lots of security guards, cleaners and fast food waiters out there for whom the new style of employee relations is far from a reality.

1.5 *Given the debate on the move towards individualism and away from collectivism in the past 20 years, how would you account for the rise in interest in teamwork?*

At first sight this does seem something of a paradox. However, it does seem that part of our definition of collectivism as the individual subordinating the spirit of self-reliance to the collective interests of the work group is consistent with the notion of working in teams. This may be seen as a new form of collectivism, particularly if decision-making power is given to the team. Therefore, to some extent, they work outside the boundaries of traditional management direct control – direct control that may be checked by collective representation. In recent years the self-managed team as a work unit has been at the forefront of efforts by management to move towards a model of employee relations consistent with the unitarist perspective based on the notion of a strong culture and commitment of the employee to the goals of the organisation.

CASE 1   The arrival of Zonka in the UK[1]

Zonka is a large manufacturer of consumer electronics. It established itself in South Korea in the 1980s and has grown to the point where it is one of the largest manufacturers of consumer electronics in South East Asia. It has five manufacturing plants in South East Asia and employs over 7000 employees. Twenty per cent of the employees are in managerial, administrative and technical jobs; the remainder are production operatives. Zonka is owned partly by the South Korean government and partly by a large public holding company based in Hong Kong. The company's commercial record in recent years has been impressive, owing largely to its expertise in production and marketing. It has achieved 50 per cent annual growth since 1993 and has cultivated a strong export market in developing countries in South Asia, particularly India. This is due mainly to the cost advantage the South Koreans have over their main competitors, the Japanese. However, Zonka is ambitious for further growth. The markets of South East Asia, particularly the Chinese market, offer further opportunities. However, these markets offer restricted profit opportunities. Zonka's main strategic objective for the next five years is to follow in the footsteps of other Korean companies and enter the European market and increase profits through this initiative. In particular, Zonka sees enormous growth in the European TV and DVD markets, consequent upon the projected widespread take-up of digital TV in the first decade of the twenty-first century.

Zonka considered the strategy of selling its TVs and DVDs to established European manufacturers and retailers in order that these companies might sell the appliances under their own brand names. This presents to Zonka the advantages of no set-up costs and guaranteed sales, but carries the disadvantage of lower profits and dependence on a few large customers. The alternative strategy was to set up a manufacturing facility in Europe. Zonka felt sufficiently confident about its brand and its expertise in production and marketing to adopt this strategy. Consideration was given to establishing a factory in the Netherlands until the final decision was taken to locate the new factory in the UK. The site chosen was a large greenfield site in a growing town in the South Midlands of England. The site was chosen because it had good transport links and the promise of a large potential workforce, which would supply the sort of skills that Zonka needed. The financial assistance given by the local authority also influenced Zonka's decision.

This story begins at the point in the development of Zonka Manufacturing (UK) Ltd, where key appointments have been made. The General Manager, Production Manager, Finance Manager and HR Manager have all been appointed. Their task is to purchase and install the technology needed to assemble the products, develop distribution mechanisms, and recruit and train the workforce. Initially Zonka Manufacturing (UK) Ltd will assemble DVDs in the UK plant only from parts made by Zonka in South Korea. The product research and development and design will be done in South Korea, albeit with assistance from UK experts. The marketing and sales for Europe will be conducted in the UK by Zonka Sales (UK) Ltd.

Initially Zonka Manufacturing (UK) Ltd will operate two 8-hour shifts in the UK factory: 06.00–14.00 and 14.00–22.00. The shifts will be shared equally between the operatives: that is, all staff will be expected to work an equal amount

---

[1] The organisation and the people working within it are fictional.

of 06.00–14.00 and 14.00–22.00 shifts. It is estimated that 300 operatives will be needed in addition to approximately 40 clerical and supervisory staff who will perform such duties as material control, transport, accounting, management information and personnel. It is envisaged that the workforce will be mainly female, young and, therefore, inexperienced at working in an environment similar to that of Zonka Manufacturing (UK) Ltd.

The HR Manager has advised the General Manager that it may be wise to recruit a core of permanent employees to begin the operation and supplement this core with a large body of operatives employed by a staffing agency. This would provide an element of security were sales demand not to be quite what is envisaged in the early months. Recruiting operatives is the first priority of the HR Manager, Kate Ryan. In addition, she needs to recruit and train HR staff to assist her. Clearly this is only the first task that Kate and her staff will need to perform.

Previous to joining Zonka Manufacturing (UK) Ltd, Kate Ryan was in the financial services industry. Consequently she has brought a fresh mind to the company. She has been given a certain amount of latitude to design the HR policies and procedures in the way she thinks fit. However, she is expected to work within the guiding principles of Zonka's philosophy. These guiding principles are contained in a briefing pack sent to Kate by the Director of HR in Zonka, South Korea. They are:

1 Employment in the company is based on the philosophy of democracy. Therefore, all employees are to be treated with equal respect, irrespective of their status within the company. All Zonka Manufacturing (UK) Ltd employees are to be called 'members' and share in a profit plan where all can enjoy the fruits of the organisation's success. Zonka Manufacturing (UK) Ltd will be a single-status company with the same terms and conditions for all employees.

2 There will be open communication between management and employees. Management will conduct the business in such a way that, as far as is consistent with the normal rules of trading, no secrets are kept from the workforce. There will also be a strong commitment to employee involvement. No major decisions affecting the future of Zonka Manufacturing (UK) Ltd will be made without staff being involved in the making of those decisions.

3 As part of the commitment to employee involvement Zonka Manufacturing (UK) Ltd is prepared to share the management of employee relations with one trade union. As far as possible this should follow the model where the employees are represented by a 'company union', which works in partnership with the management of Zonka Manufacturing (UK) Ltd.

4 Zonka Manufacturing (UK) Ltd will have a strong commitment to employee development. There will be training opportunities for all staff to develop themselves in their current job. At the same time the company is committed to the principle of lifelong learning, and will assist employees to develop themselves for future opportunities both within and outside Zonka Manufacturing (UK) Ltd.

5 Zonka Manufacturing (UK) Ltd wishes to be an 'upper quartile payer' in the local area surrounding the manufacturing site. This is so that high-quality staff may be attracted and retained, and should also reflect the fact that many staff will have to work at non-social times.

6 At the same time as offering good-quality terms and conditions, employment at Zonka Manufacturing (UK) Ltd will be based on the philosophy of meritocracy. All employees will be treated with courtesy, respect and generosity. In return employees will be expected to perform to a high standard at all times. Those employees who are deemed, through the company's performance management scheme, to be effective will be rewarded more generously than those who are less effective. All employees who consistently fall below the high work standards set by the company will be given every chance to improve their performance, but the company will not hesitate to conduct disciplinary action against those who do not improve.

Kate found these guiding principles from the Director of HR in South Korea helpful in giving her a start. But she realised that an awful lot of detailed work was necessary if these were to be converted into workable HR policies and procedures.

Questions

1 What policies would Kate Ryan need to draft in order to convert the guiding principles from the Director of HR in South Korea into workable HR policies and procedures?

2 What are likely to be the characteristics of the psychological contract that will exist between Zonka Manufacturing (UK) Ltd and its individual employees?

3 Which perspective on employee relations does the Director of HR in South Korea seem to have adopted in designing the guiding principles?

4 The guiding principles from the Director of HR in South Korea contain several contradictions between the principles of individualism and collectivism. What are they? To what extent do you feel that these can be reconciled in practice?

Chapter 2

The changing context and nature of the employment relationship

At the end of this chapter you should be able to:

■ explain the main changes that have occurred in the wider environment within which work occurs;

■ relate these changes to the way in which work is organised;

■ appreciate why and how the nature of the employment relationship has changed and is continuing to change.

2.1 Introduction

The employment relationship between employee and employer does not occur within a vacuum (Blyton and Turnbull, 1998). Rather, this relationship is influenced and affected by a host of factors associated with the way in which work is organised and the wider context within which work takes place. As we can see from Figure 2.1, these factors can be subdivided into three major elements:

■ the wider environments within which work occurs;
■ the organisation of work subsystem;
■ the sequence of events within these over time.

The first of these, the wider environments, embraces a wide range of interrelated influences drawn from the political, economic, technological and social environments within which work is located. These environments are able to both stimulate and constrain the organisation of work subsystem. For example, political actions such as legislation for a national minimum wage may constrain an employer's reward policy, which in turn will influence the relationship with their employee. In contrast, the introduction of information and communication technologies may enable work to take place at new locations, thereby altering the way in which work is organised and the employment relationship.

The organisation of work subsystem is itself a product of the wider environment. Gallie *et al.* (1998) highlight four key areas where changes in the way work is organised have occurred that impact upon the employment relationship. These are:

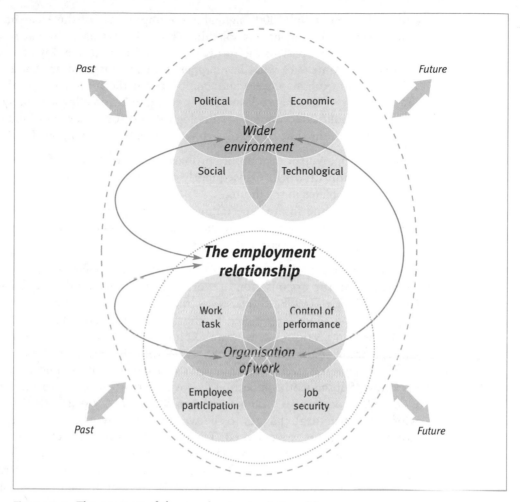

Figure 2.1 **The context of the employment relationship**

- the work task;
- the control of performance;
- employee participation;
- job security.

Salamon (2000) argues that any changes will have an impact at all levels of the employment relationship. These include the organisation (for example work group, section, department and sometimes site), the industry (for example automobile manufacturing), the national (for example the United Kingdom) and the supranational (for example the European Union). Within each of these levels, factors will impact upon each other (horizontally), influencing both how work is organised and the employment relationship. In addition, the factors in each level will also have an external (vertical) impact upon other levels, again influencing both the organisation of work and the employment relationship.

Our third element, time, is represented by the double-headed arrows linking the employment relationship and its wider environments to both the past and the future

(Figure 2.1). Salamon (2000) highlights the importance of this element, emphasising that present employment relationships are each part of a sequence of events that stretches from the past to the future. Therefore current employment relationships occur in the context of what has happened in the past and are conditioned by the aspirations of both employees and employers for the future. Within the wider environments, or at the macro level, employment relationships are likely to adjust in response to political, economic, technological and social developments over time. At the micro level, the time context is evident in two ways (Salamon, 1998):

- current employment relationship problems are the product of earlier actions in the organisation of work. Consequently their solutions will, as elements change, become problems in the future;
- the attitudes and future expectations of actors in the employment relationship are conditioned, at least in part, by their individual and collective experiences of what has happened in the past in the organisation of work.

In this chapter we are concerned with exploring how elements of these wider environments and the organisation of work subsystem have influenced and resulted in what Gallie *et al.* (1998: 2) refer to as 'the restructuring of the employment relationship' with particular reference to the United Kingdom (UK). To this end, we commence, in Section 2.2, with an exploration of the wider environments within which employment relationships are set. Within this, we consider the impact of the political, economic, technological and social environments and how they have altered over time. Subsequently, in Section 2.3, we narrow our focus to the organisation of work. This commences with a discussion of the theory of the flexible firm, against which the structural changes to the way in which work is being organised in the twenty-first century are explored. The implications of these changes in the employment relationship for both employers and employees are then considered in Section 2.4. The chapter concludes with a summary in which we highlight the key issues relating to the changing context and nature of the employment relationship.

2.2 Changes in the wider environments within which work takes place

There are no doubts in the minds of many commentators that we are living in a period of unparalleled change in the world of work, and that this is being shaped by powerful society-wide forces. Although there is debate as to whether or not these changes are as transformational as those brought about by the Industrial Revolution and the transition from feudalism, it is clear that both managers' and employees' experience of recent change is increasing. Surveys of British managers for the Institute of Management show the proportion of managers experiencing change at work in the preceding year rising from 57 per cent in 1997 to 67 per cent in 1999 (Worrall and Cooper, 1999). Warhurst and Thompson (1998) highlight an increasing convergence between business and academic commentators' views about such changes and their impact upon work and workplace. At a macro level, they argue, these commentators focus upon the advent of a 'post-industrial, information or knowledge economy'

(Warhurst and Thompson, 1998: 1). This emphasises the rise of the service sector and decline of manufacturing alongside the emergence of what is commonly termed the *information age*. Technological and information resources are expanding more rapidly than ever before, and competition between organisations is intensifying, resulting in the need to drive down costs. Increasingly such competition is at a global level. At the same time organisations are having to change their ways of working. Within the UK, for example, public sector organisations are being compelled to embrace the ideology of the marketplace and adopt new managerial practices.

Projecting from these changes, some commentators, such as Handy (1990, 1996), talk of an optimistic future in which work will be more autonomous and creative for the majority. As part of this, careers will become more varied, individuals taking responsibility for ensuring that new employment opportunities will benefit their career paths. Others appear more pessimistic, talking about the dehumanisation of work (Ritzer, 1998) and threats to traditional employment packages (Bridges, 1995). Whichever viewpoint you subscribe to, one thing is certain: the wider context within which work takes place is changing, and this is influencing both the way in which all our work is organised and, ultimately, all our employment relationships.

The political environment

The impact of the political environment and in particular governmental influences on the employment relationship are discussed in detail in Chapter 6. However, in outlining the changes in the wider context for work, it is important that an overview of the political environment is included. As part of the political process governments establish the formal and informal rules within which the employment relationship operates. As the 'third actor' in the employee relations system (Poole, 1986: 99), governments, through legislation, set frameworks for subjective value judgements on fairness and equity, power and authority, and the rights of the individual rather than the collective. These cover issues ranging from discrimination and equality, such as the Race Relations (Amendment) Act 2000, to the rights for representation by a recognised trade union in the workplace (Employment Relations Act 1999). In addition, as both direct and indirect employers, they demonstrate their ideological preferences through the mix of organisations that are in the public sector and the approach they choose to manage the employment relationship. Consequently, government's economic and social policies constrain the general environment providing sets of rules within which employment relationships operate.

Within the UK, successive governments' policies have played a key role in 'defining' social problems and 'setting the agenda' for employee relations (Winchester, 1983: 105). Salamon (2000) argues that this influence on employee relations can be seen in three main areas:

- government's power and authority to change the rules of the employee relations system;
- government's direct and indirect control of organisations within the public sector and the associated potential to demonstrate their preferred model;
- the influence of government's social and economic policies on the general environment within which employment relationships are conducted.

Changing governments and associated political ideologies have inevitably exerted different influences upon the employment relationship over time. The period of both Labour and Conservative governments in the United Kingdom during the 1960s and 1970s has been termed one of 'consensus' politics (Salamon, 2000: 121) in which a corporatist approach was adopted. During this period up to 1979, successive administrations in formal consultation with trade unions and employers intervened in the economy with the aim of managing demand, thereby maintaining full employment.

After the election of a Conservative administration in 1979 the government's strategy changed, drawing direction from a free market *laissez-faire* ideology. Throughout the period to 1997, a principal aim was to promote individualism, self-reliance and private enterprise (Millward *et al.*, 2000). This was mirrored in other European countries. The role of government in economic planning was reduced significantly, relying instead on market forces. This was supported by legislation to reduce the powers of trade unions and deregulate employment, thereby emphasising flexibility of labour (Sparrow and Marchington, 1998). Over this period successive Conservative governments sought to limit the impact of the European Union (EU) on the operation of the UK labour market and labour flexibility, including opting out of the Social Chapter of the Maastricht Treaty 1992.

The election of a 'New Labour' government in 1997 heralded a move back towards a more consultative approach by government to managing the employment relationship. The Employment Relations Act 1999 reintroduced some additional protection for employees, such as for those dismissed while undertaking lawfully organised industrial action as well as providing support for this in the event of a claim for recognition by employees (Department of Trade and Industry, 2000). In addition, the Social Chapter of the Maastricht Treaty was adopted and a national minimum wage established. However, legislation from previous Conservative administrations concerned with enabling labour flexibility and curbing the powers of trade unions to promote individual actions was not repealed. Thus although New Labour appeared to be consulting more frequently with both employers and trade unions, it did not seek to re-establish the formal mechanisms of the 1960s and 1970s.

■ The economic environment

Globalisation

Developments in the world economy over the same period have increasingly been described using terms such as *globalisation* and *internationalisation* (Blyton and Turnbull, 1998). However, we should note that globalisation is not a new phenomenon. Companies such as Ford have had a multinational presence for many years, in this case producing cars outside the USA since the 1920s. What is new is the pace at which organisations in the more recently industrialised countries, principally Japan and other Far Eastern economies, have established production facilities across the world, and the scale on which this is occurring. Such organisations have extended their influences through alliances, joint ventures and partnerships (Blyton and Turnbull, 1998), and through the increasing financial interdependence between different countries' economies (Leat and Woolley, 1999). Over 80 per cent of world trade is now attributed to multinational corporations, the top 200 multinational corporations controlling approximately one-third of global production (United Nations Conference on Trade and Development, 1994; cited in Leat and Woolley, 1999).

Consequently, the world of work is controlled increasingly by multinationals. Traditionally, UK companies have invested more overseas than any country other than the USA. Although this pattern is changing, with both Japan and France also accounting for higher proportions of the world total of outward investment than the UK in the period 1989–94, the UK is still a net investor abroad. Eurostat figures show that for 1997 UK companies invested over £35.1 billion compared with an inward investment of £21 billion (cited in Leat and Woolley, 1999). This inward investment by foreign companies to the UK represents the highest foreign direct investment for any EU member state (Eurostat figures cited in Leat and Woolley, 1999). As a consequence there are over 1000 multinational corporations in the UK employing approximately 50 per cent of the UK's working population (Leat and Woolley, 1999).

The implications of globalisation for the employment relationship are numerous. Much of the foreign direct investment into the UK in the 1990s appears to have been due, at least in part, to its evolution towards a low wage, low investment in employees economy (Blyton and Turnbull, 1998). This has presented favourable terms and conditions of employment (to the employer) relative to the rest of the EU as not only are the wage costs lower, but non-wage costs such as holiday pay, sick pay, pension contributions and vocational training are also less. Conversely, it has presented a potential danger within the EU as, in order to be able to attract investment for their home industries to compete, economies may be pulled down to the lowest level rather than up to a minimum accepted standard (Blyton and Turnbull, 1998). However, while noting that this was the pattern in the 1990s, recent EU economic forecasts suggest that wage growth in the UK is high, even when relatively strong economic growth compared with the rest of the EU is taken into account (European Commission Directorate-General for Economic and Financial Affairs, 2000c). This suggests a reduction in the differential outlined above.

Direct foreign investment also brings new ideas about management processes and employee relations practices. Within the UK these have included single union and no-strike agreements, company uniforms for all, and non-unionism. Consequently, there has been pressure on other firms to adopt what is seen as 'best practice'. Foreign management has also highlighted weaknesses of the host country's management. For example, within the UK the level of productivity at Japanese car companies was repeatedly quoted as being almost a third higher than that of their UK counterparts (Turnbull, 1991).

The rise of private service sector employment

Within the UK, the Institute of Management surveys of British managers over the period 1997–99 (Worrall and Cooper, 1999) suggest that over three-quarters of British managers now believe that the business environment within which their organisation is operating is either stable or growing. However, the overall proportion hides sectoral differences, managers in the private service sector being most likely to consider that the environment within which their organisation is operating is growing.

Millward *et al.* (2000) emphasise that the employment relationship is likely to vary according to the type of goods produced or services delivered and whether or not the organisation is under public or private ownership. We have already alluded to the impact of ownership when we referred to government's use of the public sector to demonstrate its preferred model of employee relations. Within the UK, public sector organisations have been characterised as good employers with more joint regulation procedures and centralisation of bargaining structures when compared with private sector organisations. In contrast, private sector organisations have often been characterised as large manufacturing organisations, being highly unionised with collective practices. This parody ignores the opposite reality of low trade union membership in many private sector service organisations, such as those involved in hotels and catering. Thus, as suggested by Green (1992), changes in the industrial composition and ownership of organisations are also likely to affect the overall nature of the employment relationship.

In 1980, the first full year of the Conservative administration, Millward *et al.* (2000) report that 25 per cent of all Britain's workplaces were engaged in private manufacturing, employing some 38 per cent of the working population. A further 43 per cent of workplaces were engaged in private sector services such as hotel and catering or finance, employing 26 per cent of those in work. From this we can calculate that 68 per cent of workplaces were in the private sector, employing 64 per cent of the working population. During subsequent successive Conservative governments the number of workplaces involved in manufacturing and the number of people they employed both declined. As we can see from Figure 2.2, the decline in manufacturing jobs was particularly marked during the recession of the early 1980s, the proportion of manufacturing workplaces falling to 21 per cent and the proportion employed in manufacturing to 27 per cent by 1984 (Millward *et al.*, 2000). Since this time the

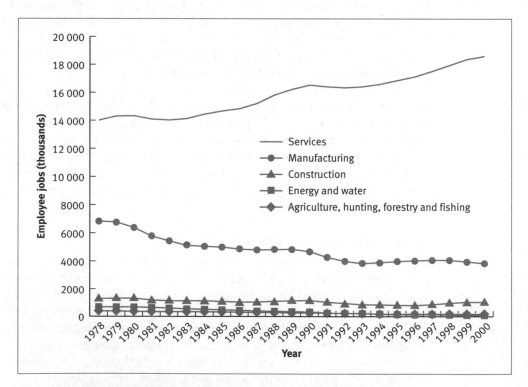

Figure 2.2 **Number of employee jobs by industry in the UK 1978–2000**
Source: Developed from Office for National Statistics (2001)

number of jobs has continued to fall (Figure 2.2), some 18 per cent of workplaces involved in manufacturing employing some 25 per cent of the working population (Millward *et al.*, 2000). Such a decline is by no means unique to Britain, but it is unusual in its composition. Whereas in other EU countries decline in manufacturing employment has often been due to productivity gains – *positive deindustrialisation* – in Britain the decline represents an actual loss of output – *negative deindustrialisation* (Blyton and Turnbull, 1998).

Figure 2.2 also highlights how the number of service sector service jobs was left relatively unscathed in the UK by the recession of the early 1980s. However, subsequent to this the service sector has grown. As we can see from Figure 2.3, this was most rapid in the banking, finance and insurance industries and to a lesser extent in distribution, hotels and restaurants – in other words, the private service sector. The private service sector experienced relatively rapid growth during the second half of the 1980s so that by 1990 it accounted for some 49 per cent of workplaces and 38 per cent of the working population (Millward *et al.*, 2000). This was due, in part, to the Conservative government's privatisation of public utilities such as water, gas and telecommunications. In addition the introduction of compulsory competitive tendering to public sector organisations such as local authorities and health authorities resulted in external and private contractors being used to provide services that would previously have been provided 'in-house'. Not surprisingly, the number of public administration, education and health jobs in the UK showed only limited growth during this period and the 1990s.

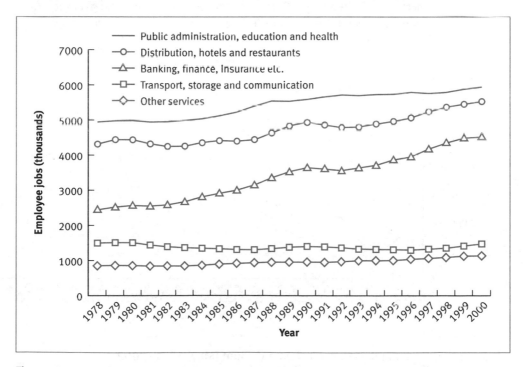

Figure 2.3 **Number of service sector employee jobs in the UK 1978–2000**
Source: Developed from Office for National Statistics (2001)

Although the private services sector, like manufacturing, was affected by the recession of the early 1990s, it has continued to grow in terms both of the proportion of workplaces and of the workforce it encompasses. In the first full year of the New Labour government administration (1998) private sector services accounted for some 54 per cent of workplaces and 44 per cent of all those in employment. In contrast, the public sector accounted for 28 per cent of workplaces and 32 per cent of the working population (Millward *et al.*, 2000). Such growth in the private services sector is not unique to Britain. The private service sector is the only net creator of jobs in most developed countries (Blyton and Turnbull, 1998).

Unemployment

Within the UK, levels of unemployment had traditionally followed the economic cycle, the underlying unemployment trend remaining static at around 2 per cent (Salamon, 2000). However, the late 1970s marked a change in this pattern, levels in subsequent decades being much higher. Precise comparisons over time using government figures of the period are difficult. Alongside numerous definition changes (Fenwick and Denman, 1995) there have been changes in the social environment such as increased participation by women in the labour force and rapid expansion of student numbers in further and higher education. Fortunately, the Office for National Statistics (King, 2000) has reworked these data to produce a time series of the number of claimants that is consistent with current definitions. As we can see from Figure 2.4, using the current definition the number of claimants increased steadily from the mid 1970s subsequent to the oil price rises and associated economic setbacks. By the late 1970s, the ONS calculates that the average number of claimants was just over 1.1 million or 4.3 per cent of the workforce.

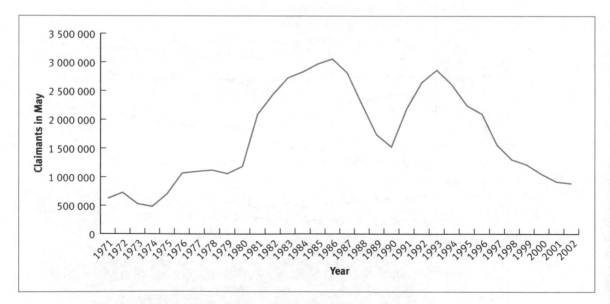

Figure 2.4 UK seasonally adjusted claimant count (May) 1971–2002

Note: All these data are consistent with definitions of claimants as of May 2002
Source: Developed from unpublished data provided by Office for National Statistics (2002b)

By 1986 the number of claimants had risen to over 3 million, representing 11 per cent of the workforce (Office for National Statistics, 2002b). Despite relatively rapid economic growth in the second half of the 1980s, claimants fell only to 1.6 million, before rising again during the recession of the early 1990s. By January 1993 more than 2.9 million people were registered as claimants, over 10 per cent of the workforce (Office for National Statistics, 2002b). Subsequent to 1993 unemployment within the UK has declined, government figures recording an annual average of just under 1 million claimants in 2001 representing 3.4 per cent of the workforce. However, this decline hides considerable changes in the experience of unemployment for the workforce.

In 1995, 52 per cent of all those on Britain's unemployment register who found a job were unemployed again within a year (12 per cent in less than 4 weeks). For these workers employment has become 'a much more precarious affair with insecurity, redundancy, temporary contracts and unemployment contributing to an overall experience of a fragmented, rather than a unified, working life' (Noon and Blyton, 1997: 32–3). Experience of redundancy and unemployment in Britain is now widespread, and the threat of redundancy is ever present. Most workers are no longer protected by trade unions or the certainty of seniority, career hierarchies or the last in, first out (LIFO) principle (Blyton and Turnbull, 1998).

Within the EU as a whole, the incidence of long-term unemployment among workers appears to be similar to that in the UK. For example, in 1999, 53 per cent of those unemployed in the UK had been so for a year or more compared with 57 per cent in the EU as a whole. However, these figures also hide an overall increase in the likelihood of multiple spells of unemployment (European Commission Directorate-General for Economic and Financial Affairs, 2000b). Thus, although unemployment has declined in recent years, the proportion of the workforce who have experienced it has increased. This has a major impact on employees' feelings of job security, an issue that is discussed later in relation to the social environment.

Thus, alongside globalisation of organisations, there has been a restructuring of employment. In particular there has been an increase in the proportion of the workforce employed in the private service sector and a corresponding decrease in employment in private sector manufacturing and the public sector. Within Britain, decline in manufacturing employment has been due to reductions in manufacturing output. However, this is not typical of other EU countries, where decline in manufacturing employment is more likely to have been due to productivity gains. In contrast, growth in employment has occurred in areas that traditionally have been less regulated by governments and less organised by trade unions. Over the same period perceived job security has declined, the number of the workforce who have experienced unemployment and/or redundancy growing.

■ The technological environment

Since the 1970s, the impact of new technologies upon the wider context within which work takes place has been considerable and continues to grow at an ever increasing rate. Indeed, we sometimes forget that the first personal computers (PCs) became available only in the mid 1970s when companies like Apple, Tandy and Commodore introduced low-cost, typewriter-sized computers (Beekman, 1994).

Initially, in the late 1970s and 1980s, the focus was upon using microelectronics to automate routine tasks previously undertaken by people in both manufacturing and office work. However, in the 1990s, automation was supplemented by systems that spread work over time and geographically, using distributed communication technology (Greenbaum, 1998). Control and coordinating functions were also supported more fully through the availability of better information, particularly at the level of sending, storing and receiving messages, documents and files.

Evidence of the growth in use of technology in Britain, and in particular the use of automation in manufacturing and computerisation of office tasks, is provided by Workplace Employee Relations Surveys' data (Millward *et al.*, 2000). In 1984 under half (44 per cent) of manufacturing establishments surveyed were using microelectronics in applications such as machine control and automated handling and storage. By 1998 the proportion (of those workplaces that had also been surveyed in 1990) using microelectronics was 87 per cent, use among larger manufacturing companies being almost universal. The impact of this was highlighted during a recent consultancy project we undertook for a UK chemicals manufacturer. As part of this project we visited one of the manufacturing facilities and were amazed by the extent to which production was computer controlled. Less than 20 per cent of employees were working directly in the manufacturing process, the majority being in maintenance and support roles.

Growth in the use of micro technology for office-based tasks has been even more significant. In 1984, only a quarter (25 per cent) of workplaces surveyed had word processors on site. By 1990 over three-fifths (62 per cent) of workplaces had word processors, small workplaces being less likely to have them than large; when these workplaces were interviewed again in 1998, some 90 per cent had this technology. These figures Millward *et al.* (2000) believe approximate to a crude but reasonable estimate of the extent of use of new technologies in British workplaces.

The pace of adoption of such technical change has, to a certain extent, been slowed by the need to fit the design of the technology to the work being carried out (Greenbaum, 1998). More recent changes have facilitated the embedding of control and coordination into computer software and network technology. For checkout operators using electronic point of sale (EPOS) equipment, clerical operators working at computers or customer services personnel working in call centres, new technology has supported greater centralised monitoring of timekeeping and performance (Blyton and Turnbull, 1998). For example, the amount of time that call centre operatives take to answer each telephone call and deal with the customer is recorded, providing supervisors with information to monitor and control performance (Warhurst and Thompson, 1998). However, for other jobs the use of new technology has allowed the transfer of process control from supervisors to work groups. Here employees undertake tasks that would previously have been done by their supervisors, such as ordering materials in a just-in-time production process.

Technology has also had an impact on the context and nature of work for managers. For example, the Institute of Management survey of British managers in 1999 (Worrall and Cooper, 1999) found that 1 in 20 managers 'hot desked', using a desk, telephone and computer connections as and when required rather than having their own, personal workspace at the office. Eighty-two per cent of managers in the same survey ranked the PC as the most essential tool to their job, followed by email

(72 per cent) and the mobile telephone (53 per cent). As for those in more junior jobs, new technologies had changed the nature of their work. Former discrete tasks such as drafting and then typing a letter had been combined into a single job, undermining traditional job boundaries.

At the same time telecommunications technology has offered organisations increased freedom to locate work anywhere. Within the UK, call centres have been located in areas of relatively high unemployment and where the regional accent has been shown by research to be pleasing to customers (Richardson and Marshall, 1996). Global availability of computer applications such as Microsoft's Office XP combined with almost instantaneous data transfer mean that data manipulation tasks can be dispersed geographically and subsequently recombined and managed through information accumulated in the software systems. Fax, voice mail, email and Internet standards mean that labour can be supported by the same technology and take on characteristics such as those found in Europe and the USA throughout the world (Greenbaum, 1998). Your telephone request for support from your Internet provider may be dealt with by a person in Ireland or, in the future, in Bangalore rather than the UK. Relocation elsewhere in the world has become closer to being feasible for some tasks, although not yet quite at the level of the 'flip of an electronic switch' hypothesised by Greenbaum (1998: 129). It can be argued that the associated uncertainty caused by this relative ease of transfer of work has a negative effect on job security and perhaps on wage increases.

Thus the actual effects of new technologies on the nature of work and jobs have varied considerably between work contexts (Blyton and Turnbull, 1998). New jobs have been created and other existing jobs have disappeared or have been amalgamated. Use of new technologies has enabled greater autonomy for some knowledge workers such as university lecturers. Such people had usually already exercised some autonomy prior to the use of technology. For other workers, such as call centre operatives, technology has enabled greater control (Kinnie *et al.*, 2000). It has also resulted in changes in workers' skills. Greenbaum (1998) argues that although workers using new technology would probably be considered to have upskilled jobs, their wages and working conditions would not reflect this enhancement. Rather, new technology has resulted in new jobs that have both gained and lost skill elements, the gains not always outweighing the losses.

self-check question	2.1 Think back to your last visit to a supermarket. In what ways does micro technology affect the environment within which work is taking place?

◼ The social environment

The development of the welfare state within the UK after the Second World War embodied the beliefs that the strong in society should support the weak, and that the state should take responsibility both for provision of education, health and other social services and for ensuring equality of access. Building upon these ideals, the 1960s saw a challenge to previously accepted values, attitudes and institutions such as the involvement of women in the workforce. In particular, developments in education, in conjunction with economic prosperity, full employment and the creation of a consumer market through advertising, resulted in a workforce with increased expectations in both reward and participation in decisions. The decline in economic prosperity and accompanying high unemployment in the late 1970s coupled with government policies in the 1980s and 1990s negated many of these developments. The consistently higher levels of unemployment and reductions in public expenditure on benefits and social services meant that there was less available for the 'weak' when their demands were increasing. This heightened the differentials between those that had relatively secure, well-paid work and those who were either unemployed or in temporary or part-time, low-paid work. At the same time traditional assumptions associated with the Protestant work ethic were being undermined as secure, adequately paid employment was no longer readily available. Rather, working life was and is now increasingly characterised by:

- a series of jobs interspersed with periods of unemployment;
- the probability that some of these jobs will be either temporary contracts and/or part time (Salamon, 2000).

Of particular importance within these social changes has been the increase in female participation, especially within part-time work. UK labour force survey data illustrated in Figure 2.5 highlight the increase in female participation and in particular a narrowing gender gap. Projections indicate a further narrowing of this gap between males and females (Office for National Statistics, 2002a). Such employment has been predominantly in the service sector and part time (Blyton and Turnbull, 1998). Related to this are changing social attitudes. A survey in the early 1990s (Liff, 1995) highlighted the fact that nearly two-thirds of the British population felt that women

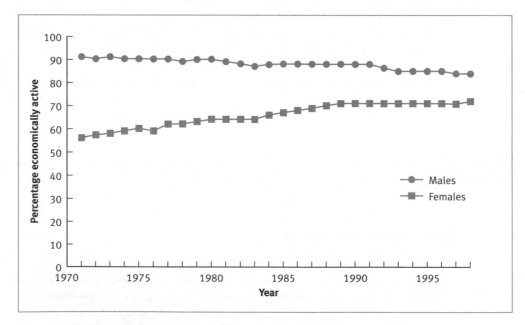

Figure 2.5 UK economic activity rates by gender 1971–98

Source: Developed from Office for National Statistics (2002a)

should work part time while their children were at school. However, although women's presence is greater than ever before, their relative standing is lower, with under-representation in managerial positions still existing (Millward *et al.*, 2000). A most significant part of this change has been the increase in dual-earner households. In most of these the man's career has taken precedence, the woman playing a supportive role and adding paid employment to her household work. However, non-traditional dual-career households, in which the woman's career is considered equally important or takes precedence, are increasing in frequency (Hakim, 1996).

Participation in further and higher education increased rapidly in the 1990s, approximately one-third of all school leavers now attending a higher education institution. At undergraduate degree level, growth has been particularly rapid in subjects such as business and administration studies and information technology, the former accounting for 35 700 or 11 per cent of all applicants accepted for undergraduate degree courses starting in 2001 (UCAS, 2002). Although participation has resulted in a better-educated workforce, it has also removed a substantial proportion of young people from the labour market. In contrast to the increasing participation in education, investment in formal training and vocational qualifications within the UK has been relatively limited. Sixty-four per cent of the UK workforce have no vocational qualifications compared with 26 per cent in Germany (Blyton and Turnbull, 1998).

In an *ad hoc* Europe-wide survey of employees conducted by the EU in 1999 (European Commission Directorate-General for Economic and Financial Affairs, 2000b) some 33 per cent of UK employees' present jobs were classified as 'unskilled', the equal highest proportion (with Spain). The overall proportion of unskilled jobs for the EU as a whole was 21 per cent. An *ad hoc* survey of industry employers conducted by the EU (European Commission Directorate-General for Economic and Financial Affairs, 2000a) also revealed above EU average (28 per cent) proportions of unskilled employees for the UK (39 per cent). However, in this survey, Danish, Irish and Spanish employers reported above UK proportions of unskilled employees. The same survey highlighted the fact that, throughout the EU, employers expected their need for unskilled workers to decline in the future.

Despite this, the figures for the proportion of those employed in the UK who had received training were all below that for the EU as a whole. In particular, only 45 per cent of UK employees had received training in the past 2 years compared with 60 per cent of employees EU-wide (European Commission Directorate-General for Economic and Financial Affairs, 2000b). The Institute of Management surveys of British managers (Worrall and Cooper, 1999) suggest that the receipt of training is dependent upon level within the organisation. These surveys show that the percentage of managers receiving formal training in the past 12 months is increasing, 82 per cent of all managers receiving at least some formal training in 1999. This proportion is highest for public sector organisations (92 per cent) and lowest for family-owned businesses (74 per cent).

Notwithstanding the Working Time Directive (IDS, 1999), there are fewer constraints on employers' freedom to manage working time in the UK than in the rest of the EU. Moreover, the legal framework was made more permissive in the late 1980s under the Conservative government. According to EU surveys of employees the average weekly contracted working hours in the EU per week were the same in both 1994 and 1999 – 35 hours. This is very similar to the figure recorded by both surveys for the UK, 34 hours (European Commission Directorate-General for Economic and Financial Affairs, 2000b). However, UK responses to the question 'How many hours per week do you work at present?' reveal a marked contrast to the EU average. In 1999 some 36 per cent of respondents in the UK worked 34 hours or less per week compared with 25 per cent of all EU respondents. Conversely similar proportions of respondents in the UK (30 per cent) and the EU as a whole (27 per cent) worked 41 or more hours per week, suggesting a far greater use of part-time workers in the UK than in the EU in general (European Commission Directorate-General for Economic and Financial Affairs, 2000b). Within the EU, part-time workers in manufacturing account for only 5 per cent of employees compared to 15 per cent in the service sector. However, there are significant between-country variations. Within the UK the proportion of part-time jobs in manufacturing doubled between 1994 and 1999 and is now 'three times above the community level' (European Commission Directorate-General for Economic and Financial Affairs, 2000a: 2). Evidence from the UK supports this, highlighting the relatively rapid rate of increase when compared with full-time permanent employment. Figures from the 1998 Workplace Employee Relations Survey show that part-time workers now account for a quarter of all jobs in workplaces of 25 or more employees. In addition, part-timers formed the majority of the workforce in 26 per cent of workplaces surveyed (Cully *et al.*, 1999). These part-time workers are predominantly female.

Institute of Management surveys of British managers over the period 1997–99 (Worrall and Cooper, 1999) suggest that these aggregate figures on working time disguise wide variations in hours worked. These surveys suggest that, although a declining percentage of British managers are often or always working in the evenings (49 per cent) or at weekends (32 per cent), some 75 per cent are working over their contracted hours. These proportions vary directly with seniority, fewer junior than senior managers claiming to often or always work in excess of their contract hours. Linked to this finding, 66 per cent of British managers felt that the number of hours they were working was having an adverse effect on their health, 68 per cent thought it was adversely affecting their productivity, and over 79 per cent felt it was having an adverse impact on their partners and children (Worrall and Cooper, 1999). Not surprisingly, perhaps, over half (52 per cent) of those responding to the 1999 Institute of Management survey of British managers (Worrall and Cooper, 1999) felt that their organisation did little to help them balance their home and work commitments. This, combined with the earlier evidence, suggests that many managers did not feel positive about their employment relationships.

2.3 Changes in the organisation of work

Our discussion of the wider environment within which work occurs has served to highlight a broad range of changes. As we have already alluded, these have had an effect on the organisation of work, with consequent implications for the employment relationship. Gallie *et al.* (1998) in their book *Restructuring the Employment Relationship* highlight four key areas where changes have occurred in the organisation of work. These, they believe, are central to employees' experiences of the employment relationship. Gallie *et al.* (1998: 25) refer to these areas as *structural factors*, namely:

- the characteristics of the work task;
- the way in which performance is controlled;
- the participation of employees in wider organisational decision-making;
- job security and the polarisation of the workforce into core and a periphery.

Overarching the realities of employees' experiences represented by these four structural factors is a considerable body of academic theory and debate arising from Atkinson's (1984, 1985) work on the flexible firm. This theory is based principally at the organisational level. It is concerned with the way organisations use labour and, in particular, issues associated with job-based flexibility. Within this section, we consider first the theory and debate associated with the flexible firm and job-based flexibility. Then we consider the structural realities of such flexibilities for the employment relationship, basing our discussion around each of Gallie *et al.*'s (1998) four factors in turn.

■ The theory of the flexible firm and job-based flexibility

Research by Atkinson in the 1980s raised the profile of issues associated with organisational labour flexibility. These were captured in his model of the flexible firm (Figure 2.6), in which he split employees into those who are core to the organisation and those who are peripheral. This division is based upon the nature of employees' skills, the relative need by the organisation for these skills, and the availability of such skills in the labour market. By reducing or increasing its peripheral workforce, it is argued, an organisation can adjust to changes in demand. Whereas this means the organisation can offer a high degree of security to its core workforce, the converse is true for the peripheral workers, who will have little or no job security. Similar models have been proposed subsequently, although none has generated as much debate (Taylor, 1998). Worthy of mention, however, is Handy's (1990) development of Atkinson's ideas. In this, Handy argues that, in the future, jobs for those who are core to the organisation will decline rapidly, with the result that many skilled people will have to be employed as peripheral workers. These people, Handy (1990: 146) argues, are likely often to combine part-time work for a range of organisations into the equivalent of a full-time job, operating a *work portfolio*.

Within the model of the flexible firm, Atkinson identifies four types of job-based flexibility that organisations might seek from their labour force. These are functional, numerical, financial and distancing flexibility. The first of these, *functional flexibility*, offers the flexibility to redeploy employees quickly to match tasks required. This, he argues, is achieved through the use of workers core to the organisation and through employing workers from external groups such as subcontractors. Core workers have secure employment with the organisation and are likely to have been trained by the organisation to have a variety of specific skills and experience that cannot be bought in easily. In contrast, workers employed or subcontracted from external groups have specialist skills that are not specific to the organisation and can be bought in as and when required, the organisation deciding the functions they require at the time. The use of such workers is increasingly common in shortage occupations such as information and communications technology workers. Writers about such occupations comment on a 'steady haemorrhaging of permanent employees into the IT contract market' (Harvey and Kanwal, 2000: 104). In times of economic growth, contracting opportunities

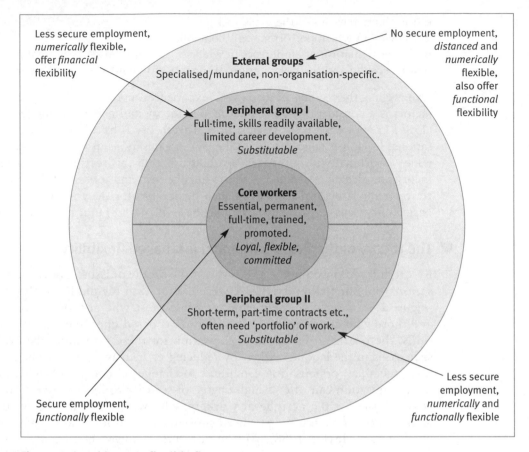

Figure 2.6 **Atkinson's flexible firm**
Source: Developed from Atkinson (1984, 1985)

exceed the supply, resulting in high labour turnover and skills shortages. In periods of recession, cuts in IT budgets and projects put 'on hold' mean redundancies pushing people into the peripheral labour force.

Atkinson uses the term *numerical flexibility* to refer to an employer's ability to change the number of hours worked by employees in line with fluctuations in organisational demand for their labour. This, he argues, is achieved through the use of two distinct groups of peripheral employees as well as external groups. The first group of peripheral employees (Peripheral group I, Figure 2.6), are those employed on a full-time basis by the organisation, such as production-line workers. Although such workers are full time, they have less security than core employees as their jobs either are de-skilled or do not require organisation-specific skills. In addition, high turnover in this group facilitates numerical adjustments. The second group of peripheral workers (Peripheral group II, Figure 2.6) consists of employees on temporary and part-time rather than full-time contracts. These include students working part time while studying for their degrees, the nature of their contract facilitating numerical flexibility for the employer. External groups, such as subcontractors' own employees, provide a third group of workers who can be used when required by the organisation for specific pieces of work, thereby providing numerical flexibility, as well as the functional flexibility referred to earlier.

Financial flexibility, commonly termed 'pay flexibility' (Atkinson and Meager, 1986) is used by Atkinson to refer to the way in which organisations allow pay to reflect differences in supply and demand for different groups in the labour market. This, he argues, can also be used to support functional and numerical flexibility. Peripheral group I workers' financial reward can, although they are full time, be more easily adjusted to reflect the organisation's need for labour. In contrast, the short-term and part-time contracts for Peripheral group II employees provide numerical (discussed earlier) and financial flexibility through both the amount these workers are paid and whether or not they are contracted.

Atkinson's fourth type of flexibility, *distancing flexibility*, occurs when subcontractors are used to replace employees, thereby distancing the worker from the organisation. In effect contracts *for* a service replace contracts *of* employment, thereby enhancing numerical flexibility. Within this subcontracting process the organisation decides the functions it requires from subcontractors and how much it is willing to pay at the time. In many organisations subcontractors are used to provide both specialist services such as fire alarm testing and regular services such as office cleaning. Through doing this the organisation uses the specialist skills of its subcontractors' employees to gain numerical and in some cases financial and functional flexibility. Such flexibility can also be used as a recruitment and selection tool, allowing the employer to 'try out' people prior to offering them a permanent contract.

Since its publication, Atkinson's model has been the subject of a range of criticisms and debate (Pollert, 1991; Millward *et al.*, 2000). These can be placed in two distinct groups: first, the purpose of the model and, in particular, whether it is a tool for analysing changes or a model of what is actually happening; second, the difficulties in defining core and periphery within real-life organisations. The research evidence on which these criticisms are based suggests that, although organisations have become more flexible in the way they use workers, their disaggregation of the workforce does not conform very closely to Atkinson's model (Sparrow and Marchington, 1998). In reality, there appears to be very little specific use of core–periphery strategies *per se*. Organisations appear to have precise but differing flexibility requirements for different jobs, which they address on a job-by-job ad hoc basis. In addition they appear to be using different forms of job flexibility, both separately and in combination, as part of a deliberate wider HR strategy (Mayne *et al.*, 1996).

Building upon Atkinson's ideas (outlined earlier), Sparrow and Marchington (1998) identify seven discrete but parallel flexibilities around which organisations may structure employment relationships. Although there are obvious parallels between these and Atkinson's job-based flexibilities, these discrete flexibilities offer more precision and enable us to understand more clearly how flexibilities can be related to individual posts (Table 2.1). Each can be considered a discrete area of flexibility that an organisation can pursue within a post. However, when examining this table we need to be mindful of the mutually supportive nature of these flexibilities. For example, financial flexibility can be used to encourage functional flexibility by rewarding workers according to the range of skills they possess. Sparrow and Marchington (1998: 18) argue that each flexibility tends to be 'associated with a different "battle" or struggle between interested parties' within the employment

Table 2.1 Discrete flexibilities and associated 'battles'

Discrete flexibility	Nature of the 'battle'	Equivalent Atkinson's flexibility
Functional (varying the tasks workers undertake)	**The roles and competences that are deemed appropriate for the job**: for example, the need for a multiskilled individual, new core competences, or cross-business process skills; alternatively, the need to work across existing demarcation lines	Functional
Numerical (varying numbers)	**Ownership of the employment relationship**: for example, the need for a job to be within the core internal labour market rather than being outsourced or performed by the peripheral labour market	Numerical
Temporal/working time (varying number and timing of hours worked)	**Employee presence on the job**: in particular, the need for a continual employee presence to enable the job to be fulfilled, as opposed to using flexitime, nil hours overtime and the like	
Financial (varying pay and reward)	**Reward–effort bargain between employer and worker**: for example, the best balance between the reward and delivery of performance, and the use of benefits other than pay	Financial/pay
Cognitive (varying the form of psychological contract)	**The mental frame of reference and level of cognitive skills required to perform the job effectively**: in particular, the mental and cultural frames of reference required and the nature of the psychological contract	Distancing
Organisational (varying the form of the organisation)	**The form and rationale for the organisation in which the job fits**: for example, the appropriateness of a joint venture or temporary alliance or 'adhocracy'	
Geographical/locational (moving people/varying workplace)	**Ideal location for the job and its constituent tasks**: in particular, the latitude available for changing locations, using homeworking or virtual teams	None

Source: Developed from Sparrow and Marchington (1998); Atkinson (1984, 1985)

relationship. The nature of the 'battle' for each flexibility can be expressed as a series of aspects of the employment relationship over which agreement needs to be reached between employers, employees and their representatives (Table 2.1).

The use of the seven discrete flexibilities (Table 2.1), either individually or in combination, to provide labour flexibility has advantages and disadvantages for both organisations and workers. We have summarised these in Table 2.2. Even a cursory examination of this table suggests that there are more benefits for the organisation than for workers. It is therefore not surprising that much of the literature on labour

Table 2.2 **Advantages and disadvantages of labour flexibility**

	Advantages	*Disadvantages*
For organisations	■ Can match work provisions more closely with customer/product demand ■ Reduces fixed costs (e.g. home workers need less office space) ■ Can aid recruitment and retention ■ Increases productivity (shorter hours mean people less likely to be tired/stressed) ■ Reduces absence and turnover	■ Increased training costs ■ Higher direct costs (e.g. part-timers) ■ Management of the 'flexible' workforce ■ Communication difficulties ■ More complex administration
For workers	■ Can combine work more easily with other non-work interests ■ Greater job satisfaction ■ Improved motivation ■ Less tiredness	■ Unequal treatment in terms of pay and benefits (but less so owing to European Union legislation) ■ Reduced career development opportunities ■ Limited training opportunities ■ 'Psychological contract' is threatened ■ Increased job insecurity ■ Increased stress

Source: Developed from Emmott and Hutchinson (1998)

flexibility argues that it is overall of greater benefit to organisations. Research by Creagh and Brewster (1998) has identified examples of good practice in flexible working, such as the creative use of job shares and part-time work to permit a better balance between professional and family life. However, Legge (1998) implies that such good practice is not widespread, highlighting some of the dilemmas associated with flexible working.

Part-time work, as outlined in the previous section, tends to be clustered towards lower-paid jobs with less responsibility. Legge (1998) argues that, if an individual accepts part-time work because full-time work is impracticable, then they are unlikely to be a free agent or powerful bargainer in the labour market. Consequently, the reward for part-time work within a particular organisation may be influenced by this power relationship and in particular the need to reduce labour costs.

With regard to temporary, fixed-term and agency-type contracts Legge (1998) argues that, although these offer employers benefits, they do little for employees. From an employer's perspective, such contracts offer the only practical option where funding is dependent upon fixed-term grants or is uncertain, if the employer is to avoid unnecessary redundancy costs. Second, they allow the employer to reduce headcount formally; and, third, they can be used to reduce direct employment costs directly, by using agency-employed staff at cheaper rates than directly employed equivalents. For workers, Legge (1998) argues that the benefits of such contracts are few. Alongside job insecurity there are costs of unemployment if there is discontinuity between contracts or securing another job. Such jobs generally have fewer associated benefits such as leave or training. Although it has been argued that this is purely a function of the economic marketplace within which employers and workers find themselves, you may wish to reflect on the comment of one employment agency director, who stated: 'There is a close relationship between E and F in the alphabet. E is for exploitation and F is for flexibility' (Purcell and Purcell, 1996; cited in Legge, 1998: 291).

self-check question	**2.2** Many organisations expect employees to work regularly beyond their contract. What are the relative benefits of this expectation for employee and organisation?

■ The characteristics of the work task

Three main, and apparently conflicting, theses have been advanced with regard to the changing characteristics of the work task (Gallie *et al.*, 1998). The first of these argues that there has been a long-term trend of rising skill levels as societies become more industrialised. Associated with this is a decentralisation of decision-making as employees gain more control and discretion, and work experience improves. The second puts the contrary view that there has been a long-term trend of erosion of skill levels, with concomitant degradation of work experience as employees lose control. Finally, it has been suggested that experiences of the work task and associated skill changes differ substantially between different segments of the labour market, leading to a polarisation of employment experiences. This concern with the skill content of work is based upon the premise that there is a direct relationship between skill levels and the quality of working life and, in particular, between the level of discretion that employees can exercise in their work and the intrinsic quality of that work.

Gallie *et al.* (1998) argue from their own survey data that the qualifications required for jobs increased over the 1986–92 period, as did the period needed to gain the skills required for effective job performance. This they found was especially the case for semi- and unskilled manual workers. Even those workers who did not change jobs found that more skills were demanded. The dominant trend was therefore towards an increase of skills, although this appeared to be due mainly to requirements for new skills brought about by restructuring of work tasks. Alongside this there was a marked decentralisation of decision-making. Sixty-five per cent of respondents believed they had experienced an increase in responsibility, whereas only 8 per cent felt it had decreased. Again, the most marked changes were for semi- and non-skilled manual work and for lower non-manual jobs. Despite this, Ritzer (1998) argues as part of his McDonaldisation thesis that for many of these employees these changes still mean that work is characterised by a production line logic. Such employees are supposed to memorise scripts so that they follow not only corporate rules in what they do but also in what they say. At the same time, although task discretion may have increased most for skilled manual workers, it has declined for everyday decisions made by professional workers (Gallie *et al.*, 1998) such as bank managers. In these cases human decision-making, such as granting a loan, has often been replaced by computer-based expert systems.

Some 82 per cent of those surveyed by Gallie *et al.* (1998) who felt their skills had increased also felt responsibility had increased. In addition, there was a strong relationship between skill increase and variety in the job. They found that increases in skills had 'a consistent and powerful effect in improving job quality within each occupational class' (Gallie *et al.*, 1988: 40). However, this also led to a marked increase in the pressures associated with work. Thus although these findings support the optimistic hypothesis outlined earlier, there is also evidence to support the more pessimistic analysis of a degradation of the work experience due to the sharp intensification of work pressures.

The way in which performance is controlled

Supervision remains the dominant form of control, most employees being conscious of its influence on their performance (Gallie *et al.*, 1998). However, although the importance of control of work effort has been growing overall, this hides a number of different patterns. Managers and professional workers have experienced a loosening of direct supervision whereas manual workers have experienced a tightening. Technical control, where people are constrained by the system of pacing work and incentives based on work pace, has increasingly been used for manual workers. In contrast, bureaucratic controls, such as performance management systems and progression, have been used more frequently for non-manual and especially professional workers, replacing, at least in part, direct supervision.

Thus both task discretion and control within the workplace have increased. The use of technical control such as machine-based pacing and monitoring has not been linked to task discretion. Rather, the higher the level of control through administrative procedures, the greater the amount of task discretion given to employees (Gallie *et al.*, 1998). Not surprisingly, therefore, employers have been more likely to apply technical control to manual workers such as those on production lines, especially where tasks are undertaken with the aid of computers. Conversely, employers have been more likely to apply bureaucratic control through prescribed administrative procedures to non-manual workers, especially those higher in the organisational hierarchy. Once again, Gallie *et al.* (1998) found that this is more likely where work is undertaken with the aid of computers.

Participation of employees in wider organisational decision-making

The main modes of employee participation and changes in its nature are discussed in more detail in Chapters 7 and 8. However, it is useful to explore briefly the main changes and their implications for the organisation of work. The two most widespread forms of participation are *direct participation* and *trade union representation*. Direct participation, where employees are involved personally in decisions that go beyond their immediate work task, affects approximately a third of the workforce. There is some evidence that this has declined since the mid-1980s (Gallie *et al.*, 1998). Trade union membership has also declined over the period (Millward *et al.*, 2000). The net result of this is that the capacity of employees to affect their employment conditions appears to have diminished over time. However, improved organisational communication means that they may have become better informed about organisational activities. In contrast to these trends, Gallie *et al.* (1998) found that, where employees had opportunities for direct participation, they were more favourably disposed to technical and organisational change.

■ Job security and the polarisation of the workforce into core and periphery

Job security

As outlined in Section 2.2, the proportion of the labour force at risk from a spell of unemployment has been rising. For males, this increase in job insecurity is considerable. However, for females, the pattern is more stable, although still increasing (Millward *et al.*, 2000). Gallie *et al.* (1998) argue that this is due to their likely employment in part-time work. Overall, the risk of people finding themselves unemployed is determined by the demand for their skills in the labour market and the nature of the particular sectors in which they are employed. Manual occupations have a much higher risk of becoming unemployed, and, although there was limited change in the relative vulnerability of manual and non-manual employees up to 1992, the relative proportion of people in non-manual jobs has increased. Consequently, the number of non-manual workers who are unemployed has increased. Subsequent to a period of unemployment, further unemployment is more likely than before. Those who are unemployed are generally only able to obtain jobs that are insecure and offer little prospect for personal advancement or development.

It may be thought that declining job security is simply a feature of the twenty-first century, which is not important as people have come to accept a lack of security as normal. However, this decline is contrary to what most people want from their jobs. For over 75 per cent of people being in a secure job has been consistently ranked as either important or very important, whatever their age (Ladipo, 2000). There is therefore an apparent conflict between the value placed on security by employees and what is happening to the employment relationship.

---

self-check question

2.3 Imagine you are advising a young person who is looking for her or his first job. Which one of the following features would you say is the most important, and which next? Give reasons for your choices.

- good conditions;
- good starting pay;
- interesting work;
- promotion opportunities;
- secure job.

The flexible workforce

Rapid expansion of a flexible workforce is a central theme in the literature on the changing structure of employment, and was a desired outcome of legislative changes in the 1980s and 1990s. Data from the 1998 Workplace Employee Relations Survey (Cully *et al.*, 1999) suggest that only a quarter of UK organisations use a functionally flexible core of trained employees, adaptable in the tasks they can undertake. Rather, organisations use non-standard employment contracts to gain flexibility (Millward *et al.*, 2000). Gallie *et al.* (1998) argue that within Britain two groups constitute the growing flexible labour force: part-time workers and workers employed on direct short or fixed-term contracts. In addition there are those in temporary employment by agencies, those undertaking freelance work, and home and outworkers (Millward et al., 2000). In addition, flexibility is provided by permanent employees of other firms subcontracted to undertake work for the organisation. Although the number of part-time workers has grown since 1980 (Millward et al., 2000), the use of temporary workers was relatively stable in the 1980s (Gallie et al., 1998). During the 1990s this has grown by 31 per cent (Emmott and Hutchinson, 1998), in particular with regard to employees on short, fixed-term contracts and the use of temporary workers from agencies (Millward et al., 2000).

A key assumption of the flexibility literature we reviewed earlier has been that part-time and temporary workers fulfil similar functions for employers in terms of flexibility (Atkinson, 1984, 1985). However, research by Gallie et al. (1998) suggests that this is not the case. Part-time workers are predominantly female and employed principally in service industries such as retail and finance, and public services such as education, medical services and welfare (Millward et al., 2000). They tend to occupy jobs of relatively low skill content and are less likely to have received recent training to increase their skills. Despite this, Gallie et al. (1998) found that the trend was for the skills gap between part-time and full-time workers to be diminishing, although part-time workers were still at a severe disadvantage. The level of discretion that part-timers could exercise in their work diminished over the period 1984–92, and they were less likely to be offered opportunities for self-improvement. Part-time workers are less well paid even after taking into account the low skill levels of such jobs, and they have fewer fringe benefits and a far more pessimistic view of career opportunities. In addition they are less likely to belong to a trade union (Millward et al., 2000).

Evidence from Gallie et al.'s (1998) survey suggests that part-time workers are in relatively stable organisational environments, with few pressures upon them for greater flexibility in patterns of working (temporal flexibility). Performance rewards for part-timers are significantly less likely (pay flexibility), these workers being far more likely to be covered by pay systems that make no attempt to relate pay to individual performance. In addition, part-timers tend to work relatively rigid hours when compared with full-timers, suggesting limited temporal flexibility for employers. Job security of part-time workers is dependent upon the number of hours worked. Consequently, those working under the minimum hours for statutory formal protection often have none (IDS, 1999). Gallie et al. (1998) suggest that, despite this lack of formal protection, the great bulk of the part-time workforce experiences relatively high job security. The picture of part-time workers therefore does not correspond to theories of a peripheral labour force particularly well in relation to offering high levels of numerical and functional flexibility. Although part-time employees appeared to be aware that they were less protected in the legal sense, in practice Gallie et al. (1998) found that they were more likely to feel that their current jobs were more secure than those of full-timers. Work history data supported this observation for women, part-time work for this group being no more likely to lead to unemployment than full-time work.

Temporary workers were defined by Gallie et al. (1998) as those who believed their job was considered by their employer to be temporary, either short term (less than 12 months) or for contract workers between one and three years. These people tended to be employed in leisure and personal services, health and (particularly) education, construction and energy/water. Those workers on short, fixed-term contracts were found to have very similar skill levels to the permanent workforce when looking at the distribution by class of employment. By contrast, short-term temporary workers, often from employment agencies, were less skilled and far less likely to have received training. Despite this, the training gap between short-term temporary workers and permanent employees had diminished significantly since the mid-1980s (Gallie *et al.*, 1998). Short-term temporary workers experienced significantly lower work pressure and were provided with much lower levels of work interest. For longer-term contract workers work pressures were the same as for the permanent workforce.

Freelance workers, home workers and outworkers were not included in Gallie *et al.*'s survey. However, research by Millward *et al.* (2000) suggests that the incidence of the use of freelance workers, although relatively low, is increasing. In contrast the use of home workers and outworkers is low and appears to have changed little.

A sizeable proportion of more highly skilled contract workers in Gallie *et al.*'s (1998) survey saw their jobs as offering reasonable opportunities for upward mobility, whereas short-term temporary workers saw themselves as trapped in current positions. Both types of temporary work contributed to a strong sense of job insecurity. However, there was no sign of increasing polarisation between the permanent and the peripheral workforce. If anything, the short-term temporary workers were beginning to have a better view of their prospects, whereas the permanent workforce felt less secure. Short-term temporary workers experienced a strong sense of entrapment, whereas contract workers perceived their current contract would provide a bridge to better work.

The 1998 Workplace Employee Relations Survey (Cully *et al.*, 1999) also indicates other ways in which organisations are organising labour to provide numerical flexibility. Around 90 per cent of workplaces were found to contract out at least one service to an external provider. On average, four services were contracted out, the most common being building maintenance (61 per cent), cleaning (59 per cent), transport of documents or goods (39 per cent), and training (38 per cent). In over a third of workplaces this work would have been undertaken directly by the organisation's employees five years previously.

self-check question	**2.4** How do part-time workers differ from temporary workers in terms of the flexibility they offer organisations? What are the reasons for this?

2.4 The nature of the employment relationship

As we have highlighted in the previous sections of this chapter, organisations in the Western world have faced intensified competition, increased market volatility and uncertainty, and an increasing pace of technological change. Within the UK this has been accompanied by government attempts to increase labour market flexibility. Consequently, organisations have become more lean (Kinnie *et al.*, 1998), changing the nature of the employment relationship and employing fewer people on traditional or standard contracts. Europe-wide surveys such as the EAPM (Mayne *et al.*, 1996) and the Cranet-E (Friedrich and Kabst, 1998) suggest that, throughout Europe, organisations are becoming more flexible in their use of labour. Evidence from the UK's 1998 Workplace Employee Relations Survey (Cully *et al.*, 1999) indicates that the majority of workplaces have employed labour on fixed-term contracts or temporary workers within the last five years. These organisations are, in effect, achieving numerical flexibility by adjusting the size of their workforce in line with demand. In contrast, functional flexibility is less widespread (Cully *et al.*, 1999).

These changes have had far-reaching impacts upon the ways in which employees view the employment relationship. Employees are now less likely to be represented collectively by a trade union. They now work in a permanent state of change and are likely to experience periods of both employment and unemployment. Employment stability – the length of time an average employee stays with a given employer – has declined (Sparrow, 2000), suggesting a change in the psychological contract. Whereas workers had previously tended to stay with the same employer throughout their careers, perhaps changing occupations, they are now more likely to change employer and stay in the same occupation. Consequently, for people at the start of their careers such as graduates, loyalty is more likely to be to their occupation than to their employer. For older employees who have stayed with the same employer, downsizing and delayering have altered the way in which the employment relationship is viewed. Perceived job insecurity has increased: in particular, employees who have experienced job loss believe all subsequent job opportunities are less secure (Sparrow, 2000). This sense of job insecurity has both heightened employees' need for employability within the wider labour market and reduced their levels of trust of employers. Two main themes are associated with these changes to the employment relationship: the changing nature of the psychological contract between employer and employee, and the employee's employability in the wider marketplace. It is to these that we now turn.

The psychological contract

As highlighted in Section 2.3, employees are feeling less secure in their employment relationships with employers. In particular, the feeling of security engendered by the perception of a job for life is being replaced by a feeling of perceived impermanence. Not only do employees feel insecure about continued employment in a particular job with a particular employer or a different job with the same employer; they are also less secure about employment in general. The first two of these are likely to be reflected in the psychological contract between employer and employee. This is a concept we deal with in more detail in Chapter 1.

Employability

There is no one definition of employability, but a review by Hillage and Pollard (1999) suggests that, for the individual, employability has three key strands:

- the ability to 'gain' initial employment, and hence the need to ensure that skills, careers advice and an understanding of the world of work are embedded in the education system;
- the ability to 'maintain' employment and move between jobs and roles within the same organisation, and hence the need to be able to meet new job requirements;
- the ability to 'obtain' new employment by moving between organisations and being independent in the labour market.

In addition, they argue that employability is also about the quality of such work in relation to people's skill levels and personal desires.

From these strands it is apparent that the skills an individual possesses are likely to be key in both gaining and maintaining employability, and in particular the ability of that individual to obtain new employment by moving between organisations. As we have already seen, the level of skills within the UK is far lower than elsewhere in the EU, suggesting that employability of individuals is likely to be lower.

Employability of individuals is also likely to be linked to the nature of their status in the labour market. As well as individuals' skill levels, personal circumstances such as caring responsibilities are likely to affect employability. External factors such as the nature of the economy and the type of job openings available are likely to be important. Here we have seen that, relative to the rest of the EU, the UK had positioned itself as a low-wage, low-skill economy. However, as we noted, since the late 1990s wage rates have been rising relative to the rest of Europe without a concomitant increase in skills or productivity. This suggests that the advantages associated with this position are declining.

Thus at first glance the employment relationship within the UK appears, in comparison with the rest of Europe, to be focused upon employees who are relatively unskilled. For these workers, employability is due to their acceptance of relatively low wages. Consequently, such employees are vulnerable where unemployment is concerned. They have limited employability assets, as not only are their skills limited but, from an employer's perspective, each is easily substitutable as many others have similar skills. You will, however, remember that this is a massive oversimplification. Employees' skill levels and employers' investment within them vary considerably between organisations and levels within organisations. Within the UK, surveys suggest that those in managerial posts are more likely to receive some formal training, this being most likely for those in public sector organisations (Worrall and Cooper, 1999; Millward *et al.*, 2000). Thus these employees' employability is, in terms of Hillage and Pollard's (1999) strands, being enhanced.

2.5 Summary

- The employment relationship does not occur in a vacuum but is influenced by and impacted upon by a host of other factors. These are associated with the way in which work is organised, the wider context within which work takes place, and the sequence of events within these over time.
- At present the world of work is experiencing rapid change shaped by powerful society-wide forces. These changes can be looked at in terms of:
  - the political environment and the role of successive governments;
  - the economic environment and issues such as globalisation, the growth of private sector employment and unemployment;
  - the technological environment and the impact of information and communication technologies;
  - the social environment including increasing female participation in the labour force and changing social attitudes.

- These society-wide forces are resulting in changes in the way work is organised and, in particular, in the more flexible use of labour by organisations. This has been characterised as the polarisation of the workforce into a core and a periphery, and has considerable implications for:
  - the characteristics of the work task;
  - the way in which performance is controlled;
  - the participation of employees in organisational decision-making;
  - issues associated with job security.

- Consequently, the nature of the employment relationship is changing. Fewer people are employed on traditional or standard contracts, and they are increasingly working in a permanent state of change. Employment stability has declined and workers are more likely to change employers and to experience periods of unemployment. Associated with this are changes in the nature of the psychological contract and a rise in the importance of employees' employability in the wider marketplace.

References

Atkinson, J. (1984) *Flexibility, Uncertainty and Manpower Management*, Institute of Manpower Studies Report No. 89, Brighton, Institute of Manpower Studies.

Atkinson, J. (1985) 'Flexibility: planning for the uncertain future', *Manpower, Policy and Practice*, 1, 26–9.

Atkinson, J. and Meager, N. (1986) *New Forms of Work Organisation*, Institute of Manpower Studies Report No. 121, Brighton, Institute of Manpower Studies.

Beekman, G. (1994) *Computer Currents, Navigating Tomorrow's Technology*, Redwood, CA, Benjamin/Cummings.

Blyton, P. and Turnbull, P. (1998) *The Dynamics of Employee Relations* (2nd edn), Basingstoke, Macmillan.

Bridges, W. (1995) *Jobshift: How to prosper in a workplace without jobs*, London, Nicholas Brealey.

Creagh, M. and Brewster, C. (1998) 'Identifying good practice in flexible working', *Employee Relations*, 20:5, 490–503.

Cully, M., O'Reilly, A., Millward, N., Forth, J., Woodland, S., Dix, G. and Bryson, A. (1999) *The 1998 Workplace Employee Relations Survey: First Findings* [online][cited 23 June 2002] Available from <http://www.dti.gov.uk/er/emar/ffind.pdf>

Department of Trade and Industry (2000) *Employment Relations Act 1999: Summary of the Act* [online][cited 23 June 2002] Available from <URL:http://www.dti.gov.uk/er/actsumm5.pdf>

Emmott, M. and Hutchinson, S. (1998) 'Employment flexibility: threat or promise', in Sparrow, P. and Marchington, M. (eds), *Human Resource Management: The new agenda*, London, FT Pitman, pp. 229–44.

European Commission Directorate-General for Economic and Financial Affairs (2000a) *European Economy: Supplement B: Business and Consumer Survey Results*, No. 1, January.

European Commission Directorate-General for Economic and Financial Affairs (2000b) *European Economy: Supplement B: Business and Consumer Survey Results* No. 3, March.

European Commission Directorate-General for Economic and Financial Affairs (2000c) *European Economy: Supplement A: Economic Trends*, No. 1/2, April.

Fenwick, D. and Denman, J. (1995) 'The monthly claimant unemployment count: change and consistency', *Labour Market Trends*, 13:8, 397–400.

Friedrich, A. and Kabst, R. (1998) 'Functional flexibility: merely reacting or acting strategically?', *Employee Relations*, 20:5, 504–23.

Gallie, D., White, M., Cheng, Y. and Tomlinson, M. (1998) *Restructuring the Employment Relationship*, Oxford, Clarendon Press.

Green, F. (1992) 'Recent trends in British trade union density: how much of a compositional effect?', *British Journal of Industrial Relations*, 30:3, 445–58.

Greenbaum, J. (1998) 'The times they are a'changing: dividing and recombining labour through computer systems', *in* Thompson, P. and Warhurst, C. (eds), *Workplaces of the Future*, Basingstoke, Macmillan, pp. 124–41.

Hakim, C. (1996) *Key Issues in Women's Work*, London, Athlone.

Handy, C. (1990) *The Age of Unreason*, London, Arrow.

Handy, C. (1996) *Beyond Certainty*, London, Arrow.

Harvey, C. and Kanwal, S. (2000) 'Self-employed IT knowledge workers and the experience of flexibility', *in* Purcell, K. (ed.), *Changing Boundaries in Employment*, Bristol, Bristol Academic Press, pp. 104–32.

Hillage, J. and Pollard, E. (1999) 'Employability: developing a framework for policy analysis', *Labour Market Trends*, 17:2, 83–4.

IDS (1999) *IDS Brief 628: Employment Law Review 1998*, London, Incomes Data Services Macmillan.

King, J. (2000) 'Seasonal adjustment review of the claimant count and Jobcentre vacancies series', *Labour Market Trends*, May, 219–24.

Kinnie, N., Hutchinson, S. and Purcell, J. (1998) 'Downsizing: is it always lean and mean?', *Personnel Review*, 27:4, 296–311.

Kinnie, N., Purcell, J. and Hutchinson, S. (2000) 'Managing the employment relationship in telephone call centres', *in* Purcell, K. (ed.), *Changing Boundaries in Employment*, Bristol, Bristol Academic Press, pp. 133–59.

Ladipo, D. (2000) 'The demise of organizational loyalty', *in* Purcell, K. (ed.), *Changing Boundaries in Employment*, Bristol, Bristol Academic Press, pp. 186–208.

Leat, M. and Woolley, J. (1999) 'Multinationals and employee relations', *in* Hollinshead, G., Nicholls, P. and Tailby, S. (eds), *Employee Relations*, London, Financial Times Pitman Publishing pp. 93–131.

Legge, K. (1998) 'Flexibility: the gift wrapping of employment degradation', *in* Sparrow, P. and Marchington, M. (eds), *Human Resource Management: The new agenda*, London, FT Pitman, pp. 286–95.

Liff, S. (1995) 'Equal opportunities: continuing discrimination in a context of formal equality', *in* Edwards, P. (ed.), *Industrial Relations: Theory and practice in Britain*, Oxford, Blackwell, pp. 461–90.

Mayne, L., Tregaskis, O. and Brewster, C. (1996) 'A comparative analysis of the link between flexibility and HRM strategy', *Employee Relations*, 18:3, 5–24.

Millward, N., Bryson, A. and Forth, J. (2000) *All Change at Work? British employment relations 1980–1998 as portrayed by the Workplace Industrial Relations Survey series*, London, Routledge.

Noon, M. and Blyton, P. (1997) *The Realities of Work*, Basingstoke, Macmillan.

Office for National Statistics (2001) *Employee Jobs by Industry 1978–2000: Social Trends 31* [online] [cited 23 June 2002]. Available from <http://www.statistics.gov.uk/statbase/tsdataset.asp?vlnk=3470&More=Y>

Office for National Statistics (2002a) *Economic Activity Rates by Gender, 1971 to 1998: Social Trends 30* [online] [cited 23 June 2002]. Available from <http://www.statistics.gov.uk/statbase/xsdataset.asp?vlnk=5099&More=Y>

Office for National Statistics (2002b) United Kingdom seasonally adjusted claimant count consistent with current coverage, Office for National Statistics unpublished tables [email to authors: online]

Pollert, A. (1991) 'The orthodoxy of flexibility', *in* Pollert, A. (ed.), *Farewell to Flexibility*, Oxford, Blackwell, pp. 3–31.

Poole, M. (1986) *Industrial Relations: Origins and patterns of national diversity*, London, Routledge & Kegan Paul.

Richardson, R. and Marshall, J.N. (1996) 'The growth of telephone call centres in peripheral areas of Britain: evidence from Tyne and Wear', *Area*, 34:3, 308–17.

Ritzer, G. (1998) *The McDonaldization Thesis*, London, Sage.

Salamon, M. (1998) *Industrial Relations* (3rd edn), London, Prentice Hall.

Salamon, M. (2000) *Industrial Relations* (4th edn), Harlow, Financial Times Prentice Hall.

Sparrow, P. (2000) 'New employee behaviours, work designs and forms of work organization: what is in store for the future of work?', *Journal of Managerial Psychology*, 15:3, 202–18.

Sparrow, P. and Marchington, M. (1998) *Human Resource Management: The new agenda*, London, FT Pitman.

Taylor, S. (1998) *Employee Resourcing*, London, Institute of Personnel and Development.

Turnbull, P. (1991) 'Buyer–supplier relationships in the UK automotive industry', *in* Blyton, P. and Morris, J. (eds), *A Flexible Future? Prospects for Employment and Organization*, Berlin, Walter de Gruyter, pp. 169–89.

UCAS (2002) *Annual Datasets: Subject dataset, UK 2001* [online] [cited 23 June 2002]. Available from <http://www.ucas.co.uk/figures/archive/download/index.html>

Warhurst, C. and Thompson, P. (1998) 'Hands, hearts and minds: changing work and workers at the end of the century', *in* Thompson, P. and Warhurst, C. (eds), *Workplaces of the Future*, Basingstoke, Macmillan, pp. 1–24.

Winchester, D. (1983) 'Industrial relations research in Britain', *British Journal of Industrial Relations*, 20, 100–27.

Worrall, L. and Cooper, C.L. (1999) *The Quality of Working Life: 1999 survey of managers' changing experiences*, London, Institute of Management.

self-check Answers

2.1 *Think back to your last visit to a supermarket. In what ways does micro technology affect the environment within which work is taking place?*

Your answer will obviously be dependent upon the supermarket you have visited. However, you are likely to have talked about the electronic point of sale (EPOS) scanning of goods you have purchased at the checkout. This has meant that, because all goods are barcoded, it is no longer necessary for someone to price them individually, or for the checkout operator to read the prices and key them into the cash register. In addition, it means that stock control is undertaken automatically rather than manually; a computer program signals to the distribution warehouse when further items require delivery. Consequently, just-in-time deliveries can be made and the amount of goods stored in stockrooms rather than on the shelves can be reduced to a minimum. In some supermarkets purchases are also recorded by the computer against the customer's supermarket loyalty account. This means that detailed market research on purchasing habits is, in effect, undertaken automatically. EPOS also means that work rates of all checkout operators can be monitored automatically, rather than by a supervisor being present.

You may also have talked about the payment methods of electronic funds transfer at point of sale (EFTPOS). This reduces the amount of cash held by supermarkets and the amount of backroom staff needed to process cheques and cash, as much of the work is done automatically.

2.2 *Many organisations expect employees to work regularly beyond their contract. What are the relative benefits of this expectation for employee and organisation?*

Whenever an employee works beyond contract, it has been argued that she or he is, in effect, providing the employer with free labour. Working beyond contract can benefit the organisation in terms of numerical flexibility as it does not need to employ additional people. It can also benefit the organisation in terms of temporal or working time flexibility if the employee is present at times outside her or his contracted hours, or works additional hours. Where employees are asked to undertake tasks outside their normal duties, this can also provide the organisation with functional flexibility.

The benefits for the employee are perhaps less obvious. However, if she or he is paid for this work then an obvious benefit is the financial reward. Employees can use such additional work to demonstrate their commitment to the organisation, and may derive a greater sense of job security from having undertaken it. In addition, and probably of equal importance, some people actually like their jobs and enjoy working beyond contract.

2.3 *Imagine you are advising a young person who is looking for her or his first job. Which one of the following features would you say is the most important, and which next? Give reasons for your choices.*

Your answer will be personal to you. However, you might wish to compare your answer with colleagues. UK research reported in Ladipo (2000) has shown that whether people were brought up in the 1980s, the 1960s, the years immediately after the Second World War, or the years immediately before the Second World War their responses were remarkably similar. For people brought up in the 1980s the percentages of people choosing each of the features as either 'most' or 'next most' important was:

- secure job   72%
- interesting work   46%
- promotion opportunities   34%
- good conditions   27%
- good starting pay   20%

2.4 *How do part-time workers differ from temporary workers in terms of the flexibility they offer organisations? What are the reasons for this?*

Part-time workers differ considerably from temporary workers in terms of the flexibility they offer organisations. In general, part-timers tend to occupy jobs of relatively low skill content and are less likely to have received recent training to develop their skills. These jobs tend to be principally in the service industries (retail and finance) and in the public services such as education, medical services and welfare. As individuals, they offer organisations relatively little functional or temporal flexibility. However, in aggregate their part-time nature allows organisations to use them for greater flexibility in patterns of working (both temporal and functional).

In contrast, temporary workers can offer organisations far more flexibility. Those on short-term contracts (less than one year) often have very similar skill levels to those of permanent workers in equivalent jobs. They therefore can provide numerical as well as functional and temporal flexibility. Those from agencies are far less skilled and less likely to have received training but still offer numerical flexibility. In addition, they may be used to provide financial flexibility by being paid less for the same work.

Contract workers on longer-term contracts are often highly skilled and can offer organisations functional flexibility. For such workers, the longer-term nature of their contracts means that numerical flexibility is only in the longer term.

CASE 2   Ben's Garage[1]

Background

Ben's Garage is one of two garages with a mainstream car manufacturer's franchise owned by a local company. Over the years it has built up a reputation based upon good service, most of its customers having purchased two or more cars from the garage and subsequently using the garage for servicing. The site consists of a show-room, a workshop and a parts operation. The showroom and workshop attract primarily private drivers, whereas the parts operation supplies both trade and private customers as well as the garage's workshop. For the past five years, the garage has kept these three aspects of its work entirely separate. Employees of each of the three areas consider themselves skilled in their particular area. In addition, each now operates as a separate cost centre, reporting individually on turnover, margin and return on assets.

Showroom

Sales success has been based on good service to a loyal customer base. Although the showroom is relatively small, the garage prides itself on being able to obtain most cars for customers wishing to take a test drive. Sales enquiries are generated from personal recommendation, passing trade and repeat purchases. The sales staff receive a basic salary and commission for each car they sell. The busiest times are between midday and 2 p.m., and after 4 p.m. on weekdays and all day Saturday. In addition, the garage is considering opening the showroom on Sunday afternoons.

Workshop

Nearly all bookings are taken by telephone. The customer's phone call is taken by one of the two part-time workshop receptionists. One receptionist works three hours in the morning (8–11 a.m.), the other works three hours in the afternoon (3–6 p.m.). When the garage is busy, or there is additional clerical work, the receptionists are requested to work additional hours. On the day of the service, the customer brings in their vehicle and checks in at the workshop reception. Should the receptionist be busy or not available the customer has to wait. At check-in the receptionist confirms details, and sorts out a loan car if required. This takes about 8 minutes. About 80 per cent of customers check in their cars

---

[1] The garage and the people working within it are fictional.

▶

before 10 a.m. Subsequently the workshop receptionist may telephone customers for authorisation for additional work. In addition, he will check with the parts operation for the availability of items for repair work etc. When the customer returns to collect his/her car the receptionist goes through the work carried out and takes the payment.

All workshop staff, except receptionists, are paid a monthly salary. This is dependent upon skills and length of service. Receptionists are paid at the end of each week for the hours they have worked.

Parts operation

This has a separate entrance and caters for two groups of external customers (trade and private) as well as the workshop. Trade customers tend to telephone or fax to order parts, which are subsequently delivered by a self-employed contract van driver. Private customers tend to call in to purchase the parts required. Although a stock of parts is held, those not available can be ordered on a next-day basis. All parts operation staff are paid a monthly salary. This is less than those employed in the workshop owing to the skills required. The contract van driver is paid on the basis of journeys made. This means that, if no parts are delivered, he receives no pay.

Staffing structure

Showroom	Workshop	Parts operation
Sales manager (Brendan)	Workshop manager (Tim)	Parts manager (Dick)
3 salespersons	2 receptionists (part time) 6 mechanics	2 staff (1 contract van driver)

This case study is based around a typical Monday morning, and as usual the telephone in Workshop Reception is ringing. Tim reaches across and grabs it at the tenth ring.

DICK Hello, is that Tim?

TIM It is indeed. What's up in Parts then?

DICK I've got a bit of a problem, Tim....

TIM Well, I didn't think you were calling just to chat about the match...

DICK Look, one of my two staff has just called in sick, and we're a bit stretched. Have you got anyone you can spare?

TIM Spare? Not likely! It's a madhouse here, and will be until ten o'clock – but if you can wait 'til then I'll get someone to go over.

DICK Ten o'clock's fine – the parts truck never arrives before 10.30. [*Dick's relief is evident.*] I owe you a pint, Tim.

Oh, and before you go, what about tomorrow? Steve said he'd be off for the next few days. Could I have your bloke until he's back? Same arrangement? Just after ten?

TIM Look, I'm not sure; he says the work is boring… and I might need him back around four o'clock for the evening rush; but yes, OK – provisionally, although don't bank on it for certain!

Just after lunch the garage's Managing Director is passing by Parts reception and notices one of Tim's mechanics behind the counter. He sees Tim….

MANAGING DIRECTOR Tim! What's going on? I've just seen one of your mechanics in Parts reception!

TIM Dick's a man short, so he asked if I could help him out; the guy's only been over there for part of the morning.

MANAGING DIRECTOR Hum, you're obviously overstaffed if you can afford to allow highly skilled mechanics to do menial work… also, why on earth is your receptionist still here? It's gone half past one!

Questions

Examine the information in the scenario and the graph of customer arrival rates (Figure 2.7) and waiting times for visits to the workshops (Figure 2.8).

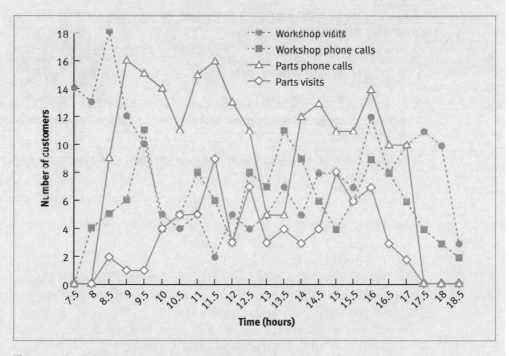

Figure 2.7 **Weekly customer arrival rates**
Source: Survey of customer arrival rates over a representative period

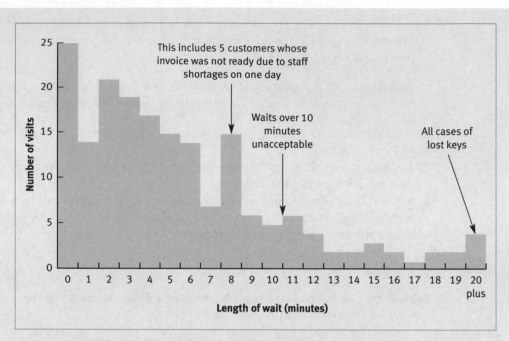

Figure 2.8 **Waiting time for visits to workshop: previous week**
Source: Survey of customer arrival rates last week

1 What do these tell you about the need for labour flexibility at Ben's Garage?

2 What hinders this taking place?

3 What recommendations would you make regarding the use of people resources at Ben's Garage?

4 What, if any, are the implications of your recommendations for employers and employees?

Part Two

Regulating the employment relationship

Chapter 3

The role of power, justice and culture in the regulation of the employment relationship

At the end of this chapter you should be able to:

■ define the concept of power and analyse its use in organisations;

■ explore the role of power in the regulation of the employment relationship;

■ define the concept of organisational justice and analyse its significance in organisations;

■ explore the role of justice in the regulation of the employment relationship;

■ define the concept of culture and explain its importance to understanding the employment relationship;

■ explore the role of culture in the regulation of the employment relationship.

3.1 Introduction

This chapter considers a range of concepts that are integral to the conduct of the employment relationship. These are *power, organisational justice* and *culture*. More traditional employee relations textbooks either have taken these three concepts for granted, or have virtually ignored them altogether. Related concepts to those in this chapter that have featured in some earlier texts are *equity* and *fairness*. Although these concepts undoubtedly reside at the centre of the employment relationship, they may be seen as lacking analytical precision and are sometimes used as little more than synonyms. Fairness lies at the heart of justice, and organisational justice theory may be seen as a development from earlier equity theory. Consideration of theories of organisational justice and power offer much greater analytical development and depth through which to explore the employment relationship. In relation to context, it has been usual to include at least one chapter in an employee relations textbook that examines a number of external contextual variables, related to economic, political, social and legal factors and perhaps others as well. This book includes such a chapter. However, it has been less usual to include an extended discussion related to the importance of organisational culture in particular.

This chapter is designed, or least intended, to cover these aspects. It seeks to examine the role of power, justice and culture in the regulation of the employment relationship. Power pervades this relationship, and, rather than implicitly refer to aspects of power, Section 3.2 reviews a range of approaches to and definitions of organisational power. This leads to a consideration of power relations in the employment relationship. The concept of organisational justice has led to the development of three overlapping theories that have been subject to a considerable level of research that relates to the employment relationship. The development of these theories provides a rich analytical framework to explore and to relate to the subject of this book in Section 3.3. Section 3.4 seeks to demonstrate how the culture of an organisation affects both the formulation and the use of power in organisations, and helps to shape perceptions about organisational treatment and justice. A case study is included, based on reported experiences in a real organisation, which explores the relationship between power, organisational justice and culture in the employment relationship.

3.2 The role of power in the regulation of the employment relationship

Power is an integral part of the employment relationship. R. Martin (1992: 2) wrote: 'Orthodox industrial relations scholars have recognized the central importance of power.' More recently, Rose (2001: 4) commented that 'the employment relationship is ... characterised by power relationships between employer and worker.' Yet in spite of such clear statements about the role and importance of power in the employment relationship, it has often been overlooked as a subject of discussion in many previously published employee relations textbooks (Kelly, 1998). Kirkbride (1992) refers to the concept of power often being used in a 'taken-for-granted' way in the employment relations literature. Nevertheless, as Townley (1994: 1) states: 'Whether explicitly acknowledged, or not, the experience of work is located in, and constituted by, power relations.'

■ Attempting to define power and recognising its use in organisations

Our purpose here will therefore be to describe and discuss the principal ways in which power has been defined, and to consider, albeit succinctly, its use in organisations. This will allow us to develop a discussion about the nature of power relations in the employment relationship.

A frequent starting point in terms of defining power is the work of Weber (1978) and of Dahl (1957). Weber's definition of power stressed the ability of a person to get others to do what he or she wants, including acting against their will. Dahl's definition says that one person has power over another to the extent that this second person does something that he or she wouldn't do otherwise. These definitions of power may be seen as emphasising behavioural control, and they stress the notion of one person having 'power over' others (Lukes, 1986; Hardy and Clegg, 1996). Earlier work in the field of employee relations by Fox (1974) appears to recognise and follow this approach to power. Fox (1974: 14) wrote that: 'Power ... enables the few to minimise the discretion of the many in the making of decisions deemed by the few to be important for their purposes.' Fox goes on to state that the likely outcome of the use of such power will be to create employment relations that are characterised by distrust. The original use of this power will, according to Fox, be based on distrust and will in turn lead to the reciprocation of distrust by those who are subject to it.

However, the limitation of a person's discretion to act according to his or her own will (even where this is feasible) does not have to rely on the overt use or behavioural exercise of power. More subtle or covert forms of power may be used to limit discretion and action. Dahl's work, and that of other researchers on power in the 1950s and 1960s, focused on community-centred decision-making processes in the USA. It led to the finding that participation was open to all of those affected by such decisions. This is the ideal position of a fully participative democracy. Others recognised, however, that participation in decision-making processes might be restricted to particular groups in society. Similarly, the range of issues to be subject to participative decision-making processes might also be restricted. These issues were therefore likely to be restricted to matters that didn't threaten the position of those elite groups who already enjoyed a position of power. Schattschneider (1960) referred to this outcome as the *mobilisation of bias*. In this way, the issues and grievances of some groups will not be considered and will remain outside any formal decision-making processes. Schattschneider saw organisations as being based on the mobilisation of bias, with the outcome that participation either would not be allowed, or would be controlled, in respect of the issues of particular groups within an organisation.

Bachrach and Baratz (1962) identified what they labelled as a *second face of power*, based on Schattshneider's idea of the mobilisation of bias. For them the investigation of power needed to commence by seeking to understand the mobilisation of bias in an organisation. This could be done by analysing the dominant values and political procedures of the organisation, with a view to understanding which groups in the organisation benefited from the bias that would be revealed and which groups were disadvantaged by it. This second face of power is essentially a restrictive one, preventing or reducing the effective and meaningful participation of some groups in an organisation. In this sense the notion of what was called *non-decision-making* is at least as important as decision-making in terms of understanding the nature and dynamics of power in organisations. Those who control 'non-decision-making' can effectively maintain the status quo and the existing structures of power within an organisation.

In this way, those who control the ability of others to raise issues or grievances that would conflict with the status quo exercise power. This amounts to control over the organisational agenda and over those issues that may be debated openly or bargained over. Bachrach and Baratz (1970) refer to a number of strategies that those in power may use to achieve this control. A dissenting voice either may be prevented from being raised at all, or may be restricted to nothing more than a covert utterance, or if raised openly it may be checked from advancing to any organisational decision-making forum, or it may be rejected at such a stage.

Lukes (1974) argued that there is another dimension of power that is important to its understanding. The work of Dahl and that of Bachrach and Baratz, which Lukes respectively termed the *one-dimensional view* and *two-dimensional view* of power, both focus on 'actual behaviour' and 'actual, observable conflict' (Lukes, 1974:

21–2). Lukes recognised, however, that conflict is not necessary to exercise power and that power may be used to avoid the incidence of overt conflict. Indeed, the incidence of overt conflict and attempts to use power openly may actually indicate a position of weakness rather than one of strength:

> ... very often, it is not those groups which have most frequent recourse to overt use of coercion who have most power; frequent use of coercive sanctions indicates an insecure basis of power. (Giddens, 1968: 261, cited in Barker and Roberts, 1993: 197)

The more effective use of power will involve preventing this type of outcome. Power can thus be seen as a potential and latent capacity rather than something that needs to manifest itself openly, in order to exist. Lukes develops this idea in his suggestion that:

> ... is it not the supreme and most insidious exercise of power to prevent people, to whatever degree, from having grievances by shaping their perceptions, cognitions and preferences in such a way that they accept their role in the existing order of things, either because they see or imagine no alternative to it, or because they see it as natural and unchangeable, or because they value it as divinely ordained and beneficial. (1974: 24)

In this way, Lukes' *three-dimensional view of power* suggests that power may be used to alter or shape the views of those affected so that their 'real interests' are excluded or suppressed by those who exercise it (Lukes, 1974, 1986). Such an outcome would create a *hegemonic* effect (Clegg, 1989), where the interests of those who exercise power would be universally accepted by all, leading to a situation where this informed and shaped an organisation's culture.

The implications of this view of power have been criticised on the grounds not only that the identification of 'real interests' is highly problematic, but that these will be shaped by the conditions in which a person finds herself or himself. Thus, although some may consciously or unconsciously accept the values projected through the prevalence of power, this may also be seen as reflecting their best interests in such circumstances. However, even in this case there is scope to question whether such an acceptance is real or self-serving and how this affects behaviour as a consequence. In addition, there is scope to question whether those affected universally share perceptions about prevailing conditions. Such perceptions may vary, for example, between participants in different areas of an organisation, between women and men, between those in different occupational groups and so forth (e.g. see the discussion in Barker and Roberts, 1993). Where this type of fragmentation occurs, this is likely to prevent the development, or reduce the prevalence, of an ideological and cultural hegemony based on the existence of latent power.

This discussion points to the sociological relationship or dualism between structure and agency (e.g. Townley, 1994). *Structure* refers to the existence of factors such as the ownership and control of resources that help to determine people's attitudes, behaviour and the nature of power relations. *Agency* refers to the voluntary nature of human action based on will and the exercise of choice. Barker and Roberts (1993: 210) state that the 'debate over the theory of power (became) stuck in the gravitational pulls between individual action and social structure.' However, they use

Benton's (1981) work that considers how interests are identified and the nature of conflicts that arise in this process to develop this debate. Benton points out that people's interests in practice are unlikely to be straightforward and simple. These are likely to be characterised by conflicting identifications, loyalties and beliefs. The tension between structure and agency is therefore open to intervention. Those who exercise power have the scope to intervene actively to shape, for example, employees' perceptions about their interests. Power may therefore be exercised deliberately to shape perceptions of interests, attitudes and behaviour. Such a position appears to support the structural determination of 'interests' through the exercise of power, but also implicitly recognises the existence of human agency and the conflicts to which this can lead. Bachrach and Baratz (1970) identified a number of types of power that may be exercised, and these are shown in Box 3.1.

Box 3.1   **Types of power**

- *Force*. Power is exercised through ensuring an absence of choice, where those affected are aware of this action and its originator.
- *Manipulation*. Power is exercised through ensuring an absence of choice, where those affected are unaware of this action and its originator.
- *Coercion*. Power is exercised through the threat of sanctions in the case of non-compliance.
- *Influence*. Power is exercised without implying the use of threats.
- *Authority*. Power is exercised when one person recognises another's instruction as being based on some form of legitimacy and procedural reasonableness.

Source: Adapted from Bachrach and Baratz (1970)

So far, we have tended to define and use power in a negative way. The 'power terms' in Box 3.1 refer to a number of negative uses of power, related to the use of force, manipulation and coercion. These reinforce the notion of someone or something having 'power over' a person or a group, etc. Use of power in this way may be unrecognised, related say to Lukes' three-dimensional view, or may be more overtly exercised, related to the use of force or coercion and backed up by the threat or use of sanctions. These forms suggest the idea of a *zero-sum* approach to power, with winners and losers, where the interests of some (however determined) are supported over those of others (e.g. Mumby, 2001). This leads to notions of domination and potential resistance. In relation to the overt exercise of power in an organisational context, management would rely on a 'command–obedience relationship' (Lukes, 1986: 3). We recognised earlier that the use of more subtle forms of power, related to its conscious or unconscious acceptance, is likely to be more effective. One way in which power may be exercised and accepted is related to the final concept listed in Box 3.1. We therefore now consider the concept of authority and the notion of legitimate power in organisations.

Organisational strategy determines the purpose and goals of an organisation. To achieve this, an organisation will need to establish a formal organisational structure composed of a necessary range of roles and relationships including hierarchical ones. Those who hold positions of responsibility within such a structure are granted formal authority, which may be seen as a legitimised form of power. The intention is that their authority will be recognised and accepted by those with whom they inter-act, including those in subordinate positions (e.g. Morgan, 1997). This approach is linked to Talcott Parsons' concept of power as being a *system resource* (Lukes, 1986). The fulfilment of social or organisational goals requires and legitimises a situation whereby some people enter positions of authority over others in order to achieve these goals. In theory, this type of rational–legal authority will be limited to the formalised functions of a postholder in an organisational structure. It would not extend to power exercised in a more discretionary way. This approach essentially characterises the operation of organisations as bureaucracies, where work is con-ducted according to systems of rules. However, as we consider in the following subsection, managers may seek to exceed their authority by engaging in forms of dis-cretionary power, while those subject to rules may also use these to gain control in relation to their job performance.

The exercise of authority and other organisational characteristics such as an organ-isation's structure and culture are therefore 'invariably saturated and imbued with power' (Hardy and Clegg, 1996: 629). This has not prevented strands of the literature viewing the exercise of power by management as being legitimate while seeing its use by others outside the formal organisation as illegitimate, reflecting a unitarist perspec-tive as discussed in Chapter 1. Where a unitarist perspective prevails, the pursuit of goals other than those sanctioned by the organisation, as well as any conflict associ-ated with these demands, will be seen as dysfunctional. In more critical strands of the literature this narrow approach to defining what is 'legitimate' power in organisations is seen as promoting only the interests of organisational elites and reinforcing the structural nature of power (see the discussion in Hardy and Clegg, 1996).

The work of Foucault provides an alternative and yet relevant approach for under-standing the nature of power in organisations. Foucault saw power as pervading every social relationship rather than emanating from particular sources in a downward direction. Each individual is seen as a vehicle of power and as a result power should be viewed not just as a centralised entity but as something that circulates through all social networks (Foucault, 1980). Foucault's analytical emphasis is therefore placed on understanding *relationships of power* rather than seeing power as something that is possessed by a relative few and exercised over the remainder. In this way, 'power is relational: it is not a possession' (Townley, 1994: 7). This places emphasis on a micro-level of analysis, and on analysing the practices and techniques used in everyday life to understand the ways in which power relations affect our lives.

Foucault treated power and knowledge as interrelated concepts; hence what he terms *power/knowledge*. Put simply, power requires knowledge, and knowledge pro-vides a basis for power. This leads to power potentially being seen as 'positive and creative, not just negative and repressive' (Townley, 1994: 8). This power/knowledge linkage led to his conceptualisation of *disciplinary power*: 'power is conceived of as a technique which achieves its strategic effect through its disciplinary character' (Clegg, 1989: 153). Foucault's analysis identified practices, or *disciplines*, that 'create both knowledge and power. Disciplines are techniques designed to observe, monitor, shape and control behaviour' (Townley, 1994: 5). A central theme related to this under-standing is that of *surveillance*: 'Foucault sees the methods of surveillance and assessment of individuals, which were first developed in state institutions such as prisons, as effective tools developed for the orderly regimentation of others...' (Clegg, 1989: 153). According to this approach, disciplinary power provides a regulatory means of effective control that operates through various forms of surveillance at, and assessment of, work. This suggests the means to ensure behavioural compliance. Disciplinary power may even lead to the internalisation of surveillance behaviours where the subject obediently disciplines himself or herself (Clegg, 1989). This ultimately suggests some form of psychological compliance. This approach therefore appears to provide an alternative way to conceive of power, related to its diffuse, pervasive, potentially internalised and continually recreated nature, rather than something that is just centralised, external and essentially stable.

This brief discussion of several, often conflicting, theories of power has been intended to provide an overview of its nature and use in organisations. Although power remains a highly problematic and contested concept, this discussion has nevertheless illustrated that it is an important theme to seek to understand in terms of studying the employment relationship. We therefore turn to discuss the nature of power relations in the employment relationship, which will allow us to apply and consider further some of the ideas introduced above.

self-check question	3.1 Think of an organisational situation with which you have some familiarity. How does power manifest itself in this situation, and what types of power are exercised?

■ Power relations in the employment relationship

Townley (1994: 13) states that the central issue in the employment relationship is 'the indeterminacy of contract, the naturally occurring space between expectation and deliverance of work'. Each employee or worker may be seen as representing a particular capability and a capacity to work. The realisation of these attributes is the objective of effective management. However, the nature of this capability and the extent of this capacity may be contestable areas for discussion and negotiation, and they indicate a forum for the exercise of power. Whereas managers will seek to formulate expectations and targets about work, individual employees will develop views about their willingness to conform to these expectations and to accede to forms of managerial control. They will also form perceptions about the nature and fairness of their organisational treatment. Edwards (1995: 13) states that: 'expectations about standards of performance have to be built up during the process of production.' These factors suggest the scope to exercise some level of discretion in the employment relationship. Employees will thus be able to exercise some control over the conduct of their work and the level of their effort in terms of what they do and how they do this. Whereas management will attempt to find ways in which to control the conduct of work, employees will also seek to exercise, or to find new ways of maintaining, some level of discretion.

In the previous section we referred to the distinction between *legitimate* and *illegitimate* forms of power. Authority conferred by holding a position in a formal organisation is seen as a legitimised form of power. Attempts by employees to exercise some discretion over the conduct of their work, or job controls, have been equated with the use of unauthorised or illegitimate power. This distinction also points to the incidence of *actual* power, as opposed to the exercise of formal authority. Past organisational research identified the basis (or bases) for the exercise of this type of power. Early research in this area found that groups of workers who possess particular technical knowledge or sets of competence that are not easily substitutable, and which are exercised in the context of high interdependence, where their role is central to the achievement of production, will be in a position to exercise such power (e.g. Thompson, 1956; Mechanic, 1962).

Power is also generated through the ability to exercise control in situations of uncertainty. For example, Crozier's famous study (1964) identified the maintenance workers in a French state-owned factory as holding power because of their ability to exercise control in relation to the production process. Given the bureaucratic systems in place in the organisation, machine breakdowns were the major remaining source of uncertainty relating to production. Based on the system of rules operating in this organisation, this gave these maintenance workers a position of considerable discretionary power over both production workers and production supervisors. These maintenance workers were able to defend their privileged position in relation to this particular task. Production supervisors were not able to check on maintenance or exercise control over these workers, given the nature of the organisation. Their central position in relation to resolving uncertainty in this system therefore gave them considerable power.

The development of the 'strategic contingencies theory of intra-organisational power' (Hickson *et al.*, 1971) recognised that uncertainty, substitutability and centrality were key variables affecting the nature of power in organisations (Mumby, 2001). Power will vary between organisational sub-units according to their relationship to these variables. The most powerful parts of an organisation will be those that are central to its working, whose work is not easily substitutable and least dependent on other parts, and which are best able to deal with factors that create uncertainty (e.g. Hardy and Clegg, 1996). Although these parts of an organisation may themselves be characterised by internal differences, strengths and weaknesses, these factors may nevertheless confer power on some who work within them in relation to those who work in other parts of an organisation. The nature of such power is likely to devolve on managers as much as, or perhaps more than, other types of workers.

A related theory of power is known as the *resource dependency theory*. This views the relative power of organisational sub-units and individuals as depending upon their possession and use of scarce resources. Many potential bases of power resources have been listed, and Hardy and Clegg (1996) comment that these are potentially infinite in the absence of the identification of possible contexts. Perhaps the best known is that of French and Raven (1959), who identify five that are common and important and which relate to influence on individuals. These are reward, coercive, legitimate, referent and expert power. We summarise these in Box 3.2.

As indicated in the discussion above, there are potentially numerous bases of power, including those that exert influence on organisational groups as well as on individuals. For example, Hardy and Clegg (1996) also refer to the power that derives from control over information and contacts with senior managers. Morgan (1997) includes in his list of power resources the formation and use of networks and interpersonal alliances. We have already referred to other bases, such as the ability to manage or exploit uncertainty.

| Box 3.2 | **Bases of power** |

- *Reward power*. Power based on the ability to reward, for example in relation to pay rises, whose strength increases with magnitude and expectation
- *Coercive power*. Power based on the ability to punish, for example in relation to dismissal, whose strength depends on the magnitude of the punishment and its likelihood
- *Legitimate power*. Power based on the internalisation of values that indicate the legitimate right of another person to influence a subject's behaviour and the obligation to accept this. This is the same as authority, discussed above
- *Referent power*. Power based on the identification of a person with another, or with a group leading to a desire to join or maintain membership
- *Expert power*. Power based on the knowledge of a person, or another's perception of this, in relation to a given area

Source: Adapted from French and Raven (1959)

However, although factors such as being best able to deal with uncertainty, low substitutability and centrality may confer a degree of labour power on some employees, other variables will affect its realisation. Most obviously, the incidence of product market competition and rising levels of unemployment will be likely to weaken the realisation of labour power. Even without such external environmental influences, employees may not be aware that they possess such power, or they may not have the motivation to attempt to use it. The recognition and realisation of power is likely to be related to the development of group cohesion and consciousness among employees, as we saw in relation to the case of the maintenance workers reported above (Kelly, 1998).

More fundamental than this perhaps is the fact that employees will have a number of interests in relation to their role as workers, and that although some of these may be seen to oppose those of their employers, others will not, requiring at least some form and level of cooperation. A number of different shared, or common, interests between employees and employers may be identified. These will include a shared interest in relation to the economic need to generate income from work. Given that performance standards need to be devised and revised during the process of production, some level of cooperation as opposed to simple compliance will also be necessary. In more general terms, Blyton and Turnbull (1998: 31) recognise that many people 'identify with and define themselves in relation to their work.' Work may therefore provide a form of intrinsic motivation, a means of identification and a sense of purpose.

Some interests will therefore be shared, or at least overlap, but the nature of the employment relationship will nevertheless be contradictory and antagonistic (Edwards, 1986, 1995). According to Edwards, it will be contradictory because management need to provide employees with some level of autonomy to be able to benefit from their creative capabilities, while at the same time exercising various forms of control over them. Antagonism will follow from the use of managerial strategies designed to optimise the generation of surplus value from employees' labour and minimise their discretion (Edwards, 1995). In overall terms, and on a day-to-day basis, cooperation between employers, or managers, and employees will be necessary to realise the interests of both, particularly in the face of uncertainty, although the actual conduct of the employment relationship is likely to be characterised by what Edwards (1986) terms *structured antagonism.*

In spite of the structured antagonism that underpins the employment relationship, shared or common interests and the need for cooperation will have implications for the identification and use of employees' discretionary power. The presence of interests that are common with those of employers, as well as the existence of employees' interests that conflict with one another, suggests that these will have a moderating effect on the use of discretionary power. It also suggests a situation of greater complexity in reality, compared with the rather notional scenario of conflict arising from the identifiable and distinct interests of employers on the one hand and employees on the other. This situation will also have implications for the use of power by employers and management. Given the messy scenario where the employment relationship is in practice characterised by the occurrence of forms of antagonism and conflict but where there is also a need to ensure some level of employee consent and cooperation, there will be an active need to seek the latter. Edwards (1995: 11) cites Alan Fox's (1966: 14) phrase that 'cooperation needs to be engineered.' We discuss the role of managerial strategies to exercise control and to seek cooperation further in Chapter 4. However, we conclude this part of our discussion by specifically discussing the nature of employers' power.

Employers will have some interests in common with those who work for them, as well as a measure of shared dependence where the parties in the relationship each provide something that the other cannot, but they will also have other interests that are clearly identifiable and discrete. Employers will possess power and exercise control as the owners of the assets of an organisation, or as their agents. Although the owners or agents of such assets may be equivocal about the nature and extent of power conferred in this way, ownership will be likely to focus and shape their beliefs and values, particularly in relation to any challenge to their sense of legitimacy and authority. Using the concept of power in an aggregated sense, there are frequent references in the literature to the balance of power between the parties involved in the employment relationship. Reference is sometimes made to the balance of power shifting between the parties involved depending on factors such as the level of employment or a willingness on the part of unionised employees to engage in industrial action. However, this type of analysis has been questioned because of the underlying asymmetry of power based on the ownership of organisational resources. Such asymmetry of power related to ownership leads to the dominance of organisational elites, whose power is either drawn directly from the ownership of these resources, or arises because of their relationship to those who own them.

In this way, Hardy and Clegg (1996) suggest that any focus on the *balance of power* within an organisation is likely to be related only to the superficial aspects of organisational politics rather than to its deeper foundations. One way in which employees have sought to counter this underlying asymmetry of power has been to form and join trade unions, and we consider the power resources of trade unions later in this book, particularly in relation to their relative decline over recent decades. This discussion is located in Chapter 5 and also in Chapter 6.

The studies and theories to which we have referred in this section indicate that power relations pervade employment relationships. It is not possible to reduce the role of power in these relationships to a simple prescription. Our discussion has instead been intended to convey something of the complexity of this issue, while attempting to provide a systematic review of the theories of power that have been developed. We shall explore aspects related to this discussion in subsequent chapters, although we now turn to discuss the role of justice in the regulation of the employment relationship.

self-check question

3.2 Think of an organisation with which you are familiar.

Which functional groups in this organisation appear to be able to use their knowledge or situation as a power resource over and above the authority formally granted to them? What are the particular bases of their power?

3.3 The role of justice in the regulation of the employment relationship

Organisational justice theory (Greenberg, 1987) focuses on perceptions of fairness in organisations. It seeks to categorise and explain the views and feelings of employees about their own treatment and that of others within an organisation. Cropanzano and Greenberg (1997) point out that organisational justice theory is descriptive in nature. It does not seek to prescribe how justice may be achieved. Instead, it is concerned with understanding the subjectively held perceptions of employees that result from the outcomes of decisions taken in an organisation, the procedures and processes used to arrive at these decisions, and their implementation.

Organisational justice has developed to offer theories in relation to each of these issues. Employees' perceptions about the outcomes of decisions taken in an organisation and their responses to these form the basis of *distributive justice* (Homans, 1961; Leventhal, 1976). Perceptions about the fairness of the processes used to arrive at, and to implement, organisational decisions form the basis of two types of justice theory – *procedural justice* and *interactional justice* (e.g. Cropanzano and Greenberg, 1997). We consider each of these types of organisational justice in turn to understand their role in the regulation of the employment relationship.

■ Distributive justice

Organisational decisions affect the allocation of resources and the nature of outcomes in organisations. Distributive justice is concerned with perceptions of fairness about organisational allocations and outcomes. In this sense, the concept of distributive justice provides the basis of an analytical framework that can be used to understand the perceptions of those affected in relation to many different types of organisational allocation and outcome.

Perceptions about the fairness of organisational allocations and outcomes will be largely reactive in nature (Greenberg, 1987). Homans (1961) conceived of distributive justice as arising from the outcomes of a social exchange in relation to inputs previously made. Perceptions about fairness will be based on a subjective assessment of outcomes in relation to the costs incurred or investments made in an exchange. For example, others would see a promotion as fairer where they perceived this as recognition of the appointed person's experience, previous effort, achievement, and suitability for the intended role. Such an allocation would be likely to be seen as unfair where it arose simply as the result of favouritism.

Adams (1965) proposed that feelings of inequity would arise where the ratio of a person's outcomes in relation to their inputs from an exchange was perceived as disproportionate, as the result of a comparison with others. The significance of this comparison with others and the ways in which this may be formulated are discussed below. This theory allows for the recognition of positive and negative forms of inequity. Perceptions of unfairness may lead to positive inequity, where the person experiencing this state feels that others had a greater claim to a particular reward or outcome compared with himself or herself. It has been suggested that this may lead to the person feeling guilty. A person experiencing this state may undertake a revaluation of their contribution, to alleviate this feeling. This might lead them to think their contribution is worth more than they did so originally! On the other hand, perceptions of unfairness may lead to negative inequity, where those experiencing this reaction feel that they had a greater claim to a particular reward or outcome in relation to others who receive this benefit, leading to feelings of anger and possibly alienation. A number of potentially adverse behavioural reactions may follow from this perception, such as reduced job performance, embarking on the use of withdrawal behaviours such as absenteeism, and reduced cooperation (Folger and Cropanzano, 1998).

More generally, different allocations of resources or rewards between occupational groups may adversely affect perceptions of fairness in relation to their differential treatment. For example, there are likely to be negative perceptions about distributive justice where outcomes such as redundancies and increases in workload are seen to affect some groups of workers disproportionately in relation to others (Brockner, 1992). This type of scenario is likely to lead to perceptions of inequity and distributive injustice. It emphasises that distributive justice may be applied to situations where organisational outcomes, such as involuntary job losses or increased workload, are negative and where there is an issue about the distribution of such outcomes. Punishments or other negative outcomes for those adversely affected (such as disciplinary action or failure to achieve a performance-related pay rise) may also generate perceptions of unfairness and negative inequity, where these are perceived by the subject of the decision as unjust.

A key question relates to the causes of perceptions about distributive justice: what factors influence employees' perceptions about whether an outcome is seen as fair or unfair, and whether such perceptions are strongly or weakly felt? As we referred to earlier in relation to the development of distributive justice, perceptions will be largely based on comparisons with others (Adams, 1965; Greenberg, 1987; Cropanzano and Greenberg, 1997). In this way, perceptions about outcome fairness will not be simply related to an absolute measure, such as the more money or better treatment that a person receives, but will also be based on one or more social comparisons. These are termed *referent standards*. This raises a supplementary question about how referent standards are chosen. A number of bases of such standards have been advanced in the literature. An important basis is likely to be comparisons made with specific others working nearby. For example, an employee may seek to compare her or his treatment with co-workers by observing the way in which they are treated. This type of comparison is likely to be important in relation to the allocation of tasks and the setting of performance targets. This comparison may be more generalised so that the referential standard becomes an external group (Greenberg, 1987), allowing generalised comparisons to be made with those who work elsewhere, in relation to a person's occupational group or a similar type of organisation. This type of comparison may be important in terms of relative pay levels, leading to perceptions about external equity related to comparative levels of reward. More generally still, an employee may make a comparison with a broader social or societal norm or expectation.

The basis on which organisational decisions are made may also help to explain why employees see some organisational outcomes as unfair. A number of bases have been identified in the literature (Leventhal, 1976; Lerner, 1977; Greenberg, 1987; Cropanzano and Greenberg, 1997). These include allocations based on the principle of equity, where contribution is recognised and used to decide the nature of an allocation; equality, where an allocation is shared irrespective of contribution; and needs, where an allocation may be divided unequally based on greatest need. Many organisational decisions are ostensibly based on the principle of equity, although employees observing such allocations may perceive that published business-related criteria do not match their judgements about effective prior performance. This is likely to lead to perceptions of unfairness in relation to resulting outcomes. Where the principle of equity is used in situations requiring a high degree of group cohesion, the result is likely to be detrimental where any resulting unequal allocation of resources is felt to be unjustified by those affected (Deutsch, 1975; Greenberg, 1987). The use of the equity principle is also likely to lead to perceptions of unfairness where employees' economic needs to maintain organisational membership are threatened by an outcome such as selecting redundant staff only according to an organisation's pursuit of cost minimisation. This is particularly likely to be the case where some staff have a reduced need to work and are willing to leave voluntarily, provided that they receive a reasonable level of redundancy compensation (Brockner and Greenberg, 1990).

Organisational communication may play at least some role in helping to alleviate some negatively held perceptions about outcomes, by providing an explanation for the decision underpinning an outcome. This leads us to a consideration of procedural justice.

Procedural justice

Assessments of organisational justice depend not only on perceptions about the fairness of allocations and outcomes but also on perceptions about the procedures used to arrive at such decisions. Procedural justice is concerned with perceptions of fairness about the procedures and processes used to arrive at decisions. Since the conceptual development of procedural justice in the mid-1970s (e.g. Thibaut and

Walker, 1975; Leventhal, 1976), the importance of this concept for many aspects of human resource management has been recognised (Folger and Cropanzano, 1998). A key finding emerges from numerous studies conducted in different areas of decision-making that affect people in organisations: decisions based on procedures that are perceived as fair are more likely to be accepted by those they affect, than decisions arising from procedures that are not perceived as fair (Cropanzano and Greenberg, 1997). Genuinely fair procedures and processes are also likely to moderate the impact of negative reactions that arise from decisions leading to undesirable employee outcomes. For example, whereas the use of redundancies is likely to generate negative reactions, Brockner (1990) concluded that genuine procedures to help those being made redundant should help to generate a perception of fairness amongst those who remain in employment. This type of impact has been termed a *fair-process effect*, where perceptions about the fairness of the process help to promote an acceptance of the outcomes even where these have adverse implications (Folger *et al.*, 1979; Folger and Cropanzano, 1998).

Organisational studies designed to understand the dynamics of procedural justice have focused on the related concepts of *voice* (Folger, 1977) and *process control* (Thibaut and Walker, 1975). These concepts are linked to the scope for the subjects of organisational decision-making to participate in the process of arriving at, including being able to influence, the decisions that are made. Participation or voice allows those affected to exercise some degree of process control, or personal influence, in relation to the process of reaching a decision (Thibaut and Walker, 1975; Greenberg and Folger, 1983). The ability to exercise process control has been linked to a number of positive attitudinal and behavioural reactions. Davy *et al.* (1991) found that process control positively affects perceptions about fairness and job satisfaction, which in turn influence levels of commitment to the organisation and intention to stay. Other positive attitudinal and behavioural reactions have been reported in the literature arising from perceptions about procedural justice and the exercise of process control, including improved trust in management and some evidence for increased job performance (for a review of sources see Cropanzano and Greenberg, 1997).

Leventhal's (1976, 1980) work details other facets that have been found to promote procedural justice. These relate to the following list:

- the consistent application of organisational procedures between individuals and across an organisation;
- the avoidance of self-interest in the application of procedures;
- accuracy in their use based on reliable information;
- scope to evaluate the application of procedures and alter outcomes where necessary;
- allowing for the representation of differing interests during their use; and
- the adoption of ethical standards through their use.

Representation of differing interests during the application of organisational procedures is related to the concept of voice, although many of these other facets suggest a stage beyond the process of applying such procedures. These facets therefore point towards and suggest a link with the theory of interactional justice, which we discuss next (Folger and Cropanzano, 1998).

■ Interactional justice

Perceptions about procedural justice, related to the way in which decisions are made, may be differentiated from justice considerations arising from their implementation. There are two principal aspects to this differentiation. The first of these relates to different stages of the process. Initially, perceptions about procedural justice will arise in relation to the scope for those who are likely to be affected by a decision to be able to exercise voice and to engage in some level of process control. Those affected may develop perceptions about whether the decision-making procedure is just or unjust, depending on whether they are able to exercise voice and whether this is seen to be effective. This perception may inform the way in which they continue to perceive the remainder of the process. However, perceptions of fairness developed at this stage may be altered by the subsequent implementation of the decisions that are made.

The second aspect of this differentiation therefore relates to the way in which decisions are applied in practice. Decision-makers may intend their decisions to be interpreted and applied in a particular way. However, those charged with applying decisions might interpret and implement them in a way that contravenes the original intention of the decision-makers. This may be related to a lack of clarity about what was intended, or because of other reasons such as contravention of Leventhal's (1976) principles relating to the avoidance of self-interest and the adoption of ethical standards on the part of the implementers. In reality, these principles are idealistic and even where broadly followed in practice are likely to lead to a range of interpretations. However, where principles such as consistency of treatment and post-implementation evaluation are not adequately applied, it may be that biased implementation leads to perceptions of unfairness and injustice.

Interactional justice (Bies and Moag, 1986) is thus concerned with perceptions about the fairness of the interpersonal treatment received by those affected during the implementation of decisions. This has been identified as being composed of two principal elements relating to the explanations and justification offered for decisions made, and the level of sensitivity of treatment of those affected during the implementation of decisions. Justification of organisational decisions through effective explanations has been found to produce an effect similar to that of process control: justification has been related positively to procedural fairness and, in turn, to intention to stay (Daly and Geyer, 1994). This may be explained through the finding that employees are more likely to accept a decision, even an unfavourable one, when given an adequate and genuine reason for it (Brockner et al., 1990; Brockner and Wiesenfeld, 1993; Daly and Geyer, 1994). Similarly, the way in which people are treated during a period of implementation has also been found to affect their perceptions about the fairness of the process (Folger and Cropanzano, 1998). This suggests a clear role for line managers in relation to the development of their subordinates' perceptions about fairness. Part of this will involve communicating decisions, providing reasons for these, and consulting about their impact on the future nature of work with those affected in the area that they manage. The nature of the way in which affected employees are treated is therefore likely to have a significant impact on the perceptions that they form about the fairness not only of the process of implementation but also of the decisions that underpin this process.

self-check question
3.3 Think of a decision that has been taken in an organisational situation with which you have some familiarity, or indeed in another social situation of which you are aware. What were your reactions to this decision and to the way in which it was arrived at and carried out? Analyse these by using the three strands of organisational justice theory.

3.4 The role of culture within the employment relationship

Culture is one of the most widely written about concepts in management literature, typified by writers such as Handy (1993), Peters and Waterman (1995), Tayeb (1996) and Hofstede (2001). Messages relating to organisational culture from these and a vast range of other publications have been summarised as twofold by Hendry (1995): first, organisational culture matters, and the right culture can lead to improved performance; second, organisational culture is a tangible phenomenon, which can be managed and will impact upon all aspects of the organisation, including the management of the employment relationship. In addition, publications focusing on national cultures highlight the importance of understanding the implications of these for human resource practices in both multinational firms and uninational firms employing a multicultural workforce. Within this they argue that the national cultures within which an organisation is situated and from which its workforce are drawn will have a major influence on the organisation's culture. This implies that although it might be possible for an organisation to manage some aspects of its own culture and thus its impact upon the employment relationship, external influences such as national cultures will also have an impact.

In this section we have chosen to use Brown's (1998: 9) definition as the basis of our discussion:

> Organisational culture refers to the patterns of beliefs, values and learned ways of coping with experiences that have developed during the course of an organisation's history, and which tend to be manifested in its material arrangements and in the behaviours of its members.

This definition uses the term *culture* collectively to refer to more than a single set of beliefs and values within any one organisation. Through doing this the possibility of more than one culture coexisting within an organisation is acknowledged, as is the possibility of a multinational organisation having differing cultures in different countries owing to the influences of national cultures. By implication, this means that we have adopted a combination of J. Martin's (1992) differentiation and integration perspectives on the study of culture. These will be discussed as part of our consideration of frameworks for understanding cultures. Following this we shall consider typologies of culture and the implications of these for managing the employment relationship.

■ Frameworks for understanding cultures

Work by Schein (1992) and Hofstede (2001) emphasises that cultures manifest themselves in many ways. Some of these are visible and therefore relatively easy to discern when studying an organisation but, because of their shallow or superficial nature, the true meaning is difficult to decipher. These manifestations are Hofstede's *symbols*, *heroes* and *rituals* and Schein's *artefacts* (Figure 3.1). The deepest levels of culture (Hofstede's *values* and Schein's *basic underlying assumptions*) are invisible and, as a consequence, extremely difficult to discover. They provide what Argyris (1995: 21) terms the *theories in use* upon which the more visible practices or artefacts of culture are built. Hofstede (2001: 10) refers to these values as the *core* of culture. Such values are likely to have become so taken for granted that there would be little variation in them within a culture or subculture (Schein, 1992). They will be communicated to new members, thereby transferring the culture. If these basic underlying assumptions are strongly held then group members will find behaviour on any other premise inconceivable. For this reason employee relations practices that run counter to these underlying assumptions are unlikely to find support within the organisation. Similar considerations also need to be made in relation to national cultures. For example, different cultures attach different values to different types of reward and the extent to which reward should be individual or collective. Reflecting upon this, Schneider and Barsoux (1997) contrast the relative importance of financial and non-financial incentives between cultures. They compare the Swedish preference for time off with monetary rewards with Japan, where many employees take only half their 16-day holiday entitlement.

Between the deepest and shallowest levels Schein (1992) introduces *espoused values*. These are values connected with moral and ethical codes, and determine what people think ought to be done, rather than what they necessarily will do. Often organisations present a particular view of their culture through formal documents, such as annual reports, mission statements and speeches by senior managers. These predict much of the behaviour that is observed at the practice or artefact level, especially with regard to what people *say*, but they may conflict with what people *do* (Schein, 1992). In research we undertook in an English county council there appeared at first to be almost universal acceptance of management's desire to create a 'can do' culture, and the intention to improve its levels of public service. However, subsequent in-depth interviews revealed that those who felt they had been treated

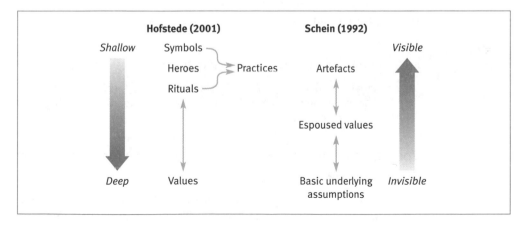

Figure 3.1 A comparison of Hofstede's and Schein's representations of cultures

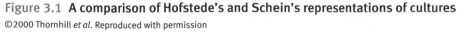

unjustly were only espousing the new culture, their behaviours reflecting their basic underlying cynicism about the new culture (Saunders *et al.*, 2002).

J. Martin (1992) identifies three perspectives for looking at organisations' cultures. These she termed *integration*, *differentiation* and *fragmentation*. The integration perspective implies that all members of an organisation share a common culture, and there is consensus regarding the beliefs held and the behaviours expected. This concept of one culture is easy to comprehend, but our discussion of the nature of power relationships between employees and managers earlier in this chapter suggests that it is unlikely to exist in its purest form. Although there may be some aspects of the way in which people in organisations behave and beliefs that are accepted by everyone, it is unlikely that all the beliefs and behaviours of those who exercise power will be universally accepted. Rather, employees and their representatives are likely to have different beliefs about some aspects of the employment relationship. Martin terms this perspective *cultural differentiation*, arguing that, for this, within-organisation manifestations of culture will be inconsistent. Only subcultures, perhaps formed round different work groups such as shopfloor workers and management, will exist with consensus being found within as opposed to between these groups. Martin's fragmentation perspective offers a further, if somewhat extreme, alternative to the other two. Within this researchers argue that they can detect very little cultural consensus in what they are studying other than around time-specific sensitive issues such as an imminent downsizing. Inevitably, these issues will change over time and, as a consequence, cultures are ambiguous and uncertain.

In reality, therefore, the idea of an integrated whole-organisational culture in which all members hold precisely the same beliefs is unlikely to occur in practice. Rather, organisations will exhibit only some organisation-wide cultural consensus and consistency. In addition there will be differentiation between groups of employees. Our research at the global nylon manufacturer Dupont's Gloucester site (Thornhill *et al.*, 2000) emphasises this, highlighting how some employees had embraced the 'trust culture' introduced by management as part of a change process. Although these employees were now taking responsibility for their own actions, others, in particular production workers, still believed that this was not part of their job. This example also emphasises that culture is not a static entity, but rather an organic process that is created, sustained and changed by people (Bate, 1995).

---

self-check question

3.4 Think of an organisation with which you are familiar.

    a What do you think are the main artefacts of its culture?

    b Can you distinguish any subcultures within the organisation using different artefacts?

■ Typologies of cultures and their implications for managing the employment relationship

Over the last 30 years a large number of typologies of both national and organisational cultures have been developed. These provide differing overviews of the variations that exist between cultures and some indication of the associated dimensions. Although these typologies are not applicable to all organisations or nations, they provide a series of idealised types through which to begin to understand aspects of cultures and subcultures and explore the implications of these for the employment relationship. To this end we begin by considering national cultures.

The influence of national cultures

As we suggested earlier, one of the influences upon an organisation's culture is the national culture within which it is located. Within the literature, there is a long-standing discussion as to whether national cultural differences and their impact are declining or increasing. This is known as the *convergence–divergence debate*. Those favouring the convergence view argue that the rapidly increasing use of technology and the growing numbers of multinational organisations will result in a convergence of organisational configurations in terms of strategy, structure and management (Senior, 2002). As a consequence the impact of national cultures on organisational cultures will decline as organisations have no national allegiance, only an international common purpose (Ohmae, 1994). In contrast writers like Tayeb (1996) and Hofstede (2001) argue that, despite the growth in multinational organisations, between-country differences in language, religious beliefs, laws, political systems, education and the like will mean that their cultures will diverge. Consequently, organisations will need increasingly to be aware of differences in national cultures, their influence upon the organisation's culture or subcultures and the implications for the organisation's policies and procedures. Our discussion in Chapter 2 highlighted how advances in telecommunications technology were increasingly enabling organisations to locate work anywhere, thereby taking advantage of economic differences between countries. The management of such changes in the location of work also needs to take account of cultural differences between countries. These will influence both the culture of organisations operating within these countries and the employment relationship within these organisations. In addition an increasingly culturally diverse workforce within countries such as the UK further emphasises the need to understand the implications of national cultures for organisational employee relations practices.

The best-known work on national cultures has been undertaken by the Dutch academic Geert Hofstede, the most recent version being published in 2001. In this Hofstede focuses on the differences and similarities between national cultures using five dimensions based upon survey data drawn from employees of IBM worldwide, first in the 1960s and continuing through the next three decades. These are power distance, individualism/collectivism, masculinity/femininity, uncertainty avoidance and Confucian dynamism.

Power distance relates to the extent to which less powerful employees accept that power is distributed unequally. Thus within low power distance countries such as the UK, Sweden and Denmark, inequalities between people are likely to be minimised and consultative decision-making is likely to be used. In contrast, in high power distance countries such as Malaysia and the Philippines, inequalities are considered desirable and there are greater differentials between employers and senior managers in terms of pay and privileges.

Individualism/collectivism refers to the extent to which individuals are orientated to themselves and their immediate family rather than wider, strong, cohesive in-groups that offer protection in exchange for unquestioning loyalty. In high-individualism countries, such as the USA and the UK, contracts of employment are based on mutual advantage in which employer-provided training and good physical conditions are taken for granted and are hence relatively unimportant. For low-individualism countries, such as Pakistan and Indonesia, contracts with employers tend to be viewed in moral terms like a family relationship. Consequently, hiring and promotion decisions are more likely to take into account the employee's in-group. The provision of training, and the like, is less likely to occur, and where it does it is unlikely to be taken for granted.

The *masculinity/femininity* dimension refers to the extent to which assertiveness and decisiveness are prioritised over more caring values such as nurturing and concern for quality of life, Hofstede's label attributing these to specific genders. In 'masculine' countries, such as the UK and Italy, managers place greater emphasis on competition and high performance. Employment disputes tend to be resolved by conflict, and there is often a stronger ethos of living to work. In more 'feminine' countries, such as Sweden and the Netherlands, conflicts tend to be resolved by compromise and negotiation, and there is often an ethos of working to live.

Uncertainty avoidance relates to the extent to which people feel threatened by ambiguous or unknown situations. In low uncertainty avoidance countries, such as the UK and Hong Kong, there is greater tolerance of risk and ambiguous situations, and people are likely to be motivated by achievement and by esteem. For high uncertainty avoidance countries, such as Portugal and France, there is a fear of ambiguous situations, and people are more likely to be motivated by security and esteem.

Hofstede's final dimension, *Confucian dynamism*, captures the long- or short-term orientation of culture. Countries with a high long-term orientation, such as China and Japan, emphasise the adaptation of traditions to a modern context, are sparing with resources, and stress perseverance. In contrast, countries with a low long-term orientation, such as the USA and the UK, tend to have less respect for traditions, place lower emphasis on the importance of social and status obligations, approve conspicuous consumption, and demand quick results.

Table 3.1 notes the relative scores on Hofstede's dimensions of national culture for selected countries. Hofstede has emphasised that although his work, and that of others such as Laurent (1983), on upper and middle managers has focused on the nature of national cultures, these nations are largely a creation of the twentieth cen-

Table 3.1 Relative scores on Hofstede's dimensions of national culture for selected countries

Country	Power distance	Individualism/ collectivism (high=individualism)	Masculinity/ femininity (high=masculinity)	Uncertainty avoidance	Confucian dynamism (high=long term)
Germany (West)	Low	High	High	Moderate	Moderate
Hong Kong	High	Low	Moderate	Low	High
Japan	Moderate	Moderate	High	High	High
Netherlands	Low	High	Low	Moderate	Moderate
Pakistan	Moderate	Low	Moderate	Moderate	Low
Sweden	Low	High	Low	Low	Moderate
Taiwan	Moderate	Low	Moderate	Moderate	High
UK	Low	High	High	Low	Low
USA	Low	High	High	Low	Low

Source: Developed from Hofstede (2001)

tury. Indeed, within the past two decades, we have seen the dissolution of the Soviet Union and Yugoslavia into constituent countries and the reunification of Germany. Despite this, differences between countries in language, education and laws mean that national cultures are still powerful forces in shaping the patterns of beliefs, values and learned ways of coping with experiences for employees within organisations.

self-check question	**3.5** Examine Table 3.1. Use Hofstede's dimensions to suggest how the view of employee relations of a Japanese company setting up a manufacturing operation in the UK might differ from that of a potential UK workforce.

The influence of organisational cultures

Our exploration of Hofstede's work on national cultures has further emphasised the importance of power and the way it is exercised for the management of the employment relationship. However, it has also highlighted the importance of other factors such as the importance of the way in which conflicts are resolved and justice is seen to be done. Alongside this it has also emphasised that the tolerance of employees of uncertainty, the focus on the individual or the collective, and whether the time orientation is over the shorter or longer term, are also likely to influence the way in which the employment relationship operates.

Structural views of organisational culture inevitably use structural artefacts or symbols as outward expressions of an organisation's culture. Of these, the most widely known and influential is probably Handy's (1993) typology. This was developed in the 1970s from work by Harrison (1972) and is concerned with how authority is exercised within an organisation and is the basis for power. These artefacts through which power is expressed can be used to help explore the likely cultural implications for managing the employment relationship. Handy proposes four main types of organisational culture: power, role, task and person. He argues that although these types do not have a high level of rigour, the differing power structures they encapsulate impact upon the way the organisation does things – in other words the organisation's ways of coping with experiences that have developed during the course of its history.

In a *power culture*, Handy argues, there is a single source of power from which rays of influence spread out. The internal organisation of power is highly dependent upon trust, empathy and personal communication for its effectiveness. Authority comes from the resources controlled and the leader's charisma. This means that the strength of the culture comes from the willingness of employees to defer to the leader and, presumably, accept her or his power. Within such a culture, Handy argues that employees are unlikely to be concerned about taking risks or issues of job security. In contrast, power in a *role culture* comes from the bureaucracy (rules and procedures) and the logic and rationality of the way functions/specialisms are organised. Position power and to a lesser extent expert power are therefore the main bases for authority, and such organisations attract employees who value security and predictability.

Power in a *task culture* is based upon employees' expertise rather than their charisma. This is likely to necessitate a different approach to managing the employment relationship, as flexibility and adaptability are valued, and authority is based upon the employee's ability rather than their position or seniority until a crisis occurs. When this happens, such cultures can, Handy argues, quickly change into a power or role culture with rules or procedures or internal political influences becoming the dominant way of managing employees. Within Handy's fourth type, the *person culture*, power and authority lie within each of the individual members, and rules and procedures are of minimal importance. This, Handy argues, occurs in very few organisations and represents a group of people who decide that it is in their own interests to come together as a group rather than individually. Later work by Pheysey (1993) has linked task and person cultures in particular with processes of support and achievement used within organisations, thereby emphasising the importance of culture in motivating and controlling employees.

Work by Quinn and McGrath (1985) uses the nature of information exchange within organisations to distinguish between different organisational cultures. Within their typology the focus is on how things are done rather than the status that these processes give to both individuals and groups within the organisation. As part of their work, they argue that the manner in which these transactions are conducted (the artefact) is governed by a set of norms, which reflect the basic underlying assumptions within the organisation. From this they identified four generic cultures determined by these dominant beliefs: rational or *market* culture, ideological culture or *adhocracy*, consensual or *clan* culture, and the hierarchical culture – *hierarchy*. Although there is a concern about the nature and use of power within these, they also appear to have some parallel with Hofstede's individualism/collectivism and masculinity/femininity dimensions.

A *market culture* is directive and goal orientated, with individuals being judged according to their output and achievement. The 'boss' is firmly in charge of the organisation, and their competence is the basis of authority. Decisions are made decisively and compliance is guaranteed by employees' contracts. In contrast, within an *adhocracy* individuals are judged according to their intensity of effort rather than achievement. Authority in an adhocracy is maintained by charisma, and power comes from referring to organisational values. Decisions are taken intuitively.

Authority in the *clan culture* is based upon the informal status of organisation members. Decisions are made participatively, and employees comply because they have shared in the process by which these were reached. Individuals are evaluated in terms of the quality of relationships they enjoy with others and are expected to show loyalty to the organisation. In a *hierarchy culture* authority is vested in the rules, and those with technical knowledge exercise power. Decisions are made on the basis of factual analysis, and leaders are conservative. Compliance of employees is maintained by surveillance and control, and they are evaluated against formally agreed criteria. They are expected to value security. Thus the artefact of the nature of transactions within an organisation provides a means of helping to distinguish the underlying culture.

The typology of organisational culture of Deal and Kennedy (1982) is explained through artefacts related to the importance of the marketplace. They identify four generic cultures based upon the interaction of two marketplace factors: the degree of risk associated with companies' activities, and the speed at which company and employees receive feedback on their decisions and strategies (Figure 3.2). The latter factor, speed of feedback, can be argued to incorporate aspects of the short- or

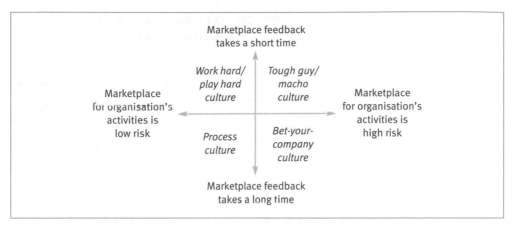

Figure 3.2 Deal and Kennedy's typology of organisational culture
Source: Developed from Deal and Kennedy (1982)

long-term orientation of the culture – Hofstede's Confucian dynamism dimension. Whilst Deal and Kennedy recognise that organisations will not fit into any one of their four cultures perfectly, they argue that this framework is useful in helping managers to identify their own organisation's culture(s).

Within *tough guy/macho cultures* the focus is on speed and the short term, which places enormous pressures on employees to take risks and get results quickly. As a result internal competition, tension and conflict are common, suggesting both masculine and individualist dimensions in which employees are unlikely to make a long-term commitment to the organisation. *Work hard/play hard cultures* also focus on short-term feedback for performance, but at the same time each individual action is unlikely to have high risks for the organisation as a whole.

Bet-your-company cultures are associated with risk, but feedback takes a long time. As a consequence decision-making tends to be top down, and there is a strong respect for authority, technical competence and cooperative working linking to power distance and uncertainty avoidance dimensions. The *process culture* is a low-risk and slow feedback culture, which operates well in a known predictable environment with employees receiving relatively little feedback on their work and memos and reports seemingly disappearing into a void. Those employees who remain in such organisations tend to be orderly, punctual and attentive to detail.

Managing the employment relationship as cultural artefact

Organisational culture is therefore likely to influence and be reflected in the way that an organisation manages its employment relationship. This in turn will have been influenced by external factors including the national cultures within which it operates. Earlier in this section we defined an organisation's culture in terms of artefacts, espoused values and basic underlying assumptions. Artefacts as the most visible of these often have symbolic value for employees over and above their normal associations. Most of this book focuses upon the relationship between management and employees, but it is worth considering that the manifestations of this relationship can also be thought of as cultural artefacts.

Within an organisation, aspects of the way in which the employment relationship is managed are likely to have strong symbolic associations for employees. These may manifest themselves in particular procedures or policies, such as a partnership agreement between an organisation and a trade union (Chapter 6) or an avoidance of redundancy procedure (Chapter 12), but are likely to be based upon the underlying basic assumptions of that organisation. From these sources, individuals are likely to obtain the information that they need to understand how the employment relationship operates within the organisation and what forms of behaviour are acceptable and unacceptable. In addition, the way in which employee relations are managed may also provide a focus for identification or loyalty such as a bargaining group or perhaps a trade union with which they can identify.

Considering an organisation's culture in the way that we have in this chapter suggests that it is as an objective entity, and in particular 'something an organisation has' (Legge, 1994: 405), which manifests itself visibly in the organisation's features and behaviours, including its systems, procedures, policies and processes. In doing this we are considering culture as one of a number of variables that an organisation has, such as the set of psychological predispositions that employees possess that lead them to act in certain ways (Schein, 1992). This implies that culture is a distinct influencing variable that needs to be understood in managing the employment relationship.

3.5 Summary

- This chapter has examined the role of power, justice and culture in the regulation of the employment relationship.
- Power is a problematic concept to define, and yet the theories of power that have been advanced lead to a number of insights when applied to organisations and to the employment relationship. The employment contract, in its broadest sense, is one that is constructed through the course of the employment relationship and thus provides scope to act as a forum for the exercise of power. Power may be seen to pervade this relationship. There are potentially many bases of power, some of which are seen as legitimate, but there are also others that indicate 'actual power', which are generally labelled as illegitimate. However, the realisation and exercise of forms of labour power are likely to be moderated by a number of variables. These include the need to develop forms of cooperation in the employment relationship. The basis of employers' power may be seen to include interests that are clearly identifiable and discrete. References to the 'balance of power' between employers and employees, and shifts in this, are seen to be superficial, given the underlying asymmetry of power that exists because of structural factors that favour employing organisations.
- Organisational justice theory focuses on perceptions of fairness. It is concerned with understanding the subjectively held perceptions of employees that result from the outcomes of decisions taken in an organisation, the procedures and processes used to arrive at these decisions, and their implementation. Distributive justice is concerned with perceptions of fairness about organisational allocations and outcomes. Perceptions about fairness will be based on comparisons made with others. Perceptions of unfairness are likely to lead to adverse psychological and behavioural

reactions. Assessments of organisational justice also depend on perceptions about the procedures used to arrive at such decisions, or procedural justice. Decisions based on procedures that are perceived as fair are more likely to be accepted by those they affect, than decisions arising from procedures that are not perceived as fair. Genuinely fair procedures and processes are also likely to moderate the impact of negative reactions that arise from decisions leading to undesirable employee outcomes, leading to the notion of a 'fair process effect'. Finally justice considerations also arise from the implementation of organisational decisions. Interactional justice is composed of two principal elements relating to the explanations and justification offered for decisions made, and the level of sensitivity of treatment of those affected during the implementation of decisions.

■ Organisational and national cultures will impact on the nature of the employment relationship. Strongly held beliefs and values will affect the nature of the employee relations policies and practices that are established in an organisation. However, there may be a distinction between espoused policies and the way in which these operate in practice. Organisational cultures are likely to be differentiated, with a range of subcultures existing in an organisation. These will impact on the nature and conduct of the employment relationship. The attributes of national cultures will also affect facets of the contract of employment and the employment relationship, although this is likely to occur in a way that is taken for granted by those within a particular culture. A number of organisation culture typologies have been outlined in order to consider the implications of each type for the nature and management of the employment relationship. Organisational culture will thus influence and be reflected in the way that an organisation manages the employment relationship.

References

Adams, J.S. (1965) 'Inequity in social exchange', *in* Berkowitz, L. (ed.), *Advances in Experimental Social Psychology* Vol. 2, New York, Academic Press, pp. 267–99.

Argyris, C. (1995) 'Action science and organizational learning', *Journal of Managerial Psychology*, 10:6, 20–6.

Bachrach, P. and Baratz, M.S. (1962) 'Two faces of power', *American Political Science Review*, 56, 947–52.

Bachrach, P. and Baratz, M.S. (1970) *Power and Poverty: Theory and practice*, New York, Oxford University Press.

Barker, R. and Roberts, H. (1993) 'The uses of the concept of power', *in* Morgan, D. and Stanley, L. (eds), *Debates in Sociology*, Manchester, Manchester University Press, pp. 195–224.

Bate, P. (1995) *Strategies for Cultural Change*, Oxford, Butterworth-Heinemann.

Benton, T. (1981) 'Objective interests and the sociology of power', *Sociology*, 15, 161–84.

Bies, R.J. and Moag, J. (1986) 'Interactional justice: communication criteria of fairness', *in* Lewicki, R., Sheppard, B. and Bazerman, M. (eds), *Research on Negotiation in Organizations* Vol. 1, Greenwich, CT, JAI Press, pp. 43–55.

Blyton, P. and Turnbull, P. (1998) *The Dynamics of Employee Relations* (2nd edn), Basingstoke, Macmillan.

Brockner, J. (1990) 'Scope of justice in the workplace: how survivors react to co-worker layoffs', *Journal of Social Issues*, 46:1, 95–106.

Brockner, J. (1992) 'Managing the effects of layoffs on survivors', *California Management Review*, Winter, 9–28.

Brockner, J. and Greenberg, J. (1990) 'The impact of layoffs on survivors: an organizational justice perspective', *in* Carroll, J.S. (ed.), *Applied Social Psychology and Organisational Settings*, Hillsdale, NJ, Lawrence Erlbaum Associates, pp. 45–75.

Brockner, J. and Wiesenfeld, B. (1993) 'Living on the edge (of social and organizational psychology): the effects of job layoffs on those who remain', *in* Murnighan, J.K. (ed.), *Social Psychology in Organizations*, Englewood Cliffs, NJ, Prentice Hall, pp. 119–40.

Brockner, J., DeWitt, R.L., Grover, S. and Reed, T. (1990) 'When it is especially important to explain why: factors affecting the relationship between managers' explanations of a layoff and survivors' reactions to the layoff', *Journal of Experimental Social Psychology*, 26, 389–407.

Brown, A. (1998) *Organisational Culture* (2nd edn), London, Financial Times Pitman Publishing.

Clegg, S.R. (1989) *Frameworks of Power*, London, Sage.

Cropanzano, R. and Greenberg, J. (1997) 'Progress in organizational justice: tunnelling through the maze', *in* Cooper, C.L. and Robertson, I.T. (eds), *International Review of Industrial and Organizational Psychology*, Vol. 12, Chichester, Wiley. *Reprinted in* Cooper, C.L. and Robertson, I.T. (eds) (2001), *Organisational Psychology and Development*, Chichester, Wiley, pp. 243–98.

Crozier, M. (1964) *The Bureaucratic Phenomenon*, Chicago, University of Chicago Press.

Dahl, R. (1957) 'The concept of power', *Behavioral Science*, 2, 201–15.

Daly, J.P. and Geyer, P.D. (1994) 'The role of fairness in implementing large-scale change: employee evaluations of process and outcome in seven facility relocations', *Journal of Organizational Behaviour*, 15, 623–38.

Davy, J.A., Kinicki, A.J. and Scheck, C.L. (1991) 'Developing and testing a model of survivor responses to layoffs', *Journal of Vocational Behaviour*, 38, 302–17.

Deal, T.E. and Kennedy, A.A. (1982) *Corporate Culture: The rites and rituals of corporate life*, Reading, MA, Addison-Wesley.

Deutsch, M. (1975) 'Equity, equality and need: what determines which value will be used as the basis for distributive justice?', *Journal of Social Issues*, 31:3, 137–49.

Edwards, P. (1986) *Conflict at Work*, Oxford, Blackwell.

Edwards, P. (1995) (ed.), *Industrial Relations Theory and Practice in Britain*, Oxford, Blackwell.

Folger, R. (1977) 'Distributive and procedural justice: combined impact of "voice" and improvement on experienced inequity', *Journal of Personality and Social Psychology*, 35, 108–19.

Folger, R. and Cropanzano, R. (1998) *Organizational Justice and Human Resource Management*, Thousand Oaks, CA, Sage.

Folger, R., Rosenfield, D., Grove, J. and Cockran, L. (1979) 'Effects of "voice" and peer opinions on responses to inequity', *Journal of Personality and Social Psychology*, 37, 2243–61.

Foucault, M. (1980) *Power/Knowledge: Selected Interviews and Other Writings 1972–1977*, New York, Pantheon.

Fox, A. (1966) *Industrial Sociology and Industrial Relations*, London, HMSO.

Fox, A. (1974) *Beyond Contract: Work, Power and Trust Relations*, London, Faber & Faber.

French, J.R.P. and Raven, B. (1959) 'The bases of social power', *in* Cartwright, D. (ed.), *Studies in Social Power*, Ann Arbor, MI, University of Michigan, pp. 150–67.

Giddens, A. (1968) 'Power in the recent writings of Talcott Parsons', *Sociology*, 2, 257–72.

Greenberg, J. (1987) 'A taxonomy of organizational justice theories', *Academy of Management Review*, 12:1, 9–22.

Greenberg, J. and Folger, R. (1983) 'Procedural justice, participation, and the fair process effect in groups and organizations', *in* Paulus, P.B. (ed.), *Basic Group Processes*, New York, Spinger-Verlag, pp. 235–56.

Handy, C. (1993) *Understanding Organisations*, London, Penguin.

Hardy, C. and Clegg, S.R. (1996) 'Some dare call it power', *in* Clegg, S.R., Hardy, C. and Nord, W.R. (eds), *Handbook of Organization Studies*, London, Sage, pp. 622–41.

Harrison, R. (1972) 'Understanding your organization's character', *Harvard Business Review*, 50: May–June, 119–28.

Hendry, C. (1995) *Human Resource Management: A strategic approach to employment*, Oxford, Butterworth-Heinemann.

Hickson, D.J., Hinings, C.A., Lee, C.A., Schneck, R.E. and Pennings, J.M. (1971) 'A strategic contingencies theory of intraorganizational power', *Administrative Science Quarterly*, 16:2, 216–29.

Hofstede, G. (2001) *Culture's Consequences: Comparing values, behaviours, institutions and organisations across nations*, Thousand Oaks, CA, Sage.

Homans, G.C. (1961) *Social Behavior: Its elementary forms*, New York, Harcourt Brace Jovanovich.

Kelly, J. (1998) *Rethinking Industrial Relations Mobilization, Collectivism and Long Waves*, London, Routledge LSE.

Kirkbride, P. (1992) 'Power', *in* Hartley, J. and Stephenson, G.M. (eds), *Employment Relations: The psychology of influence and control at work*, Oxford, Blackwell, pp. 67–88.

Laurent, A. (1983) 'The cultural diversity of Western conceptions of management', *International Studies of Management and Organization*, 13:1–2, 75–96.

Lerner, M.J. (1977) 'The justice motive: some hypotheses as to its origins and forms', *Journal of Personality*, 45, 1–52.

Leventhal, G.S. (1976) 'Fairness in social relationships', *in* Thibaut, J.W., Spence, J.T. and Carson, R.C. (eds), *Contemporary Topics in Social Psychology*, Morristown, NJ, General Learning Press, pp. 211–39.

Leventhal, G.S. (1980) 'What should be done with equity theory?', *in* Gergen, K.J., Greenberg, M.S. and Willis, R.H. (eds), *Social Exchanges. Advances in theory and research*, New York, Plenum, pp. 27–55.

Lukes, S. (1974) *Power: A radical view*, London, Macmillan.

Lukes, S. (1986) *Power*, New York, New York University Press.

Martin, J. (1992) *Cultures in Organizations: Three perspectives*, New York, Oxford University Press.

Martin, R. (1992) *Bargaining Power*, Aldershot, Gower.

Mechanic, D. (1962) 'Sources of power of lower participants in complex organizations', *Administrative Science Quarterly*, 7:3, 349–64.

Morgan, G. (1997) *Images of Organization*, Thousand Oaks, CA, Sage.

Mumby, D.K. (2001) 'Power and politics', *in* Jablin, F.M. and Putnam, L.L. (eds), *The New Handbook of Organizational Communication*, Thousand Oaks, CA, Sage, pp. 585–623.

Ohmae, K. (1994) *The Borderless World: Power and strategy in the interlinked economy*, London, HarperCollins.

Peters, T.J. and Waterman, R.H. (1995) *In Search of Excellence*, London, HarperCollins.

Pheysey, D.C. (1993) *Organizational Cultures: Types and transformations*, London, Routledge.

Quinn, R.E. and McGrath, M.R. (1985) 'The transformation of organizational cultures: a competing values perspective', *in* Frost, P.J., Moore, L.F., Louis, M.R., Lundberg C.C. and Martin, J. (eds), *Organizational Culture*, Beverly Hills, CA, Sage, pp. 315–34.

Rose, E. (2001) *Employment Relations*, Harlow, Financial Times Prentice Hall.

Saunders, M.N.K., Thornhill, A. and Lewis, P. (2002) 'Understanding employees' reactions to the management of change: an exploration through an organisational justice framework', *Irish Journal of Management*, 23:1, 85–108.

Schattschneider, E.E. (1960) *The Semi-Sovereign People*, New York, Holt, Rinehart and Winston.

Schein, E.H. (1992) *Organizational Culture and Leadership* (2nd edn), San Francisco, Jossey-Bass.

Schneider, S.C. and Barsoux, J.L. (1997) *Managing Across Cultures*, London, Prentice Hall.

Senior, B. (2002) *Organisational Change* (2nd edn), Harlow, Financial Times Prentice Hall.

Tayeb, M.H. (1996) *The Management of a Multicultural Workforce*, Chichester, Wiley.

Thibaut, J. and Walker, L. (1975) *Procedural Justice*, Hillsdale, NJ, Erlbaum.

Thompson, J.D. (1956) 'Authority and power in identical organizations', *American Journal of Sociology*, 62, 290–301.

Thornhill, A., Lewis, P., Millmore, M. and Saunders, M.N.K. (2000) *Managing Change: A human resource strategy approach*, Harlow, Financial Times Prentice Hall.

Townley, B. (1994) *Reframing Human Resource Management: Power, ethics and subjects at work*, London, Sage.

Weber, M. (1978) *Economy and Society: An outline of interpretive sociology* (ed. Roth, G. and Wittich, C.), Berkeley, CA, University of California Press.

self-check Answers

3.1 *Think of an organisational situation with which you have some familiarity. How does power manifest itself in this situation, and what types of power are exercised?*

Inevitably the organisation you are thinking of is unlikely to be one with which we are familiar. However, you will be likely to have considered the manifestation of power within this organisational context along one or more dimensions. Following the discussion in the chapter you will probably have evaluated the way in which power is exercised over others and the extent to which the organisation is participative (democratic) or non-participative (authoritarian). Where the organisation appears to be more participative you may have considered the scope of that participation. Which issues are open to decision-making and which are in the realm of 'non-decision-making'? You may have also considered the extent to which conflict is present or absent, the nature of any conflict, and the reasons for this. To what extent is power used overtly or covertly? The use of power may of course vary within the organisation and between different participants in similar roles.

Your conclusions about the way in which power manifests itself within this organisational setting will be linked to the types of power that are used. You may have found it useful to draw on the types listed in Box 3.1. However, you may have also developed the depth of your analysis by thinking about the practices and techniques used in this setting that demonstrate the exercise of power. This may have also led you to think about the difference between power that is accepted as legitimate and that which is seen as discretionary or personal.

There are a number of ways to respond to this question, and the main point perhaps is to start to relate the analysis in the chapter to an organisational setting with which you have some familiarity, to test these ideas.

3.2 *Think of an organisation with which you are familiar.*

Which functional groups in this organisation appear to be able to use their knowledge or situation as a power resource over and above the authority formally granted to them? What are the particular bases of their power?

This question will again require you to conduct an analysis that is specific to an organisation known to yourself. Your answer will therefore be specific to this context. However, you will be likely to have drawn on a number of the concepts briefly outlined and discussed in the chapter. These are likely to include the following:

- the nature of the technical knowledge of the group or groups that you have identified;
- their central role in the organisational system;

■ the difficulty of finding an alternative way of conducting the work that they undertake (which may be due to technical or political reasons); and

■ their ability to deal with uncertainty, or perhaps their ability to create it.

You may have also drawn on other bases of power to recognise the power resources of the functional group or groups that you have analysed.

3.3 *Think of a decision that has been taken in an organisational situation with which you have some familiarity, or indeed in another social situation of which you are aware. What were your reactions to this decision and to the way in which it was arrived at and carried out? Analyse these by using the three strands of organisational justice theory.*

Your reactions to this decision and the processes of making and implementing it may be broadly positive or negative, or may reflect a shift between these two types of reaction. Organisational justice theory allows you to analyse your reactions by examining these in relation to the outcomes of the decision that was taken in the organisation, the procedures and processes used to arrive at this decision, and its implementation. Your feelings may therefore be positive or negative in relation to all three aspects, or they may reflect different reactions in relation to each aspect. For example, the decision may have initially led you to react negatively, but knowledge about the procedure used to arrive at this may have helped to moderate your view. Alternatively, the decision making procedure may have appeared fair, but the way in which the decision was implemented may have led you to feel negative. These are just examples of how you may have reacted. The value of organisational justice theory is that it provides a fairly simple but effective means of understanding reactions. As such it is a useful tool to explore and understand employees' reactions in the employment relationship.

3.4 *Think of an organisation with which you are familiar.*

a *What do you think are the main artefacts of its culture?*

b *Can you distinguish any subcultures within the organisation using different artefacts?*

Inevitably the organisation you are thinking of is unlikely to be one with which we are familiar. However, the following discussion of a small sample of a university's cultural artefacts may give some clues to the nature of your answer.

a Within the university, the main artefacts of the culture include the learning centre (library), and the lack of any reserved car parking spaces. The naming of the library as a 'learning centre' is a strong symbol of the importance of learning within the university; the lack of reserved car parking spaces is a symbol of the egalitarian nature of the culture. Other artefacts, which are perhaps less visible, include written documents such as the student charter (explaining amongst other things students' rights to high-quality teaching), the ethical code, and the plagiarism policy. The former of these again emphasises the learning culture within the organisation, and the latter two point to the university's ethical beliefs of not causing harm to others and fairness.

b Different subcultures also exist within the university between, for example, academic and support staff as well as between different departments. Academic and support staff are, for example, represented by different trade unions (NATFHE and Unison respectively) and have different conditions of service. Some departments focus predominantly on undergraduate teaching whereas others, such as the Business School, deliver courses to both undergraduate and postgraduate students.

3.5 *Examine Table 3.1. Use Hofstede's dimensions to suggest how the view of employee relations of a Japanese company setting up a manufacturing operation in the UK might differ from that of a potential UK workforce.*

The UK scores lower on the power distance dimension than Japan. According to Hofstede, this suggests that potential UK employees will be less likely than Japanese employees to accept uneven distributions of power within the workplace and will expect more consultative decision-making. Potential UK employees are also less likely to be happy with large pay and reward differentials than Japanese employees.

Hofstede's research suggests that UK employees are likely to be more individualistic than Japanese employees. This suggests that the potential UK employees are more likely to view their contract of employment from an individual perspective of their own exchange relationship with the organisation.

Both UK and Japanese employees are likely to place emphasis on performance at work, both having scored towards the masculine on Hofstede's masculinity/femininity dimension. This means there are less likely to be differences in the view of employee relations in this area.

However, Hofstede's work highlights the fact that UK and Japanese employees differ markedly on uncertainty avoidance. This suggests that potential UK employees are likely to have a lower level of uncertainty avoidance, and implies that they are less likely to be motivated by long-term job security. This means that the reward package developed is likely to differ from that which would be developed for Japanese employees.

Finally, Hofstede's work highlights the fact that Japanese employees are likely to have a longer-term view than their UK employees. This may be reflected in the focus on longer-term targets rather than quick results more normally expected in UK organisations.

| CASE 3 | **Power, justice and culture in Publicservice.org[1]** |

Publicservice.org exists to provide a specific range of services in a given geographical area, and obtains most of its funding from the state. The nature of these services is not particularly important in relation to the purpose of the case study. One aspect of organisational context that is important is the role of government in terms of establishing initiatives that need to be implemented and targets to be achieved, and as a source of funding.

Employees point to an increasing number of government initiatives and related priorities that affect them. They are also aware of the implications of this governmental intervention in relation to the services that they provide and the expectations that are associated with this. Some employees commented that it was increasingly difficult to sustain the effort that was required to cope with the initiatives that were being introduced. One employee stated, 'I feel that there is a loss of professional control; we are expected to do more and more but it is increasingly difficult to cope even where you give up your own time.' Another thought that the organisation had become increasingly reactive in its planning as it sought to introduce new initiatives. One

---

[1] The organisation and the people working within it are fictional.

employee felt that there was a danger of creating additional bureaucracy to cope with these initiatives. Another believed that the organisation's decision-making and policies were increasingly being skewed by the need to respond to these central government initiatives, not least because the attainment of additional resources was tied to the achievement of centrally determined standards. This person also commented that important information for the implementation of the initiatives with which they were involved was centrally devised and often took a considerable period of time to arrive. As a result of these changes, several employees felt that the level of resources available and the demands made upon them were becoming an acute issue. Those in areas where new initiatives were being implemented indicated in particular that the workload associated with this often resulted in staff feeling anxiety and stress.

Employees often recognised that the 'difficulties' the organisation faced and the stress evident within it were caused by a lack of resources and the advent of government initiatives that were outside management's control, but many nevertheless felt that management was rather remote. One person commented that 'Management sometimes appear to have little idea about what is really going on.' This belief broadly typified that of several others. Higher tiers of management were referred to as being 'remote', 'distant', 'unaware' and 'rarely seen'. An employee commented that, 'They don't really understand the work, the pressures, and the diversity needed.' Many felt that management didn't reciprocate the level of commitment to staff that employees were offering to the organisation to help to fulfil its goals related to service.

Although management was felt to be 'remote' and 'distant', they were nevertheless praised by many for their attempts at top-down communication. However, some commented that, although top-down communication had improved over the recent past, there was insufficient attempt to promote 'pathways of communication from the bottom up'. One commented that management was engaging in 'rhetoric'; others said that they wished to feel more involved and to receive more support. Another stated that 'management are good at "talking the talk", but I'd like to see them "walking the talk" much more; coming to find out how they can help us and how we can help the organisation.' In spite of these comments about the role of management in general, which generally referred to more senior managers, many stated that their line managers were very supportive in terms of helping them to cope with the changes that were introduced as well as with their high workloads.

Management was seen as being driven by external forces, and many employees perceived that organisational planning was restricted to the organisation's most senior managers. One commented that 'the corporate plan is the product of the senior management team'. This led to a feeling that while 'some policies appear to be well worked through, others seem pretty unrealistic and baffling in terms of the decisions made and their practical effects.' An employee summed up the views of several with the comment that 'little notice is taken of front line staff when decisions are taken.' This often led to other comments associated with frustration and even anger. One person said, 'Decisions are taken without much thought for the effect that these will have on people at the sharp end of delivery. These are often associated with a message such as, you are the expert, you need to deal with this....' Another commented that 'decisions are taken that affect my work but no one bothers to talk to me about this before the decision is taken. This has happened a couple of times and I feel quite demoralised about it.'

This situation was associated with reports that rumours frequently circulated about future plans and decisions. In this sense, the attempts that were being made to cascade communication from the top and throughout the organisation were strongly welcomed by most employees. However, these attempts were associated with problems. Those who worked in facilities that were physically distant from the central location of the organisation, as well as many who worked in departments where services were delivered, complained that they often did not receive the same level of communication about organisational developments as those who worked 'in the centre'. Many commented that they were so busy that they had little time to search available internal media to obtain news about the organisation. In particular the organisation had recently established an intranet, which was used to convey a wide range of information to employees who had access to a personal computer.

There was a general feeling that employees would value the opportunity for face-to-face consultation to a far greater extent than was apparent in the organisation. Many also felt that there was scope for more local decision-making. One person commented that 'I rarely feel that my experience and feelings as a practitioner are taken into account in relation to the decisions that affect our work, but with so many government targets and political issues, I wonder if that will ever be possible?'

Questions

1 How would you analyse the nature of power relations in Publicservice.org?

2 How may the three facets of organisational justice theory be applied to the case study organisation to help to analyse the perceptions of employees?

3 How would you characterise the organisational culture of Publicservice.org?

Chapter 4

Managerial approaches and the role of managers in regulating the employment relationship

At the end of this chapter you should be able to:

- explain the strategies that managers utilise in order to attempt control of the activities of employees;

- categorise these broad control strategies as distinct management styles;

- understand the ways in which these management styles are constantly undergoing change to match changed organisational contexts;

- identify constraints upon management decisions in the management of the employment relationship;

- identify the main factors that influence the choice of management style.

4.1 Introduction

It is likely that most people, if asked what they thought the subject of industrial relations is about, would probably mention strikes and trade unions. It is unlikely that many would think immediately of the role of managers in employment relations. Yet even the most ardent union sympathiser would acknowledge that in the past few years managers have played a more important role in the conduct of the employment relationship. Chapter 5 tells a clear story of the decline of trade union influence throughout Europe and North America. In many industries, for example national newspapers and coalmining, the once dominant role of the unions has been ceded to management. But control of the employee relations agenda is not a phenomenon of the late twentieth century. The origins of unions in the nineteenth century reveal that the reason for their foundation was a response to the often draconian conditions imposed by employers as characterised in Victorian novels by writers such as Charles Dickens.

In general, trade unions are responsive bodies, responding to the agenda set by managers. This may not always be true in all circumstances. Industrial relations folklore is full of stories of the printing unions, for example, dictating to employers not only how employees should be managed but also whom those employees should be:

selection was from the ranks of union members by union officials. Unions at the workplace also frequently take the initiative over ensuring health and safety standards are met. But the last two decades have seen management growing in confidence throughout Europe, and as a result grabbing the initiative from unions in the control of the employment relationship both at the workplace and in national policy matters. This has been due to a number of factors. Not the least of these, as Chapter 2 details, has been the need for organisations in the developed countries to meet the challenge of overseas competitors with higher productivity.

This chapter is about the way in which managers manage the employment relationship in order to achieve what is their fundamental employee relations objective: to ensure that employees perform their roles in the most efficient and effective way possible in order for the organisation's goals to be met. It starts with a consideration of the notion of management control (Section 4.2) – the broad strategies managers adopt to achieve their fundamental employee relations objectives. The debate then moves on to examine a well-known typology of management styles (Section 4.3). In particular, we review the appropriateness of this typology to the way in which the employment relationship is being managed at the start of the twenty-first century. Part of this review is an explanation of the declining impact of collective employment relations at the workplace and the growth of employment relations without trade unions (Section 4.4). The final part of the chapter (Section 4.5) examines the factors that influence the choice of strategy and style adopted by managers.

4.2 Management control strategies

In Chapter 1 we discussed the different ways of thinking about the employment relationship. One of these ways, *pluralism*, assumes that the relationship between employers and employees has the potential for conflict, as the parties seek fundamentally different things from the relationship. Thus the relationship is founded on the principle of what Blyton and Turnbull (1998: 84) call *structured antagonism*. Most of us enter employment not because of a heartfelt desire to serve the community or to fulfil our personal ambitions (albeit that these factors often assume considerable importance as interest in the job grows), but because of economic necessity. It follows from this that many of us would rather be doing something else than selling our labour to our employer. This is where the notion of management control assumes importance. Put simply, if we would rather spend our time at work doing what we want to do, or at least doing what our employer wants us to do in the way *we* want to do it, then managers need to devise ways of making us do what *they* want us to do.

Friedman (1977) talks of two types of strategy that managers use to exercise authority over what he calls labour power: responsible autonomy and direct control. *Responsible autonomy* attempts to mobilise labour power by giving employees the opportunity to have control over their own work situations in a manner that benefits the organisation. In order to achieve this managers give employees status, authority and responsibility. Managers seek to win employee loyalty and attempt to get employees to adopt the goals of the organisation. By contrast, *direct control* involves close supervision of employees – a harsher regime of discipline characterised by threats of, say, pay reduction or dismissal. It also entails minimising the individual responsibility given to employees. As Morgan (1997) notes, direct control is part of the approach that sees the organisation, and its employees, as machine-like. It has somewhat militaristic overtones, and in industry owes much to the work of F.W. Taylor, the father of scientific management (1911). The following quotation captures the spirit of scientific management perfectly:

> Set goals and objectives and go for them.
> Organise rationally, efficiently and clearly.
> Specify every detail so that everyone will be sure of the jobs that they have to perform.
> Plan, organise and control, control, control.
> (Morgan, 1986: 33)

A regime of direct control is hardly an attractive proposition for an employee. For the past 20 years it has also been somewhat unfashionable. Employers have realised that greater productivity is possible using a strategy of responsible autonomy. This is very much the Theory Y approach of McGregor (1960), which assumes that human beings welcome the opportunity to take responsibility for their working lives, or, to use the modern terminology, to be empowered. This school of thought is that of the human relations school. The assumptions on which their writing is based are summarised below:

- individuals have needs to satisfy in organisations; they do not exist in order to satisfy the purposes of the organisation;
- organisations and individuals both bring needs to the relationship. When they fit then both prosper;
- democratic leadership is the best way to ensure such a fit;
- openness and participation is the best way to demonstrate such leadership.
  (Fineman and Mangham, 1987)

More recently, Walton's (1985) views have been influential. He advocates that managerial policies of mutuality (where employers and employees share goals and agree on the means to achieve these goals) rather than direct control will elicit employee commitment, which in turn will yield both better economic performance and greater human development.

What managers practising strategies of direct control and responsible autonomy

---

self-check question   **4.1** How valid do you think is Walton's claim that managerial policies of mutuality rather than direct control will elicit employee commitment, which in turn will yield better economic performance?

---

have in common is that they both assume that their particular strategy will yield the best results in terms of organisational performance. When we think about management control we tend to think about direct control, but if the purpose of responsible autonomy is to elicit more effective employee performance as Walton suggests, then it is equally controlling. It is just that it has a face that is rather more acceptable in the twenty-first century.

Blyton and Turnbull (1998) make the point that the application by management of a particular control strategy is not as straightforward and unproblematic as is suggested here. First, it implies that managers choose a strategy in a rational, deliberate manner. However, we are warned by some commentators (e.g. Mintzberg and Waters, 1989; Whittington, 1993) that strategy formulation often emerges as a result of a pattern of management actions over time rather than from a formal, deliberate process. As we shall see later in this chapter, much employment relations activity is cast in the mould of fire-fighting, not cool, logical strategy formulation. The second reason why management strategy in employee relations is not as straightforward as the control debate implies is that managers clearly do not have unfettered choice in the control strategy they adopt. As Blyton and Turnbull (1998: 85) note: 'control is the product of past and present struggles' and a 'contradictory array of structures and practices is inevitably the outcome.' Consequently, the problematic nature of control strategy choice becomes even more complex. Different strategies may be adopted with different sets of employees over different issues. The same employees may be subject to seemingly contradictory strategies. Japanese companies operating in Europe provide good examples of these seeming contradictions: for example, imposing tight individual discipline while at the same time encouraging employee involvement (see Bassett, 1987).

These broad control strategies are useful in helping us to think about the way in which managers ensure that their power in the employment relationship is used in such a way that the organisation benefits. But they originate from the labour process literature, which tends to assume that the employment relationship is based on a distinct imbalance of power, where the greater power rests with managers. This implies that managers are in the driving seat in choosing the strategy to adopt, albeit they are constrained by history.

But, as Chapter 3 notes, in many situations the greater power does not rest with managers. In the twenty-first century most jobs in the developed economies are based upon the use of knowledge rather than the exercise of manual labour. The more specialised this knowledge (e.g. computer experts) the more the power balance shifts in favour of the managed rather than their managers. You may argue that such situations lend themselves to the exercise of strategies of responsible autonomy. This may be so. But many of us would not recognise either being controlled directly, through threat and coercion, or being empowered as part of a strategy of responsible autonomy. So what is needed is a more detailed way of thinking about the way in which managers seek to manage the employment relationship. For example, we need a way that recognises that many of the decisions that affect our working lives are based on the notion of *shared power*. Such decisions are neither made by managers nor imposed upon us without consultation. Nor are they made by us having being empowered to do so by our managers. They are made jointly by managers in consultation or negotiation with trade unions or other collective bodies representing employees. We also need to consider the management of the employment relationship in such a way that the methods used in decision-making are examined.

For this it is more helpful to look at the work of commentators who have categorised in more detail the way in which the employee relationship is managed. It is to the concept of management style that we now turn.

4.3 Management styles in employment relations

Purcell and Gray (1986: 213) define management style in employee relations as 'the preferred way of dealing with employees individually or collectively'. In this chapter we use the well-known typology of Purcell and Sisson (1983) as a starting point and a structure for a detailed examination of employment relations management. Purcell and Sisson drew their fivefold typology from the original work of Fox (1974), whose work on unitarism and pluralism we considered in Chapter 1.

Before analysing this typology we must emphasise that categorising management styles in employment relations in this way has its weaknesses. They are clearly ideal types. By this we mean that the description may over-simplify reality and not capture the complexity of what really goes on in organisations. This complexity becomes evident when you try to attach a 'label' to the management style of a particular organisation. Often what emerges is a hybrid, where some aspects of one type of style are evident together with aspects of others. Kessler and Purcell (1995) offer further warnings. First, there may be a distinction between the style preferred and the practice adopted. Second, there may be no clear preferred style other than simple 'muddling through' (although we do consider this as part of the typology). Third, different styles may be adopted in respect of different categories of employee. This is not to say that a typology of management styles is worthless. Far from it. What it does is allow us to order our analysis and possibly define a distinctive style adopted in a particular organisation. Concluding what something is *not* may allow us to define what it *is*.

Purcell and Sisson (1983) divide their five styles of managing employment relations into those managers who are:

- traditionalists;
- sophisticated paternalists;
- sophisticated moderns (constitutionalists);
- sophisticated moderns (consultors);
- standard moderns.

We summarise the typology of management styles in Table 4.1. We now examine each of these in turn.

Traditionalists

This is where you may expect to find the greatest evidence of direct control. Purcell and Sisson (1983: 113) emphasise the likely opposition to trade unions of such employers, and suggest that these are the sort of employers 'whose treatment of employees is overtly exploitative.' Such employers have a view of employees as simply labour: to be treated as a factor of production (Blyton and Turnbull, 1998) much as they would treat plant and machinery. The dominant rationale behind the use of such an approach to employment relations is that of cost minimisation. Thus the employer in the traditionalist mould would typically pay less than average wages, invest little in training, provide poor working conditions, and provide little job security. Such employers are typically to be found most readily in such service industries as hotel and catering and hairdressing and in garment manufacturing. Indeed, the image often

Table 4.1 **Management styles in employment relations**

Title	Characteristics	Most likely to occur in:	Possible examples
Traditionalists	■ Exploit employees ■ Treat labour as a factor of production ■ Driven by cost minimisation ■ Little attention to employee involvement ■ Anti-union	■ Hotel and catering ■ Garment manufacturing	■ See text for examples of employers reported to TUC 'bad bosses hotline'
Sophisticated paternalists	■ Non-union ■ Generous treatment of employees ■ Sophisticated HR policies, including employee involvement, training, career management ■ Unitarist	■ High technology ■ Creative industries (e.g. advertising)	■ Marks and Spencer ■ Hewlett-Packard
Sophisticated moderns (constitutionalists)	■ Reluctantly recognise trade unions ■ Formal, detailed collective agreements ■ Win–lose attitude to bargaining ■ Pluralist	■ Manufacturing ■ Engineering	■ Ford
Sophisticated moderns (consultors)	■ Willingly recognise trade unions ■ Unions enjoined in the management of the employment relationship ■ Bargaining seen as a joint problem-solving exercise ■ HR policies to engender employee commitment	■ Companies with relativelylow labour costs as proportion of total costs ■ Japanese-owned companies	■ ICI ■ Hitachi ■ Nissan ■ Dupont
Standard moderns	■ Recognise trade unions, albeit with ambivalent attitude ■ Fire-fighting approach to employee relations	■ Heavy manufacturing and engineering companies with long tradition of unionisation ■ Conglomerate, multi-product companies that have grown through acquisitions and diversification	■ Lucas ■ British Aerospace

Source: Adapted from Purcell and Sisson (1983), Purcell and Gray (1986), Blyton and Turnbull (1998) and authors' own research

conjured up is the 'sweat shop', where workers produce articles of clothing on piece-work at very low wage rates in dreary, or even dangerous, physical conditions.

You may think that such employers are rare in these more enlightened times, but this is not so. The TUC were so concerned about such employers that in 1997 they set up a 'bad bosses hotline'. This received nearly 5000 calls in five days from employees who reported that they were dissatisfied with low pay and poor conditions (BBC Online, 1997). Particularly telling examples were:

- a firm in North East England where the boss simply cancelled Christmas;
- staff in a Lincolnshire factory who have to wait half an hour with their hands up before being given permission to go to the toilet;
- a store manager in Yorkshire and Humberside who threw objects at someone who spoke up for the staff;
- a boss in the North West who deliberately left pornography lying around the office;
- a North East England company that sacks its workers if they go off sick.

Other workers report hourly wages as low as £1 (this was prior to the introduction of the National Minimum Wage) and long hours. Dundon *et al.* (1999) report the instance of a motor company in the North West of England who stopped the wages of, and eventually dismissed, a garage mechanic who lost two fingers in an industrial accident at work.

The TUC General Secretary, John Monks, is quoted as saying:

> I think this is just the tip of the iceberg... Nothing makes the case better for effective employment rights and for giving staff the right to be heard through union recognition, than these cases. (BBC Online, 1997)

Although the TUC expected that low wages and long hours would be the most common complaint, early calls to the hotline cited bullying as the employees' major concern. Neither were the callers exclusively those workers who one would expect to be the most likely to be exploited – that is, those with little power. One third of callers said they worked in white-collar jobs, while one in four was a manager.

Guest and Hoque (1995) refer to such traditionalist employers as the *bad* and the *ugly*. The former category of employers typically spends little time on such practices as employee involvement and communication, training and quality enhancement. The same will be true of 'ugly' employers, but they will pursue a 'deliberate strategy to deprive workers of many of their traditional rights including a voice of any sort' (Guest and Hoque, 1995: 3). Nearly one third of the 119 employers in their research (all of which were non-union) were defined as either bad or ugly as a result of their responses to questionnaires on their employment relations practices. Guest and Hoque also asked the companies in their sample to report on 'HR and employee relations outcomes' (e.g. workforce commitment, quality of staff employed, quality of work, staff flexibility, industrial disputes, absenteeism and labour turnover). The bad employers emerged as having the poorest HR outcomes and the ugly employers the worst employee relations outcomes. It may be that the actual picture is somewhat bleaker than that portrayed in this research. The sample was concentrated in the manufacturing sector although it may be expected that an equally grim, or even worse, picture may have emerged in the service industry. In addition, the questionnaire was self-completed by the employers and, as Guest and Hoque (1995: 11) admit, 'we must accept the possibility that some respondents put an optimistic gloss on some of the results.'

The image of the 'bad and the ugly' employer or the harsh Victorian capitalist employer is slightly at odds with the predominant management style in France. However, we have included this in the traditionalist category as it is characterised as the practice of direct authority by the senior managers of the organisation, who do not expect the legitimacy of this authority to be questioned (Lane, 1989). Typically, the Président-Directeur Général enjoys a highly powerful position in French organisation. This is reflected in the strong element of direct control that is exercised throughout the organisation. Employees typically have little say in what goes on as management jealously guard their prerogative to make decisions. In addition, there is 'a low level of concern for those affected by decision-making' (Lane, 1989: 105). Consequently, management does not seek worker commitment to the organisation, merely their obedience.

We are naturally cautious about generalising management style in this way. However, the authoritative study by Hofstede (1980; 2001) to which we referred in Chapter 3 reinforces Lane's claims. He found considerable employee acceptance of the propositions that management decision-making was autocratic or paternalistic; that employees were afraid to disagree with their managers and they did not prefer a consultative decision-making style in their managers. Hofstede concluded that the *power distance ratio* (which essentially measures inequality of power in the organisation) of French managers was much higher than that of British and German managers and nearer to that of Turkey, Colombia and Hong Kong.

◼ Sophisticated paternalists

Like the traditionalists, the sophisticated paternalists adopt an essentially unitary stance. Unlike the traditionalists, however, they are not normally termed 'bad' or 'ugly' employers. Indeed, they are generally thought to be good employers because they look after their employees in a paternalistic way. They would normally pay above-average wages for their sector and provide good working conditions. They normally pursue a promote-from-within policy. This offers career opportunities to employees, many of whom would join the organisation in a junior capacity. Personnel policies would typically be advanced, with considerable attention paid to training and employee involvement. However, the sophisticated paternalist employer would not recognise trade unions for employee representation or collective bargaining purposes. That is not to say that they are necessarily anti-union in the same way as the traditionalist. The aim of their personnel policies is to engender commitment, enthusiasm and loyalty in their employees. The intention is that the employees see no need for causes to be taken up by a trade union.

The archetypal employer in the sophisticated paternalist mode, despite its recent trading difficulties, has long been Marks and Spencer:

> From the start, Marks and Spencer was known for its caring attitude towards staff, pioneering the provision of benefits ranging from hot lunches to healthcare. One of the principles on which the company was built – and now a core value – was to 'foster good human relations with customers, suppliers and staff'. (Whitehead, 1999)

This is reinforced by the company's staff training literature, which articulates the guiding principles behind the personnel policies. These are (Turnbull and Wass, 1998: 101):

- good human relations – treat workers as individuals with respect and honesty;
- good communications – open and honest at all levels;
- equal opportunities – full and fair regardless of sex, race, age or disability;
- good conditions of employment – high standards and a share in the company's success.

There is evidence that Marks and Spencer is keen to shed its overly paternalistic image in the wake of its recent problems. It has developed a new vision, a new structure for HR, has emphasised the empowerment of line managers in an attempt to shed its centralising tendency and, importantly, puts its faith in performance management (Crabb, 2002). None the less, Marks and Spencer is often cited as one of the organisations practising what has become known as *human resource management* (HRM), or more particularly what is often called *soft* HRM. In this HRM variant employers treat their employees as valued assets rather than 'labour'. Consequently, they are prepared to invest in these assets through good-quality training. They develop policies such as communication (another aspect of employee relations that the company is seeking to improve) and participation to secure the motivation and commitment of their employees. The emphasis in soft HRM is on the 'human' aspect of HRM, whereas the stress in the 'hard' version is on treating employees as a 'headcount resource' to be treated in 'as rational a way as any other factor of production' (Storey, 1992: 29). That is not to say that the sophisticated paternalist management style is concerned with simply the idea of being a 'good employer'. Employers such as Marks and Spencer believe that having good-quality employees is an important element in ensuring that they provide good-quality service to the customer, as the following quotation from a Marks and Spencer senior executive demonstrates:

> Quality customer service is emerging as the marketing tool of the nineties. Quality service depends on having friendly, knowledgeable staff who deal face to face with the customers. These staff are the front-line troops and their importance cannot be over-estimated. (Stanley, 1998)

Earlier in this chapter we warned against the temptation to categorise these management styles in an uncritical way: that the reality was inevitably more complex than this typology suggests. This is particularly true when we consider the sophisticated paternalists. We noted that one of the reasons for caution was that there may be a distinction between the style preferred and the practice adopted. In the case of the sophisticated paternalist it may be that there are managers who use the language of the 'soft' HRM school but the practices of the 'hard' variety. After all, it is much more acceptable as a manager to talk to employees in terms of your desire to treat them as an asset than it is to tell them they are thought of as purely a 'headcount resource'. Sisson and Marginson (1995) note how the language of 'soft' HRM finds its way into the everyday language of many managers although the reality may be somewhat different from the terms used. Therefore, for example, total quality management means 'doing more with less'; lean production means 'mean production'; 'right sizing' means redundancy; and 'emphasising the individual' means undermining trade unions.

self-check question   **4.2** What do you think may be some of the disadvantages for the employer of pursuing a management style based on sophisticated paternalism?

There is a nagging feeling that sophisticated paternalism is an ideal that is easy to espouse but difficult to practise, particularly in the intensively competitive market conditions in which most employers now find themselves. Such conditions are likely to tempt organisations to pursue cost minimisation strategies, which calls into question the soft HRM, 'investing in people as an asset' model. For example, most personnel managers will say that the first budget to be cut in hard times is that for training. As Turnbull and Wass (1998) note, there is an inherent contradiction between control over and cooperation from the organisation's employees. Hard conditions are likely to promote hard HRM responses.

■ Sophisticated moderns (constitutionalists)

The major difference between the sophisticated moderns and either the traditionalists or the sophisticated paternalists is that they recognise trade unions. Purcell and Sisson (1983) subdivide the sophisticated moderns into two categories: constitutionalists and consultors. They note that constitutionalists are more likely to be found in North America whereas consultor is the more prevalent style in Europe.

Constitutionalist managers are inclined to have a similar set of values to the traditionalists. That is, they would prefer to run the organisation without the presence of trade unions. They see unions as an unwelcome intrusion upon management prerogative. However, unlike the traditionalists, they are not able to translate these values into practice. This is because they are often very large organisations operating in areas of the economy where there is a tradition of employees joining unions and where union organisation is particularly strong.

The employer usually placed in this category is Ford. Ford satisfies the criteria for allocating employers specified by Purcell and Gray (1986). It is a single-industry employer with mass or large batch production requiring a large unit in which to operate. Labour costs form a high proportion of overall costs, and Ford operates in a highly competitive product market. Moreover, it has a history of, at best, grudging acceptance, at worst antipathy towards trade unions, which stems from the anti-union attitudes of the American founder, Henry Ford. According to Beynon (1984: 43):

> The idea of working men questioning his prerogatives as an owner was outrageous. He would have none of it. He refused to be involved in Roosevelt's New Deal and the provision that the National Reconstruction Agency had for employee representation.

Ford was quoted as saying:

> We will never recognise the United Auto Workers or any other union. Labour union organisations are the worst things that ever struck the earth, because they take away a man's independence. (Beynon, 1984: 43)

So the constitutionalists reluctantly accept trade union recognition as inevitable because they accept, if not welcome, the view that employment relations are pluralist. Given this inevitability, the constitutionalist employer will 'make the best of a bad job' by using the situation to ensure that, as far as possible, conflict at the workplace is minimised and the least possible constraints are imposed upon management in both operational and strategic decision-making. Thus the employee relations goals are stability and control and the institutionalisation of conflict. By this last phrase we mean that conflict is handled through recognised, formal, democratic channels rather than being allowed to spread unchecked throughout the organisation in an undisciplined way. This is achieved through codified agreements that are reached through negotiation. Chapters 7 and 9 cover collective and individual grievance procedures, which are essential ways in which possible conflict is kept within agreed limits.

Purcell and Gray (1986) note that the collective agreements that are the fundamental elements of the constitutionalist management style need to be highly specific in their content. This is important given the quasi-legal nature of this management style. There should be as little scope for different interpretations as possible. Purcell and Gray also stress the importance of care being given to the administration of such collective agreements at the point of production. At Ford, and indeed any similar organisation, the management imperative is to keep production moving. This, therefore, is the central objective of employment relations management.

However, at Ford there are signs that the basis for employment relations is changing. In 1999 the company and the trade unions struck a Modern Operating Agreement that effectively replaces the so-called Blue Book, a 200-page bible that has specified working practices at the company's Dagenham plant for decades (*The Independent*, 1999). This agreement features new labour mobility and multi-skilling, a reduction of overtime through more flexible working times, more flexible holiday rotas, and new measures to curb absenteeism. But the agreement came too late to save car production at Dagenham. The last Fiesta was made at the site in 2002 (the site is now used for diesel engine production) as the company switched production to other European sites, fearing the investment that would have been required at Dagenham to achieve the necessary productivity levels (BBC Online, 2002).

■ Sophisticated moderns (consultors)

Sophisticated modern consultors have much in common with the sophisticated paternalists, except for the important difference that the consultors recognise trade unions. Unlike the constitutionalists, their attitude to trade unions is not one of grudging acceptance of the inevitability of recognition. It is more positive, founded on the principle that workplace unions can help in the management of the employment relationship. This help may be particularly important when management want to introduce significant change, for example in working patterns. Unions act as a 'voice' of employees, and therefore serve as a convenient channel of communication with the workforce. Moreover, they perform a valuable function to assist management in selling perhaps unpalatable messages to employees.

As the label 'consultor' suggests, the dominant approach is to enjoin unions in the conduct of employment relations rather than drive through changes in the face of anticipated opposition from unions. One way of summarising the differences between the two approaches is to use Walton and McKersie's (1965) distinction between distributive and integrative bargaining. They describe *distributive* bargaining as being concerned with the resolution of issues of difference and disagreement between the parties when one party's goals are in basic conflict with the goals of the other party. The annual pay negotiation may be an obvious example of this, where management wish to contain costs and trade unions wish to raise the standard of living of their members. By contrast, *integrative* bargaining relates to the joint solving of a problem that will be to the advantage of both parties. Here, there is no fundamental conflict between the two parties, and therefore some degree of integration of the parties' goals is possible. An example here may be health and safety arrangements, where a safe working environment is in the interest of employers and employees. At the risk of over-simplification, we may say that the constitutionalists have a distributive approach to employment relations and the consultors an integrative approach. Sophisticated paternalism is concerned with solving problems rather than settling disputes (Purcell and Sisson, 1983).

The constitutional approach suggests that managers will give trade unions as little information as is consistent with management objectives. By contrast, information is the cornerstone of the consultors' management style. Their aim is to take employees and their unions along with their plans, particularly in the case of organisational change. This may well include involvement in long-term strategic plans. In addition, Purcell and Gray (1986) note that the consultors are likely to introduce a range of policies designed to promote the commitment of employees to the organisation and its goals. These include profit sharing and share option schemes (see Chapter 10), team briefings, and other communication activities and problem-solving groups dedicated to, for example, the enhancement of product quality. We should point out, however, one important caveat to the consultors' style. Despite the high level of employee and trade union involvement in management decision-making, the right to make the final decision rests with management.

Blyton and Turnbull (1998), in their adaptation of Purcell and Gray's (1986) management style typology, give the example of the UK based/Japanese-owned companies as consultors. Much was written about the so-called 'new style agreements' between single unions and UK based/Japanese-owned companies in the 1980s (e.g., Wickens, 1987; Bassett, 1987). This was seen as an attempt to mirror the seemingly unitarist arrangements that the giant Japanese corporations operate in Japan. These new-style agreements consist of a package of employment measures that are designed to promote harmonious employment relations and guarantee the sort of high productivity for which Japanese companies are renowned. This package usually comprises:

- an agreement that recognises a single union to bargain on behalf of all employees (or *company members* as they are often called);
- *flexible working arrangements*, concerning both the tasks that employees perform and the time at which they perform these tasks;
- *single-status terms and conditions of employment*, meaning that, for example, the same payment and sick pay arrangements apply to all employees, irrespective of their position in the company;
- a high level of *employee participation and involvement* in the decision-making of the company;

- a *no-strike agreement*, in which the company and the union agree that there shall be no lock-out or industrial action in the event of a dispute;
- *pendulum arbitration*, meaning that in the event of a dispute that is referred to the arbitrator for a decision (see Chapter 7) the arbitrator is obliged to find in favour of the last offer by the company or the trade union. A compromise solution is not to be recommended by the arbitrator. This is the cornerstone of the no-strike agreement, which effectively means that there will be no strikes.

You may notice that the first four of these elements of the 'new-style agreements' are now part of the fabric of employment relations, in part as a consequence of the publicity surrounding these 'new' agreements and the significant increases in productivity that Japanese companies seemed to deliver. Even the fifth, no-strike agreements, is very much in line with the spirit of the partnership agreements that are receiving so much publicity at the beginning of the twenty-first century.

The 1998 Workplace Employee Relations Survey (Cully *et al.*, 1999) notes that of the workplaces in the survey that recognised trade unions (53 per cent), 43 per cent recognised only one union (albeit that this may not necessarily mean that the union covered all employee categories). The 1990 survey (Millward *et al.*, 1992) indicates that the equivalent figure was 36 per cent (29 per cent contained members who performed both manual and non-manual jobs). This may be due, in part, to the merger of unions, meaning that only one union performs the function that was previously fulfilled by a number that have merged (for example, COHSE, NALGO and NUPE merged to form Unison). But there is no doubting the advantages that single unionism presents to employers. Principal among these are the reduced amount of time that management has to spend dealing with multiple unions, and the removal of the possibility of unions mounting higher claims in the wake of deals settled previously with fellow unions. Dealing in a cooperative way with one union offers a more consultative way forward than multi-unionism. The prospect of stable, harmonious employment relations practices is central to improving performance and output in Japanese companies (Bassett, 1987). They allow companies 'to concentrate on production, not on *ad hoc* solutions to keep it going' (Bassett, 1987: 90). Despite the reservations the trade union movement has about single union representation, the likelihood is that their popularity among employers will continue to grow.

Chapter 2 details the rise in popularity of more flexible working arrangements. Central to the 'new style agreements' has been those concerned with the ability of management to allocate a wide variety of tasks among employees, for example machine operators conducting their own simple machine maintenance, thus breaking down the tight boundaries traditionally placed around jobs by so-called *demarcation*. Tailby (1999) warns against exaggerating the extent to which more flexible working arrangements have become widespread. However, there is little doubt of the importance of greater functional flexibility in many organisations. This, of course, is entirely consistent with the existence of a single union at the workplace, covering all employees, irrespective of their status or job function. Traditionally it was one of the objectives of some unions to preserve tight job boundaries in order to protect the exclusivity of the skill of their members and therefore preserve their members' bargaining power.

Differing contractual arrangements for manual and non-manual workers have been prevalent historically in most European countries. Price and Price (1994) note research evidence to suggest this is changing, albeit slowly, and the reasons for this change: principally, increasing democracy at the workplace, the effect of technology blurring manual and non-manual distinctions, functional flexibility and the growth of commitment-seeking HRM techniques. A report by EIRR (1995) suggests that the blue/white collar divide has virtually disappeared in France, Italy, The Netherlands, Portugal and Spain. Considerable moves to harmonisation are evident in Germany, Malta, Norway and Switzerland but it has further to go in the UK, Belgium, Austria and Denmark.

self-check question	**4.3** What terms and conditions of employment (other than payment methods and sick pay) have traditionally been different for white- and blue-collar workers?

However, the significance of single-status terms and conditions of employment for a consultative style of employee relations management is much less than arrangements for participation and employee involvement. Chapter 8 details the changes in the extent to, and the ways in, which employers have involved employees in recent years. This has seen a movement away from the traditional management–union joint consultative committee towards other forms of involvement. The company joint council operated by Nissan (Blyton and Turnbull, 1998: 220–1) is a good example of this. This council comprises elected employees who are both union and non-union members, and nominated individuals (e.g. the chair and secretary and the personnel director). The council has three functions: to act as a consultative forum for business issues, to act as the final decision-making body for the in-house grievance procedure, and to be the sole forum for the negotiation of terms and conditions of employment. The council differs from the normal consultative and bargaining machinery in that all council members, elected or nominated, are obliged to act in the best interests of Nissan, not in the interests of their constituents.

The 1998 Workplace Employee Relations Survey notes that while the amount of traditional joint consultative committees has declined over the past two decades, there has been emphasis on other forms of employee involvement. Management is now more likely to communicate to employees through newsletters and management–employee meetings, at which there is an increased tendency to share business information. Suggestion schemes are more prevalent, as is the opportunity to participate in the company's fortunes through share ownership schemes (see Chapter 10).

All this suggests that the sophisticated modern emphasis would seem to be moving in the direction of the consultors. In this, UK organisations are following in the footsteps of their German counterparts, who have adopted this style for decades.

Van Ruysseveldt and Visser (1996) contrast the German with the UK and French styles of employee relations and conclude that it is integrative. The organisations that represent the interests of German employers and employees act as social partners seeking consensus and operate within an employee relations framework that is characterised by formal structures and procedures. The German system of employee relations is best known for the high degree of worker participation at organisation and workplace level. There are mandatory works councils (*Betriebsträte*) elected by and from all workers, union and non-union. Employers are legally obliged to give the councils information and consult with them over a wide range of issues. They monitor the law and collective agreements although they are not allowed to bargain collectively or take industrial action. The information and co-decision-making rights of employees are underpinned in larger companies by a supervisory board (*Aufsichtsrat*), one third of the members of this board being elected by employees. It is important to bear in mind the high degree of legal regulation of this aspect of German employment relations. Both the structures and processes are legally regulated and enforceable, so, as Van Ruysseveldt and Visser (1996: 129) point out: 'each party is forced to take account of the demands, wishes and interests of the other.'

■ Standard moderns

Those who have enthused about the increasingly 'strategic' nature of employee management would expect the opposite of the standard modern style. Here, managing employment relations is seen as a major issue for consideration only when it is a problem. As with both types of sophisticated moderns, trade unions are recognised, although the management attitude to dealing with unions is likely to be ambivalent. Unlike the sophisticated moderns, there is no clear employment relations strategy. The approach is ad hoc, pragmatic, incoherent and based on fire-fighting. Even within the same organisation, the approach may differ between sites and workplaces. This stems from the different reactions of operational managers, who are predominantly responsible for employee relations management. Blyton and Turnbull's (1998) adaptation of the management style typology notes that standard moderns are most likely to have a long tradition of unionisation and be found in conglomerate, multi-product companies that have grown through acquisitions and diversification. Such companies are typically to be found in engineering and heavy manufacturing (e.g. Lucas, Rover, British Aerospace).

It is tempting to think, with all that has been written about HR strategy in recent years, that the standard modern style would be on the wane. But in the UK, at least, this is not the case. There appear to be three principal explanations for this:

- The relative unimportance traditionally attached to employee management matters by UK managers. This is clearly related to the regard for short run financial considerations to take precedence over longer-run investment, in particular, people (Bach and Sisson, 2000).
- The constant tension that exists between management and employees. The former, as we pointed out at the start of this chapter, need to devise ways of making employees do what managers want them to do. But in seeking control over the employment relationship, managers must simultaneously pursue the cooperation of their employees. This delicate tension is always manifest to some degree in the employment relationship, as Chapter 1 records in more detail.
- The constant state of change, in ownership, structures, procedures and personnel of many large organisations. This is hardly conducive to a consistent approach to management policies, particularly in areas that are not in the mainstream of management activity.

4.4 Managing without unions: small and medium-sized non-union employers

The management style typology may be criticised as being too biased towards organisations recognising trade unions. After all, only the traditionalists and the sophisticated paternalists do not recognise unions. The former category consists of 'bad and ugly' (Guest and Hoque, 1995) employers, and the latter perhaps may be thought of as something of an ideal. It is extremely difficult to assess the proportion of employers who fall into these two camps. But let us be charitable and say that the majority of small employers are not traditionalists. We may say with greater confidence that there is a small minority of employing organisations that are sophisticated paternalists, although there is evidence of growth in the use of so-called *high commitment management practices* (such as employee communication, employee involvement, or profit sharing), particularly in larger workplaces, in workplaces that are part of larger organisations, and in the public sector (Cully *et al.*, 1999).

This suggests that there are many employers who are not covered by the management style typology: those who do not recognise unions and who are neither the 'bad and ugly' nor 'ideal' employers. The majority of employers fitting these criteria are small and medium-sized firms (SMEs). These are generally thought to have between 10 and 499 employees (Kinnie *et al.*, 1999). This is an area of the economy that has been largely ignored in employee relations research (Wilkinson, 1999). Table 4.2 illustrates the point that non-unionism is much more likely to be found in SMEs than in large organisations. Only 13 per cent of small employers (10–99 employees) recognise unions, whereas nearly three-quarters of large organisations (10 000+ employees) have such arrangements. (The corresponding figure for workplaces is bound to be higher because this includes workplaces in the public sector, such as local government maintenance depots, where there is near-universal trade union recognition.)

Table 4.2 **Trade union presence by workplace and organisation size and economic sector**

Workplace size	Recognised trade union present (% of workplaces)
25–49	39
50–99	41
100–199	57
200–499	67
500 +	78
Organisation size	
Less than 100	13
100–999	29
1000–9999	58
10 000 +	73
Private sector	25
Public sector	95

Source: Cully *et al.* (1999: 92)

This raises the question: what is the predominant management style in non-union SMEs? The answer, according to McLoughlin and Gourlay (1994), is that there is not one. Their research was in the high technology sector only. When one considers the fact that businesses with 0–49 employees account for over 99 per cent of UK businesses and 45 per cent of non-governmental employment (Wilkinson, 1999), and the enormous variety of small firms in the UK, it is reasonable to assume that their conclusion stands for the whole of the small firm sector. But that is not to say that no patterns regarding management style emerge from research evidence.

McLoughlin and Gourlay (1994) found no systematic application of the sort of HRM techniques associated with sophisticated paternalism. Nor did they find support for the 'bad and ugly employer' thesis. The reality was somewhere in the middle. They found considerable variation in the way in which employees were managed in small non-union firms. The greatest determinant of management style was a degree of dependence on the scarce skills of employees – not surprising in the high-technology sector. This led to a pragmatic and highly individualised approach to managing the employment relationship. This was particularly evident in pay determination, communications and grievance handling. McLoughlin and Gourlay concluded that there was a sort of 'benevolent autocracy' at work in the organisations they studied:

> ...there was recognition of the dependence upon employees with scarce labour market skills which were essential to the business. In such instances, management style... recognised the need to 'carry the support of employees' if business objectives were to be achieved. Even if the methods for achieving this were highly informal, if not rudimentary, they did not amount to the unhindered or unconstrained exercise of the managerial prerogative. (McLoughlin and Gourlay, 1994: 155)

The reference to informality, and therefore unpredictability (Wilkinson, 1999), is consistent with other evidence. Cully et al. (1999) note that small businesses tended to have a less formal approach to managing the employment relationship than small workplaces that were part of large multiple organisations. They were less likely to have personnel expertise in house or sophisticated personnel techniques such as performance appraisal, incentive pay schemes or structures for representing the views of employees. As Cully et al. (1999: 273) report: 'Owner-managers generally took the view that they were there to take the decisions, and this was reflected in the way they ran their businesses.'

For further evidence of the predominant style of managing the employment relationship in small firms it is necessary to look in more detail at the practice of personnel techniques. This is provided in useful detail by the 1998 Workplace Employee Relations Survey (Cully et al., 1999). One of the most publicised deficiencies in the UK is the relative lack of investment in training. This is particularly the case in small firms (see Wilkinson, 1999, for a summary of research evidence). The 1998 Workplace Employee Relations Survey notes that only 17 per cent of small businesses provided training for most of their employees in the 12 months prior to the survey (Cully et al., 1999). Of course, the resources to provide the training may be less plentiful in small firms than in their larger counterparts. But it is reasonable to assume that small firm owners and managers conclude that the short-run gains of 'getting the product out of the door' outweigh the longer-run gains of a workforce with enhanced skills, particularly as those employees may decide to work elsewhere in the future.

Employee involvement seems to be another approach that is less favoured in small firms. The 1998 Workplace Employee Relations Survey (Cully *et al.*, 1999) found that less than 23 per cent of small firms involve their employees in such activities as problem-solving groups. This is somewhat confusing in the light of the picture in regard to employee communication. Only 22 per cent of small businesses had no team briefings, regular whole workforce meetings, systematic use of the management chain or newsletters. The most prevalent form of communication was the meeting with the whole workforce, something that is possible with a relatively small number of employees. This casts doubt on the typicality of this revealing quote from a personnel manager interviewed in a small firm case study by Dundon *et al.* (1999: 258):

> [Communicating with employees] ...can be a dangerous thing. [The current system of withholding information is] a strategy that has been built up over the years and is used to keep the employees on their toes.

It might be expected that pay systems in small firms would be less sophisticated than in larger ones. The 1998 Workplace Employee Relations Survey (Cully *et al.*, 1999) provides confirmation. Less than one-half of small employers had incentive pay schemes. As many small firms are family owned, or have a single working owner, it may be expected that profit-related pay would not be popular. This proved to be so. Only 20 per cent of small firms reported having such schemes compared with 58 per cent of small workplaces that were part of multiple organisations. Only 13 per cent of small firms had individual or group performance-related pay schemes. The predominant mode of incentive scheme was the cash bonus, perhaps for the reason that such schemes are simple to operate. The picture regarding pay determination was clear. Just 1 per cent of small businesses determined the pay of their non-managerial employees by collective bargaining. By contrast, 67 per cent of firms decided employees' pay unilaterally by managers. Only 13 per cent of small firms determined the pay of non-managerial employees solely by individual negotiation.

The impression of informality and lack of procedural sophistication is confirmed by examination of procedures for performance appraisal, grievance, disciplinary and equal opportunities procedures (Table 4.3).

The figure of 32 per cent of small employers operating performance appraisal may be treated with caution. The term 'formal' is open to interpretation. Our experience is that some managers may deem a brief, informal chat with an employee about her

Table 4.3 Incidence of performance appraisal, formal procedures for dealing with individual grievances and disciplinary cases and equal opportunities policies in small businesses

Procedure or policy	% of workplaces
Formal performance appraisal for at least 60% of non-managerial employees	32
Formal individual grievance procedure	68
Formal disciplinary and dismissals procedure	70
Equal opportunities policy	19

Source: Cully *et al.* (1999: 263)

performance to be a 'formal appraisal'. That three out of ten small employers do not have formal grievance and disciplinary procedures is more telling than the statistic that seven out of ten have such procedures. Given the obligation to have such procedures and publicise their presence to employees (see Chapter 9), this renders an enormous amount of small employers vulnerable to employment tribunal claims that they may have difficulty defending. Given the theme of informality, it is not surprising that only 19 per cent of small firms had equal opportunities policies. Of those that did not, the majority thought that such a policy was unnecessary or they had not thought of introducing one. A substantial proportion of small firms without such a policy said that 'they either had a policy and it wasn't formalised or that it was in the process of being formalised or that they aimed at being an equal opportunities employer regardless of having a policy' (Cully *et al.*, 1999: 264). This seems to promise little for the employment prospects of under-represented groups in this important sector of the economy. This conclusion is reinforced by the 1998 Workplace Employee Relations Survey finding that informal approaches to recruitment dominate in small businesses, with great reliance being placed on the recommendations of other employees.

One important reason for the lack of sophistication in the management of the employment relationship in small firms is suggested in the case study of Dundon *et al.* (1999) of a small commercial truck dealer. Here, managers outside the family circle tended to be time-served ex-mechanics or sales reps. Dundon *et al.* report one manager as recalling.

> The problem with motor trade managers is that they've had very little training – particularly in people and communication skills – they've got very rough and ready management skills. (Dundon *et al.*, 1999: 255)

---

self-check question
  4.4 What other reasons may there be for a lack of formal personnel procedures in small firms?

So we are left with an impression that the employment relationship in small, non-union firms is somewhat unpredictable. At its best it may contain much of the sophisticated paternalist; at its worst it may resemble the traditionalist. What is clear is that the absence of collective representation for employees means that they are very much subject to the preferences of their managers.

4.5 The factors that influence the choice of strategy and style adopted by managers

It is too simple to assume that managers have a 'free choice' of the style of employment relations they adopt. In most organisations managers have the legacy of history, which influences the general philosophy and value system that shapes everyday policy and practice. The values of the founder are a clear example of this, as the case of Henry Ford mentioned earlier in this chapter illustrates. Even in start-up organisations on greenfield sites managers have to operate within a particular international, national and industry context. This chapter ends with a brief consideration of factors that influence the choice of strategy and style adopted by managers. The first set of factors is *contextual*.

In all countries the conduct of the employment relationship is governed to some degree by the amount and nature of legislation that impacts upon it. You will, for example, have noticed the legal requirement for German companies to have formal arrangements for employee participation. Similarly, in Germany and France there are highly regulated systems of industrial training. In addition, collective agreements are legally enforceable in many European countries, but not in the UK. The voluntary system in the UK, where employers and employees and their representatives have been largely free to work out their own way of managing the employment relationship, means a greater variety of management styles may be adopted. You will be aware, however, that the impact of EU legislation (for example, the adoption by the UK of the National Minimum Wage and the Working Time restrictions) will do much to create uniformity in working arrangements across Europe.

Sisson and Marginson (1995) note the reliance on multi-employer bargaining in many European countries. Chapter 7 notes that such arrangements have become much less widespread in the UK. The presence of multi-employer bargaining means that management is more likely to belong to an employers' association that negotiates industry-wide on pay, hours and holidays as well as training, employment security and work methods. Although such deals are highly centralised, there is still scope for workplace bargaining over the finer detail of how the industry-wide arrangement is implemented. Such reliance on multi-employer bargaining means that a role for trade unions is apparent at workplace level, thus reducing the ability of management to choose a deliberately non-union strategy.

The second set of factors that influence the choice of employment relations strategy and style adopted by managers relate to characteristics of *the organisation itself*. These are structural, and are suggested largely by the discussion in the chapter.

The first of these relates to the *size* of the organisation. It is clear from the discussion earlier in this chapter that the small organisation is likely to be less formal and sophisticated in its management style. But this is only part of the story. The 1998 Workplace Employee Relations Survey (Cully *et al.*, 1999) notes that workplace and organisational size is related to a number of variables. Among these are:

- *Trade union recognition*: 39 per cent of workplaces with 25–49 employees recognise a union compared with 78 per cent of workplaces with more than 500 employees.
- *Joint consultative committees (JCCs)*: 80 per cent of organisations with fewer than 100 employees had no JCC compared with 20 per cent of organisations with more than 10 000 employees.
- *Collective bargaining*: 11 per cent of private sector workplaces with 25–49 employees determined the pay of non-managerial employees by collective bargaining compared with 43 per cent of private sector workplaces with 500 or more employees.
- *Employee involvement*: 26 per cent of organisations with 25–49 employees reported non-managerial employees participating in problem-solving groups compared with 47 per cent of organisations with 10 000 or more employees.

So the picture is clear: the larger the workplace and the organisation, the more likely it is to have formal employee relations procedures. Sisson and Marginson (1995: 100) provide a persuasive explanation for this:

Other things being equal, the larger the organisation, the more complex the management task. The more complex the management task, the greater the need for rules and procedures to achieve consistency of behaviour on the part of individual managers. The greater the need for rules and procedures, the greater the need for workers and workers' representatives to accept their legitimacy.

To reinforce Sisson and Marginson's argument, the 1998 Workplace Employee Relations Survey (Cully *et al.*, 1999) reports that 17 per cent of workplaces with 25–49 employees had an HR specialist at the workplace compared with 88 per cent of workplaces with more than 500 employees.

The discussion on non-union small businesses earlier in this chapter also suggests the importance of *ownership of the organisation* as a factor that influences the choice of employment relations management strategy and style adopted. The owner-manager small business is particularly associated with a highly unitarist, paternalist view of employment relations, which sees trade unions as an intrusion into the running of a business that is seen very much as the owner's own creation. But this says nothing about two important differences between organisations in the private and public sectors, and those operating in the UK that are owned by larger organisations based overseas.

The tradition of trade union organisation in the UK public sector is still strong, despite the decline in trade union influence in recent years. The 1998 Workplace Employee Relations Survey (Cully *et al.*, 1999) notes that the proportion of employees who are union members in public sector workplaces was more than double that in the private sector. Ninety-five per cent of public sector workplaces have at least one recognised union on site, the equivalent figure for private sector workplaces being 25 per cent. Here again, managerial style and strategy in the public sector are considerably more constrained than in the private sector. That said, those traditions are under threat from two sides: first, the declining importance of the public sector throughout Europe as former public sector organisations (such as water, gas and telecommunications) are privatised; second, the increased temptation for managers to bypass traditional employee relations structures, even though they remain in place.

Overseas-owned companies operating in the UK had a particularly distinctive set of characteristics according to research conducted by Marginson *et al.* (1993). As compared with UK-owned companies:

- they tended to have relatively high levels of expenditure on employee training;
- they used a wider range of methods of employee communication;
- they were more likely to use upwards and two-way forms of communication;
- they were more likely to provide information on investment plans to employees;
- they were less likely to utilise forms of financial participation.

We illustrate some of the characteristics of management strategy and style in the case study of Prosperous Life at the end of this chapter.

4.6   Summary

- Management seek to control the efforts of its employees through two principal control strategies: direct control and responsible autonomy.
- The style of management of employee relations adopted in organisations may be categorised as traditionalists, sophisticated paternalists, sophisticated moderns (constitutionalists), sophisticated moderns (consultors) and standard moderns.
- The management style typology may be criticised as being too biased towards organisations recognising trade unions. The majority of small and medium-sized organisations are non-union, and the management strategy and style adopted in these tends to be unpredictable.
- The choice of strategy and style adopted by managers tends to be influenced by a number of factors, among which are legislation and organisational size and ownership.

References

Bach, S. and Sisson, K. (eds) (2000) *Personnel Management: A comprehensive guide to theory and practice* (3rd edn), Oxford, Blackwell.

Bassett, P. (1987) *Strike Free*, London, Macmillan.

BBC Online (1997) 'Employees moan on the 'phone', [online] [cited 22 December] Available from <http://news.bbc.co.uk/hi/english/business/newsid%5F41000/41714.stm>

BBC Online (2002) 'Dagenham: end of the line', [online] [cited 19 February] Available from <http://news6.thdo.bbc.co.uk/hi/english/business/newsid_745000/745577.stm>

Beynon, H. (1984) *Working for Ford* (2nd edn), Harmondsworth, Pelican.

Blyton, P. and Turnbull, P. (1998)*The Dynamics of Employee Relations* (2nd edn), Basingstoke, Macmillan.

Crabb, S. (2002) 'Thrill of the purchase', *People Management*, 10 January, 26–31.

Cully, M., Woodland, S., O'Reilly, A. and Dix, G. (1999) *Britain at Work*, London, Routledge.

Dundon, T., Grugulis, I. and Wilkinson, A. (1999) 'Looking out of the black-hole: non-union relations in an SME', *Employee Relations*, 21:3, 251–66.

EIRR (1995) 'Blue- and white-collar status survey, part three', *European Industrial Relations Review*, No. 263, December.

Fineman, S. and Mangham, I. (1987) 'Change in organisations', *in* Warr, P. (ed.), *Psychology at Work* (3rd edn), London, Pelican, pp. 314–34.

Fox, A. (1974) *Beyond Contract: Work, power and trust relations*, London, Faber.

Friedman, A. (1977) *Industry and Labour: Class struggle at work and monopoly capitalism*, London, Macmillan.

Guest, D. and Hoque, K. (1995) 'The good, the bad and the ugly: employment relations in new non-union workplaces', *Human Resource Management Journal*, 5:1, 1–14.

Hofstede, G. (1980) *Culture's Consequences: International differences in work-related values*, Beverly Hills, CA, Sage.

Hofstede, G. (2001) *Culture's Consequences: Comparing values, behaviours, institutions and organisations across nations*, Thousand Oaks, CA, Sage.

Kessler, I. and Purcell, J. (1995) 'Individualism and collectivism in theory and practice', *in* Edwards, P. (ed.), *Industrial Relations: Theory and practice in Britain*, Oxford, Blackwell, pp. 337–67.

Kinnie, N., Purcell, J., Hutchinson, S., Terry, M. Collinson, M. and Scarborough, H. (1999) 'Employment relations in SMEs: market-driven or customer-shaped?', *Employee Relations*, 21:3, 218–35.

Lane, C. (1989) *Management and Labour in Europe*, Aldershot, Edward Elgar.

Marginson, P., Edwards, P.K., Armstrong, P., Purcell, J. with Hubbard, N. (1993) *The control of industrial relations in large companies: an initial analysis of the second company level industrial relations survey*, Warwick Papers in Industrial Relations, 45, Industrial Relations Research Unit.

McGregor, D. (1960) *The Human Side of Enterprise*, New York, McGraw-Hill.

McLoughlin, I. and Gourlay, S. (1994) *Enterprise Without Unions: Industrial relations in the small firm*, Buckingham, Open University Press.

Millward, N., Stevens, M., Smart, D. and Hawes, W.R. (1992) *Workplace Industrial Relations in Transition*, Aldershot, Dartmouth.

Mintzberg, H. and Waters, J. (1989) 'Of strategies deliberate and emergent', *in* Asch, D. and Bowman, C. (eds), *Readings in Strategic Management*, Basingstoke, Macmillan, pp. 4–19.

Morgan, G. (1986) *Images of Organisation*, Newbury Park, CA, Sage.

Morgan, G. (1997) *Images of Organisation* (rev. edn), Newbury Park, CA, Sage.

Price, R. and Price, L. (1994) 'Change and continuity in the status divide', *in* Sisson, K. (ed.), *Personnel Management: A comprehensive guide to theory and practice in Britain* (2nd edn), Oxford, Blackwell, pp. 527–61.

Purcell, J. and Gray, A. (1986) 'Corporate personnel departments and the management of industrial relations: two case studies in ambiguity', *Journal of Management Studies*, 23:2, 205–23.

Purcell, J. and Sisson, K. (1983) 'Strategies and practice in the management of industrial relations', *in* Bain, G. (ed.), *Industrial Relations in Britain*, Oxford, Blackwell, pp. 95–120.

Sisson, K. and Marginson, P. (1995) 'Management: systems, structures and strategy', *in* Edwards, P. (ed.), *Industrial Relations: Theory and practice in Britain*, Oxford, Blackwell, pp. 89–122.

Stanley, J. (1993) 'Quality and service at Marks and Spencer', *in Company Information: Quality and service*. Cited in Turnbull, P. and Wass, V. (1998) 'Markist management: sophisticated human relations in a high street retail store', *Industrial Relations Journal*, 29:2, 98–111.

Storey, J. (1992) *Developments in the Management of Human Resources*, Oxford, Blackwell.

Tailby, S. (1999) 'Flexible labour markets, firms and workers', *in* Hollinshead, G., Nicholls, P. and Tailby, S. (eds), *Employee Relations*, London, Financial Times Pitman Publishing, pp. 457–504.

Taylor, F.W. (1911) *Principles of Scientific Management*, New York, Harper & Row.

The Independent (1999) 'Ford deal with unions saves Dagenham and 25,000 jobs', 22 April.

Turnbull, P. and Wass, V. (1998) 'Markist management: sophisticated human relations in a high street retail store', *Industrial Relations Journal*, 29:2, 98–111.

Van Ruysseveldt, J. and Visser, J. (1996) *Industrial Relations in Europe: Traditions and transitions*, London, Sage.

Walton, R. (1985) 'From control to commitment in the workplace', *Harvard Business Review*, 2: March/April, 77–9.

Walton, R. and McKersie, R. (1965) *A Behavioral Theory of Labour Negotiations*, New York, McGraw-Hill.

Whitehead, M. (1999) 'A time for buy-in', *People Management*, 3 June, 54–6.

Whittington, R. (1993) *What is Strategy and Does it Matter?*, London, Routledge.

Wickens, P. (1987) *The Road to Nissan: Flexibility, quality, teamwork*, Basingstoke, Macmillan.

Wilkinson, A. (1999) 'Employment relations in SMEs', *Employee Relations*, 21:3, 206–17.

self-check Answers

4.1 *How valid do you think is Walton's claim that managerial policies of mutuality rather than direct control will elicit employee commitment, which in turn will yield better economic performance?*

This is an extremely difficult question to answer. It sounds like common sense. After all, employees who are treated 'well' are likely to respond in such a way that they may be more inclined to put their hearts into their jobs than those who are treated 'badly' (note the quotation marks, which indicate the value-laden way in which we have used these terms). But even if you accept this (and this is by no means straight-forward), does it necessarily mean that more 'committed' employees will lead to better economic performance? There are many other factors that may militate against better economic performance, such as poor-quality products, an economic recession, or unforeseen product competition. Walton's claim has strong face validity, but we are dealing here with human behaviour, and perhaps the most predictable thing about that is its sheer unpredictability.

4.2 *What do you think may be some of the disadvantages for the employer of pursuing a management style based on sophisticated paternalism?*

There is no doubt that the claim to be a 'good employer' means that the organisa-tion has an awful lot to live up to, and there is an air of inevitability about the fact that many employees will be disappointed when their expectations are not met. Despite the rhetoric, the reality is that organisations are driven by business impera-tives, and these create situations where short-run needs contradict the essentially long-term perspective of sophisticated paternalism. An obvious example of this is the employer who needs to cut costs and therefore declares redundancies despite the implicit (if not necessarily explicit) promise of job security. Both Marks and Spencer and IBM (another oft-quoted example of sophisticated paternalism) faced this situa-tion in the 1990s. So perhaps sophisticated paternalism is an ideal that is difficult to live up to in practice.

4.3 *What terms and conditions of employment (other than payment methods and sick pay) have traditionally been different for white- and blue-collar workers?*

White-collar workers have traditionally enjoyed:

■ better pension arrangements;
■ longer holidays, with choice of time at which holidays taken;
■ a shorter working week;
■ time off with pay for personal reasons (e.g. dental appointments);
■ use of company facilities (e.g. telephone);
■ the lack of necessity to 'clock in' upon arrival for work;
■ no pay deduction for lateness;
■ more predictability of earnings;
■ greater career opportunities;
■ better car park and canteen facilities.

4.4 *What other reasons may there be for a lack of formal personnel procedures in small firms?*

You may have suggested a number of these in addition to those mentioned in the main text. There is less likely to be a personnel specialist. He or she will see the need for such procedures and have expertise to draft them. The level of legal regulation in the UK is such that, even if the law has been broken (e.g. unlawful discrimination), it does not specify that formal procedures should be in place to reduce the likelihood of this happening. The absence of trade unions means that there is often no pressure on employers to introduce procedures. But perhaps the main reason is the view that some employers see their employees as simply a cost to be minimised rather than an investment to be protected and nurtured.

CASE 4   Prosperous Life[1]

Prosperous Life is part of a major industrial group and is one of the largest life assurance and pensions company in the UK. It employs over 3500 people. The company's product range comprises life insurance, unit trusts, pensions and mortgages. Prosperous Life was founded in 1971 and grew rapidly with high profits throughout the 1970s, 1980s and 1990s. Prosperous Life's head office is located in a large commercial and industrial town in the South of England.

This case concentrates on the client services division at head office. This division provides an administrative service to clients and sales force. The principal functions of the division are the receipt and processing of policy applications and the provision of a pre- and after-sales service to salespersons and clients. The division is structured into groups, arranged by function (e.g. pensions), each of which is headed by a group manager. Beneath the group manager there are a team of operations managers, each of whom has responsibility for a team of work controllers, client services administrators and support administrators. In a recent inspection by the industry regulator the division was congratulated for the level of commitment to achieving quality.

Working life at Prosperous Life is conducted at a hectic pace. The company's founders set this pace with their combination of flair and hard work. These are qualities that remain today and are reflected in *The Prosperous Life Approach*, which was originally published in the early 1980s. This remains a significant document because it is issued to all employees. The principles enshrined in the booklet mirror the language used by many employees. The opening paragraph in the document encapsulates the essence of Prosperous Life's organisational culture:

> Prosperous Life is a refreshingly different place to work compared with most other companies. This 'difference' is demonstrated by the high level of enthusiasm, effort and commitment to be found amongst our people. These are rare attributes in today's business world, and they do set us apart from most other organisations... The key beliefs of the Prosperous Life approach are: commitment to service; demanding and caring and positive management (by providing clear direction, sound leadership and providing the support required to get results).

---

[1] The organisation and the people working within it are fictional.

Much of *The Prosperous Life Approach* is taken up with a full explanation of what is meant by 'demanding and caring'. The document emphasises the role of hard work in Prosperous Life but gives equal significance to the intention to reward hard work in a generous manner. There is similar stress placed upon the importance of respect for the individual, who is to be treated in a manner 'exactly as we would like to be treated ourselves'. At Prosperous Life there is no collective employee representation, either by trade union or by staff association. However, much emphasis is given in the document to the desire of the company to arrange employees in small work teams.

However, 'demanding and caring' means different things to different people:

> I think that the company wants to get more out of people. It wants more of them to put in the longer hours and harder work, to show more commitment and ambition. This isn't spelled out, but people read between the lines to get the message. (Administrator)

Working extra hours at Prosperous Life is a particularly potent symbol of commitment. Not that this is entirely voluntary. Guidance notes for merit pay point out that there is a certain 'norm' in terms of the amount of effort needed to achieve the results required of the job. Typically this will involve senior staff needing to work extra hours in order to achieve these results. A more junior employee, full of Prosperous Life enthusiasm and confidence, gave some indication of the strength of the demanding and caring values:

> People in the town say the 'Prosperous wring you dry'. There is some truth in that because they do expect a lot but give a lot in return.

Many employees speak of the way that people behave at Prosperous Life. Employees are portrayed as being 'positive'. In remarking on the infectious nature of this, one employee said that 'you sort of get dragged along by it'. An operations manager commented on the 'buzz of enthusiasm around the place'. A personnel manager spoke of the way in which new ideas are taken up by Prosperous Life managers with great enthusiasm. A senior administrator spoke of the 'brash American feel' to the organisation.

Part of the logic of hard work is necessitated by the policy of carrying no surplus staff. One administrator spoke of the fact that often, as people left, they were not replaced, thus putting pressure on those who remained. Another operations manager talked with pride about how redundancies had always been virtually non-existent – a consequence of the low staffing level policy. There is little doubt about the deliberate nature of this policy. It was summed up neatly by one manager, who commented that it was a cost-cutting policy based on 'understaffing and overpaying'.

Prosperous has distinctly meritocratic values. It is a fact of life at Prosperous Life that people expect and receive recognition for success. As one administrator put it:

> Here at Prosperous there is a constant atmosphere of how to win, how to be successful...you have to be quite tough to survive here, they put a lot of pressure on you...

This message was reinforced by a poster that appeared on several office walls:

> MAKE SURE YOU'RE IN A WINNING
> POSITION IN THE HIGH PERFORMANCE
> CHALLENGE: PROSPEROUS LIFE

There is little doubt that Prosperous Life has many employees who are very competitive. This is hardly surprising, given that many managers talked of this being one of the attributes sought at selection. Several managers talked of the importance of recognition in the context of paying for individual job performance. The general feeling was that money was a short-lived incentive; the real incentive in Prosperous Life was 'a pat on the back'. But it was felt to be so much better if that 'pat on the back' was in public. As one senior manager put it:

> There are a lot of very achievement-oriented people in Prosperous. They want others to see that they have been given a grade higher or they have a bigger car – it's public recognition that's more important to them rather than salary...

In view of the meritocratic nature of Prosperous Life and the competitive values of its employees it is predictable that the company has a very clear view of the type of employee it wishes to recruit. Managers have different ways of expressing the same message: that Prosperous Life seeks to recruit performance-conscious employees. A series of adjectives are usually used to portray the merits of the ideal employee: adaptable, young, meritocratic, motivated, ambitious, driving – people who will 'fit in' with the Prosperous way of doing things.

Another strong value at Prosperous Life is the intolerance the company has for poor performers. An operations manager talked of how she hated giving rises to people who she thought were not performing at their best. This same manager talked about so-called 'dead wood' at Prosperous Life. This phrase is commonly used to portray someone who doesn't share the same thrust and ambition as the typical Prosperous employee. It is not meant to imply that this category of employees consists wholly of poor performers; indeed their job performance is in general considered adequate. But this is an illustration of the standards that are set at Prosperous Life.

The manager in the client services division at Prosperous Life is different from the traditional UK manager. He or she (they are almost equally divided by gender) is characterised by an attention to management *processes*, as well as outputs. The management of people is seen by group managers as vitally important.

A telling image is that of the 'new style' manager. This is reflected in the comments of one manager:

> The job of the Prosperous manager is quite different from ten years ago. There have been changes in technology, organisational structure and management style. Ten years ago the job of the manager was 80 per cent technician, 20 per cent people manager. Now it is the reverse.

But perhaps the best summary of 'new style managerialism' at Prosperous Life came from an operations manager who had obviously given the matter a great deal of thought:

> I don't know anything at all about the technical side of the jobs that my people do. I think that it's my job to manage them. I do that through talking to them about what they do and making sure that everything is right for them to do their jobs. If you treat them correctly you'll get that back 20 times over from them. They'll want to do it for you. Before I was a manager I thought that the way to do it was to get stuck in and help the staff like the way my previous manager helped me... but I see now that that's not my job, except in emergencies... I couldn't do it anyway, I don't know their jobs... and I simply haven't got the time.

Prosperous Life managers tend to be, as one operations manager put it, Prosperous Life 'born and bred'. Most have been with the company for the majority of their careers.

Few in the client services division have strong academic qualifications. This same operations manager thought that there were no graduates among the management team of which she was a part. Neither does the company attach much importance to management qualifications. The company's view is that 'it is what you can do that is important, not what you know'. It is possible to deduce that this may be a deliberate strategy to 'lock' managers into the company. This is based on the assumption that a lack of qualifications makes key employees less likely to seek employment outside the company.

The management career at Prosperous Life is one that typically seems to start in the mid- to late twenties and end in the early forties. The management cadre is typically recruited from school or after two or three years with another financial services organisation, and is very ambitious. Therefore there is a need to promote them young to retain their services. Allied to this is the concept of management burn-out. The need to improve performance each year means that management in Prosperous Life is a very high-pressure occupation. It is assumed that by their early forties Prosperous Life managers would not be able to sustain the level of commitment that the organisation demands.

Questions

1 To what extent do you think that the way in which employees are managed at Prosperous Life reflects a deliberate control strategy and, if so, what are the components of this strategy?

2 In the light of Purcell and Gray's management style typology, how would you categorise the management style in Prosperous Life's client services division?

3 What factors are necessary to support and maintain the approach to the management of employees at Prosperous Life?

Chapter 5

The role of trade unions and employers' associations in regulating the employment relationship

At the end of this chapter you should be able to:

■ define the purpose of trade unions and employers' associations and analyse their roles and functions;

■ analyse the changing structure and nature of trade unionism;

■ analyse recent trends in trade union membership and recognition, and consider the implications of these for the future unionisation of the workforce;

■ evaluate the promotion of partnership in the workplace;

■ analyse the role and activities of union officials and workplace representatives, including those engaged on health and safety duties.

5.1 Introduction

This chapter commences by exploring the purpose and functions of trade unions, in Sections 5.2 and 5.3. It then seeks to explain the structure of trade unionism and the way in which this is changing in Section 5.4, exploring some of the implications that have arisen from the nature of trade unionism in Britain. These implications relate to mergers between unions, multi-unionism in the workplace, the emergence of a small number of proportionately large unions, the development of single union agreements, and single table bargaining. Section 5.5 discusses the role and functions of the Trades Union Congress in Britain and of the European Trade Union Confederation. Section 5.6 defines the nature of employers' associations in Britain, discusses their changing functions, and describes the role of the Union of Industrial and Employers' Confederations of Europe.

Recent trends relating to trade union membership and recognition are examined in Section 5.7. This section explores employers' attitudes to unionisation, the advent of union derecognition in the 1980s and 1990s, and the ways in which unions responded to declining levels of union membership and recognition through this period. This establishes the context for discussion of the introduction of the statutory recognition of trade unions in 2000, and this section discusses the initial impact of this change. Section 5.8 explores the nature of partnership approaches in the workplace and the impact that this may have on union membership and recognition. The case study at the end of this chapter, based on the TUC Partnership Institute, permits this approach to be explored in greater detail. Sections 5.9 and 5.10 describe the role of trade union officials and workplace representatives, and the involvement of union representation in health and safety committees. This final section also briefly outlines the nature and functions of the Health and Safety Commission and Health and Safety Executive.

5.2 Defining the purpose of trade unions

You may have asked yourself the following questions. How relevant are trade unions in the early twenty-first century? More particularly, what are they for? If you have had similar thoughts to these, you will not have been alone. The role of trade unions has always been subject to question, and they have often operated in an environment characterised by at least some degree of hostility. The work of Allan Flanders, an important theorist of industrial relations, helps us to understand the nature of reactions to trade unions over a long time span. In 1961, Flanders wrote that,

> Increasingly the unions are accused of being out of date, of clinging to restrictive practices that have outlived their usefulness, of failing to adapt their organisation to present needs, of being ... unresponsive to the challenges that contemporary society presents. (1975: 13)

These comments were related to the context of that time, but they may resonate in the current period in relation to calls for employment modernisation and greater flexibility. In 1968, Flanders asked the question, 'What are trade unions for?' (Flanders, 1975: 38–47). His response is still highly relevant today in helping us to answer this question and, in so doing, to define, and understand the purpose of, trade unions.

Flanders believed that the primary responsibility of a trade union was to protect the welfare of its members. Its membership will have come together in the union because they will have recognised some level of common interest. The union offers a means to identify and give voice to such common interests, and to require some level of collective discipline and action to protect or pursue them. In conventional terms this means defending and where possible improving the terms and conditions of employment of the union's membership. In even more concrete terms, Flanders wrote that unions 'are out to raise wages, to shorten hours, and to make working conditions safer, healthier and better in many other respects' (1975: 41). In seeking to achieve these outcomes, their purpose is sectional, which means that they promote 'the interests of the section of the population they happen to organise' (Flanders, 1975: 41). In doing so, the purpose of trade unions is to engage in the regulation of the employment relationship. For Flanders,

> The constant underlying social purpose of trade unionism is participation in job regulation. But participation is not an end in itself, it is the means of enabling workers to gain more control over their working lives. (1975: 42)

Much of this analysis reflects the earlier definition of trade unions by the labour movement historians Sidney and Beatrice Webb. The Webbs defined a trade union as 'a continuous association of wage earners for the purpose of maintaining or improving the conditions of their working lives' (1920, cited in Clegg, 1979: 182). The idea of being a continuous association indicates a state of permanence. Flanders recognised that, for this to be the case, trade unions also needed to be dynamic organisations. In order to be dynamic, trade unions require an active core of membership, for many who are members of a union do not take an active part in their affairs. Trade unions are also affected by the environment within which they operate. Many trade unions have developed to become numerically large before losing the bulk of their membership through commercial, industrial or technological events. A current example of this in the UK is the National Union of Mineworkers. Many unions in the past, faced with a diminishing level of membership, have sought a defensive merger with another, more numerically strong union. We shall return to some of the implications of this later in the chapter.

Acts of Parliament since the nineteenth century have sought to define the purpose of trade unions. The current definition is contained in the Trade Union and Labour Relations (Consolidation) Act 1992. Section 1 of this Act defines a trade union as an organisation, whether temporary or permanent, that consists wholly or mainly of workers whose main purpose is the regulation of relations between these workers and employers or employers' associations. The law goes further in terms of identifying those organisations that may legally call themselves trade unions. In order to be recognised legally in the UK, the Certification Officer must officially list a trade union. Many statutory rights for trade unions, their officials and members are available only to unions certified as being independent. A trade union will be able to obtain a Certificate of Independence from the Certification Officer only if it is able to demonstrate that it is not under the control, or financial influence, of any employer. The Certification Officer is appointed by the Secretary of State for Trade and Industry. Box 5.1 briefly describes the functions of this official.

However, even a legal definition does not fully represent the complex nature of what trade unions are for and how they function in practice. Blackburn and Prandy (1965: 119) recognised that 'trade unionism is not an "all or nothing" quality, but one which can exist in varying degree.' They developed the concept of *unionateness*

Box 5.1   Functions of the Certification Officer

The home page of the website of the Certification Officer says that this statutory official is responsible for:

- keeping lists of trade unions and employers' associations;
- receiving and examining the annual returns from these organisations;
- investigating complaints about trade union elections and alleged breaches of union rules;
- making sure that the statutory requirements established for mergers between trade unions and between employers' associations are properly observed;
- overseeing the finances and political funds of these organisations;
- certifying those trade unions that meet the criteria of independence.

Source: Adapted from Certification Officer's website at <http://www.certoffice.org>

to characterise differences between trade union policies and activities as a means of measuring the extent to which such an organisation is 'a whole-hearted trade union, identifying with the labour movement and willing to use all the powers of the movement' (Blackburn, 1967: 18). Blackburn and Prandy (1965) and Blackburn (1967) identified a number of elements of unionateness. These relate to the following questions, first about a trade union's identification and affiliation:

- Does the organisation call itself a trade union?
- Has it been listed as a trade union?
- Is it affiliated to the Trades Union Congress?
- Is it affiliated to the Labour Party?

Second, about the way in which it functions:

- Does it operate independently of any employer?
- Is its principal purpose to engage in collective bargaining and other forms of job regulation to protect the interests of its members?
- What forms of industrial action are its members prepared to use to pursue their interests? Are they prepared to engage in strike action?

These elements are useful to identify the degree of unionateness of a trade union. Where the answer to all, or nearly all, of these questions is 'yes' in respect of a particular trade union, this would indicate a high degree of unionateness. For example, the four largest trade unions in the UK (see Table 5.3) – UNISON, Amicus, the Transport and General Workers' Union and GMB – would each be categorised as highly unionate. Some organisations combine the role of being a professional association with that of a trade union. For example, in the Health Service a number of professional health bodies are also listed and certified as independent trade unions as they fulfil the function of regulating the employment relationship of their members with the employers of these people. These include the British Medical Association, the Royal College of Midwives, and the Royal College of Nursing of the UK. These organisations fulfil some of the criteria in the list above and therefore demonstrate an intermediate degree of unionateness. Where the answer is 'no' to many of the questions listed above, this would indicate a low degree of unionateness.

However, the reality may be more complex than it first appears in some cases. The Certification Officer's list of trade unions for March 2002 includes several that are referred to as being staff associations within specific employing organisations, although they have also met the criteria established to receive a certificate of independence as a trade union. These particular staff associations are therefore likely to demonstrate a higher degree of unionateness than may at first be evident from looking at their name. As Farnham and Pimlott (1995) recognised, several trade unions commenced their existence as staff associations and then developed a higher degree of unionateness through broadening their membership base, or by merging with external unions. The Certification Officer's Annual Report in 2000 provides two examples of this type of development. The banking and finance union, UNIFI (see Table 5.3), was created in May 1999 as the result of the amalgamation of three employee organisations: the Banking Insurance and Finance Union (BIFU); Unifi, the staff union of Barclays Bank; and the NatWest Staff Association. The second example was the merger of several company-based staff associations, many of which already had certificates of independence, into the Manufacturing, Science and Finance Union (now itself part of Amicus: see Table 5.3). These examples indicate how degree of unionateness develops for many trade unions during the course of their existence.

Any attempt to define what a trade union is for therefore needs to consider all of the dimensions to which we have referred. The definitions cited above are useful in general terms, but it is nevertheless important to recognise that the specific purpose and values of one trade union may vary, albeit perhaps only slightly, from that of another. To return to the work of Flanders briefly, he argued that the best way of seeking to define the purpose of trade unions is to examine their behaviour: 'to infer what they are for from what they do' (Flanders, 1975: 41).

5.3 The functions of trade unions

The primary function of trade unions is related to the regulation of the employment relationship. Other related functions include recruiting new members and retaining existing ones, pursuing issues for particular groups of members, providing member services, pursuing institutional goals related to the development of the union (or perhaps even its survival), and realising some measure of personal fulfilment for those who work for it. We shall discuss each of these. We start briefly with the recruitment and retention of members, and broaden this particular discussion to explore the relationship between levels of membership and the nature of union power.

■ Recruiting new members and retaining existing ones: building union density and union power?

A key function of trade unions relates to their efforts to build and retain membership. Although the power of a trade union cannot be measured simply in relation to the size of its membership, its ability to attract members from particular groups of workers will be important to influence employers to recognise the union to act for these members. This is an obvious although important point. Millward *et al.* (2000) recognise that levels of membership and employer recognition of unions mutually reinforce each other, so that a high level of membership will encourage recognition, and in turn this will encourage employees to join a recognised union. Employees joining a trade union expect to benefit from the greater protection and scope for improvement that its collective resources offer, in comparison with remaining outside its membership. However, these benefits need to be evident and to outweigh any costs of joining.

Unions that build up high levels of membership density, whereby the considerable majority of those eligible to join actually do so, should be able to exercise much greater power and influence, where other circumstances are also favourable, than poorly organised groups. In theory, the power of union and individual should be enhanced together in these circumstances. Batstone (1988), in discussing the power resources of trade unions, suggested that these are composed of two basic factors. These relate to the power resources of individual workers and the ability of a union to combine these resources and to mobilise, or use, them.

The level of power that workers may exercise depends on their scarcity value in the production process or the provision of services, the extent to which they are required given the state of the labour market, their ability to disrupt production or service provision, and their political influence (Batstone, 1988). Some workers will be able to exercise a higher level of power than others, when 'measured' in relation to these elements. For example, highly skilled workers will possess much greater scarcity value in relation to lower-skilled ones in the same industry, although the state of the labour market may adversely affect this value where demand is depressed. Batstone's (1988) second factor, relating to a union's ability to combine workers effectively and to use their power resources, indicates that level of membership by itself will not ensure the realisation of this power. Mobilisation of potential power resources will depend not only on level of membership but also on the extent to which members identify with, are committed to and involved in realising the goals of the union. Underpinning this will be the extent to which a union is effectively structured and defined by a clear strategy around which members may identify. The action taken by the members of the Fire Brigades Union (FBU) in 2002 indicates an example of a clear aim and strategy around which its membership coalesced. Batstone (1988) also recognised that the role and attitude of the state will affect union power, and we return to this aspect in a later section of this chapter when we look at the role of the Trades Union Congress.

■ Regulating the employment relationship

Clegg (1979) summarised the four principal ways in which the employment relationship is regulated. *Collective bargaining* involves trade unions and managers jointly regulating aspects of the employment relationship, although the exact level at which this activity takes place and its scope will vary (see Chapter 7). *Employer regulation* or *managerial regulation* relates to aspects of the employment relationship being decided unilaterally by either employers or managers respectively. *Trade union regulation* involves an attempt by a union to determine particular conditions unilaterally and to impose these on an employer. *Statutory regulation* relates to those aspects of the employment relationship governed by legislation. Within organisations more than one of these forms of regulation may operate, perhaps emphasising the different organisational levels at which the employment relationship is regulated. In addition, particular forms of legal regulation will affect aspects of the employment relationship, for example in relation to equality of opportunity and health and safety at work. Statutory regulation will also affect classes of workers such as those covered by the national minimum wage.

It has been widely recognised that collective bargaining is the key method used by trade unions to protect or improve the interests of their members (e.g. Thornley *et al.*, 2000). Collective bargaining is discussed in detail in Chapter 7, so we will only refer to it briefly at this point in order to recognise it as a major union function. The term developed from the fact that union organisation of employees led to the collective representation of their interests to employers and involved the process of bargaining at which each side sought to apply pressure, including contemplating forms of industrial action, to seek to resolve differences between them. In the past, collective bargaining was the predominant method used to determine many aspects of the employment relationship; however, its use has reduced significantly in the UK.

Millward *et al.* (2000) report on the reduced coverage of collective bargaining during the last two decades of the twentieth century. In 1984, 86 per cent of employees in unionised workplaces employing 25 or more people had their pay and conditions determined through collective bargaining. In terms of all workplaces employing 25 or more people, 70 per cent of employees were covered by collective bargaining in 1984. By 1998, 67 per cent of employees in unionised workplaces of this size were covered by collective bargaining. In terms of all workplaces with 25 or more employees, by 1998 only 40 per cent of employees were covered by collective bargaining. This reduced coverage was also accompanied by a narrowing of the range of subjects that were subject to collective bargaining (see Chapter 7 for further discussion of the reduced scope of bargaining). However, the recent increase in trade union recognition deals (discussed later in this chapter) may indicate the end of this downward trend.

Trade union recognition and collective bargaining also lead to other forms of employee representation that help to regulate the employment relationship. Collective bargaining is likely to lead to two types of collective agreement. The first type leads to agreements about *substantive issues* such as levels of pay, hours and patterns of work and contractual entitlements such as annual leave. The second type leads to agreements about a range of *procedural issues* to deal with problems that arise during the course of employment. These will be likely to include agreed procedures for handling collective disputes, individual grievances and disciplinary actions, as well as in relation to other areas where trade union representation is permitted. Procedural agreements will also cover arrangements for bargaining and facilities for union representatives at the workplace. Trade unions will also gain rights in relation to the disclosure of information for collective bargaining purposes and in relation to consultation (see Chapter 10).

Trade unions can therefore seek to regulate or influence aspects of the employment relationship through a number of means including collective bargaining, joint consultation and individual representation. As we recognised earlier, individual unions are also likely to focus on particular objectives, and this will affect the way in which they function. These objectives may be promoted by the nature of environmental factors that affect the industrial or occupational sectors within which the union operates. For example, UNISON, which is the largest union in Britain (see Table 5.3), is currently focusing on the ownership of public services in the UK through its 'Positively Public' campaign, aimed at 'keeping the public services public'. It is against the creation of Private Finance Initiatives (or PFIs) and public–private partnerships (or PPPs), which it believes are against the public interest as well as the interests of its members (IRS, 2002a). Public campaigning such as this indicates that trade unions may also engage in a broader range of activities with the aim of seeking to regulate the employment relationship through such indirect means.

■ Pursuit of issues for particular groups of members and the provision of services for all members

Recently, trade unions have focused more on issues affecting particular groups of members. IRS (2002a) report that the TUC has promoted a range of diversity and equal opportunities work-related issues. These include issues related to the treatment of women, gay and lesbian workers, part-time employees, and disability and racism in the workplace. The Union of Shop, Distributive and Allied Workers, or USDAW, whose membership is approximately two-thirds female, has been promoting a range of issues that relate particularly to its female members. These issues include equal and low rates of pay, part-time working, harassment and maternity rights (IRS, 2002a). Through the pursuit of these types of issue, unions attempt to influence and regulate the employment relationship, albeit in relation to particular groups of members and in specific areas that relate closely to their personal experiences of work.

Unions have also sought to widen their appeal by offering a range of non-traditional services to existing members that may also encourage non-members to join. These have included a range of financial services such as insurance, loans, mortgages and purchase discounts, offered in association with financial services organisations, and access to legal advice. The success of these additional services in attracting members is open to evaluation.

■ Institutional and personal goals

It is common to refer to a trade union and its members, as opposed to a union being composed of its members where the two would be thought of as indivisible. References to organisations in general make the same assumption. All organisations are composed of people, and when we refer to a distinction between the two it is likely that we are tacitly referring to 'the organisation' as being the group within it who exercise greatest power over its strategy and structure. In this way, all organisations including trade unions can be seen as being composed of different sets of interests, rather than all within an organisation or union somehow sharing the same set. We have already considered the idea of a trade union as being a continuous association, indicating some sense of permanence. Trade unions, as we shall consider further in the next section of this chapter, have had to adapt through the course of time in order to survive. Some unions had to abandon exclusive policies so that they could broaden their membership base in order to survive, or so that they could merge with another union whose membership was more inclusive in relation to different occupations and levels of skill. However, such a change may indicate the dilution of some members' interests in order to secure the wider goal of maintaining the union into a future period.

The continuation of a union in a particular form, the pursuit of broader principles of trade unionism, or the nature of a union's direction may therefore conflict with the interests of members at particular points in time. These issues will indicate conflict between sections of a union's membership and its leadership. One of the authors recalls a regional official of a large union in the early 1980s recounting that 'when the union was on the defensive it had to encourage its members, whereas when it experienced periods of militancy it had to try to constrain them!'

Participation in the operation of a union's functions offers opportunities to individual members to take part in types of activity that most would not experience otherwise. Unions require organisational structures that encompass workplace, local and national levels. This creates opportunities for union members to become involved as workplace-based representatives (usually on a part-time basis); or district, divisional, regional or national officials depending on the particular structure of a union; or even to aspire to nationally elected office as general secretary, or deputy general secretary, of their trade union for one or more terms of office. These activities offer the opportunity to participate in, for example, employee representation at a range of levels and for different purposes, the recruitment of members, health and safety matters, negotiation and bargaining, policy-making and implementation, and the management of the union's affairs. Participation in such activities may therefore offer scope for development and personal fulfilment (although not all experience of union affairs leads to positive outcomes!). The capabilities of those involved and the way in which these activities are conducted will also have a direct relationship to the internal efficiency of the union and to its external effectiveness in terms of its overall scope to exercise influence in the regulation of the employment relationship.

---

self-check question

5.1 How may the other trade union functions discussed above be related to a union's primary function to become involved in the regulation of the employment relationship?

5.4 The changing structure of trade unionism in Britain

■ Number of trade unions

Table 5.1 shows the number of trade unions and level of membership in Great Britain over recent years.

Table 5.1 **Number of trade unions and level of membership: Great Britain, 5 year intervals, 1975–2000**

Year	Number of unions	Membership (millions)
1975	446	11.7
1980	467	12.6
1985	391	10.8
1990	306	9.8
1995	260	8.0
2000	221	7.8

Source: Adapted from Certification Officer's Annual Reports

The number of trade unions decreased steadily over the course of the twentieth century. At the beginning of the twentieth century there were 1323 unions (Donovan, 1968), whereas at the start of the twenty-first century there were 221 unions listed in Great Britain. This reduction was accompanied by the increasing concentration of membership in a few, proportionately very large, unions. By 2000, the 16 largest trade unions in Great Britain accounted for just under 6.5 million members out of a total membership of 7.9 million, or 82 per cent of all union members (Whybrew, 2001) (see also Table 5.3). This demonstrates a situation in the UK of a small number of large unions and a much larger number of smaller ones. However, trying to categorise these different unions according to which groups of workers they organise is problematic.

■ Classifying trade unions

The way in which trade unions developed and evolved in the UK became a source of frustration for those who have tried to classify them into meaningful analytical categories. A number of bases for organising different types of workers in unions have been identified. These organising bases, or boundaries, form the traditional way of classifying unions into types. These are shown in Table 5.2, together with the generic name given to each type of union organisation.

Table 5.2 Traditional classification of trade unions

Organising basis or boundary	Generic union name
Within an employing organisation	Company unionism Employment unionism
Within a craft or group of skills	Craft unionism
Within an occupational group	Occupational unionism
Within an industry	Industrial unionism
According to a religious or political affiliation	Ideological unionism
Based on inclusion, not bound by any of the above	General unionism (Class unionism)

We shall briefly consider each of the categories listed in Table 5.2.

Company unionism and employment unionism

Company unionism generally refers to a union that is not only restricted to organising within a particular employing organisation but also sponsored or even controlled by it. This strategy has been used to restrict recognition to the company union, and the only encouragement to join a union will be limited to membership of this organisation. Employing organisations resorting to this approach in the past have actively discouraged membership of any independent trade union. The term company unionism has therefore been used in a pejorative way to indicate an inferior form that is not independent of the employer and which is controlled or influenced by this organisation to prevent conflict from occurring, at least overtly.

A potentially less negative form of union organisation restricted to those in the employment of a particular concern has been termed *employment unionism* (Turner, 1962). We noted earlier that several unions or staff associations that only organise within one company and that bear its name have obtained certificates of independence in the UK. The key to this single-employer form of employee organisation is therefore the degree to which the union is independent of the employer rather than the fact that membership is restricted to within the company.

Craft unionism

The power of *craft unions* rested on the organisation of highly skilled workers who were central to the production process in which they were employed (Chapter 3). These skilled workers were able to limit the supply of new labour through their exclusive position in being able to train and pass on their skills to entrants to the particular craft. However, the exclusiveness of many different craft unions was eroded through time by industrial and technological changes. Technological changes allowed employers to develop new production processes that permitted them to use other workers with lower levels of skill, thereby displacing craft workers. The rise of the car industry through the twentieth century provides an example of this type of development, although examples of skill displacement continue to occur as new technology allows for the replacement of particular groups of workers. Many craft unions, such as the Amalgamated Engineering Union (now part of Amicus), either had to open up their membership to groups of lesser-skilled workers to survive, or had to merge with another union, or face extinction. These developments meant that craft unions lost the basis of their power in the labour markets within which they organised.

Occupational unionism

Occupational unions, like craft ones, organise workers who undertake the same type of job. This involves organising an occupational group across employment boundaries. In some cases this will involve a union organising an occupational group who work within the same industry or sector. In this way, the National Union of Teachers or the National Association of Schoolmasters and Union of Women Teachers recruit teachers irrespective of their employer. Some occupations spread across industrial sectors, and an occupational union will expand its recruitment across these industrial boundaries. For example, Unison organises those in similar types of 'support' jobs who work in local government, education or the health service. The scope of organisation for this type of union therefore spreads *horizontally* across employers and industrial boundaries.

Industrial unionism

Industrial unionism adopts a different basis for the way in which it seeks to organise workers and build a union movement. Its strategy is based on organising all workers within a particular industry irrespective of their occupation or level of skill. These unions have been characterised as being '*vertically*' oriented in terms of their approach to building membership. This model of, or approach to, unionism has never been firmly established in Britain. Some industries have witnessed the existence of a dominant union, in terms of membership levels, but these unions have never established exclusive rights to organise all workers in a particular industry. For example, the National Union of Mineworkers was the dominant union in the British coal industry, but other unions existed to organise and represent supervisory and managerial grades of employees. Similarly, the former National Union of Railwaymen, now part of the National Union of Rail, Maritime and Transport Workers, faced competition to organise train drivers from the Associated Society of Locomotive Engineers and Firemen.

The early model of trade unionism in Britain was based on the creation of craft unions, around which the early general unions sought to organise lower-skilled groups of workers irrespective of the industry in which they were employed. This historical basis has subsequently affected the shape of trade unions in Britain. This may be contrasted with the situation in Germany, where the structure of trade unionism was reshaped after the Second World War. This led to the creation of 16 industrially based unions affiliated to the German Trade Union Confederation, Deutscher Gewerkschaftsbund (DGB). This union federation incorporated members from across the range of occupational levels in each industry, although smaller union federations also formed for white-collar workers (the DAG) and civil servants (DBB), as well as the Christian Federation of Trade Unions (CGB). In spite of these other federations, the DGB operated as the predominant union grouping for all occupations. However, in response to membership losses, several of the industrial unions affiliated to the DGB embarked on a series of mergers from 1996, with the result that German trade unions have taken on a multi-sectoral approach, with a smaller number of unions operating across various industries. Even with this development, however, at the level of the company or the workplace the principle of a single union remains (Jacobi *et al.*, 1998).

Ideological unionism

Political affiliations and religious beliefs have also shaped the basis of trade union organisation in some European countries. These considerations have been superimposed on top of the other dimensions of union structure discussed in this section. For example, trade unions in France and in Italy have traditionally been influenced by ideological and, to some extent, religious beliefs and aligned according to political affiliations. This has led to the fragmentation of the union movements in these countries (e.g. Goetschy, 1998; Regalia and Regini, 1998). These dimensions affecting the shape of trade unions have not been so evident in Britain, although see the discussion later relating to the determinants of union mergers.

General unionism

General unionism, in theory, is designed to be open to any grade of worker, or occupation, across any industrial sector. The earliest attempts at general unionism, in the nineteenth century, were designed to organise all grades of worker as a political class. However, any attempt to develop *class unionism* was abandoned by the later, more successful generation of general unions that developed, as these general unions made agreements with other unions, including craft ones, to regulate the scope of their organising activities (see example, Turner, 1962).

■ The nature of trade unionism in Britain

As a result of these different approaches to the development of trade unionism in Britain, compounded by several decades of union mergers, growth and decline, and industrial and technological changes, the nature of trade unions in Britain presents a somewhat unclear picture. In the 1960s, Turner (1962: 240–1) noted that many unions 'including certain of the biggest are now virtually unclassifiable.' He went on to comment that, 'The difficulty in confining such unions to a category is partly that the categories themselves often fail to yield a sharp jurisdictional definition in practice.' For example, it is often difficult to offer a precise definition of particular industries and occupations. In the period since Turner wrote these comments, unions in Britain have continued to merge and, as we discussed earlier, to form proportionately larger bodies that have often been referred to as *super-unions*. In this way, many of the largest unions in Britain may best be thought of as multi-sectoral employee organisations, recruiting a range of occupations at different grades in a way that has been shaped by a number of historical reasons. Table 5.3 shows the membership of the 15 largest trade unions in the UK in 2001, which account for 82 per cent of all union members. Box 5.2 briefly describes the sectors within which each of the four largest unions organise, together with some indication of the types of workers they recruit.

Table 5.3 Membership of the 15 largest trade unions in the UK, 2001

	Union	TUC affiliated	Membership
1	Unison: The Public Service Union	Yes	1 272 470
2	Amicus[a]	Yes	1 079 185
3	Transport and General Workers' Union	Yes	858 804
4	GMB	Yes	683 860
5	Royal College of Nursing of the United Kingdom	No	334 414
6	Union of Shop, Distributive and Allied Workers	Yes	310 222
7	National Union of Teachers	Yes	286 245
8	Communication Workers' Union	Yes	284 422
9	Public and Commercial Services Union	Yes	267 644
10	National Association of Schoolmasters and Union of Women Teachers	Yes	255 768
11	Graphical Paper and Media Union	Yes	200 008
12	Association of Teachers and Lecturers	Yes	178 697
13	UNIFI	Yes	160 267
14	Union of Construction Allied Trades and Technicians	Yes	114 854
15	British Medical Association	No	111 055

[a] Amicus was created on 1 January 2002 from a merger of the Amalgamated Engineering and Electrical Union and the Manufacturing Science and Finance Union. The table shows the combined membership for the year 2001–02.

Source: Adapted from Certification Officer's Annual Report of 2001–02: see Cockburn (2002); and ⟨http://www.tuc.org.uk/tuc/unions_list.cfm⟩

Box 5.2 illustrates a complex pattern of organising activities for the four largest trade unions in the UK. Each of these unions is the result of several or many mergers through time. Some of the other 15 largest unions have a narrower organising focus, within particular occupational groups, industrial or employment sectors. However, attempting to apply a categorical label to several of these unions is still problematic (see Table 5.2). This is due partly to the problem of being able to define a particular industry or occupation adequately. Irrespective of this definitional problem, however, most of these unions attempt to recruit across a range of occupations and employment sectors, and none can be said to have an exclusive right to organise all workers within a particular industry.

So why is the nature of trade unionism in the UK 'messy' in terms of the attempts that have been made to categorise it? One obvious reason is that it has a relatively long history that reflects its struggle to develop as well as the subsequent way in which it has done so in practice, as we noted above. It is also the product of real events and real people, rather than existing for convenient academic categorisation. The resultant pattern of trade unionism in the UK has often led to the issue of *multi-*

Box 5.2   Main trades and sectors within which each of the four largest UK unions organises

UNISON: The Public Service Union

Local government, health care, the water, gas and electricity industries, further and higher education, schools, transport, voluntary sector, housing associations, police support staff.

Amicus

Manufacturing, engineering, energy, construction, IT, defence aerospace, motor industry, civil aviation, chemicals and pharmaceuticals, steel and metals, shipbuilding, scientists, technologists, professional and managerial staff, electronics and telecommunications, tobacco, food and drink, textiles, ceramics, paper, professional staff in universities, commercial sales, the voluntary sector, financial services, NHS.

Transport and General Workers' Union

Administrative, clerical, technical and supervisory; agriculture; building, construction and civil engineering; chemical, oil and rubber manufacture; civil air transport; docks and waterways; food, drink and tobacco; general workers; passenger services; power and engineering; public services; road transport commercial; textiles; vehicle building and automotive.

GMB

Civil air transport, security, AA, aerospace, defence, clothing, textiles, food production and distribution, retail, hotel, catering, chemicals and process, construction, building supplies, furniture and timber, local government, NHS, care, education, engineering, offshore, shipbuilding, energy, utilities.

Source: Trades Union Congress at <http://www.tuc.org.uk/tuc/unions_list.cfm>

---

unionism, and the mergers that occurred between unions have taken place for a number of reasons, some of which may not appear to the external observer to be entirely objective. We now discuss briefly the nature of and reasons for union mergers in the context of the UK, to help to understand the nature of trade unionism in Britain, and the nature and issue of multi-unionism, before briefly looking at the advent of single-union agreements over recent years.

Union mergers

Union mergers are regulated by the Trade Union and Labour Relations Act 1992 and by other statutory regulations. These statutory instruments define two types of union merger. The first of these involves a *transfer of engagements*, where a union agrees to transfer its membership into another union, following a postal ballot of all of its members that is subject to independent scrutiny and which produces a favourable vote. The second of these involves an *amalgamation*, where the members of two or more unions vote by the required majority in each case to merge their memberships into a new union. The statutory regulations that govern union mergers are principally designed to facilitate these changes and to protect the interests and rights of the members involved (Cockburn, 2002).

Union mergers have been a continuing feature of trade unionism in Britain. Undy *et al.* (1981) produced a threefold categorisation to explain the reasons for mergers between trade unions. One of these categories covers a *defensive merger*, where a union suffering from membership decline and reduced income merges with another union that is more powerful. A second category covers a *consolidating merger*, where a union seeks to consolidate its organising position through a merger with another union. The third category covers an *expansionist merger*, where a union merges with another in order to expand its membership and to organise in an industry or amongst an occupation that is new to it. A general motive underlying each of these reasons for merging is the desire to retain or enhance a critical level of power that stems from collective organisation. Without this, a union's purpose to engage in the regulation of its members' employment relationships will be diminished.

IRS (1992a) identified a number of reasons for the union mergers that were taking place in the 1990s. These included financial, industrial, organisational, political and technological reasons as well as a competitive effect. Declining membership at this time reduced union income from subscriptions, pushing some unions towards merger. Conversely, mergers offered greater economies of scale and cost-effectiveness to the larger unions that resulted. The decentralisation of collective bargaining (see Chapter 7) that was increasingly occurring in this period added to unions' costs because they needed to train and resource local union officials and workplace representatives (discussed later in this chapter) to undertake this work. Industrial and technological changes were also affecting traditional boundaries between particular occupations and between grades of skill. Such changes threatened previously understood recruitment boundaries between unions for members, as well as creating new opportunities leading to increased competition between these unions. These factors helped to push some unions towards merger.

However, not all of the union mergers that resulted did so for such rational reasons. Some mergers have taken place over time for reasons that are more political. Consequently, many merged unions have been seen as being politically to the 'right', 'centre' or 'left' of the trade union movement. In some cases, political alignment may be seen to have taken precedence over the industrial logic of the situation, where there was a more obvious alternative partner for merger. IRS (1992a) also recognised that some mergers have caused some smaller unions to seek a merger for themselves for fear that they will be left vulnerable to a hostile merger at a later date.

Table 5.4 lists the major recent mergers that have taken place in the UK.

Multi-unionism

The Royal Commission on Trade Unions and Employers' Associations (Donovan, 1968) recognised two types of *multi-unionism*. The first type involved the situation where each occupational group in a workplace is organised by a different union. This situation was recognised as being common at that time in Britain, given the absence of industrial unionism. The second type involved a situation where two or more unions compete 'for membership within a given group of workers' (Donovan, 1968: 179). This second type of multi-unionism was seen as less desirable. The Report of this Royal Commission discussed a number of possible solutions to the issue of multi-unionism. These included promoting industrial unionism, although this was not seen as practicable given the entrenched position of the existing unions in Britain

Table 5.4 **Recent major union mergers in the UK**

Merged union	Former unions	Year of merger	Membership strength, 2001
Unison – The Public Service Union	National and Local Government Officers' Association (NALGO), National Union of Public Employees (NUPE) and Confederation of Health Service Employees (COHSE)	1999	1 272 470
Amicus	Amalgamated Engineering and Electrical Union (AEEU) and Manufacturing Science and Finance Union (MSF)	2002	1 079 185
Communication Workers Union	Union of Communication Workers (UCW) and National Communications Union (NCU)	1995	284,422
Public and Commercial Services Union	Civil and Public Services Association (CPSA) and Public Services Tax and Commerce Union (PTC)	1998	267 644
Graphical Paper and Media Union	National Graphical Association (NGA) and Society of Graphical and Allied Trades (SOGAT)	1991	200 008
UNIFI	Banking, Insurance and Finance Union (BIFU), Unifi and NatWest Staff Association	1999	160 267

by this time. Two other possible solutions were discussed. These were seen as complementary and involved 'agreements between unions on recruiting rights and negotiating rights' and 'many more mergers between unions' (Donovan, 1968: 182).

In spite of union merger activity over recent decades, multi-unionism is still evident in the workplace. The Workplace Employee Relations Survey of 1998 found that while 43 per cent of unionised workplaces with 25 or more employees had one union present, 57 per cent had two or more unions present. One quarter of unionised workplaces with 25 or more employees had four or more unions present. As nearly half (47 per cent) of workplaces with 25 or more employees were reported as not having any unions present in 1998, it is useful to look at union presence and multi-unionism in relation to this proportion. In this way, the WERS data show that while 47 per cent of workplaces of this size did not have any union present, 23 per cent had one union present and the remaining 30 per cent had two or more unions present (Cully *et al.*, 1999). Not all of the unions present were recognised, however. Of the 53 per cent of all workplaces of this size where a union was present, 45 per cent had a recognition agreement and the other 8 per cent did not recognise a union. The average number of unions at workplaces of this size where unions were present in 1998 was 2.4 (Millward *et al.*, 2000).

There are a number of ways in which the potentially adverse effects of multi-unionism can be reduced. One of its potentially adverse effects relates to conflict between unions in respect of the second type of multi-unionism, where unions compete for members from within the same group of workers. Union mergers may eliminate this type of conflict, where the unions involved merge. However, the nature of union mergers, as we noted above, has not always been based on industrial grounds. IRS (1992a: 13) commented that 'mergers may coexist with enhanced inter-union competition for members.' Although this may only occur in particular cases, it demonstrates that union mergers do not necessarily eliminate inter-union competition and conflict, given the underlying nature of unionism and the types of merger that result in particular cases. Another potentially adverse effect of multi-unionism can be the development of fragmented structures for collective bargaining (Cully *et al.*, 1999), whether at the workplace or at a higher level of bargaining. To overcome this effect, significant proportions of employing organisations have promoted the use of single-union agreements or single-table bargaining. We now discuss the use of these strategies in this context.

Single-union agreements and single-table bargaining

Single-union agreements, as defined below, developed in the 1980s. They were most often associated with the establishment of new production plants on 'greenfield' sites, often involving inward investments by foreign-owned companies, and where union recognition was new. In a *single-union agreement*, one union represents all relevant employees for collective bargaining and representation purposes. However, the price of being recognised as the single trade union sometimes involved competing unions going through a 'beauty contest', perhaps with the effect of undercutting one another to gain the sole right of recognition in the workplace concerned. Single-union agreements also became associated with the following terms:

- union support for the organisation's goals;
- single-status employment;
- flexible working arrangements, multiskilling and the eradication of demarcation boundaries between jobs;
- training to promote multiskilling, flexibility and team working;
- initiatives to promote employee involvement, with a company or staff council to deal with both consultation and negotiation issues composed of employee representatives who may not be union members;
- a no-strike clause and binding arbitration for the resolution of disputes incorporating the principle of pendulum arbitration, where the arbitrator has to decide between the management's offer and the union's claim rather than seek to reach a compromise deal (e.g. IRS, 1992b).

These single-union agreements were seen to avoid multi-unionism and the problems that may arise in relation to inter-union competition and conflict, and to promote a culture that emphasised the company, flexibility, cooperation and consensus. However, the recently elected joint General Secretary of Amicus, Derek Simpson, has written about the operation of some single-union agreements in less than complimentary terms. He is quoted in IRS (2002c: 2) as follows:

> Many deals did not recognise the role of shop stewards, nor the right of the trade union to negotiate over pay on behalf of the members. We had the farcical situations of shop stewards denied time off for trade union duties under a single union agreement, no access to staff in order to recruit and, most ridiculous of all, pay negotiations conducted with a company-appointed staff council with no role for the union.

The nature of single-union agreements may vary in practice, but the comments above indicate the way in which managerial power over the employment relationship was exercised in some of these arrangements.

An alternative means to avoid fragmented bargaining structures where a number of unions are already recognised in a workplace involves the introduction of *single-table bargaining*. This strategy copes with the presence of several recognised unions by bringing these around a single table to negotiate jointly. This avoids not only the fragmentation of bargaining but also the associated past tendency to make claims characterised by 'leapfrogging', where one union sought to improve on the previous deal made by another union on the basis of maintaining traditional wage differentials (e.g. Gall, 1994). The WERS data indicate that, where collective bargaining was used to determine pay settlements in 1998, 77 per cent of such workplaces were using single-table bargaining. This compares with 40 per cent in 1990. Millward *et al.* (2000: 203) comment that, 'This shift, most marked in the public sector, but still very pronounced in the private sector, possibly represents one of the most striking changes in the nature of British industrial relations in the 1990s'.

5.5 Trades Union Congress and European Trade Union Confederation

■ The Trades Union Congress

The Trades Union Congress, or TUC, describes itself as 'the voice of Britain at work'. Founded in 1868, it is the representative body of the trade union movement in the UK, with approximately 70 affiliated unions that collectively represented about 6.7 million workers, or roughly 85 per cent of those who were members of a union, in 2002. In this way, the TUC is a secondary organisation, representing unions that have decided to affiliate to it. Kessler and Bayliss (1998: 184) refer to the TUC as being 'the servant of its affiliated unions and not their master'. The majority of its income is derived from the fees paid by these unions. Table 5.3 shows that all but two of the 15 largest unions in the UK are affiliated to the TUC. These two unions are the Royal College of Nursing and the British Medical Association.

Box 5.3 summarises the key functions of the TUC.

The way in which the TUC seeks to operationalise these functions is expressed in the organisational objectives that it publishes. The TUC's objectives for 2003 are summarised in Box 5.4.

The TUC has experienced a number of significant changes since 1980. These have affected its internal organisation and its relationship with the government in particular. The TUC conducted a number of reviews from 1980 into its internal organisation that led to significant changes in its operating structures and staffing. The traditional policy-making body of the TUC has been its annual Congress, which meets each September for a period of four days. Affiliated unions send delegates to Congress on a proportionate basis. This annual meeting considers a range of motions, or resolutions, that, if agreed, form the basis of the work of the TUC for the following year. In between the annual Congress, policy-making is entrusted to the TUC's General Council, which meets every two months. This is

| Box 5.3 | **Functions of the TUC** |

- The TUC is the means through which British trade unions formulate common policy positions about issues that affect them as a whole.
- It provides an important means to lobby government about trade union, employment, economic and social issues.
- More broadly, the TUC campaigns about issues that affect people at work.
- It also conducts research related to these issues.
- The TUC provides the means through which unions are represented on different public bodies in the UK, in the European Union and at the International Labour Organisation of the United Nations. It also develops links to other trade union bodies internationally, and is a member of the International Confederation of Free Trade Unions (ICFTU).
- It operates education and training programmes for union representatives through its network of staff in England, Scotland and Wales. Accredited programmes are organised for workplace representatives, safety representatives and pension scheme trustees.
- The TUC helps to promote cooperation between unions and to resolve disputes where these arise.
- The TUC has also been active in developing financial and some other services for union members.

Source: Adapted from the TUC website at ‹http://www.tuc.org.uk/›

| Box 5.4 | **Objectives of the TUC for 2003** |

- Securing improved workplace rights and raising public awareness of the need for these.
- Campaigning for high-quality public services that are provided from within the public sector and resolving issues about the pay and conditions of those who provide these services.
- Promoting the European Social Model and engaging in issues related to the enlargement of the EU and the euro referendum.
- Promoting trade unionism and working with unions to organise those in work through various initiatives.
- Raising awareness about pensions reform and promoting new pensions policies.
- Promoting equality though initiatives including publicity about the continuation of pay discrimination, involvement in legislation about equality issues, continued anti-racism work, and highlighting age discrimination.
- Working with national and international trade union organisations to consider and coordinate approaches to a range of international economic and labour issues.
- Working at regional and sectoral levels to improve the effectiveness and influence of the trade union movement.
- Promoting and spreading the partnership model of industrial relations, easing tensions between trade unions relating to membership and recognition, and ensuring greater coordination between them.
- Developing the services of the TUC for affiliated unions and strengthening relations between them.

Source: Summarised and adapted from the TUC website at ‹http://www.tuc.org.uk/the_tuc/tuc-5927-f0.cfm›

also broadly representative of the unions that are affiliated to the TUC. The composition of the Council is structured according to a number of sections that permit representation from:

- different-sized unions (calculated on a sliding scale, with 6 seats for a union of 1.2 million members or more);
- women members (for whom 4 seats are specifically reserved from amongst unions with fewer than 200 000 members); and
- black members (for whom 1 seat is for a member from a union with over 200 000 members; 1 seat is for a member from a union with under 200 000 members; and 1 seat is reserved for a woman).

In 1994, an Executive Committee of the TUC was established. This meets monthly to oversee the implementation of policy and its development, and to manage the financial affairs of the organisation as well as to deal with any urgent matters that arise. The General Council decides the membership of the Executive. The TUC employs over 200 people, who are organised into seven departments, about 100 of whom are located at its headquarters in the centre of London. There are also offices in Glasgow for the TUC of Scotland and Cardiff for the Wales TUC, in Birmingham, Bristol, Leeds, Liverpool, London and Newcastle for the six Regional Councils in England, and in Brussels.

The 1980s and 1990s also saw changes to the TUC's relationship with the government. There was a significant reversal of the corporatist approach that had developed since 1945, which manifested itself in the creation of a number of tripartite bodies that brought government, employers and the trade unions together to consider a range of important economic, industrial and social issues. The Conservative governments of 1979–1997 espoused a non-interventionist approach that was anti-corporatist (see Chapter 6). However, they did intervene to introduce a range of legislation that codified many trade union activities and that was not seen as sympathetic to the aims and methods of trade unionism. They also operated a policy of seeking to reduce public expenditure, and introduced cash limits in the public sector that effectively operated as an indirect form of policy on incomes (see Chapter 6; Kessler and Bayliss, 1998). Relative salaries in many public sector occupations declined as a result.

Many of the tripartite bodies, where the TUC enjoyed representation, were gradually abolished through the period of these Conservative governments. The National Economic Development Council (NEDC), which had been chaired by the UK's prime minister, had its activities reduced in 1987 before being abolished in 1992. In the area of training policy a succession of tripartite bodies were abolished through the 1980s: the Industrial Training Boards (ITBs), the Manpower Services Commission (MSC), and its successor the Training Commission. These were replaced by the employer-led Training and Enterprise Councils (TECs) (see Chapter 6). Kessler and Bayliss (1998: 196) indicate that tripartite representation continued only for those bodies whose 'function ... is hardly conceivable except on a tripartite basis'. These bodies include the Health and Safety Executive (HSE) and the Advisory, Conciliation and Arbitration Service (ACAS) (see Chapters 2, 6 and 7). More generally, the TUC found that the frequency and quality of its meetings with government departments had diminished.

The return of a Labour government in 1997 resulted in a change of attitude to the role of trade unions in the UK. Chapter 6 outlines several of the ways in which this change has been demonstrated. In particular this includes the restoration of trade union rights at GCHQ, ending the UK's opt-out from the Social Chapter of the Treaty of Maastricht, and statutory recognition of trade union rights, where the majority of employees are in favour (see Chapter 7). However, these changes have not led to a return to the old corporatist approach, or to the more widespread use of tripartism. As the quotation of Tony Blair's words in Chapter 6 indicates, the view of the government has been that governing the country and running the unions are and should be seen as discrete matters. This suggests the continuation of a more limited role for the TUC, although it would also be unwise to exaggerate the level of its pre-1979 influence when it enjoyed a wider range of representation in some of the consultative structures that had been established to advise and inform government.

The European Trade Union Confederation

John Monks, General Secretary of the TUC from 1993 to 2003, was the sole nominated candidate to become the General Secretary of the European Trade Union Confederation from 2003. The ETUC was established in 1973, 'to provide a trade union counterbalance to the economic forces of European integration', according to its website (ETUC, 2002). Following political changes in central and eastern Europe, a number of trade union bodies have recently joined the ETUC, so that in 2002 its membership stood at 76 national trade union confederations from 35 countries, together with a further 11 European industry federations, giving it representation of some 60 million members. The ETUC is recognised by the European Union, the Council of Europe and the European Free Trade Association as the representative body of the trade union movement at the European level. The principal objectives of the ETUC are to:

- influence the direction of European-level legislation and policy-making through representations to the institutions of the EU and by participating in consultation processes including at the EU's Economic and Social Committee;
- engage in the regulation of employment with employers at the European level through the European social dialogue process. The ETUC and UNICE (discussed below) are recognised by the EU as Social Partners and are permitted to negotiate framework agreements at the European level. This has resulted in three such agreements relating to parental leave, part-time work and fixed-term contracts, which are now part of EU legislation following ratification by the EU's Council of Ministers;
- campaign for employment rights through trade union action, including the organisation of demonstrations within European cities to promote trade union causes (ETUC, 2002).

5.6 Employers' associations and the Union of Industrial and Employers' Confederations of Europe

■ Defining employers' associations

Like trade unions, employers' associations are defined in law. The current definition is contained in the Trade Union and Labour Relations (Consolidation) Act of 1992. Section 122 of this Act defines an employers' association as an organisation, whether temporary or permanent, that consists wholly or mainly of employers whose main purpose includes the regulation of relations between these employers and workers or trade unions. Associations in particular industries operate as both trade and employers' organisations, so that their functions cover commercial representation as well as the regulation of the employment relationship.

The Certification Officer's report for 2002 lists 94 employers' associations covering England, Scotland and Wales. However, as listing is a voluntary matter, this report notes that a further 90 employers' associations had submitted an annual return to the Certification Officer in line with their statutory requirement to do so although these organisations had not applied to be listed. The largest employers' associations include the Engineering Employers' Federation (EEF), which is made up of 16 member associations that have several thousand organisations in their collective membership; the National Farmers' Union, with 137 492 members in 2002; the National Federation of Retail Newsagents, with 21 855 members; the Federation of Master Builders, with 13 450 members; the Freight Transport Association, with 10 996 members; and the Retail Motor Industry Federation, with 9710 members. Many employers' associations cover, or predominantly cover, very small employing organisations, with fewer than 20 employees, and fairly small ones, with 20–500 employees. Notable among these associations is the Federation of Small Businesses, with over 174 000 members.

As these data indicate, an employers' association may operate as a national federation of other associations, such as the EEF. Conversely, it may operate as a local association of employers, which may or may not be associated to a national federation. An example of the former case, where an employers' association is part of a national federation, is the EEF West Midlands Association, with 991 members in 2002. Alternatively, an association may represent the employers in a particular industry without adopting a dual structure: for example, in addition to the cases listed above, the Chemical Industries Association had 166 members in 2002. Specialist associations also exist in particular industries, such as the Vehicle Builders and Repairers Association in the motor industry and the Newspaper Society in publishing. Employers' associations also exist in the public sector, such as the Representative National Organisation of Employers of Local Authority Staff, the Association of Colleges, and the Universities and Colleges Employers' Association (see Cockburn, 2002).

■ The changing role and functions of employers' associations

Traditionally, the principal role of an employers' association has been to represent its members at multi-employer collective bargaining with recognised trade unions, which generally led to industry-wide collective agreements for terms and conditions of work. As Chapter 7 outlines, the incidence of multi-employer bargaining has declined considerably in recent years (Cully *et al.*, 1999). This has raised a question about the continuing role of employers' associations. However, they have managed to adapt to place greater emphasis on other functions and to serve the needs of smaller employing organisations in particular, who often do not have the resources to invest in specialist functions within their own businesses, as we outline in the following paragraphs.

Although multi-employer bargaining continues in some industries, employers' associations now place much greater emphasis on providing advisory services to their members, representing these in a number of ways and operating disputes procedures when required. Employers' associations are able to invest in the specialist provision of these services, which smaller employing organisations in particular would not have the resources to be able to provide for themselves. IRS (2002b) report that employers' associations provide advice to their members on a wide range of topics. These include advice on health and safety, employment law, disciplinary, equal opportunities, pay, welfare, recruitment, change and partnership matters. They are also able to organise and offer training courses and consultancy, for which additional fees are likely to be payable.

Employers' associations are also able to invest resources to represent the interests of their members to a range of other organisations. A key role for employers' associations is to lobby government at both national and local levels. IRS (2002b) found that 90 per cent of its sample of employers' associations represented the interests of their members to government departments. Representing the interests of members to the departments and institutions of the EU was also found to be highly important (IRS, 2002b). Employers' associations also provide a means to represent the common interests of their members to the trade unions recognised within an industry, even where multi-employer bargaining no longer takes place.

Employers' associations provide other services for their members including advice and representation in relation to employment tribunal cases, the operation of disputes procedures, provision of model policies for members to adopt or adapt, dissemination of current employment issues, and the opportunity for networking within the membership (e.g. IRS, 2002b). Employers' associations have had to adapt to structural changes, related to industrial change and the levels at which collective bargaining occurs in many industries and occupational sectors, but they have been able to secure an important role, particularly in relation to serving the specialist needs of smaller employing organisations. These associations may also be affiliated to employers' organisations that have a wider remit and that help to represent employers' interests at the European level. In this way, many employers' associations are members of the Confederation of British Industry (CBI), which in turn is a member of UNICE.

■ Union of Industrial and Employers' Confederations of Europe (UNICE)

The Union of Industrial and Employers' Confederations of Europe, or UNICE, describes its role as the 'the voice of business in Europe'. Founded in 1958, its membership is made up of 34 business federations from 27 countries in Europe. Its mission is to promote the common interests of the businesses that are represented by its member organisations, to influence the decision-making processes at the European level so that these take account of business needs, and to represent its member organisations at the European social dialogue process.

It wishes to see 'improving labour market flexibility' and 'a well functioning internal market, including less and better legislation' (UNICE, 2002). Based in Brussels, it is recognised by the EU as one of the Social Partners that are permitted to negotiate framework agreements at the European level. There are two other employers' organisations that are also recognised as partners in the European social dialogue process. These organisations are the European Centre for Public Enterprises and Services of General Economic Interest (CEEP) and the European Association of Craft, Small and Medium-Sized Enterprises (UEAPME).

UNICE announced in late 2002 that the Social Partners in the European social dialogue process (ETUC, CEEP, UEAPME and UNICE) had agreed their programme of work for the period of 2003–2005 to cover 19 industrial relations and employment regulation issues (UNICE, 2002).

self-check question	**5.2** What can an employers' association do to help an individual employer?

5.7 Trade union membership and recognition

■ Trade union membership

Table 5.1 shows levels of union membership in Great Britain at five-year intervals between 1975 and 2000. Union membership peaked at just over 13.2 million members in 1979. This equated to approximately 57 per cent of those in employment at this time (although union density amongst the actual workforce would have been lower as not all union members were in employment). By 2000, union membership had fallen to 7.8 million people, a decline of approximately 40 per cent, so that only 29 per cent of those in employment were union members. In fact, trade union membership in Great Britain has remained around 7.8 million since 1997, according to the Certification Officer's annual reports.

The Labour Force Survey (LFS) reveals data about union densities in Great Britain, although this only considers the union status of those in employment (Brook, 2002). *Union density* is the unionised workforce expressed as a percentage of potential membership. Union densities may be calculated in relation to the total in employment, or for particular industries, sectors, occupations and workplaces, or in relation to individual and job-related characteristics, as we now describe. In 2001, according to the LFS, 29 per cent of employees were members of a union in Great Britain. There was a slight variation according to gender: 30 per cent of males in employment were members and 28 per cent of females. Young employees were significantly less likely to join a union: only 5 per cent of those under 20 years of age were members in 2001. In contrast, 38 per cent of those in employment aged 40–49 years old were members. According to the LFS classification, 30 per cent of black or black British employees were union members in 2001, 29 per cent of white employees,

25 per cent of Asian or Asian British employees and 22 per cent of Chinese and other ethnic groups. Employees with a degree or other higher education qualification were more likely to join a union in comparison with employees generally. In contrast, those with GCSEs as their highest qualification or employees without any qualifications were less likely to join a union.

Length of service is also positively related to union membership. In 2001, only 12 per cent of employees with less than one year's service were union members. In contrast, 45 per cent of employees with 10–20 years' service were members, rising to 60 per cent of those with 20 years' service or more. The very high proportion of managers and supervisors who are union members in the public sector means that, in aggregate terms, these groups are more unionised than non-managers or non-supervisors (managers, 30 per cent; supervisors, 37 per cent; other employees, 27 per cent). Those in permanent employment are more likely to be union members (30 per cent density) than those in temporary employment (19 per cent density). This is also the case for those in full-time employment (32 per cent density) in comparison with those in part-time employment (20 per cent density).

Significant differences in union densities exist in relation to industrial sector and size of workplace. Fifty-nine per cent of those employed in the public sector were union members in 2001; in the private sector, union membership was just 18 per cent. Within the private sector there are also some noticeable differences: union densities remain relatively high amongst those employed in energy and water (53 per cent) and transport and communication (37 per cent), but are much lower for those employed in hotels and catering (4 per cent), wholesale and retail jobs (12 per cent) and construction (14 per cent). People employed in the same industrial classification, for example in education and in health, are far more likely to be union members if they work in the public sector than in the private sector. In workplaces employing fewer than 25 people, only 15 per cent of employees were union members in 2001, whereas 36 per cent were members in workplaces employing 25 or more (Brook, 2002).

A number of reasons have been advanced to account for the decline in trade union membership between 1979 and 1997. Metcalf (1991: 22) stated that changes in union membership are

> determined by the complex interaction of five factors: the macroeconomic climate, the composition of jobs and the workforce, the policy of the state, the attitude and conduct of employers, and the stance taken by unions themselves.

Chapters 2 and 6 discuss how some of these factors changed during this period. Studies of the decline of trade union membership have emphasised different factors. Carruth and Disney (1988) and Disney (1990) place emphasis on the role of macroeconomic factors in this decline, with high unemployment and real wage growth acting to depress union density. In contrast, Freeman and Pelletier (1990) place emphasis on the role of changes in labour law in the UK during the Conservative governments of the 1980s to explain the reduction in union density during that period. Yet other studies have placed emphasis on changes in the composition of jobs and the workforce during this period to explain this decline (e.g. Millward and Stevens, 1986, 1988). Metcalf (1991) rejects the idea that only one of these factors could largely explain the decline in union membership and density that occurred in the UK in the period to 1997. His view is that,

It seems much more plausible that macroeconomic factors, industry composition, and industrial relations law *each* played a part: the authors [of the various explanations advanced] are all *partly* right.' (Metcalf, 1991: 23) (original emphasis)

He also places emphasis on the roles and attitudes of employers and the unions in this decline.

■ Employers' attitudes to unionisation, union recognition and derecognition, and how unions responded: from 1979 to the late 1990s

The policy of an employer towards unionisation is an important factor in determining level of union membership (e.g. Metcalf, 1991; Millward *et al.*, 2000). According to the WERS series, unions were present in 54 per cent of British workplaces in 1998, having declined from 73 per cent in 1984 (Millward *et al.*, 2000). *Union presence* is defined as one or more union members in a workplace. The presence of unions also varies by sector. In 1998, union presence was 97 per cent in the public sector, 42 per cent in private sector manufacturing and 35 per cent in private sector services (Millward *et al.*, 2000). However, as Metcalf (1991: 25) stated, 'recognition is the fulcrum on which membership moves.' According to the WERS series, trade union recognition declined significantly through the 1980s and 1990s. In 1984, unions were recognised in 66 per cent of workplaces. By 1998, this had fallen to 42 per cent of workplaces. In the public sector there was some reduction in recognition for the purpose of collective bargaining, so that unions were recognised in 87 per cent of this sector in 1998. This reduction in the public sector is largely explained by a small number of structural changes, such as the ending of the national pay bargaining system for teachers by the government in 1987 and the establishment of a pay review body to recommend pay increases (Millward *et al.*, 2000).

Recognition fell much more significantly in the private sector between 1980 and 1998. Half of workplaces in the private sector recognised unions in 1980; by 1998 this had fallen to a quarter of private sector workplaces (Millward *et al.*, 2000). Millward *et al.* (2000: 97) comment that,

> The decline in the incidence of union recognition from 1980 onwards was thus almost a wholly private sector phenomenon. From 1990 onwards it was entirely so.... Manufacturing and service industries were equally affected. Almost all of the broad industrial sectors experienced a substantial fall in union recognition between 1990 and 1998.

As with the decline in union membership discussed above, there is more than one reason for this decline in union recognition. Linkages are also evident to the reasons presented above for the decline in union membership. For example, industrial restructuring led to the closure of many organisations in 'mature' and 'declining' industries. These older and generally larger employing organisations in the private sector had traditionally granted union recognition. They were composed mainly of full-time, male workers who undertook manual work, of which a high proportion were union members. By the late 1990s, the relative decline of this type of workplace meant that Millward *et al.* (2000) were able to report that these no longer stood out as the bedrock of union representation and recognition in relation to other categories of workplace. By the late 1990s, smaller establishments and organisations were also significantly less likely to recognise unions than larger ones, as were younger workplaces than older ones. While union recognition was diminishing in the declining parts of the economy in particular, it was not being replenished in the new and developing sectors. The reduction in union presence, reported above, to only 42 per cent in private sector manufacturing and 35 per cent in private sector services workplaces in Britain by 1998 appears to provide evidence for this: without union members being present, recognition will not occur.

The decline in recognition also occurred because of union derecognition in some employing organisations that altered their policy towards trade unions. Claydon (1989: 215) defines derecognition 'as a decision to withdraw from collective bargaining in favour of other arrangements for regulating employment relations.' His study of derecognition in Britain in the 1980s found that this should not be equated with deunionisation, where unions are not given any rights to organise or operate within an employing organisation (Claydon, 1989). Derecognition took a number of forms along two dimensions, breadth and depth. *Breadth of derecognition* contains three categories:

- general, where the union's bargaining rights on behalf of all employees are withdrawn;
- grade specific, where these rights are withdrawn in respect of a particular grade of employee in an organisation;
- plant specific, where bargaining rights are withdrawn at a particular plant, establishment or workplace (Claydon, 1989).

Depth of derecognition refers to the nature of the bargaining and representation rights that are withdrawn. Depth in this context contains four possibilities or categories, where derecognition:

- is partial, so that a union loses bargaining rights in respect of pay determination but retains these rights for other issues;
- involves the union losing its status as a bargaining agent, so that it loses all bargaining rights but still retains the right to be consulted and to represent individual members in respect of grievances etc.;
- involves the union losing its status for all collective issues, so that it retains representation rights only in respect of matters affecting individual members.
- involves the union losing all rights over collective issues and individual representation. This amounts to deunionisation (Claydon, 1989).

Studies of derecognition in the 1980s and 1990s nevertheless found that this was a limited phenomenon. For example, Claydon (1996) identified 170 cases for the period between 1984 and 1993, with the greatest concentration occurring between 1988 and 1993. In the period to 1988, cases of derecognition occurred most often in the publishing, paper and print industries (12), followed by cases involving companies operating in ports, shipping and transport (11), and 6 cases each in broadcasting and communications, petroleum and chemicals, and food manufacture (Claydon, 1996). In the period between 1988 and 1993, Claydon (1996) identified 112 cases, with the greatest number still in publishing, paper and print (25), followed by cases in the metal, engineering and vehicle industries (16), and 15 cases each in the petro-leum and chemicals, and the wholesale, retail and distribution industries. Gall and McKay's study (1994) identified just under 400 cases between 1988 and 1994. Their study confirms the relatively high level of cases in the industries identified above, with the National Union of Journalists, Graphical, Paper and Media Union, Transport and General Workers' Union and Amalgamated Engineering and Electrical Union most frequently confronted by cases of derecognition.

Claydon (1996) identified two broad approaches to union derecognition. The first of these involves management acting in a *reactive* way to the decline in union mem-bership by seeking to derecognise the union or unions involved. Millward *et al.* (2000) report from the WERS series data that managers interviewed who had been involved in cases of derecognition justified these in just over half of cases by saying that union membership had declined or union activity was absent. The second approach to union derecognition involves management acting in a *purposive* way to get rid of unions from the regulation of the employment relationship. Claydon (1996) describes how this approach often involved an incremental strategy to elimi-nate union presence by allowing areas of weak unionisation to wither in an organisation and targeting hard or strong areas of union membership, particularly where these existed in a strategically important area of the production process. Such targeting appears to have been associated with organisational restructuring, downsiz-ing and the announcement of redundancies, contracting-out of some functions, and the introduction of incentives to encourage employees to sign up to individual con-tracts that eradicated the need for collective bargaining (e.g. Claydon, 1996).

Although cases of derecognition are important in terms of understanding the way in which the regulation of the employment relationship for some groups of employees has changed, its incidence in the 1980s and 1990s was limited. By the late 1990s, it appears to have declined significantly, so that the ACAS Annual Report of 1999–2000 reports only one case of full union derecognition (ACAS, 2000), and the Report of 2000–2001 refers only to two cases of partial derecognition (ACAS, 2001).

Union strength and managerial policy are seen as important determinants of dere-cognition. Claydon (1989, 1996) concluded that a crucial factor in many cases of derecognition was union strength, as measured by membership density in an organisa-tion, support for the union from members and the resources available externally to support the union at the workplace. Whereas these indicators of union power, where evident, may be countered by a highly determined and well-resourced employing organisation and its management, the existence of reasonably effective unionisation in many workplaces may have reduced attempts at union derecognition. Conversely, the policy of management in many organisations is likely to have been sufficiently accept-ing of union recognition not to invest in the effort to derecognise, especially in a period when unions were weakened. This presents a complex scenario where both union strength and its relative weakness may potentially avert union derecognition. The crucial factor may therefore be the attitude and policy of an employing organisa-tion's management. Management may support the regulation of the employment relationship through collective relations, it may accept this on pragmatic grounds, or it may oppose this, sometimes, given particular circumstances, being prepared to attempt to operationalise this opposition. Of course, within particular employing organisations this situation is likely to be more complex, perhaps with support for the collectivisation of some employment relationships but not others, or with some managers supporting union presence and others opposing. A weakened union presence may be accepted in particular cases, although where the legitimacy of union presence is threatened, derecognition may follow. This has happened in cases where national collective bargaining arrangements have ceased and the legitimacy for union recognition has consequently reduced in workplaces where its strength was low, leading to cases of derecognition (e.g. Metcalf, 1991; Claydon, 1996; Millward *et al.*, 2000).

Trade unions responded to their membership losses in a number of ways. These included continuing to recruit members in traditional areas, attempting to recruit in new areas, attempting to broaden the appeal of the union by offering new services, resisting attempts at derecognition, entering single-union agreements, and engaging in union mergers. We have already considered some of these strategies. Many single-union agreements were seen to offer too many concessions to employers. A union entering this type of arrangement gained recognition and the sole right to recruit amongst an organisation's workforce, but its attractiveness to potential members may have been decreased by the terms of the agreement that gave it single-union status. Unions also broadened the range of services offered to members, although these remain marginal to their core functions of engaging in the regulation of the employment relationship, including the negotiation of pay increases and the promotion and protection of employees' rights (e.g. Waddington and Whitston, 1997).

Unions were active in the recruitment of new members as a means to counter membership losses. While total union membership declined by about 40 per cent between 1979 and 1997, unions were nevertheless investing considerable resources to recruit new members. Some unions continued to recruit large numbers of new members, although their membership levels still show an overall decline. The largest union in Britain in 1979 with two million members, the Transport and General Workers' Union (TGWU), continued to increase its recruitment though the 1980s, with 245 000 recruits in 1988 alone (Metcalf, 1991). In overall terms, however, the TGWU continued to lose members through the 1980s and 1990s, standing at just 858 804 members in 2001 (see Table 5.3). This equated to a loss of about 59 per cent of its level of membership in 1979. Metcalf (1991) also referred to the Union of Shop, Distributive and Allied Workers (USDAW) losing about one-quarter of its membership each year in the 1980s. In 1979, the membership of USDAW stood at just over 460 000; by 1996 this had declined to about 282 000, although by 2001 it stood at about 310 000, a loss of about one-third in terms of its overall level of membership between 1979 and 2001. Although both of these unions lost members in overall terms, the fact that they were able to recruit large numbers of new members demonstrates scope to expand membership in sectors where union density is low or volatile. Both of these unions also have fairly open approaches to recruitment (see the discussion earlier).

Other unions with scope to improve the density of membership in the industry, employment sector or occupation within which they organised were also able to recruit large numbers of new members. Some unions were able to increase their levels of membership against the trend of overall decline between 1979 and 1997. The teacher unions and the Royal College of Nursing of the United Kingdom (RCN) were able to stand out against the trend of overall decline. Notably, the membership of the RCN increased from about 160 000 in 1979 to 334 000 by 2001. Conversely, unions with a relatively closed approach to recruitment, or which organised in a declining industry or employment sector, suffered losses that were closer to the overall trend or greater than the trend. The most notable case in this respect is the National Union of Mineworkers, which had a quarter of a million members in 1979, but which was reduced to a few thousand members by the mid 1990s.

One further strategy that helped some unions to respond to membership losses was to merge with another union. Table 5.4 outlines a number of mergers that helped each of the unions formed to become one of the largest in Britain. These include Unison, Amicus, the Communication Workers' Union, the Public and Commercial Services Union, the Graphical, Paper and Media Union, and UNIFI. These mergers helped these unions to consolidate their organising positions and to provide a resource base for expansion in particular cases. Throughout the 1980s and 1990s unions ran various campaigns aimed not only at increasing membership levels in general but also at targeting particular groups who were less well represented. Although recruitment gains were made, these campaigns were not always successful. For example, the campaigns organised under the auspices of the TUC in Manchester and at the Docklands in London were described as 'relative failures' (IRS, 1993). Despite the efforts made to recruit new members and the relative success achieved in some cases, union membership declined significantly between 1979 and 1997, as we recognised above.

■ The impact of statutory recognition: union recognition from 2000

As we noted above, the return of a Labour government in 1997 resulted in a change of attitude to the role of trade unions in the UK. The Employment Relations Act of 1999 introduced provisions for the statutory recognition of trade unions, which were implemented on 6 June 2000. These provisions are outlined in Chapter 7, together with a brief description of the role of the Central Arbitration Committee (CAC), which is the independent body provided with statutory powers to adjudicate on applications related to statutory recognition and derecognition (Table 7.2). This statutory recognition procedure complements the traditional route to recognition, where unions approach an employer, to be either rebuffed or voluntarily accepted. The opportunity to use a statutory route to gain recognition is clearly seen as being advantageous for trade unions, provided that the qualifying conditions are not too onerous (see Chapter 7).

In fact, according to Gall and McKay (1999), the trend away from derecognition had already begun to change in the mid-1990s, with cases of union recognition exceeding cases of derecognition in Britain. Following the implementation of legislation for the statutory recognition of unions in June 2000, the incidence of union recognition in employing organisations increased significantly, as Table 5.5 shows.

In addition to the 450 recognition agreements reached voluntarily during the first full year after the introduction of provisions for the statutory recognition of trade unions, a further 20 cases were approved statutorily through the CAC (TUC, 2002a). According to these data, the average number of union recognition agreements, through both voluntary and statutory means, was 39.2 per month during the period from November 2000 to October 2001, indicating a significant increase on the

Table 5.5 **Cases of union recognition, 1996–2001**

Period	Number of months	Number of voluntary agreements	Average number per month during period
January–December 1996	12	110	9.2
January 1997–February 1998	14	81	5.8
March 1998–October 1999	20	109	5.5
November 1999–October 2000	12	159	13.3
November 2000–October 2001	12	450	37.5

Source: Adapted from TUC (2002a)

1990s. Agreements reached voluntarily provided for full recognition in 94 per cent of these cases, according to the TUC. This included recognition for collective bargaining in relation to pay, hours of work and holidays, member representation and time off for union duties. These agreements were reached with a range of private sector organisations and involved 23 unions, with Amicus involved in 136 cases, the GMB in 109 cases, the Graphical, Paper and Media Union in 72 cases, TGWU in 58 cases, Unison in 20 cases, and the National Union of Journalists in 19 cases (TUC, 2002a). Some of these recognition agreements involved more than one union.

The statutory provisions that were introduced have undoubtedly bolstered the increased trend in cases of voluntarily agreed recognition. David Yeandle, deputy director of employment policy at the Engineering Employers' Federation, comments in *IRS Employment Review* that,

> ... there seems little doubt that the existence of the statutory procedure – and sometimes the threat of its use – has led to a number of organisations adopting a different approach to union recognition ... (resulting) ... in an increasing number of voluntary recognition agreements being reached.... (IRS, 2002d: 2)

This early period since statutory recognition raises questions about whether unions will only regain recognition in some areas where they lost it previously, whether their attempts to gain recognition will slow after an initial period of activity, and whether union membership will increase in response to wider recognition. Unions will also need to build membership and gain recognition in areas where they have traditionally been weak, or where they have lost their presence as we described earlier, especially as unions were present in only 54 per cent of British workplaces in 1998. The provisions for statutory recognition also exclude employers with fewer than 21 employees, relieving these employers of attempts by unions to gain recognition backed by this means. Conversely, the TUC (2002a) reports that, where voluntary agreements have been reached, these have been prompted not only by the existence of these statutory provisions but also through successful union campaigns to promote membership and recognition in these workplaces. In this way, these statutory provisions may provide a focus around which some recovery may take place, leading to greater numbers of union recognition agreements and some improvement in the overall level of union membership.

5.8   Partnership approaches in the workplace: the way forward?

Another means to promote trade unions in the workplace and union membership is through partnership agreements. Union recognition agreements may be reached as the result of management realising that it has no choice where a union is able to apply successfully for statutory recognition. This may mean that recognition is granted somewhat reluctantly, even though this attitude may change. Partnership agreements are likely to commence from a different basis. They are more likely to develop in organisations where unions are already recognised and where management and union wish to develop or restructure the nature of their relationship. Traditional union–employer relationships may be based on an adversarial model of interaction. Partnership in this context is based on a joint commitment, by the union as well as management, to work for the successful development of a business or employing organisation. This implies a model of mutual gain, where employees benefit from collective representation, and the interests of the business are enhanced by the release of added value from this relationship. The TUC believes that union membership and recognition will be promoted through the process of working in partnership with employing organisations in this way. It has established a TUC Partnership Institute to help to promote the dissemination of workplace-based partnership. The TUC has also defined six key principles for partnership, which help to make clear its rationale for this approach. These are outlined in Box 5.5.

This approach emphasises a model for mutual gain that may allow it to be differentiated from more traditional approaches to trade union recognition and collective representation. It also allows partnership to be differentiated from the approach taken to single-union agreements in the 1980s. Earlier we quoted the views of Derek Simpson, the joint General Secretary of Amicus, about the nature of many of these single-union agreements in the 1980s. In these comments, he goes on to say that,

> When I say I will renegotiate agreements that do not meet the needs and aspirations of our members, I mean I want to close the book on the dark days of the 1980s and replace them with a redefined template for partnership. ... We only seek a fair deal for our members and meaningful partnerships with their employers. (IRS, 2002c: 2)

The extent to which partnership agreements deliver mutually beneficial gains, help to develop union membership and recognition, and meet the needs and aspirations of union members will need to be evaluated as this approach develops. Some employers and employers' organisations may attempt to promote the idea of partnership with the workforce without seeking to recognise or work with trade unions. In 1998, the Institute of Personnel and Development issued a 'position paper' that stated:

> IPD believes it is entirely sensible that, where a majority of employees in a relevant business unit want to have a trade union recognised, the employer should reach such an agreement. However, it seems to IPD that 'partnership' has more to do with an approach to the relationship between employers and employees, individually and in groups, than it has to do with trade unions as such. (IPD, 1998: 8–9)

Partnership may be associated more with a unitarist approach to the management of the employment relationship in the strategy of some organisations than with the development of a pluralist approach that actively involves trade unions. Kelly (1996,

---

> Box 5.5　**The TUC's principles for partnership**
>
> *Principle 1: Joint commitment to the success of the enterprise*
>
> Effective partnerships will be developed where both unions and employers understand an organisation's strategy and are committed to its success. This requires the replacement of any adversarial approach to regulating the employment relationship.
>
> *Principle 2: Recognition of respective legitimate interests*
>
> Genuine partnerships will recognise the legitimate existence of different interests and views between unions and employers. Arrangements are required to resolve these differences in an atmosphere of trust.
>
> *Principle 3: Commitment to security of employment*
>
> Partnership needs to embrace employment security to complement the existence of forms of flexibility in the workplace. Flexibility should not be used at the expense of employment security. This will mean restricting the use of compulsory redundancy and developing employability where appropriate.
>
> *Principle 4: Focus on the quality of working life*
>
> Partnership should provide opportunities for employees to participate in the making of decisions that affect their working lives and for improved terms and conditions of work. It should also broaden the scope of organisational issues that are considered jointly by unions and employers.
>
> *Principle 5: Transparency and sharing of information*
>
> Partnership is based on transparency and the sharing of information at an early stage, with opportunities for meaningful consultations to be conducted with unions and employees.
>
> *Principle 6: Mutual gains and adding value*
>
> Effective partnerships will lead to improved organisational performance, terms and conditions, and develop employee involvement, commitment, and mutual gains.
>
> *Source*: Adapted from ‹http://www.tuc.org.uk/pi/partnership.htm› and related material (TUC, 2002b)

1998) has observed that hostility to union presence has developed in the recent past, and that 'It is, after all, difficult for a union to construct a partnership with an employer who would prefer that the union simply did not exist' (Kelly, 1998: 63).

self-check question　**5.3** What opportunities exist for trade unions to recover some of their losses of the last two decades, and what factors may threaten any such recovery?

5.9　Union officials and workplace representatives

Different types of union official manage trade unions. In the British context in particular, those who manage union affairs may be divided into two main types. The first type that unions employ are generally referred to as *full-time officials*. These officials work at national or regional level. This organisational arrangement is similar to that of the TUC described above. The chief officer of most unions is referred to as its General Secretary. For example, the Graphical, Paper and Media Union (GPMU), the eleventh largest union in the UK in 2001 with 200 000 members (Table 5.3), has an organisational structure that includes a general secretary, deputy general secretary, general president, national officer(s) with particular sectoral responsibilities, and financial secretary to manage its affairs (GPMU, 2000). These officers are elected by the union's membership. The GPMU also employs industrial officers who may work at the union's head office or in its regions. This union is organised into 10 regions, covering Great Britain and the Republic of Ireland. Within these regions, the union is organised into branches, which are run by a number of branch officials including a chairperson or president, secretary, committee members, auditors and health and safety advisor, elected by the branch membership. At company level, where there are two or more GPMU members a union chapel is formed, and the member who oversees this is known as the father/mother or clerk of the chapel (GPMU, 2000).

Lay officials or *workplace representatives* make up the second type of union official. The existence of these representatives provides an important indication of trade union strength at the workplace. They provide an important means of representing the interests of union members to management not only because of their locational proximity but also because they share a close understanding of the issues of the particular employment relationship. Workplace representatives are formally accredited to represent the interests of the members of a recognised trade union in an employing organisation and thus are recognised by its management for this purpose. They are employed by this employing organisation, within which they are very likely to receive time off from their normal duties to operate as workplace representatives. They can be differentiated from other union officials at national and regional levels where these are employed by the union itself. Workplace representatives of different unions may be known by different terms including shop stewards, corresponding members or staff representatives. The senior workplace representative of a union may be referred to as its convenor, or as we saw in relation to the example of the GPMU the father/mother or clerk of the chapel.

Workplace representatives may be involved in a range of union activities, which may be classified into two main categories. The first of these relates to the functions that they carry out on behalf of the trade union as an *external organisation*. This principally involves:

- recruiting other eligible employees to join the union;
- promoting the benefits of membership to potential and actual members;
- receiving information from the union externally and communicating this to members within the workplace;
- making contact with other workplace representatives, and with branch, regional or perhaps national officials for advice and assistance in relation to casework, negotiating and dispute situations;
- reporting any breaches of agreement to branch, regional or perhaps national officials.

The second category relates to involvement in union processes at the *workplace*, which principally involves:

- representing the interests of members to the management of an employing organisation to endeavour to promote or protect these, and to respond to the treatment of members by management;

- protecting and promoting members' interests in relation to health and safety at work (discussed below);
- advising and representing members in relation to discipline and grievance cases (see Chapter 9);
- negotiating about pay and conditions of work where this is devolved to workplace level (see Chapter 7);
- engaging in the process of joint consultation at the workplace (see Chapter 8);
- involvement in collective disputes where these arise at the workplace;
- reporting outcomes to members, consulting with them and encouraging them to become more active in the union.

However, the proportion of workplaces with union representatives fell significantly between 1980 and 1998. In 1980, union representatives were present in at least 53 per cent of workplaces with 25 or more employees; by 1998 this had fallen to 33 per cent. Non-union representatives were reported in a further 41 per cent of such workplaces in 1998. The remaining quarter of such workplaces did not have any workplace representatives (Millward *et al*, 2000).

In 1998 union representatives were present in 74 per cent of workplaces with 25 or more employees that recognised trade unions. Private sector services organisations of this size that recognised unions were least likely to have union representatives (58 per cent), whereas they were present in 93 per cent of private sector manufacturing firms that recognised unions. The WERS data also show that whereas there was a decline in the proportion of workplaces with union representatives in the 1980s, their presence stabilised in the 1990s in organisations with recognised unions (Cully *et al.*, 1999; Millward *et al.*, 2000).

In 1998 each union representative in the workplace represented an average of 29 members compared with 32 members in 1990, although this varied significantly depending on workplace size and industrial sector (Cully *et al.*, 1999; Millward *et al.*, 2000). In organisations with 25–49 employees, the average number of members represented by each union representative was 17. This compares with 53 members per union representative in organisations with 500 or more employees (Cully *et al.*, 1999). These data in the last three paragraphs indicate that although the presence of union representatives is restricted to a smaller proportion of organisations than in 1980, there nevertheless remains a reasonably well-organised infrastructure of workplace representatives in organisations where unions are recognised (see Godfrey and Marchington, 1996; Millward *et al.*, 2000).

| *self-check question* | **5.4** This chapter has referred to a number of different ways of identifying trade union power. What determinants of trade union power have been identified in the chapter? |

5.10 Health and safety committees and union representation

The Health and Safety Regulations of 1996 mean that all employing organisations in the UK should now consult with employees or their representatives about health and safety matters. This consultation may take place in different ways. These include the use of health and safety committees and consulting directly with safety representatives. Slightly fewer than 4 out of 10 workplaces had health and safety committees and in marginally less than 3 out of 10 workplaces consultation took place directly with safety representatives in 1998 (Cully *et al.*, 1999; Millward *et al.*, 2000).

However, although legislation has promoted the development of workplace representation for the purpose of health and safety consultation, the most recent WERS data suggests that unions appointed representatives to health and safety committees in only about one-third of cases by 1998 (Millward *et al.*, 2000). The Health and Safety Commission's guide to the health and safety system in Great Britain (HSC, 2002: 32) states that, 'in workplaces where trade unions are recognised, the unions have the right to appoint safety representatives to act on the employees' behalf in consultations with their employer....' As Millward *et al.* (2000) suggest, in those organisations where they are recognised but do not have representatives, unions are not able to establish these in practice. The right to appoint representatives exists, but in practice the lack of workplace-based strength does not allow this to occur. It also appears to indicate an area in which the presence of non-union representatives has become more evident.

■ The Health and Safety Commission and Health and Safety Executive

At national level in the UK the Health and Safety Commission (HSC) and the Health and Safety Executive (HSE) are the two principal governmental organisations responsible for the regulation of health and safety at work. The Health and Safety at Work etc. Act 1974 led to the establishment of these two institutions. The HSC is a tripartite body consisting of 10 commissioners whose role is to introduce arrangements for the health, safety and welfare of people at work and for the public from the way in which businesses and organisations operate. The functions of the HSC include proposing new laws, regulations and standards, promoting research and training, providing information and advice, and maintaining the Employment Medical Advisory Service. The HSE is appointed by the HSC, with government approval and advice, and assists the Commission. The HSE is responsible for the enforcement of health and safety law. It operates through a board that is composed of several directorates. Its staff of approximately 4000 is organised within these directorates and includes inspectors, scientists, technologists, medical experts, policy advisors and lawyers (HSC, 2002; HSE, 2002).

5.11 Summary

- Trade unions may be defined in relation to their functions to protect their members' welfare and to participate in job regulation with employers. Unions may be differentiated according to their degree of unionateness.
- Other union functions include recruiting new members and retaining existing ones, pursuing issues for particular groups of members, providing member services, and pursuing institutional goals related to the union's development, or even its survival.
- The number of trade unions in Britain has steadily declined. By 2000 the 16 largest trade unions in Great Britain accounted for almost 6.5 million members out of a total membership of 7.9 million, or 82 per cent of all union members. The development of trade unionism in Britain makes classification problematic, although many unions may be described as multi-sectoral in terms of the scope of their organising activities.

- Union mergers and multi-unionism are continuing features of trade unionism in Britain. Recent employer strategies to overcome problems of multi-unionism include the introduction of single-union agreements and single-table bargaining.
- The Trades Union Congress, or TUC, is the representative body of the trade union movement in the UK, with approximately 70 affiliated unions that collectively represented about 6.7 million workers, or roughly 85 per cent of union members in 2002. The TUC has experienced a number of significant changes over the last two decades.
- With the decline in the incidence of industry level or multi-employer collective bargaining, many employers are no longer members of employers' associations. Many employers' associations continue to function by placing much greater emphasis on advisory services for their members and servicing the needs of small employers in particular.
- Trade union membership fell significantly between 1979 and 1997, although this has since stabilised. However, the incidence of union presence and union recognition in employing organisations, particularly in the private sector, also declined significantly in this period.
- The introduction of statutory recognition of trade unions and the promotion of partnership agreements by the TUC and its affiliates offer these unions some hope to expand their membership and the incidence of union recognition.
- This chapter also describes the role and activities of union officials and workplace representatives including those engaged on health and safety duties.

References

ACAS (2000) *Annual Report, 1999–2000*.

ACAS (2001) *Annual Report, 2000–2001*.

Batstone, E. (1988) 'The frontier of control', *in* Gallie, D. (ed.), *Employment in Britain*, Oxford, Blackwell, pp. 218–47.

Blackburn, R.M. (1967) *Union Character and Social Class*, London, Batsford.

Blackburn, R.M. and Prandy, K. (1965) 'White-collar unionization: a conceptual framework', *British Journal of Sociology*, 16:2, 111–22.

Brook, K. (2002) 'Trade union membership: an analysis of data from the autumn 2001 LFS', *Labour Market Trends*, 110:7, 343–54.

Carruth, A. and Disney, R. (1988) 'Where have two million members gone?', *Economica*, 55:1, 1–19.

Claydon, T. (1989) 'Union derecognition in Britain in the 1980s', *British Journal of Industrial Relations*, 27:2, 214–24.

Claydon, T. (1996) 'Union derecognition: a re-examination', *in* Beardwell, I.J. (ed.), *Contemporary Industrial Relations: A critical analysis*, Oxford, Oxford University Press, pp. 157–74.

Clegg, H. (1979) *The Changing System of Industrial Relations in Great Britain*, Oxford, Basil Blackwell.

Cockburn, D. (2002) *Annual Report of the Certification Officer, 2001–2002* [online] [cited 19 November] Available from <http://www.certoffice.org/annualReport/pdf/2001-2002A.pdf>

Cully, M., Woodland, S., O'Reilly, A. and Dix, G. (1999) *Britain at Work as Depicted by the 1998 Workplace Employee Relations Survey*, London, Routledge.

Disney, R. (1990) 'Explanations of the decline in trade union density in Britain: an appraisal', *British Journal of Industrial Relations*, 28:2, 165–78.

Donovan, T. N. (1968) *Royal Commission on Trade Unions and Employers' Associations* (Cmnd. 3623), London, HMSO.

ETUC (2002) 'About the ETUC' [online] [cited 26 November] Available from <http://www.etuc.org/en/about_etuc>

Farnham, D. and Pimlott, J. (1995) *Understanding Industrial Relations* (5th edn), London, Cassell.

Flanders, A. (1975) *Management and Unions: The theory and reform of industrial relations*, London, Faber & Faber.

Freeman, R. and Pelletier, J. (1990) 'The impact of industrial relations legislation on British union density', *British Journal of Industrial Relations*, 28:2, 141–64.

Gall, G. (1994) 'The rise of single table bargaining in Britain', *Employee Relations*, 16:4, 62–71.

Gall, G. and McKay, S. (1994) 'Trade union derecognition in Britain, 1988–1994', *British Journal of Industrial Relations*, 32:3, 433–48.

Gall, G. and McKay, S. (1999) 'Developments in union recognition and derecognition in Britain, 1994–1998', *British Journal of Industrial Relations*, 37:4, 601–14.

Godfrey, G. and Marchington, M. (1996) 'Shop stewards in the 1990s: a research note', *Industrial Relations Journal*, 27:4, 339–44.

Goetschy, J. (1998) 'France: the limits of reform', *in* Ferner, A. and Hyman, R. (eds), *Changing Industrial Relations in Europe* (2nd edn), Oxford, Blackwell, pp. 357–94.

GPMU (2000) *Rules of the Graphical, Paper & Media Union*, Bedford, GPMU.

Health and Safety Commission (2002) *The Health and Safety System in Great Britain*, HSE Books and available at <http://www.hse.gov.uk/aboutus/hsc/index.htm>

Health and Safety Executive (2002) 'About us' [online] [cited 12 December] Available from <http://www.hse.gov/aboutus/index.htm>,
<http://www.tuc.org.uk>,
<http://www.tuc.org.uk/tuc/unions_list.cfm>

IPD (1998) *Employment Relations into the 21st Century*. IPD position paper, London, Institute of Personnel and Development.

IRS (1992a) 'Unions respond to membership losses', *Employment Review 519*, London, Industrial Relations Services, September, pp. 13–15.

IRS (1992b) 'Single-union deals in perspective', *Employment Review 523*, London, Industrial Relations Services, November, pp. 6–15.

IRS (1993) 'New union recognitions embrace over 60,000 workers', *Employment Review 545*, London, Industrial Relations Services, October, p. 2.

IRS (2002a) 'What do unions want – apart from a pay rise?', *Employment Review 746*, London, Industrial Relations Services, February, pp. 14–16.

IRS (2002b) 'Stormy waters ahead for employers' associations?', *Employment Review 748*, London, Industrial Relations Services, March, pp. 7–13.

IRS (2002c) 'Trade unions: Expert view: Goodnight sweetheart', *Employment Review 761*, London, Industrial Relations Services, October, p. 2.

IRS (2002d) 'Trade unions: Expert view: The limits on union organisation remain', *Employment Review 745*, London, Industrial Relations Services, February, p. 2.

Jacobi, O., Keller, B. and Muller-Jentsch, W. (1998) 'Germany: facing new challenges', *in* Ferner, A. and Hyman, R. (eds), *Changing Industrial Relations in Europe* (2nd edn), Oxford, Blackwell, pp. 190–238.

Kelly, J. (1996) 'Union militancy and social partnership', *in* Ackers, P., Smith, C. and Smith, P. (eds), *The New Workplace and Trade Unionism*, London, Routledge.

Kelly, J. (1998) *Rethinking Industrial Relations*, London, Routledge.

Kessler, S. and Bayliss, F. (1998) *Contemporary British Industrial Relations* (3rd edn), Basingstoke, Macmillan.

Metcalf, D. (1991) 'British unions: dissolution or resurgence?', *Oxford Review of Economic Policy*, 7:1, 18–32.

Millward, N. and Stevens, M. (1986) *British Workplace Industrial Relations 1980–1984*, Aldershot, Gower.

Millward, N. and Stevens, M. (1988) 'Union density in the regions', *Employment Gazette*, 96:5, 286–95.

Millward, N., Bryson, A. and Forth, J. (2000) *All Change at Work?*, London, Routledge.

Regalia, I. and Regini, M. (1998) 'Italy: the dual character of industrial relations', *in* Ferner, A. and Hyman, R. (eds), *Changing Industrial Relations in Europe* (2nd edn), Oxford, Blackwell, pp. 459–503.

Thornley, C., Ironside, M. and Seifert, R. (2000) 'UNISON and changes in collective bargaining in health and local government', *in* Terry, M. (ed.), *Redefining Public Sector Unionism*, London, Routledge, pp. 137–54.

TUC (2002a) *Focus on Recognition, 2002*, London, TUC.

TUC (2002b) *TUC Partnership Institute* [online] [cited 12 December] Available from <http://www.tuc.organisation.uk/pi/partnership.htm>

Turner, H.A. (1962) *Trade Union Growth, Structure and Policy*, London, Allen & Unwin.

Undy, R., Ellis, W., McCarthy, W. and Halmos, A. (1981) *Change in Trade Unions*, London, Hutchinson.

UNICE (2002) UNICE website [online] [cited 12 December] Available from <http://unice.org/unice/Website.nsf/>

Waddington, J. and Whitston, C. (1997) 'Why do people join unions in a period of membership decline?', *British Journal of Industrial Relations*, 35:4, 515–46.

Webb, S. and Webb, B. (1920) *The History of Trade Unionism 1666–1920*, London, Longman.

Whybrew, E.G. (2001) *Annual Report of the Certification Officer, 2000–2001* [online] [cited 12 December] Available from <http://www.certoffice.org/annualReport/pdf/2000-2001.pdf>

self-check Answers

5.1 *How may the other trade union functions discussed above be related to a union's primary function to become involved in the regulation of the employment relationship?*

The effectiveness of a union depends, to varying degrees, on each of the functions outlined and the way in which these are seen to support one another. One dimension of union power is related to its membership. The level of, as well as the 'qualities' exhibited by, its membership will affect the willingness of employers to recognise and to bargain with a union. This has recently been reinforced by the conditions that underpin the statutory recognition of trade unions, discussed in Section 5.7 and Chapter 7. Level of membership also affects the union's resource base, which will in turn affect its ability to pursue a range of agendas for members and to arrange services that appeal to these members. Conversely, the pursuit of interests that relate closely to the experiences and concerns of employees at work should help to attract them into membership. The effectiveness of a union also depends on the existence of an active core of members, especially those who put themselves forward to become workplace representatives and full-time officials. Through these examples, we can recognise that the effectiveness of a union is bound to the way in which its functions mutually support one another.

5.2 *What can an employers' association do to help an individual employer?*

Employers' associations may negotiate with trade unions in multi-employer collective bargaining structures where these continue to be used to determine levels of pay and conditions of employment. They may also devise and operate formal procedures for resolving disputes and advise in relation to difficulties with pay settlements.

Employers' associations also provide advice on a wide range of issues including those related to employment legislation, health and safety and other employee relations and personnel matters. This is likely to include the dissemination of information and model procedures to members. Advice in relation to employment tribunal cases and representation at these may be provided. They may also provide consultancy services and offer training courses. Employers' associations also offer the specialist capability to represent members' interests to government, at local and national levels and at the European level, sometimes via other employers' organisations. This final function indicates the importance of pressure group activity.

5.3 *What opportunities exist for trade unions to recover some of their losses of the last two decades, and what factors may threaten any such recovery?*

The principal opportunities outlined in this chapter for unions to recover some of their losses relate to the introduction of the statutory recognition of trade unions and the development of partnership agreements. The incidence of union recognition had already started to rise at the beginning of this decade, and partnership agreements have been introduced in a number of organisations. The TUC reports that union recognition has been gained not only because of the existence of these statutory provisions but also because of successful campaigns to develop membership at particular workplaces. However, a number of questions may be raised in relation to these strategies. These include whether unions will only regain recognition in some areas where they lost it previously, whether their attempts to gain recognition will slow after an initial period of activity, and whether union membership will increase in response to wider recognition or where partnership agreements are reached.

A number of factors threaten the prospect of a union recovery. A number of key measurements indicate the way in which unions were adversely affected during the 1980s and 1990s. Union density in relation to total employment stood at only 29 per cent in 2000, with total union membership at about 7.9 million. According to the WERS data series, unions were present in only 54 per cent of British workplaces in 1998, and recognised in only 42 per cent, with recognition in the private sector standing at just 25 per cent. Significant variations within the private sector indicate areas where unions struggle to promote recognition and membership. Even within workplaces where unions are recognised, union activity may be low, and in 1998 union representatives were present in only 74 per cent of such workplaces with 25 or more employees. These factors indicate that any recovery is likely to be limited or slow, and it may be focused in particular parts of the economy and amongst specific sectors of employment.

5.4 *This chapter has referred to a number of different ways of identifying trade union power. What determinants of trade union power have been identified in the chapter?*

The power of a union will depend on the level and nature of its membership as well as on other factors. A union's ability to attract members from particular groups of workers will be important to influence employers to recognise the union, although the attitude of an employer is likely to have a moderating effect in terms of the decision taken by many employees about whether to join. Unions that build up high levels of membership density should be able to exercise much greater power and influence, although other circumstances need to be favourable. This recognises that union power is based on factors other than the level of union membership, although this is an important, underlying factor. Other factors relate to the power resources of individual workers and the ability of a union to combine these resources to mobilise, or use, them. The power resources of workers are related to their scarcity value in the production process or the provision of services, the extent of demand for their type of labour, and their ability to disrupt production or service provision. A union's power will also depend on its ability to combine workers effectively to use these power resources. Mobilisation of potential power resources will also depend on the extent to which members identify with, are committed to and involved in realising the goals of the union. Underpinning this will be the extent to which a union is effectively structured and defined by a clear strategy around which members may identify. Traditionally, the power of craft unions was also defined by the ability of skilled workers to limit the supply of new labour through their exclusive position in being able to train and pass on their skills to entrants to the particular craft. The existence of representatives and activity in the workplace also provides an important indication of trade union power.

CASE 5   The TUC Partnership Institute

The TUC launched its Partnership Institute in January 2001, with the aim of developing partnerships between unions and employing organisations that will improve employee relations. Partnerships are designed to develop a joint focus that improves people's working lives and the performance of the businesses for which they work. The TUC believes that partnership in the workplace is capable of producing a range of benefits both for employees and for the organisations that employ them, as well as in terms of promoting union membership and organisation.

The TUC believes that a successful approach to partnership is based on six principles (TUC, 2002b). These are:

- *Joint commitment to the success of the enterprise.* Effective partnerships will be developed where both unions and employers understand an organisation's strategy and are committed to its success. This requires the replacement of any adversarial approach to regulating the employment relationship.
- *Recognition of respective legitimate interests.* Genuine partnerships will recognise the legitimate existence of different interests and views between unions and employers. Arrangements are required to resolve these differences in an atmosphere of trust.
- *Commitment to security of employment.* Partnership needs to embrace employment security to complement the existence of forms of flexibility in the workplace. Flexibility should not be used at the expense of employment security. This will mean restricting the use of compulsory redundancy and developing employability where appropriate.
- *Focus on the quality of working life.* Partnership should provide opportunities for employees to participate in the making of decisions that affect their working lives and for improved terms and conditions of work. It should also broaden the scope of organisational issues that are considered jointly by unions and employers.

▶

■ *Transparency and sharing of information.* Partnership is based on transparency and the sharing of information at an early stage, with opportunities for meaningful consultations to be conducted with unions and employees.

■ *Mutual gains and adding value.* Effective partnerships will lead to improved organisational performance, terms and conditions of work, and develop employee involvement, commitment, and mutual gains.

The TUC Partnership Institute is based at its National Education Centre in north London and is composed of a small team of staff supported by a larger group of associates. The Director of the TUC Partnership Institute, Linda Kelly, is responsible for its strategic direction. The TUC's Economic and Social Affairs Department is also responsible for promoting partnership to employers, government and the unions as well as conducting research into this concept. An Advisory Board to the Partnership Institute has been established. Chaired by Professor William Brown of Cambridge University, this is composed of union, employer, academic and other representatives.

The TUC Partnership Institute provides a range of support to promote the development of partnership at work. This includes the provision of advice, diagnostic assessment, training and consultancy about partnership working to both unions and managers. The Partnership Institute recognises that the introduction of partnership working is likely to be problematic, often changing the behaviours and attitudes of those involved for this to be successful. Success in this context requires the development of trust between those involved and their commitment to the approach of partnership, as well as the sustained operationalisation of these attributes in practice. Underpinning the approach to partnership is a commitment to joint decision-making and problem-solving. The TUC Partnership Institute states:

> In our view, partnership is about real joint decision making and problem solving, it is about unions having more influence in the workplace, and employees exercising greater control over their immediate working environment. (TUC, 2002b)

The agenda for partnership encompasses consideration of business strategy, the organisation of work, collective bargaining and issues that affect the quality of working life.

The consultancy work undertaken for the Partnership Institute includes running workshops for union representatives and managers and developing partnership agreements. The provision of training covers the development of skills required for partnership working, including those related to information sharing, developing consensus and jointly solving problems. Training is offered to organisational managers and union representatives, and where this is undertaken jointly it may help to develop a partnership culture within the organisation. The Partnership Institute also uses a diagnostic approach to assess the nature of working relationships between organisational managers and union representatives and the way in which these impact on performance and quality of working life, which may also be benchmarked to other organisations. This allows positive attributes of union–employer relationships to be identified, as well as areas where these could be developed. Independent consultants who demonstrate impartiality in their work with unions and organisational managers are used to provide these services (TUC, 2002b).

The TUC Partnership Institute recognises that there will be a number of aspects that will be common in all cases for partnership to work effectively. These include:

- building a common understanding of the situation and the need for change;
- the establishment of trust between those involved;
- developing an open approach to information and channels for effective communication;
- allowing unions to become more involved in decision-making and developing the participation of employees in respect of operational decisions that affect their work;
- establishing partnership working as part of the culture of an organisation (TUC, 2002b).

Questions

1 Based on your reading of the chapter as well as the case study, how does the TUC's approach to partnership relate to previous approaches to promote unionisation in the workplace?

2 How would you evaluate the prospects for the success of this approach?

Chapter 6

The role of government in regulating the employment relationship

At the end of this chapter you should be able to:

- outline the roles of government in regulating the employment relationship and its basis for power;

- distinguish between political ideologies and discuss the approaches each is likely to adopt to manage the employment relationship;

- discuss how successive United Kingdom governments have managed the employment relationship;

- appreciate the influence of the European Union on this.

6.1 Introduction

Governments, through the political process, help to shape the formal and informal rules within which the employment relationship operates. As the *third force* in the employment relations system (Poole, 1986: 99), governments set both the legal context and the frameworks for subjective value judgements on fairness and equity, power and authority, and the rights of the individual rather than the collective (Salamon, 2000). Other forces at national level are the trade unions, represented by the Trades Union Congress (TUC); and the employers, represented by employers' organisations such as the Confederation of British Industry (CBI) and the Local Government Association. Because of their law-making role, only governments can change statutory regulations directly. These legal regulations are also influenced by governments' economic and social policies, which constrain the general environment within which the employment relationship operates. In addition, governments, as both direct and indirect employers, demonstrate their ideological preferences for the employment relationship through the mix of organisations that are in the public sector and the approach they choose to manage both employers and employees.

Within this chapter we are concerned principally with the impact of successive governments and their ideologies on policies, legislation and value judgements and how these affect the employment relationship within the United Kingdom. For example, if economic policies are directed to creating full employment and maximising economic growth, in general this may weaken the bargaining power of the employer relative to employees. In such a situation, demand for labour is likely to be high, causing scarcity and therefore causing wages to rise. Conversely, if policies are directed to restraining economic growth, then demand for labour is likely to fall, resulting in general in increasing unemployment. In this situation, the bargaining power of the employer is strengthened owing to an oversupply of potential employees (Gennard and Judge, 1999). If government legislation restricts the rights of trade unions, such as the range of legislation consolidated in the Trade Union and Labour Relations (Consolidation) Act 1992 and the Trade Union Reform and Employment Rights Act 1993, then the bargaining power of the employer is likely in general to be strengthened. In contrast, if legislation is more favourable to employees or trade unions, such as the Employment Relations Act 1999 and the Employment Act 2002, employers' power is likely in general to be reduced. Inevitably, as suggested by these examples, when governments change so do their political priorities and public policies. As we shall see in this chapter, some of these priorities and policies, such as equal opportunities, last for a considerable time owing to general political and public consensus about them. Others have a more limited duration. In addition, UK governments' policies are shaped increasingly by distinctive supranational employment relations systems, in particular legislation from the European Union's (EU) parliament (Jensen *et al.*, 1999).

This chapter develops our brief overview of the impact of government and the political environment on the employment relationship in Chapter 2. We commence in Section 6.2 by examining the relationship between the UK government and the state and exploring the roles that governments can utilise in regulating the employment relationship. Subsequently, in Section 6.3, we outline the range of political ideologies that governments can adopt, exploring in particular their implications for the nature of trade unions' power. Building upon these concepts, the changing role of successive UK governments in regulating the employment relationship is discussed. In doing this we begin in Section 6.4 with an overview of what is often referred to as the post Second World War period of political consensus up to 1979. In Section 6.5 we then consider the 'new relationship' between government, trades unions and employers of successive Conservative governments led by Margaret Thatcher and John Major from 1979 to 1997. In Section 6.6 we assess the implications of the post-1997 New Labour government's 'Third Way'. Alongside these UK developments, we also discuss the growing influence of the EU on the regulation of the employment relationship, particularly in recent years. We conclude the chapter with a case study in which the influence of government upon employment within a major UK outsourced services company is explored.

6.2 An overview of government's roles and basis of power

■ The roles of government

There is considerable agreement amongst commentators that governments set the wider economic and social framework within which the employment relationship operates, but the precise outcomes of individual government's fiscal, monetary and social policies are more varied. Taking an overview, Gennard and Judge (1999) argue that all governments have the role of economic manager and, although ideologies and policies may differ, the objectives are broadly similar whichever political party is in power. They define these as:

- price stability;
- full employment;
- economic growth;
- balance of payments surplus;

and argue that the relative priorities given to each are dependent upon the government in power. For example, as we shall see, the UK Labour governments between 1974 and 1979 emphasised full employment, whereas Conservative governments between 1979 and 1997 emphasised price stability. In contrast, the New Labour governments since 1997 have emphasised macroeconomic (price) stability and employment opportunities for all, tackling the supply-side barriers to economic growth (Gamble and Kelly, 2001). Poole's (1986) categorisation of government strategies into the areas of employment levels, relationships at work and the distribution of economic reward highlights at the aggregate level the strategies with which these objectives might be achieved. The first of these, *employment levels*, includes aspects such as job creation and protection. The second, *relationships at work*, incorporates issues of industrial democracy such as trade union rights and collective bargaining as well as legislation relating to individuals such as discrimination and employment rights. The third covers the *distribution of economic reward*, including issues such as low pay and the rate of pay increases. The pursuit of these objectives may also be constrained or enabled by EU legislation, directives and rulings of the European Court of Human Rights. The different ways in which each of Gennard and Judge's four objectives is pursued can therefore be seen in the strategies that different governments have adopted and the ways in which these are operationalised.

Work by Farnham and Pimlott (1995) emphasises two key roles for government in operationalising these strategies. These they characterise as defining through example the meaning of model employer and acting as industrial peacekeeper. Historically, successive UK governments have accepted responsibility to act as what they consider a *model employer*. Through this desire to provide exemplars of good practice, employees of government institutions were among the first to receive pensions, holidays, training and security of employment. With regard to the second role, of *industrial peacekeeper*, there was until recently a long tradition of governments taking steps to seek satisfactory outcomes to major strikes, in particular intervening directly to help settle large-scale industrial disputes.

The 1979–97 Conservative government's free market ideology led to the model employer being defined in terms of practices developed by the private sector. Farnham and Pimlott (1995) suggest that, under this, the model employer became one in which managers were in positions of indisputable authority, and employees had only a consultative and supporting role. Pay determination was based on individual performance and appraisal, and new technologies and working practices were expected to be accepted by employees without opposition or complaint. In addition, the government no longer took the role of industrial peacekeeper, intervening to help settle disputes. Rather, the two sides were allowed to resolve the dispute and market forces were used to achieve a sense of reality. After the 1997 election, New Labour focused upon incorporating the range of EU minimum standards affecting working conditions and terms of employment as well as, most notably, introducing a minimum wage. However, its tone of government has been one of softening private sector market principles, rather than suggesting a different model employer. At the time of writing, the New Labour government has yet to face major industrial unrest. However, their pro-market stance and retention of the majority of trade union legislation suggests that a full return to the role of industrial peacekeeper is unlikely.

Government and the state

Within the UK, the state comprises a wide range of governmental institutions that surround the government (Figure 6.1). The government can therefore be viewed as at the centre of a range of state institutions, operating within a political mechanism whose authority is backed by the legal system (Salamon, 1999). However, governments are elected for a particular term with a maximum of five years, and so, unlike the state, are transient in nature. In addition the differing ideologies of the political parties mean there is potential for changes in government policy and strategy.

Government policies are operationalised by the state, which shapes and regulates the structures and interactions that make up society. The transitory nature of governments means that some of the agencies of the state will be of limited duration. This may be because the government agency is associated with a specific short-term policy decision and so has a limited natural life, such as the Conservative government's Standing Commission on Pay Comparability (1979–80). Alternatively, a change in government may result in a new ideology within which there is no part for that agency. In 1986, as part of the strategy to make employing people economic, the

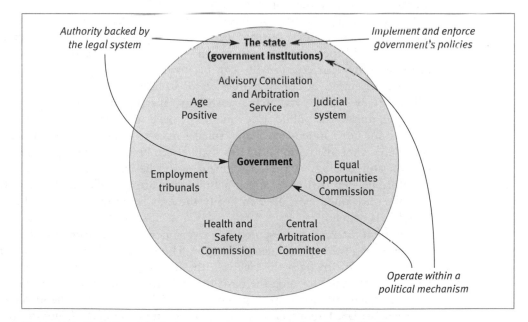

Figure 6.1 **Relationship between government and state institutions**

Conservative government restricted the role of wages councils, subsequently abolishing them in 1993. There is also potential for governments to redefine the boundaries of agencies. In particular this may occur if an agency is forced to support the government's espoused views rather than being allowed to act independently. For example, in 1993 the Conservative government removed the duty of the Arbitration and Conciliation Advisory Service (ACAS) 'to encourage collective bargaining' thereby ensuring that its work was brought more into line with government's legislation. This had little to do with any form of encouragement for trade union activity.

self-check question

6.1 Re-examine Figure 6.1. Name three other state institutions that are likely to influence the employment relationship. The UK Government's website *ukonline* may be of help here: <http://www.ukonline.gov.uk>

■ The basis of governmental power

The basis of a government's power to manage the employment relationship is based upon what Salamon (2000: 284) terms its *representative position*. In other words, power is derived from being elected through a democratic process to represent the people. Within this, a government's position needs to be considered in the light of three different, although overlapping, assumptions about the nature of the interests they represent:

■ national;
■ sectional;
■ capitalist.

These three interests also highlight three constraints on the ways in which governments can influence the employment relationship.

In representing the first of these, the *national interest*, a government will argue that it occupies a neutral position between the conflicting interests of employers and employees and their representatives. On the basis of this, government's intervention in the employment relationship can be justified on the grounds of protecting the interests of employees or of employers or upholding the wider interests of society when threatened by particular pressure groups (Farnham and Pimlott, 1995). For example, during the public sector manual worker disputes of the winter of 1978–79, the Labour government used the armed forces to collect refuse. However, what is considered as in the national interest is likely to be dependent upon the political persuasion and ideology of the government using the justification for its actions. It can therefore be seen that government actions in relation to the employment relationship will be constrained by a need to justify these as being in the national interest, however this is defined.

Sectional interests represented by government can be argued to have been legitimised through the government's election. These interests will have come together as a political party to fight the election, the ideology upon which their election campaign was founded forming the basis for legislation and other governmental policies. Such sectional interests were apparent and widely discussed in the ideological affinity between the UK Labour Party and the trade unions and the Conservative Party and employers in the second half of the twentieth century. Although it can be argued that these relationships declined considerably in the last decade of the twentieth century, the experiences of the post Second World War period (discussed later) indicate clearly how governments are constrained by sectional interests.

Representation of the *capitalist* or *employers' interest* is considered by Salamon (2000) to occur irrespective of the ideology of the political party in power. He bases this on the argument that, whatever the political beliefs of the party in power, government is constrained by the need for both economic stability and the confidence of employers in the government. Without these, any government is unlikely to be able to maintain its own power and be re-elected (Blyton and Turnbull, 1998). One underlying assumption of this argument is that government needs the support of industry more than industry needs the support of government. Indeed, it is worth reflecting that, with increasing globalisation, it is possible for multinational organisations, such as motor vehicle manufacturers, to negate or reduce the impact of any government intervention in the employment relationship by transferring all or part of their operations to another country. Government responses justified as being in the national interest are therefore more likely to be linked to the interests of employers than of employees. For example, government support for industrial action could damage employers' confidence in government and in the long-term economic stability. It would therefore not be considered as in the wider interests of society; rather it would be seen as sectional, selfish and irresponsible.

6.3 Political ideologies, trade union power and the employment relationship

As long ago as the reign of Elizabeth I, government intervened in the employment relationship by fixing wages (Farnham and Pimlott, 1995). Indeed, it was not until the early stages of the Industrial Revolution in the UK that governments began to adopt a less interventionist role in economic and industrial affairs. Political theory identifies two distinct ideologies with regard to governments' role: *laissez-faire* (or liberalist) and *corporatist*. These can be plotted as extremes on a continuum ranging from *laissez-faire* to corporatist (Figure 6.2). A *laissez-faire* ideology is characterised by a free market economy within which competition for goods, services and labour is the basis for regulating society. The emphasis is on each individual being responsible for her or his well-being rather than this being provided by the state. The direct role of government in the employment relationship has been termed *passive* within a *laissez-faire* ideology. However, it can also be considered to be coercive, as legislation is used to minimise disruptive action by employees, thereby upholding and supporting managers in their right to manage.

At the other extreme the corporatist or interventionist ideology is based on a belief that social and economic aspects of life are interrelated and that political influence and regulation should be used to manage the employment relationship. In particular, government should accept responsibility and take a direct role in protecting individuals from social problems arising from the marketplace and in improving their quality of life. This means that the operation of the marketplace must be constrained through interventionist regulation to allow social justice. In addition, there may be a desire for consensual government.

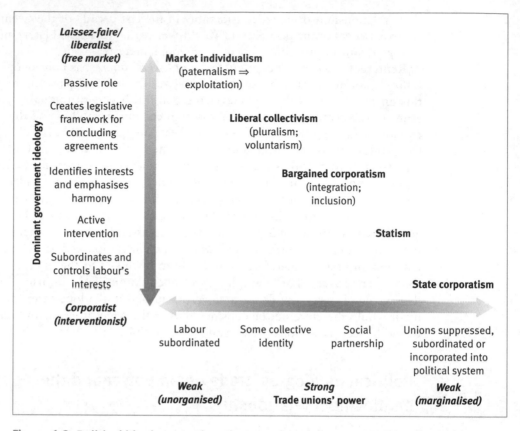

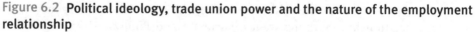

Figure 6.2 **Political ideology, trade union power and the nature of the employment relationship**

These ideological extremes form one axis of a widely used analytical framework to explore government influences on the employment relationship. Integrated within this framework are the relative power of trade unions and the reasons for this power. In Figure 6.2 this is represented by the horizontal axis. Moving from left to right along this axis, labour is subordinated initially because trade unions are weak and unorganised. As labour is organised into autonomous trade unions, its collective identity grows and social partnerships between government and trade unions are established. Consequently, the power of trade unions becomes stronger. Moving to the right, suppression or regulation of trade unions or their subordination or incorporation into the political system results in their being marginalised in the employment relationship, with little real power.

self-check question

6.2 Outline the key beliefs of the *laissez-faire* and corporatist ideologies. For each, note the key implications for a government's management of the employment relationship.

At the top left of Figure 6.2, *market individualism* occurs when the government has a *laissez-faire* ideology and trade union power is weak. In such circumstances, employees are relatively unorganised and subordinate to a market within which they are little more than a commodity to be bought and sold. As in the UK for much of the nineteenth century, property rights and in particular the ownership of capital and income inequalities are legitimised. Government policy is directed to protecting the rights of the employers to manage, as they consider appropriate, rather than protecting employees against managerial excesses. Consequently the nature of the employment relationship is dependent upon individual employers, and can range from benevolent paternalism to exploitation. The former of these is evident in company towns built by industrialists for their employees, such as the Cadbury Brothers' Bournville (now part of Birmingham) and Lever Brothers' Port Sunlight (near Liverpool). Over the first half of the twentieth century, market individualism in the UK gradually gave way to *liberal collectivism*. Through this period the growth in trade union power and employees' collective identity was accommodated and indulged by the dominant employers' interest as a way of absorbing pressure for change from employees.

Liberal collectivism, like market individualism, occurs when the government has a *laissez-faire* ideology. However, in this situation, there is a need to accommodate greater collective economic power and strength of employees through trade unions, particularly with regard to negotiating basic terms and conditions of employment. Consequently, the government may intervene to create a legislative framework within which employers and trade unions can reach agreement. In doing this, government may adopt a *voluntarist* approach, allowing trade unions and employers to decide on their own matters concerning the management of the employment relationship. Alternatively, it may adopt a *pluralist* approach, based on the belief that power is not and cannot be concentrated. In the latter approach the government acts as a neutral arbiter, accommodating some of the interests of different groups within the employment relationship, choosing between different policy alternatives on the basis of the arguments and what they judge to be likely to be most popular (Rose, 2001).

Bargained corporatism occurs only when trade union power is strong and is based upon the ideas of social partnership and maintaining harmony through trade-offs or 'bargains' between different interest groups. Within this ideology, corporatism refers to the domination of society by large organisations whose activities and relations are planned and coordinated, rather than being determined by marketplace competition or conflict (Rose, 2001). At the organisational level, bipartite social partnerships are developed between employers (management) and trade unions while, at a national level, a tripartite relationship is developed between government, trade unions and employers (Salamon, 1999). In its simplest form, government involves both trade unions and management by consulting frequently about the strategy on both employment and wider social and economic issues. In more advanced forms, as in Scandinavia, the tripartite relationship is formalised through decision-making with various quasi-governmental bodies. In return, employers and trade unions are expected to cooperate in the achievement of this strategy, including maintaining stability in the employment relationship.

Within the UK, the 1960s saw an increasing need for more government management of the economy to ensure both full employment and low inflation. Salamon (2000) argues that this resulted in a movement from a liberal collectivist towards a bargained corporatist approach to regulating the employment relationship based upon social partnership between trade unions and government. This emphasised mutual interests and inclusion and was, particularly under Labour governments, characterised by discussions between government, employers and trade unions on economic and social issues and union acceptance of wage restraint through both voluntary and statutory incomes policies. Although not just the preserve of Labour governments, this has often been referred to as 'beer and sandwiches at No. 10' as Labour prime ministers such as Harold Wilson and James Callaghan met with trade union leaders at 10 Downing Street. Within this relationship governments were able to offer additional things that could not have been achieved in employer–trade union bargaining such as social policy reforms, changes in employees' rights and changes in economic policy. It did, however, differ from statism as the unions were in social partnership, rather than being weak and marginalised, or state corporatism where the interests of labour are suppressed, subordinated or incorporated into the political system.

Statism, like bargained corporatism, has a corporatist governing ideology. However, here it is combined with industrially weak trade unions. In order to redress the balance of power between employers and employees the government intervenes in the employment relationship, legislating to establish terms and conditions for employees. Consequently, trade unions are more likely to be focused upon political than employment-related activities (Salamon, 1999).

Finally, at the bottom right of Figure 6.2, *state corporatism* occurs when a corporatist ideology, often involving long-term dominance, is combined with politically subordinated or suppressed trade unions. In countries where this exists, such as the former communist countries of Eastern Europe and some of the tiger economies of South-East Asia, control over all aspects of the employment relationship is through the political system rather than the free market forces associated with the *laissez-faire* ideology. Under such an ideology, it might be argued that exploitation of labour by the state could exist.

In this section, we have outlined briefly the nature of government intervention during the nineteenth century and the period up to the Second World War. However, there is a need to consider the remaining half of the twentieth century and the first few years of the twenty-first century in more detail so that we can understand better the nature of the employment relationship and government's role within it. In order to do this we have subdivided the post Second World War period into:

- the postwar settlement, 1945–79;
- the new relationship, 1979–97;
- the Third Way, 1997 onwards.

Building upon the interrelated concepts of political ideology and trade union power already outlined, we now explore the role of government in the UK employment relationship for each of these periods.

6.4 The postwar settlement, 1945–79

■ Overview

In the period after the Second World War until 1979, there was considerable political consensus within the UK. Successive governments drew their approach to regulating the economy, interacting with trade unions and in handling the employment relationship from a bargained corporatist ideology. This consensus was founded on five interrelated factors:

- the need for government to set a good example as a model employer;
- public support for collective bargaining;
- the voluntarist belief of a minimum of state and legal interference in employment relations;
- the commitment of government to full employment policies;
- the close involvement of the TUC, and the CBI after its formation in 1965 by Royal Charter, with government in management of the economy.

Not surprisingly, given their ideology, successive governments favoured collectivist values and action, emphasising the importance of cooperation, shared beliefs and values and the need of the state to achieve collective improvements. Individualism, it was claimed, led to selfishness and a society divided between rich and poor (Farnham and Pimlott, 1995).

Adoption by the state of the role of model employer was based on the implicit understanding that, as long as government and senior management discharged their responsibilities to be good employers, employees and their union representatives would accept a reciprocal obligation to avoid industrial conflict (Winchester, 1983). Being a good employer embraced a wide range of activities. These included recognition of trade unions and joint determination of terms and conditions of employment including pension schemes, sick pay and workplace procedural agreements in areas such as discipline and grievance handling. In addition it encompassed the acceptance of collective bargaining for determining pay and conditions (predominantly at a national level), widespread use of joint consultation procedures, and ensuring that pay of public sector employees was broadly comparable with that of the private sector. By 1979 the government was acknowledged as a model employer throughout its public sector institutions. These employed some 7 449 000 people in areas such as the Civil Service, local government, police, fire and National Health Services, national defence and education, power, telephones and water utilities and nationalised industries such as rail (Kessler and Bayliss, 1998).

In regulating the economy, successive governments of this period adopted Keynesian policies to provide full employment and economic stability. These were, in essence, based on the ideas developed by economist John Maynard Keynes (1997) in the 1930s, and argued that:

- levels of unemployment are determined by the total demand for goods and services within the economy;
- during periods of high unemployment, governments should stimulate demand by lowering taxes and interest rates (fiscal and monetary policy) and increasing their own (public) expenditure on public works;
- policies to stimulate demand will create extra employment, thereby increasing individuals' spending power;
- increased spending power will, in turn, increase demand for goods produced in the private sector;
- increased demand for private sector goods will lead to private sector employers taking on more labour, thereby increasing spending power and demand once again;
- if repeated throughout the economy, greater spending power and demand will result in a reduction in unemployment.

This meant that, when unemployment rose, the government should inject more spending power into the economy by increasing public expenditure and/or cutting taxes.

The postwar settlement between 1945 and 1979 can be divided into two subperiods. The first, between 1945 and the Donovan Commission Report of 1968, can be characterised as voluntarism with, not surprisingly, little legislation affecting the employment relationship. Subsequent to this, the second subperiod is characterised by increased government intervention in the way the employment relationship was managed. It is to these that we now turn.

■ From 1945 to the Donovan Commission Report (1968)

During the 1945–68 period there was relatively little legislation directly affecting the employment relationship (Box 6.1). Employees' rights were derived primarily from their contracts of employment and trade union immunity from the Trades Disputes Act 1906, the Trades Disputes Act 1965 being introduced to protect trade union members from legal liability for intimidation of employers by threatening strike action. However, this period saw an increase in labour unrest brought about by increasing pressures in the labour market. Trade union membership was expanding, there was near full employment and, linked to this, employees' aspirations for higher salaries were growing. At the same time, employers needed to improve productivity and alter working practices to meet increasing demand for goods and services. These pressures resulted in employers breaching industry-wide national agreements on pay and other issues, replacing them with organisation and local-level collective bargaining. The resultant conflict between industry and organisation-level collective bargaining led to the Labour government charging the Donovan Commission to analyse the UK system of industrial relations.

Box 6.1	Summary of major UK legislation affecting the employment relationship, 1945–79
Act	**Key features**
Trades Disputes Act 1965	■ Protected trade union members from the tort of intimidation by threatening strike action.
Equal Pay Act 1970	■ Legislated that all women's contracts had an implied equality clause if this was not already specifically contained in the contract. This meant women's contracts were no less favourable than those of a man engaged in like work or work rated as equivalent.
	■ If discriminated against, women could take their cases to an employment tribunal to seek redress.
Industrial Relations Act 1971	■ Removed most legal proceedings arising out of industrial disputes from ordinary courts, placing them under the National Industrial Relations Court.
	■ Introduced new ground for legal proceedings – unfair industrial practice – thereby reducing trade union immunity.

Box 6.1	Continued

Industrial Relations Act 1971 (continued)

- Replaced Registrar of Friendly Societies with Registrar of Trade Unions and Employers' Associations with whom trade unions and employers' associations could be registered if their rules and procedures conformed to standards laid down in the Act.
- Limited trade union immunities to unions registered under the Act.
- Empowered the Secretary of State to order a cooling-off period where an industrial dispute threatened the economy or public health or safety.
- Assumed that written collective agreements between employers and employees were legally enforceable unless they expressly contained a disclaimer.
- Introduced statutory support for trade unions seeking recognition.
- Introduced an employee's right to his or her job, regardless of contract, after a certain length of service, and the right to claim for unfair dismissal.

Health and Safety at Work etc. Act 1974

- Established the Health and Safety Commission and the Health and Safety Executive.
- Extended protection of law on health and safety to include 8 million workers not previously covered.
- Placed statutory duties on employers, self-employed and employees in achieving acceptable safety standards at work.

Trade Union and Labour Relations Act 1974

- Repealed much of the Industrial Relations Act 1971, re-establishing trade union immunities back to the position established by the Trades Disputes Act 1906.

Sex Discrimination Act 1975

- Promoted equal treatment of men and women in employment, education and provision of goods and services.
- Covered discrimination against women and men and on the grounds of marital status at all stages of the employment relationship.
- Exempted small firms of five or fewer employees.

Trade Union and Labour Relations (Amendment) Act 1976

- Extended trade union immunity to the breach of all contracts for which trade unions were responsible when they called their members out on industrial action, thereby giving trade unions freedom to encourage their members to take secondary industrial action.

Race Relations Act 1976

- Made indirect and direct discrimination unlawful on the grounds of colour, race, nationality or ethnic or national origin in employment (and other areas).
- Act did not apply to the police or public services.

The Donovan Commission (1968) recommended that there should be voluntary reform in which both management and trade unions accepted the reality of organisation-level bargaining and the need for this to be made more formal. In particular, the recommendations focused on the development of formal substantive agreements between employers and trade unions. These agreements were to be initiated by management. However, the reforms suggested did not proceed fast enough, prompting both the Labour and the Conservative parties to produce legislative proposals to speed up the process.

Post Donovan Commission (1968) to 1979

Upon election, the incoming Conservative government's proposals resulted in the Industrial Relations Act 1971 (Box 6.1). This proposed a comprehensive legal framework, assuming that both written and collective agreements between employers and employees were legally enforceable unless they expressly contained a disclaimer. Trade union immunities from being sued for damages caused by strike action were limited through the concept of unfair industrial practices. If the unions committed these, those affected now had the right to sue. The 1971 Act was resisted by the trade unions and, in reality, had very little effect, largely because employers did not put its provisions into practice (Edwards et al., 1998). The Act lost credibility and, when the Labour government was elected, it returned the law on trades disputes to what it had been previously through the Trade Union and Labour Relations Act 1974. However, one significant feature that was maintained was the provisions against unfair dismissal. These restricted employers' freedoms to dismiss employees and, although modified by subsequent legislation in the 1980s, have not been fundamentally altered.

The Trade Union and Labour Relations (Amendment) Act 1976 extended trade union immunity to breach of all contracts for which trade unions were responsible when they called their members out on industrial action. This meant that trade unions could pursue secondary action. For example, action could now be taken against an employer with whom the trade union had no dispute but who might be a key customer. Through this action, the trade union hoped the secondary employer would put pressure on the employer involved in the main dispute to settle on more favourable terms (Gennard and Judge, 1999). Other employment-related legislation was consistent with the ideology of voluntarism, supporting the establishment of health and safety standards (Health and Safety at Work etc. Act 1974) and equal opportunities (Equal Pay Act 1970; Sex Discrimination Act 1975; Race Relations Act 1976).

During the 1970s, the establishment of the Advisory, Conciliation and Arbitration Service (ACAS) further facilitated third-party intervention in industrial disputes. This operated in addition to the Central Arbitration Committee, which had originally been established as the Industrial Court in 1919. Established by Royal Commission in 1974, ACAS was placed on a statutory basis in the Employment Protection Act 1975. Through this service, mediation and arbitration was, and is, undertaken by an independent person selected jointly by the parties to the dispute from a list of competent arbitrators provided by ACAS. Successive governments worked alongside the TUC and the Confederation of British Industry (CBI) in what is often referred to as a *tripartite governmental process*. The process became so highly developed that, regardless of the political party in power, it continued. However, in general terms

Labour governments had better relationships with the TUC, whereas Conservative governments had better relationships with the CBI.

Towards the end of this period the basis upon which the postwar settlement existed began to be challenged owing to high inflation and associated wage claims. Attempts were made by successive governments to limit wage settlements in both the public and private sectors by creating labour markets that were more competitive and by using low public sector wage settlements as an example of what could be achieved. Despite involvement of both the CBI and the TUC, these attempts were seen by some as a deliberate attempt to shift the balance of power away from the trade unions in favour of the employers. Public sector resistance to declining real incomes and standards of living relative to the private sector resulted in large-scale industrial disputes by certain groups of employees including local authority manual workers, post office workers, electricity workers and coalminers. The most prominent of these were the national mineworkers' strikes of 1972 and during the winter of 1973–74. The Conservative government went to the electorate in the midst of the 1974 strike on the issue of who governed the country, an election that the Conservatives, under Edward Heath, lost.

The incoming Labour government was elected with the miners' strike still in progress, at least partially on the basis that it knew how to get on with the trade unions. However, it had only a small majority. Prices were now rising rapidly owing to the quadrupling of oil prices by OPEC (Organisation of Petroleum Exporting Countries) and wage settlements were being concluded at extremely high levels (for example teachers 27 per cent, nurses 30 per cent) to compensate for restraints and anomalies of the previous Conservative government (Kessler and Baylis, 1998). The government renounced the Conservative government's incomes policy and, in order to manage the situation, agreed a *Social Contract* with the TUC. This avoided the compulsion of earlier policies of wage restraint, instead being based on a quasi-contractual agreement between government and the TUC. In exchange for limiting wage increases to annual claims for compensation for rises in the cost of living, the government agreed to extend rights for individual workers and trade union rights (Employment Protection Act 1975; Trade Union and Labour Relations (Amendment) Act 1976), provide tax concessions, increase public expenditure, and take other measures to reduce unemployment (Edwards *et al.*, 1998; Kessler and Baylis, 1998).

The Social Contract received strong support from some trade union leaders, such as Jack Jones of the Transport and General Workers' Union, and succeeded initially in bringing down both wage and price inflation through reductions in real pay (Kessler and Bayliss, 1998). However, despite rising unemployment (Figure 2.4), it proved impossible to limit wage settlements in the private sector, and the government's ability to manage the economy and its role as a model employer was called into question. Resistance to pay increase limits grew, culminating in a series of disputes, particularly by public sector manual workers, in what became known as the 1978–79 *Winter of Discontent*. Strikes in essential services, including refuse collection and hospitals, resulted in a dramatic rise in the number of working days lost (Figure 6.3), giving the impression that the government had lost control and was unable to manage the economy.

In 1979 the Labour government tried to deal with public sector unrest by establishing the Standing Commission on Pay Comparability chaired by Hugh Clegg. This was to look into pay comparability between public and private sectors. However, the

Figure 6.3 **Working days lost and stoppages 1977–2000**
Source: Developed from Davies (1999, 2001)

results of the election later that year suggested that the government had lost public support for its management of the economy, strikes in essential services damaging its credibility. The Labour government was defeated in 1979, and a new era for employers was ushered in under Margaret Thatcher, who had campaigned on the basis of curbing the power of trade unions. The elected Conservative government allowed the Standing Commission to complete reports already in progress on nurses, teachers, local authority manual workers and National Health Service manual workers, and agreed to honour the awards suggested. However, the cost of doing so reinforced the new administration's hostility to this form of pay bargaining (Kessler and Bayliss, 1998). In 1991 the Standing Commission was abolished, the principle of comparability being replaced subsequently by the criterion of *ability to pay* for public sector pay determination (Edwards *et al.*, 1998).

6.5 The new relationship, 1979–97

The strikes of the 1978–79 Winter of Discontent reinforced the need for a different governmental approach to trade unions. Within the new Conservative government right-wing groups led by Sir Keith Joseph popularised a new type of relationship between government and trade unions. This challenged the liberal collectivist values, shifting sharply towards a market individualist ideology in which the needs of individuals to follow their own talents and abilities and energies within a broad unobtrusive framework of law were paramount (Farnham and Pimlott, 1995). However, despite the new government's approach being overtly anti-corporatist, some commentators (for example Edwards *et al.*, 1998) argue that the 1980s did not

represent a widespread move to accept individualism. Concern about class inequality remained largely as it had been, the change being that now people did not believe there were any real means of dealing with the problem of unemployment and so mass protest seemed out of place.

Policies adopted by the Conservative government were developed from the ideas of monetarism such as those put forward by Milton Friedman and others in the 1970s. Unlike Keynesian economists, who identified unemployment as the major economic problem, monetarists considered that it was inflation. In particular they argued that (Rose, 2001):

- high levels of government expenditure lead to rapid growth in the supply of money circulating in the economy;
- this excessive monetary growth is caused in part by government borrowing, the Public Sector Borrowing Requirement (PSBR), being used to finance budget deficits;
- if the supply of money grows more quickly than the production of goods and services then inflation will result as there is money to purchase more goods and services than are available;
- increasing inflation increases expectations of future inflation rates being even higher, resulting in still higher wage demands and settlements and a wage price inflationary spiral with increased unemployment as the competitiveness of firms declines;
- to prevent inflation, the increase in overall purchasing power needs to match the rate of increase in the output of goods and services in the economy as a whole;
- if this increase in economy-wide purchasing power exceeds the increase in the supply of goods and services in the economy as a whole, spending power (demand) must be decreased by raising interest rates and reducing government (public) expenditure.

Therefore, according to monetarists, the key to reducing unemployment and controlling inflation is enhancing the ability of the economy to increase the supply of goods and services to the market, while preventing excessive monetary growth. They argue that creating an environment conducive to private enterprise can do this. In particular it creates incentives for individuals to work and for firms to invest, produce, and employ, liberalising product markets, privatising publicly owned companies, reducing taxation and deregulating labour markets (Gennard and Judge, 1999). Not surprisingly, therefore, the Conservative government's employment relations policy was characterised by a rejection of ideals related to the postwar consensus, and in particular by:

- replacement of the government by the private sector as model employer;
- privatisation of nationalised industries and parts of the public sector economy;
- increasing legal control of trade unions and their activities and a clear anti-trade union ideology;
- abandoning the government commitment to full employment policies;
- almost total exclusion of the TUC and the CBI from government economic policy-making.

self-check question 6.3 In what ways do the ideas of monetarism differ from those of Keynesian economics?

Conservative government changes, which affected the employment relationship, were a combination of pre-planned strategy and opportunistic reactions to events (Edwards *et al.*, 1998). In particular, their employment relations policies were integrated with their economic policies of free working of markets and the need to minimise state interference. Scope for lawful industrial action was to be reduced, trade unions were to be allowed to be sued for damages, and the rights of those not taking part in industrial action increased. National training policy was also reformed, with most Industrial Training Boards being abolished in 1981 and the Manpower Services Commission in 1988. Training was now employer-led, with no statutory underpinning (Keep and Rainbird, 1995). Tactically, a step-by-step approach rather than a once and for all change was adopted. Consequently, there were a large number of Acts (see Box 6.2).

Box 6.2	Summary of major UK legislation affecting the employment relationship, 1979–97

Act	Key features
Employment Act 1980	<ul><li>Introduced the distinction between primary and secondary industrial action, removing immunity from civil action for secondary industrial action except for specified purposes.</li><li>Allowed employers to start legal proceedings against individuals who they considered were acting unlawfully in industrial action.</li><li>Restricted the right to picket to employees picketing their own workplace, union officials joining members they represented, and workers dismissed by that company.</li><li>Stopped trade unions with closed shop agreements from expelling individuals or refusing admission. Widened acceptable grounds for individuals' refusal to join to include conscience and deeply held personal beliefs. Non-union members at the time any new closed shop agreements came into force were no longer compelled to join.</li></ul>
Employment Act 1982	<ul><li>Introduced narrower definition of trade dispute outside which strikes would not be immune from legal action. Disputes had to relate *wholly or mainly* to terms and conditions, discipline, dismissal or bargaining machinery.</li><li>Allowed trade unions to be sued for damages and their funds sequestrated where unlawful industrial action was authorised or endorsed by a responsible person or body within the union.</li><li>Further restricted the closed shop so that it was now unfair for an employer to sack an employee where there was a closed shop agreement unless the closed shop had been approved by ballot during preceding 5 years.</li><li>Allowed damages to be awarded against both employer and trade union in respect of unfair treatment.</li></ul>

Box 6.2	Continued

Trade Union Act 1984
- Forced unions to elect executive councils by secret ballot from a members' register.
- Allowed unions immunity from being sued only if industrial action was approved through secret ballot as part of which members were informed that by taking industrial action they would be breaking their contracts of employment.
- Forced unions to hold political fund secret ballot every 10 years if they wanted to hold a political fund and engage in political activities.

Wages Act 1986
- Method of payment open to employer's choice, or negotiation where trade union recognised.
- Limited power of wages councils so they no longer applied to workers aged under 21 and could only set minimum wage and one-premium wage within strict guidelines.

Sex Discrimination Act 1986
- Removed exemption of small firms (five or fewer employees) given in the 1975 Act.
- Extended scope of 1975 Act to include retirement, dismissal, promotion, demotion, transfer or training and amended Equal Pay Act 1970 in same way.

Employment Act 1988
- Outlawed unions' right to discipline members for ignoring a call for industrial action after a ballot in favour of such action.
- Outlawed industrial action designed to maintain a 100 per cent union membership agreement and all dismissals for non-union membership.
- Forced unions to elect secretaries and presidents by secret ballot from a members' register; all ballots now had to be postal.
- Appointed a Commissioner for the Rights of Trade Union Members with powers to assist union members taking or contemplating legal action against their union.

Employment Act 1990
- Abolished pre-entry closed shops, meaning that workers could no longer be refused employment on the grounds of non-membership or membership of a union.
- Outlawed industrial action by workers of an employer not party to a trade dispute except where such action met lawful picketing requirements.
- Made unions liable for all industrial action, including action not officially sanctioned by the union, unless they had taken specific measures to repudiate that action.
- Allowed employers to dismiss employees taking unofficial industrial action with no claim for unfair dismissal.
- Outlawed industrial action in support of workers dismissed for taking unofficial action.
- Extended the role of Commissioner for the Rights of Trade Union Members.

▶

Box 6.2	Continued

Trade Union and Labour Relations (Consolidation) Act 1992	■ Consolidated existing provisions outlined above for collective employment law.
Trade Union Reform and Employment Rights Act 1993	■ Further restricted industrial action ballots to being postal, and requiring 7 days' notice if union was to have immunity from legal repercussion. Union also required to give employer 7 days' notice prior to taking action. ■ Created Commissioner for Protection Against Unlawful Industrial Action to assist members of the public who, as a result of unlawful industrial action, are likely to be prevented from receiving goods and services, to stop the action via the High Court. ■ Forced unions to get written consent from members every 3 years for their subscriptions to be deducted from salaries. ■ Outlawed unions taking disciplinary action against a member leaving and unions refusing membership to a member of another union. ■ Amended Transfer of Undertaking of Prior Employment (TUPE) regulations to include public and not-for-profit sectors' employees.
Disability Discrimination Act 1995	■ Provided protection from discrimination in employment for disabled employees and job applicants to firms of 20 plus employees.
Employment Rights Act 1996	■ Consolidated existing provisions outlined above for individual employment law.

In the period 1979–97 successive Conservative governments sought to impose individualistic values by creating an enterprise culture in which individuals were to be encouraged to seek business success and keep the rewards they gained. Enterprise was to be tested in the free market and not impeded by what they termed the monopoly of trade union power. Individuals were encouraged to identify with market and commercial success rather than collective trade union values. People previously living in local authority (now predominantly housing association) houses were encouraged to become property owners through right-to-buy legislation (Housing Act 1985), and privatisation of nationalised industries such as gas (1986) and electricity (1990 and 1991) helped widen share ownership and profit sharing (Figure 6.4). Legislation formalised the governments' determination to redress the balance of power in the employers' favour, both reducing employment protection and outlawing what it considered inappropriate use of trade union power. Employment protection was no longer seen as minimum standards but rather as a burden upon business, bringing the government into conflict with EU social policy. Although some aspects of these governments' agendas, such as those relating to industrial action and trade union regulation, were not curbed by EU directives and rulings from the European Court of

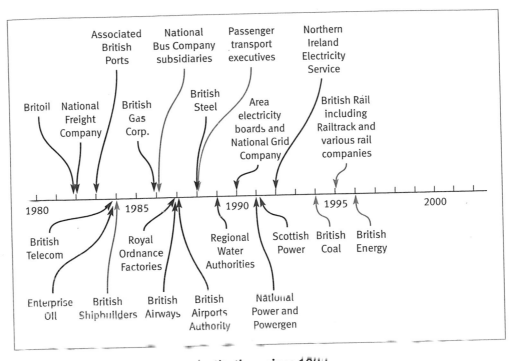

Figure 6.4 Major government privatisations since 1982

Note: Arrows in blue refer to year privatisation commenced

Justice, in other areas limits were placed. These are outlined later. At the same time levels of unemployment within the UK rose from under 1.1 million in 1979 to a high of nearly 3.1 million in 1986 (see Figure 2.4) and, in a climate of widespread redundancies, industrial action became a more considered activity. Indeed, it seems likely that, as suggested by Edwards *et al.* (1998), the introduction of these legislative changes was assisted by fear of unemployment and the belief by many employees that their trade unions were powerless to protect them.

The shift towards a market individualist ideology meant that the Conservative government did not consider the role of model employer as part of its remit. Within weeks of their taking office the public sector and, in particular, local government was no longer seen as an ideal. Now it was 'criticised by ministers who claimed it was wasteful, profligate, irresponsible, unaccountable, luxurious and out of control' (Newton and Karran, 1985: 116). Indeed, commentators argue that 'by the early 1990s it was difficult to detect what the model employer role of the government was, other than being hostile to trade unionism and national collective bargaining' (Farnham and Pimlott, 1995: 215). Despite this, the Conservative governments' views of the key features of an ideal employment relationship have been suggested. This 'ideal' is based upon the premise that managers should be in positions of indisputable authority, with employees taking only a supportive and consultative role within organisations. Pay determination is based upon individual performance and personal appraisal. An additional feature is that new technologies and working practices are expected to be accepted by employees without opposition or complaint (Farnham and Pimlott, 1995). Given that, over the 1979–97 period, there was con-

siderable privatisation of nationalised industries alongside the contracting-out of much public sector work to the private sector, it can be argued that, as suggested earlier, government's role model for employers was now the private sector.

Throughout the 1980s, Conservative governments pursued a policy of privatisations of over 15 major public sector organisations. These included the British Gas Corporation, British Telecom, the British Airports Authority and Britoil (Figure 6.4). In the 1990s, British Rail and British Coal were privatised. Within the public sector, work was increasingly contracted out to the private sector. The Local Government Planning and Land Act 1980 required local authorities to invite competitive tender for certain work normally undertaken by their own employees in direct service organisations. This was extended by the Local Government Act 1988, incorporating a much wider range of activities including refuse collection, cleaning of buildings and maintenance and management, into what is now known as *compulsory competitive tendering.*

Employment legislation between 1979 and 1997 was characterised by an increase in frequency and an incremental approach (Box 6.2). These Acts in general had a deregulatory focus, reducing trade union power, reinforcing the employer prerogative and emphasising the individual rather than the collective. Successive Conservative governments became less favourably disposed to collective bargaining, arguing that employees should be rewarded as individuals. Trade union strength was considered to stem from legal immunities in relation to industrial action and the coercive power of the closed shop. Consequently, legislation was introduced to counteract this.

The influence of the closed shop, whereby all employees had to belong to a trade union, was reduced by the Employment Act 1980, the Employment Act 1988 made dismissal of any employee on the grounds of trade union membership automatically unfair. Subsequently the Employment Act 1990 made all forms of closed shop unlawful.

Union leaderships were seen as unrepresentative of the views of an implicitly more moderate membership, and so legislation was also passed prescribing more democratic procedures. The Trade Union Act 1984 required secret ballots every 5 years for the election of union executive members. The Employment Act 1988 extended this to cover all union presidents and general secretaries, stipulating that ballots should be postal and scrutinised independently. At the same time rights were legislated for individual members, including the right not to be disciplined for refusing to take part in industrial action.

In contrast to pre-1979, the traditional role of employers' federations in national wage bargaining was discouraged, the argument being that wage differentials should reflect scarcity of labour. In 1980 statutory recognition procedures introduced as part of the Employment Protection Act 1975 were abolished, as were the procedures to extend collectively bargained rates of pay to comparable groups of workers. In 1986 statutory minimum protection by wages councils for all workers under the age of 21 was removed and other powers of wages councils were reduced. The Trade Union Reform and Employment Rights Act 1993 abolished wages councils with only agricultural industry retaining any statutory regulation of pay. In contrast, wage negotiations at operating unit level were encouraged, as the ability to pay and scarcity of labour factors could more easily be taken into account and the 'going rate' argument discouraged (Gennard and Judge, 1999).

Individual employment rights were also reduced by the adjustment of the qualifying period of employment from 6 months to 2 years and of procedural rules relating

to unfair dismissal and eroding working women's maternity rights. The Employment Act 1988 continued this emphasis on deregulation, repealing a range of laws that restricted employment of women and regulated young people's hours of work.

Industrial action was increasingly restricted through legislation. Picketing away from the pickets' own workplace and secondary industrial action (by workers whose employer was not party to the dispute) other than in tightly defined circumstances were made unlawful by the Employment Act 1980. The Employment Act 1982 defined a trade dispute more tightly and exposed unions to injunctions and damages in cases of unlawful industrial action. Subsequently the Employment Act 1984 made it unlawful for unions to authorise or endorse industrial action without a secret pre-strike ballot. After the Employment Act 1990 all secondary industrial action was unlawful, union liability included industrial action organised by shop stewards, and employers were able to dismiss selectively any employee taking unofficial industrial action. (See Chapter 9 for more on industrial action legislation.)

Conservative governments adopted a new approach to regulating industrial disputes rather than using the traditional method of seeking compromise. These, with their focus on mediation and opportunities for compromise, were rejected as being a sign of weakness. Instead, the government was willing to pay substantial indirect financial costs to defeat public sector unions. For example, the miners' strike of 1984–85, which led to a reduction in capacity for coal by two-thirds, is estimated to have cost £5 billion (Adeney and Lloyd, 1986). Disputes such as the printers with News International at Wapping (1986), the miners in 1984–85 and the teachers (1986) were allowed to continue until one side had won – in every case the employers. Within public sector disputes, state employers were encouraged to adopt a more abrasive and confrontational style of management.

Thus rather than continuing the role of industrial peacekeeper, the government adopted economic policies that led directly to strikes, particularly in the public sector (Farnham and Pimlott, 1995). After a long-running dispute with teachers, they imposed new contracts of employment and pay increases on teachers. This ended their system of national collective bargaining through the Teachers' Pay and Conditions Act 1987. Legislation, consolidated in the Trade Union and Labour Relations (Consolidation) Act 1992, was passed that restricted the rights of trade unions to (Box 6.2):

- take industrial action with immunity to disputes between workers and their own employer;
- picket;
- operate closed shops;
- run their own internal affairs as they wished;
- collect and maintain funds for political purposes.

This further undermined the traditional collectivist practices of trade unions and, in combination with other trade union and employment relations policies of the four successive Conservative governments, shifted the emphasis of public policy and workplace practices towards individualist values and the enterprise culture.

During the 1980s the number of strikes fell, albeit with fluctuations, the very high number of working days lost in 1984 being due to the miners' strike of that year (Figure 6.3). During the 1990s there were further substantial falls in the number of

strikes. This is likely to have been for four interrelated reasons. First, between 1979 and 1986 the number of unemployment claimants rose to over 3 million, remaining above 2 million until 1997 other than in 1989 and 1990 (Figure 2.4). This, when combined with high numbers of redundancies (Chapter 12) and relatively low inflation, is likely to have reduced employees' expectations of wage increases. Second, the number of people employed in industries prone to striking – in particular, mining – also declined, reducing the bargaining power of these industries and thus their tendency to strike. At the same time the numbers employed in new service industries without a history of industrial action rose from 14.3 million in 1979 to 17.6 million in 1997 (Figure 2.2). Finally, although there is no evidence to suggest that legislation made workers less willing to take industrial action, Edwards (1995) argues that it indirectly shaped assumptions about the desirability and efficacy of action. (See Chapter 9 for more on the decline in strike action.)

Throughout the 1979–97 period there was a clear tension between the EU and successive Conservative governments. In 1989 the UK government refused to sign the Community Charter of the Fundamental Social Rights of Workers (the Social Charter). A compromise was reached, whereby other member states could use EU institutions to introduce binding legislation within the social field but such legislation would not apply to the UK. This was achieved using a separate Social Policy Agreement, which listed the social issues upon which Member States could legislate. This legislation was attached to a Social Policy Agreement annexed to the Treaty of Maastricht 1992, the whole treaty being incorporated as a *social chapter* into the Treaty of Rome. Consequently, 'the term "the UK opt-out from the Social Chapter" came into being' (Gennard and Judge, 1999: 106). Despite this, some commentators (such as Edwards *et al.*, 1998) believe that, although the UK successfully opted out of many social measures, the impact may have been more formal than real. For example, the European Works Councils Directive 1994, although not formally applied to the UK until 1999, required companies based elsewhere in the EU with the requisite number of employees to establish employee works councils in respect of their employees. These companies also established works councils for their UK employees.

Elsewhere the EU acted as a restraint on the UK government's deregulatory ambitions (Edwards, 1995). For example, the EU's Transfer of Undertakings Directive 1977, whereby employees' rights were protected when there was a change of employer following a change of ownership, was incorporated into UK law as the Transfer of Undertakings and Protection of Employment (TUPE) Regulations only in 1991, excluding public sector workers. In 1992 the European Court of Human Justice confirmed that the 1977 Directive applied in both private and not-for-profit sectors. This was particularly significant in the UK context for public sector work contracted out to the private sector, as it required existing contracts of employment to continue. An amendment was incorporated into the Trade Union Reform and Employment Rights Act 1993 (Box 6.2). The Sex Discrimination Act 1986 was introduced because the 1975 Act did not comply with the EU's Equal Treatment Directive 1976. Similarly, the European Court of Human Rights dismissed the UK's challenge of the EU Working Time Directive 1993, in November 1996. This led to the Working Time Regulations 1998, which implemented the Directive introducing conditions for hours worked, rest and annual leave entitlements and made special provision for night workers (Incomes Data Services, 1999). Although eventually implemented

under the New Labour government, these were in direct contradiction to the Conservative government's deregulatory framework.

Thus, during the 1979–97 period, successive Conservative governments' legislation and rhetoric encouraged individualisation and depoliticisation of employment relations (Farnham and Pimlott, 1995). After 1979, attempts by government to control pay increases were abandoned in favour of economic policies of deflation and strengthening market forces and the supply side of the economy. Collectivist values and institutions were rejected in favour of the individual interests of employees and employers, and a desire to develop a greater personal relationship between the two. Employees were encouraged to loosen their allegiance to collectivist values of traditional trade unionism in favour of personal commitment to and involvement in the commercial objectives and values of the organisation employing them. Personal links were strengthened further by use of a range of incentives including share ownership schemes, profit-related pay, private health care and performance-related pay, alongside management schemes to increase the personal involvement and commitment of employees to their work and their employer.

6.6 The Third Way, 1997 onwards

In their election campaign the Labour party differentiated itself from the pre-1997 Labour party, emphasising that it was New Labour. As the political arm of the trade union movement, Labour had traditionally sought to defend and advance the interests of workers within the economy and the replacement of capitalism by socialism. Yet, in order to be elected, it needed to show that it would govern in the wider democratic interest, could run the economy, and could secure the cooperation of employers. The structural weakness of the trade unions by the mid-1990s allowed the party to position itself openly for the first time as pro market and pro business, endorsing most of the employment relations reforms of the 1980s and early 1990s (Box 6.2). At the same time it committed itself to a distinctly social democratic agenda within the field of employment, focusing on individuals' employment rights such as a minimum wage and a *New Deal* to increase employment and reward relatively low-skilled work (Gamble and Kelly, 2001). This agenda was apparent in a range of pledges in its election manifesto relating to trade unions and their role in the employment relationship. These focused upon:

- establishing a national minimum wage;
- the restoration of trade union rights at GCHQ (Government Communication Headquarters), Cheltenham;
- ending the UK's opt-out from the Social Chapter of the Treaty of Maastricht 1991;
- statutory recognition of trade union rights, where the majority of employees were in favour;
- the ending of trade unions' need to obtain written consent from members every 3 years for their subscriptions to be deducted from salaries;
- some protection for dismissed lawful strikers.

Once in government, New Labour's approach soon became labelled as the *Third Way* (Blair, 1998). This reconciled a liberalist ideology's emphasis on economic

efficiency and dynamism with a more corporatist concern for equality, integration and social inclusion. Four values were identified by Tony Blair (1998) as summarising the Third Way. These are:

- *equal worth* – all human beings are equal and should be treated as such;
- *opportunity for all* – concerned with opportunities, not outcomes;
- *responsibility* – people not only claim rights from the state but also accept the responsibilities that go with these;
- *community* – the structures and organisations that support individual opportunity and ground responsibility in meaningful relationships.

Within such an egalitarian approach, outcomes could be assured only if people's assets were more equally distributed. Education and training were therefore important to New Labour, as they enable assets to be distributed more equally and help reduce income inequalities. New Labour's election objectives of growth, fairness and jobs were pursued through ensuring minimum standards affecting working conditions, terms of employment and a minimum wage. These standards were justified in terms of the need for efficiency and quality (Clift, 2001). However, although there was (and is) no egalitarian commitment to redistribution and equality of outcome, there is a commitment to social justice. This relies on ensuring minimum standards and equality of opportunity.

Since 1997 New Labour's economic policy has had two strands: the first relates to macroeconomic stability and the second to the provision of employment opportunities for all by tackling supply-side barriers to growth. These have been developed in the context of a positive engagement with the EU, in particular signing up to the Social Chapter of the Treaty of Maastricht in 1997 (which became operational in 1999) and moving towards economic and monetary union (Gamble and Kelly, 2001). Longer term policies for raising economic performance and personal prosperity and for better public services also centre on supply-side reforms. Here strategy has relied heavily on incentives to workers and employers through reforming the welfare state and, in particular, making it financially worthwhile to be in work – in other words, making work pay. This approach is based upon the argument that raising the labour supply will allow sustainable higher employment without inflationary pressures (Glyn and Wood, 2001). However, as Glyn and Wood (2001) comment, this ignores the regional geographic concentration of those without work. Alongside this, education policy has assumed major importance as a policy tool, education being regarded as central to improving individuals' employability. An early example of this was government's New Deal to help young unemployed people into jobs or training, funded by the £5.2 billion windfall tax on the privatised utilities announced in 1997. The 1998 budget introduced working families' tax credits, raising tax thresholds for the less well off and guaranteeing a minimum weekly income of £180 to a family with one full-time worker.

Welfare reforms have been complemented by efforts to raise standards in education and promote a lifelong learning strategy, the latter emphasising how learning continues throughout adult life rather than just in schools. Although some have argued that this is predominantly rhetoric (e.g. Glyn and Wood, 2001), it has included innovations such as the University for Industry scheme and, until they were closed in 2002, Individual Learning Accounts. These are intended to help individuals

to invest in upskilling and reskilling throughout their careers. Over time, it appears that the corporatist approach to such initiatives is gradually being abandoned, the emphasis increasingly being placed on the responsibilities of individuals and employers for training.

Despite restoring trade union recognition rights to GCHQ employees, New Labour has also reassured employers that trade unions' legal immunities would not be reinstated. This is one of the most significant continuities with the previous Conservative governments (Glyn and Wood, 2001). In addition, calls for renationalisation have continued to be rejected, the government favouring public–private partnership and most recently, in the case of the rail network, a government-backed 'not for dividend' company (Osborne, 2002). Alongside this, there has been a drive through the Private Finance Initiative (PFI), originally introduced by the Conservatives in 1992, to bring private sector capital into the public sector.

This means that business is now involved in public sector infrastructure projects including education and health. Within the UK, 150 such projects were agreed between 1997 and 2000 with a capital cost of £20 billion, additional projects worth a further £20 billion being expected over the period 2000–03 (Ball et al., 2001). However, while successive governments have argued that this is a good deal for the public purse offering cost-effective, innovative design, and operating and mainte nance cost savings, research by Ball et al. (2001) suggests that this value for money argument is less clear. They also question whether the PFI is, in reality, facilitating significant amounts of additional investment into the public sector.

A clear, pro-business rhetoric has been adopted by New Labour within which the trade unions appear to be downgraded. Trade unions no longer determine Labour governments' employment relations policy and the old demarcation between industrial and political authority is no longer recognised by political party leaders. Rather, New Labour seeks to promote more collaborative working between business and trade unions through initiatives such as the Partnership at Work fund (Department of Trade and Industry, 2001b). It appears that the majority of key unions have accepted New Labour's economic and social policies and the replacing of voluntarism by legal rights often based upon European Union legislation, such as many of those provided in the Employment Relations Act (Box 6.3) (Ludlam, 2001).

New Labour's influence on the employment relationship can also be seen in its support for European Union employment-based legislation. Most significant of these has been the adoption of the Social Chapter of the Treaty of Maastricht, which provides for 12 fundamental rights for workers, relating to (Rose, 2001):

- their freedom of movement between member states;
- adequate protection for employment and remuneration;
- improvement of working conditions;
- adequate social protection and social security;
- freedom of association (the right to join or not to join trade unions);
- adequate and continuing vocational and job training;
- equality of treatment for men and women;
- information, consultation and participation of workers on key workplace issues;
- health and safety at the workplace;
- protection of children and adolescents at work;

- access of elderly persons to labour markets (age discrimination);
- access of disabled people to labour markets (disability discrimination).

This was formalised by the Treaty of Amsterdam 1998, which introduced a new 'chapter' to the Treaty of Rome relating exclusively to employment. This was signed by all member states including the UK, many of the rights being transposed into UK law as part of the Employment Relations Act 1999 (Box 6.3). In addition to the fundamental rights outlined above, the 1998 Treaty encouraged social dialogue on issues such as employment, the right to work, working conditions, social security and accident prevention. It also contained an employment charter committing the EU to take into account the need to achieve sustainable employment opportunities when taking decisions relating to its commercial and economic objectives.

Box 6.3	Summary of major UK legislation affecting the employment relationship, 1997 onwards
Act	**Key features**
National Minimum Wages Act 1998	■ Introduced a statutory national minimum wage of £3.60 an hour before deductions for all workers. Was £3.20 for employees aged 18–21 and £3.20 for accredited trainees aged 22 plus in first 6 months of training. ■ Excludes voluntary workers, armed forces, and prisoners.
Employment Relations Act 1999	■ Established new procedures for recognition of trade unions in organisations employing 21 or more people if that is the wish of the majority of the workforce. ■ Prohibited employers from discriminating by omission against employees on basis of trade union membership or non-membership or activities. ■ Simplified law on industrial action, in particular with regard to disclosing to employers the names of employees balloted, and providing greater scope for the courts to disregard small accidental failures in organisation of ballots. ■ Replaced existing maternity and parental leave provisions so now include a minimum of 18 weeks' maternity leave in line with pay for all women, additional maternity leave after 1 year's service, 3 months' parental leave for mothers and fathers, guaranteed job back or its equivalent at the end of parental leave. ■ Extended protection for employees taking lawful industrial action, making it unfair to dismiss employees in action lasting less than 8 weeks and unfair for longer disputes unless the employer has taken all reasonable procedural steps to resolve the dispute. ■ Revised duties of ACAS to include dispute prevention as well as resolution.

Box 6.3	Continued

Learning and Skills Act 2000
- Established Learning and Skills Council (LSC), bringing responsibility for all post-16 learning, other than higher education, under one state institution.

Employment Act 2002
- Revised existing maternity and parental leave provision so mothers now entitled to 6 months' paid maternity leave and 6 months' unpaid; fathers entitled to 2 weeks' paid paternity leave.
- Established a duty for employers to consider requests for flexible working arrangements from parents with young children.
- Introduced minimum requirements for internal discipline and grievance procedures.
- Implemented EU directive on fixed-term work.
- Provided time off for trade union learning representatives to ensure adequate training to carry out their duties.

The Working Time Regulations 1998, which implemented the 1993 EU Working Time Directive, appear to have had little effect on most organisations. Research reported by the European Industrial Relations Observatory (2002) has found that long hours are still worked consistently by a minority of employees, facilitated by voluntary exemptions. In addition it appears that the regulations are of little concern to most employers and employees.

There have been four major Acts (Box 6.3) since New Labour came to power, predominantly concerned with individual employment rights rather than those of trade unions. The first of these, the National Minimum Wages Act 1998, was the result of the deliberations of the Low Pay Commission, who had been charged with recommending at what level the minimum wage should be set. Within its manifesto, the Labour Party (1997) had stated that it 'must be sensible' and 'not harm competitiveness'. Initially set at £3.60 an hour, it has subsequently been increased, the 2001 rate being £4.10 an hour with a further increase to £4.20 in October 2002 (Department of Trade and Industry, 2001a). It is estimated that in 1998, the year before its introduction, some 1.5 million employees were paid less than the minimum wage (IRS, 2002). These people were employed predominantly in retail, health and the hotel and catering industries. However, political considerations, and in particular the fear of appearing to favour union power and corporatism, have stopped discussion of wage bargaining (Glyn and Wood, 2001).

New Labour's focus upon the individual employee was emphasised in the Department of Trade and Industry's (1998) White Paper *Fairness at Work*. This became the Employment Relations Act 1999, extending employment rights for individuals as well as conferring some rights on trade unions as collective bodies. After almost two decades of no legal support for trade union recognition within the UK, the Act enabled employees to have a trade union recognised by their employer where the majority of the relevant workforce wished. Under the Act, one or more independent trade unions seeking recognition must apply to the employer in writing, after which the employer has 10 days to respond. If the employer does not respond, or rejects the

request, the trade union can apply to the Central Arbitration Committee for a decision. If, instead, the employer indicates that while not accepting the request they are willing to negotiate regarding the recognition of a bargaining unit, a negotiation period of 28 days is available. If these negotiations fail then the claim is referred to the Central Arbitration Committee to decide on the appropriate bargaining unit.

Despite this, the predominant focus of the Act was on individuals' employment rights rather than on trade unions (Box 6.3). In particular, it incorporated a wide range of family-friendly policies set out in the social chapter of the Treaty of Maastricht, such as increasing maternity leave for all employees from 13 to 18 weeks and introducing a statutory right to 3 months' parental leave for all employees (Box 6.3). Individual employees' rights in the event of dismissal have been extended by reducing the qualifying period of employment from two years to one and raising the maximum amount of compensation that could be claimed from £12 000 to £50 000. Additional legislation (Public Interest Disclosure Act 1998) has protected employees who have made disclosures such as about a criminal offence, failure to comply with legal obligation, endangering health and safety from dismissal, selection for redundancy or victimisation on that ground.

Although New Labour seems to embrace EU employment legislation, there is some evidence that the government has sought to amend or veto the directives such as the Working Time Directive. Here New Labour has sought to exempt voluntary work hours above the 48-hour maximum limit and to exempt employers from keeping detailed records of employee overtime. On the basis of this it has been argued that New Labour is trying to claim both credit from employees and trade unions for social welfare improvements and support from employers in their fight to dilute the impact of legislation (Glyn and Wood, 2001).

In its manifesto for the 2001 General Election New Labour promised to maintain a light touch to employment regulation and improve skills and training, especially vocational learning (Cooper, 2001). Much of the focus on improving skills and training could already be seen in the operationalisation of the Learning and Skills Council established by the Learning and Skills Act 2000 (Box 6.3). The LSC is responsible for all post-16 education and training, excluding higher education, but including further education, work-based training, adult and community learning and school sixth forms (Department for Education and Employment, 2001). Among its priorities is maximising the contribution of education and training to economic performance, further highlighting the government's use of education as a tool to improve people's employability.

Subsequent to its election to a second term of office, New Labour has begun to reorganise the institutions of state, including those that have an impact upon the employment relationship (UK online, 2001). In particular a new Department for Work and Pensions (DWP) has been established. This department combines the employment and disability responsibilities of the former Department for Education and Employment with the welfare and pensions responsibilities of the former Department of Social Security. A new Department for Education and Skills (DfES) replaces the Department for Education and Employment, having responsibility for education, training and lifelong learning. It therefore seems that New Labour's linking of welfare and employment is likely to continue, with continued prominence being given to Third Way values such as opportunity for all and social responsibility.

The Employment Act 2002 continues the emphasis on issues of social responsibility, supporting

> the Government's commitment to create highly productive, modern and successful workplace through fairness and partnership at work... deliver[ing] a balanced package of support for working parents, at the same time as reducing red tape for employers by simplifying rules governing maternity, paternity and adoption leave and pay, and mak[ing] it easier to settle disputes in the workplace. (Department of Trade and Industry, 2002: 1)

In particular it increases statutory entitlements to paid and unpaid maternity leave, introduces paid paternity leave to fathers, and introduces a new statutory right to time off for trade union learning representatives to ensure they are adequately trained to carry out their duties. It also implements the EU directive on fixed-term work, providing fixed-term employees with rights to be paid the same as similar permanent employees.

Thus New Labour's third way provides a distinctive alternative to the voluntarist approach to employment relations of the 1979–97 period. This has been replaced by what Gamble and Kelly (2001) term a social democratic approach, within which there is an accepted legal structure for employment relations with an emphasis on individual rights. There is some evidence that the TUC and major unions share much of New Labour's economic and political assumptions. Ludlam (2001) argues that trade unions wish to act as agencies in, for example, training, pensions and legal representation, and – perhaps more importantly – are looking to use this for new recruitment opportunities. In addition, if these prospects fail, or relations with New Labour deteriorate, he questions whether there are viable political alternatives for unions. Without doubt, the relationship between Labour and the trade unions has changed from the old tripartite corporatist approach. Addressing the TUC Annual Congress in 1999 Blair asserted that 'in many ways we have a better, clearer relationship than ever before between trade unions and Labour... You run the unions. We run the government. We will never confuse the two again. (cited in Glyn and Wood, 2001: 56)

Looking to the future, at a European level, a central issue is likely to be determining the balance between policies that protect employees and those that create jobs, particularly where, as in the UK, lower labour costs and limited employee protection have been used as a source of competitive advantage. Trade unions are inevitably concerned that, without some form of harmonisation of employment protection, working arrangements and pay, employees will suffer as multinational organisations simply transfer the work on the basis of the lowest labour costs (Salamon, 2000). This has implications for downsizing and plant closures, such as General Motors' closure of its Vauxhall plant at Luton. However, EU countries that provide the greatest employment protection may keep jobs because of the costs associated with transferring them, whereas countries with less protection lose them, although this reason is denied strenuously. In addition, there is likely to be further employment legislation in response to EU directives. In particular, the Anti Discrimination Framework Directive 2000 will require comprehensive legislation prohibiting discrimination at work on the grounds of sexual orientation, religion or belief and age, and as a consequence will require amendments to the Disability Discrimination Act 1995 (Silkin, 2001). Issues relating to religion and sexual orientation will need to be incorporated into UK law by December 2003, and those relating to age and disability by December 2006.

self-check question

6.4 Design a table that outlines briefly how government attitudes differed between the postwar settlement (1945–79), the new relationship (1979–97) and the Third Way (1997 onwards) with regard to:

a full employment;
b state ownership of industries;
c public expenditure and taxation;
d legislation affecting trade unions and employees;
e involvement of the TUC in regulating the economy.

6.7 Summary

- Through the political process governments establish the formal (legal) and informal rules within which the employment relationship operates. These rules are influenced by government economic and social policy, which constrains the general environment within which the employment relationship operates. In addition, government, as both direct and indirect employer, demonstrates its ideological preferences.

- Government's power to manage the employment relationship is based upon its mandate from the electorate. The state implements and enforces government policies, operating within the political mechanisms, their authority being backed by the legal system.

- Two distinct political ideologies can be identified: *laissez-faire* and capitalist. The former is characterised by a free market economy within which competition for goods and services provides the basis for regulation. The latter is characterised by a marketplace that is constrained by regulation to allow social justice. When integrated with ideas about the relative power of trade unions, an analytical framework can be devised through which to explore government influences on the employment relationship.

- Within the UK, post Second World War government influences on the employment relationship can be divided into three distinct periods:
  - the postwar settlement of 1945–79, which was a period of considerable political consensus within which successive governments based their approach to regulating the economy, interacting with trade unions and handling the employment relationship on a bargained corporatist ideology;
  - the new relationship between 1979 and 1997, during which successive Conservative governments replaced the ideology values of the postwar consensus with a market individualist ideology that increased legal control of trade unions and abandoned the commitment to full employment policies;
  - New Labour's Third Way from 1997 onwards, which reconciled a *laissez-faire* ideology's emphasis on economic efficiency and dynamism with a more corporatist concern for equality, integration and social inclusion.

- The European Union's influence on UK employment relations has increased, particularly since the adoption of the Treaty of Maastricht in 1998. This treaty provides for fundamental rights for workers as well as encouraging social dialogue on issues such as employment, the right to work, working conditions and social security.

elf-check question

6.5 Use the websites of the Department of Trade and Industry ⟨http://www.dti.gov.uk/er/⟩, the European Industrial Relations Observatory ⟨http://www.eiro.eurofound.ie⟩ and the Institute of Employment Rights ⟨http://www.ier.org.uk/⟩ to update and expand your knowledge of:

a recent UK government employment-related legislation;

b EU directives and their impact on UK employment-related legislation;

c trade union views on recent EU and UK employment-related legislation.

References

Adeney, M. and Lloyd, J. (1986) *The Miners' Strike 1984–5*, London, Routledge.

Ball, R., Heafey, R. and King, D. (2001) 'Private Finance Initiative – a good deal for the public purse or a drain on future generations?', *Policy and Politics*, 29:1, 95–108.

Blair, T. (1998) *The Third Way: New politics for the new century*, London, Fabian Society.

Blyton, P. and Turnbull, P. (1998) *The Dynamics of Employee Relations* (2nd edn), Basingstoke, Macmillan.

Clift, B. (2001) 'New Labour's Third Way and European social democracy', *in* Ludlam, S. and Smith, M.J. (eds), *Labour in Government*, Basingstoke, Macmillan, pp. 52–72.

Cooper, C. (2001) 'Statesmen of intent: employment and the three manifestos', *People Management*, 7:11, 12–13.

Davies, J. (1999) 'Labour disputes in 1998', *Labour Market Trends*, 107:6, 299–312.

Davies, J. (2001) 'Labour disputes in 2000', *Labour Market Trends*, 109:6, 301–14.

Department for Education and Employment (2001) *Learning and Skills Council* [online][cited 6 November 2001] Available from ⟨http://www.dfes.gov.uk/a z/PrintFriendly_LEARNING_AND_SKILLS_COUNCIL.html⟩

Department of Trade and Industry (1998) *Fairness at Work*, London, The Stationery Office.

Department of Trade and Industry (2001a) *A Detailed Guide to the National Minimum Wage*, London, The Stationery Office.

Department of Trade and Industry (2001b) *Partnership at Work* [online][cited 12 November 2001] Available from ⟨http://www.dti.gov.uk/partnershipfund/guidance.htm⟩

Department of Trade and Industry (2002) *Employment Bill 2001* [online][cited 1 July 2002] Available from ⟨http://www.dti.gov.uk/er/employ/index.htm⟩

Donovan Commission (1968) *Report of the Royal Commission on Trade Unions and Employers Associations*, London, Her Majesty's Stationery Office.

Edwards, P. (1995) 'Strikes and industrial conflict', *in* Edwards, P. (ed.), *Industrial Relations: Theory and practice in Britain*, Oxford, Blackwell, pp. 434–60.

Edwards, P., Hall, M., Hyman, R., Marginson, P., Sisson, K., Waddington, P. and Winchester, P. (1998) 'Great Britain: from partial collectivism to neo-liberalism to where?', *in* Ferner, A. and Hyman, R. (eds), *Changing Industrial Relations in Europe*, Oxford, Blackwell, 1–54.

European Industrial Relations Observatory (2002) *2001 Annual Review for the UK* [online] [cited 1 July 2002] Available from ⟨http://www.eiro.eurofound.ie/2002/01/feature/UK0201168f.html⟩

Farnham, D. and Pimlott, J. (1995) *Understanding Industrial Relations* (5th edn), London, Cassell.

Gamble, A. and Kelly, G. (2001) 'Labour's new economics', *in* Ludlam, S. and Smith, M.J. (eds), *New Labour in Government*, Basingstoke, Macmillan, pp. 167–83.

Gennard, J. and Judge, G. (1999) *Employee Relations* (2nd edn), London, Chartered Institute of Personnel and Development.

Glyn, A. and Wood, S. (2001) 'Economic policy under New Labour: How social democratic is the Blair government?', *The Political Quarterly*, 72:1, 50–66.

IDS (1999) *IDS Brief 628: Employment law review 1998*, London, Incomes Data Services.

IRS (2002) 'Floor covering: the minimum wage survey', *IRS Employment Review* No. 750, pp. 19–25.

Jensen, C.S., Madsen, J.S. and Due, J. (1999) 'Phases and dynamics in the development of EU industrial relations regulation', *Industrial Relations Journal*, 30:2, 118–34.

Keep, E. and Rainbird, H. (1995) 'Training', *in* Edwards, P.K. (ed.), *Industrial Relations*, Oxford, Blackwell, pp. 515–42.

Kessler, S. and Baylis, F. (1998) *Contemporary British Industrial Relations* (3rd edn), Basingstoke, Macmillan.

Keynes, J.M. (1997) *The General Theory of Employment, Interest and Money*, London, Prometheus books.

Labour Party (1997) *Labour's Business Manifesto: Equipping Britain for the future*, London, Labour Party.

Ludlam, S. (2001) 'New Labour and the unions', *in* Ludlam, S. and Smith, M.J. (eds), *New Labour in Government*, Basingstoke, Macmillan, pp. 111–29.

Newton, K. and Karran, T. (1985) *The Politics of Local Expenditure*, London, Macmillan.

Osborne, A. (2002) 'Fiasco over Railtrack costs £21bn', *The Daily Telegraph*, 28 June, 1–2.

Poole, M. (1986) *Industrial Relations: Origins and patterns of national diversity*, London, Routledge and Kegan Paul.

Rose, E. (2001) *Employee Relations*, Harlow, Financial Times Prentice Hall.

Salamon, M. (1999) 'The state in employee relations', *in* Hollinshead, G., Nicholls, P. and Tailby, S. (eds), *Employee Relations*, London, Financial Times Pitman Publishing, pp. 179–208.

Salamon, M. (2000) *Industrial Relations: Theory and practice* (4th edn), Harlow, Financial Times Prentice Hall.

Silkin, L. (2001) 'European countdown on legislation affecting UK employment law', *People Management*, 7:16, 17.

UK online (2001) 'Post-election changes to government departments' [online] [cited 5 November 2001] Available from <http://getting.ukonline.gov.uk/post-election/post-election.htm>

Winchester, D. (1983) 'Industrial relations in the public sector', *in* Bain, G.S. (ed.), *Industrial Relations in Britain*, Oxford, Blackwell, pp. 155–78.

self-check Answers

6.1 *Re-examine Figure 6.1. Name three other state institutions that are likely to influence the employment relationship.*

Your answer to this question will inevitably be dependent upon the three state institutions that you choose. However, ones that are more common include the following:

- *Commission for Racial Equality (CRE)*. The CRE's duties are to work towards the elimination of racial discrimination, to promote equal opportunity and good relations between people of different racial groups, and to monitor the workings of the Race Relations Act 1996. Within this, the Commission has both powers of investigation and powers to draw up codes of practice to eliminate discrimination in the workplace.
- *Department for Education and Skills (DfES)*. This department has responsibility for education, training and lifelong learning.
- *Department for Work and Pensions (DWP)*. The DWP is responsible for the modernisation of work- and benefit-related services for people of working age and older people. It includes the Employment Service and the Benefits Agency.
- *Learning and Skills Councils (LSC)*. The LSC became fully operational on 1 April 2001. It replaced the Further Education Funding Council and the Training and

Enterprise Councils (TEC), and is responsible for all post-16 education and training excluding higher education. The LSC was given a number of key priorities by the New Labour government. These include maximising the contribution of education and training to economic performance.

■ *Police force*. As part of the public sector the way in which the police are treated as employees has been used by successive governments to indicate both what they consider to be model employment practice and the importance of law and order. The police have been used to enforce government legislation relating to the employment relationship such as that relating to picketing (Trade Union and Labour Relations (Consolidation) Act 1992).

6.2 *Outline the key beliefs of the* laissez-faire *and corporatist ideologies. For each, note the key implications for a government's management of the employment relationship.*

A *laissez-faire* ideology is characterised by a free market economy within which competition for goods, services and labour is the basis for regulating society. Individuals are responsible for their own well-being rather than this being provided by the state. Consequently, government's direct management of the employment relationship is likely to be very limited other than, perhaps, legislating to minimise distortions. By doing this the government upholds and supports managers in their right to manage.

In contrast a corporatist ideology is characterised by the belief that social and economic aspects of life are interrelated, and that political influence and regulation should be used to manage the employment relationship. Consequently the government should accept responsibility for and take a direct role in protecting individuals from social problems arising from the marketplace and in improving their quality of life. This means that the government must intervene to constrain the operation of the marketplace and allow social justice. In addition, there may be a desire for consensual government through mechanisms of social partnership.

6.3 *In what ways do the ideas of monetarism differ from those of Keynesian economics?*

Keynesian economics argues that unemployment is the major economic problem facing governments, whereas monetarists consider that it is inflation.

Keynesian economics argues that rising unemployment is due to declining demand for goods and services within the economy. In contrast, monetarism argues that increasing unemployment is due to a wage–price inflationary spiral, which causes the competitiveness of firms to decline.

Keynesian economics argues that, during periods of high unemployment, governments should stimulate demand by lowering taxes and interest rates (fiscal and monetary policy) and increasing their own (public) expenditure on public works. In contrast, monetarism focuses upon reducing spending power in the economy as a whole by raising interest rates and reducing government expenditure.

6.4 *Design a table that outlines briefly how government attitudes differed between the postwar settlement (1945–79), the new relationship (1979–97) and the Third Way (1997 onwards) with regard to:*

a *full employment;*
b *state ownership of industries;*
c *public expenditure and taxation;*

    d legislation affecting trade unions and employees;
    e involvement of the TUC in regulating the economy.

	Postwar settlement (1945–79)	New relationship (1979–97)	Third Way (1997 onwards)
Full employment	Maintenance of full employment and the welfare state	Abandonment of commitment to full employment and focus on control of inflation	Raising labour supply to allow sustainable high employment without inflationary pressure
State ownership of industries	Continuing state ownership of industries nationalised between 1945 and 1951	Denationalisation of state-owned industries and return to private ownership	Limited denationalisation of state-owned industries; use of public–private partnerships and 'not for profit' private companies instead of privatisation or renationalisation
Public expenditure and taxation	High levels of public expenditure; high tax burden	Levels of public expenditure reduced; tax burden through direct taxation reduced	Public expenditure increased slightly; tax burden through income tax not raised; other forms of personal taxation increased, and benefits such as minimum wage help wealth redistribution
Legislation affecting trade unions and employees	Continuation of voluntarist traditions of industrial relations	New trade union laws reducing immunity from industrial action and picketing and restricting the closed shop; measures aimed at depoliticising industrial relations such as political levy and political fund; policies to weaken collective organisation and industrial action	Majority of trade union legislation kept; Employment Relations Act 1999 introduced mandatory recognition procedures and better employment protection; however, focus more on individual employment rights than on trade unions
Involvement of TUC in regulating the economy	Involvement of Trades Union Congress (TUC) in government decisions affecting the welfare state and the management of the national economy	Exclusion of the TUC from the governmental policy-making process	TUC acknowledged but kept at a distance

6.5 Obviously what you find has yet to be written! However, we hope you find these sites useful.

CASE 6 Employee relations at Vertex[1]

Vertex is a major UK supplier of outsourced services, which focuses on the management of customer interactions. It provides a wide range of customer relationship management (CRM) outsourcing capabilities such as multi-channel contact (call) centres using telephone, Internet, mail and fax, billing services and debt management and the implementation and management of change. Some 20 UK public and private sector organisations outsource CRM to Vertex; contracts include the London Borough of Ealing's benefits administration service, Littlewoods' Bet Direct telephone betting service, and Virgin Trains' rail enquiries and ticket booking service thetrainline.com.

Created in 1996, when North West Water (one of the privatised regional water authorities) merged with Norweb (the privatised North West Area Electricity Board) to form United Utilities plc, Vertex is a wholly owned subsidiary. It has a turnover of over £300 million and employs approximately 8000 people (Vertex, 2001a). Employees are based both within host organisations across the UK and at the company's head office in Greater Manchester. By 2001 Vertex was dealing annually with over 110 million customer phone calls and contacts and printing and sending out 60 million bills and documents. It was also processing some 92 million payments collecting over £6 billion.

In 1996 the newly created company needed to bring together two distinct and different employee representation practices. The trade union at North West Water, Unison, had already been derecognised and replaced by a non-union model of individual employee contracts. In contrast, Norweb's administrative employees who were transferring to Vertex were still represented by Unison, with employee relations following a traditional collective bargaining model. Vertex decided to adopt a non-union model. According to Paul Glover, the trade union representative at the time of writing, this was because of memories of painful and non productive industrial relations. In contrast, Vertex's human resources (HR) department says that the non-union model was adopted because it offered the easiest way of moving all staff in the new company to the same terms and conditions, together with the perception that trade unions would inhibit the necessary degree of change in the new company. However, both Unison and Vertex's HR department agree that the non-union model was chosen because the constraints imposed by collective bargaining were, at that time, considered bad for the business (Walsh, 2001). In particular, at that time collective bargaining arrangements were not considered positively by organisations from whom Vertex was trying to win contracts to provide customer services.

The newly formed Vertex offered every employee the opportunity to sign an individual contract worth a 5 per cent pay increase, increased holiday entitlement for some and a 7.5 per cent bonus. This equated to a 15 per cent pay rise (Walsh, 2001). Perhaps not surprisingly, Unison found it virtually impossible to persuade members not to sign away their trade union's negotiating rights. Ninety-five per

[1] The assistance of Janie Hazelwood and Tony Stark (Vertex) in the preparation of this case is gratefully acknowledged.

cent of Vertex's employees, who had previously been employed by Norweb, gave up their collective bargaining rights in exchange for personal contracts. Despite this, few employees actually resigned their trade union membership.

Writing in 2001, Walsh comments that this derecognition of the trade union (Unison) could easily have been the end of collective bargaining at Vertex, the company prospering under its chosen non-union model of employee relations. However, this was not the case. Trade union officials were among those nominated and subsequently elected by the workforce as employee representatives on the company-wide employee consultation forum. Rather than using the forum destructively, they acted responsibly and gained respect. In particular, when Vertex changed its reward strategy in 1998, the representatives elected to the forum contributed constructively to the consultation, influencing the outcome positively.

By 1998 a change in UK government and commercial pressures had begun to suggest that Vertex should consider restoring trade union recognition. The *Fairness at Work* White Paper had included rights for trade unions as collective bodies, in particular proposing legal support for union recognition. Vertex was finding it difficult to win contracts for outsourced operations from local authorities, despite the constructive relationship with their employees' trade union, Unison, which also represented public sector workers. Mike Jeram, Unison's national secretary for energy and the utilities, believes that 'Vertex realised that it would be better to have the unions on board' (Walsh, 2001: 35). The human resources department therefore decided to initiate discussions on a return to collective bargaining using the *Fairness at Work* White Paper to provide both the mechanisms and the language for this process.

As part of 'fairness at work' discussions Unison asked Vertex for recognition as the trade union representing employees. In response, Vertex put together a joint working group consisting of managers and trade union representatives to explore the matter. The working group devised a draft form for a potential partnership agreement to deal with future changes in the workplace. This was put to the company's board and subsequently to a ballot of the main group of Bolton office employees, the customer service representatives formerly employed by Norweb. Of the 75 per cent of Bolton customer service representatives who voted, 89 per cent were in favour of the agreement and of union recognition. However, team leaders, who were balloted separately, voted marginally against the partnership agreement. A recognition agreement with the trade union, Unison, was signed in late 1999. However, before Vertex would proceed voluntarily towards a partnership agreement with Unison they needed to be sure that they were creating the right form. Thus although the partnership agreement's guiding principles had been agreed in advance of the ballot they still needed to be developed in detail.

On 25 January 2000 Vertex and Unison signed a partnership agreement that covered all customer service representatives and administrators and certain specialist roles within the Bolton operation. This was prefaced with eight guiding principles:

- The business and the trade unions agree to try to achieve and maintain an industrial relations climate of mutual trust and cooperation.
- We also share a common interest in the success of the business.

- We recognise the need for both managers and staff to be flexible in their outlook and receptive to change.
- The business recognises the right of staff to belong to a trade union and the right of unions to represent their members.
- The unions recognise the right of management to manage the business in an effective and efficient manner.
- Representatives within the employment relations structure recognise their responsibility to reflect the views of all staff, not just those of trade union members, or a particular group of interests.
- There is a common understanding that the objective of this agreement is to look forwards, not backwards. We start from where we are and aim to improve.
- It is jointly recognised that there is a place for both a consultative and a negotiating framework. The business recognises the need to strengthen the existing Consultative Framework to ensure that both Forums are fully effective.

(Vertex Data Science Ltd and Unison, 2000: 1)

Subsequently Vertex and Unison bid to the Department of Trade and Industry for Partnership Fund money to support the development and application of their partnership agreement, money being awarded in March 2000 (Department of Trade and Industry, 2001). The work part-funded by this money brought together managers and trade union representatives from across Vertex to explore the potential for a shared business agenda (Vertex, 2001c), and has resulted in the partnership agreement being extended and lifted to a more strategic level. It has focused upon identifying and resolving key business issues such as pay progression, diversity, flexible working and integration of Vertex's formal consultation process with unionised collective bargaining.

Both Vertex and Unison argue that union recognition and, in particular, their partnership approach to managing the employment relationship have already had considerable benefits. As examples they cite public sector, and in particular local authority, contracts they have won. These have included managing and delivering the benefits administration service for the London Borough of Ealing from the council's current premises, using over 100 employees whose employment was transferred to Vertex (Vertex, 2001b). For these and other new contracts Vertex has involved its own trade union in the bidding process. Consequently employers, with highly unionised workforces, have gained confidence that work they outsource is unlikely to suffer from poor employee relations and industrial disruption. In addition, employees being transferred from local authorities to Vertex under TUPE (Transfer of Undertakings of Prior Employment) regulations are able to contact Vertex's union representatives about the process directly and received reassurances. At the same time joint trade union and management subgroups on areas such as 'pay and progression' and 'dignity at work' have developed new pay schemes and greater cultural understanding in the workplace respectively. These it is believed have also helped employee retention (Walsh, 2001). In October 2001 Vertex won the Chartered Institute of Personnel and Development's People Management Award for its partnership success.

Questions

1 To what extent do you believe the political climate in 1996 was supportive of Vertex's desire for employees to give up their collective bargaining rights and the introduction of individual contracts?

2 Outline how the election of New Labour in 1997 and subsequent legislation has supported Vertex's return to collective bargaining.

3 To what extent do the eight guiding principles that preface Vertex and Unison's Partnership Agreement (2000) reflect New Labour's ideals for relationships between employers and trade unions?

References

Department of Trade and Industry (2000) 'Partnership at Work: Announcement of the successful projects in the first round of the Partnership at Work Fund' [online][cited 12 November 2001] Available from <http://www.dti.gov.uk/partnershipfund/success.htm>

Vertex (2001a) 'About us: Key facts' [online][cited 12 November 2001] Available from <http://www.vertex.co.uk/aboutus/keyfacts.html>

Vertex (2001b) 'Delivering best value: Case study – London Borough of Ealing and Vertex' [online][cited 12 November 2001] Available from <http://www.vertex.co.uk/pdf/ealing.pdf>

Vertex (2001c) 'Vertex wins 2001 CIPD People Management Award' [online][cited 12 November 2001] Available from <http://www.vertex.co.uk/news/press_releases/2001/251001_cipd.html>

Vertex Data Science Ltd and Unison (2000) 'A partnership agreement between Vertex Data Science Ltd – Customer (Energy) Business and UNISON', Unpublished partnership agreement.

Walsh, J. (2001) 'A happy reunion', *People Management*, 7:22, 32–6.

Chapter 7

Regulating the employment relationship through collective bargaining

At the end of this chapter you should be able to:

- define collective bargaining and explain its purposes;

- analyse the content of a collective bargaining agreement;

- explain the structure of collective bargaining;

- examine the coverage of collective bargaining in the UK and other developed economies;

- explain the legal significance of collective bargaining and outline statutory procedures for trade union recognition;

- analyse the major changes in the collective bargaining levels;

- analyse the process of negotiating and understand its relevance to collective bargaining;

- examine the incidence of industrial action and procedures for containing this;

- identify the role of ACAS in employee relations dispute resolution.

7.1 Introduction

In his celebrated book on British industrial relations Clegg (1979) argued that collective bargaining was so important that the study of industrial relations was essentially the study of collective bargaining. Indeed, the back cover of his book states that 'an appreciation of the structure and working of collective bargaining is the most important key to understanding industrial relations as a whole.' Clegg's justification for this view was that collective bargaining related to all the dealings between employers and managers on the one hand and trade unions, shop stewards and employees on the other over the 'making, interpretation and administration of employment rules' (Clegg, 1979: 4). Much has changed since 1979, not the least of which has been the declining influence of trade unions at the workplace, as is detailed in Chapter 5, and the consequent reduction in collective representation. But it would be wrong to assume that collective bargaining is no longer an important way in which the employment relationship is regulated. As the twentieth century ended, approximately one-half of UK employees still had their pay determined by the collective bargaining process. In the public sector in particular, collective bargaining is still the most important way in which terms and conditions of employment are decided.

Like many other aspects of employment relations, collective bargaining has undergone significant change in recent years, and we illustrate the most important of these changes in this chapter. The chapter covers a definition and the purposes of collective bargaining (Section 7.2), the collective bargaining agreement (Section 7.3), collective bargaining structure (Section 7.4), coverage of collective bargaining (Section 7.5), legal issues in relation to collective bargaining (Section 7.6), and major changes to the levels at which collective bargaining takes place (Section 7.7). However, the purpose of the chapter is not to give a historical account. We set out to explain the importance today of collective bargaining in regulating the employment relationship for many employees, many of whom have little idea of its relevance to their working lives.

In addition to an examination of collective bargaining the chapter covers the process of negotiation (Section 7.8) as well as sections on industrial action (Section 7.9) and the role of ACAS as a third party intervening with a view to resolving disputes to prevent industrial action (Section 7.10).

7.2 Collective bargaining: definition and purposes

Collective bargaining may be defined as:

> ... a voluntary, formalised process by which employers and independent trade unions negotiate, for specified groups of employees, terms and conditions of employment and the ways in which certain employment-related issues are to be regulated at national, organisational and workplace levels.

In Chapter 3 we argued that the possession and use of power is the lifeblood of employment relations. This is nowhere more evident than in collective bargaining, which is essentially an exercise in power sharing between employers and employees. In many, particularly smaller, organisations managers make unilateral decisions about the conduct of the employment relationship, for example deciding the pay levels of individual employees (see Chapter 4). Similarly, employees may impose their own decisions (for example, beginning to clear up in a retail store before the store closes). Collective bargaining concerns the joint determination of such decisions. This suggests, of course, that recognition for full collective bargaining rights is the goal of all trade unions. But the enthusiasm with which managers participate in collective bargaining will be more variable. So there is likely to be a continual tension between trade unions, who want to extend the range of issues subject to joint regulation, and managers, who may wish to retain their prerogative to make unilateral decisions on issues that they see as legitimately within their domain.

In Chapter 1 we described the importance of differing frames of reference in analysing the employment relationship. Burchill (1997: 4) describes collective bargaining as the pluralist concept *par excellence*. Collective bargaining embodies the recognition that employers and employees have separate and often conflicting interests: collective bargaining is the mechanism by which these conflicting interests may be reconciled. Moreover, as Blyton and Turnbull (1998) point out, it gives the conduct of employment relations greater predictability by providing formal channels through which potential conflicts may be aired. These channels are part of the permanent apparatus of employment relations, so collective bargaining can be seen as a continuous process. Managers may raise proposals that they want to negotiate (such as the introduction of more flexible working hours). Trade unions may accede to these after negotiated modifications. Alternatively, trade unions may raise issues that they want to resolve (such as the need for a formal redundancy policy). The definition above notes that collective bargaining is a formalised process in that there are clear rules laid down about the way in which bargaining is to be conducted. We go into greater detail about the content of a collective bargaining procedure and the process of negotiating later in this chapter.

Our definition of collective bargaining notes that the process is about determining terms and conditions of employment for specified groups of employees and the ways in which certain employment-related issues are to be regulated. This immediately highlights the distinction between what are called substantive and procedural terms of collective agreements. *Substantive terms* concern the content of employment terms, e.g. pay and hours of work. These are the aspects of collective agreements that we would most readily recognise. *Procedural terms* of the collective agreement, on the other hand, set out the rules and procedures to be used by both sides in regulating the conduct of the employment relationship and the bargaining arrangement. At the risk of over-simplification, substantive terms may be said to be about the *what* of the collective agreement and procedural terms about the *how*. Box 7.1 lists some of the aspects of employment terms and conditions which come under these two headings.

It is perfectly valid to ask why this distinction between substantive and procedural terms is important. The answer is that they lead us into an important discussion about the various functions of collective bargaining, which we hope will reinforce the conceptual and practical importance of collective bargaining in regulating the employment relationship.

Chamberlain and Kuhn (1965) list these three functions as:

- *The market function.* This may be seen as a marketplace where employers and employees meet together to negotiate the price at which labour will be bought and sold. This relates to the price at which labour will be supplied to the company by its present and future employees. You can see that this relates most directly to the substantive terms of the collective agreement.
- *The governmental function.* This views collective bargaining as a political process in which 'the bargaining relationship may... be viewed as a continuing "constitution" in which the collective agreement is the body of law, determined by the management/union negotiators as the legislature, and executive authority is vested in management who must exercise it in accordance with the terms of the constitution' (Salamon, 2000: 332).
- *The decision-making function.* This perspective sees collective bargaining as a way in which employees, through the trade unions, participate in the decisions that affect their working lives, which, argued the Donovan Commission (1968), is the right of all citizens in a democracy. As such, it serves as a constraint upon the power of managers who may otherwise impose decisions unilaterally upon employees.

> **Box 7.1   Examples of substantive and procedural terms of the collective bargaining agreement**
>
> *Substantive terms*
>
> - *Pay* (e.g. salary and wage basic rates, gradings, method of pay, overtime and shift premia, special payments for working unsociable hours, bonuses, allowances for travel or special clothing)
> - *Hours of work* (basic working hours, shiftwork patterns, flexihours, meal breaks)
> - *Holidays* (basic entitlement, service entitlement, holiday pay)
> - *Health and safety* (protective clothing, injury benefits, eye tests)
> - *Welfare* (canteen facilities, sports and social clubs)
> - *Pensions* (contributions, benefits)
> - *Training* (entitlements, payment of fees, time-off provision)
>
> *Procedural terms*
>
> - *Individual grievances*
> - *Collective disputes* (stages, third-party intervention by conciliation or arbitration)
> - *Disciplinary issues*
> - *Redundancies* (consultation, methods of selection)
> - *Equal opportunities* (recruitment and selection, training, promotion)
> - *Negotiating* (frequency, participants)
> - *Joint consultation* (issues, committee structure)

These three functions of collective bargaining should not be thought of as mutually exclusive. For example, one of the arguments managers may make against collective bargaining is the time that decision-making takes when it is subject to joint regulation. They would argue that this indirectly affects the price of labour, in that higher productivity may not be achieved as quickly as it would were they able to introduce, say, changes in working practices without consultation or bargaining. What Chamberlain and Kuhn's categorisation does is emphasise that collective bargaining is both an economic and a political process. It is from this that it derives its significance.

self-check question   **7.1** What advantages do you think managers may derive from collective bargaining?

7.3   The collective bargaining agreement

Having outlined some abstract points about collective bargaining, we think it is appropriate at this stage to introduce you to a sample collective agreement (Box 7.2). This will allow us to make several important points, with the advantage of being able to cross-refer to a concrete example.

Box 7.2	Agreement between Bristow Helicopters Ltd and Amicus

Scope of the agreement

To the exclusion of all other trade unions, Bristow Helicopters Ltd recognises Amicus ('the union') as having sole recognition and negotiation rights for all UK-based staff employed by Bristow Helicopters Ltd and British Executive Air Services Ltd (together referred to as 'the company') excluding all pilots and aircrew, engineering staff at the grade of director, chief engineer, deputy chief engineer, manager (departmental, engineering, engineering operations, design, logistics, quality assurance, technical services, type engineering) or equivalent positions but not excluding senior shift supervisors. At British Executive Air Services Limited this would currently exclude from this agreement senior maintenance engineers and quality assurance superintendents.

Further exclusions include staff at the grade of director, chief accountant, manager (contracts, commercial, general, personnel, computer, shipping and transport, systems development, deputy personnel) or equivalent positions.

General principles

The objectives of this agreement are to work in partnership and in line with the partnership criteria annexed hereto:

- to develop and maintain the objectives of the company, its employees and customers;
- to promote and maintain mutual trust and cooperation between the company, the employees and the union; (and)
- to establish procedures by which matters affecting these relationships can be dealt with effectively and speedily.

Both the company and the union are agreed on the need:

- to support a business committed to the highest level of quality, productivity and competitiveness;
- to make such changes to technology and working practices as will maintain this commitment;
- to avoid any industrial action;
- to respond flexibly and quickly to changes in demand for the company's services;
- to maintain open and direct communication with all employees on matters of mutual interest and concern; (and)
- for the effective training of union representatives, including the provision of reasonable paid time off. The company will discuss with the union the facilities that are required at the bases to ensure that the representative role can be performed adequately.

Company consultative council

The company will establish a single company consultative council which will address communications and consultation issues relevant to the company's operations and to its employees. The consultative council will include employees and union representatives.

The consultative council will operate to generate awareness and contribution from employees to the company's strategic development, its performance within an evolving commercial climate and to many significant changes that may be required in the best interests of the company.

▶

Box 7.2	Continued

Negotiations

The parties agree to negotiate on pay (defined as basic pay, executive, professional and training allowances, location allowance and increments), hours (defined as shift patterns and normal hours of work) and holidays. Any negotiations will be conducted solely by specially convened meetings between the company and the union. No cost-incurring claims will be made separately from the negotiating forum.

Both the company and the union are totally committed to resolving negotiation issues or any other potentially conflicting situations as far as possible without recourse to external agencies. Only after the company chief executive and the union general secretary have both agreed to refer the situation to ACAS would the service become involved.

If agreement still cannot be reached between the company chief executive and the union general secretary both the company and the union will be free to consider what action they consider appropriate.

Consultation

The company will consult with the union on issues relating to pensions. The company will consult with the union on redundancy criteria and redundancy pay where a potential redundancy situation arises.

Confidentiality

Both parties agree not to discuss or communicate any issue in respect of which negotiation is to take place or is taking place or any other issue which may be the subject matter of discussion or communication between the parties from time to time, with any third party (which for the avoidance of doubt shall include any form of media) other than their own advisers.

Enforcement

Both parties agree that this agreement is not legally binding as between the parties.

Term of the agreement

This agreement will remain in place until a new version is agreed by both parties. Either party may terminate the agreement at any time following the presentation in writing to the other party of three calendar months' notice.

Source: Bristow Helicopters Ltd. Reproduced with the permission of Bristow Helicopters Ltd and Amicus.

7.4 The structure of collective bargaining

A useful way of analysing the structure of collective bargaining is to use the well-known framework of categorising the structural features as levels, units, agents, scope and form.

■ Bargaining levels

Collective bargaining may take place at a number of levels. It may be conducted at national, single-employer level (e.g. Ford, Tesco) or multi-employer industry level (e.g. higher education). It may be at regional or district level (e.g. NHS), or at the level of the organisation. Even at organisational level it may be that there are local-level agreements that apply to certain workplaces in the organisation. In the example in Box 7.2 it is clear that this is an agreement that applies to the single employer and is conducted mainly at national level. So the individual employee's contract of employment will contain terms and conditions that originate from the national collective agreement.

There has been a decline in the significance of multi-employer national agreements and a consequent move to decentralise bargaining activity in recent years as organisations have sought to make their collective bargaining more responsive to their general management strategies. We go into more detail on this later in this chapter.

Bargaining units

This refers to the group of employees to be covered by a particular collective agreement. In the example in Box 7.2 you will notice that this applies to all UK-based staff employed by the company excluding all pilots and aircrew, engineering staff at the grade of director, chief engineer, deputy chief engineer, manager (departmental, engineering, engineering operations, design, logistics, quality assurance, technical services, type engineering) or equivalent positions but not excluding senior shift supervisors, as well as further exclusions including staff at the grade of director, chief accountant, manager (contracts, commercial, general, personnel, computer, shipping and transport, systems development, deputy personnel) or equivalent positions.

In our own organisations there are two main bargaining units covering academic and non-academic staff. Traditionally, common interests have determined the suitability of bargaining units. These interests derive from the nature of the working conditions of the group of employees, their qualifications and training, and features of the employment contract. They may also relate to the wishes of the particular employees to belong to a specific union or the present collective bargaining arrangements. In addition, they may reflect such management-determined features as the organisation's structure, both functionally and geographically (Farnham, 1997).

In large complex sectors such as the NHS and local government there are numerous bargaining units covering such diverse employee groups as porters, occupational therapists, gardeners and social workers. However, such arrangements are not typical of workplace collective bargaining arrangements. Of the 45 per cent of workplaces in 1998 that recognised unions for bargaining purposes, only 28 per cent conducted negotiations with multiple bargaining units (Cully et al., 1999).

Bargaining agents

The agent is the organisation appointed to represent the bargaining units. This is the trade union (or, possibly, independent staff association). It follows that the greater the number of bargaining units in the organisation, the greater the possibility of a number of bargaining agents. So, in the NHS there are over 40 trade unions (Burchill, 1997). In our own organisation there are two agents: NATFHE and Unison, representing academic and non-academic staff respectively. But in 41 per cent of the workplaces that recognised trade unions in 1998, such as Bristow, only one union was recognised.

A further 31 per cent conducted single-table bargaining (Cully *et al.*, 1999), where various union representatives are brought together round a so-called *single table* in order to conduct one set of negotiations for all employee groups.

self-check question **7.2** What are the arguments for and against single-table bargaining?

Bargaining scope

This is a key element of bargaining structure. Scope defines the subjects to be covered in the collective agreement and the way in which they will be covered. In our example in Box 7.2 the matters for negotiation (pay, hours and holidays) and consultation (pensions and redundancy) are clearly stated. The intention is to limit the scope for negotiation and consultation to these issues, with remaining matters to be the subject of discussion in the company consultative council.

Bargaining form

This simply refers to the form in which the collective agreement is expressed. The formal, written agreement in Box 7.2 is clearly necessary in a large disparate organisation. If such agreements are drafted in quasi-legal form it reduces the possibility of misinterpretation. But this is a national agreement. We made the point earlier that such national agreements may be supplemented by workplace agreements over issues relating only to specific employees. It is quite likely that these may be informal and unwritten, or confirmed by internal memo.

7.5 Coverage of collective bargaining in the UK and other developed economies

In Chapter 5 we noted the decline in trade union membership and workplace recognition. It is not surprising, therefore, to see that there has been a similar decline in the incidence of collective bargaining. In the early 1970s collective bargaining covered 80 per cent of all male and 70 per cent of all female UK manual workers and over 60 per cent of both male and female non-manual workers (Blyton and Turnbull, 1998). Cully *et al.* (1999) estimate that in 1984, 70 per cent of all UK employees were covered by collective bargaining; by 1990 that figure had fallen to 54 per cent, and in the 1998 Workplace Employee Relations Survey it had fallen to 41 per cent of all employees. They go on to report that the fall had been experienced in all sectors of the economy. In the public sector the decline had been from 80 per cent to 63 per cent of all employees; in private manufacturing the fall was from 51 per cent to 46 per cent and in private services from 33 per cent to 22 per cent.

Table 7.1 illustrates the pattern of collective bargaining found by the 1998 Workplace Employee Relations Survey (Cully *et al.*, 1999). Significant patterns emerge in Table 7.1. The first is the greater popularity of collective bargaining in the public sector. As a result of the greater likelihood of public sector workplaces

Table 7.1 Method of pay determination for non-managerial employees, by workplace size and sector in 1998

	Multi-employer collective bargaining (% of employees)	Single-employer collective bargaining (% of employees)	Workplace collective bargaining (% of employees)	Determined by managers or some other method (% of employees)
Private sector				
25–49 employees	4	5	2	89
50–99 employees	4	9	3	84
100–199 employees	10	11	7	72
200–499 employees	5	13	14	68
500+ employees	2	25	16	57
All private sector workplaces	5	14	9	72
Public sector				
25–49 employees	30	11	0	59
50–99 employees	30	19	0	51
100–199 employees	37	15	1	47
200–499 employees	43	20	1	36
500+ employees	35	16	6	43
All public sector workplaces	35	16	3	46
All workplaces	14	15	7	64

Source: Adapted from Cully *et al.* (1999: 108)

determining pay through collective bargaining, 54 per cent of employees in the public sector had their pay determined in this way. This was due largely to multi-employer agreements as in higher education and local government. In the private sector the equivalent figure was 28 per cent. This disparity between public and private sectors has existed since the early part of the twentieth century. In 1916 the Whitley Committee Report on the Relations between Employers and Employees designed a formal centralised collective bargaining structure that was to serve as a model in the public sector, and to some extent the private sector, and which, despite attempts at modification, endures to this day. Thus collective bargaining has been encouraged in the public sector, as it has been seen as delivering several decades of orderly employment relations. This has been aided by the structure of employment in the public sector, which until recent years has been characterised by 'largely monopolistic public corporations which are the sole buyers of labour' (Farnham and Pimlott, 1995: 159). Clearly, the size of workforces employed by this type of organisation, and their bureaucratic mode of organising, lent itself to highly centralised collective bargaining.

The second significant pattern to emerge from Table 7.1 is that the larger the workplace, the greater chance there is that pay is determined by collective bargaining. This may be for two reasons. First, the statistics in Table 7.1 refer to workplaces, not organisations. Many of the small workplaces in the sample would be, for example, branches of large retail organisations or small depots belonging to large public authorities. Collective bargaining is less likely to happen at this level than at single employer or multi-employer level. This is demonstrated clearly in the public sector data, where there is little evidence of workplace bargaining. The second reason is demonstrated in the private sector data. In Chapter 4 we commented on the informality and unpredictability of employment relations in small and medium-sized enterprises (SMEs). They are less likely to have personnel experts to conduct bargaining, and have less sophisticated pay schemes and structures for representing the views of employees. Collective bargaining is evident only in those private sector workplaces with more than 500 employees where 4 out of 10 employees have their pay collectively determined.

Coverage of collective bargaining in the UK is less widespread than in many other countries. It is greatest in Denmark and Sweden. In these countries there is both high bargaining coverage and union membership density. This reflects some of the characteristics of the so-called Nordic (Denmark, Sweden, Finland and Norway) model of industrial relations (Kjellberg, 1998). These countries have been ruled by social-democratic governments that have promoted a spirit of compromise between employers' associations and trade unions. Kjellberg describes the Nordic model as both centralised and decentralised. Nordic union confederations have traditionally had a significant role in national bargaining for manual employees. At the same time, there has been a meaningful role for unions at workplace level, where they pursue some of the activities that are the province of bodies such as works councils in other European countries. This active workplace role ensures a high level of union density.

The decline in collective bargaining coverage in the UK has been mirrored in many other European countries (Bean, 1994). This is due to several factors. First, there is the change in the *structure of the labour market*, which was covered in detail in Chapter 2. Collective bargaining is the natural consequence of trade union recognition, which, as Chapter 5 has shown, has declined substantially in the UK. This, in turn, is related to union membership levels which have also plummeted (see Chapter 5). The decline in those industries, such as steel and coal, characterised by collective regulation is directly reflected in the reduction in bargaining coverage. The second factor is *union derecognition by employers*. There is some evidence of this phenomenon in the late 1980s and early 1990s, particularly when organisations open new sites (Brown *et al.*, 1995) (see Chapter 5). It is unclear whether this was part of a deliberate strategy adopted by some managers to marginalise trade unions or a consequence of fading employee interest in collective representation leading to collective bargaining arrangements falling into disuse. A third possible explanation is the growth of *individualised pay arrangements*, which we detail in Chapter 10. The principle of rewarding employees on the basis of their individual contribution to the organisation is one that sits uneasily with collective bargaining with its 'same rate for all' philosophy. A fourth reason, which accounts for part of the apparent decline in the UK public sector, is the replacement of collective bargaining by *pay review bodies* for significant groups such as teachers and nurses. Fifth, there is the possibility that the further development of individual labour law offering employees, for example, minimum wage protection, dismissal, redundancy and anti-discrimination rights may create a perception among non-union members of the *limited value of union membership*. The sixth possible reason is the *withdrawal of legal assistance* to trade unions in claiming recognition. We deal with this, and its reintroduction, in the next section.

7.6 Legal issues relating to collective bargaining

One of the reasons why there has been a major decline in collective bargaining coverage in the past 20 years has been the lack of support for trade unions in claiming recognition from the employer for collective bargaining purposes. Essentially, it has been the decision of the employer whether or not to enter into collective bargaining arrangements with a trade union. However, during the 1970s there was some legal support for unions who could demonstrate to an employer that there was sufficient demand for union representation at the workplace from that employer's employees who were also the union's members. However, one of the first pieces of legislation hostile to trade unions from the incoming Thatcher government in 1979 saw the abolition of legal support for unions in claiming recognition. The Employment Relations Act 1999 reintroduced measures similar to those that had existed through the 1970s.

■ Legal support for trade union recognition

Should a claim for recognition from a trade union to an employer not lead to a voluntary agreement the law has a role to play. The Employment Relations Act 1999 provides that in certain circumstances a trade union (or trade unions) may make an application to the Central Arbitration Committee (CAC) for a declaration that it should be recognised to conduct collective bargaining regarding pay, hours and holidays on behalf of a group or groups of workers employed by an employer in a particular bargaining unit. The functions of the CAC are outlined briefly in Box 7.3.

Box 7.3 Functions of the Central Arbitration Committee

The Central Arbitration Committee:

- is a permanent independent body with statutory powers whose main function is to adjudicate on applications relating to the statutory recognition and derecognition of trade unions for collective bargaining purposes, where such recognition or derecognition cannot be agreed voluntarily;
- has a statutory role in determining disputes between trade unions and employers over the disclosure of information for collective bargaining purposes;
- deals with claims and complaints regarding the establishment and operation of European Works Councils in Great Britain;
- provides voluntary arbitration in industrial disputes.

If the CAC receives an application from a trade union or unions, it must first decide whether it can accept the application. It does this by applying a number of admissibility tests. These tests include whether or not the trade union has 10 per cent of the workforce in its proposed bargaining unit in membership, and whether or not a majority of workers in the proposed bargaining unit would be likely to support recognition of the trade union. Where the CAC decides it can accept the application, and where the bargaining unit proposed by the trade union in its originating application has not been agreed with the employer, the CAC must next decide whether or not the proposed bargaining unit is the appropriate one. The CAC does this by considering primarily whether or not what is proposed is compatible with effective management. If the CAC decides a different bargaining unit is the appropriate one, it must next consider whether or not the application remains valid. It does this by reapplying to the bargaining unit it has determined a number of the tests it applied to the bargaining unit proposed by the trade union in its originating application.

Where the CAC decides that the application remains valid, and over 50 per cent of the appropriate bargaining unit are members of the applicant union(s), the CAC may declare that the union(s) should be recognised. Alternatively, where the CAC is satisfied that the interests of good industrial relations require a secret ballot to be held, or for other specified reasons, the CAC may still decide to hold a ballot even though the union(s) has/have majority membership in the appropriate bargaining unit. If the CAC is unsatisfied that the applicant union(s) has/have majority membership in the appropriate bargaining unit, it must always arrange for a ballot to be held before deciding whether or not to grant recognition. Where a ballot is held, the CAC will grant recognition where a majority of participants in the ballot, and at least 40 per cent of the workers constituting the appropriate bargaining unit, vote in favour.

◼ The lack of legal enforceability of collective agreements

Although there is now some support for trade unions in claiming recognition for collective bargaining purposes, it is important to note that collective agreements, such as that in Box 7.2, are not legally enforceable. However, the terms and conditions of employment that flow from the collective agreement are legally binding in the individual's contract of employment. This emphasises the voluntary nature of collective bargaining in the UK.

There are potential problems with legal enforcement of collective agreements. As we have noted, agreements are defined at different levels. Whereas it may be straightforward for an industrial court to interpret a national-level formal agreement, it may be much less so with a workplace-level informal and, possibly, unwritten agreement. But, more importantly, legal enforceability may inhibit the flexibility of collective bargaining arrangements. As we suggested earlier, collective bargaining is a dynamic, continuous process. Collective agreements, say on benefits and working hours, are not usually for a fixed time period. They are reviewed and renegotiated as and when the parties think it is appropriate. Fixing a lifetime period for the collective agreement could have two effects: making it less responsive to changing circumstances, and focusing renegotiation, and therefore possible dissent, into a clearly defined time frame – that is, when the agreement is shortly to expire.

The UK is unusual in that there is no legal enforceability of collective agreements. Hollinshead and Leat (1995) note that there is usually a fixed time period to agreements in other countries, with penalties or remedies applying in the event of non-performance of the contract during its lifetime. It is common for parties to not have the right to renegotiate or apply pressure to change the substantive terms of the agreement (so-called *disputes of interest*), although it may be possible to engage in a dispute over the interpretation or implementation of the procedural element of an existing agreement (so-called *disputes of right*). For example, in Germany and Sweden agreements are legally binding; disputes of interest are unlawful during the life of the agreement, and disputes of interest may not be the subject of industrial action but must be resolved by mediation/conciliation or be settled by the labour courts.

7.7   Major changes in the collective bargaining levels

We indicated earlier that in recent years there has been significant change in not only the prevalence of collective bargaining but also the level at which it has been conducted. In this section we examine two major, interrelated trends: the decision by many organisations to withdraw from national level multi-employer bargaining, thereby accepting responsibility themselves for bargaining with trade unions, and the trend within organisations to devolve the responsibility for much bargaining activity from the centre to workplaces.

■ Multi-employer bargaining

Salamon (2000: 347) defines national multi-employer agreements as being 'negotiated between national trade unions and employers' associations' and covering 'employees of a given description in a specified industry or sub-industry'. In our example of the 'new' university sector we pointed out that there are two bargaining units: academic and non-academic staff. Therefore there are two national agreements in operation forged by two different unions (NATFHE and Unison) in conjunction with one employers' association, the Universities and Colleges Employers' Association (UCEA). Salamon (2000) notes that such agreements apply only to those organisations where the employer is a member of the relevant employers' association, although any similar organisation may decide to adopt the relevant terms and conditions of employment flowing from the agreement. In such cases, however, the employer does not have access to the dispute resolution facilities offered by the employers' association. (We examine dispute resolution procedures later in this chapter.)

Until recently, national multi-employer bargaining was the dominant model in the UK and continental Europe. It affords both management and unions significant advantages (Box 7.4).

It is interesting to examine the list of relative advantages to employers and trade unions in Box 7.4 and consider which points are the most persuasive to the respective parties at the beginning of the twenty-first century. In our view the advantages to unions considerably outweigh those to employers. The basis of our argument is the relative weakness of unions now as opposed to their heyday in the 1960s and 1970s. The majority of the union advantages listed above involve either the reduction of operating costs or the prospect of increased income: broadly the strategic position one would expect from any organisation facing commercial difficulties. On the other hand, the list of employers' advantages seems much less convincing. Two of these refer to the concerns employers may have about trade union 'opposition'. These are less relevant in a climate of reduced union influence. In addition, employers are much less concerned about the effect of competing with one another through differential wage and salary costs. This is for two reasons. First, because the more competitive

---

Box 7.4   National multi-employer bargaining

Advantages to employers

- More concerted response to trade union organisation
- Reduces chances of employers competing with one another through differential wage and salary costs
- Eliminates need for smaller employers to spend negotiating time and possess negotiating expertise
- Reduces trade union role at the workplace

Advantages to trade unions

- Enhances bargaining strength
- The negotiation of acceptable minimum standards for an industry's employees
- Increases chances of gaining recognition from employers not already part of a national agreement
- Rationalisation of resources
- Demonstrable relevance to industry employees thereby enhancing recruitment prospects

---

business climate of recent years has meant that employers must compete with one another rather than participate in 'comfortable' non-competitive agreements. The major UK clearing bank sector, where multi-employer bargaining ceased in the late 1980s, is a good example of such a situation. The second reason is that many employers have been concerned much more with increasing the productivity of their employees rather than simply with reducing labour costs, following the advice of Pfeffer (1998).

Given the relative importance to the parties of these advantages it is hardly surprising that the incidence of national multi-employer bargaining has declined considerably in recent years. Cully *et al.* (1999) track this decline by comparing the UK Workplace Employee Relations Surveys in 1980 and 1998. This is shown in Table 7.2.

Table 7.2 **The proportion of workplaces with recognised trade unions in which the pay of some or all employees originated from multi-employer bargaining: 1980 and 1998**

Year	Public services (%)	Private manufacturing (%)	Private services (%)	All workplaces (%)
1980	81	57	54	68
1998	47	25	12	34

Source: Cully *et al.* (1999: 228)

Clearly there has been a marked decline in all three main sectors of the economy, with the most dramatic decline being in private services. But the 1998 Workplace Employee Relations Survey charts an even more significant decline in multi-employer bargaining when, as we note earlier in this chapter, one considers that the proportion of employees covered by collective bargaining at any level has declined from 7 out of

10 to 4 out of 10 in a similar period. Cully *et al.* (1999) note that in 1980 multi-employer bargaining impacted upon 43 per cent of all workplaces (not just those, as in Table 7.2, where trade unions were recognised), but by 1998 that figure had fallen to 14 per cent. The proportion of private sector workplaces affected by multi-employer bargaining had fallen to just 4 per cent. This allows Cully *et al.* to draw the conclusion that private sector workplaces had virtually abandoned the practice of joining together to regulate terms and conditions of employment, meaning that multi-employer bargaining is now largely a public sector phenomenon in the UK.

We have given some indication as to the reasons for the decline in multi-employer bargaining in the private sector. The increased level of product market competition has driven organisations to examine ways of making their expenditure on labour costs more effective. We noted earlier the example of banking, where multi-employer bargaining was firmly entrenched. The greater flexibility offered to individual banks through withdrawing from multi-employer bargaining has enabled them to introduce pay systems more attuned to their perceived individual needs (see Thornhill *et al.*, 2000: Ch. 5). Banking is one of a number of industries that abandoned multi-employer agreements. Others include road passenger transport upon the deregulation of the industry, journalists in national and provincial newspapers and independent television technicians, to facilitate the introduction of new technology, and engineering (Kessler and Bayliss, 1998) as a result of a protracted dispute over the length of the working week. The decline in the public sector has been largely a consequence of the break-up of formerly large monopoly organisations into separate companies, notably in water supply, electricity supply and railways (see Thornhill *et al.*, 2000: Ch. 7).

We mentioned earlier the role that employers' associations played in multi-employer bargaining. Not surprisingly, their significance in employment relations has diminished in recent years in line with the decline in multi-employer bargaining. The functions of employers' associations are:

- negotiating collective agreements with trade unions;
- assisting members in resolving employee relations disputes;
- advising and assisting members on employee relations matters; and
- representing members' views to government.

In the 1984 Workplace Employee Relations Survey, 22 per cent of workplaces were in membership to employers' associations. By 1998 this had declined to 18 per cent, although in the largest workplaces (500+ employees) the figure remained at the 1984 level (Cully *et al.*, 1999).

Decentralising collective bargaining

The decline of multi-employer agreements means that many employers such as Tesco and Lloyds TSB now bargain singly with their respective trade unions. In addition, many organisations have embarked upon a process of pushing the responsibility for collective bargaining down to the level of the site or even the department (see Figure 7.2).

self-check question   **7.3** What arguments would you use to persuade senior managers of the virtues of single-employer bargaining?

There is little doubt that the move to decentralise bargaining within the organisation has been management inspired. We suggested earlier that this has been a strategic response to the desire to reduce labour costs and increase labour flexibility. The move to decentralised bargaining has developed at the same time as many organisations have decentralised their organisational structures to divide their organisations along geographical, functional or product lines. For any manager being held responsible for the profit performance of a particular unit of his or her business it follows that that manager would want to control costs as far as possible. An important part of gaining control of costs is to control salary and wage costs, either through influencing directly the size of the pay bill or through ensuring that changes are made to working practices to ensure the workforce work more productively. Clearly, this is much easier for the manager bargaining directly with the employees' representatives rather than having centralised bargains imposed.

Undoubtedly, giving local managers greater control over their costs has been a major impetus for decentralising bargaining. The local manager is given much more flexibility. This flexibility is apparent in several ways:

- It allows local managers to take advantage of local labour market conditions. There is a compelling logic to this when it is realised that, under centralised bargaining arrangements, a manager operating in a locality with a high cost of living will be tied to paying the same wage rates as the manager in a low-cost area. This is the principle behind the long-established London weighting allowance. But high living costs are apparent in many areas. In addition, the local manager may be operating in an area where it is hard to recruit because of a buoyant external labour market. In such circumstances it is important to ensure there is the flexibility to make pay rates sufficiently attractive for potential recruits. However, differential pay rates within the organisation may have the effect of creating barriers to recruitment in the internal labour market (employees already in the organisation), thereby perhaps prejudicing longer-term employee development.

    At this point it is worth noting the opposition that trade unions have to the principle of decentralised bargaining. This has been most apparent in the NHS and education. Destroying national bargaining strikes at the heart of the traditional trade union principle of *rate for the job* based on notions of fairness, the *going rate*, comparability and cost of living. But decentralised bargaining is very much in tune with market-led thinking. In the UK the Conservative governments of the 1980s championed decentralised bargaining. They were firmly 'committed to the belief in the supremacy of the free market ... [in which] national level collective bargaining is seen as an inefficient interference with the operation of markets' (Fatchett, 1989: 255).

- It allows local managers to match rewards to business performance. Again it may seem entirely logical that a key determinant of the manager's bargaining position should be the business unit's ability to pay. This is clearly a market argument that may work in favour of employees if the business unit is prospering.

- It allows local managers to negotiate change at the local level. We noted earlier the provision that many organisation-level agreements have for some issues to be negotiated at local level. Therefore, the trend to decentralised bargaining represents nothing new. However, this facility does present managers with a significant opportunity to influence the performance of their unit. The 1998 Workplace Employee Relations Survey (Cully *et al.*, 1999), however, warns against overstating the prevalence of non-pay bargaining at local level, as it was pay that dominated workplace bargaining.

■ In addition, bargaining at local level presents management with the advantage that any industrial action flowing from a breakdown in negotiations is likely to be restricted to that site. But there are potential disadvantages. There is always the possibility of leap-frogging claims, where employee representatives in one unit see the deal negotiated at another site and use this as a bargaining lever to extract a comparable deal. Local bargaining consumes a good deal of management time, and may necessitate the employment of specialist expertise. It also means that there is a lack of control from the centre, although the possibly harmful effects of this may be mitigated by the use of policy guidelines from the central personnel department.

Before leaving the topic of decentralisation it is important to emphasise that the movement to decentralised bargaining is not solely one way. It presents advantages to local managers, but it can create costly precedents (Blyton and Turnbull, 1998). In such circumstances there is a pressure to move away from purely local arrangements. This is what Kessler and Bayliss (1998) noted in their research:

> So, from management's point of view, decentralisation of collective bargaining is not a simple story: some firms have gone further than others, some have yet to decentralise, some have drawn back, some have found that the appropriate level for decentralisation is not the same in all parts of the firm, and some have found that the nature of the product and the technology of its production are a determining influence. Even so, the general trend in management has been, and continues to be, a preference for more decentralised bargaining, although within a firmly controlled, centrally determined financial budget and/or central guidelines. (Kessler and Bayliss, 1998: 122)

7.8 Collective bargaining and the process of negotiating

So far in this chapter we have concentrated on the structure of collective bargaining. We now turn to the key process in collective bargaining: that of negotiating.

> Negotiation is a process whereby two or more interested groups seek to reconcile their differences through attempts to persuade the other group to move from their initial position, with the overall aim of reaching an agreement. (Pilbeam and Corbridge, 1997: 123)

Of course, negotiating is not exclusively a feature of collective bargaining. It has several other formal applications in employment relations. It is utilised at the level of the individual employee to settle pay or to reconcile differences. This latter application may give rise to a formal grievance being raised, which may result in negotiating a solution involving managers, employees and trade union representatives. However, it is the use of negotiating in collective bargaining with which we are concerned in this section.

Negotiating in collective bargaining has several distinct features:

- It is an intentional event involving face-to-face meetings between the parties set up to bargain over issues that need resolution. For example, the agreement in Box 7.2 states that 'any negotiations will be conducted solely by specially convened meetings between the company and the union. No cost-incurring claims will be made separately from the negotiating forum.'

- It always ends in a conclusion. You will note from the definition above that the overall aim is to reach an agreement. However, that is not always the result. A vitally important part of the collective agreement is provision for action in the event of the parties not agreeing. In the Bristow agreement (Box 7.2) you will notice that in the event of disagreement assistance is sought from a third party, in this case ACAS, although a consequent failure may see either party taking 'whatever action they consider appropriate' to settle the issue. The point to stress here is that, by whatever means, a resolution is reached. (We go into more detail on disputes in the next section.)

- The relationship between the parties normally must continue after negotiating has ended. Gennard and Judge (2003) stress the differences between employee relations negotiating and normal commercial negotiations. Unlike sales negotiations, where the negotiator probably sees the client infrequently, or maybe only once, negotiators in collective bargaining often have to work with each other every day. Therefore the promotion of an antagonistic relationship is not in anybody's interests. This acts as a considerable constraint on the conduct of negotiations. It suggests that a *win–win* outcome, where all parties are satisfied, is the ideal outcome. Consider, for example, if management were to succeed in 'putting one over' on the union side. The normal response would be for the union side to harbour a grudge, which would lead to their adopting 'getting back' behaviours in the next round of negotiations. Such a cycle of points-scoring is hardly conducive to harmonious collective employee relations.

- It is based on the power relationship between the parties. Chapter 3 has gone into considerable detail on the relative power of the parties to the employment relationship. It would be foolish to pretend that this was always equal and that a win–win outcome was always possible. However, what is important to continued effective employee relations is that both parties consider the needs of each other in negotiations. As Torrington and Hall (2002: 634) note: the greater the power differential, the more negative the attitudes.

The three stages of negotiations

It is customary for those writing about the process of negotiating to portray the process as progressing through a series of stages. This is useful because it facilitates an understanding of the various subprocesses and allows some order to be imparted into what is often a pretty disorderly business. However, you should not think that negotiations always move smoothly through these three stages. In practice, negotiators move back and forth between, and within, the stages, particularly if progress is unsatisfactory. Here we call these three stages *preparing to negotiate*, *negotiating*, and *concluding negotiations*.

Preparing to negotiate

This is a vital stage of the negotiating process. It will include:

- assembling all the facts pertinent to the negotiations (this may include the going rate of pay in the industry and/or detailed costings of different levels of settlement);
- setting negotiating aims and objectives, and forecasting the aims and objectives of the other side.

This is often portrayed as having an *ideal position* (that which you would ideally like to be the outcome), a *realistic position* (less than ideal, but a position that you would be willing to settle for), and a *fallback position* (that you are unwilling to fall below). At the same time, you will attempt to predict the ideal, realistic and fallback positions of the other side. This can be summarised usefully by means of what Gennard and Judge (2003) call an *aspiration grid*. Let's say, for example, that you are negotiating a change to a package of terms and conditions with the union negotiators. This may be based on the union claim for a 3 per cent increase to the basic pay rate, an increase in pay rate for weekend working from normal rate × 1.25 to normal rate × 1.5, 2 days' extra holiday per year, and payment for company clothing laundered at home. The normal outcome of such negotiations is a compromise package where components of the package are traded against one another. You, the management side, will not want to concede certain components but are quite happy to concede others. The same will apply to the trade union side. An aspiration grid for the above example may look like Figure 7.1.

An X indicates that the party is not prepared to trade that item, whereas an O indicates the opposite. If both parties have an X against the same item in their fallback column then it may be anticipated that there will be no grounds for agreement. In Figure 7.1 there is some scope for agreement, as there is no coincidence of Xs in either the management or union fallback columns. However, management is not prepared to trade the increases to basic rate against other components although the union *is* prepared to trade this. But the union is not prepared to trade either the increase in weekend working rate or the extra holiday claim. Only the laundry allowance (which may have been put in deliberately as the 'easily disposable' issue), on the face of it, leaves scope for agreement. Drafting an aspiration grid helps both parties to define their negotiating aims, anticipate the aims of the other side, and

Possible solutions	Management Ideal	Realistic	Fallback	Trade union Fallback	Realistic	Ideal
3% increase to basic pay	X	X	X	O	O	X
Weekend working: normal × 1.25 to normal × 1.5	X	X	O	X	X	X
2 days' extra holiday	X	O	O	X	X	X
Laundry allowance	X	O	O	O	O	X

Figure 7.1 **A sample negotiating aspiration grid**

Source: Adapted from Gennard and Judge (2003: 319)

estimate the information required to advance their positions, and gives a general guide as to the expected structure of the negotiating session.

Deciding the composition of the negotiating team and the roles of the team members
If thought is not given to who in the team does what, the consequence is likely to be a free for all, with the scope for intra-team disagreement that plays into the hands of the other party. Gennard and Judge (2003) suggest that the team will comprise a *leader*, who will be expected to be the main spokesperson in the team and control the direction of her team; a *note-taker*; an *observer*, who watches and listens; and a *strategist*, who checks progress against the defined negotiating aims and objectives. In fact, it may be that this is where the negotiations begin. Negotiating goes on at a number of levels within the framework of negotiations. As well as intra-team negotiating (there may well be disagreements between team members about what constitutes satisfactory progress), the negotiators have to sell their ideas to their principals (senior managers and trade union members), who have to live with the consequences of the agreements.

Anticipating the arguments and counter-arguments of the other party
We have already mentioned the importance of anticipating the negotiating aims and objectives of the other party. It will also be helpful to anticipate how they are likely to pursue those objectives. They will have done their preparation too, so thinking through how they will advance their cause will help you to counter their arguments.

Negotiating

Starting the meeting and making proposals
It would normally be management that initiates the meeting by clarifying its purpose and outlining the management case. Alternatively, it may be that the proposals come from the union side. In either case it is important that the side receiving the proposals is absolutely clear about what is being proposed. The proposing side may ask the other side for their immediate response to the proposals in order that a broad picture can be gained as to the way forward for the meeting. This will establish such common ground that exists and the areas where there is no agreement.

Exchanging ideas and agreeing
This is the key phase of the negotiating encounter, where proposals are considered, counter-proposals are made, and the real bargaining takes place. Effective negotiating consists of such key behaviours as:

- listening carefully to what is being said (and what is not being said);
- questioning to clarify what is being said;
- testing understanding to ensure that this is shared between the parties;
- summarising progress to date;
- seeking agreement to proposals;
- bringing in other people in the team who may have valuable contributions to make.

A particularly important part of the negotiating stage is to seek adjournments periodically. This will help each side to check progress, discuss counter-proposals that have been put by the other side, define its own proposals, and check with its principals their level of satisfaction on progress to date.

Concluding negotiations

Assuming agreement has been reached, the final stage is to agree what has been agreed and prepare a written confirmation of the agreement. Agreeing what has been agreed sounds obvious, but it can promote a resumption of negotiations if there is confusion. It is better to confirm agreement at this stage than wait until the final written report is circulated, when disagreement would lead to the negotiating meeting being reconvened.

Gennard and Judge (2003) recommend that the written agreement should contain the following:

- an identification of the parties to the agreement;
- the date when it was agreed;
- what was agreed;
- the date when it will be implemented;
- how disputes over interpretation or application will be resolved;
- its duration;
- signatures of representatives of the parties to the agreement.

This section has adopted a rather positive tone and assumed that negotiations usually end in agreement. But this is not always the case. In Section 7.10 we consider what happens in the event of failure to agree.

7.9   Industrial action

Often dispute resolution procedures are rather more involved than that outlined in our sample procedure in Box 7.2. A more detailed procedure exists in a financial services organisation where we conducted research. In this case, in the event of an initial disagreement a further meeting is held at the request of either party. This is attended by an executive from the company, who assists in resolving the point of issue. In the event of further failure to agree, an ACAS conciliation officer may be called upon to assist the parties in arriving at their own solution to the disagreement (for more detail on the role of ACAS as a third party in employee relations disputes see Section 7.10 below). Should this not lead to agreement the issue may be referred to a mutually acceptable independent arbitrator proposed by ACAS. In these situations, the principle of *pendulum arbitration* applies. This is where the arbitrator's terms of reference will be to find in favour of either the company or the union: a compromise solution will not be recommended. Section 7.10 explains in more detail the various activities of ACAS including collective conciliation and arbitration.

The importance of clear procedures in the event of a failure to agree is highlighted by the procedure in our financial services example. The existence of arbitration, the results of which either party is morally and constitutionally, if not legally, obliged to accept, means that industrial disputes are outside the scope of the agreement. So this agreement is, in essence, a no-strike agreement in the same way as were the much-heralded agreements in Japanese-owned UK sites such as Toshiba and Hitachi in the 1980s. This may be one of the reasons why the incidence of industrial action in the UK has declined so dramatically in recent years. In fact 1997 saw the lowest number

Table 7.3 **Stoppages in progress: UK, selected years, 1980–2000**

Year	Working days lost (000s)	Working days lost per 1000 employees	Workers involved (000s)	Stoppages	Stoppages involving the loss of 100 000 working days or more
1980	11964	520	834	1348	5
1984	27135	1278	1464	1221	11
1988	3702	166	790	781	8
1990	1903	83	298	630	3
1991	761	34	176	369	1
1992	528	24	148	253	0
1993	649	30	385	211	2
1994	278	13	107	205	0
1995	415	19	174	235	0
1996	1303	57	364	244	2
1997	235	10	130	216	0
1998	282	12	93	166	0
1999	242	10	141	205	0
2000	499	20	183	212	1

Source: Davies (2001)

of working days lost through disputes since records began. Similarly, the number of stoppages in 1998 was a record low, as Table 7.3 illustrates. Although a rise was recorded in 2000, over one-half of the days lost were due to one dispute.

Similarly, the 1998 Workplace Employee Relations Survey (Cully *et al.*, 1999: 126) asked workplaces about the incidence of industrial action. Only 2 per cent of workplaces reported any industrial action during the past year. 5 per cent noted that there had been no action during the past year, but some in the past 5 years, and 93 per cent replied that there had been no action in the past 5 years.

There are several possible reasons for this notable decline in recorded industrial action. Many of these are suggested in other chapters of this book. Edwards (1995) attributes the decline to five main factors: changes in employment structure; the economic environment; improved employee relations; improved means of dispute resolution; and legislation on industrial action.

■ Changes in employment structure

Chapter 2 charts the decline in the number of workers employed in manufacturing and the rise in the number employed in the service industries. It is in the former that strike activity has been more prevalent. Edwards (1995) cites three main industries as being particularly strike-prone: coalmining, dock work and car manufacturing. Indeed, in the case of coalmining Edwards has done some startling analysis. He took the average number of days lost due to strikes per UK coal employee and calculated how many strikes would have occurred in the period 1986–90 had the industry employed as many workers as it did in 1971. He calculated that there would have been 300 more strikes had employment been at the 1971 level. This would have increased the number of strikes by approximately 40 per cent.

It is not simply that workers in the service sector are less likely to want to strike. It is that they have less support for any action they may wish to take. Crucially, this usually means that they work for employers who do not recognise a trade union prepared to take up a dispute on behalf of embittered employees. The fact that days lost in industrial action are days for which the employee is not paid is also a highly significant factor, as many employees in the service sector are not high earners. As Clegg (cited in Blyton and Turnbull, 1998) noted, strikes are more prevalent when workers have not only the motivation but also the opportunity and the means.

The economic environment

The evidence to support the proposition that workers are less likely to strike in times of economic recession and high unemployment is less clear-cut. High unemployment levels in the 1980s and early 1990s would seem to account for workers being less prepared to risk losing their jobs through expressing discontent. But there is also the argument that high inflation leads to workers wanting to maintain real wage levels and using the strike weapon to achieve this end (Edwards, 1995). Recession may also mean low levels of wage increases and dissatisfaction by workers expressed through strikes. Wage rates and earning levels have consistently been the main cause of working days lost due to industrial action in the UK (Davies, 1999).

Improved employee relations

Edwards (1995: 448) suggests that 'better industrial relations' may mean three things: an increase in the level of employee commitment and cooperation; a reassertion by management of its right to manage, leading to workers being frightened of strike action; and changes to the technical organisation of work (for example more robotisation in factories, meaning less dirty, boring jobs) coupled with a reduced emphasis on pay systems such as piecework (see Chapter 10), which was often seen as a cause of unrest. There may be some substance in the third of these suggestions, but the first two are so generalised that it is of little value pursuing them. That said, the 1998 Workplace Employee Relations Survey (Cully et al., 1999) does offer some evidence that most UK employees are generally reasonably satisfied with their lot. In general, harmonious employment relations seemed to be the norm and a high proportion of employees expressed themselves satisfied with their job, albeit not with their pay.

However, we must be careful in assuming that measures of industrial action and survey evidence tell us everything about the health of employment relations. Such evidence usually refers to what is called *organised industrial action*. This may take the form of collective action promoted by the trade union. As well as strikes this may involve a withdrawal of employee cooperation with management, working to rule (that is, sticking to the details of the job description), overtime bans and go-slows. In the same way management may exercise sanctions by unilaterally imposing revised terms and conditions of employment, locking out employees from the works, hiring replacement workers for strikers (for example News International when it moved from Fleet Street to Wapping), and closing the works (for example Timex in Dundee).

But much industrial action is covert. This may be termed *unorganised individual action*. This is where the individual employee expresses dissatisfaction through such means as absenteeism, lateness, poor-quality work, thieving, or sabotage, or by simply leaving. This may be rationalised by the disgruntled employee as 'getting back' at the employer, and as such is as potent as organised collective action. It may also be that there is an element of collusion within work groups where employees agree among themselves to cover for each other as individuals take unauthorised absences.

Improved means of dispute resolution

We have already noted the significance for dispute resolution of disputes procedures in recognition agreements. In addition to this internal dispute resolution procedure, legislation added another. One of the most persuasive arguments accounting for the decline in strike action in the late 1980s and 1990s is the legislative programme undertaken by successive Conservative governments to curb the ability of trade unions to promote strike action. One of these measures made it necessary for trade unions to conduct secret ballots of those members likely to be affected by a strike in order to secure their agreement to take strike action. Edwards (1995) argues that there is little conclusive evidence to show that this did reduce the number of strikes. However, there are at least two reasons to assume that the secret ballot provision will lead to the avoidance of strikes. The first is that the necessity to have a vote leads to a *cooling-off* period where respective positions may be carefully considered. The second is that a vote in favour of a strike may persuade management of the determination of their employees and therefore the legitimacy of the proposed action. We now go on to consider the post-1980 legislation in more detail.

Legislation

When employees strike (or take other forms of industrial action) they will normally break their employment contract. If trade unions or their officials organise such action they are, in effect, interfering with the performance of employment contracts. They may also be interfering with the performance of the employer's commercial contracts. Under common law it is unlawful to break a contract, or interfere with the performance of a contract, or threaten to do either of these things. Without some legal protection, this places the trade union in a highly vulnerable position. It means that every time it organised a strike it would face legal claims from the employer. This may be a claim for damages to compensate for losses incurred (such as lost profit) or a request for an injunction to prevent the industrial action from taking place.

For most of the twentieth century trade unions enjoyed a high level of protection from such legal action. This took the form of the so-called *statutory immunities*. By the late 1970s the organisation of virtually all forms of industrial action was protected by these statutory immunities. In addition, unions enjoyed a special privilege in that they could not be the subject of legal action in their own right; such action was against their principal officers. (This was changed in 1982.)

The incoming Conservative government in 1979 was dedicated to trimming the power of trade unions. It embarked upon a legislative programme that meant that unions would have to pass a number of stringent tests if they were to claim immunity from legal action being taken by the employer in the event of industrial action. We note below the most significant of these tests.

In order to be lawful, industrial action must:

- *relate wholly or mainly to the contemplation or furtherance of a trade dispute*. A trade dispute must be wholly or mainly about employment-related matters such as pay and conditions. It cannot be about, say, political matters such as a protest about government policy that may have to be carried out by the employer (unless it impinges upon employment conditions). Moreover, the trade dispute must be between workers and their own employer.
- *have been the subject of a properly conducted secret ballot*. The ballot must offer all affected employees the opportunity of voting by post and be subject to independent scrutiny. A majority of those voting must be in favour of industrial action. Any action must take place within 4 weeks of the ballot, and the employer must be given 7 days' notice of both the ballot and the planned industrial action.
- *not be secondary action*. Secondary action refers to industrial action taken by workers whose employer is not a party to the trade dispute to which the action relates. This is usually called *sympathy action*, where workers of one employer (for example train drivers) take sympathy action in support of a separate dispute between workers and a different employer (for example council workers).
- *not be 'unofficial'*. It is quite possible, of course, that workers can simply 'walk off the job' irrespective of any role that may be played by trade union officials. In such circumstances the union officials must repudiate the action of the union's members in writing if they do not want to be associated with the action and render the union liable to legal action taken by the employer. This legislation is supported by the provision that for industrial action to be lawful it must not:
- *be in support of any employee dismissed while taking unofficial industrial action.*
- *not involve unlawful picketing*. When pickets attempt to persuade people not to go into their workplace, or not to collect or deliver goods, they may be interfering with the performance of those workers' contracts of employment, and they may also be interfering with the performance of the employer's commercial contracts. The fact that the industrial action itself may be lawful does not necessarily mean that the picketing is lawful. For picketing to be lawful the pickets must be at or near their own place of work, and the purpose of the picketing must be peacefully to obtain or communicate information or peacefully to persuade a person to work or not to work. Those breaking the criminal law by violent or threatening behaviour on picket duty or obstructing the highway enjoy no protection from the law. In addition the Code of Practice on Picketing (HMSO, 1980) recommends that no more than six pickets should be on duty at any workplace entrance.

We note above the significance of the secret ballot legislation for the reduction in the number of stoppages in recent years. Two of the legislative changes have wider importance for the trade union movement. First, the outlawing of secondary industrial action strikes at the very heart of trade unionism. The most famous UK strike of all, the 1926 General Strike, was a triple alliance of the miners, railwaymen and transport workers. Such solidarity may not be a feature of modern social life, but there is a powerful symbolic significance in the outlawing of expressions of solidarity. Of more contemporary significance is the effect of secondary action legislation on an economy where so many large industries have been broken up. The rail industry is a good example. In 2000, employees of Connex, one of the post-British Rail train operating companies, took strike action in support of a 35 hour week and all allowances to be consolidated into basic pay and, therefore, pensionable. Prior to the secondary action legislation it is reasonable to assume that such a dispute would quickly have spread through all the train operating companies, since drivers would have identified a common cause. If one unplanned employee relations consequence of breaking up large companies is that the government was able to operate 'divide and rule' among the unions, this secondary action implication lent considerable reinforcement.

The second legislative change which has had wide significance for the trade union movement concerns picketing. Television screens in the 1970s and 1980s were full of powerful images of mass picketing at such workplaces as coalmines and newspaper depots. Such was the theatre of collective industrial relations. But it was a play of which the public tired, particularly after the 1979–80 Winter of Discontent. The legislation reflected public opinion. Such is the background we must understand when we look at the data on strikes today.

7.10 Third-party intervention: the role of ACAS

ACAS is funded by the Department of Trade and Industry and is a non-departmental body that is fully independent and impartial. It employs around 800 staff, based at offices throughout Britain. ACAS is headed by a Chair and overall guidance is provided by the ACAS Council made up of 12 members ranging from union members to academics. Both the Chair and the Council members are part-time and appointed by the Secretary of State for Trade and Industry. As Chapter 6 notes, ACAS has a key role in assisting in the resolution of industrial disputes. Although this is the emphasis of the section it is important to note that ACAS has a wider role to play in employee relations. This role involves preventing and resolving industrial disputes, resolving individual disputes over employment rights, providing impartial information and advice on employment matters, and improving the understanding of industrial relations. Box 7.5 gives a comprehensive account of the range of activities pursued by ACAS.

Box 7.5 ACAS service standards

Preventing and resolving collective disputes

ACAS provides assistance to parties seeking settlement of collective disputes on employment issues by way of conciliation, mediation or arbitration. ACAS can also assist in preventing and resolving problems at work by providing advisory mediation. ACAS has no powers to secure the acceptance of its assistance or to impose any solution for an issue in dispute. Before providing assistance ACAS encourages parties to make full use of any agreed procedures they may have for negotiation and the settlement of disputes.

Advisory mediation

Advisory mediation enables ACAS to work jointly with employers, employees and employee representatives to help overcome problems which threaten to damage the employment relationship or which constitute a major obstacle to organisational effectiveness.
  We will:

■ discuss fully the nature of the problems and what help might be provided and, where appropriate, be ready to suggest alternative sources of assistance;

Box 7.5	Continued

- explain our role and working methods and agree clear terms of reference;
- provide advisory mediation only when there is joint participation of the employer, employees and/or their representatives.

Collective conciliation

This is a voluntary process whereby employers, trade unions, and worker representatives can be helped to reach mutually acceptable settlements of their disputes by an impartial and independent third party.

We will:

- offer assistance where no request has been made where we consider it appropriate;
- provide appropriate assistance for as long as a dispute continues;
- explain to the parties that they alone are responsible for their decisions and any agreements reached.

Arbitration and mediation in disputes

Arbitration involves the parties jointly asking a third party to make an award which they undertake to accept in settlement of the dispute. Mediation involves the third party making recommendations as a basis for settlement. ACAS will normally agree to arrange arbitration or mediation only when it has not been possible to produce a conciliated settlement.

We will:

- maintain a panel of independent, impartial and skilled arbitrators and mediators from whom we make appointments;
- assist parties to agree clear terms of reference for arbitration or mediation;
- explain to parties that arbitration is to settle the issue between them and they are committed to accepting an award.

Resolving individual disputes

ACAS conciliation officers have a statutory duty to attempt to conciliate settlements of disputes where complaints have been or could be made to an industrial tribunal under most employment protection legislation. Conciliators offer to assist both parties involved in a dispute to reach a voluntary settlement without the need to go to an employment tribunal hearing.

We will:

- write to or telephone applicants and (as necessary) respondents, or their named representatives, giving information about the conciliation process together with a named contact and an offer to conciliate and take prompt further action as soon as requested by either party or, if no request is received, when it is useful to do so;
- keep the parties informed about the options open to them and their possible consequences whilst not expressing an opinion on the merits of a case;
- seek to promote reinstatement or re-engagement, if the complaint is of unfair dismissal, before any other form of settlement;
- not disclose information, given to a conciliation officer in confidence, to any other party unless required to do so by law;
- encourage the parties to consider the consequences of proposed settlement terms and to seek further advice if necessary;
- encourage the parties to record the terms of a settlement in writing as quickly as possible.

▶

| Box 7.5 | Continued |

Providing information and advice and promoting good practice

We provide a country-wide telephone enquiry service ready to respond to queries from individuals on virtually all employment matters (other than job vacancies, health and safety and training), including the rights, protections and obligations which employment law provides. We do not provide legal advice for particular cases. In certain circumstances we can provide more extensive advisory assistance and we also publish advice and promote good industrial relations practice.

Advisory assistance

Where an enquiry is too complex to deal with in a telephone conversation, we will

- suggest an appropriate ACAS or other publication, or
- suggest an appropriate ACAS conference, seminar, or workshop, or
- arrange a meeting at a mutually agreeable time and place, or
- see personal callers promptly or make an appointment with a named member of staff,
- suggest other sources of help, such as trade unions, employers' associations and Citizens Advice Bureaux, the Commission for Racial Equality and the Equal Opportunities Commission.

Publishing advice and promoting good practice

We will use our experience of working with organisations and the results of any research we carry out to promote good industrial relations practice. In particular we will provide:

- conferences;
- seminars;
- small firms workshops;
- advisory booklets, handbooks, occasional papers and other publications.

Source: ‹www.acas.org.uk›

Much the most important third-party intervention by ACAS is *collective conciliation* where employers, trade unions and worker representatives are helped by ACAS to reach mutually acceptable settlements of their disputes. ACAS dealt with over 1300 such requests in 2001–02, with the result of its intervention being a settlement or progress towards a settlement in 89 per cent of cases. The majority of these cases were about pay (44 per cent) with trade union recognition accounting for 27 per cent of cases. Forty-seven per cent of the requests for collective conciliation were received jointly from employers and trade unions, 31 per cent from trade unions, and 12 per cent from employers (ACAS, 2002).

Mediation, where ACAS makes recommendations as a basis for settlement, was less prevalent than conciliation as a form of third-party intervention in 2001–02 although there were over 500 such projects. Here 31 per cent of the cases were about disputes over communication, consultation and employee involvement; 24 per cent were about collective bargaining arrangements; 23 per cent concerned organisational effectiveness and change handling; and 13 per cent were about pay.

As arbitration involves the parties to disputes handing power to the third party it is hardly surprising that arbitration is much less popular than conciliation or mediation as a form of dispute resolution. Sixty-eight cases of ACAS arbitration were recorded in 2001–02 with approximately two-thirds concerning pay issues and the remainder the settlement of disputes involving dismissal and discipline (ACAS, 2002).

7.11 Summary

- Collective bargaining is defined as: 'a voluntary, formalised process by which employers and independent trade unions negotiate, for specified groups of employees, terms and conditions of employment and the ways in which certain employment related issues are to be regulated at national, organisational and workplace levels'. It has three functions: market, governmental and decision-making.
- The structure of collective bargaining can be analysed in terms of the levels at which it operates, the units and agents involved, the scope of the agreements, and the form they take.
- There has been a significant decline in the coverage of collective bargaining in the UK and, to a lesser extent, in other developed economies.
- There is now some legal support for trade unions claiming recognition rights for collective bargaining. However, collective bargaining in the UK is essentially voluntary in nature, and agreements are not legally enforceable although the content of collective agreements is normally incorporated into individual contracts of employment.
- Many employers have withdrawn from national level multi employer bargaining and devolve the responsibility for much bargaining activity to workplace level.
- The three stages of negotiation are preparing to negotiate, negotiating, and concluding negotiations.
- There has been a significant decline in the incidence of industrial action in recent years due to changes in employment structure, improved employee relations processes, improved means of dispute resolution, and legislative changes.
- ACAS performs a number of employee relations functions, including intervention in the resolution of collective disputes.

References

ACAS (2002) *Annual Report 2001–2002*, London, Advisory, Conciliation and Arbitration Service.

Bean, R. (1994) *Comparative Industrial Relations: An introduction to cross-national perspectives*, London, Routledge.

Blyton, P. and Turnbull, P. (1998) *The Dynamics of Employee Relations* (2nd edn), Basingstoke, Macmillan.

Brown, W., Marginson, P. and Walsh, J. (1995) 'Management: pay determination and collective bargaining', *in* Edwards, P. (ed.), *Industrial Relations: Theory and practice in Britain*, Oxford, Blackwell, 123–50.

Burchill, F. (1997) *Labour Relations* (2nd edn), Basingstoke, Macmillan.

Chamberlain, N. and Kuhn, J. (1965) *Collective Bargaining*, New York, McGraw-Hill.

Clegg, H. (1979) *The Changing System of Industrial Relations in Britain*, Oxford, Basil Blackwell.

Cully, M., Woodland, S., O'Reilly, A. and Dix, G. (1999) *Britain at Work*, London, Routledge.

Davies, J. (1999) 'Labour disputes in 1998', *Labour Market Trends*, June, 299–313.

Davies, J. (2001) 'Labour disputes in 2000', *Labour Market Trends*, June, 302.

Donovan, T.N. (1968) *Royal Commission on Trade Unions and Employers' Associations 1965–1968*, Report Cmnd. 3623, London, HMSO.

Edwards, P. (1995) *Industrial Relations: Theory and practice in Britain*, Oxford, Blackwell.

Farnham, D. (1997) *Employee Relations in Context*, Wimbledon, Institute of Personnel and Development.

Farnham, D. and Pimlott, J. (1995) *Understanding Industrial Relations* (5th edn), London, Cassell.

Fatchett, D. (1989) 'Workplace bargaining in hospitals and schools: threat or opportunity for the unions?', *Industrial Relations Journal*, 20:4, 253–9.

Gennard, J. and Judge, G. (2003) *Employee Relations* (3rd edn), Wimbledon, Chartered Institute of Personnel and Development.

HMSO (1980) *Code of Practice: Picketing*, London, HMSO.

Hollinshead, G. and Leat, M. (1995) *Human Resource Management: An international and comparative perspective*, London, Pitman.

Kessler, S. and Bayliss, F. (1998) *Contemporary British Industrial Relations* (3rd edn), London, Macmillan.

Kjellberg, A. (1998) 'Sweden: restoring the model?', *in* Ferner, A. and Hyman, R. (eds), *Changing Industrial Relations in Europe*, Oxford, Blackwell, pp. 74–117.

Pfeffer, J. (1998) 'Six dangerous myths about pay', *Harvard Business Review*, May–June, 109–19.

Pilbeam, S. and Corbridge, M. (1997) 'Employee relations skills', *in* Farnham, D. (ed.), *Employee Relations in Context*, Wimbledon, Institute of Personnel and Development, pp. 123–54.

Salamon, M. (2000) *Industrial Relations: Theory and practice* (4th edn), Hemel Hempstead, Prentice Hall.

Sisson, K. (1987) *The management of collective bargaining: an international comparison*, Oxford, Blackwell; cited by Blyton, P. and Turnbull, P. (1998) *The Dynamics of Employee Relations* (2nd edn), Basingstoke, Macmillan.

Storey, J. and Sisson, K. (1993) *Managing Human Resources and Industrial Relations*, Buckingham, Open University Press.

Thornhill, A., Lewis, P., Millmore, M. and Saunders, M. (2000) *Managing Change: A human resource strategy approach*, London, Financial Times Prentice Hall.

Torrington, D. and Hall, L. (2002) *Human Resource Management* (5th edn), London, Prentice Hall.

self-check Answers

7.1 *What advantages do you think managers may derive from collective bargaining?*

There are several potential advantages. First, there is the time and cost saving to be enjoyed by managers who have to deal with only a limited number of union officials (perhaps only one) rather than conduct negotiations with numerous employees at an individual level. You may counter this by saying that managers may decide key employment issues without employee involvement. But this may lead to charges of inconsistency, with one employee being treated more favourably than another. This is another potential advantage. The larger the organisation, the more the need for consistency in procedures and, arguably, the greater consistency and fairness that will result if the interests of employees are fully taken into account when procedures are defined.

Another potential advantage for managers is that collective bargaining gives greater legitimacy, in the eyes of employees, to decisions about their working lives (Blyton and Turnbull, 1998). In the short term this, of course, means that managers are able to achieve the sort of changes they wish. In the longer term this leads to more effective employment relations, since employee resistance is much less likely. Related to this is the argument that, by agreeing to bargain over some issues, employees are signalling their willingness to compromise over possibly contentious issues. Moreover, the willingness to bargain over some issues is an implicit agreement that other issues are the subject of management prerogative (Sisson, 1987).

7.2. *What are the arguments for and against single-table bargaining?*

Storey and Sisson (1993) summarise these as follows.

Arguments for:

- Saves time through having to deal with only one set of negotiations.
- Reduces the possibility of inconsistencies of application of procedures across bargaining units.
- Reduces the possibility of one union promoting a higher claim in order to leap-frog the deal achieved by a union in a previous set of negotiations.
- Enhances the move towards harmonisation of terms and conditions of employment, in particular between blue- and white-collar employees.
- Reinforces the notion of unions and management working together in partnership to forge harmonious employment relations.

Arguments against:

- The cost of 'levelling up' terms and conditions of employment.
- Loss of opportunity to 'play one group off against another' (Storey and Sisson, 1993: 207).
- Danger that negotiations spend too much time on specific issues that affect a minority of (possibly powerful) employees.
- Loss of identity of individual trade unions.

7.3. *What arguments would you use to persuade senior managers of the virtues of single-employer bargaining?*

Salamon (2000) suggests that a more positive approach to the management of employment relations is possible. This comes from the more direct control that managers have over their own employment relations destiny. They control pay costs rather than have these imposed upon them by a multi-employer deal. This means that they can integrate pay policy with other HR policies and strategies with a view to improve organisational performance. In addition, you could argue that both management and employee representatives are likely to be more committed to a bargain they have struck. This is particularly important in deals that involve changes in working practices. The commitment of employees is vital in order that such change may be effective.

CASE 7	Bargaining for change at Magnox Electric plc[1]

Magnox Electric plc employs over 3000 staff in managerial, professional, technical, industrial and administrative roles. Most of the staff are employed in 10 nuclear power stations in different parts of the UK. Magnox Electric is one of the electricity generating companies that was part of the Central Electricity Generating Board (CEGB) that existed in the UK until the privatisation of the electric supply industry in the Thatcherite reforms of the public sector in the 1980s and early 1990s. In 1990 the industry was divided into four main private sector companies: National Power, Powergen, Nuclear Electric, and the National Grid. The area electricity boards were sold within the commercial sector.

The collective bargaining arrangements that existed under the Central Electricity Generating Board were, in the words of Magnox Electric's industrial relations manager Philip Parker,

'typically 1970s in that they were multi-employer (including CEGB, the Electricity Council and the area boards, each of which was a separate employer in its own right), highly proceduralised and characterised by an extremely complex set of formal arrangements with several trade unions.'

There were different bargaining and consultation arrangements for different groups of staff, with joint committees that operated at national, district and works level.

The post-1990 period saw a reform of the collective bargaining arrangements. Each of the four main generating companies set up separate arrangements. Nuclear Electric, the forerunner of Magnox Electric, developed an industrial relations strategy that consisted of two main principles. The first of these was the removal of management grades from formal bargaining. The terms and conditions of these managers were defined in personal contracts. The second principle was the development of *single-table bargaining*, whereby all the separate joint committees for bargaining and consultation were merged into one. This had the effect of reducing the size of the book of joint regulations from 200 pages to 30. This was accompanied by a *framework agreement*, which included harmonised terms and conditions for most employee groups.

According to Philip Parker the relationship between the employer and the various trade unions in the electricity supply industry has always been good, even during the 1990s, which saw dramatic reductions in the number of staff (Nuclear Electric, for example, reduced headcount from 14 500 to 8000). This has been due to a shared concern by all in the industry to reflect a public service ethos by demonstrating the highest possible concern for safety and to 'keep the lights on'. In addition, the nuclear electric industry is one that is particularly sensitive to adverse publicity. This had had the effect of ensuring that all involved in the industry 'pull together'.

The conflict-free relationship between the employer and the trade unions was enhanced by a significant decrease in the power of trade unions in the 1990s. This decrease was due to two main factors: the general decline in influence of trade unions in the UK economy, and the creation of an internal market in electricity supply as a result of the creation of separate companies in the industry that were in

---

[1] The assistance of Philip Parker (Magnox) in the preparation of this case is gratefully acknowledged.

competition with one another. This second factor limited the ability of trade unions to threaten discontinuity of production. Such a disruption would leave the way open for a competitor to supply customers and prejudice the commercial viability of the company threatened with disruption.

In 1996 Nuclear Electric demerged into separate operating companies, and Magnox Electric plc was created. This resulted in a further reform of collective bargaining and consultation arrangements and the creation of the Magnox Joint Council (MJC). This joint body comprises members from the employer and five trade unions:

- TGWU;
- Unison;
- GMB;
- Prospect (formerly EMA and IPMS);
- Amicus (formerly AEEU and MFS).

The recognition agreement between Magnox Electric and the five unions that defines the activities of the MJC covers virtually all the company's staff, the exception being the managerial grades. The collective bargaining scope of the MJC is covered by four main headings. These are:

- issues that are the subject of joint negotiation: these are the traditional items such as pay, holidays, sick pay, shift allowances and work pattern payments, discipline procedures and maternity rights;
- issues that are jointly agreed but that are not necessarily the subject of joint negotiation: such issues include the application of working time regulations and consultation on the use of subcontractors;
- issues that are the subject of joint consultation 'in good faith': examples here include policies on stress management, drugs and alcohol abuse, equal opportunities, organisational and manpower changes and harassment;
- discussion on 'wider business issues': this category may include anything that may be relevant to employee interests, such as business planning, strategic objectives, safety strategy, and general 'stakeholder dialogue'.

The recognition agreement also includes details on time off for trade union duties for trade union officials and a procedure for the settlement of differences, although, according to Philip Parker, this is never used. An important plank in this settlement of differences procedure is that work will continue even in the event of a dispute. This is seen to be imperative in the light of health and safety strictures and the agreement under which nuclear sites are licensed. The procedure allows for either side to refer a disagreement to a third party for conciliation or, eventually, for arbitration.

The effective working relationship between Magnox Electric and the trade unions through the MJC has led to the creation of what Philip Parker has called 'the most significant agreement in the history of the industry'. This is the *Lifetime Partnership Agreement*. The Lifetime Partnership Agreement is a response to the unique circumstances of the nuclear power station industry. Power stations have a planned lifespan of 20–30 years with a lengthy period of defuelling and decommissioning when they cease to generate electricity. Consequently, stations progressively need fewer staff to operate them, with the resultant need for redundancies. From the point of view of redundancy management this situation at least has the virtue that redundancies can be planned for years ahead. But management need to retain the services of key staff during the defuelling and decommissioning phases. Moreover, those staff need to be motivated to produce a high level of professionalism consistent with the concern for health and safety. This means that redundancies need to be conducted in a manner that engenders the commitment of staff. According to Philip Parker, 'management and unions saw this as an opportunity to learn from what happened in the coal-mining industry and learn from the mistakes made in that industry.'

The climate that exists in Magnox Electric is obviously one of uncertainty. Although cessation of electricity generation in power stations is certain, the dates of such cessation may be sooner than expected in some stations. In addition, the rate and pattern of staff dispersal cannot always be predicted with the certainty that staff would prefer. The company also stress in the Lifetime Partnership Agreement that job content is likely to change considerably. Therefore flexibility and skill development must play an important part in the agreement.

The Lifetime Partnership Agreement, which covers all permanent staff and runs from 2002 to 2010, consists of seven elements:

■ redundancy and severance arrangements;
■ faster pension build-up;
■ counselling support;
■ learning support;
■ outplacement support;
■ co-operation, flexibility and performance; and
■ model organisational change principles.

Redundancy and severance arrangements

The agreement makes clear that the emphasis is on retaining staff for much of the period but that redundancies are inevitable at major change points. Voluntary redundancy will be encouraged, but staff who are asked to leave at the end of the organisational change process will be consulted, as will trade unions. Moreover, selection for redundancy will be against fair and transparent criteria. The redundancy terms are generous. Staff with up to 6 years' service receive 6 months' salary. Staff with between 6 and 22 years' service receive a month's salary for each year's service, with a maximum of 22 months. Accrued pension benefits are available from the age of 50.

Faster pension build-up

The company will set up ways in which staff can build up their pension benefits faster than in the past, to improve their financial position in retirement. The aim is to support staff who will not be able to earn the pension benefits that would have been available to them had the employment lasted longer.

Counselling support

The company is setting up independent professional financial counselling support for staff and their families. This will be devoted in particular to personal finances and pension issues.

Learning support

This will take two forms: learning support for skills aimed at enhancing the performance of the organisation, and opportunities for personal development and growth. The latter element is a particularly significant element of the Lifetime Partnership Agreement. It provides professional career counselling and the creation of a personal learning account, which enables staff to have financial support and extra paid leave to allow the learning of new skills. These new skills do not have to be linked to the individual's job at Magnox.

Outplacement support

In addition to the provision under the heading of learning support the agreement provides for funds to be made available for outplacement/further training. This may include individual counselling, development of job search skills, CV preparation support, interview skills training, and advice on self-employment.

Cooperation, flexibility and performance

This part of the Lifetime Partnership Agreement emphasises the need for cooperation by trade unions and staff in achieving the following objectives: rapid adaptation to a changing business environment, the development of broader skills; new approaches to resourcing business activities; and a full contribution to the high performance standards. The agreement also notes the management expectation that future pay settlements must reflect broader public sector pay arrangements and the cost of the benefits package under the Lifetime Partnership Agreement.

Model organisational change principles

The key features of this final element of the agreement are:

- a first stage of counselling where any organisational change affects staff. This will include future organisation, advice on relocation opportunities, opportunities elsewhere and full details of the release package;
- an HR planning exercise assessing staff suitability for remaining posts using fair and transparent criteria. The outcome of the assessment process, along with outcome of the previous counselling stage, will form the basis of selection for the next stage;
- an independent review of selection proposals;
- a second stage of counselling, where staff are informed of the outcome of the selection process;
- the opportunity to appeal against selection decision;
- the deferment of some final decisions to allow for the potential redeployment of staff members who are prepared and suitable to move to other business units.

▶

The Lifetime Partnership Agreement ends with an expression of the wish that in 2010 those signing the agreement will be able to say that motivated staff were treated well; the right people had been retained and recruited; change had been accomplished in a cost-effective way; a good relationship between management and trade unions was evident; those staff leaving the organisation felt they had been treated well; and, finally, that a good organisational legacy is in place.

Questions

1 What do you think are the advantages to Magnox Electric of the simplified bargaining arrangements that prevailed upon the fragmentation of the industry?

2 What are the necessary preconditions for the creation of an agreement similar to the Lifetime Partnership Agreement?

3 What would be your argument against the trade union 'traditionalist' who asserted that the Lifetime Partnership Agreement was against the interests of the five unions' members?

Chapter 8

Regulating the employment relationship through employee participation and involvement

At the end of this chapter you should be able to:

- define and differentiate terms used in relation to employee participation and employee involvement;

- recognise philosophical differences between employee participation and employee involvement, and analyse their differing aims;

- examine forms of employee participation and employee involvement, and evaluate differing strategies underpinning the use of methods such as employee communication and joint consultation;

- evaluate attitudes towards the use of employee participation and employee involvement;

- analyse the role of European legislation for the future of employee participation and employee involvement.

8.1 Introduction

Concepts related to employee participation and employee involvement have a long history. Sometimes these concepts have been used in an undifferentiated way, which generates a degree of complexity and even confusion. Our aim in this chapter is to analyse the relationship between employee participation and employee involvement, in order to be able to differentiate between their aims and intended outcomes. Section 8.2 commences this discussion.

Section 8.3 focuses on the nature of employee participation and its occurrence in practice. Section 8.4 focuses on the nature of employee involvement and its use in organisations.

Differentiating between employee participation and employee involvement is made more difficult by the fact that some of the methods used to achieve either approach overlap in relation to their terminology. It is therefore necessary to differentiate between forms of information provision, communication and consultation to be able to understand how these techniques may be used to support either approach (Section 8.5). Section 8.6 analyses developments emanating from the European Union for the future of employee participation and employee involvement. After studying this chapter, we hope that you will be able to relate the aims and practices associated with employee participation and with employee involvement to other aspects of the management of the employment relationship. A case study exploring these approaches within an organisation is included at the end of the chapter.

8.2 Understanding the terminology of and philosophical differences between employee participation and employee involvement and their differing aims

Over several decades a number of terms or concepts have emerged that categorise approaches to the participation of employees in relation to the making and implementation of organisational decisions that affect them. These terms include *employee* or *worker participation* and *employee involvement*. An agreed set of definitions does not exist through which we may understand and differentiate these terms. In some cases, these terms are used as synonyms. For example, Marchington *et al.* (1992: 7) reported that 'the [British] Employment Department ... consider[ed] the terms "employee participation" and "employee involvement" to be synonymous.' This is partly understandable in terms of the way in which participation and involvement may be used in relation to one another. For example, to participate voluntarily is likely to lead to a feeling of involvement, and a sense of involvement is likely to lead to some level of participation.

However, a significant conceptual simplification is created if we think of employee participation and employee involvement as synonymous concepts, or if we simply see one as an input and the other as an outcome. The range of definitions that have been advanced through the course of time suggests that participation and involvement should not be treated as a single concept (Wall and Lischeron, 1977). Instead, employee participation and employee involvement strategies will be designed to pursue different aims and outcomes. This was recognised by Brannen (1983: 13), who understood that if these concepts are merged, this would imply that: 'individuals or groups may influence, control, be involved in, exercise power within, or be able to intervene in decision-making within organisations.' Processes or outcomes such as *influence*, *control*, *involvement*, the *exercise of power* and *interventions in decision-making* imply many different types of practice and intention. Even where an umbrella term has been used to consider different forms of participation, such as by Eldridge *et al.* (1991) who asked, 'Whatever happened to industrial democracy?', significant distinctions are evident in the resulting analysis related to the exercise of power and control and the nature of employee influence.

Consideration of some definitions for employee participation and employee involvement respectively allow us to start to recognise important differences that exist between these concepts in relation to the exercise of power, the locus of control, the nature of employee influence, and the driving force behind each approach in practice. These are set out in Box 8.1.

These definitions indicate a contrast between employee participation and employee involvement. This contrast is evident in relation to a number of dimen-

---

Box 8.1 Definitions of employee participation and employee involvement

The Royal Commission on Trade Unions and Employers' Associations (Donovan, 1968: 257) included a brief chapter on 'Workers' participation in management', and referred to this as 'participation by workers and their representatives, over and above issues dealt with in collective bargaining, in decisions concerning the running of the undertaking'.

Brannen (1983: 16) said that 'workers' participation is about the distribution and exercise of power, in all its manifestations, between the owners and managers of organisations and those employed by them. It refers to the direct involvement of individuals in decisions relating to their immediate work organisation and to indirect involvement in decision-making, through representatives, in the wider socio-technical and political structures of the firm.'

Hyman and Mason (1995: 21) used participation to 'refer to State initiatives which promote the collective rights of employees to be represented in organisational decision-making, or to the consequence of the efforts of employees themselves to establish collective representation in corporate decisions, possibly in the face of employer resistance.'

In contrast, the CBI defined employee involvement in 1988 (cited in Kessler and Bayliss, 1998: 125) as 'a range of processes designed to engage the support, understanding and optimum contribution of all employees in an organisation and their commitment to its objectives'.

In 1991, the CBI and the then Department of Employment launched an initiative called 'Managing for Success – Improving business performance through employee involvement'. This described the purpose of employee involvement as being to 'promote business success through a combination of practices and systems designed to secure the maximum awareness and commitment of all employees in an enterprise to its objectives' (CBI/EDG, 1991).

The Chartered Institute of Personnel and Development and the Industrial Participation Association developed an Employee Involvement Code, dating back to 1982, one of whose aims was to 'generate commitment of all employees to the success of the organisation' (IPM/IPA, 1982).

---

sions. These relate to the promotion of participation or involvement, its intended purpose, the exercise of power, locus of control, and the nature of employee influence. Further dimensions related to the practice of employee participation and employee involvement have been identified that help to differentiate between these approaches. These relate to the scope, level and form of employee participation or involvement (e.g. Marchington *et al.*, 1992). We shall now explore each of these sets of dimensions to differentiate between these approaches, first in relation to employee participation and then in relation to employee involvement.

8.3 Employee participation

■ Promotion of participation

Employee participation has been promoted in three principal ways. Participation has been promoted by the State; at a supra-governmental level by the European Union (EU); and more generally through the activity of trade unions and workforce agitation. We shall consider the promotion of employee participation by the EU in a later section in this chapter, when we look at the establishment of European Works

Councils and the requirement for structures to be set up within organisations for the purpose of informing and consulting employees within Member States. The discussion that follows considers the attitude of the British State to employee participation over recent decades and its status in UK employing organisations as a result, as well as its attempted promotion more generally through activities by trade unions and groups of employees.

This discussion initially focuses on events in the 1970s, as this was a 'high-water mark' for employee participation in the context of the UK. Following the return of a Labour government in 1974, a Committee of Inquiry chaired by Lord Bullock was established in 1975 to consider how 'a radical extension of industrial democracy in the control of companies by means of representation on boards of directors' could be achieved (Bullock, 1977: v). This was to be designed to incorporate trade union representation as an essential element of this form of employee participation.

Before this period in the UK, the idea of this type of employee participation had not received such State support. The reference in Box 8.1 to the Royal Commission on Trade Unions and Employers' Associations between 1965 and 1968, chaired by Lord Donovan, is revealing in the sense that the ensuing report included only one chapter (of just 10 paragraphs) out of 16 that explicitly considered employee participation. The report acknowledged the importance of this aspect of industrial relations, but gave two reasons for considering this matter only briefly:

> First, we are agreed that any changes which might be made in order to facilitate and encourage such participation should be subsidiary to our main proposals for the reform of collective bargaining; and, secondly, we have been unable to agree upon changes which might be expected to have the desired effect. (Donovan, 1968: 257)

A significant reason underpinning the lack of agreement about how to promote employee participation in company decision-making at this time (Brannen *et al.*, 1976) was the prevalence of the view that had been advanced by the eminent industrial relations academic, Hugh Clegg (1951, reproduced in McCarthy, 1972: 74), that 'trade unions [are] an Opposition which can never become a Government.' Participation in corporate decision-making, according to this view, would have significantly compromised what was seen as the essentially oppositional role that the trade unions needed to play.

Having stated that employee participation essentially required board-level representation for employees and trades unions, the Bullock Committee suggested how this should be implemented, as we outline briefly below. However, this proposal for board-level employee participation was highly contested. The Committee actually produced two reports: a main report signed by its trade union and academic members, who constituted a numerical majority, and a minority report signed by its employers' representatives. The main report recommended the introduction of employee representatives onto redefined company boards, in private sector organisations over a certain employment size, in equal numbers to shareholder board members, with a third group of directors to be co-opted through agreement between these employee and shareholder representatives.

Those signing the minority report disagreed not only with the recommendations in the main report but also about the remit given to the Committee. They believed that

'"Industrial democracy" is a term which can all too easily be applied to a wide range of developments, some good, some in our view, bad. ... Certainly it is unwise to impose "democracy" on those who are unwilling or unready to receive it' (Bullock, 1977: 171). However, the views expressed in the minority report were but a 'pale reflection' of the depth of feeling of many British employers against the proposals being made for corporate-level employee participation at this time (Cressey *et al.*, 1985: 2). This was in spite of the fact that the authors of the main report promoted their recommendations in terms of a model of participation that they believed would incorporate employee interests with those of employers in order to produce greater efficiency:

> Sooner or later, we believe, this is a decision which will have to be taken... We believe the change in attitude of the TUC and their willingness to accept a share of responsibility for the increased efficiency and prosperity of British companies offer an opportunity to create a new basis for relations in industry which should not be allowed to pass. ... For if we look beyond our immediate problems it appears to us certain that the criterion of efficiency in the world of tomorrow ... will be the capacity of industry to adapt to an increasing rate of economic and social change. (Bullock, 1977: 161)

This aim of incorporation of employee interests with those of employing organisations is one view of the intended purpose of employee participation. We shall consider this and other views in more detail below.

A White Paper on Industrial Democracy was subsequently published in 1978. This proposed establishing a two-tier board structure with a statutory right for employee representatives, following an employee ballot, to sit on an envisaged policy (as opposed to a management) board in companies with over 2000 employees (Cressey *et al.*, 1985). However, with the return to power of a Conservative government in 1979 these proposals for a statutory approach to participation were eschewed. The stated preference of this government was to leave any arrangements for participation as a voluntary matter for companies to make decisions about how they might wish to involve employees (e.g. Kessler and Bayliss, 1998). This remained the view of the Conservative governments throughout the 1980s and 1990s.

The result of this failed attempt in the 1970s and the continued espoused policy of voluntarism throughout the 1980s and 1990s meant that the UK did not develop a statutory framework for employee participation. Only two countries in the EU at the beginning of this century did not have a statutory framework for consultation or participation – Ireland and the UK. We return to consider the recent establishment of such a statutory framework – albeit limited to information and consultation rights – in the section below that examines recent developments in the EU.

Of course, other forms of employee participation had long existed below company board level. The Bullock Committee's main report (1977) believed that such forms were necessary, and that these would be complementary to their proposals for statutory employee participation on company boards. Participation at below board level was seen in this report as any form that permitted employees, or more particularly trade unions, jointly to regulate issues affecting employment in an organisation. Three main categories relating to participation at this lower level have usually been identified. *Collective bargaining* has traditionally been seen as the primary means of joint regulation and participation. *Consultation* that effectively allows for some sort of veto over particular management proposals has also been seen as an important means to permit participation. Finally, the *provision of information* has been seen as necessary for participation but not as a form in its own right, according to Bullock.

The strength of the trade unions, at least in general terms, was seen as great enough in the 1970s to promote the development of employee participation at below board level. However, over the next two decades the reduced power of the trade unions and the diminishing scope and effectiveness of collective bargaining (discussed in Chapter 7) reversed their ability to promote employee participation at this level.

■ The intended purpose of participation, nature of employee influence, exercise of power and locus of control

In the definitions cited above and discussion so far, employee participation has been used to emphasise some degree of power sharing and regulatory ability in relation to organisational decision-making, by (or on behalf of) a group of employees. However, even within analyses that consider only employee participation (as opposed to involvement) there are different views about the extent of power sharing and therefore the nature of employee influence and the locus of control. In broad terms, participation can be used to describe a range of situations where employees exercise either less than equal power over decision-making in comparison with management, or equal power, or even greater power than management where workers determine the outcome (Brannen, 1983).

The latter scenario is often referred to as *workers' control* (e.g. Coates and Topham, 1970; Eldridge *et al.*, 1991). These alternative situations indicate a very different approach to and outcome from employee participation in each case. A question has also been raised about the types of decision that may be open to employee influence. It is therefore useful to discuss a number of dimensions of employee participation that have been identified, to be able to analyse different types of participation in practice. These dimensions relate to the degree or depth, scope, level and form of employee participation (e.g. Schuchman, 1957; Poole, 1975; Marchington, 1980; Marchington *et al.*, 1992; Blyton and Turnbull, 1998). We shall now consider these four dimensions and use them to analyse types of employee participation.

Degree of participation relates to the extent of employees' influence, or the level of their control, over the way in which a decision is reached. As indicated in the previous paragraph, this may vary along a continuum that ranges from no influence through to control over a particular decision. In between these two extremes lie a number of possibilities. One of the earliest attempts to categorise these possibilities (Schuchman, 1957) recognised a number of key points along such a continuum. In ascending order of influence, these are rights to receive information, raise objections, make suggestions, be consulted, reject a proposal either temporarily or permanently, make a decision jointly with management, and exercise sole control over a decision (Poole, 1975; Marchington, 1980). The first four points of this continuum indicate a low level of participation, as we now consider.

As we referred to above, the Bullock Report (1977) recognised that the provision of information, although necessary for participation, should not be seen as a form in its own right. Any right to raise objections or make suggestions, although permitting some level of employee influence, does little to alter management's power to determine any decision. The Bullock Report also recognised that the nature of consultation varied, and believed that only those forms that permit some sort of veto over particular management proposals should be seen as a means to permit participation. For such reasons, these activities (providing information through to non-veto forms of consultation) have been seen as being promoted by management to encourage 'cooperation' (Schuchman, 1957; Poole, 1975; Marchington, 1980) (see Figure 8.1). In terms of our differentiation here between employee involvement and employee participation, these activities would be manifestations of the former rather than the latter. Participation in this sense must therefore be seen as commencing from the point where employees have a right either to veto a proposal advanced by management or to be involved in the conception of proposals from their earliest formulation (see Figure 8.1). Consequently, *joint regulation* and/or *co-determination*, indicating the exercise of equal power, are usually used as terms to indicate employee participation in decision-making.

Pateman's (1970) categorisation differentiates between three degrees of participation indicated by *full*, *partial* and *pseudo* approaches. Only the first is seen as proper participation. Joint regulation or co-determination would be an example of full participation in decision-making. Non-veto forms of consultation and similar activities exemplify partial participation, indicating the exercise of less than equal influence over decision making in comparison to management. Managerial activities, such as the dissemination of information (discussed later), that seek to persuade employees about decisions that have already been made are seen as pseudo participation. Pseudo participation in this categorisation would again be analogous to employee involvement.

However, even if we have reached an understanding about what is meant by participation in relation to the degree of influence conferred by such activity, there is still a weakness inherent in this approach related to the types of decision that may be open to such employee influence. In this way, participation in some decisions may apparently

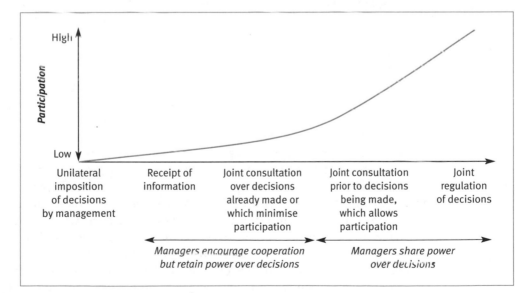

Figure 8.1 **Degree of participation**

confer a high level of influence; however, the limited nature of these decisions in rela-tion to the functioning of an organisation may result in the maintenance of a high level of managerial control and a low level of employees' control. Examples of this would include full participation in relation to choosing the employee of the year or the charg-ing policy about parking at work but only partial or pseudo participation in relation to matters of a more strategic or direct operational nature. The *scope* of the decisions that are subject to employee participation is therefore a critical aspect in assessing the nature of employees' influence and the locus of control in an organisation.

The scope of decisions that might be subject to employee participation may be placed into one or more different categories that in turn help us to understand the nature of employees' influence and control in a given organisation. For example, Marchington (1980) and Marchington *et al.* (1992) differentiate between the scope to participate in decision-making about strategic, operational and individual task issues. Scope to engage in decision-making about task matters, perhaps through col-lective bargaining, while providing a significant means for participation will, however, prove to be considerably different from the scope to participate in strategic decision-making in the way envisaged in the Bullock Report (1977; see also Kessler and Bayliss, 1998). Of course, in practice participation may range across more than one of these domains, as well as none. It is therefore important to identify not only whether participation exists but also the range of activities included in a given organ-isation in order to be able to assess the nature of employees' influence.

This provides a link to the *levels* at which employee participation may take place within a particular organisation. We recognised above that participation has been associated with employee influence at the strategic decision-making level of an organisation, through some form of representation at board level. Such representa-tion may occur at main board level, or at the subsidiary board of an operating unit within a multidivisional type of organisation. For the Bullock Committee, representa-tion at such strategic decision-making boards was the key to employee participation. Other types of employee participation at a lower level within an organisation were seen as being complementary. Such other forms, referred to above and discussed in detail below and elsewhere in this book, include collective bargaining and participa-tion through works council style representation.

The significance of employee participation occurring at board level has been recognised in the literature. Poole (1975) and Brannen (1983), for example, elabo-rated on the significance of participation occurring at a strategic level. It has been recognised that, where participation only occurs at an operational level, whether in a division, business unit or department, its scope is likely to be limited significantly by decisions taken at a higher strategic level. It has also been recognised that participa-tion may occur at such strategic and operational levels but be restricted to particular issues, such as health and safety, the transfer of undertakings, redundancies or the management of pension funds, because specific statutory rights underpin its use in these areas. It is also important to recognise that, even where participation has occurred at a strategic level in the UK context in a limited number of cases in the past, its scope has been limited *in practice* by a range of logistical and attitudinal problems (see Brannen *et al.*, 1976; Brannen, 1983; Cressey *et al.*, 1985; Eldridge *et al.*, 1991). For example, greater management familiarity with, and in-depth knowl-edge of, strategic matters, as well as their control over information, gives them a significant advantage over employee representatives. This is an issue that we return to when we discuss the practice of European Works Councils below.

As we have recognised, employee participation is likely to manifest itself in the *form* of formal and elected representation on established organisational decision-making bodies, such as board-level participation, or on other specially convened bodies such as works councils, or through the machinery established for collective bargaining. It is therefore likely to be indirect to the majority of employees whose interests are being represented at these decision-making bodies. Those who hold such representative positions may be personally known to those whom they represent, or they may be fairly distant from them in the sense of being elected as professional trade union officials who have little day-to-day contact with an organisation's workforce.

Through these dimensions, it is possible to differentiate employee participation from employee involvement (discussed in detail below). We shall use these dimensions in our discussion of employee involvement to compare its aims in relation to those for employee participation. These dimensions also provide a means to analyse practices across a range of countries, of which we shall include a discussion about developments in the European Union later in this chapter. However, it is important that we examine the extent to which employee participation, according to this differentiation, is seen in action in the current UK context.

Participation in practice

There is little evidence of employee participation at the level of corporate decision-making in the UK context in the early twenty-first century, in the way envisaged in the Bullock Committee's main report in 1977. References to such forms of participation are historical and refer to experiments in the steel industry and in the Post Office, as well as to a small number of other cases (e.g. Brannen *et al.*, 1976; Eldridge *et al.*, 1991). There are nevertheless employee representatives on the corporate boards of some organisations in the public sector/services. For example, if you are reading this chapter as a student at a university or a college, there are likely to be student and employee representatives on its governing body. However, the proportion of student and employee representatives in relation to the total number of people sitting on this body is likely to be small, suggesting a limited degree of participation.

The prevalent forms of employee participation in the UK context centre on the existence of collective bargaining, joint consultation arrangements and works councils. The extent of these forms, as well as their depth and scope, has been reported through the Workplace Employee Relations Survey (WERS) series (e.g. Millward *et al.*, 1992; Cully *et al.*, 1999; Millward *et al.*, 2000) and the Employment in Britain research programme (Gallie *et al.*, 1998). Collective bargaining is explored in Chapter 7. However, it is worth briefly considering some of the available data about collective bargaining, to understand the extent of employee participation that this process permits through scope for joint regulation of aspects of the employment relationship.

Millward *et al.* (2000) report that the coverage of collective bargaining has reduced significantly over the past two decades. In 1984, 86 per cent of employees in unionised workplaces employing 25 or more people had their pay and conditions determined through collective bargaining. In terms of all workplaces employing 25 or more people, 70 per cent of employees were covered by collective bargaining in

1984. By 1998, only 67 per cent of employees in unionised workplaces of this size were covered by collective bargaining. In terms of all workplaces with 25 or more employees, by 1998 only 40 per cent were covered by collective bargaining. Complementary data taken from employee perceptions about levels of union influence over decision-making at the workplace have been produced by Gallie *et al.* (1998). They report (1998: 101) that 'while 63 per cent believed that the unions had either a great deal or a fair amount of influence over pay, only 25 per cent thought this was true for the way in which work is organised.' Given the reduced presence of unions and generally lower membership densities in workplaces by 1998 compared with earlier years, particularly in the private sector (Millward *et al.*, 2000), this indicates a somewhat limited scope for collectively based forms of employee participation. The possibility for participation in decision-making will be constrained both by the restricted presence and strength of unions in the workplace and by limitations placed on their scope to negotiate about broader issues affecting their members even where they are present.

Given the limited extent and scope of employee participation through collective bargaining, we now consider whether forms of consultation offer some means to participate in the regulation of the employment relationship. Cully *et al.* (1999) report that 53 per cent of all workplaces with 25 or more employees in the 1998 WERS had some form of joint consultative arrangement. These take different forms in relation to the organisational level at which consultation occurs. Seventeen per cent of all workplaces of this size were reported as only having a workplace-based consultation committee. Twenty five per cent only have access to a committee at a higher organisational level to facilitate consultation across the organisation. Eleven per cent had arrangements both at individual workplace level and at a higher level to permit consultation to occur across the organisation. Smaller organisations, measured by number of employees, were found to be less likely to engage in formal consultation (80 per cent of organisations employing less than 100 were reported as not having a committee, whereas the opposite was the case for organisations employing over 10 000 employees). Formal consultation arrangements are also much more prevalent in the public, as opposed to the private, sector. Over half of private sector organisations did not have such an arrangement (57 per cent), whereas less than one-fifth of public sector organisations were without a consultative committee (18 per cent). Cully *et al.* (1999) also found that the attitude of management towards employee consultation and the existence of unions was positively related to the likelihood of formal consultation arrangements existing within organisations.

A key question for our consideration is the extent to which these consultation committees permit participation, or at least some level of influence, in the regulation of the employment relationship. Earlier WERS data covering the 1980s (Millward *et al.*, 1992) indicate that about 3 out of 10 consultative committees engaged in both consultation and bargaining. The incidence of bargaining, as opposed to just consultation, was reported as being twice as frequent in the public sector and in private sector manufacturing, compared with private sector services in this period. These sectors (the public sector and private sector manufacturing) were also the ones where union organisation was likely to be more prevalent (Millward *et al.*, 1992).

The 1998 Workplace Employee Relations Survey also offers some information about the extent to which consultative and employee representative arrangements provide a forum for participation through negotiation of issues raised. In organisations where consultative arrangements exist, Cully *et al.* (1999) found that employee participation was restricted in both degree and scope. Negotiation, as opposed to just consultation, occurred only as a minority activity in relation to each of nine issues discussed with survey participants (including pay and conditions, handling grievances, health and safety, and pay systems). In about half of the organisations where consultation occurred, it was reported that there was an absence of any negotiation. The number of issues subject to negotiation in relation to the nine discussed averaged only 1.1 in organisations where there were union representatives and 0.9 where there were non-union representatives (Cully *et al.*, 1999).

From these findings, we may conclude that formal participation in the regulation of the employment relationship is constrained in the current climate. Cully *et al.* (1999) offer two factors to explain this conclusion, which relate to our earlier discussion. First, scope to participate in decisions that affect many workplaces is constrained by the fact that many of these are taken at a higher organisational level, reducing the potential for local managerial as well as employee influence. It was at this higher organisational decision-making level that the political attempt to introduce employee participation in the UK in the 1970s failed. Second, managerial attitudes to employee participation may not be favourably disposed towards joint regulation of the issues that the workforce would like to influence in respect of the decisions to be made. The main report from the Bullock Committee sought to promote participation at the strategic level through a rationale based on achieving the incorporation of employee interests with those of their employing organisations, and through envisaged gains related to greater efficiency and adaptation to change (see page 251 above). However, its means to achieve this, through power sharing, did not find favour with employers, as we recognised above. The power-sharing nature of participation clashed with the unitary conception of governance that appears to be the preferred approach of most employing organisations. For reasons related to this preference, Ramsay (1977) believed that, whenever employing organisations had acquiesced with forms of employee participation in the past, this had been motivated by a desire to offer some degree of influence in order to contain a potentially more fundamental challenge to management's control. His *cycles of control* thesis suggests that management have been willing to adopt a pragmatic approach to forms of employee participation during periods of labour shortages and unrest. Once the period of labour market problems had subsided, management allowed these participative activities to disappear or become trivial.

Ramsay's thesis to explain periods of employee participation principally as the result of a subtle managerial strategy to accommodate tensions arising from labour shortages and unrest has been criticised (e.g. Ackers *et al.*, 1992). The forms of employee involvement that we now consider are motivated by a different and wider managerial strategy than the temporary accommodation of labour market tensions. Hyman and Mason (1995) and Blyton and Turnbull (1998) recognise that employee involvement strategies are not so much about coping with labour market issues, but are a means to address tensions created by competitive product markets, where a key HR strategy is to optimise employee commitment and contribution. We therefore now move to examine employee involvement.

8.1 Think of an organisational situation with which you have some familiarity.

What forms of employee participation, if any, exist in this organisation?
What authority promotes the existence of these forms of employee participation?
Evaluate the practice of these forms of employee participation using the dimensions of
degree or depth, scope, level and form.
What practical problems exist in relation to the exercise of employee participation?

8.4 Employee involvement

■ Promotion of employee involvement

In contrast to the promotion of employee participation as a means of sharing some degree of power in relation to organisational decision-making, employee involvement is promoted by management on a voluntary basis to influence employees' attitudes and workplace behaviours. This approach was supported, in the UK context, by the Conservative governments of the 1980s and 1990s (e.g. CBI/EDG, 1991). These Conservative governments supported the philosophy of voluntarism, aimed at allowing management to introduce forms of involvement as they saw fit rather than having a standard model imposed from some external source. In this way, this support was also a reaction against attempts by the European Commission to promote forms of employee participation. Michael Howard, the Conservative Secretary of State for Employment in the early 1990s, summed up this view in a speech to promote involvement:

> Those who have practical experience in the day-to-day business of industrial relations in this country know that our voluntary approach is the most effective one because it means that firms are free to establish the arrangements which are best suited to their own individual circumstances. A specific model of consultation imposed by community-wide legislation would destroy the flexibility which we believe is essential for effective employee involvement. (Howard, 1991: 14).

■ The intended purpose of involvement, nature of employee influence, exercise of power and locus of control

The nature and purpose of employee involvement has been characterised along a number of dimensions. These allow it to be clearly differentiated from the concept of participation discussed above. One of these dimensions relates to its underpinning philosophy. As we saw in the quotation from Michael Howard's speech in 1991, the philosophy of involvement is related to a free market, non-interventionist stance. Management is promoted as knowing best, and according to this view should be allowed to introduce those initiatives that it wishes to, without outside intervention. Voluntarism is a form of self-determination and is related to non-intervention. This position of managerial ascendancy is also strongly unitarist. The definitions of employee involvement in Box 8.1, with their emphasis on employee awareness of, support for, and commitment and contribution towards organisational objectives, emphasise the underpinning unitary and managerialist nature of involvement initiatives as a further key dimension.

Another dimension flows from this recognition. For the unitary nature of employee involvement to be realised, it is designed primarily as a set of initiatives to appeal to and address employees as individuals. The concept of involvement is an essential component of a range of other individually focused human resource strategies, such as performance and reward management (see Chapter 10).

A further dimension is related to the level at which involvement initiatives are designed to operate within an organisation. These are focused either at the task and workgroup level, or at the corporate level but limited to the provision of information directly to employees rather than being related to any form of power sharing, or more generally through forms of financial involvement. These dimensions are summarised in Table 8.1. We explore these dimensions further through a discussion of the analytical framework that we used above to analyse participation, this time related to employee involvement.

Table 8.1 Dimensions of employee participation and involvement

Participation	Involvement
Fostered by trade unions and through interventionist-style governmental and European Union regulation	Fostered by employers/managerial interests on a voluntary basis, supported by free-market style governments
Pluralist and rights-centred	Unitarist and business-centred
Collectivist in nature	Individualist in nature
Intended to gain representation via employee representatives, who may be members of trade unions	Intended to generate employee commitment and contribution to their employing organisation
Indirect means of participating for most employees	Directly focused on employees, bypassing indirect employee forums in many cases
Power centred, with the aim of achieving operational and strategic influence	Task-centred and focused also on generating communicative and/or financial involvement

Employee involvement initiatives are designed to generate no more than a low or localised *degree* of employee influence. As we recognised in the discussion above about participation, possible involvement through the dissemination of information, communication, the making of suggestions or consultation (see Table 8.2 below for a list of methods for each of these categories) offers employees only very limited influence over decision-making. These are all limited in relation to the degree of power conferred on employees. Although there may be some degree of employee influence exercised through one or more of these means, management's right to make decisions is not subject to any formal means of joint decision-making, and employees do not exercise any right of veto. This is consistent with the essentially unitarist nature of such strategies, where the underlying belief is in the existence of common interests between employees and their employer. With management left to identify what that common interest may be, the intention behind such involvement initiatives is to develop employee cooperation, commitment and contribution, not to share power (e.g. Schuchman, 1957; Poole, 1975; Kessler and Bayliss, 1998).

The involvement initiatives referred to in the above paragraph, ranging from information dissemination to consultation, are labelled as *communicative involvement* by Gallie *et al.* (1998: 96). This allows them to differentiate these initiatives from those that they term *direct participation*. For Gallie *et al.* (1998: 90), 'direct participation is most likely to occur with respect to relatively local decisions about work organisation, since these are the types of decisions where management is particularly likely to benefit from employees' technical knowledge.' This type of involvement is therefore concerned with the granting of some localised employee influence over the way in which work is scheduled and undertaken. The rationale for such task-level involvement, recognised in the Gallie *et al.* quotation, is related to managerial attempts to generate greater efficiency (such as through the reduction of supervisory time) and effectiveness (by tapping into the know-how of employees). Geary (1994) identifies ways in which task involvement may be achieved, including through the use of semi-autonomous work groups, team working and quality management techniques to involve employees. It is important to recognise that granting employee discretion over aspects of work is capable of leading to a higher level of employee influence in comparison with communicative involvement, albeit that any such influence will be very localised and may be more illusory than real. This type of direct involvement is often referred to as *empowerment*, and has been recognised as being a difficult concept to realise in practice, given the nature of the employment relationship in many real-life instances (e.g. Geary, 1994; Marchington, 1995; Cunningham *et al.*, 1996). We return to this issue below when we discuss employee involvement in practice.

The *scope* of decisions that might be subject to employee involvement is therefore limited to task-level issues, indicating a sharp contrast to the nature of decisions that are intended to be subject to employee participation. The scope to become involved in strategic and operational, as opposed to individual task, issues (e.g. Marchington *et al.*, 1992) is restricted to the receipt of information, engagement in communication, opportunities to make suggestions and perhaps also to engage in consultation. This is again consistent with the underpinning unitary approach that drives this strategy, whether this is explicitly recognised and expressed or not. Management strategy in relation to decisions taken at strategic and operational *levels* is to offer scope to receive information about these and perhaps to be able to discuss them, but not to engage in the decision-making process when such decisions are being made. In this sense, involvement is about creating awareness and understanding of strategic and operational issues, with a view to engendering cooperation, commitment and contribution, through the explanation and justification of decisions made by management.

In broad terms, this indicates two principal *forms* of involvement so far: *task-level involvement* and *communicative involvement*. In addition, there is a need to recognise a third form of intended employee engagement with corporate objectives through *financial involvement*. Financial involvement seeks to link some proportion of an employee's reward to organisational performance through schemes such as profit-related pay and employee share ownership. The Conservative governments of the 1980s and 1990s sought to encourage the widespread development of schemes for financial involvement through an extension of related tax relief. This had a considerable impact during this period in terms of the number of schemes that were introduced, with over 2 million employees being covered by such arrangements.

The effectiveness of each of these approaches to employee involvement, in terms of altered attitudes and behaviours, is likely to be dependent on a number of factors, and is a far from simple matter to assess. An important part of any assessment of employee involvement in practice is likely to include employee perceptions about managerial actions and style of leadership. This is likely to be a significant way of assessing whether managerial strategies to engender employee involvement are perceived as marginal, 'bolt-on' approaches, or as a more fundamental and genuine approach to influence and perhaps change the culture of an organisation positively. For this reason, *managerial style* has been judged to be an integral component of involvement, and is recognised to have an important relationship to perceptions about employee involvement in practice (e.g. Marchington, 1992; Storey, 1992; Guest *et al.*, 1993). We may therefore treat managerial style as a means to affect employee involvement, even though it may be seen as a somewhat diffuse and less tangible form of involvement. Conversely, by ignoring managerial actions and style of leadership, an organisation may invest in forms of communicative and task-level involvement but fail to develop any sense of credibility in relation to these where its prevailing style of management is seen as being incongruent with the aims of such initiatives.

In summary, we have identified a number of important principal forms of employee involvement. Related to these, the earlier definitions of employee involvement in Table 8.1 referred to *a range of processes* and *a combination of practices and systems*. These processes, practices and systems may be listed under the principal categories or forms that we have discussed above. Table 8.2 presents these categories of employee involvement, and lists related forms that are associated with each category, together with a brief management rationale.

■ Employee involvement in practice

Millward *et al.* (2000: 136) conclude that by 1998 'there had been a major shift from collective, representative, indirect and union-based voice, to direct, non-union channels.' We review the forms that this major shift took using the typology outlined in Table 8.2, by analysing reported developments in the use of communicative involvement through the provision of downward information and two-way communication, task involvement and financial involvement.

Forms of communicative involvement measured in the Workplace Employee Relations Survey series demonstrate that these continued to develop in terms of their use across the 1980s and 1990s (Cully *et al.*, 1999; Millward *et al.*, 2000). In relation to the provision of information to employees, two-thirds of workplaces provided information about their financial position in 1998. Similarly, over 6 out of 10 organisations composed of multi-site operations provided information to their employees about their financial position. Managers provided information about investment plans to employees in just over half of organisations in 1998. Managers in 6 out of 10 workplaces also provided information to employees about staffing plans in 1998. Only about one in six organisations across all sectors did not provide any of these types of information to their employees according to this survey data. Of particular interest, the 1998 survey data reveal that the increase in the provision of information directly to employees was most pronounced in unionised organisations. Forty-nine per cent of unionised workplaces provided information to employees about their

Table 8.2 **Categories and forms of employee involvement**

Main categories of employee involvement	Examples of related forms	Management's likely rationale
Communicative involvement: information provision/ downward communication	Team briefing; other briefing groups; corporate newspapers, journals and reports aimed at employees; videos; audiotapes; email; recorded telephone briefings	To provide information; uniform messages; to be educative or re-educative
Communicative involvement: problem-solving involvement and upward, two-way communication	Briefing groups with feedback and managerial response loops; quality circles; quality action teams; quality improvement teams; suggestion schemes; employee surveys	Explicit access to employees' experience and skills; gain cooperation and opinions
Communicative involvement: consultation	Joint consultation committees, working parties or groups; staff forums	Providing information and testing reactions
Task involvement at job and work organisation levels	Job redesign: job enlargement and job enrichment. Work reorganisation: team working; (semi) autonomous working groups; 'empowerment'. See also problem-solving involvement	To be re-educative; providing greater levels of motivation and satisfaction; empowering
Financial involvement	Employee share ownership plans; profit-related pay; performance-related pay; bonus schemes	To be re-educative; providing incentives and promoting effort
Managerial actions and style of leadership	Participative managerial style; being visible; accessible and informal; creating credibility; ensuring actions in line with key messages	To provide support; encourage positive working relationships and trust; reduce barriers

Sources: Developed from: CBI/EDG (1991); Ackers *et al.* (1992); Marchington (1992); Storey (1992); Guest *et al.* (1993); Marchington (1995); Kessler and Bayliss (1998); Thornhill *et al.* (2000)

financial position, investment and staffing plans, compared with just 27 per cent of non-union workplaces that provided all three of these types of information (Cully *et al.*, 1999; Millward *et al.*, 2000). One of the principal means of disseminating information is through the issue of organisational newsletters. By 1998, half of organisations were found to be distributing these to employees, with Cully *et al.* (1999) noting that smaller organisations (with fewer than 1000 employees) were also increasingly using this method (just under one-third). This means of disseminating information to employees remained most common in large organisations and in the public sector.

Direct communication of a more two-way nature has been measured in the WERS series through the incidence of regular meetings between senior managers and employees, meetings or briefing groups involving more junior managers and employees, and other forms of problem-solving communication (Cully *et al.*, 1999; Millward *et al.*, 2000). It has been estimated that, by 1998, regular meetings between senior managers and employees occurred in just under half of workplaces, having risen from one-third in 1984. By the late 1990s, it has also been estimated that about two-thirds of workplaces were using team briefing or briefing groups on a regular basis. The increase in the use of briefings over the 1990s has been particularly concentrated in private sector workplaces without recognised unions and joint consultation arrangements (Millward *et al.*, 2000).

The use of problem-solving groups in the workplace also increased significantly over the 1990s, rising from 35 per cent of workplaces in 1990 to just under half by 1998 (Millward *et al.*, 2000). Suggestion schemes were operating in one-third of workplaces in 1998 (Cully *et al.*, 1999). The increasing use of problem-solving groups and suggestion schemes over the 1990s, as well as the greater incidence of workgroup-level systems for briefing employees, may also be seen as an indication of managerial attempts to broaden the extent of task-level involvement during this period.

Gallie *et al.* (1998) found that the use of communicative involvement was positively associated with the presence of particular organisational characteristics. These include the incidence of higher skill levels in the organisation, the use of new technology, which may itself facilitate greater direct communication, and organisational size as we noted above. They also found that forms of communicative involvement are more likely to be more developed in organisations with systems of performance and reward management. This approach to management involves performance appraisal, the establishment of targets and setting performance-related pay, with effective communication being seen as a necessary prerequisite for this approach to work (see Chapter 10).

Forms of financial involvement also continued to be used at the end of the 1990s. Of the two principal forms briefly described above, schemes for profit-related pay were the most widely used during the 1990s, with arrangements for profit-sharing being used to some extent in 44 per cent of private sector workplaces with over 25 employees in 1990 and in 46 per cent of such workplaces in 1998. Employee share ownership schemes were also evident in about one-quarter of the private sector by 1998 (Cully *et al.*, 1999).

---

self-check question

8.2 Think of an organisational situation with which you have some familiarity.

What forms of employee involvement, if any, exist in this organisation?
Who is responsible for promoting these forms of employee involvement?
Evaluate the practice of these forms of employee involvement.
What practical problems exist in relation to the exercise of employee involvement?

8.5 Common terms but different intentions: differing roles for communication, information and consultation

Our discussion of employee participation and employee involvement has recognised that there are common terms used in relation to each approach, but with the intention of achieving a different purpose. For example, the provision of information in relation to employee participation is seen as being a prerequisite to the sharing of power. In relation to employee involvement, information provision is aimed instead at generating employee attitudes that are congruent with those espoused by managers and the organisational goals that they wish to achieve, as well as providing knowledge-based workers in particular with necessary data (e.g. Townley, 1994; Marchington and Wilkinson, 2000).

Any requirement placed on management to provide information to employees, their representatives or trade unions is known as *disclosure of information*. Management may be obliged to disclose information through having entered into a recognition and/or collective agreement with one or more trade unions. Effective collective bargaining is likely to rely on the disclosure of some management information, and disclosing a high level of information may help to promote a more integrative approach to bargaining (see Chapter 7) (Salamon, 1992, 2000). Such disclosure may be in relation to negotiations that generally cover the regulation of the employment relationship, or it may be more narrowly focused, for example in relation to specific organisational changes that have been made the subject of some form of employee participation, such as restructuring and redundancies.

Perhaps the most widespread obligation on employers in this respect stems from their statutory requirement to disclose information. Townley (1994) provides a brief résumé of this statutory requirement, commencing with the initial and unfulfilled proposal for the disclosure of information in 1969, through a series of legislation dating from the early 1970s. This includes the Health and Safety at Work etc. Act 1974 and the Employment Protection Act 1975, as well as the 1977 ACAS Code of Practice, which promoted the disclosure of information to trade unions for the purpose of collective bargaining. More recently, the statutory requirement to disclose information has grown, boosted by legislation emanating from the European Union requiring the disclosure of information to, as well as consultation with, employee representatives. This includes the European Works Councils, Acquired Rights, Collective Redundancies and Health and Safety Framework Directives. EU directives such as these have led to legislation in the UK including the Collective Redundancies and Transfer of Undertakings (Protection of Employment) (Amendment) Regulations 1995 and the Health and Safety (Consultation with Employees) Regulations 1996. These regulations have spread the right to information disclosure and consultation into non-union situations (e.g. Hall, 1996; Terry, 1999). We return to the role of EU legislation in promoting disclosure of information in the following section.

In contrast to enforced disclosure, *dissemination of information* refers to a situation where an organisation voluntarily informs its employees about any matter affecting itself. This is the type of information provision and communication linked with employee involvement, aimed at developing employees' identification with, as well as commitment and contribution to, their employing organisation. This approach is also intended to optimise work effectiveness. However, its achievement in practice is likely to be problematic. Linked to this, strategies based on the dissemination of information and communication may be poorly conceived and inadequately implemented, as we now discuss.

Part of the rationale behind any strategy to disseminate information may be to 'educate' employees about the economic circumstances of their employing organisation, thereby shaping their attitudes to generate expectations that are seen by management as being more realistic. This type of strategy is therefore also intended to assert the authority of managers and to improve organisational effectiveness (Townley, 1994). However, lowering employee expectations and seeking to improve effectiveness in the same period, for example, is likely to be a very difficult mix to achieve and sustain. The outcome of this strategy from an employee perspective may be the adoption of an instrumental approach to work and/or a position of passive compliance (Marchington and Wilkinson, 2000). Employment relationships based on employee compliance are generally judged to be inappropriate, particularly in relation to competitive environments where commitment to an organisation is seen as likely to aid competitive advantage (e.g. Walton, 1985). Forms of information dissemination and communication that seek to generate commitment to an organisation therefore need to recognise employees' interests, their reactions to any changes occurring around them, and the organisation's responsibility to and for its employees.

Different writers have variously labelled the distinction between these two approaches to information dissemination and communication. Townley (1994) refers to the former approach as being designed to have an educative function and to the latter approach as being part of a strategy to engender commitment. Salamon (1992, 2000) refers to the former approach as having corporate-centred aims and the latter approach as having employee-centred aims. These two sets of labels are clearly complementary and conceptually useful in conjunction with one another. Townley (1994) argues that the 'educative' (and corporate-centred) approach to communication is likely to be based on the exercise of managerial power but is unlikely to be integrated with other human resource policies. Conversely, the commitment-based communication strategy will not only be more employee-centred, emphasising a cooperative and joint problem-solving approach, but is also more likely to be part of an integrated human resource strategy. The distinction being drawn here is akin to the difference in managerial style between an authoritarian approach and a more sophisticated human relations strategy (see Chapter 4) (e.g. Purcell and Sisson, 1983; Purcell and Gray, 1986).

Another set of distinctions can be drawn around the use of joint consultation. We have already recognised that consultation that allows some degree of joint decision-making is distinct from forms that do not permit this type of outcome. Marchington (e.g. 1988, 1994) has developed a typology of four models of consultation, each of which demonstrates a distinct purpose. These are labelled as:

- the non-union model;
- the marginal model;
- the competitive model;
- the adjunct model (Marchington, 1988).

Marchington analyses each of these models in relation to the presence of trade unions and collective bargaining, so that the *non-union model* of consultation is fostered in organisations to resist any attempt at unionisation and the collectivisation of the employment relationship. An employer's strategy in this approach may combine an educative function, through the provision of information about the enterprise to influence the attitudes of employee representatives on the committee, with a more sophisticated approach, by responding to employee concerns in the hope of preventing any momentum to unionise.

In the *marginal model* consultation is seen as being unimportant, because unions are established and other fora exist for collective bargaining and employee participation. However, there may be some motivation for retaining this type of consultative arrangement because of its symbolic value (to show corporate concern), or because it provides a means to absorb the time of employee representatives and unions without the organisation having to concede much by the way of tangible outcomes.

The third type of model of consultation potentially accords greater value for an organisation in the sense that it is used to *compete with collective bargaining*. Issues of substance will be discussed with union representatives through this type of consultative arrangement, with the intention of creating an educative forum to persuade these representatives about the economic circumstances of the organisation and to move their perceptions towards those of management. In conjunction with this approach to enjoin union representatives in management thinking, the organisation is also likely to deploy employee involvement initiatives directly at its employees to justify managerial actions and to gain commitment. Success in this strategy will perhaps reduce the necessity for negotiation, moderate demands made when collective bargaining occurs, and possibly reduce its scope.

In the fourth type of model, consultation is not used to supplant collective bargaining but to operate alongside it in a meaningful way. As an *adjunct to collective bargaining*, this model of consultation provides a means to cover those issues that are not dealt with through negotiation. This model is likely to exist in workplaces where union organisation is not only strong but also where there are particularly competent union representatives who are less prone to accept attempts by management to affect their perceptions and alter their attitudes. A key point to emerge from Marchington's typology is that management may actively use forms of consultation to pursue their own aims, rather than simply agree to take part in this at the behest of a recognised trade union.

These alternative approaches to information and communication, and models of consultation, demonstrate not only a fit with our earlier discussion about employee participation and employee involvement, but also the existence of different strategies that the parties to the management of the employment relationship may adopt in particular circumstances. Marchington (1994) recognises, for example, that changing circumstances may alter the nature of the model of consultation that is used at different points in time. A consultation committee may commence its existence as a means to prevent unionisation but later be used to compete with the functions of a union if one subsequently gains recognition. In contrast to this situation, a consultative committee that functioned effectively as an adjunct to collective bargaining may become marginal where unionisation itself withers in a workplace. These potentially changing scenarios demonstrate the dynamic nature of the employment relationship in many workplaces over time and the scope for change to occur in a number of ways. The principal type of change that we have witnessed so far, of course, in the recent past relates to the growing use of forms of employee involvement. However, a question may be posed about the future in respect of the nature of both employee involvement and employee participation.

self-check question **8.3** In relation to the organisational situation that you used for the self-check questions above:

What types of information are disclosed to employees and what types are disseminated?
What do you think is management's rationale for disseminating particular types of information?
Where employee consultation is evident in this organisation, how does this relate to the typology described above, and is there any evidence that the purpose of consultation has changed, or is changing?

8.6 The role of the European Union for the future of employee participation and involvement

The reported decline of forms of employee participation and growth of employee involvement, as discussed above, indicate one trend towards employer-led initiatives. However, there is also some evidence for the development of partnership agreements in the regulation of the employment relationship (see Chapter 5). Unions also continue to have at least some presence in about half of workplaces with 25 or more employees and to be recognised in about 4 out of 10 organisations of this size, within which about two-thirds of employees are covered by collective bargaining (Millward *et al.*, 2000). These data indicate that some forms of employee participation will continue into the future and will be a significant feature of the employment relationship for many people.

A major stimulus to promote certain forms of employee participation comes from recent European Union social legislation. Several EU Member States have a tradition of employee participation of the type that has caused a high level of resistance from British employing organisations. Earlier we charted the attempt in the 1970s to introduce some form of statutory board-level representation into the UK context. This attempt failed. In contrast, about two-thirds of European Union Member States have introduced statutory board-level representation to some extent. Some countries, such as Denmark, Germany and the Netherlands, have two-tier board structures, with employees being represented on a higher-level supervisory board. Statutory requirements vary between countries depending on the nature of their enabling legislation, with the requirement for this type of employee participation being dependent on factors including a minimum organisational size, the nature of its ownership and legal form, and industrial sector. For example, some countries, such as Greece and Ireland, confine this type of statutory employee participation to state enterprises. The extent of employee participation also varies from minority level representation to *full parity* co-determination, where employees make up half of the supervisory board (e.g. IRS, 1990; Brewster *et al.*, 2000).

Recent legislation from the EU is being used to promote forms of employee participation at below board level. The Member States except the UK adopted the Community Charter of Fundamental Social Rights, known as the Social Charter, in December 1989. This included recognition of the need for rights to information, consultation and participation relating to matters such as technological and organisational change and redundancies (e.g. Kessler and Bayliss, 1998). We referred earlier to a number of EU directives that have led to legislation in Member States to enact particular requirements for information disclosure and consultation. These include directives relating to European Works Councils, Acquired Rights and Collective Redundancies. Of particular significance in the UK context, the regulations that finally led to the intended implementation of the latter two Directives, in 1995, introduced the right to information disclosure and consultation in non-union situations in respect of collective redundancies and the transfer of undertakings (Hall, 1996; Terry, 1999).

The European Works Councils (EWCs) Directive was adopted in 1994 and came into force in September 1996. Initially, this was introduced into 17 of the 18 Member States of the European Economic Area (EEA), with the exception of the UK. Its provisions were designed to affect *Community-scale* companies, defined as those having at least 1000 employees within these Member States, with 150 or more employees in each of at least two such countries. Affected companies are obliged to set up a European Works Council (EWC) within a given period following a properly constituted request and subsequent negotiation in order to provide information to and consult with their workforce, through representatives, on a transnational basis. The process of establishing an EWC may be triggered by a company's central management or by a request from 100 or more employees or their representatives in at least two Member States.

Initially, during the two years between September 1994 and 1996, Article 13 of the Directive permitted companies to reach a voluntary agreement for the establishment of an EWC. As this route to establishing an EWC exempted companies from the specific provisions of the Directive, allowing the parties greater scope when negotiating an agreement, there was an initial flurry of activity, with some 450 EWCs being set up by 22 September 1996 (IRS, 2000a). An analysis of 386 Article 13 EWC agreements (Marginson *et al.*, 1998; IRS, 1998a) found that these varied from the statutory provisions of the Directive in respect of four principal aspects. Voluntarily agreed EWCs were often found to cover a broader geographical area than just EEA countries, and to include the UK; however, some agreements imposed an employment size threshold below which direct representation on the EWC from that country's operations would not be allowed. Some voluntarily agreed EWCs also established structures at divisional level in the company, where these divisions operated across EEA countries, rather than set up a corporate level or group-wide structure in line with the statutory requirement of the Directive. Most voluntarily agreed EWCs were also established as joint management–employee councils rather than following the Directive's statutory provision for the establishment of employee-side-only EWCs. Although the Directive does not specifically grant trade unions a role, unions nevertheless became signatories to the establishment of just under half of voluntarily agreed EWCs. Of particular interest, the involvement of trade unions was associated with the establishment of joint management–employee EWCs rather than the German model of employee-only councils. Although all voluntarily agreed EWCs were concerned with receiving information and consultation, some 4 per cent were also given the right to make recommendations and proposals, and a further 2 per cent were granted negotiating rights (Marginson *et al.*, 1998; IRS 1998a, 1998b).

Of the EEA Member States, the UK was not directly covered by the 1994 EWCs Directive because of its opt-out from the Social Chapter of the 1991 Maastricht Treaty of the European Union, negotiated by John Major's Conservative government. However, many of the voluntarily agreed EWCs negotiated through Article 13 included British workforces. Indeed, it has been reported that, of the 250 companies with operations in the UK that agreed to set up Article 13 EWCs, only seven excluded their British workforce (Marginson *et al.*, 1998; IRS, 1998a). Many of these companies were British owned and headquartered but were still affected by the Directive because of the size and nature of their operations in other EEA Member States. Cressey (1998) reports the TUC finding that over 50 British-based companies agreed to set up Article 13 EWCs. These companies include many well-known names such as Barclays Bank, British Airways, BT, Coats Viyella, Courtaulds, GKN, ICI, Marks and Spencer, NatWest Bank, Pilkington, Scottish and Newcastle, and Unilever (a fuller list is shown in Wills, 1999). We return to the ending of the UK opt-out from the Social Chapter below.

After 22 September 1996 the Directive came into effect and the procedure for introducing EWCs changed. The creation of EWCs in the 17 EEA Member States was then governed by the Directive (or more specifically its transposition into national law). Article 5 required that a request to establish an EWC should become the subject of negotiation by setting up a *special negotiating body* (SNB) of employee representatives to reach agreement with management. An agreement has to fulfil the requirements laid down in Article 6 about the coverage of the EWC, its composition, functions, meetings and facilities (IRS, 1999a). Negotiations may continue for a period of up to 3 years, after which if agreement is not forthcoming the Directive provides for the establishment of a statutory EWC model in the company. This provision clearly acts as an incentive to reach agreement. Similarly, when a company's employees make a valid request for a council to be set up but its central management refuses to enter negotiations within 6 months, this statutory EWC model will also be applied.

Since 1996 the rate at which new EWCs have been created has slowed. The number of transnational organisations potentially affected by the 1994 EWCs Directive is thought to be about 1200. IRS (2000a) estimates that the total number set up by early 2000 is about 600, including those established under Article 13. Negotiations to set up new EWCs will also be in progress. Table 8.3 shows some of the range of companies that are reported to have established an EWC under Article 6.

The UK's opt-out from the Social Chapter and from this Directive was ended in 1997, with the return of a Labour government. An EWC 'extension' directive was formally adopted in December 1997, which gave affected organisations 2 years to reach a voluntary agreement in line with Article 13 of the original Directive. This was subsequently transposed into UK law through the Transnational Information and Consultation of Employees Regulations 1999, closely following the requirements of the Directive outlined above (IRS, 1999b).

The statutory functions of an EWC relate to the disclosure of information and consultation. This will be of a transnational nature and may be intended to supplement and enhance arrangements to undertake consultation within the national or local settings of a company's operations. The need for these linkages to occur in practice has been recognised in order to promote EWCs as a meaningful way of consulting with employees, although their ability to facilitate this in the way that they

Table 8.3 Some organisations reported as establishing EWCs under Article 6

Air France	France	Air transport
Akzo Nobel	Netherlands	Chemicals
American Express	USA	Financial services
BTR	UK	Engineering
Bosch	Germany	Engineering
Cadbury Schweppes	UK	Confectionery
Campbell Bewley	Ireland	Food
Carlsberg	Denmark	Beverages
Cummins	USA	Diesel engines
Dalgety	UK	Food and agricultural
General Electric	USA	Plastics and power systems
Glaxo Wellcome	UK	Pharmaceuticals
Heineken	Netherlands	Brewing
IBM	USA	IT
Michelin	France	Rubber and tyres
Nissan	Japan	Motor manufacturing
Nortel	Canada	Telecommunications
Sara Lee Douwe Egberts	USA	Food and personal
Swedish Match	Sweden	Matches and tobacco

Source: IRS / ETUC

are currently being run has been questioned, as we discuss below. Certainly, by intention, the nature of envisaged information disclosure is designed to allow employee representatives to get closer to corporate-level issues. The Directive envisages that EWCs will be provided with information about substantial matters affecting employees' interests, including company performance and prospects, production and sales, investments, the employment situation, organisational changes, introduction of new working methods or production processes, production transfers, mergers, closures or cutbacks and collective redundancies. Consultation may cover any of these aspects.

However, the extent to which the operation of EWCs is advancing employee participation is open to question. Cressey (1998) points to trade union awareness that EWCs are restricted in their capacity to promote employee participation because they are limited to a consideration of corporate-level issues. Wills (1999) believes that management interest in establishing EWCs, particularly in relation to Article 13, has been driven by their attempts to use these councils as a vehicle to promote their own agenda and vision, and to help to build a European corporate culture. She also points to a strategy in some companies where an EWC has been used to create a competitive situation between unions and non-unionists to represent employee interests. This may suggest scope to develop a typology similar to that of Marchington (1988, 1994) described above. The effectiveness of EWCs may also be limited by the way in which they are constituted. The European Trade Union Confederation (ETUC) would like to see the employment size thresholds for the establishment of EWCs reduced. The Directive requires only that EWCs meet on an annual basis, although exceptional circumstances, such as relocations, closures or collective redundancies, may require that additional meetings occur. The ETUC also believe that the procedures for information disclosure and consultation need to be made more effective. In addition, consulting with representatives on a transnational basis, while allowing links to corporate management and to other national unions and company operations (Cressey, 1998), may make this process appear remote to the majority of a company's workforce.

In their proposals the European Trade Union Confederation include the following suggestions for the reform of EWCs to improve their effectiveness from the trade union perspective:

- Information needs to be more continuous and to be provided in good time.
- Consultation should take place well before management takes decisions, to enable employees' views to be considered.
- Meetings other than the existing annual information and consultation meeting need to be planned 'with a view to reaching agreement' on matters discussed.
- Representatives on EWCs need to be given greater rights, including access to training, time off work, and the resources to disseminate information from EWC meetings to lower-level employee representatives, to establish linkages to these structures.
- Representatives need to be able to meet together outside the formal EWC meeting and to be allowed greater access to expert assistance, including enjoining union officials (see IRS, 2000b).

These proposed extensions to the operation of EWCs would alter the nature of the process towards one that was more power centred and away from a narrowly defined information-sharing and consultation remit. They are not supported by the European employers' organisation, UNICE. Employee participation clearly remains a topical issue that exercises the minds of various stakeholders to this process.

self-check question	**8.4** How would you analyse the position of EWCs in relation to the dimensions used to analyse employee participation and employee involvement, relating to degree or depth, scope, level and form?

The extension of statutory information and consultation rights to the national level has been at issue in the EU since late 1998, when the European Commission adopted a draft Directive on this matter. This statutory extension was finally resolved when a Directive for the provision of information to and consultation with employees' representatives within Member States was agreed in February 2002 (2002/14/EC). This agreement was partly reached when it was accepted that a long timetable would be allowed to transpose this Directive into national legislation. This was because Ireland and the UK do not already have national-level systems for employee information and consultation. Consequently, Member States do not have to transpose this Directive into national legislation before March 2005, and it does not have to be implemented for all affected organisations, depending on their size, until 2007 or 2008. However, once it is implemented in practice, affected organisations will have to provide information about their activities and economic situation and also undertake consultation in respect of their employment situation (including threats to employment) and on decisions likely to introduce substantial changes to the organisation of work or contractual relations. Such consultation will have to take place with a view to reaching agreement about the introduction of substantial changes to the organisation of work or contractual relations.

8.7 Summary

- This chapter has differentiated between the concepts of employee participation and employee involvement. Employee participation is used essentially as a power-centred concept, fostered by trade unions and through governmental and European Union regulation. Employee involvement is recognised as a unitarist and business-centred concept, fostered by employer and managerial interests, designed to generate employee commitment and contribution.

- Participation takes three principal forms: board-level representation; joint regulation of employment issues; and joint consultation, where this allows an employee veto over particular managerial proposals. The nature and extent of employee participation may be analysed through four dimensions that relate to its degree, scope, level and form.

- In the UK, collective bargaining remains the most widespread means of permitting some degree of employee participation, although this has reduced significantly over the past two decades. The scope of such bargaining has also been reduced. The scope for participation through forms of employee consultation is also limited.

- In contrast, there has been a significant shift to forms of employee involvement in the UK over the past two decades. These include a range of channels that are focused directly towards employees, including forms of communicative involvement, task-level involvement and financial involvement. Employee involvement will also be affected and moderated by managerial actions and styles of leadership.

- There are differing strategies underpinning the use of methods such as employee communication and joint consultation in relation to the pursuit of employee participation or employee involvement. This emphasises the need to differentiate between these approaches and to understand the purpose of communication, information-sharing and consultation strategies in practice.

- Recent legislation emanating from the European Union has helped to promote some forms of limited employee participation, notably in relation to the introduction of European Works Councils in affected organisations and through the impending development of a national system for informing and consulting employees. Although these measures establish systems for consultation, the degree of participation permitted through these approaches falls short of power sharing and joint regulation.

References

Ackers, P., Marchington, M., Wilkinson, A. and Goodman, J. (1992) 'The use of cycles? Explaining employee involvement in the 1990s', *Industrial Relations Journal*, 23:4, 268–83.

Blyton, P. and Turnbull, P. (1998) *The Dynamics of Employee Relations*, Basingstoke, Macmillan.

Brannen, P. (1983) *Authority and Participation in Industry*, London, Batsford Academic.

Brannen, P., Batstone, E., Fatchett, D. and White, P. (1976) *The Worker Directors: A sociology of participation*, London, Hutchinson.

Brewster, C., Mayrhofer, W. and Morley, M. (2000) *New Challenges for European Human Resource Management*, Basingstoke, Macmillan.

Bullock, A. (1977) *Report of the Committee of Inquiry on Industrial Democracy* (Cmnd 6706), London, HMSO.

CBI/EDG (1991) *Managing for Success*, launch issue, April, London, CBI/EDG.

Clegg, H.A. (1951) *Industrial Democracy and Nationalization*, Oxford, Blackwell.

Coates, K. and Topham, A. (1970) *Workers' Control*, London, Panther Books.

Cressey, P. (1998) 'European works councils in practice', *Human Resource Management Journal*, 8:1, 67–79.

Cressey, P., Eldridge, J. and MacInnes, J. (1985) *Just Managing: Authority and democracy in industry*, Milton Keynes, Open University Press.

Cully, M., Woodland, S., O'Reilly, A. and Dix, G. (1999) *Britain at Work as Depicted by the 1998 Workplace Employee Relations Survey*, London, Routledge.

Cunningham, I., Hyman, J. and Baldry, C. (1996) 'Empowerment: the power to do what?', *Industrial Relations Journal*, 27:2, 143–54.

Donovan, T.N. (1968) *Royal Commission on Trade Unions and Employers' Associations 1965–1968* (Cmnd 3623), London, HMSO.

Eldridge, J., Cressey, P. and MacInnes, J. (1991) *Industrial Sociology and Economic Crisis*, London, Harvester Wheatsheaf.

Gallie, G., White, M., Cheng, Y. and Tomlinson, M. (1998) *Restructuring the Employment Relationship*, Oxford, Clarendon Press.

Geary, J.F. (1994) 'Task participation: employees' participation enabled or constrained?', *in* Sisson, K. (ed.), *Personnel Management: A comprehensive guide to theory and practice in Britain* (2nd edn), Oxford, Blackwell, pp. 634–61.

Guest, D., Peccei, R. and Thomas, A. (1993) 'The impact of employee involvement on organisational commitment and "them and us" attitudes', *Industrial Relations Journal*, 24:3, 191–200.

Hall, M. (1996) 'Beyond recognition? Employee representation and EU law', *Industrial Law Journal*, 25:1, 15–27.

Howard, M. (1991) Speech to the Department of Employment and CBI Conference on Employee Involvement, Monday 22 April, London.

Hyman, J. and Mason, B. (1995) *Managing Employee Involvement and Participation*, London, Sage.

IPM/IPA (1982) *Employee Involvement and Participation Code*, London, IPM.

IRS (1990) *Employee Participation in Europe*, EIRR Report No. 4, London, Industrial Relations Services.

IRS (1998a) 'An analysis of Article 13 EWC agreements', *European Industrial Relations Review 296*, London, Industrial Relations Services, September, 16–18.

IRS (1998b) 'EWCs are achieving new and effective forms of employee-interest representation', *IRS Employment Trends 669*, London, Industrial Relations Services, December, 2.

IRS (1999a) 'Article 6 agreements in focus', *European Industrial Relations Review 305*, London, Industrial Relations Services, June, 25–8.

IRS (1999b) 'UK draft EWCs legislation', *European Industrial Relations Review 307*, London, Industrial Relations Services, August, 28–9.

IRS (2000a) 'European Works Council update', *European Industrial Relations Review 316*, London, Industrial Relations Services, May, 20–2.

IRS (2000b) 'Commission issues EWCs report', *European Industrial Relations Review 317*, London, Industrial Relations Services, June, 19–22.

Kessler, S. and Bayliss, F. (1998) *Contemporary British Industrial Relations* (3rd edn), Basingstoke, Macmillan.

Marchington, M. (1980) *Responses to Participation at Work*, Farnborough, Gower.

Marchington, M. (1988) 'The four faces of employee consultation', *Personnel Management*, May, 44–7.

Marchington, M. (1992) *Managing the Team: A guide to successful employee involvement*, Oxford, Blackwell.

Marchington, M. (1994) 'The dynamics of joint consultation', *in* Sisson, K. (ed.), *Personnel Management: A comprehensive guide to theory and practice in Britain* (2nd edn), Oxford, Blackwell, pp. 662–93.

Marchington, M. (1995) 'Involvement and participation', *in* Storey, J. (ed.), *Human Resource Management: A critical text*, London, Routledge, pp. 280–305.

Marchington, M. and Wilkinson, A. (2000) 'Direct participation', *in* Bach, S. and Sisson, K. (eds), *Personnel Management: A comprehensive guide to theory and practice in Britain* (3rd edn), Oxford, Blackwell, pp. 340–64.

Marchington, M., Goodman, J., Wilkinson, A. and Ackers, P. (1992) *New Developments in Employee Involvement*, Employment Department Research Series No. 2, London, HMSO.

Marginson, P., Gilman, M., Jacobi, O. and Krieger, H. (1998) *Negotiating European Works Councils: An analysis of agreements under Article 13*, Report prepared for the European Foundation for the Improvement of Living and Working Conditions and the European Commission.

McCarthy, W.E.J. (ed.) (1972) *Trade Unions*, Harmondsworth, Penguin Books.

Millward, N., Bryson, A. and Forth, J. (2000) *All Change at Work?*, London, Routledge.

Millward, N., Stevens, M., Smart, D. and Hawes, W.R. (1992) *Workplace Industrial Relations in Transition: The ED/ESRC/PSI/ACAS surveys*, Aldershot, Dartmouth.

Pateman, C. (1970) *Participation and Democratic Theory*, Cambridge, Cambridge University Press.

Poole, M. (1975) *Workers' Participation in Industry*, London, Routledge & Kegan Paul.

Purcell, J. and Gray, A. (1986) 'Corporate personnel departments and the management of industrial relations: two case studies in ambiguity', *Journal of Management Studies*, 23:2, 205–23.

Purcell, J. and Sisson, K. (1983) 'Strategies and practice in the management of industrial relations', *in* Bain, G.S. (ed.), *Industrial Relations in Britain*, Oxford, Blackwell, pp. 95–120.

Ramsay, H. (1977) 'Cycles of control: worker participation in sociological and historical perspective', *Sociology*, 11:3, 481–506.

Salamon, M. (1992) *Industrial Relations: Theory and practice* (2nd edn), Hemel Hempstead, Prentice Hall.

Salamon, M. (2000) *Industrial Relations: Theory and practice* (4th edn), Harlow, Financial Times Prentice Hall.

Schuchman, A. (1957) *Co-determination, Labor's Middle Way in Germany*, Washington DC, Public Affairs Press.

Storey, J. (1992) *Developments in the Management of Human Resources*, Oxford, Blackwell.

Terry, M. (1999) 'Systems of collective employee representation in non-union forms in the UK', *Industrial Relations Journal*, 30:1, 16–30.

Thornhill, A., Lewis, P., Millmore, M. and Saunders, M. (2000) *Managing Change: A human resource strategy approach*, Harlow, Financial Times Prentice Hall.

Townley, B. (1994) 'Communicating with employees', *in* Sisson, K. (ed.), *Personnel Management: A comprehensive guide to theory and practice in Britain* (2nd edn), Oxford, Blackwell, pp. 595–633.

Wall, T.D. and Lischeron, J.A. (1977) *Worker Participation*, London, McGraw-Hill.

Walton, R.E. (1985) 'From control to commitment in the workplace', *Harvard Business Review*, 85:2, 77–84.

Wills, J. (1999) 'European Works Councils in British firms', *Human Resource Management Journal*, 9:4, 19–38.

self-check Answers

8.1 *Think of an organisational situation with which you have some familiarity.*
What forms of employee participation, if any, exist in this organisation?
What authority promotes the existence of these forms of employee participation?
Evaluate the practice of these forms of employee participation using the dimensions of degree or depth, scope, level and form.
What practical problems exist in relation to the exercise of employee participation?

Inevitably, the organisation you are thinking of is unlikely to be one with which we are familiar. However, in relation to the series of questions posed, you will be able, perhaps following some enquiry, to find out whether some form of participation exists at board level, or at a lower level related to joint regulation or collective bargaining of particular terms and conditions of employment. You will also be able to find out whether any form or forms of joint consultation exist within the organisation.

In relation to the authority that promotes any employee participation, you will be able to find out whether this is underpinned by legislation, or through prior trade union recognition and agreement within the organisation. The degree of participation will inform you about the extent of employees' influence in relation to organisational decision-making, and the scope of participation will provide you with information about which types of decision are subject to this influence. Consideration of the levels at which participation occurs within the organisation will allow you to understand how this works in practice, as will consideration of the forms that participation takes.

Using these dimensions to analyse and evaluate participation within an organisation should help you to consider what practical problems exist in its usage. These may, for example, relate to a sense that participation forms are somewhat remote and that they do not affect most employees' working lives. There may also be a management attitude that this is something that they are forced to engage in and which they seek to use for their own purpose. Alternatively, where participation exists in your organisation, you may have reached the conclusion that in overall terms it is accepted as part of the operation of the organisation and is valued by those engaged in or affected by its practice.

8.2 *Think of an organisational situation with which you have some familiarity.*
What forms of employee involvement, if any, exist in this organisation?
Who is responsible for promoting these forms of employee involvement?
Evaluate the practice of these forms of employee involvement.
What practical problems exist in relation to the exercise of employee involvement?

Reference to Table 8.2 will have provided you with a checklist to use to identify the forms of employee involvement that exist within your organisational context. It may be interesting to identify the relative usage of involvement forms within this organisation, using the categorisation offered in Table 8.2. Involvement also includes, or is affected by, the nature of managerial actions and styles of leadership, and it may therefore be interesting to evaluate the extent to which the use of forms of involvement is congruent within the organisation.

It is likely that you will have identified that management is responsible for promoting employee involvement within the organisation. Hopefully, you will have been able to identify the levels of management at which specific forms of involvement are promoted. Again, recognising that involvement also includes, or is affected by, the nature of managerial actions and styles of leadership, it will be significant to recognise that, if involvement is to be engendered within an organisation, it will need to be promoted by all levels of management.

This recognition will hopefully help you to evaluate the practice of employee involvement within the organisation. You may have found it useful to use Tables 8.1 and 8.2 to evaluate employee involvement in your organisational context.

The comments above allude to possible practical problems arising from any attempt to promote employee involvement. Practical problems may arise in particular ways: for example, they may occur where the use of forms of communicative involvement is not reinforced by managerial actions within the organisation (see Table 8.2). There may also be a number of espoused aims for employee involvement within an organisation (see for example Table 8.1), although these may not be transferred into organisational practice, perhaps being 'crowded out' by other organisational imperatives related to cost pressures, resource allocation pressures and competition. Alternatively, employee involvement may be evaluated as a valuable component of organisational culture and the management of the employment relationship.

8.3 *In relation to the organisational situation that you used for the self-check questions above:*
What types of information are disclosed to employees and what types are disseminated?
What do you think is management's rationale for disseminating particular types of information?
Where employee consultation is evident in this organisation, how does this relate to the typology described above, and is there any evidence that the purpose of consultation has changed, or is changing?

You are very likely to have found that the types of information that are disclosed to employees are related to those required by legislation. For example, this will include those related to business transfers, collective redundancies and health and safety matters. Those types of information that are disseminated to employees relate to a broader range of subjects about which management voluntarily wishes to inform the workforce. The rationale for disseminating such information is likely to be related to an educative, or re-educative, purpose designed to shape attitudes and expectations, and consequently to affect employee behaviour.

Your response to the third question in this series will also depend on the organisational context that you have used to explore and answer it. Hopefully, however, you will be able to relate the use of consultation in this context to Marchington's typology related to the non-union model, the marginal model, the competitive model and the adjunct model. You may also be able to recognise how the purpose of consultation is changing, or has changed, within this organisational context.

8.4 *How would you analyse the position of EWCs in relation to the dimensions used to analyse employee participation and employee involvement, relating to degree or depth, scope, level and form?*

Degree of participation will be determined by the extent to which employee representatives are able to influence organisational decision-making. The purpose of EWCs is to receive information and to be consulted rather than to engage in negotiation. The extent to which EWCs may be able to influence decision-making will depend on the nature of the consultation process in practice, its timeliness, and the capabilities of those representing employee interests. Reform of the type requested by the ETUC may increase the degree of participation that EWCs permit in organisational decision-making. The potential scope for participation granted to EWCs appears to be extensive, although of course this will be limited by the nature of their engagement in decision-making. The Directive envisages that EWCs will be provided with information about substantial matters affecting employees' interests, including company performance and prospects, production and sales, investments, the employment situation, organisational changes, introduction of new working methods or production processes, production transfers, mergers, closures or cutbacks, and collective redundancies. Consultation may cover any of these aspects. However, consultation at the EWC level will be related to transnational corporate matters and will need to be underpinned by effective national level consultation, as well as by coordination between these levels. As EWCs work on the basis of an indirect, representational form of employee participation at a transnational level, there is also a danger that they will appear to be somewhat remote to most employees. This impression is likely to be reinforced by the relative low frequency of their meetings.

CASE 8 — Participation and involvement at The Grange Community School[1]

The Grange Community School is located on the eastern edge of Bristol, in Warmley. Its 885 pupils are drawn from the urban fringes of north-east Bristol, including Kingswood. The Grange is controlled by the South Gloucestershire Local Education Authority, and was threatened with closure in recent years. The Grange has a teaching staff of 58, who together with about 30 support staff are led by the headteacher, Steve Colledge.

Steve Colledge became headteacher at The Grange in early 2002, and the other members of its senior management team were also appointed to their posts during this year. These comprise a deputy headteacher, who is responsible for staffing, staff development and operational management issues, and two assistant heads, who are responsible for curriculum and teaching matters, and pupils and learning respectively. These other members of the senior management team were appointed to their posts from within the staff of the school. The fifth member of The Grange's senior management team, its director of resources, has responsibility for the support staff who work at the school.

Teaching at The Grange is organised into nine academic faculties. The assistant head for curriculum and teaching has line management responsibility for the nine heads of faculty. Within each faculty there are about six academic members of staff, together with faculty-based support staff such as technicians. Like many other secondary schools, The Grange also operates a house-based system for pupils, which is concerned principally with pastoral care. There are four such houses at The Grange, each run by a head of house, who is responsible to the assistant head for pupils and learning. The Grange also runs a sixth form, managed by a head, which offers a range of AS/A2 level subjects that cater for the 45 per cent of pupils who stay on at the school.

[1] The assistance of Steve Colledge in the preparation of this case is gratefully acknowledged.

Like all schools, The Grange is subject to a range of environmental influences and pressures that impact on the way it is managed and its scope for development. Central government continues to lay stress on improving standards in education. To this effect, the Department for Education and Skills generates a range of information, consultation documents and proposals for legislation. More locally, local education authorities have a range of concerns that are outlined in statutory obligations and an education development plan. Each school also has a governing body, which helps to shape its direction and provides a source of guidance and accountability for its management.

In addition, the main terms and conditions of employment of those who teach in the maintained schools sector in England and Wales are determined by the School Teachers' Review Body (STRB). This was established in 1991 to consider and report on the conditions of employment of school teachers in England and Wales. The establishment of this review body saw the ending of collective bargaining between the employers' body and trade unions in this sector of education. The STRB produced its eleventh report in 2002, which made a number of recommendations about the pay and career structure of classroom teachers, performance thresholds for progression onto the upper pay scale for teachers, the pay of heads, deputies and assistants, and other issues (Vineall, 2002). This report was presented to the Prime Minister and the Secretary of State for Education and Skills, who then decide whether to accept and implement each of the recommendations made. In arriving at its recommendations, the STRB consults with a range of organisations including the trade unions representing school teachers and head teachers.

Although the trade unions no longer engage in collective bargaining to determine the pay and conditions of those they represent, they are able to participate in more local-level discussions about conditions of employment through joint standing consultative committees at local education authority level.

The existence of these forms of intervention to determine conditions of employment affects the scope for and nature of employee participation and involvement in schools. Steve Colledge refers to this as 'working within someone else's set of rules'. The scope to reach a school-based agreement on particular issues is tempered by the existence of nationally determined conditions, such as those that affect the nature of teacher contracts. Nevertheless there is a need for the management of a school to offer leadership in respect of its development and an expectation by those involved that this will be offered. The senior management of a school will need to identify the expectations of government and the opportunities that these provide, and to identify how it should respond to specific government initiatives. This will include identifying what the school needs to do, what its targets will be, when these need to be met, and how to achieve them. This might include responding to the offer of government grants, applying to become a specialist school, or attaining progressive educational standards. There is also a need to recruit and retain high-quality staff, which requires a recruitment and retention strategy at a time of teacher shortages.

Within this framework of intervention and regulation there is scope for determined and effective leadership, and for employee involvement and participation, in the running of schools. At The Grange some degree of participation occurs through meetings that involve some negotiation about conditions within the school between

Steve Colledge and representatives of three teacher unions – the Association of Teachers and Lecturers (ATL), the National Union of Teachers (NUT), and the National Association of Schoolmasters Union of Women Teachers (NASUWT). Steve Colledge meets with union representatives on a regular basis to inform and consult them about developments in the school. He is willing to meet with them to present options about change and to talk these through before making a decision. Such discussions with the representatives of these teacher unions tend to occur around 'a single table', where they meet together with Steve Colledge, although there is also scope for individual discussion. There is also scope for the district representative of one or more of these teacher unions to visit the school to discuss aspects of the performance of the teaching contract, such as the level of cover required. Steve Colledge also meets with support staff, some of whom are members of Unison (see Chapter 5), to keep them informed and to consult with them as a group. In addition to these union-based forms of employee participation, there is also provision for some degree of employee participation through the election of two teachers and one member of the support staff employed at The Grange to its governing body. However, these staff governors do not sit as representatives of any trade union and are not expected to consult formally with the rest of the staff about the views of and decisions taken by the governing body.

An attempt is made to weave employee involvement into the management and operation of the school. The organisation of work in the school is based on the principle of a number of overlapping teams. These include the senior management team, faculty-based teams and house-based teams. At the faculty level within the school, the heads of faculty are seen as a key group to influence its effectiveness and development. Most heads of faculty are recent appointments and are sent on a range of training courses to become familiar with new educational initiatives. They hold faculty meetings of their staff every three weeks to discuss the work of their areas and to consider how to respond to new initiatives. Heads of house also hold team meetings at the school. Minutes from these meetings are circulated with the school. Meetings of the heads of faculty and the heads of house are also held, sometimes jointly, to consider initiatives and to evaluate progress. A member of the senior management team of the school attends these meetings. Meetings between the senior management team and these groups of heads are also held. More generally, meetings involving all academic staff in the school are held eight times a year. Support staff attend some of these meetings, with additional meetings being held specifically for this group.

The use of these types of meeting to seek to involve staff at a range of levels within the school requires a delicate balance to be reached in relation to the nature of its leadership. The senior management team of The Grange has attempted to develop a style of leadership where the resulting agenda is not seen to be dominated by it. There is nevertheless a need to offer leadership, particularly in relation to the options open to the school that arise from the external initiatives and challenges that affect its future. Members of the school's senior management team are allowed time within their schedule of work to meet with heads of faculty and of house to listen to and understand different points of view and to discuss matters. This also provides an opportunity to identify misconceptions and to discuss these.

▶

The role of the senior management often involves understanding the direction of change, interpreting what this will mean for the way the school operates, and promoting involvement from staff to help to meet this need for change. Involvement is encouraged in this context by asking heads what they would like to do to meet a target rather than imposing a means to achieve this. There are also a growing number of 'toolkits' for faculties to use regarding the Key Stage 3 strategy, teaching and learning in the foundation subjects and the OFSTED model for self-evaluation. Discussion about such ideas leads to reflection and the possible modification of a proposal, and avoids the imposition of a strategy from above to bring about change. Steve Colledge also promotes the idea of sitting down with anyone who objects to a change, or who requires convincing, to discuss this with them. This consumes both time and energy but provides the opportunity to ask them whether they have seen the documentation that originated the need to consider change and how they would seek to approach this need.

Questions

1 How does the context of the education system in the maintained schools sector affect the scope for and nature of employee participation?

2 How would you evaluate the nature of employee involvement at The Grange?

Reference

Vineall, T. (2002) *School Teachers' Review Body: Eleventh Report 2002* (Cm 5353), Norwich, The Stationery Office Limited. Available through the website of the Office of Manpower Economics: <http://www.ome.uk.com/stp_review.cfm> (Crown copyright).

Chapter 9

Regulating the employment relationship through grievance and discipline

At the end of this chapter you should be able to:

- define grievance and discipline;

- identify the sources of grievance and discipline cases;

- describe the advantages of treating grievance and discipline in a systematic manner;

- identify the content of grievance and discipline procedures;

- explain why grievance and discipline may not be conducted in a formal, rational manner.

9.1 Introduction

In Chapter 1 we explained that the pluralist perspective on employee relations stressed the inevitability of conflict. Chapter 7 dealt with the manifestation of conflict at a collective level and how collective bargaining procedures may be used to regulate this conflict. This chapter is about conflict at the level of the individual employee.

Throughout this book we have attempted to portray the employment relationship as an essentially simple concept. The employer and employee enter into a contract in which both have needs, both material and psychological. For most of us, most of the time, these needs are met. If they are not, either we, as employees, resign or our employer dismisses us. But these are extreme consequences of employer or employee needs not being met. It is more likely that we reach a compromise where both our needs are more or less met most of the time. This is often the result of an implied, unstated understanding reached over a period of time. However, this understanding need not be implied and unstated. It may be based on systematic efforts to resolve differences based on coherent employee relations procedures. This is where grievance and discipline procedures and processes are valuable.

Torrington and Hall (1998) make the point that grievance and discipline are matters from which line managers often prefer to shy away. Consequently, the onus is often upon the HR specialist to become involved in grievance and, particularly, discipline issues. Conducting grievance and discipline cases effectively is important because, as Chapter 11 makes clear, the result of doing so ineffectively can mean the appearance of managers and HR specialists in an employment tribunal explaining and defending their actions. This may be unavoidable, but the existence and observance of effective procedures lessens the chances of what is a harrowing experience for both employers and employees.

In this chapter we define grievance and discipline (Section 9.2), and consider the origins, legal background and causes of employee grievances (Section 9.3). In Section 9.4 we examine grievance procedures. In Section 9.5 we turn our attention to discipline issues and in Section 9.6 we consider why grievance and discipline practices are often not conducted in a formal, rational manner.

9.2 Grievance and discipline defined

It will be evident on occasions in this chapter that there is sometimes an unclear distinction between grievance and discipline issues. Consequently we make it clear at the outset of the chapter how each is defined.

■ What is a grievance?

An employee may raise a grievance about any issue that concerns the relations between her and her employer. The issue may affect her conditions of employment, or those of several of her colleagues in the organisation, when that issue contradicts the provisions of a collective agreement or the individual contract of employment. The grievance may stem from her feeling that works rules are being misapplied, that laws are being disregarded, or that the general custom and practice that applies to her job is being ignored. Therefore it is apparent that grievances may originate from a host of sources. We look at these sources later.

Torrington and Hall (1998) clarify the meaning of employee relations grievances by drawing the distinction between dissatisfaction, complaint and grievance:

■ *Dissatisfaction* is anything over which employees are unhappy, irrespective of whether this unhappiness is openly expressed. You may read this and say to yourself: 'Some people spend all their working day moaning. For them, unhappiness at work is a natural condition.' This is a fair point. After all, paid employment for many is something imposed by economic necessity rather than the subject of free choice.

■ *Complaints* are spoken or written dissatisfactions of which supervisors or managers are made aware. As such they are more formal than general everyday moans.

■ *Grievances* are complaints that are presented formally to management or a union official through the use of a recognised procedure.

Of course, these terms are not mutually exclusive. For example, general dissatisfaction about the way in which managers ask employees to work non-standard hours may give rise to a series of complaints about a specific example of this practice. This employee discontent is elevated to the status of a grievance when an employee protests formally, citing an abuse of the collective agreement or the individual contract of employment. This example illustrates how a grievance may be an individual grievance (one employee protesting about the implementation of the contract of employment) or the first stage of a collective dispute involving all employees covered by a particular collective agreement on the flexibility of working hours. Obviously a collective dispute is far more likely in an organisation where a recognition agreement with a trade union exists. In a unionised environment a grievance may become a collective dispute only if the union decides to make it so (see Chapter 7), but even in a non-unionised environment it is not impossible for employees to group together and raise a collective or group grievance. To sum up, grievance is a formal complaint, made by an individual or a group about an aspect of the way in which he, she or they have been treated.

■ What is discipline?

Discipline may be defined as 'action instigated by management against an employee who fails to meet reasonable and legitimate expectations in terms of performance, conduct or adherence to rules' (Pilbeam and Corbridge, 2002: 415).

We deal with matters of discipline later in the chapter, but now we continue with an analysis of the grievance process.

9.3 Origins, legal background and causes of grievance

The necessity for employers to cater for employee grievances was initially imposed under the Industrial Relations Act 1971. This followed the conclusion by the 1968 Donovan Commission that employee relations could be improved with clear, user-friendly procedures. This employee right is now part of the Employment Rights Act 1996, which states that all employees are entitled to know the identity of the person to whom they should initially apply in the event of a grievance and what consequent steps may be taken in this event. Most UK organisations have grievance procedures. In the 1998 Workplace Employee Relations Survey, 91 per cent of workplaces had a formal procedure in place for dealing with grievances raised by non-managerial employees (Cully *et al.*, 1999).

■ The causes of employee grievances

As with any dispute, it is often quite difficult to pinpoint with certainty the actual cause of an employee grievance. If the aggrieved employee were to note down all the underlying causes of his dissatisfaction it might lead to quite a complex set of interrelating factors. Yet if that same employee were asked, say, in an exit interview why he was leaving he might say that it was due to one overriding cause, for example salary. This was the general conclusion drawn by Salipante and Bouwen (1990) from a study of people with grievances in Belgium and the USA. They group the primary sources of employee conflict into three categories:

- Environmental sources
  - Economic terms and conditions of employment. This may relate to levels of pay but also may have its source in the *wage–effort* bargain. In short, employees may feel that they are being paid too little for what they do.

- Physical job conditions.
- The job may be too demanding, or insufficiently demanding, given the abilities of the employee.
- Poor economic condition of the company.
■ Sources related to goals, means of achieving goals and inequities of treatment
  - Ideological differences of interests, goals and means. An example would be an employee who 'blows the whistle' on her employer about an aspect of the employer's policy of which she disapproves strongly.
  - Differences over goals and how these may be achieved.
  - Perception of inequity as a consequence of organisation policy, procedure or the decisions of an individual.
  - Perceptions of inequity stemming from organisational policy or procedure and mismatch with career expectations.
■ Sources related to relationships between individuals, groups or organisations
  - Institutional relations (employees versus management; trade union versus management; union versus union).
  - Sexual and racial prejudice.
  - Interpersonal or intergroup rivalries.
  - Personality conflicts and personal problems.

In Salipante and Bouwen's (1990) research only about 20 per cent of the respondents described the source of the conflict as a substantive issue (such as pay). Over two-thirds attributed the source to relationships between individuals, groups and organisations.

self-check question	**9.1** Why do you think that you might present the reason for your dissatisfaction, complaint or grievance as a coherent, perhaps single, issue, when the reality may be much more complex?

A study of grievance procedures in 72 UK public and private sector workplaces by IRS (1997) found that the most important sources of employee grievances are:

■ introduction of new work practices;
■ disciplinary action taken;
■ interpretation of terms and conditions of employment;
■ staffing levels;
■ personal issues;
■ discrimination;
■ grading;
■ bullying;
■ health and safety;
■ pay;
■ sexual harassment.

This list emphasises the point made above that it is too simplistic too see these factors as discrete items. The introduction of new work practices, for example, may be tied up with the interpretation of terms and conditions of employment and staffing levels. Many organisations have sought to reduce costs in recent years by reducing staffing levels. This has usually meant that staff who remain are asked to adopt new work practices by, for example, learning new skills and therefore becoming more flexible. This has the effect of revising the contract of employment because employees are carrying out different duties, perhaps at different times and in a different location, from those detailed in the original contract of employment. An employee grievance raised in such circumstances may be valid, both morally and legally. The law books contain many cases where the employee claims constructive dismissal on the basis that the employer has breached the contract of employment to such an extent that the employee is justified in resigning claiming constructive dismissal (see Chapter 11 for more detail on this legal provision). In fact, constructive dismissal may be seen as the final point of appeal for any aggrieved employee because such cases are heard in the industrial courts under the jurisdiction of statute law. An example of this may be found in the case of *Simmonds* v. *Dowty Seals Ltd* (1978). In this case a night worker was threatened with disciplinary action if he refused to work on the day shift. However, the Employment Appeal Tribunal (EAT) concluded that the company had repudiated his contract by attempting to unilaterally to change its terms. This meant that in effect Mr Simmonds had been unfairly dismissed. This case makes clear the necessity for employers to consult and negotiate over contract changes with their employees.

However, the fact that the *Simmonds* case went to the EAT shows that it was far more complex than the few words devoted to it here. When you consider that the EAT consists of High Court judges you can see that the arguments in the case were rehearsed extensively before a decision was finally reached in the employee's favour. This confirms the point made by Burchill (1997) that grievances can arise as a result of the ambiguity with which the terms of the contract of employment are defined. You will remember from Chapter 1 that employment contract terms and conditions are derived from a number of sources. Among these are organisational rules and regulations, collective and individual agreements, and custom and practice. Even when these are written, they are open to different interpretations, but often they are not written, as is the case with custom and practice.

It is predictable that disciplinary action taken occurs on the list of important sources of employee grievances, because the principle of employee appeal against disciplinary action is an important part of the disciplinary procedure, as is explained later in this chapter. Similarly, we deal with bullying and harassment later in this section.

Another useful way of categorising employee grievances, or any individual or collective dispute for that matter, is to distinguish between disputes of right and interest. Burchill (1997: 113) succinctly defines the difference between these terms:

> A dispute of right is about what an agreement actually means; a dispute of interest is about what an agreement ought to contain.

Individual employee grievances may fall into the category of either a *dispute of right* or a *dispute of interest* (or, indeed, both). For example, a dispute of right may occur over a refusal by management to allow an employee anything other than one day off with pay to attend a family wedding, following the personnel handbook offer to employees of 'reasonable time off' to attend such events. An employee grievance may be raised in the event of a second day being needed to travel 600 miles to and from the wedding. Here the dispute may turn on the meaning of the phrase 'reasonable time off'. The same personnel handbook may state that the 'normal' pay rate applies to extra hours worked at a time deemed 'unsociable hours'. A grievance may be raised about this issue which would be defined as a dispute of interest.

9.4 Grievance procedures

We hope that the preceding discussion has given you some idea of the complexity of grievance issues. Such complexity is inevitable. If disputes of right, in particular, were to be avoided, virtually all issues that might be the subject of differing interpretations would need to be formally written in such a precise manner as to be beyond dispute. Clearly this is impossible. In our view it is also undesirable, both for managers and for employees. The reason why most employment relationships 'work' is because there is give and take on both sides, something that would be threatened were every aspect of to be codified.

However, it would be wrong to assume that procedures are not a valuable feature of the employment relationship. Indeed, the 1968 Donovan Commission attributed many of the industrial relations conflicts of the 1960s to vague and long-winded procedures. In common with other employee relations procedures (that is, trade union recognition, collective bargaining, collective disputes, discipline, redundancy, equal opportunities), grievance procedures present management and employees with distinct advantages. These are summarised in Box 9.1.

Box 9.1   The advantages of a formal grievance procedure

- Provides a mechanism for employee concerns over work-related matters to be dealt with fairly and speedily before they develop into major problems and possibly collective disputes.
- Explicit recognition of the right of employees to raise grievances. It helps to formalise the conflict within agreed parameters and therefore facilitates grievance resolution within these.
- Clarifies the person with whom the initial grievance should be raised and specifies the action to be taken should an agreement not be reached at this initial level.
- Acts as a safety-valve in providing time to reflect upon the issue raised.
- Ensures greater consistency of practice across the organisation. This is particularly important in multi-site organisations where different practices would develop were a procedural framework not defined.
- Encourages the maintenance of written records that may be helpful in the event of the grievance being pursued and therefore dealt with by different participants.
- Helps to develop good employee relations practice which is important in employment tribunal cases.
- Joint development of the procedure leads to ownership of the procedure by all parties concerned with its development and enhanced determination to make it work.
- Ensures that employers meet statutory obligations.

Source: Developed from Marchington and Wilkinson (2002) and ACAS (2000b)

The most authoritative source of information for those concerned with grievance matters is the ACAS (2000a) *Code of Practice: Disciplinary and grievance procedures*. Included in the Code are the following clauses:

- It is in everyone's best interests to ensure that workers' grievances are dealt with quickly and fairly and at the lowest level possible within the organisation at which the matter can be resolved. Management is responsible for taking the initiative in developing grievance procedures which, if they are to be fully effective, need to be acceptable to both those they cover and those who have to operate them. It is important therefore that senior management aims to secure the involvement of workers and their representatives, including trade unions where they are recognised, and all levels of management when formulating or revising grievance procedures.

■ Grievance procedures enable individuals to raise issues with management about their work, or about their employers', clients' or their fellow workers' actions that affect them. It is impossible to provide a comprehensive list of all the issues that might give rise to a grievance but some of the more common include terms and conditions of employment, health and safety, relationships at work, new working practices, organisational change, and equal opportunities.

■ Procedures should be simple, set down in writing and rapid in operation. They should also provide for grievance proceedings and records to be kept confidential.

■ It is good practice for individuals to be accompanied at grievance hearings. (See below.)

■ In order for grievance procedures to be effective it is important that all workers are made aware of them and understand them and if necessary that supervisors, managers and worker representatives are trained in their use. Wherever possible every worker should be either given a copy of the procedure or provided with access to it (for example in the personnel handbook or on the company intranet site) and have the detail explained to them. For new employees this might be best done as part of any induction process. Special allowance should be made for individuals whose first language is not English or who have visual impairment or some other disability.

The Employment Act 2002 gives workers the right to be accompanied at grievance hearings by a fellow worker or a trade union official. However, this legal right applies only to grievance hearings that concern the performance of 'a duty by an employer in relation to a worker' (ACAS, 2000b). This means a legal duty derived from the contract of employment. The ACAS Code of Practice provided some useful examples of issues that may constitute an employer's legal duty to an employee. A good example concerns car parking. The employer may have no obligation to provide car parking for employees: therefore an employee raising a grievance over the lack of car parking may not have the legal right to be accompanied. However, were that employee to be disabled and need car parking facilities in order to attend the place of work, the employer's contractual duty of care would become relevant, and the worker would be likely to have a legal right to be accompanied at a grievance hearing where the issue was raised. An additional clause in the Employment Act 2002 concerns the fact that employers have a duty to give employees details of grievance and disciplinary procedures and any procedure adopted (written or otherwise) where an employee is dismissed. If employers do not comply with this requirement, compensation from a successful employment tribunal claim could be increased by up to 25 per cent (Younson, 2002).

These clauses in the Code of Practice are illustrated in the following example of a grievance procedure from one of the UK's largest financial services organisations, shown as Box 9.2.

Box 9.2 Grievance procedure: Nationwide Building Society

1 Introduction

Occasionally employees may be unhappy with the way they are being treated at work. Most situations are likely to be resolved through the normal interactions between an employee and their manager. However, where this is not possible, this procedure provides a process that enables employees to address their concerns fairly and speedily. Grievances may be raised by an individual or by a group of employees.

A grievance may be of a factual nature covering such issues as new working practices, organisational change and fair treatment. A grievance may also arise from relationships at work. Separate procedures are in place to deal with issues of harassment and bullying, and the *Harassment and Bullying Guide* provides more guidance and definitions.

Raising a grievance or having a grievance raised against you can be a difficult and distressing time. Nationwide seeks to support all parties involved in a grievance at all stages of the procedure. Any of the following may be contacted for support:

- line manager or his/her manager;
- personnel & development (P&D) consultant;
- a representative of Nationwide Group Staff Union (NGSU).

Where special appeal procedures exist, for example to deal with job evaluation or performance rating disputes, employees should follow these procedures. Concerns relating to suspicions or allegations of malpractice in the workplace can be raised confidentially using the *Procedure for Raising Concerns at Work*.

2 Principles

All employees have the right to raise a grievance about problems or concerns at work, their working environment or working relationships.

Grievances will be dealt with fairly and speedily, and any records relating to grievance procedures will be kept confidential.

Ideally, grievances should be resolved at the level at which they arise and can often be resolved quickly without the need for the formal stages of this procedure. Any employee wishing to raise a concern is encouraged to discuss it informally with their line manager. Managers have a responsibility to treat these seriously, to listen to an employee and discuss how best to deal with the issue.

If an employee feels unable to go directly to their manager, because of the nature of the concern, they should talk to their P&D Consultant or an NGSU Representative (if a member).

If an employee is unhappy with the outcome of their grievance, they have the right to refer their grievance to a higher level of management and ultimately to a Divisional Director.

A group of employees may raise a grievance. In some circumstances it may be appropriate for the group to elect a spokesperson to represent the group at meetings. However, the manager should ensure that all members of the group have the opportunity to express their concerns and to discuss the outcome of the grievance.

3 Raising grievances informally

An employee wishing to raise concerns should ask their manager for a private meeting to discuss them. If the concerns are about their line manager, employees should seek to discuss it with them, but if they feel uncomfortable in doing so they should talk to their senior manager or seek advice from P&D or an NGSU representative (if a member). Employees can talk to their P&D consultant or an NGSU representative at any time.

Box 9.2   Continued

At the meeting, the employee should explain their concerns as clearly as possible and provide any relevant supporting evidence. The manager will listen to the employee's concerns and discuss how best to resolve them. In some instances the manager may require to undertake further investigations or seek advice. In these circumstances, the manager should keep the employee informed of any progress. Although the tone of the meeting should be informal, both parties may wish to take notes of the discussions and any action agreed. All records relating to a grievance must be kept confidential. If necessary a further meeting(s) will be arranged to discuss the manager's decision about the grievance, normally within 5 working days of the original meeting. At the meeting, the manager will set out any action to be taken to address the grievance or explain clearly any reasons why further action cannot be taken.

4 Mediation

Mediation is a process that brings parties together with a view of resolving concerns under the guidance of a trained neutral third party. Mediation is suitable where all parties are willing to participate with a view to resolving the problem. If an employee feels that they would like to pursue mediation they should contact their P&D consultant or an NGSU representative. A mediator will contact them in confidence to understand the details of the concerns. They will then contact the other parties involved to explain the concerns and to see if they are willing to participate in a discussion to resolve the issues. The mediator will arrange a confidential meeting between all parties and will ensure this is conducted in a calm and constructive way. If appropriate, a follow-up meeting date may be arranged to review how things have progressed since the mediation.

5 The formal grievance procedure

If an employee feels the matter has not been resolved through informal discussions or mediation (if tried) they should raise a formal grievance. The employee should set out their grievance in writing and send it to their line manager or to their P&D consultant. P&D will review what has happened to date and check that all possible action has been taken informally. If there is no further informal action that can be taken, the formal grievance will be investigated, normally by the line manager. If an employee remains unhappy with the way their grievance has been dealt with, they can appeal to the next level of management and then, finally, to a Divisional Director.

The formal process is:

(i) Stage one

P&D will arrange with the manager to conduct an investigation into the grievance to establish and clarify the facts. Where appropriate, the investigation will include talking to other parties involved. The investigation will be completed as quickly as possible, and all parties will be kept informed of progress. A letter will be sent to both parties summarising the grievance and advising them of the support available.

When the investigation is complete the manager will invite the employee to a meeting to discuss the grievance. At least 48 hours' written notice of the meeting must be given. The meeting will be conducted by the line manager and will normally involve a member of P&D. Employees have a right to be represented or accompanied at the meeting if they so wish. If the matter is particularly complex the timescales may be extended by agreement but the employee will be kept fully informed of the progress of their grievance.

▶

Box 9.2   Continued

At the meeting:

a The employee will be invited to explain their grievance and provide any relevant evidence.

b The manager will suggest what support or action can be taken to resolve the grievance or indicate what further information or investigations they require before making a decision. Where further investigation is required a date for another meeting will be agreed.

Actions resulting from the meeting:

a The manager will confirm the outcome of the meeting and set out their decision in writing. This will be sent to the employee within 5 working days of the meeting. The employee must be told to whom they can refer their grievance if they remain unhappy with the outcome.

b The manager will also explain the decision to any other parties involved in the grievance.

c Unless there is a valid reason not to do so, action necessary to comply with the decision will be taken within 10 working days of the decision being communicated.

d Where action has been taken to address the grievance, the manager should invite the employee to a review meeting to assess if any further action is required.

(ii) Stage two

If an employee feels the matter has not been resolved at stage one of the procedure they should submit their grievance in writing to the next level of management, explaining why they are unhappy with the outcome. This should be done within two weeks of the original decision, which allows the employee time to reflect on the outcome and decide what action to take. If the employee requires assistance with the process they can seek advice from P&D or an NGSU representative. Employees can talk to their P&D consultant or an NGSU representative at any time.

The employee should provide as much detail as possible and explain clearly the reasons for their grievance. The manager should send a copy of the grievance to their P&D consultant.

The manager will invite the employee to a meeting to discuss the grievance. At least 48 hours' written notice of the meeting must be given. The meeting will be conducted by the manager and will normally involve a member of P&D. Employees have a right to be represented or accompanied at the meeting if they so wish.

In advance of the meeting, the manager will review the findings of the investigation carried out for the first hearing and will undertake any further investigation needed to validate or clarify the facts. If the matter is particularly complex the timescales may be extended by agreement, but the employee will be kept fully informed of the progress of their grievance.

At the meeting:

a The employee will be invited to explain their grievance and why they are unhappy with the outcome of stage one.

b The manager will suggest what support or action can be taken to resolve the grievance or indicate what further information or investigations they require before making a decision. Where further investigation is required a date for another meeting will be agreed.

Actions resulting from the meeting:

a The manager will confirm the outcome of the meeting and set out their decision in writing. This will be sent to the employee within 5 working days of the meeting. The employee must be told to which Divisional Director they can refer their grievance to if they remain unhappy with the outcome.

Box 9.2	Continued

b The manager will also explain the decision to any other parties involved in the grievance.

c Unless there is a valid reason not to do so, action necessary to comply with the decision will be taken within 10 working days of the decision being communicated.

d Where action has been taken to address the grievance, the manager should invite the employee to a review meeting to assess if any further action is required.

(iii) Stage three

If an employee remains unhappy with the outcome of stage two of the procedure they should submit their grievance in writing to the nominated Divisional Director, explaining why they are unhappy with the outcome. This should be done within two weeks of the original decision, which allows the employee time to reflect on the outcome and decide what action to take. The Divisional Director is the final recourse within the Society. If the employee requires assistance with the process they can seek advice from P&D or an NGSU representative. Employees can talk to their P&D consultant or an NGSU representative at any time.

The Divisional Director will review the grievance, arrange for any further investigation required to validate or clarify the facts, and invite the employee to a meeting within 10 working days. At least 48 hours' written notice of the meeting must be given. The meeting will be conducted by the Divisional Director and will normally involve a senior member of P&D. Employees have a right to be represented or accompanied at the meeting if they so wish. If the matter is particularly complex the timescales may be extended by agreement but the employee will be kept fully informed of the progress of their grievance. The Divisional Director hearing the grievance will be from a different business area to that of the employee raising the grievance and, because of the involvement of P&D throughout the process, the Divisional Director for P&D will not hear a grievance.

At the meeting:

a The employee will be invited to explain their grievance and why they are unhappy with the outcome of stage two.

b The Divisional Director will suggest what support or action can be taken to resolve the grievance or indicate what further information or investigations they require before making a decision. Where further investigation is required a date for another meeting will be agreed.

Actions resulting from the meeting:

a The Divisional Director will confirm the outcome of the meeting and set out their decision in writing. This will be sent to the employee within 5 working days of the meeting. The Divisional Director's decision shall be regarded as the final recourse within the Society.

b The Divisional Director will also explain the decision to any other parties involved in the grievance.

c Unless there is a valid reason not to do so, action necessary to comply with the decision will be taken within 10 working days of the decision being communicated.

d Where action has been taken to address the grievance, the employee's senior manager should invite the employee to a review meeting to assess if any further action is required.

6 *Issues of principle*

The outcome of any grievances, which raise issues of principle, will be the subject of consultation and discussion between management and the NGSU at the Joint Consultative and Negotiating Committee (JCNC).

Reproduced with permission.

The Nationwide procedure in Box 9.2 may be thought of as a generic procedure, capable of dealing with many general workplace situations. There are, however, special types of grievance that are best coped with by the development of special procedures. The Nationwide example cross-refers to these by making it clear that there are separate procedures in place to deal with issues of harassment and bullying. In addition, there are special appeal procedures to deal with job evaluation or performance rating disputes. In such cases employees are asked to follow these procedures. The procedure notes that concerns relating to suspicions or allegations of malpractice in the workplace can be raised confidentially using the *Procedure for Raising Concerns at Work*.

Harassment and bullying was listed earlier as being a prevalent area for grievances. We deal with this in more detail in the next section.

self-check question	**9.2** Managers and supervisors are key players in most organisations' grievance procedures. In what ways do managers threaten the fairness with which employee grievances are handled?

■ Procedures for dealing with harassment

In 1997 the TUC ran a 'bad boss' hotline to which employees were asked to report their examples of 'bad bosses'. Four out of ten of the calls were about workplace bullying (IDS, 1999). Although we don't suggest that harassment and bullying are new phenomena at the workplace, it is clear that these are becoming a cause of concern for many organisations.

Severn Trent Water Authority defines harassment as:

> ...any conduct related to age, creed, disability, nationality, race, religion, sex or any other personal characteristics which is unwanted by the individual. Harassment can also be classified as any other conduct which affects the dignity of any individual or group of individuals, at work. (IDS, 1999)

Harassment may be based on the employee's social or cultural background; race, ethnic origin or skin colour; sex or sexual orientation; religious or political convictions; membership or non-membership of a trade union; disability; age; or, indeed, the willingness of an employee to challenge harassment, leading to victimisation. Acts of harassment include unwanted physical contact (such as touching), unwanted verbal or written contact, display of pictures etc., and social exclusion (not talking to a colleague, for example).

In the IDS (1999) study of the way in which selected large UK organisations deal with harassment grievances there appeared to be two dominant approaches: *informal methods* and the instigation of *formal procedures*. The former route often involves the employee who feels that he or she is the victim talking informally to a harassment counsellor without involving managers or HR specialists. Alternatively, an external counselling service may be used. This stress upon the use of trained counsellors points up the difference between harassment issues and more general grievances. First is the essentially specialist nature of the issue. Counselling in such situations demands the sort of qualities and abilities on the part of the counsellor that many line managers (or, for that matter, HR specialists) would not possess. Second, it may be that the alleged harasser *is* the line manager, thus making the principle of 'the grievance should normally be discussed first between the employee and his immediate superior' clearly unworkable.

The informal and procedural approach is favoured in the Granada Technology Group (IDS, 1999). To attempt formal resolution of the problem the complainant is encouraged to raise the matter with the alleged harasser. This may be done with the support of a friend, colleague or manager. Alternatively, an HR specialist or a senior manager may talk to the alleged harasser (to whom, incidentally, counselling should also be offered, especially if he or she is embarrassed that particular behaviour has given offence or if the behaviour persists and the alleged harasser insists that nothing wrong is being done).

Granada's formal harassment procedure applies in the place of the normal grievance procedure. It is used when the informal route has failed, or in the first instance where the complaint is particularly serious or when the complainant prefers initially to invoke the formal procedure. The first step is a formal investigation carried out by the alleged harasser's line manager, or a member of the corporate security department where appropriate. This involves interviews with complainant, alleged harasser and any witnesses. Once the investigation is complete, a panel comprising the investigators and an HR adviser is formed. The complainant and the alleged harasser (and their representatives) attend separate meetings to face objective questioning. The panel then assesses all the evidence and decides the outcome. Granada Technology Group defines deliberate harassment as gross misconduct for which a harasser may be summarily dismissed.

It is, of course, open for alleged victims of harassment to take a case to an employment tribunal. Although sexual harassment is not yet a statutory offence, tribunals apply the concepts of sex discrimination to sexual harassment cases. The consequences of a sexual harassment claim are serious for employers. Employers are responsible in law for any acts of sexual harassment by their employees. In addition, the burden of proof at tribunals is on employers to demonstrate that sexual harassment did not take place in the workplace or that such acts did not constitute sexual harassment. As Learmond-Criqui (2002) notes, this is an alarming development for employers because there are no ceilings on awards for sexual harassment claims.

The mention above of summary dismissal leads us into the second major focus of this chapter – discipline. In it we take a similar approach to that which we have taken over grievance. We consider some of the background issues to discipline at work and examine in some detail how organisations conduct their disciplinary policy.

9.5 Discipline

Origins and legal background

Similar to the obligation for employers to cater for employee grievances, the necessity to deal formally with employee discipline was initially imposed under the Industrial Relations Act 1971. This Act created a right for many employees not to be unfairly dismissed. Chapter 11 goes into detail on the legislation. The important point to note here is that a major criterion for employment tribunals to consider when deciding whether an employee has been unfairly dismissed is the process adopted by managers in dismissing the employee. This consideration will be influenced largely by the disciplinary procedures in the organisation and the extent to which these procedures have governed the approach taken by managers. The answer to this question will play a large part in determining whether the dismissal is deemed fair and reasonable.

As with the employee's right to be informed of how grievances should be raised, so a similar right to be informed of the existence of the disciplinary procedure is contained in the Employment Rights Act 1996. The written statement of terms and conditions of employment should contain notes on any disciplinary rules in existence and the identity of the person to whom employees may apply if they wish to appeal against any disciplinary decision, and how to make such an application.

Reasons for disciplinary action

You may ask: 'How do I know what is likely to be the subject of disciplinary action and what may be defined as "acceptable" behaviour at work?' Unfortunately the answer is never simple. There are, of course, clear instances of employee behaviour that can never be acceptable: for example, seriously physically assaulting another employee. But many instances of employees failing to meet the employer's 'reasonable and legitimate expectations', noted in Pilbeam and Corbridge's (2002) definition at the beginning of this chapter, are much less clear-cut. If you are in the latter stages of reading this book you will have gathered by now that what is 'reasonable' and what is 'legitimate' varies according to the particular employment context. Swearing may be seen as normal between colleagues on the factory floor but unacceptable when important clients are being entertained in the boardroom.

Salamon (2000) notes that the employer's expectations of legitimate employee behaviour originate from three sources: *general society*, *external legislation*, and the *organisation's own rules* (see Box 9.3).

Box 9.3 The sources of employers' expectations of employees' work behaviour

General society

Personal behaviour of the employee is dictated to a large degree by the rules and norms of society. Society's rules impose on all of us the necessity to behave outside the workplace in a way that does not interfere with the safety, peace, property etc. of fellow citizens. So it is at the workplace. Fighting, stealing etc. are normally defined as gross misconduct at the workplace and render the employee liable for summary dismissal.

External legislation

Discrimination and health and safety are two areas where the law lays down strict guidelines that govern employee behaviour. This is of particular importance to employers, as they may be held liable for employee breaches of external legislation.

Organisational rules

Job performance, absenteeism and timekeeping are examples of potential discipline issues that are defined by management as opposed to societal norms or external legislation. As such they are specific to the workplace context and are defined with the effective operation of the employer's business in mind.

These three sources should not be thought of as mutually exclusive. For example, acts of racial discrimination breach not only moral (general society) and legal norms. Performing the duties for which one is paid, provided these are generally held to be reasonable and legitimate, may be thought of to be a general social norm and a common law obligation on the employee that underpins the contract of employment (see Chapter 1). It may also be expressed in specific terms in the organisation's rules. For example, progress in the salary structure is usually dependent upon acceptable job performance.

You may be wondering why we are labouring this point about the sources of employer expectations. To answer this question we return to the central theme of this book – the employment relationship. As in society at large, the organisation has to have rules to govern the behaviour of its members, processes to ensure that these rules are followed, and sanctions to be imposed if they are not. The effectiveness of this aspect of the employment relationship depends on the legitimacy granted by both managers and employees to the rules. This is normally beyond dispute in the case of the rules themselves (albeit not necessarily their application) that emanate from general society and external legislation. The main area of contention is those rules that are defined by the organisation. It is for this reason that ACAS (2000b) recommends the involvement of employees and any recognised trade unions when disciplinary procedures are introduced or revised. Survey evidence from 50 UK organisations (IRS, 1995b) suggests that they do involve their trade unions and staff associations in devising disciplinary procedures. In all the organisations surveyed by IRS where revision to disciplinary rules and procedures had taken place in the preceding 4 years, the trade union or staff association had been involved through negotiation or consultation.

Categorising the reasons why the employer may take disciplinary action tends to be the stuff of law books dealing with unfair dismissal. As such we do not wish here to duplicate what we deal with in more detail in Chapter 11. However, we think it would be helpful to list some of the main reasons, and have done so under seven categories: personal behaviour; general work conduct; discrimination; job performance; health and safety; absence; and timekeeping.

- *Personal behaviour*. We have already noted in Box 9.3 some of the more extreme examples of misconduct in this category: fighting and theft. These would normally be treated as gross misconduct (see Box 9.4). An increasingly important area is that of *substance abuse*, defined by the Institute of Personnel Management (now the CIPD) as 'problematic use of alcohol, drugs and other substances'. This is one of the examples of personal behaviour where a separate policy may need to be developed. This would put emphasis upon activities such as counselling and education before the disciplinary procedure is invoked in the late stages of the case. Failure to comply with reasonable management request may also come under this category.
- *General work conduct*. We distinguish this category from personal behaviour because general work conduct deals with those issues that relate more to work and therefore are more likely to flow from the organisation's rules rather than from general society. Examples here are unauthorised absence from the workplace, inappropriate dress, and misuse of the organisation's facilities. This final category raises another interesting potential discipline issue that is exercising the minds of both HR specialists and employment lawyers as we write this chapter – the use of the Internet for personal purposes in the employer's time and on the employer's

computers. *People Management* (1999) reports that a survey estimated that 2 million employees use the Internet at work to obtain travel information, and the same number read newspapers online. As with many other similar issues, this appears to be a very grey area.

self-check question

9.3 If you were an HR manager how would you deal with a situation where you were called upon to control the suspected abuse by employees of Internet provision in your organisation?

■ *Discrimination*. The coverage of harassment earlier in this chapter suggests that discrimination is an important reason for disciplinary action being taken against employees who behave in a discriminatory way. Indeed, 70 per cent of the 50 organisations surveyed by IRS (1995a) reported that sex and race harassment had become a common disciplinary offence. Eighty per cent listed it as an example of gross misconduct (IRS, 1995b) compared with 7 per cent that defined it as gross misconduct in a similar survey four years earlier (IRS, 1991). Equal opportunities policies normally have a clause indicating that employees found to be behaving in a discriminatory way will be subject to the disciplinary process in the same way as for other potential disciplinary offences.

■ *Job performance*. This also is an area of discipline that is receiving more attention as employers concentrate on what has become known as *performance management*. Rather like substance abuse and equal opportunities mentioned above, many larger organisations are now treating poor job performance as a specific issue that is subject to particular treatment before the general disciplinary procedure is triggered. We highlight the role of capability procedures later in this section.

■ *Health and safety*. The extent to which contraventions of health and safety regulations are an important reason for disciplinary cases will depend on the workplace. You may have worked in settings where this is a vital aspect of working life, such as restaurants or chemical factories. Even in shops and offices neglect of prescribed health and safety standards may lead to accidents that result in litigation against the employer by customers or employees.

■ *Absence* is a predictable reason for disciplinary action. This may be persistent, systematic (for example, regularly occurring after weekends), or non-reported absence. This has had increased cost implications for employers since the statutory sick pay regulations were changed in 1994 with the result that the cost of the first four weeks of absence falls on the employer.

■ *Timekeeping*. This may be as a result of the employee arriving late or leaving early. The abolition of 'clocking-in' systems in many organisations means that procedural 'backstops' are increasingly important in the event of abuse of this trust.

■ Disciplinary procedures

The document that most HR managers consult prior to drafting a disciplinary procedure is the ACAS Code of Practice (2000a). It does not, in itself, constitute statute law in that if any part of its provisions is not observed that does not render the lack of observation unlawful. However, the Code is admissible as evidence in employment tribunals. Therefore, adherence to the Code is strongly advisable.

Much the most important part of the Code of Practice is the section that details the essential features of disciplinary procedures (ACAS, 2000a). These are that procedures should:

- be in writing;
- specify to whom they apply;
- be non-discriminatory;
- provide for matters to be dealt with without undue delay;
- provide for proceedings, witness statements and records to be kept confidential;
- indicate the disciplinary actions which may be taken;
- specify the levels of management which have the authority to take the various forms of disciplinary action;
- provide for workers to be informed of the complaints against them and where possible all relevant evidence before any hearing;
- provide workers with an opportunity to state their case before decisions are reached;
- provide workers with the right to be accompanied (see also Section three [of the Code of Practice] for information on the statutory right to be accompanied);
- ensure that, except for gross misconduct, no worker is dismissed for a first breach of discipline;
- ensure that disciplinary action is not taken until the case has been carefully investigated;
- ensure that workers are given an explanation for any penalty imposed;
- provide a right of appeal – normally to a more senior manager – and specify the procedure to be followed.

The way in which the disciplinary procedure is used depends on the circumstances of each case. Should the manager suspect that the disciplinary rules have been broken there are two options available. The first is to treat it informally, as line managers would often treat a first instance of lateness. The second option is to invoke the disciplinary procedure. Such a decision is not always straightforward, and some employers 'semi-formalise' the grey area between the two positions (IDS, 2001). This may involve counselling, informal advice or cautions, but not formal triggering of the disciplinary procedure.

In the event of the disciplinary procedure being invoked there is often a three- or four-stage procedure: the emphasis of each of these stages is illustrated in Box 9.4, which details the disciplinary procedure at the computer company RM.

Box 9.4 **Disciplinary procedure: RM[1]**

Purpose and scope

This procedure is designed to help and encourage all employees to achieve and maintain standards of conduct, attendance and job performance. The company policies and this procedure apply to all employees. The aim is to ensure consistent and fair treatment for all. These procedures apply to all members of staff irrespective of sex, marital status, race or disability, religious belief or political opinion.

Principles

- No disciplinary action will be taken against any employee until the case has been fully investigated.

▶

| Box 9.4 | **Continued** |

- At every stage in the procedure the employee will be advised of the nature of the complaint against him or her and will be given the opportunity to state his or her case before any decision is made.
- At all stages the employee will have the right to be accompanied by a work colleague or a trade union representative during the disciplinary interview.
- No employee will be dismissed for a first breach of discipline except in the case of gross misconduct when the penalty will be dismissal without notice or payment in lieu of notice.
- An employee will have the right to appeal against any disciplinary penalty imposed.
- The procedure may be implemented at any stage if the employee's alleged misconduct warrants such action.
- If an offence recurs the company reserves the right to enter the procedure at any stage if the employee's alleged misconduct warrants it regardless of the time expired between offences.

Definitions

Misconduct

Misconduct would warrant either a verbal or first written warning. A non-exhaustive list of examples includes:

- poor timekeeping;
- absenteeism;
- poor performance;
- smoking in areas where it is prohibited to do so;
- overuse of company systems such as telephone, email or the Internet.

Serious misconduct

Serious misconduct may occur either on its own or because of repeated acts of misconduct or because there are mitigating circumstances surrounding a situation which would otherwise be gross misconduct. This would warrant a final written warning. A non-exhaustive list of examples includes:

- a failure to notify the company where there are no mitigating circumstances;
- threatening physical abuse;
- verbal abuse;
- refusing a manager's reasonable request;
- inappropriate use of company systems such as telephone, e-mail or the internet.

Gross misconduct

Particularly serious offences will be regarded as gross misconduct. The penalty for gross misconduct would be dismissal without notice or payment in lieu of notice. The following list provides a non-exhaustive list of examples of offences that are normally regarded as gross misconduct:

- theft, fraud, deliberate falsification of records, unauthorised possession of company property;
- fighting, assault on another person, violence or abusive behaviour;

Box 9.4 Continued

- deliberate damage to company property, reputation or interests;
- serious incapability;
- serious negligence which causes unacceptable loss, damage or injury;
- serious act of insubordination;
- a breach of the general duty to safeguard confidential information and to ensure that such information is not released to a third party except for authorised or legitimate business reasons;
- inappropriate use of data obtained through access to customers' systems through managed services contacts;
- the provision or receipt of gifts, entertainment or other personal benefits above modest requirements of business courtesy;
- the non-declaration of personal interest in any enterprise which may infringe on an employee's impartiality in any matters relevant to their duties;
- unauthorised or improper use of company vehicles;
- use of company systems such as telephone, email or the Internet for offensive or obscene purposes e.g. pornography;
- acts of incitement or actual acts of discrimination, harassment or victimisation;
- indecent behaviour;
- contravention of the company share dealing code.

Procedure

If conduct or performance does not reach acceptable standards, the line managers will decide, in consultation with personnel, whether informal counselling is appropriate or if disciplinary action is necessary. A manager or management representative at grade G or above may take disciplinary action. A personnel executive at grade G or above will also be present to ensure that the procedure is fair and consistent, although they may not always be present at verbal warnings. If after investigating the evidence it is decided that disciplinary action is appropriate the following procedure will be used:

Stage 1: verbal warning

If conduct or performance does not meet acceptable standards the employee will normally be given a formal verbal warning. He or she will be advised verbally of the reason for the warning, that this is the first stage of the disciplinary procedure and of his or her right of appeal. A brief note will be kept on his or her personal file in the personnel department, which will become spent after 6 months, subject to satisfactory conduct and performance, although this may be extended at the company's discretion.

Stage 2: written warning

If the offence is a serious one, or if a further offence occurs, a written warning will be given to the employee by his or her line manager. This will give details of the complaint, the improvement required and the timescale. It will warn that action under stage 3 will be considered if there is no satisfactory improvement and will advise of the right of appeal. A copy of the written warning will be kept on his or her personal file in the personnel department but it will be disregarded for disciplinary purposes after 12 months subject to satisfactory conduct and performance, although this may be extended at the company's discretion.

▶

Box 9.4   Continued

Stage 3: final written warning

If there is still a failure to improve, and conduct or performance is still unsatisfactory, or if the misconduct is sufficiently serious to warrant only one written warning but insufficiently serious to justify dismissal (in effect both first and final written warning), a final written warning will normally be given to the employee. This will give details of the complaint, will warn that dismissal will result if there is no satisfactory improvement, and will advise of the right of appeal. A copy of this final written warning will be kept on his or her personal file in the personnel department but it will be spent after 12 months (in exceptional cases this period may be longer) subject to satisfactory conduct and performance, although this may be extended at the company's discretion.

Stage 4: dismissal

If conduct or performance is still unsatisfactory and the employee still fails to meet the prescribed standards, dismissal will normally result. The employee will be provided, as soon as is reasonably practicable, with written reasons for dismissal, the date on which employment will terminate, and the right of appeal. If the company is satisfied that gross misconduct has occurred the result will normally be summary dismissal without notice or payment in lieu of notice.

Suspension

In some circumstances (usually in cases of alleged gross misconduct and other situations where it is thought necessary) the company may deem it appropriate to suspend an individual on full pay, normally for no more than five working days, while the company investigates the alleged offence. Any such suspension would not, in itself, constitute disciplinary action.

Appeals

An employee who wishes to appeal against a disciplinary decision should inform the line manager and personnel executive who held the disciplinary meeting within three working days of receiving the verbal warning or the written notification of the written warning, final written warning or dismissal. Written grounds for the appeal should be provided. A divisional senior manager/director will hear the appeal and their decision is final. Wherever possible, all appeals will be heard by a level of management that is higher than the level involved in the original disciplinary hearing and who have not been involved in the original disciplinary decision. At the appeal any disciplinary penalty will be reviewed but it cannot be increased.

Reproduced with permission

[1] RM is a supplier of software, services and systems to schools. It employs 1400 staff in head office and sales offices throughout the UK. This procedure was last revised in 2000.

Two further points from the ACAS literature should be noted. First, the advisory handbook (ACAS, 2000b) stresses the importance of managers keeping records on all aspects of disciplinary cases and the action taken. We recommend strongly that you visit an employment tribunal to witness an unfair dismissal case (you can visit as an ordinary member of the public). This experience will emphasise to you the importance of managers' notes. Managers are obviously key witnesses in dismissal cases and therefore they are called upon to detail actions taken as part of the disciplinary process. A complete set of notes in such circumstances is essential. Second, Paragraph 16 of the ACAS Code (2000a) emphasises the importance of managers acting 'reasonably in all the circumstances'. It goes on to say that factors that may be relevant here include 'the extent to which standards have been breached, precedent, the worker's general record, position, length of service and special circumstances which might make it appropriate to adjust the severity of the penalty'.

You may consider that this section on discipline has a distinct managerial ring to it. This is inevitable. However, it is important to clarify that the content of the disciplinary procedure and the conduct of the discipline process must afford employees certain rights that flow from principles of natural justice (Pilbeam and Corbridge, 2002: 418). Some of these are explicitly listed in the ACAS list of 'essential features' above: that is, knowledge of the alleged disciplinary breach, a preliminary investigation before any allegation is made, the opportunity for a fair hearing where the individual can explain his or her side of the story, accompaniment at any hearing, and a right of appeal to a higher authority. In addition, Pilbeam and Corbridge note that employees are entitled to know the standards expected of them (a point that is not made explicit in the procedure in Box 9.4). This is an important point, into which we go in some detail later when we consider capability procedures. This may seem an obvious point to employees in large organisations because the standards expected of them are usually explained at the commencement of employment. They may be listed in job descriptions or similar documentation. But, in a small organisation, often the employee has to infer the appropriate standards of behaviour from other employees. Not surprisingly, this sometimes goes wrong! The principles of natural justice also suggest that any mitigating circumstances should be considered, and the 'punishment should fit the crime'. Finally, Pilbeam and Corbridge propose that natural justice implies that the individual should be given the opportunity and support to improve behaviour, unless, of course, the offence is so serious that this is impracticable.

This final point raises the question of the emphasis that may be attached to the discipline process. In a study of 50 discipline procedures, IDS (1997) concluded that a change of emphasis has occurred when procedures dating from the early 1980s are contrasted with more recent examples. The older examples are more likely to stress the achievement of discipline through punishment whereas the more recent procedures emphasise the pursuit of the same ends through positive management.

■ Discipline: punishing or supporting?

In recent years, in many organisations, the demands of employers have become greater. Employers now expect higher performance standards from their employees. In the event of employers investing in their employees by providing them with good-quality training and development you may argue that this is a valid position for employers to take. After all, should not employers expect a reasonable return on their investment? But this is a far cry from the employer who raises the performance standards, finds that one of the established workers cannot meet the new standards, and uses the disciplinary process to 'get rid of' the established employee. It will be clear to you by now that the disciplinary procedure is there to protect the employee from unfair and unreasonable treatment as well as to afford the employer the opportunity of dispensing with the unsatisfactory employee.

Positive discipline (1): capability procedures

Examples of gross misconduct, fighting or theft are the colourful sides of the discipline process. But teaching employee relations to experienced managers has convinced us that a concern that is much more common for many managers is the so-called *poor performer*: the employee who, in comparison with colleagues doing similar duties, performs at a lower standard. It is natural that managers assume that the blame for such a situation lies with the employee: the employee is the problem, and the only satisfactory way of dealing with the problem is to dismiss the 'useless' employee. This may be wrong on two counts. First, it may be that the manager shares a portion of the blame for the employee's poor performance, and, second, dismissing so-called 'useless' employees without the proper disciplinary process being followed smacks of the arbitrary treatment that the legislation was introduced to stop.

The immediate problem in dealing with the poor performer is to establish whether the reason for poor performance is lack of capability or negligence. Poor performance may be evident when an employee does not have the ability to achieve the standards set by the manager, however hard that employee tries. Alternatively, the employee may possess the ability to meet the standards but, for whatever reason, is not prepared to make the effort to meet them. There is a clear need for the employer to distinguish between what the EAT termed 'sheer incapability due to an inherent capacity to function or... one of failure to exercise to the full such talent as is possessed' (Croner's, 1991: 1). This attempt to distinguish is made through the initial investigation that, for example, is detailed in the first principle of the procedure in Box 9.4 above. The EAT went on to say that 'cases where a person has not come up to the required standard through his own carelessness, negligence or idleness are much more appropriately dealt with as cases of misconduct rather than incapability' (Croner's, 1991: 1).

self-check question	**9.4** What practical difficulties do you think there may be in distinguishing between lack of capability and negligence?

You should now be clear how this may be treated as a misconduct case, but less clear about how it may be dealt with as a case of lack of capability. Many organisations now treat the issues differently in their disciplinary procedures. The capability procedure is normally an early stage of the main disciplinary procedure, which may or may not (depending upon the outcome) lead to the main disciplinary procedure being activated. Here again we use the Nationwide Building Society as an example.

The introduction to Nationwide's procedure stresses that capability is a two-way process that imposes upon managers a duty to provide appropriate support as well as requiring employees to improve performance. It points out that capability issues may arise:

■ when the employee fails to attain the standards specified in the performance agreement due to an employee's own level of ability, not where the problem is due to the Society not providing the appropriate training, support and resources;
■ due to the failure of any tests which are requirements of the job; or
■ due to the failure to retain membership/licences necessary to carry out the job. However, where this is a result of a deliberate act by the employee or a consequence of misconduct this may be managed under the Conduct Procedure.

The procedure lays emphasis upon the importance of an initial investigation. This considers:

- the performance standards set in the performance agreement;
- the actual level of performance;
- the training, support and guidance provided;
- the resources provided to enable the required standards to be reached;
- the timescales set (were these reasonable?);
- possible reasons for the performance standards not being met.

Possible outcomes of the investigation are:

- no further action is necessary;
- further action is necessary under the Capability Procedure;
- action is necessary under the Conduct Procedure.

The second of these is the most likely. The outcome is likely to be an agreement between the employee and the manager of the performance standards to be achieved, the training and support to be provided, and the timescales set for improvement. The employee is informed that if improvement is not achieved formal action will be taken.

Prior to formal action being taken, the manager responsible must provide evidence that training and support has been provided. Formal action may take two forms – an action contract with a written warning and an action contract with a final written warning. Both stages involve a hearing where the employee is given a full opportunity to explain where he or she is having difficulties with the work.

Both stages of formal action, an action contract with a written warning and an action contract with a final written warning, specify the required performance standards, the training and support to be provided, and the relevant timescales. In the event of the first formal stage not resulting in the required improvement, the employee will normally move to the second stage. Should this not generate performance improvement, the consequence may be dismissal.

At all stages the employee is given a full opportunity to explain where he or she is having difficulties with the work. Moreover, there should be constant monitoring of the employee's progress. In addition, Nationwide will consider the possibility of giving the employee alternative work more appropriate to the employee's skills and experience. In the event of this being at a lower level, the capability procedure makes clear that it may be necessary to adjust the remuneration and benefits package.

At Union Carbide in the USA a similar system of positive discipline exists (Osigweh and Hutchison, 1990). But here, prior to the final stage of dismissal, the employee is given a paid day off to consider whether to make a *total performance commitment* or to resign. This is the most significant aspect of the positive discipline system, which is based on the principle that it is always the individual who must make his or her own decision about commitment to the company and quality of job performance.

What is clear from this consideration of capability is the responsibility on the manager to ensure that sufficient assistance is given to the employee to carry out the job. The case of *Davison* v. *Kent Meters* (1975) illustrates this well. Ms Davison was dismissed for assembling nearly 500 components incorrectly. She insisted that she had followed the instructions given her by the supervisor. He, however, maintained that he had given her no such instructions and that the errors were entirely Ms Davison's fault. The tribunal ruled in Ms Davison's favour. It concluded that, if the supervisor had not given Ms Davison instructions, then he should have done! In addition, the supervisor should have checked on her performance and given her proper supervision.

Positive discipline (2): managing absenteeism

We noted earlier that a prevalent reason for disciplinary action is absenteeism. It is as major a problem in Germany as it is in the UK. The German car manufacturer Opel had been trying unsuccessfully to solve its absenteeism problem for 20 years (IRS, 1996). Several systems were employed to cure the problem before the most successful was introduced in 1995. The tone is positive, with the emphasis upon finding constructive ways of lessening absences. There are four levels of talks. The tone of these talks is dependent upon how often the employee is absent. The first three levels take place in the company of the immediate supervisor on the day of return to work.

- The first level sees the employee welcomed back to work. The employee is informed of developments since the absence, asked informally about reasons for the absence, and invited to suggest improvements to the working environment.
- The second level involves an explanation of the impact of the employee's absence on colleagues and the workload. A reminder is given of the last absence and whether it has anything to do with the workplace.
- The third level entails an explanation that further absences will have personal consequences for the employee. It is the final informal warning before official action is taken.
- The fourth level is conducted with the personnel department. In this the employee is warned of the possibility of dismissal.

Each level of talks lasts for 9 months, during which period the employee moves to the next level if absence recurs. After 9 months without absence has elapsed the talks start again at level one. There are, of course, exceptions to the system. These are illness during pregnancy, or illness due to a work-related accident; further treatment for a recognised illness; if one day of absence is taken within the 9 months since the first talk; an approved health cure; and if the employee chooses to return to work early while still classified as unfit to work.

Opel claims impressive results from the operation of the new system. At one plant alone, Rüsselheim, the reduction in absenteeism saved the company 10 million DM and cut the amount of dismissal cases by up to one-half. As the chair of the Works Council claims: 'When the formalised talk ... is led in an atmosphere of openness and motivation and the process becomes natural the (new system) will no longer be needed. Then a climate... of talking with one another rather than about one another will exist' (IRS, 1996: 28).

9.6 Grievance and discipline in practice

The bulk of this chapter is about the advantages to the conduct of the employment relationship of treating grievance and discipline in a systematic manner. As such, it assumes a highly rational approach, which stresses formal action based upon a model of good practice. However, you will be aware that in all aspects of workplace behaviour what happens in practice rarely conforms to such a model. So it is with grievance and discipline. In this final section we look briefly at the reasons why actual behaviour may depart from models of 'good practice'.

Grievance

Earlier in the chapter we drew the distinction between dissatisfactions, complaints and grievances. Despite the existence of clear procedures, the reality is that in most circumstances dissatisfactions do not turn into formal grievances. This may be because the issue is insufficiently serious. But even if it is, employees often do not wish to 'stick their heads above the parapet'. Most of us will recognise that rather than set in train a procedure that may cause us a great deal of anguish we would prefer to look for employment elsewhere.

Although this may seem like the easy way out, you will have noted before in this book the relative powerlessness of many employees in relation to their managers. This is particularly the case where employees are not organised at their workplace by a trade union, or indeed, are not members of the union. The union representative may encourage the employee to raise a grievance and lend moral and practical support, or raise it as a collective grievance on behalf of the employee if it affects a number of employees. The opposite situation to union support for the employee is the situation where employees do not even know of the existence of a grievance procedure. Despite the fact that it is a legal requirement for employers to draw the attention of their employees to the grievance procedure, we all know that not all employers are as conscientious in such matters as those whose examples have been used in this chapter. To be fair to employers, we all know that we pay little attention to such matters when we start a job, principally because we don't think that we will ever need it.

It will probably have occurred to you that, as well as employee reluctance to raise grievances, managers may be equally reluctant to encourage them. Often this may be because the manager may be the focus of the grievance. Even if this is not the case, the grievance may call into question the competence of the manager in not identifying or confronting the issue. Whatever the reason, dealing with employee grievances is a demanding and time-consuming business that most managers would prefer to avoid.

Discipline

In the same way as there is reluctance on the part of employees to raise grievances, so it is that managers are often unwilling to use the disciplinary procedure. There are a number of understandable reasons for this. The job of the manager is to 'get things done', and anything that distracts from the central purpose of the manager's job is unwelcome. Therefore, the cost to managers of exercising too harsh a disciplinary regime may be too great. This leads to custom and practice based on habitual 'blind-eye turning'. As Edwards (1994: 575) notes:

> ...informal rules may supplant formal ones. Managers may grant concessions to workers in order to meet production demands, but concessions can rapidly grow into precedents and then into relatively well-established custom and practice rules. These rules will reflect the reality of bargaining power on the shopfloor, and attempts to codify and formalise procedures are unlikely to have much effect on behaviour.

The reality of bargaining power on the 'shopfloor' (which could mean any employment setting), to which Edwards refers, suggests situations in which managers may be wary of exercising discipline for fear of reprisals by employees. This could be a result of the collective strength of employees, which may result in some form of industrial action being taken. In 1997, 2 per cent of the days lost due to industrial action were due to disputes over dismissal and other disciplinary measures (Davies, 1998). Similarly, it could be employees with key skills seeking a more 'tolerant' environment with another employer. Most managers would wish to avoid both of these situations.

You may argue that these reasons for managers not invoking the disciplinary procedure in situations where it may be warranted are based on business logic. However, anecdotal evidence from numerous managers tempts us to think that the main reason for managerial reluctance to use the discipline procedure is that most managers prefer to tell employees 'good news' rather than bad: they shy away from confrontation. Many of us can recognise this because it is unpleasant to have to tell people unpalatable things about their job performance, which may involve passing judgements about their personal behaviour. Moreover, the collection of evidence to substantiate the judgements being made can take a considerable amount of time. Therefore, it is easy to see why many managers prefer to ignore unacceptable job performance, albeit that the long-term consequences are serious. If things get so bad that the employee is eventually dismissed, the Employment Tribunal is certain to ask 'why was this issue not dealt with earlier?'. But it is not simply the absence of managerial will to confront unpleasant truths that may lead to managers not using the disciplinary procedure. It is also often a lack of managerial skill. To deliver 'bad news' in an initial disciplinary interview and end the interview in a positive way such that a performance improvement agenda is constructed involves a high degree of interpersonal skill. Despite the fact that 90 per cent of the organisations in the IRS survey (1995a) provided line manager training in discipline handling, only in one-half of the organisations is this compulsory and provided for all line managers involved.

9.7 Summary

- The legislative origin of grievance and discipline dates from 1971.
- The sources of grievance and discipline cases may be classified as environmental sources; sources related to goals, means of achieving goals, and inequities of treatment; and sources related to relationships between individuals, groups or organisations.
- Treating grievance and discipline in a systematic manner presents numerous advantages for the effective operation of the employment relationship.
- ACAS literature specifies helpful guidelines for the composition and implementation of grievance and discipline procedures.
- The emphasis in the operation of discipline at the workplace has moved from the punishment of employees to assisting them to perform more effectively.
- Grievance and discipline may not be conducted in a formal, rational manner in spite of the existence of clear policies and procedures.

References

ACAS (2000a) *Code of Practice No. 1, Disciplinary and grievance procedures*, London, ACAS.

ACAS (2000b) *Discipline at Work: The ACAS advisory handbook*, London, ACAS.

Burchill, F. (1997) *Labour Relations* (2nd edn), Basingstoke, Macmillan.

Croner's (1991) 'Capability v conduct', *Employment Digest*, No. 320, 7 October.

Cully, M., Woodland, S., O'Reilly, A. and Dix, G. (1999) *Britain at Work*, London, Routledge.

Davies, J. (1998) 'Labour disputes in 1997', *Labour Market Trends*, June, 299–311.

Davison v. *Kent Meters Ltd* (1975) Industrial Relations Law Reports, 145.

Donovan, T.N. (1968) *Report of the Royal Commission on Trade Unions and Employers' Associations: 1965–1968*, Cmnd 3623, London, HMSO.

Edwards, P. (1994) 'Discipline and the creation of order', *in* Sisson, K. (ed.), *Personnel Management: A comprehensive guide to theory and practice in Britain*, Oxford, Blackwell, pp. 562–94.

IDS (1997) *Disciplinary Procedures*, Study No. 640, December.

IDS (1999) *Harassment Policies*, Study No. 662, January.

IDS (2001) *Disciplinary Procedures*, Study No. 711, June.

IRS (1991) *Discipline at Work (2): Procedures*, Employment Trends No. 494, August, pp. 5–15.

IRS (1995a) *Discipline at Work: The practice*, Employment Trends No. 591, pp. 4–11.

IRS (1995b) *Discipline at Work (2): The procedures*, Employment Trends No. 592, pp. 5–16.

IRS (1996) 'Opel fights absenteeism', *European Industrial Relations Reports* No. 271, August, 27–8.

IRS (1997) *Handling Employee Grievances: Part 1*, Employment Trends No. 636, July.

Learmond-Criqui, J. (2002) 'For love and money', *People Management*, 30 May, 18.

Marchington, M. and Wilkinson, A. (2002) *People Management and Development: Human resource management at work* (2nd edn), Wimbledon, Chartered Institute of Personnel and Development.

Osigweh, C. and Hutchison, W. (1990) 'To punish or not to punish: managing human resources through positive discipline', *Employee Relations*, 12:3, 27–32.

People Management (1999) 'HR faces double standard charge on net crackdowns', 30 June.

Pilbeam, S. and Corbridge, M. (2002) *People Resourcing: HRM in practice* (2nd edn), Harlow, Pearson Education.

Redman, T. and Wilkinson, A. (2002) *The Informed Student Guide to Human Resource Management*, London, Thomson Learning.

Salamon, M. (2000) *Industrial Relations: Theory and practice* (4th edn), Hemel Hempstead, Prentice Hall.

Salipante, P. and Bouwen, R. (1990) 'Behavioural analysis of grievances: conflict sources, complexity and transformation', *Employee Relations*, 12:3, 17–22.

Simmonds v. *Dowty Seals Ltd* (1978) Industrial Relations Law Reports, 425.

Strathclyde Regional Council v. *Porcelli* (1986) Industrial Relations Law Reports, 134.

Torrington, D. and Hall, L. (1998) *Human Resource Management* (4th edn), London, Prentice Hall.

Younson, F. (2002) 'A lack of discipline', *People Management*, 13 June, 17.

9.1 *Why do you think that you might present the reason for your dissatisfaction, complaint or grievance as a coherent, perhaps single, issue, when the reality may be much more complex?*

There may be a number of reasons. First, it is obviously much simpler to present a single issue because it is easier to articulate and it is less likely that you will be put in the category of a constant 'moaner' for whom everything is wrong. Second, it may be possible to group a series of dissatisfactions under the umbrella of one issue. For example, you may be asked to work, unusually, at the weekend. This is the substantive issue. Yet it possibly calls into question a lack of consultation (relations with management), inadequate recompense (the wage–effort bargain), and a difference between what you expected of the job and what is being asked. Third, the grievance procedure is defined in such a way that a coherent issue is required to be the subject rather than a series of, possibly, loosely connected issues. Finally, Salipante and Bouwen (1990) argue that we redefine our private construction of our grievance into a public construction with the intention that the public definition will result in a favourable outcome for us.

9.2 *Managers and supervisors are key players in most organisations' grievance procedures. In what ways do managers threaten the fairness with which employee grievances are handled?*

As Salamon (2000) points out, in the early stages of the grievance procedure in particular, managers are often judging their own actions about whether an employee issue should be defined as a grievance. You can well imagine that many managers would be defensive in such situations and attempt to dissuade the employee from taking the matter further because it may reflect poorly on that manager. In short, the manager may effectively define the difference between a complaint and a grievance. Given the unequal power relationship that often exists between line managers and their employees, such attempts may well be successful because the employee would fear that the manager would 'have ways of achieving revenge'.

Even in the latter stages of the procedure in non-unionised organisations, where a colleague may be the accompanying representative of the employee bringing the grievance, there may be a similar element of power usage by managers in such a way that procedural fairness is threatened.

Salamon (2000) also notes that the notion of independence between different stages of the grievance procedure may well be a myth. It would be fanciful to assume that managers involved in the latter stages of a grievance case did not speak to managers who had played a part in earlier stages. There may be an element of 'closing ranks' on the part of managers, again to the detriment of procedural fairness. This may not necessarily be deliberate but based upon a shared frame of reference or a common awareness of organisational issues affecting the case, which may not be shared by the employee.

9.3 *If you were an HR manager how would you deal with a situation where you were called upon to control the suspected abuse by employees of Internet provision in your organisation?*

As this chapter has been about policies and procedures it is hardly surprising that we think that a way forward would be to develop a policy on Internet usage. This should be done in consultation with employees and/or their representatives. It seems to us that it would be too heavy-handed, and possibly quite unworkable, to ban personal use of the Internet during working hours. What is required is a high-trust approach based upon employees using their 'common sense'. If it interferes with normal work activities or if there is common sharing of 'unsuitable' material (note here how this may be a new form of harassment) then it may be appropriate to invoke the disciplinary procedure. So, once again, the disciplinary procedure may be the last resort when employees abuse the policy.

9.4 *What practical difficulties do you think there may be in distinguishing between lack of capability and negligence?*

We tend to think that it may not be as straightforward as the EAT pronouncement suggests. Negligence suggests a strong element of wilfulness. In this case the employee is deliberately negligent owing to a slipshod, couldn't care less attitude. But some cases of negligence may be the consequence of the employee not having sufficient awareness of what constitutes negligence: that is, he or she is not capable of understanding what negligence means in the context of his or her job. There is a difference between supermarket assistant A, who treats customers in a surly manner because she is having a bad day, and assistant B, who always treats customers in this manner because she doesn't know the difference between surliness and politeness. We think that the way in which you would treat these two employees would be quite different. Repeated surliness on the part of assistant A would be a misconduct case for the disciplinary procedure, whereas assistant B might well be treated as 'incapable'. There might be a case for moving assistant B to alternative work more suited to her skills and experience (for example not involving customer contact), always assuming that her employer could offer her such work.

CASE 9 — Sexual harassment in the school science laboratory

Mrs Porcelli was employed as a science laboratory technician at a school in Strathclyde. She had been in her job for 3 years. For the first two years in which Mrs Porcelli did the job she was one of three laboratory technicians. Her two immediate colleagues were both female. There was a good working relationship between the three of them. At the end of two years these female colleagues left the school and were replaced by two men: Mr Coles and Mr Reid. They enjoyed the same job status as Mrs Porcelli although they were less experienced.

There was tension between Mrs Porcelli and her two new colleagues from the outset. It seemed to her that her new colleagues were intent on hounding her out of the school.

Mrs Porcelli suffered a year of what could be described as a campaign of sustained vindictiveness and unpleasantness mounted by Mr Coles and Mr Reid

▶

against her. At the end of the year Mrs Porcelli decided that she could stand it no longer and applied successfully for a transfer to another school within the education authority.

Mrs Porcelli made a number of specific allegations. She complained that Mr Coles made a practice of deliberately concealing from her information and instructions for all the technicians emanating from the principal chemistry teacher. Mr Coles asserted that he did not need to tell Mrs Porcelli about the changes in the operation of the technicians' service that he was introducing with the consent of the principal teacher.

On one occasion Mrs Porcelli said that she returned to the technicians' room to find Mr Coles and Mr Reid clearing out a drawer and throwing her personal belongings into a black plastic sack. She also alleged that she was subjected to considerable personal abuse and obscene language when she complained to her two colleagues and tried to recover her belongings from the sack.

Mrs Porcelli asserted that Mr Coles and Mr Reid made things as difficult as possible for her to do her job. They put heavy apparatus and large storage jars in a cupboard that was too high for her to reach without a ladder. When Mrs Porcelli complained of this she alleged that Mr Reid said to her 'if you can't climb a ladder then you shouldn't be in the f*****g job.'

Mrs Porcelli alleged that Mr Coles began to subject her to sexual harassment. During morning and afternoon tea breaks she complained that Mr Coles would deliberately stare at her, following her movements about the room. She alleged that he made suggestive remarks. On one occasion he picked up a screw nail and asked her if she 'would like a screw'. On another occasion Mrs Porcelli said that he picked up a glass container shaped like a penis and asked her if she had any use for it. Mrs Porcelli alleged that Mr Coles would often turn to page 3 of the *Daily Record* and compare her physical appearance with that of the nude female depicted in the newspaper. Mrs Porcelli said that the atmosphere in the technicians' room became so unpleasant that she stopped using it during break times when her two male technician colleagues were present.

After she stopped using the technicians' room during break times Mrs Porcelli alleged that Mr Coles began to harass her in the preparation room. She said that he would come up behind her, catching her unawares, so that his body would brush against hers as she turned around. She further alleged that he behaved in an intimidating way, frequently allowing heavy doors to slam in her face when she was carrying apparatus and could not protect herself.

After Mrs Porcelli's transfer to another school she brought a case to an industrial tribunal, alleging that her employers had discriminated against her unlawfully contrary to the 1975 Sex Discrimination Act.

Source: Based on *Strathclyde Regional Council* v. *Porcelli* (1986) IRLR 134

Question

Assuming that a school has a grievance procedure but no policy for dealing with cases of alleged sexual harassment, what advice would you give to the governing body of a school in order that it may be equipped to deal effectively with any such case in the future?

Chapter 10

Rewarding the employment relationship

At the end of this chapter you should be able to:

- explain the reward objectives of employers and employees;

- identify the main methods by which employees are rewarded;

- appreciate the rapid changes taking place in reward management.

10.1 Introduction

It has not been customary for employee relations books to include a chapter on reward. This is curious, because for most of us reward is the most important outcome of the employment relationship. Indeed, it is at the very core of the employment contract because it represents the *consideration* that flows from the performance of the contract.

However, like many aspects of the employment relationship, reward is changing rapidly. What was once little more than a procedural issue, concerned with the technicalities of complex pay structures and job evaluation, is now in many organisations no longer the Cinderella topic it once was (Smith, 1993). The HRM movement has prompted many managers to think that reward has the potential to do much more than simply compensate employees for the time that they sell to their employer.

Incidentally, you will notice that we use the term *reward* rather than *pay*. As employees we expect more than pay for our efforts, so our definition of reward includes non-pay benefits, such as subsidised meals and pensions, as well as wages and salaries.

In this chapter we start by outlining the reward expectations of employers, employees and governments (Section 10.2). This concentrates on the pay element of the employment relationship outcomes, as other elements are covered elsewhere in this book. This is a particularly important section because it suggests some of the consequences for the employment relationship if these expectations are not met (Section 10.3). It also considers some of the principles, such as fairness, that underpin reward systems. The other major sections (10.4 and 10.5) consider in detail the various methods by which employees are rewarded.

10.2 The objectives of reward for the parties to the employment relationship

Employees

It would be tempting to think that as employees our objective is a simple one: to earn the biggest possible salary. However, most of us are more realistic about our earning potential, and seek a balance between what we estimate to be that potential, the level of effort we expend and inconvenience we are prepared to suffer, and our earnings. Torrington and Hall (2002) suggest that employees have a number of specific pay objectives. Here we detail four of these: purchasing power, felt-fairness, relativities and recognition.

Purchasing power

Perhaps this is the most basic objective of all: to earn sufficient money to support the lifestyle to which we aspire. From this flow many of the basic rights many of us would argue are the characteristics of a modern, democratic society: the right to decent housing, food, transport and the dignity that accompanies the ability to support oneself and one's family.

It is an objective that a substantial proportion of the workforce do not achieve. A glance at data from the 2001 New Earnings Survey (Jenkins, 2002), shown in Table 10.1, shows that 25 per cent of full-time employees in the UK earned less than £267 per week (£13,884 p.a.), and 10 per cent less than £207 per week (£10,764 p.a.). The median rate for full time employees in 2001 was £23,607 p.a.

The data for women only reveal much lower wage levels. Twenty-five per cent of full-time women earned less than £234 per week (men £297), and 10 per cent of full-time women earned less than £186 per week (men £230). Comparison of the average

Table 10.1 **Distribution of pay: Great Britain; April 2001[a] (gross weekly earnings including overtime pay and overtime hours)**

	FT men	FT women	All FT	PT men	PT women	All PT	All men (FT & PT)	All women (FT & PT)	All employees
10% earned less than	229.5	185.8	207.0	35.0	40.0	38.7	189.6	70.3	98.5
25% earned less than	296.6	233.9	267.5	60.0	71.8	69.6	272.7	132.1	193.4
50% earned less than	407.7	313.2	370.1	104.0	114.8	112.8	388.0	230.3	310.2
25% earned more than	567.5	446.4	519.8	169.0	170.4	170.1	548.2	355.8	470.7
10% earned more than	799.6	584.7	722.1	280.5	251.0	255.1	775.1	511.7	657.9

[a] Full-time employees on adult rates, whose pay for the survey period was unaffected by absence

Source: Jenkins (2002)

gross annual earnings for full-time men (£26,389) and women (£18,811) (Jenkins, 2002) shows that women earn 71.3 per cent of the median wage for men. A comparison of hourly rates in Table 10.2 reveals a similar pattern, albeit that it shows that all women (both full- and part-time) earn 76 per cent of the hourly rate for men, a figure affected by the similarity of hourly rate between part-time men and part-time women.

Table 10.2 Employees' average gross hourly earnings: men and women, April 2001; Great Britain

	FT men	FT women	FT men and women	PT men	PT women	PT men and women	All men (FT & PT)	All women (FT & PT)	All employees
Average gross hourly earnings (£) excluding overtime pay	11.97	9.76	11.18	7.69	7.03	7.13	11.82	9.06	10.66

Source: Jenkins (2002)

This comparison is unfavourable to women in spite of 25 years of the Equal Pay Act 1970, which sought to equalise pay between men and women where they are doing *like work* or if the work they do is rated as equivalent under a job-evaluated scheme, or if the work can be shown to be of *equal value*. The gap between the pay of men and women is similarly wide in other European countries. In France in 1995 the overall gap was 25 per cent and in Holland the figure is very similar (IDS, 1995).

According to *Bargaining Report* (1997; cited by Evans, 1999), between 1970 and 1975 the gap between women's and men's pay narrowed by nine percentage points. But then the pace slowed, and the gap was reduced by two percentage points in the period 1975–85, and less than six percentage points during the years 1985–95. At this rate of change, it will take 31 years before the gap is eliminated.

The effectiveness of legislation to redress the pay imbalance between men and women inevitably promotes some scepticism over whether the National Minimum Wage (NMW) in the UK will have a similarly marginal effect on the pay of low-paid workers. This was introduced in the UK in 1999. It is the natural successor to the Wages Councils, which afforded some protection to certain groups of low-paid workers. They were abolished in 1993, and were generally deemed to be ineffective (Rubery, 1995). The NMW was set at £4.20 per hour in October 2002, £4.50 per hour in October 2003 and £4.85 per hour in October 2004 for over 21 year olds. For those aged between 18 and 21, it was set at £3.60 per hour in October 2002, £3.80 per hour in October 2003 and £4.10 per hour in October 2004. This is thought to be some way below the proposed level of one-half of full-time male hourly earnings (Nichol, 1998).

The potential coverage of the NMW is considerable. It is estimated that it will cover approximately 1.9 million workers, or 8.3 per cent of the UK workforce (Nichol, 1998). This includes approximately 1.3 million women and more than 20 per cent of part-time workers (*Financial Times*, 1999).

When the NMW was first introduced in 1999, fears were expressed that it would cause wage inflation and therefore lead to job losses. For example, Business Strategies, economic consultants, predicted significant job losses in the first years of the NMW (*Financial Times*, 1999). However, the evidence from other countries does not support this. There is minimum wage protection in Australia, Belgium, Canada, France, Greece, Japan, Netherlands, New Zealand, Portugal, Spain and the USA. Yet a 1998 OECD report notes that, although there have been times when higher minimum wage rates may have cost jobs, 'sensibly set' minimum wages have contributed successfully to social policy without an adverse effect on employment (Cash, 1998). The same OECD report rebuts fears that increasing wage rates for the lower paid will lead to higher-paid employees seeking to maintain their favourable differential. The international evidence suggests that higher minimum wages lead to a more compressed earnings distribution. If this experience is replicated in the UK, it may be that the NMW will have the effect of narrowing the gap between the earnings of the low- and high-paid that is evident in Table 10.1. Consequently, this will similarly narrow the gap between the earnings of women and men. So perhaps the NMW will achieve what 30 years of equal pay legislation has failed to do. The evidence noted in the government's second annual report on the NMW (Department of Trade and Industry, 2001) suggests a consensus between government, business, unions and academics, who all agree that there has been no significant adverse impact of a statutory wage floor.

self-check question	**10.1** As an HR manager, what other arguments would you employ against your directors' allegation that the NMW will be inflationary?

Of course these favourable estimates of the benefits to the low-paid of the NMW are all based on assumptions about sufficient employees being aware of its existence and effective 'policing'. The government has run advertising campaigns for the NMW using TV, national press, local radio, youth and women's magazines. These were designed to ensure that many more employees knew about it than was the case with the rather more complex Wages Councils protection. Evidence from the government's second annual report on the NMW (Department of Trade and Industry, 2001) suggests that these efforts have been more successful. Independent research revealed that 98 per cent of employers in the five low-paying sectors, 99 per cent of low-paid workers and 90 per cent of the general public knew of the existence of the NMW, albeit not the actual rates.

However, there is no separate enforcement agency for the NMW. It is left to the combined efforts of the Contributions Agency and Inland Revenue to ensure that the rates are upheld. However, any employee who suspects the minimum wage is not being paid can go to an employment tribunal or civil court to complain, and is protected from dismissal for doing so. Inspectors who find evidence of non-compliance have wide powers of access to enter company premises and gain access to relevant employer records. In the event of an enforcement being ignored, the inspectors can apply to the employer a penalty of double the minimum wage rate per worker for each day of continuing non-payment, take a complaint to a tribunal to recover what is owed, or sue the employer through the civil courts.

In the year 2000/2001 the annual report on the NMW (Department of Trade and Industry, 2001) noted that over 7000 complaints concerning pay below the NMW were investigated. This resulted in compliance officers issuing 213 enforcement notices and 60 penalty notices. Twenty-six cases went to employment tribunal, all of which resulted in a successful outcome for the complaining worker. The total arrears owed by employers flouting the NMW was over £3 million, with an average of £418 owed to each employee concerned.

It is predictable that those earning such low pay levels possess the least bargaining power and therefore are at the mercy of their employer to a much greater degree than those earning above the median. It is also predictable that for them the employment relationship is less likely to yield non-pay benefits such as job satisfaction. However, the outlook is not all gloom for those with the least purchasing power.

Felt-fairness

The degree to which we feel that our level of pay is *fair* is a highly subjective judgement. Two people doing the same job may have quite different notions of pay *felt-fairness* (Jacques, 1961) as a result of their different backgrounds and aspirations. This is difficult to estimate, but the effects of perceived *unfairness* are much more predictable. Torrington *et al.* (2002) note that there are employees who may feel dishonest because they are overpaid. But the effects of perceived underpayment are much more serious. The employee in this situation is likely to exhibit the traditional signs of dissatisfaction, such as lateness, lack of cooperation, or absence. However, as Torrington *et al.* (2002) note, the more serious problem of resentment exists with the employee who feels underpaid and unable to move to another job. Clearly, for those employees who feel that their pay is unfair, the employment relationship is likely to be an unfulfilling one.

Relativities

The issue of felt-fairness raises the question 'fair in relation to what?'. All of us derive our judgement of what we feel to be fair from notional comparisons with other individuals and groups. These comparisons at an individual level may be related to the qualifications and experience of a colleague, or to the level of performance that we think that colleague delivers. At a group level we may feel that colleagues in a different function, or geographical region, earning more than our group have an easier life than us. At a national level, trade union negotiators use comparative data to promote the cause of their members. For example, the essential services have traditionally been an area where different employee groups have compared their earnings with one another as an important part of their pay claims. The 1989–90 ambulance workers' dispute had at its core a claim by ambulance workers that their pay had slipped behind that of the police and fire-fighters. As one ambulance worker put it:

> ...we stand shoulder to shoulder with the police and fire service on jobs, but we don't stand shoulder to shoulder on pay. And yet the ambulance service handles more emergency calls each day than either the fire or police'... (quoted in Blyton and Turnbull, 1998: 90)

Recognition

We note below the danger of assuming that pay is the simple answer to employee motivation problems. But many managers overlook the power of recognising a job well done. This is where non-pay benefits can be particularly valuable (Armstrong and Murlis, 1998). The motivational effects of a weekend trip to Paris as a reward for the completion of a successful project may be much more powerful than a cash bonus. Not only does the employee know that her efforts have been recognised, but her colleagues know too!

■ Employers

Competition

The principal reward objective for the employer is to set levels of reward to attract, retain and motivate the type of employees needed to run an effective organisation (Lupton and Bowey, 1983). The key to this is to establish the reward levels of similar organisations in the employer's area. For this purpose, employers may enlist the help of consultants, fellow HR managers in *pay clubs* (Armstrong, 1999), and even trade union officials. It is not necessarily the case that employees will always be attracted to the highest payer in a defined labour market, but the generous employer is in a strong competitive position.

Strategy or control?

Torrington *et al.* (2002) include control as one of the employer's reward objectives. In essence, this means using rewards as a tool to direct employee behaviours in a way that suits the purposes of the employer. The traditional way of doing this has been the sort of reward mechanisms, for example incentive schemes, that we detail later in this chapter.

However, in recent years there has been an ambitious drive to label everything in the field of employee relations and personnel management as *strategic*. So it is with reward. Armstrong (1999: 69) defines reward strategy as

> a business-focused statement of the intentions of the organisation concerning the development of future reward processes and practices which are aligned to the business and human resource strategies of the organisation, its culture and the environment in which it operates.

It will become evident later in this chapter that having clear objectives for the pay bill is gaining more importance in many UK organisations. This was not always so (Livy, 1988), particularly for non-manual workers. But whether making reward more 'strategic' is simply a more attractive wrapper for old-fashioned control initiatives is a moot point.

self-check question

10.2 Do you think that 'direct(ing) pay programmes to what the organisation wants to achieve' represents strategy or control?

Motivation

In a survey of employers' reasons for introducing individual performance-related pay (IPRP) (Thompson, 1992) 46 out of 48 employers said that IPRP had been introduced to motivate employees. This suggests an unproblematic causal relationship between pay and motivation. However, this relationship is a highly complex one. We cannot do justice to it here, other than to point out that employees 'tend to behave in whatever way they perceive leads to rewards they value' (Lawler, 1984). This suggests that motivation is a highly individual affair. What may motivate us may not have the same effect on our colleagues. Similarly, what may motivate us now (for example, high earnings and promotion opportunities) may not have the same effect when we are in our 50s, when we may be more concerned with the pension element of our reward package.

Given the simplistic assumptions of many employers and the complex reality of pay and motivation, it is hardly surprising that pay remains the most frequently cited reason for employee relations disputes in the UK (Davies, 1998).

Cost control

A dominating influence behind any employer's reward strategy is the need to keep a tight rein on the budget so that the organisation can afford what it pays. This is particularly important in organisations such as schools, where the ratio of labour costs to total costs is very high. Consequently, management negotiators take great care to explain the current economic position of the organisation to employees and their trade unions at the time of the annual pay review, to attempt to suppress the level of any claim. Similarly, senior managers spend time monitoring the decisions of line managers about incentive scheme payments they propose to award their employees to ensure affordability within budgets. To some extent this explains the rise in popularity of self-financing schemes such as gainsharing and profit-related pay, both of which are explained in greater detail later in this chapter.

■ Government

In recent decades governments have played a major role in pay policy, because it has been an important plank in the strategy to control inflation. This has been done in two principal ways. The first is through government's role as *employer*. In developed market economies, government acts as employer of upwards of 20 per cent of the total workforce (Hollinshead and Leat, 1995). The relationship between governments and their employees has been an uneasy one as greater productivity and accountability has been sought from public sector agencies, who have passed this pressure to their employees. Strict controls have been put on annual pay budgets, with the consequence that the pay of some employee groups has continually fallen behind inflation. The private sector has not been immune from governmental pressure on pay. At its most explicit in the UK this was a series of *incomes policies* in the 1970s (see Kessler and Bayliss, 1998), which constitute the second way in which governments have played a major role in pay policy. The influence of governments in setting private sector pay expectations should not be underestimated.

■ Trade unions

The pay objectives of trade unions may seem straightforward. As TUC General Secretary John Monks argues, 'it is only reasonable that workers are entitled to take home a living wage for an honest day's work' (Monks, 1998: 178). This may represent a share in the profits of private sector companies or a fair allocation of resources in the public sector. Not surprisingly, the trade unions have been very supportive of the introduction of the National Minimum Wage, since this, they hope, will drive up what Monks calls the 'unacceptable' level of wages for some workers.

But it would be wrong to assume that pay bargaining is the sole aim of trade unions. As the emphasis switches to unions seeking partnerships with employers, the aims are becoming wider. Monks (1998) envisages that the four main prongs of such agreements will be:

- employment security;
- employee voice;
- fair financial rewards;
- investment in training.

We note below the increasing tendency for employers to move from *rate for the job* pay systems to those which are related to the individual employee. This means that the pay bargaining role of unions changes. There is now more emphasis upon negotiating the size of the annual pay 'pot', with managers making decisions on how this pot is to be allocated. This means that the highly visible *annual pay round* battle between employers and unions may become a thing of the past. Pay negotiations will become far more complex, with pay becoming just one of a series of items on the collective bargaining agenda.

| Box 10.1 | Summary: the reward objectives of employees, employers, government and trade unions |

Employees
- Adequacy of purchasing power
- Felt-fairness
- The achievement and maintenance of relativities
- Recognition of a job well done

Employers
- To match the pay of competitor organisations
- To match the organisational strategy
- To motivate employees
- Cost control

Government
- The control of inflation

Trade unions
- The achievement of a decent living wage for all

10.3 When differing objectives are not met: industrial action over pay

We noted above that pay is the most frequently cited reason for employee relations disputes in the UK. The extent of this is illustrated in Table 10.3. You will note that in most years since 1987 pay has accounted for over one-half of the days lost due to industrial disputes.

Examination of these data leads to the question of whether it is the level of reward that is at the root of industrial disputes or the way in which the rewards are structured

Table 10.3 **Working days lost due to disputes over pay, UK, 1987–97**

Year	No. of days lost due to pay disputes	Total no. of days lost	Percentage of total days lost due to pay disputes
1987	2919	3546	82
1988	1903	3702	51
1989	3290	4128	80
1990	1098	1903	58
1991	309	761	41
1992	196	528	37
1993	150	649	23
1994	160	278	57
1995	202	415	49
1996	1063	1303	82
1997	128	235	54
1998	166	282	59
1999	166	242	69
2000	383	499	77

Source: Derived from Davies (2001)

(or, indeed, it could be both). For example, the employee may be upset at the amount of pay in his or her pay packet and the way in which that amount was arrived at, perhaps through a bonus payment that was unfairly allocated. However, care should also be exercised in placing too much faith in these data. It may be that pay is simply the tip of a much more complex iceberg of employee relations problems, and a dispute over pay is what has brought this to the surface.

So far this chapter has tended to concentrate on the amount of reward to the employee. Yet mention of the structuring of rewards leads us to the main section of this chapter. This considers the extent to which the structuring of rewards is changing to reflect a changed organisational environment. We noted earlier that reward was becoming a more strategic issue in many organisations. This has led to more ingenuity on the part of HR managers in devising reward schemes with specific aims in mind. It is to these schemes, and the thinking behind them, that we now turn.

10.4 The changing nature of reward management

University staff, and many other public sector workers, are part of a dying breed because we are rewarded in what seems to be an increasingly outdated way. Quite simply, we have a national pay scale, determined by collective bargaining, which means that our pay is determined by our grade and our length of service. This means that, when we have been in post for a number of years, we reach the top of the pay scale for our particular grade, and in the absence of promotion to a higher grade cannot earn any more salary except for the annual cost of living settlement. This type of scheme does have its virtues. It is easy to understand, it is open (that is, we can all calculate very easily how much each of us is earning), it involves no responsibility for local managers, and it means that we can move between similar institutions for career reasons not related to pay.

It is not difficult to see that the management objectives for such pay arrangements as we enjoy are rooted in the past. They belong to an era when loyalty was thought of as something to be prized. Moreover, there was an assumption that length of service meant experience that led to greater expertise in performing the job. We know from the discussion in Chapter 1 related to the psychological contract that loyalty is now less valuable, having been replaced by the desire for employee contribution. But what of the assumption that length of service = experience = greater expertise in performing the job? Of course, experience can take different forms. Ten years' experience can mean a different challenge in each of those 10 years, or it can mean each year's experience repeated 10 times. Increasingly, there is doubt about the extent to which experience does mean greater job expertise.

The example of the bank manager is relevant here. The typical bank manager's role has changed (Cressey and Scott, 1993). It has become that of a business manager, with much more emphasis upon sales. Lending decisions about retail business have been de-skilled in that information technology makes the decision for the manager by using computerised credit scoring. This is a system where various factors relating to the customer's financial circumstances are computed to give an overall credit rating. This suggests the need for managers to be less experienced. No longer does a career's experience in exercising judgement over lending decisions count if computers are making the decision. Consequently, managers can be obtained, and retained, more cheaply than their predecessors. This suggests the need for a new reward strategy for bank managers that rewards the achievement of sales and does not reward experience to the same extent as hitherto. This, of course, has the added bonus for the banks of enabling them to trim managerial labour costs.

Consequently the trend is away from pay being seen as solely determined by such factors as age, length of service and job grade. It is now more likely to be influenced by a series of considerations largely contingent upon the performance of the individual, the workgroup and the organisation. It is *contingent pay* that we are going to focus on in this chapter. We do this for two reasons. First, there are plenty of general personnel management texts that go into detail on the mechanics of pay structures (for example, the construction of pay scales, job evaluation); second, our view is that contingent pay is having a significant effect upon the employment relationship.

Armstrong and Murlis (1998: 273) define contingent pay as:

....payments related to individual performance, contribution, competence or skill or to team or organisational performance... .

We categorise contingent pay here in terms of individual schemes and those related to the team and the organisation. In the case of individual schemes we cover individual bonus schemes, individual performance-related pay (IPRP), competence-related pay, and skill-based pay. For team and organisation schemes we examine team-based pay and group incentive schemes, profit-related pay, share incentive plans, save-as-you-earn schemes and gainsharing. We must point out that making the distinction between individual and group contingent pay is one of convenience from our perspective. In reality, the boundary is blurred. For example, bonuses for quantity of sales may have an individual and a team element, as may similar schemes based on an organisation's production output.

■ Individual contingent pay

Payment by results

Payment by results (PBR) schemes are perhaps the simplest form of individual incentive scheme because they relate the pay of individuals to the quantity of their output. Such schemes have traditionally been popular in manufacturing industry for production workers. A survey in the early 1990s (Casey *et al.*, 1992) reported that approximately 60 per cent of organisations surveyed had individual bonus systems, with these being most popular among semi-skilled manual workers and sales staff. The 2001 New Earnings Survey records that 15 per cent of male workers and 12 per cent of female workers received some form of bonus payment (Jenkins, 2002).

Some PBR schemes have high basic pay, with extra achievement not rewarded to a great extent. Conversely, other schemes have low basic pay with extra achievement generously rewarded. There are other variations, but all share the Tayloristic assumptions that tasks that can be measured have quantifiable performance standards, and that money is the way to generate higher performance among workers (Roberts, 1997).

Piecework and work-measured schemes

Piecework schemes are among the most traditional forms of bonus schemes. They pay employees according to the number of 'pieces' of work produced, and still tend to be used in such industries as clothing and footwear. Most piecework schemes give employees the security of a minimum earnings level which may be set at 70 or 80 per cent of average earnings (IDS, 1999). They also often provide guaranteed payments for *downtime* when workers are unable to produce for reasons such as machine failure.

It is easy to see why job control in piecework schemes lies principally with employees. They can generate high levels of earnings by extra effort, although some may not choose to do this. Therefore levels of production, and pay, may vary greatly. It is this loss of control over production levels that may account for the fact that piecework schemes are rather limited in their use.

In work-measured schemes whole tasks, or parts of tasks, have a *standard time* defined for their completion. Bonus is related to the difference between the actual time taken to perform the task and the standard time. The worker has the incentive to complete the task in a shorter time than the standard time, allowing more to be produced and, therefore, more earned.

You may have noticed that the individual incentive schemes explained above tend to concentrate upon quantity of output. Of course, it may be that quantity-related incentive schemes are harmful to such wider organisational goals as product quality and customer service. The IDS report on bonus schemes (IDS, 1999) indicates the growth of multi-factor incentive schemes. In such schemes, there is a range of targets that reflect wider business objectives as well as financial and productivity goals. Examples of targets noted by IDS include internal service standards, turnaround or response times, fault rates, and independent customer satisfaction surveys.

Individual performance-related pay

The aspect of pay policy that has received most publicity in recent years has been individual performance-related pay (IPRP). IPRP (or, as ACAS prefer to call it, *appraisal-related pay*) is defined by ACAS as: 'a method of payment where an individual employee receives increases in pay based wholly or partly on the regular and systematic assessment of job performance' (ACAS, 1990: 2). It has been taken up with great enthusiasm in many areas of white-collar employment, for example local government and financial services. In the UK financial services industry, survey research estimated that 53 per cent of organisations base pay increases on performance or merit only (University of Bristol/ KPMG, 1994). However, surprisingly, the 1998 Workplace Employee Relations Survey (Cully *et al.*, 1999) reported that only 11 per cent of workplaces surveyed have individual IPRP schemes for non-managerial employees. This possible understatement may be related to the problem of differing definitions of IPRP.

It is not just in the USA and the UK that IPRP has become popular. In Finland, an economy not noted for flexibility in its employee relations arrangements, IPRP has been gaining ground. According to a 1997 survey conducted by the engineering employers MET, 48 per cent of blue-collar and 58 per cent of white-collar employees in engineering received some form of IPRP, nearly twice as many as in a survey carried out 6 years earlier (IDS, 1998a).

IPRP has been introduced for a number of reasons. Not surprisingly one of those most cited in the empirical research is the desire to motivate employees. We noted earlier in this chapter some of the difficulties in assuming an unproblematic causal link between pay and motivation. Research on the operation of IPRP in the Inland Revenue in the early 1990s by Marsden and Richardson (1992: 12) confirms this suspicion. They conclude: 'relatively few staff members feel that IPRP has provided them with an incentive or motivation to change their behaviour at work at all significantly.' This was particularly so with respect to the quantity and quality of work, and dealing with the public. Marsden and Richardson concede that it is possible that staff understated their level of motivational change. Consequently they asked reporting officers for their views on the extent to which IPRP had motivated staff. Their views were even more sceptical.

IPRP has also been introduced in many organisations to change the culture to reflect the 'new' values that senior managers think are necessary. Lawler (1984: 128) argues that reward systems can 'cause the culture of an organisation to vary quite widely. For example they can influence the degree to which it is seen as a human-resource oriented culture, an entrepreneurial culture, an innovative culture, a competence-based culture, and a participative culture.' Torrington (1992) echoes these sentiments. From fieldwork, studying the conclusions of other researchers and from general contacts with personnel managers and trade union officers, he concluded that IPRP is essentially a cultural initiative rather than a pay initiative, to emphasise individual enterprise and responsibility.

Germany's largest private sector employer, Siemens AG, has introduced IPRP for its managers and senior executives in order to foster a more performance-oriented culture. This is a considerable change in a company and a national employee relations system that has not been significantly innovative in pay reform (IDS, 1998b).

| *self-check question* | **10.3** How may IPRP be an effective way of changing organisational culture? |

There is also a strong thread of felt-fairness about IPRP. It is difficult to disagree with the proposition that the able and industrious employee should be rewarded for that ability and industry, and that the same level of award should not be given to the idle and incompetent. If so, you would be in sympathy with employees where such schemes have been introduced (Kessler, 1994). In general, the principle of IPRP has been applauded by employees. It is the implementation of IPRP that seems to cause problems of perceived unfairness. The employees interviewed by Procter *et al.* (1993) in an electronics plant reflected these concerns. There was evidence of favouritism, the arbitrary way in which managers applied measurement criteria, and the ways in which grades were distributed.

An important part of the operation of IPRP is that managers are put in a position where they must differentiate between the level of reward of their team members. This decision process effectively creates increased dependence of the team member on the line manager, and reduced dependence on the trade union (Kessler, 1994). Consequently, some organisations have seized this opportunity to expect greater management accountability.

ACAS (1990: 8) points out that the role of managers and supervisors is critical to the implementation of IPRP. It is they who must define the required standards of performance and behaviour, explain these to their team members, take tough decisions about assessments, communicate these decisions to team members, and defend their judgements if asked (Storey and Sisson, 1993). But often managers find this differentiation difficult, with the result that they produce statistical distributions that concentrate on the middle rank of performance, thus defeating the object of paying for differentiated performance. Kessler and Purcell (1992: 22) found evidence of the desire to 'make managers manage' in their research. They note 'IPRP is often seen as a means of forcing a manager into a direct one-to-one, usually face to face relationship with their employees'. They also observed how the pressure on managers came additionally from employees who, as one of their interviewee managers noted, 'are interested in money, and they're going to be badgering you to do it'.

This emphasis upon the relationship between the line manager and the employee means that the employment relationship changes from one where the principal actors are employers and trade unions: the parties to collective bargaining. IPRP strikes at the well-established union principle of 'the same rate for all': a move away from collectivist to individualist principles (Bacon and Storey, 1993; Storey and Sisson, 1993). Heery (1992: 3–4) argues, with support from local government case-study examples, that some employers have clear anti-union motives for wishing to introduce IPRP. He cites examples of organisations which have used IPRP as the occasion to de-recognise trade unions, although he points out that this is by no means an inevitable consequence of its introduction. In their study of IPRP in 53 Irish firms over a five-year period, Gunnigle *et al.* (1998) found evidence of IPRP as part of an increased attempt by employers to individualise the employment relationship to the exclusion of trade unions.

A likely motive for the introduction of IPRP is the weakening of collective bargaining. This can affect bargaining structure in two ways: by reducing its *scope* and its *depth*. The typical situation in which bargaining scope is reduced is where the size of the PRP 'pot' is negotiated collectively but the allocation to individual employees is at the discretion of line managers. This is favourable to the circumstances in which bargaining depth is reduced: that is, where the union is involved in consultation over the type of IPRP scheme but has limited influence over the outcomes.

A second negative outcome of IPRP for trade unions is that it is likely to reduce the perceived need of members for collective representation (Heery, 1992). This is for four reasons:

- The instrumental value of union membership may decline as the role of collective bargaining diminishes.
- The individual nature of IPRP may lead to a weakening of the collective ethos of trade unionism.
- Members may perceive IPRP as an indication of reduced management support for unions, and this may indirectly discourage membership.
- The number of employee grievances (which require union representation) may reduce if schemes meet employee aspirations for recognition and reward.

However, the IPRP implications for trade unions are not all gloom. The 1999 vote by NUT members against the introduction of IPRP in British schools provided the union with an opportunity to demonstrate its relevance to members by mobilising member support against a deeply unpopular government initiative (*The Guardian*, 1999).

Competence-related pay

We conducted research in a bank on its IPRP scheme for branch managers. Their managers set them targets that referred to *hard outputs* (such as the number of mortgages sold) and *soft processes* (for example, the way in which they led their branch team). But one of the frequent complaints of the branch managers was that it was really only the outputs that counted when performance measurement was carried out. Assessing managers were not too concerned with how the job was done provided that results were achieved. Competence-related pay overcomes this alleged weakness of IPRP by ensuring that, usually, both processes and outputs are taken into account when pay-related measurement is made.

Competence-related pay can be defined as 'a method of rewarding people wholly or partly by reference to the level of competence they demonstrate in carrying out their roles' (Armstrong and Murlis, 1998). It is predictable that interest in competence-related pay should grow, given the enormous amount of attention given to the definition of competences for purposes of selection, training and appraisal in recent years.

Armstrong and Murlis's definition of competence-related pay captures the most importance difference between competence-related pay and IPRP. This is that IPRP is essentially retrospective in that it measures performance over the past pay period (often 1 year). However, competence-related pay is more forward-looking. It identifies those competences that are likely to be associated with effective job performance.

Flannery *et al.* (1996: 92) provide a useful definition of competences. They refer to competences as 'sets of skills, knowledge, abilities, behavioural characteristics, and other attributes that, in the right combination and for the right set of circumstances, predict superior performance'. So the technical skill to do the job is clearly not enough. The successful job-holder must ally this skill (for example, introducing clients to new products) with other attributes (such as the desire to enhance the performance of the branch or team). In other words, competence-related pay is highly contextual. It also has, potentially, strong links to organisational strategy. The question that may be asked at business strategy level is: 'What competences do we want our people to demonstrate in order that we may achieve our business goals?'.

The assessing managers in the bank in which we did research would be comforted by the fact that many organisations introducing competence-related pay ally competence-related ratings with performance output measurements, the market rate for the job, and the position of the individual on the pay scale in determining salary level. This sounds like a complex process that is far removed from the collectively bargained rate for the job we noted earlier. As such, its capacity to strengthen the link between line manager and employee and weaken that between trade union and employee is at least as powerful as that of IPRP.

In the case of IPRP, we noted the arbitrary way in which managers can apply measurement criteria and the problems of a lack of felt-fairness this creates in employees. This is no less true of competence-related pay. In fact, the more the approach moves from one where identifying discernible skills and outputs is possible, the more subjective the measurement process becomes. As yet, little empirical research has been done on the operation of competence-related pay, but it would be surprising were it to uncover anything other than the same sort of employee dissatisfactions as IPRP. However, the measurement criteria themselves may be more acceptable to employees than in the case of IPRP. This is often because there is some form of employee involvement in the development of the competence statements (Armstrong and Murlis, 1998), albeit that line managers are making the assessment of the extent to which they have been demonstrated. This is unlike IPRP, where it is usually the manager who defines the performance objectives and measurement criteria, and assesses performance.

Skill-based pay

Skill-based pay is often confused with competence-related pay. However, skill-based pay is a narrower term because skills are usually defined in terms of 'the completion of training courses, satisfactory performance in a test leading to company accreditation or the attainment of NVQ levels' (Armstrong and Murlis, 1998: 324). Organisations normally introduce skill-based pay to increase the ability of employees to perform a wider range of tasks, thus assuring greater flexibility in coping with increased demands. Although it has been introduced for manufacturing jobs in organisations such as Amersham International, Pirelli Cables and Pilkington Glass (IDS, 1992), the influence of skill-based pay is spreading into white-collar jobs, for example in retailing and hotel and catering.

Skill-based pay affords the employee the opportunity to increase salary through increments to base pay. In addition, the grade structure will normally have been defined in terms of the level of skill of the employee.

As well as advantages to the employer, through the development of multiskilling, skill-based pay promises advantages to the employee. Not the least of these is the potential attractiveness of employees to alternative employers. This is particularly topical given the interest in the concept of *employability* (Hillage and Pollard, 1999) generated, in part, by the realisation that there is no longer lifetime job security.

However, skill-based pay may pose problems for employers. It is potentially very costly because of the high level of training costs and the tendency for pay levels to drift upwards by virtue of paying for skills that are not fully used. There is also the problem of demotivation of employees who have acquired all the skills 'on offer' and therefore find their desire to increase skills and salary frustrated.

Box 10.2 **Summary: individual contingent pay**

Payment by results

■ Relates pay of individuals to quantity of their output

Piecework and work-measured schemes

■ Piecework schemes pay employees according to the number of 'pieces' of work produced

■ In work-measured schemes tasks have a *standard time* defined for their completion; bonus is related to the difference between the actual time taken to perform the task and the standard time

■ Growth of interest in multi-factor schemes that reward more than output quantity

Individual performance-related pay

■ Not simple causal link between pay and motivation

■ Can be part of effort to change organisational culture

■ Has strong promise of felt-fairness

■ High level of line manager discretion

■ May be part of trade union marginalisation strategy

Competence-related pay

■ Rewards how job done as well as outputs

■ Looks to future rather than past as does IPRP

■ Measurement criteria may still be arbitrary

Skill-based pay

■ Introduced to generate multiskilling

■ Enhances employees' employability

■ High training costs for employers

10.5 Team- and organisation-contingent pay

■ Team-based pay and group incentive schemes

In recent years there has been much emphasis on the importance of people working in teams. Therefore it is hardly surprising that interest in some organisations has turned from individual IPRP schemes, and all their problems, to team-based pay. However, that interest has not been reflected in actual change. Thompson (1995) reported a rarity of team pay approaches despite the fact that team working was widespread. Thompson reasons that this seeming contradiction may have two explanations. The first is what he calls the *lag* effect. This is where organisations introduce new working practices some time before they consider linking them to pay (Thompson, 1995). The second explanation is more predictable. This, argues Thompson, is due to the *ad hoc* way in which UK organisations manage pay. Far from being strategic, pay, asserts Thompson, is being managed in a highly reactive fashion.

In team-based pay, payments, or other forms of non-financial reward, are made to team members on the basis of some predetermined criteria. These criteria may reflect some difference of individual contribution to the team's performance. Armstrong and Murlis (1998) note that the purposes of team-based pay are to:

■ deliver the message that one of the organisation's core values is effective teamwork;
■ help to clarify what teams are expected to achieve, by relating rewards to the attainment of predetermined and agreed targets and standards of performance and behaviours;
■ encourage group effort and cooperation by providing incentives and means of recognising team achievements.

Thompson (1995) identified the types of team that may be associated with team-based pay. He categorised them as *temporary* and *permanent*. An example of the former might be a team set up to open a retail store. The team would consist of employees in different functions operating at different levels in the organisation. Permanent teams might be those based on a specific function (such as HR), a process (in manufacturing plants, for example), a product market or a geographical area. What seems to be important for team-based pay to have a chance of success is that the team has a clear identity and a sense of autonomy, and consists of members whose work is interdependent and who are flexible, multiskilled and good team players (Roberts, 1997: 570).

self-check question	**10.4** What problems may there be with team-based pay?

Profit-related pay

The popularity of profit-related pay has grown considerably in recent years. It is most popular in the utilities sector (water, gas and electricity) and financial services, where 81 per cent and 80 per cent of workplaces reported its existence in the 1998 Workplace Employee Relations survey (Cully *et al.*, 1999). Overall, the survey noted that 47 per cent of private sector workplaces had profit-related pay schemes.

Profit-related pay schemes have been attractive, as it has been possible for employees to enjoy significant tax advantages. However, those were withdrawn in 2000, with the result that share option schemes, which have the capacity to enhance employee awareness of profit performance, are likely to become more popular. Two such schemes are analysed below: share incentive plans and save-as-you-earn.

Share incentive plans (SIP)

SIPs were introduced in the 2000 Finance Bill. Before October 2001 they were known as *all-employee share ownership plans* (AESOPs). SIPs provide for four types of share provision:

■ *free shares*: given by the company to employees up to £3000 in any tax year;
■ *partnership shares*: purchased by employees out of their salary before it is subject to tax or NI to a limit of £125 per month (or 10 per cent of salary, whichever is the lower);
■ *matching shares*: companies match partnership shares purchased by employees up to a limit of two matching shares for each partnership share purchased;
■ *dividend shares*: dividends may be reinvested tax-free up to a limit of £1500 per year depending on the rules in the company plan.

Employees who keep their shares in the scheme for 5 years pay no income tax or NI contributions on the shares. If the shares are withdrawn after 3 years, income tax and NI contributions must be paid on the initial market value of the shares. In addition, employees do not have to pay capital gains tax if their shares are kept in the scheme for 5 years.

SIPs offer companies a high degree of flexibility, because they may combine the four types of share provision. In addition, for the first time, companies are able to link a share ownership scheme to individual employee performance, although in an IDS study of 39 companies offering SIPs (IDS, 2001) none had yet introduced this option.

Save-As-You-Earn (SAYE) or savings-related share option schemes

The savings-related share option scheme requires a contribution from the employee. In such schemes the employee saves for a specified period of 3, 5 or 7 years. The scheme specifies that employees can buy shares at the end of the savings period with the savings fund accumulated. The price of the shares will be the market price at the start of the savings contract or at a discount agreed at the start of the contract. The shares bought at the end of the savings contract attract tax relief.

With the 3-year savings contract the employee saves a fixed amount monthly (it cannot exceed £250) and at the end of the term a cash bonus of 2.75 months' payment is added. At the end of a 5-year contract a cash bonus of 7.5 months' payment is added. At the end of the 3- or 5-year term the employee uses the amount saved and the bonus to buy shares in the company. For employees who have saved for 5 years there is the option of extending the term to 7 years, in which case 13.5 months' payments are added as a cash bonus. Employees who choose a 7-year contract do not have to make monthly contributions after 5 years but agree to leave their savings untouched for the final 2 years to qualify for the higher bonus.

The price at which employees have the opportunity to purchase shares must not be below 80 per cent of the market value at the start of the contract. This seemed to be the typical price determined by employers in an Incomes Data Services study (IDS, 1998a). At the end of the contract period employees also have the option to have their contributions returned if the share price is not favourable, rendering the scheme risk-free.

As with profit-sharing schemes, all employees who have been employed by the company for 5 years must be eligible to participate in savings-related share option schemes if the scheme is to gain Inland Revenue approval. However, 1 year appears to be a more usual minimum service period (IDS, 1998a). In 1995/96, 610 000 employees were in 1305 schemes.

Gainsharing

Gainsharing, which tends to be more popular in the USA than in Britain, is another way in which employees may share in the success created by their own efforts. In gainsharing the relationship between employees' efforts and their eventual reward is more direct than with profit-related pay. Gainsharing plans are designed so that employees share the financial results of improvements in productivity, cost saving or quality. The resultant payment is paid from costs savings generated as a result of such improvements. Employees participating in the gainsharing plan are normally part of a discernible group who have had a direct effect upon the cost savings. The gainshare plan payment to them may be made in three ways: as a percentage of base pay; as a one-off cash bonus; or as a payment per hour worked. Schuster and Zingheim (1992) make the point that the same payment would normally go to all members of the group. They are also careful to point out that the organisation must design safeguards to ensure that it derives financial value from the results generated from the project linked to gainsharing. This type of gainsharing differs from more traditional forms of gainsharing, which have operated in manufacturing under the heading of Scanlon and Rucker plans. The principal difference is that the foundation of this new type of gainsharing is the future goals of the organisation, whereas that of more traditional gainsharing plans is the historical performance standards of the participating employees. The key point here, of course, is that historical performance standards may be achieved or exceeded while the organisation's overall goals are not met.

Non-pay benefits

It is not our intention in this chapter to go into detail on the non-pay benefits that are part of the employment relationship. However, we feel it is appropriate to give due regard to these, as they play an important part in shaping the nature of the relationship.

When we think of non-pay benefits we tend to think of those in the list drawn up by Armstrong and Murlis (1998: 437–8) below:

- pension schemes;
- personal security (such as death-in-service benefits, personal accident cover, extra-statutory sick pay, other health and medical insurances, extra-statutory redundancy pay, health screening);
- financial assistance (such as loans, house purchase assistance);
- personal needs (such as holidays, childcare, career breaks, retirement, counselling, recreational facilities);
- company cars;
- other benefits (such as subsidised meals, clothing allowances);
- intangible benefits (characteristics of the organisation that make it an attractive and worthwhile place in which to work).

The last benefits in the list, the intangible benefits, are worthy of comment, perhaps because they are so often overlooked. Armstrong (1999) notes that there are five areas where employees' needs may be met by non-financial rewards: achievement, recognition, responsibility, influence and personal growth. Of these, our view is that the first two will apply to virtually all employees. Responsibility, influence and personal growth will apply to many more than we realise. All of us like to feel that we have achieved something in our work, pride being derived from a job well done. In addition, most managers realise that a simple 'thank you' and a pat on the back for a job well done has enormous motivational power. But not all employees seek greater responsibility in their jobs, or greater influence over decisions that directly or indirectly influence those jobs. This may be related to the individual's personal characteristics. But it may also be a consequence of a history of the individual's employing organisation not giving that individual the opportunity to exercise responsibility or influence. A good example of employees being given responsibility to shape the destiny of their organisation is in Semler's (1993) account of the management style in his Brazilian company. The desire of many individuals to seek opportunities for personal growth through their work is very powerful. It may seem odd that this could be termed an employee reward rather than a vital prerequisite of organisational success. Yet many individuals rate the opportunity for personal growth higher than financial reward.

Box 10.3 | **Summary: team and organisation contingent pay**

Team-based pay

- Little widespread take-up
- Important that the team has a clear identity and a sense of autonomy, and consists of members whose work is interdependent and who are flexible, multiskilled and good team players

Profit-related pay

- Widespread take-up in recent years will be curbed by withdrawal of tax benefits

Share incentive plans (SIPs)

- Consist of four types of share provision: free shares, partnership shares, matching shares, and dividend shares
- Employees who keep their shares in the scheme for 5 years pay no tax or NI contributions on shares

Savings-related share option schemes

- Require monthly savings contribution from employees
- Employees save for period of 3, 5 or 7 years
- Employees buy shares at end of savings period at price agreed at commencement of savings period
- Shares bought at end of period attract tax relief

Gainsharing

- Employees share financially in savings made as a result of their efforts
- Must be related directly to efforts of particular employee group
- Linked to organisational goals

10.6 Summary

- The parties to the employment relationship have different reward objectives.
- Employees' pay objectives are principally adequacy of purchasing power, felt-fairness, the achievement and maintenance of relativities, and recognition of a job well done.
- Employers' objectives are to match the pay of competitor organisations, to complement the organisation's strategy, to motivate employees, and to control costs. The major objective of government is to control inflation and that of trade unions is to pursue the achievement of a decent living wage for all.
- In most years since 1987 pay has accounted for over one-half of the days lost due to industrial disputes.
- Pay is increasingly becoming contingent upon the organisation's strategy and objectives and linked to the performance of the individual employee, the team and the organisation as a whole.
- An important aspect of reward is non-pay benefits.

References

ACAS (1990) *Appraisal Related Pay*, London, ACAS.

Armstrong, M. (1999) *Employee Reward* (2nd edn), London, Institute of Personnel and Development.

Armstrong, M. and Murlis, H. (1998) *Reward Management: A handbook of remuneration strategy and practice* (4th edn), London, Kogan Page.

Bacon, N. and Storey, J. (1993) 'Individualisation of the employment relationship and the implications for trade unions', *Employee Relations*, 15:1, 5–17.

Bargaining Report (1997) 'Survey, equal value', *Bargaining Report*, 174, July, cited in Evans, J. (1999) 'Pay', *in* Hollinshead, G., Nicholls, P. and Tailby, S. (eds), *Employee Relations*, London, Financial Times Pitman Publishing, pp. 332–77.

Blyton, P. and Turnbull, P. (1998) *The Dynamics of Employee Relations* (2nd edn), Basingstoke, Macmillan.

Casey, B., Lakey, J. and White, M. (1992) *Payment Systems: A look at current practice*, Research Series No. 5, Department of Employment, Policy Studies Institute.

Cash, T. (1998) 'Lessons from the international experience of statutory minimum wages', *Labour Market Trends*, September, 463–7.

Cressey, P. and Scott, P. (1993) 'Employment, technology and industrial relations in the UK clearing banks: is the honeymoon over?', *New Technology, Work and Employment*, 7:2, 83–96.

Cully, M., Woodland, S., O'Reilly, A. and Dix, G. (1999) *Britain at Work*, London, Routledge.

Davies, J. (1998) 'Labour disputes in 1997', *Labour Market Trends*, June, 299–311.

Davies, J. (2001) 'Labour disputes in 2000', *Labour Market Trends*, June, 301–13.

Department of Trade and Industry (2001) National Minimum Wage, Annual Report 2000/2001 [online] [cited 22 November] Available from <http://www.dti.gov.uk/er/nmw/ar2001.pdf>

Evans, J. (1999) 'Pay', *in* Hollinshead, G., Nicholls, P. and Tailby, S. (eds), *Employee Relations*, London, Financial Times Pitman Publishing, pp. 332–77.

Financial Times (1999) 'Pay; employers "to police selves" on minimum wage', 29 March.

Flannery, T., Hofrichter, D. and Platten, P. (1996) *People, Performance and Pay*, New York, The Free Press.

Gunnigle, P., Turner, T. and D'Art, D. (1998) 'Counterpoising collectivism: performance-related pay and industrial relations in greenfield sites', *British Journal of Industrial Relations*, 36:4, 565–79.

Heery, E. (1992) 'Divided we fall? Trade unions and performance-related pay', Paper for LSE/TUC Trade Union Seminar, 19 March.

Hillage, J. and Pollard, E. (1999) 'Employability: developing a framework for policy analysis', *Labour Market Trends*, February, 83–5.

Hollinshead, G. and Leat, M. (1995) *Human Resource Management: An international and comparative perspective*, London, Pitman Publishing.

IDS (1992) *Skill-based Pay*, Incomes Data Services Study No. 500, February.

IDS (1995) 'Equal pay still proves elusive', *Employment Europe*, No. 403, July.

IDS (1998a) *Profit Sharing and Share Options*, Incomes Data Services Study No. 641, January.

IDS (1998b) 'Moving towards performance-related pay', *Employment Europe*, No. 433, January.

IDS (1998c) 'Performance-related pay gains ground in Finland', *Employment Europe*, No. 444, December.

IDS (1999) *Bonus Schemes*, Incomes Data Services Study No. 665, March.

IDS (2001) *All-employee Share Schemes*, Incomes Data Services Study No. 712, July.

Jacques, E. (1961) *Equitable Pay: A general theory of work, differential payment and individual progress* (2nd edn), London, Heinemann Educational.

Jenkins, J. (2002) 'Patterns of pay: results of the 2001 New Earnings Survey', *Labour Market Trends*, March, 129–39.

Kessler, I. (1994) 'Performance pay', *in* Sisson, K. (ed.), *Personnel Management*, Oxford, Blackwell, pp. 465–94.

Kessler, S. and Bayliss, F. (1998) *Contemporary British Industrial Relations* (3rd edn), Basingstoke, Macmillan.

Kessler, I. and Purcell, J. (1992) 'Performance related pay: objectives and application', *Human Resource Management Journal*, 2:3, 16–33.

Lawler, E.E. (1984) 'The strategic design of reward systems', *in* Fombrun, C., Tichy, N. and Devanna, M.A. (eds), *Strategic Human Resource Management*, New York, Wiley, pp. 127–48.

Livy, B. (1988) *Corporate Personnel Management*, London, Pitman.

Lupton, T. and Bowey, A. (1983) *Wages and Salaries* (2nd edn), Aldershot, Gower.

Mabey, C. and Salaman, G. (1995) *Strategic Human Resource Management*, Oxford, Blackwell.

Marsden, D. and Richardson, R. (1992) *Motivation and performance related pay in the public sector: a case study of the Inland Revenue*, Discussion Paper No. 75, Centre for Economic Performance, London School of Economics.

Monks, J. (1998) 'Trade unions, enterprise and the future', *in* Sparrow, P. and Marchington, M. (eds), *Human Resource Management: The new agenda*, London, Financial Times Pitman Publishing, pp. 171–9.

Nichol, C. (1998) 'Patterns of pay: results of the 1998 New Earnings Survey', *Labour Market Trends*, December, 623–34.

Procter, S., McArdle, L., Rowlinson, M., Forrester, P. and Hassard, J. (1993) 'Performance related pay in operation: a case study from the electronics industry', *Human Resource Management Journal*, 3:4, 60–74.

Roberts, I. (1997) 'Remuneration and reward', *in* Beardwell, I. and Holden, L. (eds), *Human Resource Management: A contemporary perspective*, London, Pitman Publishing, pp. 506–58.

Rubery, J. (1995) 'The low-paid and the unorganised', *in* Edwards, P. (ed.), *Industrial Relations: Theory and practice in Britain*, Oxford, Blackwell, pp. 543–68.

Schuster, J. and Zingheim, P. (1992) *The New Pay: Linking employee and organisational performance*, New York, Lexington.

Semler, R. (1993) *Maverick! The success story behind the world's most unusual workplace*, London, Arrow Business Books.

Smith, I. (1993) 'Reward management: a retrospective assessment', *Employee Relations*, 15:3, 45–59.

Storey, J. and Sisson, K. (1993) *Managing Human Resources and Industrial Relations*, Buckingham, Open University Press.

The Guardian (1999) 'A stick in carrot's clothing', 9 April.

Thompson, M. (1992) *Pay and Performance: The employer experience*, Brighton, Institute of Manpower Studies.

Thompson, M. (1995) *Team Working and Pay*, Institute of Employment Studies Report No. 281, Brighton, University of Sussex.

Thorpe, R. and Homan, G. (2000) *Strategic Reward Systems*, Harlow, Pearson Education.

Torrington, D. (1992) 'Pay and performance management', Paper presented to British Psychological Society Conference, January.

Torrington, D., Hall, L. and Taylor, S. (2002) *Human Resource Management* (5th edn), Harlow, Financial Times Prentice Hall.

University of Bristol and KPMG Peat Marwick (1994) *HORATIO II: A survey of human resource practices in the retail financial services sector.*

self-check Answers

10.1 *As an HR manager, what other arguments would you employ against your directors' allegations that the NMW will be inflationary?*

You may fall back on the traditional personnel management argument that paying employees a reasonable wage is likely to ensure that they are not demotivated, even if they are not highly motivated. If you pay them far less than they think is equitable they may not voice their disapproval explicitly, but we all know that employees can 'get their own back' very effectively. This may be by leaving the organisation or, perhaps more damaging to the employer's interests, by conducting some form of implicit policy of non-cooperation.

You could also pursue the moral argument. To add weight to your argument that people should be paid a decent living wage you could cite the Social Charter. This was the statement of minimum social rights prepared by the European Commission in 1989 and rejected by the then UK government. This included a statement that employees should have the right to a fair and equitable wage, thereby enabling a decent standard of living.

10.2 *Do you think that 'direct(ing) pay programmes to what the organisation wants to achieve' represents strategy or control?*

This is a difficult question. It may be that 'strategy' is only another form of control. After all, the notion of HRM strategy has at its heart the proposition that the HR strategy can be designed and implemented with a view to changing employee behaviours (see, for example, Mabey and Salaman, 1995). This represents a view of human nature that suggests that our behaviour may be manipulated. The opposite view is that our behaviour is based on decisions we make of our own free will. This raises deeper philosophical questions, which go far beyond the scope of a book on employee relations. Our view is that there is little difference between strategy and control. It may have an acceptable 'soft' face or an unacceptable 'hard' one. But the management purpose is the same – to direct employees to behave in the manner that management desires.

10.3 *How may IPRP be an effective way of changing organisational culture?*

IPRP plays an important role in changing organisational culture through its capacity to send powerful *cultural messages* to employees. Among these are the message that the organisation is not now going to pay people simply for length of service, experience and loyalty. To rise through the pay scale employees now have to perform consistently at an above average level. Similarly, there is a message of self-reliance. This is because of the reduced role of collective bargaining in determining employees' individual salaries. IPRP means that it is up to the individual to generate pay increases. No longer can there be sole reliance on the trade union to carry out this function.

10.4 *What problems may there be with team-based pay?*

You may ask yourself how you would respond were you to be expected, albeit implicitly, to conform to performance levels that were 'just enough'. If you pride yourself on high levels of effort this might tempt you to extract yourself from the group because you felt that your earning potential might be prejudiced. Similarly, your level of felt-fairness would be low if you felt a fellow member was putting in much less effort than you. These situations would call into question the extent to which you really were a 'teamworker'.

CASE 10	**UtilityCo's new reward strategy[1]**

UtilityCo is a large provider of public utilities to the UK market. As a public utilities provider, UtilityCo was formerly in the public sector before it was privatised in the late 1980s. Although all occupational categories are represented in the UtilityCo workforce, the majority of the staff is in four main groups: engineering, technical support, contracts and general administrative support. Much of the work undertaken by UtilityCo is performed by sub-contractors working on UtilityCo's behalf.

In recent years UtilityCo's product market has been characterised by intense competition following the deregulation of the market in the late 1980s. This meant that the market was opened up to competition with the result that suppliers of, in particular, electricity, gas and telecommunication became competitors. Increased competition had two effects on organisations such as UtilityCo. First, it made them much more conscious of the necessity to sell their products rather than assume that their customers had no choice but to buy those products from the companies. For UtilityCo this led to a decision to re-invent itself as an aggressive, sales-led company rather than a public service. Second, it meant that organisations had to be increasingly aware of their operating costs in order that they might remain competitive. UtilityCo was not the only public utilities organisation that was addressing these dual concerns. UtilityCo needed to reduce its costs in order to offer competitive prices to increasingly demanding customers, government regulators and shareholders. This necessity led to the development of a strategy in which cost reduction was a cornerstone. In particular, it was felt to be of paramount importance that more value was obtained from the organisation's employees.

Obtaining more value from UtilityCo's employees was the driving force behind the new reward strategy that was introduced in 1999. The new reward strategy had been agreed in principle with the company's trade unions at the joint negotiating committee. But it was inevitable that there would be some tension experienced in its introduction since it threatened some of the traditions of the organisation guarded jealously by the unions, notably the pay system which was based on rate for the job and length of service.

For some years UtilityCo had operated a traditional pay system. The foundation of this was a conventional pay structure in which a sequence of job grades existed and jobs of broadly equivalent value were slotted into grades. A pay range was attached to each grade and pay progression was through that range which contained, typically, 10 pay points. Grades were determined by job evaluation. The HR manager at UtilityCo agreed with Armstrong (1999:209) that this structure provided an 'orderly basis for managing pay relativities'. But the perceived cost of this orderliness was a belief on the part of employees that the only means of career and pay progression was by promotion through the grade

---

[1] The organisation and the people working within it are fictional.

structure. There was an element of individual performance-related pay (IPRP), but for many employees the link between their performance and their individual reward was unclear.

The new system was based on the principle of job families. 'Job families group together a number of jobs which have some dimension of commonality defined by the organisation.... The grade structure for each family would normally cover all associated jobs from entry levels through to the most senior, providing a vertical structure' (Thorpe and Homan, 2000). All jobs at UtilityCo were grouped into eight families on six different levels. Staff who deal with customer queries in the company's call centre, for example, were placed in the job family 'sales support' at level 6 (the lowest level) whereas directors were put in the 'strategic and policy' job family at level 1

For each generic role (for example 'customer support assistant') a set of competences was defined reflecting what role holders should be able to demonstrate as a *new entrant*, *typical performer* or *high performer*. Under the new system pay was to be determined by market rate, acquisition of competences, and the achievement of individual performance targets. In addition, it was stressed by UtilityCo management that pay would be determined by job not grade. An important defining principle of the new system was that those employees who contributed more would progress faster through the pay scales than those who were typical or below typical performers. Stress was laid upon the fact that current pay and benefits were unaffected by the new system.

In her letter to all staff announcing the new job families system the HR manager echoed Armstrong (1999) in noting several advantages of the change. Principal among these were:

- employees would be better equipped to plan their own careers (within or outside the organisation) and their own training and development needs;
- broader job descriptions would give employees more opportunity to increase their skills and make their jobs more challenging;
- employees would not see grade promotions as the only way of furthering their salaries but be encouraged to think of skill acquisition as a means of career and salary progression;
- more effective employees would be able to earn more competitive salaries.

In the final analysis UtilityCo was seeking to develop a more competent and flexible workforce, better equipped to manage change and to meet the UtilityCo goal of increased efficiency and, therefore, reduced cost.

However, UtilityCo experienced some teething problems with the new strategy. These became apparent in two principal ways: the lack of use of c ompetences and the reluctance of employees to move around the organisation in the manner envisaged.

The lack of use of competences

The principle of competence acquisition is crucial to job family pay systems in general (Armstrong, 1999), and was to the UtilityCo system in particular.

Competences were essential for determining the position in the job family structure of role holders. They also helped to define position in the pay scale by allowing a judgement to be made as to whether the employee was at new entrant, typical performer or high performer level. In addition, extra pay could be earned by the acquisition of competences. Competences were, of course, an essential ingredient of the desire of UtilityCo to develop the expertise and, therefore, flexibility of its workforce. So if manager and employees were placing little emphasis upon competence acquisition and assessment this would have an important harmful effect upon the pursuit of UtilityCo's reward objectives.

In spite of the importance of competence acquisition to job family pay systems it was not achieving the impact that UtilityCo had hoped. It was useful for guiding discussions at performance appraisal interviews, but no more. The accountants, for example, thought that exams were still the way in which they could achieve career progression. In addition, many employees thought that competences were not linked to salary. But the real stumbling block was the traditional culture at UtilityCo which was still strongly rooted in former public sector norms even after many years in the private sector. This stressed the importance of grade as a status symbol among employees. It was something that everyone understood, and was a public demonstration to all that someone was successful. The consequence was that, when jobs were advertised internally, people said to themselves 'What grade is this?'

The reluctance of employees to move around the organisation

Despite the hopes of UtilityCo's managers that the new reward strategy would encourage employees to move around the organisation to seek more development, this did not appear to be happening. There was little evidence of employee interest in moving around departments in order to broaden their experience. Employees, as one manager put it, 'seemed to know what they like and like what they know'. This led to the feeling among employees that moving around to develop yourself was a management ideal but not one shared by most employees. There was particular concern over those employees who had progressed to 'high performer' or the equivalent in the 'old' system. The general opinion seemed to be that the opportunity to develop through learning new competences in different settings was insufficient incentive. It was thought that people understood the old system of promotion, but flatter structures had done away with many promotion opportunities.

There were other problems with the new strategy. Some managers thought that they were spending too much time as 'HR consultants' advising people on the competences they could acquire, and the evidence that they would need to cite to achieve advancement and on assessing that evidence.

Some of the explanations for the lack of use of competences chimed with those that could be heard in any organisation. Some employees thought that they had been on courses to learn new skills but their manager had not let them put them into practice. Others complained that if more challenging jobs were taken to grow competences it meant that it was more difficult to get a high performance award because the easier the job the easier it was for people to shine at it. Employees in specialist jobs thought that it was less easy for them to develop horizontally in such areas. Other employees thought that it was difficult to compare levels and acquisition of competences for different jobs. An example was sales support where it was easier to measure competences as they lend themselves to greater standardisation. In addition, it was thought there was a problem of people acquiring unnecessary competences, such as presentation skills, simply in order to get more money. It was interesting to note that there was still a loyalty award presented to employees who had been with the organisation for 10 years, as one manager confirmed 'irrespective of their competence'!

Some employees thought that there had been too little consultation over the job family in which they were placed. The general paucity of information about the exercise in placing employees into specific job families (for example who was going to which and why) meant that appeals were difficult because there was insufficient information on which to base an appeal.

The final point concerns an issue over which most commentators (e.g. Schuster and Zingheim, 1992) agree. This is the need for clarity and simplicity in pay systems. The presence of clarity means that changes can be communicated more easily and the system can be operated by line managers less problematically. Many UtilityCo employees and managers admired the ingenuity of the new strategy but felt it to be unduly complex.

Questions

1 What do you think should have been UtilityCo's priorities in introducing the new strategy?

2 To what extent do you agree with the view that the twin goals of reward system simplicity and designing more innovative systems are contradictory?

3 How do you think that UtilityCo can overcome some of the 'teething problems'?

References

Armstrong, M. (1999) *Employee reward* (2nd edn) London, Institute of Personnel and Development.

Schuster, J. and Zingheim, P. (1992) *The New Pay: Linking employee and organisational performance*, New York, Lexington.

Thorpe, R. and Homan, G. (2000) *Strategic Reward Systems*, Harlow, Financial Times Prentice Hall.

Part Three

Ending the employment relationship

Chapter 11

Terminating the employment relationship

At the end of this chapter you should be able to:

■ distinguish between dismissal, resignation and retirement;

■ outline and explain potentially fair reasons for dismissal;

■ describe the types of dismissal that may be considered unfair;

■ discuss the relationships between dismissal and industrial action;

■ explain the differences between wrongful and unfair dismissal;

■ outline the implications of wrongful and unfair dismissal for the employment relationship.

11.1 Introduction

All employment relationships will, eventually, come to an end. Their termination may be because the employer or employee is no longer satisfied with the employment relationship, or because the contract has come to its natural conclusion (Torrington and Hall, 1998). The termination of an employment relationship and the associated contract of employment can be instigated by the employer or by the employee for a variety of reasons. From an employer's perspective these include:

■ gross misconduct by the employee;
■ the employee's incapability or lack of qualifications in relation to her or his job;
■ redundancy as part of an organisational downsizing;
■ where continued employment of the employee would be in breach of statute;
■ some other substantial reason;

whereas from an employee's perspective the reasons include:

■ retirement for age or ill-health reasons such as mental illness;
■ resignation for a variety of possible reasons, including taking up a new contract of employment, following a partner to another geographical area, or emigration;
■ breach of contract by the employer;
■ death.

In considering these two sets of reasons for terminating an employment relationship, other distinctions are also apparent. In particular we can see that an employee can leave an organisation's employment involuntarily for reasons such as *gross misconduct* or *incapability*. Where such an involuntary requirement for an employee to leave the organisation's employment exists, the process of terminating the contract of employment is called *dismissal*. Alternatively, an employee may leave an organisation's employment voluntarily. In such instances, reasons such as 'taking up a new contract of employment' and 'emigration' emphasise that an employment relationship can also be ended voluntarily by the employee *resigning*.

Within this chapter we concentrate principally upon dismissal, considering types of dismissal and the reasons for it. Our consideration begins with an overview of the three types of dismissal – fair, unfair and wrongful – and a discussion of how employees can seek redress (Section 11.2). Subsequently in Sections 11.3–11.5, we explore each of the three types in more detail, including the relationship between dismissal and industrial action. Inevitably our discussion draws widely upon UK and European Union (EU) legislation. However, it is not the intention of this chapter to provide you with a detailed and definitive explanation of the law in relation to dismissal. There are legal texts, such as those to which we refer in the chapter, that do this. Rather, our aim is to provide an overview of the main issues associated with each of the three types of dismissal so that you can appreciate the importance of the legal dimension for the employment relationship. Within our discussion, issues of discipline and grievance are dealt with only in limited detail, as they have already been covered in Chapter 9. Similarly, we provide only a brief overview of dismissals due to redundancy or early retirement, as these are discussed in Chapter 12. We also deal briefly in Section 11.6 with issues associated with employee resignation and retirement, focusing in particular on issues associated with employee turnover and phased withdrawal from work. We conclude the chapter with a case study that looks at how issues of discipline, capability and dismissal are dealt with by Halcrow, an international infrastructure provider specialising in the transportation, water and property sectors.

11.2 Dismissal, fairness and procedures

■ The meaning of dismissal

Many people think of dismissal as simply the termination of a contract of employment by the employer. However, the actual definition stated in the Employment Rights Act 1996 is both wider and more complex. This Act states that an employee is dismissed by her or his employer if:

- the contract under which she or he is employed is terminated by the employer with or without notice;
- she or he is employed under a fixed-term contract for which the term has expired without being renewed under the same contract;
- she or he terminates the contract of employment (with or without notice) in circumstances in which she or he is entitled to do so, owing to the employer's conduct.

This means that dismissal occurs when an employee's fixed-term contract expires and when the conduct of the employer forces the employee to terminate the contract of employment, as well as when the employer terminates the contract of employment.

Organisational practice within the UK is influenced considerably by the requirements of the unfair dismissal legislation that has evolved since the Industrial Relations Act 1971. You can trace this through Boxes 6.1, 6.2 and 6.3, which summarise the major legislation affecting the employment relationship from 1945 to the present day. Recent changes were brought about by the Employment Relations Act 1999 and the Employment Act 2002. The former of these incorporated a range of policies from the Social Chapter of the Treaty of Maastricht 1992 into UK law, including the right for any employee who has completed more than a year's continuous employment in the organisation and who is under the normal age of retirement for that job not to be unfairly dismissed. The 2002 Act introduced minimum requirements for internal discipline and grievance procedures, including dismissal, and implemented the EU Directive on fixed-term work. This limited the ability of employers to use a series of fixed-term contracts to employ the same person in an essentially permanent position.

self-check question

11.1 Revisit Chapter 6, and in particular Boxes 6.1, 6.2 and 6.3. Starting with the Industrial Relations Act 1971 (Box 6.1) construct a table to provide an overview of how unfair dismissal legislation has evolved. You should use the following column headings:

Act   **Key features in relation to dismissal**

Within the UK, three distinct types of dismissal are highlighted by the legislation: fair, unfair and wrongful. The first of these, *fair dismissal*, occurs when an employer terminates the contract of employment with an employee for one or more of the five potentially fair reasons stated in the Employment Rights Act 1996. Not surprisingly, *unfair dismissal* occurs when an employer terminates the contract of employment with an employee for a reason other than one or more of the five potentially fair reasons stated in the Employment Rights Act 1996. The final type, *wrongful dismissal*, occurs when an employer terminates a contract of employment by breaching its terms and conditions.

Dismissal and redress

One consequence of dismissal-related legislation is that, where an employee seeks redress for unfair dismissal, an employer may have to prove otherwise to an independent judicial body, the Employment Tribunal (Figure 11.1). Within this the onus is on the employer to prove that the reason for dismissal was one of those permitted as fair by the 1996 Act and that he or she acted reasonably. Alternatively the employee and employer can go to voluntary arbitration. This scheme was drawn up by ACAS (Advisory, Conciliation and Arbitration Service) and came into force in England and Wales in 2001 as a result of the Employment Rights (Dispute Resolution) Act 1998. It is intended to be 'confidential, informal, relatively fast and cost efficient', and so does not consider more complex disputes (Carby-Hall, 2001: 4). Rather, it concentrates entirely on disputes arising out of the unfair dismissal law contained in the

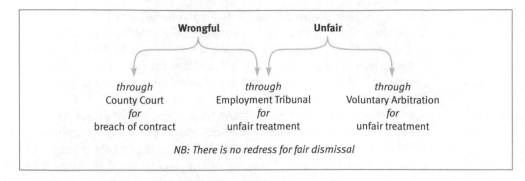

Figure 11.1 **Approaches for seeking redress after dismissal**

Employment Rights Act 1996, providing an alternative procedure to employment tribunals, where a marked increase in caseloads has resulted in long delays (Carby-Hall, 2001).

In contrast, redress by an employee for wrongful dismissal is sought through the courts. Here the onus is on the employer to justify either that the action of terminating the contract was lawful or that they were responding to an earlier breach of contract by the employee. As suggested in Figure 11.1, an employee can also seek redress for wrongful dismissal through an employment tribunal, although if this process were used, the claim would be for unfair treatment rather than for breach of contract. It is this concept of fairness in the dismissal process that we consider next, prior to exploring each of the three types of dismissal in more detail.

■ Fairness in dismissal

As you have already gathered from reading the first few pages of this chapter, the dismissal of an employee by an employer must be fair if the employee is not to seek redress. Fairness of dismissal is usually assessed sequentially by employment tribunals looking first at potential and then actual fairness. First there is a need to establish whether or not the dismissal was potentially fair – in other words, whether the reasons for the employee's dismissal were actually valid and were one or more of the five potentially fair reasons stated in the Employment Rights Act 1996 (Figure 11.3). If it is considered that these fair reasons existed then the dismissal was potentially fair. The next stage is to establish whether or not the potentially fair dismissal was fair in the actual circumstances. This decision is based around two questions (Torrington and Hall, 1998). Was the decision reasonable in the circumstances – in other words, did the employer act reasonably in treating that reason as sufficient reason for dismissing an employee? And was the dismissal carried out in line with the organisation's procedures?

Employment tribunals have looked at a variety of considerations to answer the question of whether or not the employer acted reasonably (ACAS, 2002). These include whether:

■ the employee's dismissal was a reasonable action to take in the circumstances;
■ the employer had reasonable grounds to believe that the employee had undertaken the offence concerned;

- the employer had carried out a reasonable investigation;
- the employer had followed the organisation's own procedure;
- the employee knew the allegations and was allowed to put her or his side of the story;
- the employee was allowed the right to be accompanied at the disciplinary hearing;
- in capability cases, the employee was warned and given reasonable time to improve, with appropriate training;
- in ill-health cases, the employee was consulted and her or his doctor asked for an opinion.

In addition an employment tribunal will also take into account other factors such as the employee's length of service, the size of the organisation, and consistency of treatment.

The complexity of issues associated with reasonableness and its interrelationship with other contextual factors is highlighted by the recent case of *Williams* v. *Archer* (Sapsted, 2002). In this case, the crucial issue according to the chair of the employment tribunal was Williams's refusal to sign a new confidentiality agreement after the jailing of Geoffrey Archer for perjury. During her husband's trial in 2001 Archer had received reports that Williams, her personal assistant for some 13 years, was planning to sell her story to the press. Williams denied this, arguing that she was being victimised for having made statements to the police earlier. Later that year Archer told Williams that she was no longer needed on a full-time basis because of a decline in her work commitments due to her husband's imprisonment. Williams was offered a part-time contract provided she signed a new confidentiality agreement. When Williams refused, she was offered a £9000 redundancy payment and cash in lieu of three months' salary. The employment tribunal rejected Williams's claim that she had been unfairly dismissed, stating that her employer's actions had been fair given the circumstances.

Dismissal procedures

Data from the 1998 Workplace Employee Relations Survey (WERS) emphasise that over 92 per cent of UK workplaces have procedures in place to assist with discipline and grievance including dismissal (Cully *et al.*, 1999). Cully *et al.* (1999) emphasise that this situation has long been the case, with little change since 1984, commenting that although these types of procedure are the norm, their absence is more likely in smaller workplaces. The WERS data also emphasise that almost all employees are able to appeal against management decisions to discipline or dismiss them, with only 4 per cent of workplaces not allowing this. For unionised workplaces there is an almost universal existence of formal discipline and dismissal procedures, such procedures existing in 98 per cent of such workplaces (Millward *et al.*, 2000).

The importance of such procedures for employment tribunals' assessment of fairness is highlighted by the statutory dismissal and grievance procedures set out in the Employment Act 2002, and due to come into force in mid 2003. Under the 2002 Act, all employers, whatever their size, will be obliged to follow a default statutory dismissal and grievance procedure unless one already in existence in their organisation exceeds this default. This means that, in effect, all workplaces will have such procedures by default. Employees who start work after the Act comes into force will either have the dismissal and grievance procedure set out in full in their contract, or have it referred to explicitly in their terms and conditions of employment.

With regard to dismissal the Act suggests a three-stage process (Figure 11.2), operating in conjunction with the ACAS Code of Practice (outlined in Chapter 9) and other statutory provisions discussed later in this chapter. In the first stage of the standard procedure a written statement will be used to inform both the employer and the employee of the reasons for the dismissal, disciplinary action or grievance. Subsequently, there should be a meeting between the employer and employee, prior to which both must have been given sufficient time to consider the other's written statement. At this meeting the employer must inform the employee of the decision and of her or his right to appeal. The procedure must also contain an appeal stage. This can occur after the dismissal has been imposed. Once again the employer must inform the employee of the outcome of her or his appeal. As you will probably have realised from looking at Figure 11.2, the Employment Act 2002 also provides for a shorter modified dismissal procedure in which the meeting between the written statement and appeal stages is missed out. Unfortunately, the 2002 Act is not particularly clear as to when this modified procedure should be used, although the government has indicated that the modified procedure should be used only in more extreme cases such as summary dismissal for gross misconduct (Campbell, 2002).

The Employment Act 2002 emphasises that the procedures for dismissal need to operate in conjunction with the ACAS Code of Practice and other relevant statutory provisions. The ACAS (2000) Code of Practice for disciplinary and grievance procedures (outlined in Chapter 9) provides valuable indications of what should be included in procedures prior to dismissal, whatever the reason. These are summarised by Croner (2000) as in almost all cases:

- there must be a full investigation before dismissal is contemplated;
- employees should be given full details of the disciplinary situation and an opportunity to state their views before a decision is taken;

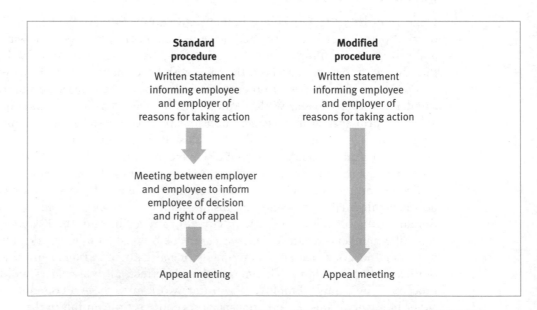

Figure 11.2 **Stages in the dismissal process set out by the Employment Act 2002**

- employees should, wherever possible, be warned of the possibility of dismissal beforehand;
- employees should have the right to be accompanied by a colleague or trade union representative in any meeting that might lead to dismissal;
- there should be a right of appeal.

Not surprisingly, failure to follow the ACAS Code of Practice, the organisational dismissal procedure as set out in the 2002 Act and other relevant statutory provisions may lead to that dismissal by an employer being automatically considered to be unfair. Despite this, the converse is not always true. Even if an organisation has followed its dismissal procedure, this will not necessarily mean that an employment tribunal considers the dismissal to be fair if the employee seeks redress.

11.3 Potentially fair reasons for dismissal

Five reasons for dismissal are stated as potentially fair in the Employment Rights Act 1996 (Figure 11.3). This means that, if an employer can show that the employee's dismissal was due to one or more of these reasons, the employment tribunal must decide whether or not the employer has acted fairly. Within the tribunal hearing, adherence to the organisation's procedure provides a positive indication that the dismissal was undertaken fairly. If the employer has acted fairly in relation to one or more of the five reasons then the actual dismissal will be considered fair. However, if the employer can be seen to have acted unfairly, such as by not carrying out a proper investigation, then the dismissal will be considered unfair.

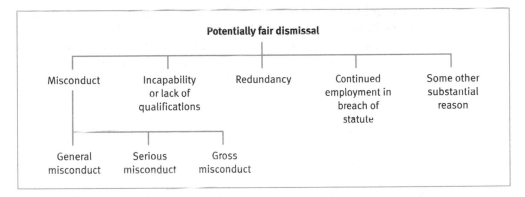

Figure 11.3 **Potentially fair reasons for dismissal**

■ Misconduct

The first of the potentially fair reasons stated in the Employment Rights Act 1996 is misconduct. General and serious misconduct are unlikely to result in summary dismissal (dismissal without notice). Initially, as discussed in Chapter 9, the organisation's disciplinary procedure will be invoked, dismissal being unlikely unless this is exhausted. In contrast, gross misconduct that destroys the employment relationship can lead to summary dismissal for the first offence (ACAS, 2002). This includes extreme versions of many of the behaviours outlined as reasons for disciplinary action in Chapter 9, including poor personal behaviour such as theft or assault, poor general work conduct such as repeated unauthorised absences, discrimination, and contraventions of health and safety regulations including the organisation's drink and drugs policies. Although you would probably agree that some of these actions, such as theft and assault, are gross misconduct, for others you may not feel this to be the case. For this reason, ACAS (2002) advises that employers should provide employees with sufficient examples in dismissal and grievance procedures to enable them to understand what constitutes gross misconduct in their workplace and the consequences of breaking these rules. ACAS (2002) states that, in cases of alleged gross misconduct, the employee should be suspended on full pay while an investigation is carried out. On completion of the investigation and of the organisation's full disciplinary procedure the employer may find that gross misconduct has occurred and then decide to dismiss the employee without notice or pay in lieu of notice.

There may, however, be situations in which the employment relationship can survive despite gross misconduct by the employee. For example, an employee who has stolen may still be employed if the employer believes that the theft was an out of character, momentary lapse and that it will not happen again. Indeed, whatever the reason, an employer may choose not to dismiss an employee but rather just issue the employee with a final written warning.

Issues associated with gross misconduct are illustrated clearly by the employment tribunal case of *O'Flynn* v. *Air Links the Airport Coach Company* (Aitkin Driver Partnership, 2002). Air Links had introduced a drink and drugs policy, including random testing, and had made it clear to all employees that a positive test result would result in dismissal. O'Flynn, one of the company's employees, knew of this policy and had not objected to it. Later, when she was selected at random for a drugs test, O'Flynn tested positive for cannabis. During the subsequent investigation she admitted to having taken cannabis and cocaine as well as other substances. As her duties included assisting drivers in manoeuvring coaches it was argued at the employment tribunal that it was important she was drink and drug free. She was dismissed by Air Links for gross misconduct. A subsequent employment appeals tribunal ruled that her dismissal was fair.

However, as we suggested earlier, the decision as to whether or not the dismissal was fair is dependent upon the circumstances of the individual case and the employer having undertaken a full investigation. In the case of *John Lewis plc* v. *Coyne* (IDS, 2001) Coyne had made unauthorised personal telephone calls using her employer's telephone, despite this being in breach of a well-known company policy. When confronted, Coyne admitted making the calls and offered to pay for them. However, in the manager's view, Coyne's conduct in breaching the policy and not offering to pay for the telephone calls until confronted was clearly dishonest, and so she was dismissed summarily. No further investigation into the nature of the telephone calls was made, because the manager felt that even one unauthorised personal call amounted to dishonesty. Subsequent investigations revealed that Coyne had made many of these 'personal' calls to a colleague who covered her work, and they were therefore work related. The employment appeals tribunal ruled subsequently that the dismissal was unfair, stating that, although in many cases there will be no doubt that actions are dishonest, in this case it was not necessarily obvious that Coyne's actions were dishonest.

Incapability or lack of qualifications

The second of the potentially fair reasons for dismissal stated in the Employment Rights Act 1996 is incapability or lack of qualifications. This includes extreme versions of job performance and absence through ill-health reasons or disciplinary action discussed in Chapter 9, as well as not having the correct qualifications. In summary, it means that if an employee lacks the skill, aptitude, physical health or correct qualifications to carry out the duties of the job then potentially there is a fair ground for dismissal. Consequentially it is potentially fair to dismiss an employee if that employee can no longer cope with the work, whatever the reason, or perhaps because standards have been raised.

Incapability can be subdivided into a number of different aspects (Snape, 1999):

- long-term illness;
- a series of short-term illnesses;
- inherent inability to undertake the job;
- poor job performance.

Inevitably, some employees may become incapable of work because of a long-term illness. Whether it is reasonable to dismiss an employee on the grounds of long-term illness is not an easy question to answer, however. It is dependent upon a range of factors, including:

- the nature of the illness;
- the length of time it has lasted, and how long it is likely to continue to last;
- whether the employee is likely to be able to return to her or his original duties;
- the need for the employer to find a permanent replacement;
- whether sick pay is still being paid.

In such cases it will be necessary to seek medical advice.

Alternatively, an employee may have a series of short-term illnesses, which when combined add up to a substantial period of absence. Again the employer will need to seek medical advice. This is illustrated by the employment tribunal case of *International Sports* v. *Thomson*, an employee who was, over a period of a year and a half, absent from work for 25 per cent of the time. The reasons given for these absences included dizzy spells, anxiety and nerves, bronchitis, virus infection, water on the knee, cystitis, dyspepsia and flatulence. The organisation's doctor had advised that there was no common link between these absences. Although medical certificates covered all these absences, she was given a warning and told that she should reduce her absence rate to less than 7 per cent, otherwise she would be dismissed. At a subsequent employment appeals tribunal, her dismissal was ruled to be fair in the circumstances (Croner, 2000).

self-check question

11.2 Jane, a primary school teacher, had an excellent employment record, having had only 3 days' sickness in the past 5 years. However, she has been on long-term sick leave for the past 6 months with chronic fatigue syndrome. A recent medical with the employer's doctor suggests that Jane is starting to recover, and she is keen to return to work. However, the nature of her illness means she is unlikely to be able to return to her post for at least another 3–4 months.

Would you advise the employer to dismiss Jane?

Incapability may also occur when the employee is inherently incapable of performing her or his job. This situation may arise if an employee is promoted and is subsequently unable to cope with the work or, alternatively, where new methods of working such as new technology are introduced and the employee is unable to adapt. In such situations the employer will have to demonstrate the employee's unsuitability to the satisfaction of the tribunal. This evidence can be undermined by, for example, the employer writing the dismissed employee an extremely positive reference. Such a lack of skill is less likely to be considered a fair reason for dismissal by an employment tribunal where the employer has contributed to it by, for instance, not allowing the employee to undertake training to improve. Employers are also normally expected to consider the option of redeployment to an alternative job before taking a decision to dismiss. Alternatively, an employee may be discovered to have a physical disability that prevents the job in question from being undertaken adequately. For example, it is not possible to be apprenticed to be an electrician if you are colour blind as this prevents you recognising colour-coded wires correctly. Providing the provisions of the Disability and Discrimination Act 1995 are followed, dismissal for such incapability can be fair.

Incapability may also occur when an employee has not performed the job to the best of her or his ability for some time. In such instances investigation is likely to highlight that it is the employee's conduct rather than an innate inability to do the job. This incapability is therefore more similar to misconduct. In such instances, Croner (2000) advises that early warnings in the disciplinary procedure should emphasise this aspect of the employee's misconduct, and that the employment relationship be based upon the requirement of each employee not to limit her or his effort.

Lack of qualifications to do the work is also a reason for dismissal, although, as pointed out by Snape (1999), this occurs relatively rarely. For a dismissal on these grounds to be upheld by an employment tribunal, the employer must show that the paper qualification such as a degree or membership of a professional institute is necessary to undertake the job, rather than just being convenient. Where the employee has claimed that she or he has qualifications that they do not have, this is simply a case of misrepresentation. However, where an employee is taken on and fails subsequently to obtain a particular qualification that is required for the job, then the employer must be seen to have acted fairly in supporting the employee to obtain the qualification. Fairness in such situations is illustrated by the case of *Al-Tikriti* v. *South Western Regional Health Authority* (Torrington and Hall, 1998). Al-Tikriti was employed as a senior registrar by the South Western Regional Health Authority. The health authority allowed registrars three attempts at passing the Royal College of Pathologists' examinations. Al-Tikriti failed on his third attempt and was dismissed. He claimed that his dismissal was unfair as he had insufficient training to pass the exams. However, the tribunal found that the training had been adequate and that the dismissal was therefore fair.

■ Redundancy

The third reason stated in the 1996 Act is redundancy. Whenever an employee's job ceases to exist it is potentially fair to dismiss that person. Although we discuss redundancy in detail in Chapter 12, there are a number of aspects that are worth highlighting here. An employee may potentially claim that dismissal for a reason of redundancy was unfair if, in reality, there was no redundancy situation or if the employer has acted unreasonably. Consequently it is important that an employer acts fairly and is seen to act fairly with regard to the possibility of redundancies. Indications of fairness include:

- a clearly stated selection procedure that has, if possible, been agreed in advance;
- giving as much notice as possible to those facing redundancy;
- consulting with individual employees at risk and considering possible redeployment;
- consulting with relevant trade unions or other employee representatives over the redundancy methods.

Continued employment in breach of statute

The fourth reason stated in the 1996 Act, that continued employment would be in breach of statute, argues that dismissal is potentially fair where an employee cannot continue to do her or his job without breaking the law. However, for this to be considered fair, the employer must prove absolutely that to have carried on employing that person would have meant breaking the law. Most often dismissal for this reason occurs after the employee has been disqualified from driving. Other common occurrences include foreign nationals whose work permits have been terminated (Torrington and Hall, 1998).

In general, then, we can see that, as with other forms of potentially fair dismissal, it is vital that the employer establishes the facts and does not dismiss the employee automatically and without ensuring that her or his view of the law is correct (Croner, 2000). In particular, for dismissal to be considered fair it is important that any legal restriction on the employee working must affect either a major or an essential part of the employee's duties, that no alternative work is available, and that other arrangements that can be made have been considered.

Given our discussion above it might seem at first that disqualification from driving for 12 months would appear to be a fair reason for dismissal of an employee for whom driving was a part of her or his duties. However, as pointed out by Croner (2000), this may not necessarily be the case. The dismissal of a warehouse employee who might occasionally have to drive his firm's delivery van would probably be considered unfair unless it was deemed essential for him to be able to drive when the need arose. Conversely the dismissal of a sales representative whose job entailed her driving in excess of 40 000 miles a year would probably be considered fair. In addition, the length of the disqualification period would have a bearing on the issue of fairness as, for shorter periods, it may be possible to reorganise driving duties to mitigate the impact of the ban. Thus, as with the other reasons for fair dismissal, it is important that the employer acts reasonably.

Some other substantial reason

The final reason given in the 1996 Act, some other substantial reason, was included to allow the full diversity of other genuinely fair dismissals rather than as a 'get out' clause (Croner, 2000). The emphasis is therefore on employers' being able to show that, in the particular circumstances, there are good economic, technical or organisational reasons for dismissal (Snape, 1999) and that they have acted reasonably. This means that, when justifying dismissal on the grounds of some other substantial reason, employers still have to show that they have investigated the circumstances fully, that other possibilities such as internal transfer, retraining or alternative work have been considered, and that they have followed their organisation's dismissal procedure.

The importance of following procedures is illustrated by the tribunal case of *Gormley* v. *Avon Lippiatt Hobbs Ltd*, a contracting firm. Lippiatt Hobbs Ltd had dismissed some employees as part of a wider rationalisation process that had also involved changes to the payment and piecework systems. The latter had resulted in a reduction of both the basic rate of pay and a lodging allowance. In this case, although the tribunal accepted the employer's evidence that there were sound business reasons for the rationalisation, the associated dismissals were still held to be unfair. The tribunal argued this on the basis that the employer had not given employees any opportunities for consultation or made use of any recognisable procedural arrangements for changing employees' contracts (IDS, 2000).

We can therefore see that a potentially fair dismissal can still be judged to be unfair if the employer is judged to have acted unreasonably within the circumstances (ACAS, 2002). The way in which reasonableness is determined therefore appears to be based upon what Torrington and Hall (1998: 247) refer to as a 'common sense approach to deciding what is fair'. Considering one of the potentially fair reasons for dismissal discussed earlier, it would therefore be unreasonable to dismiss an employee for the reason of incapability if she or he had been refused necessary training by the employer.

11.4 Unfair dismissal

As we saw when we answered self-check question 11.1, the right for an employee to claim unfair dismissal, although originally introduced by the Industrial Relations Act 1971, has been amended by subsequent Acts over the past 30 years. For example, the Sex Discrimination Act 1986 extended the scope of the 1975 Act of the same name to include discrimination in dismissal. In contrast, the Employment Act 1988 outlawed dismissal for non-union membership, and the Employment Act 1990 allowed employees to be dismissed for unofficial industrial action with no claim for unfair dismissal. Legislation in the late 1990s extended the rights of individual employees. The Public Interest Disclosure Act 1998 provided additional protection from dismissal for employees making disclosures about criminal offences, failures to comply with legal obligation and endangering of health and safety. Individual employee protection against unfair dismissal was also extended through the adoption of much of the Social Chapter of the EU's Treaty of Maastricht by the Employment Relations Act 1999. This reduced the qualifying period for claims of unfair dismissal to 1 year and extended protection for employees taking lawful industrial action.

Unfair dismissal is the most common claim made by employees in connection with the termination of their employment contract (Figure 11.4). Research by Carby-Hall (2001) highlights the fact that the number of applications made to employment tribunals for reasons of unfair dismissal, excluding redundancy, has risen, particularly since 1994. This is related partially to growing employment in small businesses

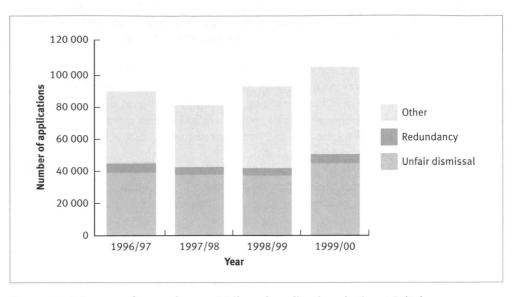

Figure 11.4 **Reasons for employment tribunal applications in Great Britain**
Source: Developed from Department of Trade and Industry (2002c)

(Department of Trade and Industry, 2002c), although as pointed out by Goodman *et al.* (1998) there are a number of other likely reasons. These include harsher disciplinary action by employers, the reduced coverage of trade unions, meaning that for an increasing number of employees a claim of unfair dismissal is their only means of redress, and employees becoming more litigious with the rise of 'no win no fee' solicitors (Carby-Hall, 2001). However, for most employers a tribunal application is a relatively rare event, with over 80 per cent of workplaces in the 1998 WERS survey having not had a tribunal claim made against them in the preceding 5-year period (Department of Trade and Industry, 2002c).

In this section we begin by outlining the situations where an employee has no right to claim unfair dismissal. Subsequently we discuss the types of dismissal that may be considered unfair, prior to exploring reasons for dismissal that are automatically considered unfair. Within our discussion, special attention is given to unfairness and dismissal within industrial action. The section closes with an examination of the costs of unfair dismissal to both the employer and the employee.

■ Situations where there is no right to claim unfair dismissal

Unless employees are claiming that they have been dismissed for one of the reasons that are *automatically unfair* (discussed later in this section), it does not necessarily follow that they have an automatic right to make an employment tribunal claim for unfair dismissal. Exploration of the legislation associated with unfair dismissal highlights seven categories of situation where employees are excluded from this right. These are where:

- employees have less than 1 year's service with their employer (unless they are claiming to have been dismissed for one of the reasons that are automatically unfair);

- employees have reached the organisation's fixed normal retirement age. Where there is no normal retirement age, then the right to claim unfair dismissal is lost at 65;
- employees are dismissed while taking official industrial action provided that the action has been going on for more than 8 weeks, sufficient attempts at dispute resolution have been made by the employer, all employees taking part in the strike on the date the dismissals took place have been dismissed, and either none or all of those dismissed have been offered their jobs back within a period of 3 months from the date of dismissal;
- employees are dismissed while taking part in unofficial industrial action;
- employees are in the police service or are people employed as a master or crew member of a fishing vessel and are paid only by a share in the profits or from the gross earnings of the vessel;
- employees are with a company that has reached a dismissal procedures agreement with an independent trade union and for whom the Secretary of State has made an order excluding them from the provisions of unfair dismissal legislation;
- employees have a contract of employment that is either illegal or is performed illegally.

When a fixed-term contract comes to an end and is not renewed, an employee is treated as being dismissed. Subsequent to the Employment Relations Act 1999 it has been illegal for employers to include waiver clauses for unfair dismissal in fixed-term contracts. Consequently an employee can claim that the dismissal was unfair provided she or he has the necessary qualifying service.

Types of dismissal that may be considered potentially unfair

Every employee, other than those excluded (as outlined above), has the right not to be dismissed unfairly, whatever her or his contractual notice period. Within this there are three types of dismissal that may be considered potentially unfair. These are illustrated in Figure 11.5. For the first two of these the employer makes the dismissal. For the third, dismissal by the employer is still considered to have occurred, as it is the employer's conduct that has caused the employee to terminate her or his contract.

The most common type of dismissal occurs when the employer terminates the employee's contract with or without notice, telling the employee that she or he has been dismissed. In order for an employee to claim unfair dismissal, it must first be

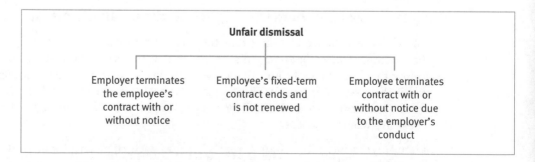

Figure 11.5 **Types of dismissal that may be considered potentially unfair**

shown that he or she has actually been dismissed. This is usually quite clear, although, if there is a dispute, it is up to the employee to prove that she or he has actually been dismissed. This may seem obvious, but there have been a number of tribunal cases in which the true meaning of the words used (either verbal or in letter form) to dismiss an employee have been debated. The 1974 tribunal case of *Futty* v. *D and D Brekkes Ltd* illustrates how conversations can be construed differently. Futty, a fish filleter, had been engaging in banter with his foreman about the nature of his job. Eventually his foreman retorted, 'If you do not like the job, f**k off' (IDS, 2001: 245). Futty claimed that this was dismissal, and found himself another job. However, D and D Brekkes denied dismissing him, arguing that such language was normal in the fish dock, and they thought that Futty would come back when he had calmed down. The tribunal found in favour of the employer, stating that the foreman's words were not a dismissal but a 'general exhortation to get on with the job', and that Mr Futty had chosen to leave.

Claims for unfair dismissal because a fixed-term contract has ended and is not renewed (Figure 11.5) are relatively rare (Snape, 1999). Technically, an employee can claim unfair dismissal if she or he is working on a fixed-term contract that has expired and not been renewed where the employee has the relevant qualifying service, as this is deemed to be a dismissal. However, within common law, fixed-term contracts are said to be terminated by the passing of time on the expiry date, so that there are no grounds for a wrongful dismissal claim if the contract has expired (IDS, 2001). Inevitably this has led to some employers attempting to get around giving people permanent contracts by employing them on a series of fixed-term contracts. The European Union's Fixed Term Employees (Prevention of Less Favourable Treatment) Regulations 2002, which came into force in the UK in October 2002 as part of the Employment Act 2002, are designed to prevent this. These regulations state that fixed-term employees are not to be treated less favourably than permanent employees who do similar work for the same employer at the same establishment. In particular, these regulations limit the scope for using a series of fixed-term contracts to employ the same person in an essentially permanent position. Where an employer renews a fixed-term contract and the employee has been working for 4 or more years under a series of fixed-term contracts it will now be deemed to be an indefinite contract. Consequently it will no longer be possible to dismiss the employee owing to the expiry of the contract.

self-check question	11.3	Why might an employer still wish to employ someone using a fixed-term rather than a permanent contract?

Constructive dismissal

When the employee terminates the contract with or without notice in circumstances in which she or he is entitled owing to the conduct of the employer, this has come to be known as a claim for constructive dismissal (Figure 11.5). However, for this claim to be upheld the employee must prove that the employer's conduct is such as to entitle her or him to terminate the contract without notice (IDS, 2000). This means that the employee must be able to claim a fundamental breach of contract. Not every breach of contract by an employer will be serious enough reason to be considered fundamental by an employment tribunal. A £10 cut in pay is obviously far more serious for an employee earning £100 a week than it is for an employee earning £1000 a week, and so would be more likely to be considered a fundamental breach.

Reasons that are automatically unfair

You may well be wondering, given there are reasons for dismissal that are potentially fair (Section 11.3), whether there are reasons for dismissal that are unfair. Legislation outlined earlier has resulted in a series of reasons for dismissal becoming regarded as automatically unfair. Where an employee is being dismissed for one of these reasons, a complaint of unfair dismissal can be brought regardless of the employee's length of service and of the reasonableness of the employer's actions, other than for unfair claims in relation to transfers of undertakings. In such situations the Collective Redundancies and Transfer of Undertakings (Protection of Employment) (Amendment) Regulations 1995 require employees to have at least 1 year's service prior to claiming unfair dismissal on a transfer of undertakings. The Department of Trade and Industry (2002a) lists reasons for dismissal that are automatically unfair as:

- in connection with membership or activities of an independent trade union;
- on grounds of pregnancy or childbirth;
- for asserting a legitimate statutory employment protection right;
- for taking legitimate action to ensure health and safety standards are observed;
- as part of or on the transfer of an undertaking where the actual transfer is the main reason for dismissal;
- for refusing to work on Sundays where the employee is a shop worker or betting worker;
- for carrying out functions as an elected employee representative, candidate for election or taking part in any election;
- for carrying out functions as an occupational pension scheme trustee;
- for reasons relating to the National Minimum Wage including carrying out functions as a workforce representative;
- for reasons relating to the Working Time Regulations 1998 including carrying out functions as a workforce representative;
- for making protected disclosures of wrongdoing or malpractice under the Public Interest Disclosure Act 1998;
- for reasons relating to the Tax Credits Act 1999;
- for taking or seeking to take parental leave;
- for taking or seeking to take time off for dependents;
- for taking lawful organised official industrial action (usually lasting 8 weeks or less);
- for exercising or seeking rights relating to trade union recognition procedures;
- for exercising or seeking to exercise the right to be accompanied or accompany a fellow worker at a disciplinary or grievance hearing;
- on grounds related to the Part-time Workers (Prevention of Less Favourable Treatment) Regulations 2000.

self-check
question

11.4 Visit the UK Department of Trade and Industry's website and access the document 'Dismissal – fair and unfair: a guide for employers' at ‹http://www.dti.gov.uk/er/individual/fair-pl714b.htm›

Use the hyperlinks in the section headed 'When is dismissal unquestionably unfair?' to explore what is meant by at least three of the reasons listed above as unquestionably unfair.

Having looked through this list you can see that it is automatically unfair to dismiss employees for taking lawfully organised industrial action lasting 8 weeks or less. Such action is known as *protected industrial action* and occurs only when the employee has been induced to take industrial action by her or his trade union and the trade union has complied with the legal requirements governing industrial action (Department of Trade and Industry, 2002b) specified in the Employment Rights Act 1996 and the Employment Relations Act 1999 (Chapter 6). However, once the trade union has repudiated the industrial action it ceases to be 'protected' two working days later. After protection has ceased, employees may be dismissed for taking what has become unlawfully organised industrial action.

It is also automatically unfair for employers to dismiss employees after 8 weeks of industrial action unless the employer has taken reasonable procedural steps to resolve the dispute. Reasonable procedural steps include actions such as offering or agreeing to start or restart negotiations or agreeing to make use of conciliation or mediation services to help resolve the dispute. In such instances an employment tribunal will decide reasonableness.

Costs of unfair dismissal

Legislation at the time of writing permits a compensatory award for unfair dismissal to an employee of up to a statutory maximum of £51,700 (IDS, 2001). However, most employment tribunal awards are much less, the median award for unfair dismissal being approximately £2,500 (Department of Trade and Industry, 2002c). Although the tribunal may also order the reinstatement of the employee, this is used in less than 0.3 per cent of all hearings (Department of Trade and Industry, 2002c). In addition the employer will face the management time and legal costs of the tribunal case as well as the cost associated with recruiting a replacement. Further indirect costs have also been highlighted, including the possible loss of contact with customers, suppliers and trade associations (Pamenter, 1994). Despite this, research reported by the Department of Trade and Industry (2002c) highlights the fact that only a minority of employers appear to be aware of indirect costs due to unfair dismissal cases. Those cited by employers include increased staff stress, adverse reputation as an employer, and damaged workplace employee relations.

Dismissal inevitably also has costs for the employee. In addition to those costs associated with making a tribunal application there are likely to be indirect costs such as associated stress. Employees who have been dismissed may also find that their future employment prospects have worsened, depending upon the reason for dismissal.

11.5 Wrongful dismissal

Unlike unfair dismissal, wrongful dismissal is not a statutory claim arising through an Act of Parliament. Rather, any dismissed employee, regardless of her or his length of service, can claim wrongful dismissal. This means that even if a person has been employed by an organisation for only a few days, she or he can still make an allegation of wrongful dismissal. Such an allegation will give rise to a civil action, which will be heard by a county court.

If an employer wrongly dismisses an employee, the employee has to bring her or his claim for damages for breach of contract within a 6-year period. In the vast majority of wrongful dismissal cases the employee's damages consist of her or his net pay together with the value of any fringe benefits such as a pension during the damages period. However, this is not a licence for the employee to print money, as the aim of such damages is to put the employee in the same position as if the contract had not been breached. Once dismissed, the employee is expected to try and reduce her or his losses by taking reasonable steps to find another job. This is known as the *duty to mitigate*. Where job search is successful, the pay and other benefits earned in the damages period must be deducted from the award of damages (IDS, 2001). If the employee fails to find new employment because she or he has not taken reasonable steps then the money that might have been earned had such steps been taken will be estimated and deducted anyway.

In claiming wrongful dismissal, an employee is arguing that the employer has unlawfully breached the contract of employment by terminating it outside its terms (Snape, 1999). Any dismissal of an employee that is in breach of contract can give rise to legal action for wrongful dismissal. Against this, an employer's defence is to show either that the contract was terminated lawfully or that they were responding to an earlier breach of contract by the employee, which itself brought the contract to an end and justified dismissal of the employee. However, for employees whose contract provides for payment in lieu of notice, or where the employee has waived the right to notice, any dismissal without adequate notice will not be wrongful, even if the employer does not make the payment in lieu (IDS, 2001).

According to Incomes Data Services (IDS, 2001), the most common breaches of contract by the employer in relation to dismissal are:

- no notice or inadequate notice being given where summary dismissal is not justifiable;
- the ending of a fixed-term contract before it is due to end;
- the ending of a fixed-task contract before the task has been completed;
- the use of disciplinary reasons where the contractual disciplinary procedures have not been followed;
- the use of redundancy reasons where the contractual redundancy procedures have not been followed.

It therefore follows that an employer can terminate a contract lawfully and avoid claims for wrongful (although not necessarily unfair) dismissal by giving the employee the notice period specified in the contract, not ending fixed-term or fixed-task contracts early or before their completion, and following contractual procedures. With regard to the period of notice, this is usually stated in the contract. For some employees this may be the same as the statutory minimum set out in the Employment Rights Act 1996 (Table 11.1). Others, such as many academics in UK

Table 11.1 **Statutory minimum periods of notice**

Length of service	Period of notice
at least 1 month	1 week
1 month to less than 2 years	1 week
2 years to less than 3 years	2 weeks
3 years to less than 4 years	3 weeks
4 years to less than 5 years	4 weeks
⋮	⋮
11 years to less than 12 years	11 weeks
12 or more years	12 weeks

universities, may have longer notice periods of either 2 or 3 months upon satisfactory completion of a probationary period. In addition, in some organisations senior or long-serving employees may be entitled to longer notice periods of up to a year. Even where a notice period is not specified in an employee's contract the statutory minimum notice period will not be applied automatically; rather there is an implied term that the notice will be of reasonable length (IDS, 2001). This may result in a longer period of notice.

As noted earlier, wrongful dismissal claims by employees are unlikely to succeed if the employee is shown to be in a fundamental breach of contract, her or his dismissal being simply the employer's response. The likely reasons for an employee being in fundamental breach of contract are in effect those for which dismissal would be considered fair (Figure 11.3). These have already been discussed in Section 11.3.

11.6 Employees' resignation and retirement

We have already discussed one form of employees terminating their employment – constructive dismissal. However, even with the increase in fixed-term contracts (Chapter 2), the vast majority of employees will terminate their own contracts either by resignation or by retirement. In this section we look briefly at these two reasons.

■ Resignation

Taylor (1998) distinguishes between resignations that are for reasons that the employer can, at least theoretically, control and those that are for uncontrollable reasons. Within the former he includes those employees who resign because of dissatisfaction with some aspect of their current employment in comparison with perceived employment opportunities elsewhere. In contrast, uncontrollable reasons include resignations resulting from ill health, relocation of a partner, and other domestic responsibilities. Morrell *et al.* (2001) point out that the turnover resulting from such resignations can be explained from both a labour market/economic and a psychological perspective. The first of these emphasises the importance of labour market and economic factors (Chapter 2) on turnover, and includes factors such as pay differentials, the level of unemployment and availability of alternative jobs. The second emphasises how individuals' predispositions to the organisation will affect their decision to resign, and encompasses aspects such as job satisfaction and their commitment (Chapter 3).

Turnover through resignation has been argued to have both positive and negative impacts on organisations. On the positive side, each resignation creates an opportunity to recruit a new employee, who can bring new ideas and methods to the organisation. However, the need to recruit, select and develop a new employee will carry associated costs. Inevitably managers will be pleased if an employee who is a poor performer resigns. However, this will not be the case if an experienced employee with key skills leaves. For these reasons, Taylor (1998) argues that organisations need to pay more attention to resignations for controllable reasons if they wish to reduce turnover levels.

Turnover rates differ markedly between sectors. For example, average annual turnover in retailing and hotels and catering within the UK has been found to exceed 35 per cent (Taylor, 1998) with some subareas such as the fast food industry being far higher. Data from the United States suggest that in this industry turnover of approximately 200 per cent per annum is not unusual (Ritzer, 1998). This is equivalent to an entire workforce turning over approximately twice a year! In contrast other sectors are much lower, the professional services sector having an average annual turnover of less than 2 per cent (Taylor, 1998). Within this general patterns are observable, turnover being higher among sales staff and those employed in routine unskilled work, and lower among managers and skilled workers. In addition, turnover tends to be more restricted in areas where there are fewer alternative job choices.

Many organisations undertake some form of exit interview or questionnaire when an employee leaves. This is based upon the premise that the data collected, when combined with data from other leavers, will allow the organisation to look for patterns in resignation reasons. Unfortunately, as pointed out by Torrington and Hall (1998), these data may not be completely accurate. The majority of those employees who resign will already have obtained another job. It is therefore likely that the reason or reasons that first caused them to search for alternative employment may be forgotten or less prominent in their minds. As part of their decisions to accept new jobs, they will have developed rational justifications as to why these new jobs are better. In addition they may still require references from the employers they are leaving, causing them to be less than forthright regarding their reasons for leaving. Despite these concerns many employers still believe that exit interviews can provide an indication of those issues that may be contributing to employees resigning.

Before concluding our discussion of resignation, we should note that an employer cannot avoid a claim for unfair dismissal by giving an employee the choice of either being dismissed or resigning. This is because the question that an employment tribunal will be considering is: Who really terminated the employment contract? For example, in the case of *Rentokil v. Morgan* (IDS, 2001) Morgan was told that he was being dismissed. He was also offered a non-negotiable severance package, including his entitlement of pay in lieu of a year's notice, on condition he signed a letter of resignation. The tribunal concluded that this was a dismissal and not a genuine resignation. This is not the same as the employee being given the choice of improving her or his performance or resigning. In this situation the employee is making a choice between performing to the level expected in the contract or resigning.

■ Retirement

In contrast to resignation, employers normally have more notice from their employees with regard to retirement. This means that succession can be planned more smoothly. Increasingly employees, rather than having an abrupt retirement after working full time to the very end, have some form of phased withdrawal. In recent years some of our colleagues have altered their contract with the university from full to part time prior to formal retirement. Others, although having retired, maintain some links through employment on a session-by-session basis. Such flexible or gradual retirement allows the organisation to continue to utilise the experience of these employees while developing its new employees. However, care needs to be taken to ensure that Inland Revenue rules on pensions and taxation are not broken.

During the 1980s and early 1990s early retirement was used widely by organisations as one of a series of methods to downsize organisations (Chapter 12). The ability of employees to afford this was, however, dependent upon the pension arrangements made by employers, and in particular the availability of enhanced pensions. This meant that redundancy costs were, in effect, switched to pension funds. As a consequence, the number of people aged 55 or over in the labour market declined (Table 11.2). However, since the mid-1990s the prevalence of early retirement with enhanced pensions has declined, especially for occupations where there is a recruitment shortage within the UK. This, combined with the harmonisation of retirement ages for men and women and recent closure or withdrawal of final salary or defined benefit pension schemes by many organisations, means that the number of older employees in the UK for 2011 in Table 11.2 is likely to be an underestimate.

Table 11.2 **Changes in the labour force 1971–2011**

Year	Males			Females		
	16–24	25–54	55 plus	16–24	25–54	55 plus
1971	3 000 000	9 700 000	3 400 000	2 300 000	5 600 000	1 700 000
1981	3 200 000	10 000 000	2 700 000	2 700 000	6 700 000	1 500 000
1991	3 100 000	11 100 000	2 200 000	2 600 000	8 500 000	1 300 000
2001	2 400 000	11 600 000	2 300 000	2 100 000	9 400 000	1 500 000
2011	2 800 000	11 200 000	2 500 000	2 300 000	9 800 000	1 900 000

Source: Developed from Office for National Statistics (2002)

11.7 Summary

- All employment relationships will, eventually, be terminated. Where an involuntary requirement for an employee to leave the organisation's employment exists, this is known as dismissal.
- Within the UK, three types of dismissal are highlighted by legislation. These are:
  - *fair dismissal* – where an employer terminates the contract of employment with the employee for one or more of the five potentially fair reasons stated in the Employment Act 1996;

- *unfair dismissal* – where an employer terminates the contract of employment with the employee for a reason other than one or more of the five potentially fair reasons stated in the Employment Act 1996;
- *wrongful dismissal* – where an employer terminates a contract of employment by breaching its terms and conditions.
- Employees can seek redress for unfair dismissal through an employment tribunal or through voluntary arbitration. Redress for breach of contract is sought through a county court.
- Unfair dismissal is the most common claim made by employees in connection with the termination of their employment contract. Legislation has resulted in a series of reasons for dismissal becoming regarded as automatically unfair. These include:
  - in connection with membership activities of a trades union;
  - for taking legitimate action to ensure health and safety standards are observed;
  - on grounds of pregnancy or childbirth;
  - for taking lawful organised industrial action (usually lasting 8 weeks or less).
- The vast majority of employees will, however, terminate their own contracts by either resignation or retirement.

References

ACAS (2000) *Code of Practice: Disciplinary and grievance procedures*, London, ACAS.

ACAS (2002) *Discipline, dismissal and grievances* [online][cited 12 July] Available from <http://www.acas.org.uk/q_a/q_a3.html>

Aitkin Driver Partnership (2002) 'Drugs: O'Flynn v. Air Links the Airport Coach Company', *People Management*, 8:9, 19.

Campbell, C. (2002) 'Employment Act: sort out your differences', *People Management*, 8:20, 18–19.

Carby-Hall, J. (2001) 'A voluntary alternative route for unfair dismissal claims: arbitration', *Managerial Law*, 43:5, 1–29.

Croner (2000) *Croner's Guide to Managing Fair Dismissal*, Kingston-upon-Thames, Croner.

Cully, M., O'Reilly, A., Millward, N., Forth, J., Woodland, S., Dix, G. and Bryson, A. (1999) *The 1998 Workplace Employee Relations Survey: First Findings* [online][cited 20 April] Available from <http://www.dti.gov.uk/emar>

Department of Trade and Industry (2002a) *Dismissal – Fair and Unfair: A guide for employers (Revision 10)* [online][cited 30 October] Available from <http://www.dti.gov.uk/er/individual/fair-pl714.htm>

Department of Trade and Industry (2002b) *Industrial Action and the Law (Revision 4)* [online][cited 30 October] Available from <http://www.dti.gov.uk/er/union/employers-pl870.htm>

Department of Trade and Industry (2002c) *Dispute Resolution in Britain: A background paper* [online][cited 21 October 2002] Available from <http://www.dti.gov.uk/er/individual/dispute.pdf>

Goodman, J., Earshaw, J., Marchington, M. and Harrison, R. (1998) 'Unfair dismissal cases, disciplinary procedures, recruitment methods and management style: case study evidence from three industrial sectors', *Employee Relations*, 20:6, 536–50.

IDS (2000) *Constructive Dismissal: Employment law supplement* (2nd edn), London, Incomes Data Services.

IDS (2001) *Contracts of Employment: Employment law handbook* (4th edn), London, Incomes Data Services.

Millward, N., Bryson, A. and Forth, J. (2000) *All Change at Work? British employment relations 1980–1998 as portrayed by the Workplace Industrial Relations Survey series*, London, Routledge.

Morrell, K., Loan-Clarke, J. and Wilkinson, A. (2001) 'Unweaving leaving: the use of models in the management of employee turnover', *International Journal of Management Reviews*, 3:3, pp. 219–44.

Office for National Statistics (2002) *Labour force by gender and age 1971–2011* [online] [cited 30 October]. Available from <http://www.statistics.gov.uk/STATBASE/Expodata/Spreadsheets/D3463.xls>

Pamenter, F. (1994) 'Alpha and omega: the effect of terminations and how to lessen their impact on the organisation', *International Journal of Manpower*, 15:6, 85–93.

Ritzer, G. (1998) *The McDonaldization Thesis*, London, Sage.

Sapsted, D. (2002) 'Lady Archer was "stingy but fair" in sacking of aide', *The Daily Telegraph*, 26 October.

Snape, R. (1999) 'Legal regulation of employment', *in* Hollinshead, G., Nicholls, P. and Tailby, S. (eds), *Employee Relations*, London, FT Pitman Publishing. pp. 268–97.

Taylor, S. (1998) *Employee Resourcing*, London, Institute of Personnel and Development.

Torrington, D. and Hall, L. (1998) *Human Resource Management* (4th edn), London, Prentice Hall.

self-check Answers

11.1 *Revisit Chapter 6, and in particular Boxes 6.1, 6.2 and 6.3. Starting with the Industrial Relations Act 1971 (Box 6.1) construct a table to provide an overview of how unfair dismissal legislation has evolved.*

Act	Key features in relation to dismissal
Industrial Relations Act 1971	Introduced employee's right to his or her job, regardless of contract, after a certain length of service, and the right to claim for unfair dismissal.
Employment Act 1980	Restricted the right to picket to employees picketing their own workplace, union officials joining members they represent, and workers dismissed by that company.
Employment Act 1982	Introduced narrower definition of trade dispute outside which strikes would not be immune from legal action. Disputes had to relate *wholly* or *mainly* to terms and conditions, discipline, dismissal or bargaining machinery. Further restricted the closed shop so that it was now unfair for an employer to dismiss an employee where there was a closed shop agreement unless the closed shop had been approved by ballot during preceding 5 years.
Sex Discrimination Act 1986	Extended scope of Sex Discrimination Act 1975 to include retirement, dismissal, promotion, demotion, transfer or training, and amended Equal Pay Act 1970 in same way.

Employment Act 1988	Outlawed industrial action designed to maintain a 100 per cent union membership agreement and all dismissals for non-union membership.
Employment Act 1990	Allowed employers to dismiss employees taking unofficial industrial action with no claim for unfair dismissal. Outlawed industrial action in support of workers dismissed for taking unofficial action.
Employment Rights Act 1996	Consolidated existing provisions, including those relating to dismissal, for individual employment law.
Employment Relations Act 1999	Replaced existing maternity and parental leave provisions including a right not to be dismissed for taking parental leave. Extended protection for employees taking lawful industrial action, making it unfair to dismiss employees in action lasting less than 8 weeks and unfair for longer disputes unless the employer has taken all reasonable procedural steps to resolve the dispute.
Employment Act 2002	Introduced minimum requirements for internal discipline and grievance procedures including dismissal. Implemented EU Directive on fixed-term work, limiting the scope for using a series of fixed-term contracts to employ the same person in an essentially permanent position.

11.2 *Jane, a primary school teacher, had an excellent employment record, having had only 3 days' sickness in the past 5 years. However, she has been on long-term sick leave for the past 6 months with chronic fatigue syndrome. A recent medical with the employer's doctor suggests that Jane is starting to recover, and she is keen to return to work. However, the nature of her illness means she is unlikely to be able to return to her post for at least another 3–4 months.*

Would you advise the employer to dismiss Jane?

As suggested in the chapter, this is a difficult situation. It is evident that, prior to this illness, Jane had an exemplary employment record. However, Jane is currently incapable of work owing to a long-term illness, which is potentially a fair reason for dismissal according to the Employment Rights Act 1996. The fairness of such a dismissal would be dependent upon the nature of Jane's illness, the fact that it has already lasted for 6 months and is likely to continue for at least another 3–4 months, and that medical advice had been sought.

Given that Jane wishes to return to work, her excellent previous employment record and the fact that a recent medical suggests she is beginning to recover, it would probably not be advisable to dismiss Jane. Rather her employer might suggest a phased return to work, with Jane teaching initially only part-time. If Jane was unable to cope with this part-time teaching, the next stage might be to consider dismissal on the grounds of incapability due to long-term illness.

11.3 *Why might an employer still wish to employ someone using a fixed-term rather than a permanent contract?*

You may well be thinking that recent legislation makes the use of fixed-term contracts far less attractive to employers. However, by employing someone using a fixed-term contract of less than 4 years, the employer will not be subject to a wrongful dismissal claim when the contract expires. Consequently, where work is likely to last only for a specified time period a fixed-term contract is still likely to be used rather than a permanent (indefinite) contract. However, adoption of the European Union's Fixed Term Employees (Prevention of Less Favourable Treatment) Regulations 2002 into UK law means that any employee employed on a fixed-term contract must not be treated less favourably than permanent employees who do similar work for the same employer at the same establishment. This means that employees on fixed-term contracts are protected against unfair dismissal, and are entitled to terms and conditions equivalent to permanent employees on a pro rata basis.

11.4 *Visit the UK Department of Trade and Industry's website and access the document 'Dismissal – fair and unfair: a guide for employers' at http://www.dti.gov.uk/er/individual/fair-pl714b.htm*

Use the hyperlinks in the section headed 'When is dismissal unquestionably unfair?' to explore what is meant by at least three of the reasons listed above as unquestionably unfair.

It is obviously not possible in the space available for us to provide answers for each of the 18 reasons listed by the Department of Trade and Industry. However, our consideration of the subsection headed 'Dismissal on the grounds of pregnancy or maternity' provides an idea of the sorts of information you are likely to find.

This states that 'a woman will automatically be regarded as unfairly dismissed if her employer dismisses her, or selects her for redundancy, because she is pregnant or has given birth to a child, or for a reason connected with her pregnancy or childbirth' (Department of Trade and Industry, 2002a). It then outlines the statutory maternity leave entitlement (18 weeks) and additional entitlements for employees who have 1 year's continuous service. The circumstances in which a woman can make a complaint of automatic unfair dismissal, regardless of length of service, are outlined. These include that the dismissal:

- is for a reason connected with pregnancy;
- is on the grounds that she has given birth and takes place during her ordinary maternity leave;
- is on the grounds that she took or sought to take or avail herself of the benefits of ordinary or additional maternity leave.

Circumstances where dismissal at the end of additional maternity leave will not be regarded as unfair by a tribunal are also outlined.

CASE 11 Discipline, capability and dismissal at Halcrow[1]

Halcrow is an international independent provider of infrastructure-based solutions and consultancy services specialising in the transport, water and property sectors. Within these sectors the company offers professional consultancy resources for the planning, design and supervision and development of projects. Halcrow is currently undertaking projects in over 70 countries (Halcrow, 2002a). Recent projects with which the company have been involved include the Channel Tunnel Rail Link, the Second River Severn Crossing between England and Wales, the Congress Public Buildings in Rome, and the Ethiopian Valleys Development Studies Authority (Halcrow, 2002b). In 2002 the company had over 3000 employees and a global network of 57 offices. Annual turnover was in excess of £150 million (Halcrow, 2002a).

The *Halcrow Staff Handbook* (2001: F1–2) outlines clearly the standards they expect from each employee and the implications of an infringement of these rules under the heading 'Discipline and Capability':

All staff are expected to achieve and maintain appropriate standards of conduct, attendance and job performance and to respect the local laws and customs of the country where they are working. They should act in a responsible and cooperative way when working for the Company, whether during working hours or not. They are expected to comply with any reasonable and lawful instruction given by management in connection with their employment and with the following rules:

(a) All staff shall comply with office rules relating to working hours and flexitime and record hours worked accurately and submit timesheet data promptly.

(b) Except in matters of domestic emergency, only business calls should be made from office telephones and staff should, where practicable, use pay phones for private calls. All calls, both incoming and outgoing, should be kept as short as possible to reduce costs and avoid congestion of the lines. Where appropriate, email or fax should be used rather than telephone.

(c) Staff shall use Internet and email facilities only for business purposes in a professional manner in accordance with the Company's policy and associated guidelines contained in Halcrow Business Procedure 740 (see Halnet).

(d) Staff shall not:

    (1) infringe the rules on smoking on Company premises, security of office premises, quality management, confidential information, health and safety, data protection or other Company matters set out in more detail elsewhere in this Staff Handbook and other Company manuals

    (2) interfere with or misuse any apparatus or facility provided for securing the health, safety or welfare of persons working in the Company's property or other places while engaged on the Company's business

    (3) undertake any paid work at their place of employment other than that for which they have been employed

[1] The assistance of Mandy Clarke (Halcrow Group Ltd) in the preparation of this case is gratefully acknowledged.

(4) report for work or undertake duties on the Company's behalf if their fitness or competence for doing so is impaired by the intake of alcohol or drugs (whether prohibited or prescribed) or other substances, in accordance with the Company's statement of policy on alcohol and drugs

(5) be in breach of the ethical code of their professional institution

(6) place or distribute any matter in printed, written or electronic form within offices or sites without the prior permission of their Responsible Director or delegate (which shall not be unreasonably withheld) (Note: Members of Staff Council may place or distribute items relating to Staff Council business)

(7) knowingly misuse any Company-provided computer equipment by making a copy of or using any data or software which is not licensed for such copying or use

(8) knowingly load into any Company-provided computer equipment data from the Internet or a diskette or other portable data storage medium emanating from outside the office without first ensuring that it has been checked for software viruses

(9) without permission disclose any confidential information relating to any company in the Halcrow Group or its clients or fail to use their best endeavours to prevent any such disclosure occurring

(10) obtain, process or disclose any personal information in breach of the Company's registration under the Data Protection Act (see Part II Section 11)

(11) commit any acts of discrimination, victimisation or harassment against any other member of staff on grounds of sex, marital status, disability, colour, nationality, ethnic or racial origins, on suspicion of being HIV positive or suffering from AIDS, nor incite others to commit such acts.

The Company will treat as misconduct any infringements of the above rules. Any action or series of actions which results in a complete breakdown of trust and confidence or which brings the Company into disrepute will be treated as gross misconduct. Examples of gross misconduct include: serious breach of the Company's policy on alcohol and drugs, failure to pass any rail industry alcohol or drugs test, physical assault, stealing, destruction, defacement or misappropriation of the Company's property, falsification of the Company's documents, unauthorised access to data held on a computer, tampering with a computer or computer program, downloading from the Internet pornographic or similar unsuitable material, sending grossly offensive email, misappropriation of the Company's funds or other serious criminal offence, gross incompetence, gross insubordination and gross negligence. Gross misconduct may result in suspension with or without pay pending investigation and formal hearing and summary dismissal without notice or pay in lieu.

The capability of staff to carry out their duties is related to their performance and attendance. Depending on the circumstances, the Company may treat poor performance or poor attendance as disciplinary offences.

The procedures for dealing with any breach of the disciplinary rules and circumstances affecting the capability of staff to carry out their duties are given in Appendix F.

Questions

1 What actions by staff does Halcrow treat as:
   a misconduct?
   b gross misconduct?

2 Why is a distinction made between misconduct and gross misconduct in the *Halcrow Staff Handbook?*

3 Why does Halcrow include the procedures for dealing with any breaches of the disciplinary rules and the circumstances affecting the capability of staff as part of the *Halcrow Staff Handbook?*

4 Use the above extract from the *Halcrow Staff Handbook* to determine how the company would be likely to treat an employee who:
   a downloaded pornography from the Internet;
   b acted in a discriminatory manner against another member of staff who was suspected of being HIV positive.

References

Halcrow (2001) *Halcrow Staff Handbook*, Swindon, Halcrow.

Halcrow (2002a) *Halcrow – about us* [online] [cited 8 November]. Available from <http://www.halcrow.com/halcrow_aboutus.asp>

Halcrow (2002b) *Halcrow – projects* [online] [cited 8 November]. Available from <http://www.halcrow.com/halcrow_capitalprojects.asp>

Chapter 12

Ending the employment relationship: organisational downsizing and workforce redundancy

At the end of this chapter you should be able to:

■ define and differentiate organisational downsizing and workforce redundancy;

■ appreciate the extent of recent organisational downsizing and workforce redundancy;

■ outline the stages and principal aspects of the regulatory framework affecting the use of redundancy;

■ analyse the implications arising from the choice of differing strategies and methods to achieve organisational downsizing and workforce redundancy;

■ evaluate the impact on the employment relationship climate of organisational downsizing and workforce redundancy.

12.1 Introduction

In the recent past, organisational downsizing and workforce redundancies have occurred widely (Section 12.3), affecting employees in organisations across all sectors of the economy. Since the 1980s an increasing amount of work has been undertaken and published that recognises the quantitative and qualitative importance of this aspect of organisational change and human resource management. A core theme running through this work has been the exploration of the impact of organisational downsizing and workforce redundancies not only on those who leave an organisation through dismissal but also on those who remain within its employment. The concept of organisational 'survivors' has been introduced in the context of the post-downsizing organisation, to explore and to explain the impact of this event on those who remain and on their subsequent performance and that of the organisation. The reactions of those who survive downsizing and redundancy have been identified, categorised and measured in a number of studies, including those cited later in this chapter. This work allows us to recognise that the nature and conduct of the employment relationship are likely to be affected by the incidence of downsizing and redundancy. However, the way in which the employment relationship is affected will vary in practice, depending on a range of factors including a number of process ones that have the effect of producing a range of potentially different outcomes.

This chapter commences by exploring and defining the concepts of downsizing and redundancy, particularly so that we may differentiate between them to further our understanding of these approaches in practice (Section 12.2). Redundancy, as the principal method used to achieve organisational downsizing, involves an interrelated set of stages, which we describe and discuss in Section 12.4. We also outline in this section the principal legal requirements that influence the conduct of these stages of redundancy. We then outline and discuss the choice of strategies that may be used to downsize, and also to decide redundancies in particular, in order to explore their potentially different implications for the future conduct of the employment relationship (Section 12.5). We extend this exploration of the implications of downsizing for the future conduct of the employment relationship by focusing on other determinants that affect the nature and strength of survivors' reactions to the occurrence of this event (Section 12.6). The case study at the end of this chapter explores the changing approach to downsizing at BT and its implications for the employment relationship.

12.2 Defining downsizing and redundancy

Downsizing and redundancy are sometimes used as alternative terms. In popular usage downsizing has been used frequently as a synonym for redundancy (Vollmann and Brazas, 1993). It is also used interchangeably with a range of other terms such as *de-recruiting*, *de-massing*, *re-engineering*, *resizing*, *restructuring*, *reorganisation* and *rightsizing*, to name but a few. The practice of organisational downsizing, where the term is used, lends support to this association with redundancy. Quality newspapers carry frequent reports about downsizing associated with redundancies, leading to the situation where terms such as those mentioned above are 'generally understood to be no more than pseudonyms for the more ubiquitous, unambiguous, but unappealing "re"-word, redundancy' (Turnbull and Wass, 1997: 44).

However, these terms can be defined as being distinct, and it is useful to treat each separately for analytical purposes. We may identify three principal ways to differentiate between downsizing and redundancy, while recognising that they are often related in practice. The first way to differentiate these concepts is related to the methods used to achieve organisational downsizing. The literature that analyses downsizing recognises that it uses *methods* other than just redundancy. Alternative methods to redundancy include the use of early retirement, natural wastage, redeployment and forms of work sharing, such as working-hours reductions and job sharing. We discuss these methods and their implications for the conduct of the employment relationship later in this chapter. In this way, downsizing can be differentiated from the narrower concept of redundancy.

The second way to differentiate these concepts relates to *organisational strategy*. Freeman and Cameron (1993) believe that downsizing should be analysed as an organisational-level concept whereas redundancy is approached at the level of the individual. Following from this differentiation, downsizing should be seen as a strategic issue whereas redundancy is an operational one. We shall return to the significance of treating downsizing as an organisational strategy after highlighting the third way to differentiate these concepts, which is related to the incidence of *legal regulation*. This third type of differentiation recognises that in many countries, for example within the member states of the EU, dismissal, of which redundancy is one form, is subject to tightly prescribed legal regulation. Downsizing, as a more nebulous concept and one that may seek to use a wider range of methods to reduce organisational headcount, may operate outside the boundaries of some of the laws that regulate dismissal. For example, natural wastage would fall outside this form of legal regulation, and some of the current ideas about some forms of work sharing (discussed in more detail later) may offer a more socially desirable means to downsize.

The legal definition of redundancy in Britain dates from the Redundancy Payments Act 1965. The current legal definition is contained in the Employment Rights Act 1996. This Act defines a redundancy as a dismissal due, wholly or mainly, to:

- the complete closure of a business;
- the closure of the employee's workplace;
- a diminishing need for employees to do work of a particular kind in the business as a whole, or at the employee's particular workplace.

Redundancy therefore relates to the need for a post or job rather than to the person who occupies it. Following the introduction of this definition, the Employment Appeal Tribunal established a simple three-stage test to determine whether an employee has been made redundant where this might be open to question (*Safeway Stores plc* v. *Burrell*, 1997). This involves asking the following questions:

- Has an employee been dismissed?
- If so, had the requirements of the employer's business for the employee or employees to carry out work of a particular kind ceased or diminished, or was this likely to be the case?
- If so, was the dismissal caused wholly or mainly by this cessation or diminution?

This definition and the related legal test, with its focus on the situation of individual employees, or groups of employees, emphasise the operational nature of redundancy.

Identifying downsizing as an organisational strategy rather than simply as an operational means to reduce an organisation's headcount allows a greater number of possible strategic objectives to be recognised and explored in relation to this concept. Exploration of these possible strategic objectives also helps to explain how a downsizing programme may fail to meet its intended organisational goals, with subsequent and significant consequences for affected workgroups and individuals (an aspect that we discuss later). Work by Cameron *et al.* (1991, 1993) has identified three possible organisational strategies to achieve downsizing:

- The first of these is the *workforce reduction strategy*, which focuses simply on reducing an organisation's headcount. This is the type of approach often referred to in newspaper reports, such as those that we mentioned above. This approach to downsizing was used by all of the organisations in the studies conducted by Cameron *et al.* (1991, 1993).
- The second approach is the *organisation redesign strategy*, which involves delayering, eliminating areas of work and job redesign, so that the amount of work is reduced as well as the organisation's headcount. This approach to downsizing was used by half of the organisations in their study.
- The third approach is the *systemic change strategy*, which, as its name suggests, is a longer-term approach intended to promote a more fundamental change. This

approach would be designed to affect the culture of an organisation, for example by promoting employee involvement and an adherence to continuous improvement, as well as introducing structural changes and workforce reductions. This was recognised to be a long-term strategy, with one-third of the organisations in their study attempting to implement it (Cameron *et al.*, 1993; Cameron, 1994b).

Downsizing may thus be implemented solely through reducing an organisation's headcount (the most popular strategy) or in combination with one or more other strategies that seek to reduce the amount of work undertaken and to bring about structural and cultural organisational change. The significance of recognising these various approaches to downsizing and their respective links to organisational strategy lies in their potentially different consequences for the organisation and their implications for the conduct of the employment relationship. A narrowly focused and short-term cost-reduction strategy is likely to result in a greater range of negative outcomes for an organisation than a more integrative, employee focused and longer-term strategy to redesign an organisation.

Definitions of downsizing have linked it with an intention to improve organizational performance (e.g. Kozlowski *et al.*, 1993). For many, improving effectiveness, efficiency, productivity and competitiveness, and thus organisational performance, is the central aim of downsizing (e.g. Freeman and Cameron, 1993; Cameron, 1994b; Kets de Vries and Balazs, 1997). This leads to the crux of the problem associated with downsizing. Shaw and Barrett-Power (1997) recognise that measures typically used to assess the effectiveness of downsizing from a corporate perspective are clearly inadequate as a means to understand and manage the impact of this process on the workgroups and individuals who survive this event. Such corporate measures will be related to profitability, productivity, investment returns, and customer satisfaction ratings. Evidence of the existence of psychological consequences at the level of workgroups and individuals, and their adverse effects on expected corporate outcomes from downsizing, is reported in the findings of a number of US-based surveys. Mishra and Mishra (1994) cite Tomasko (1992), who reported survey research that found that just one-quarter of surveyed organisations had realised their objective of improved productivity, higher investment returns, etc. A widely cited survey by the Wyatt Company of 1005 organisations found that less than half of those surveyed were able to agree that they had achieved a particular organisational objective related to a desire to reduce costs, reduce bureaucracy, improve productivity, increase investment returns, or increase profits (Cascio, 1993; Cameron, 1994a, 1994b; Kets de Vries and Balazs, 1997). Other survey work that supports this failure to achieve the intended organisational goals for downsizing is discussed in these papers. These 'corporate' measures may suggest indirectly that downsizing has had a negative impact on those who survive as employees in an organisation, and serve to highlight the presence of psychological and behavioural consequences for these 'survivors'.

We shall therefore return to and discuss the potentially different outcomes that may arise from the range of strategies that have been identified to achieve downsizing for the conduct of the employment relationship in a later section of this chapter.

12.3 Recent trends in organisational downsizing and workforce redundancy

Redundancies are one of the ways in which employees may leave their jobs (see also Chapter 11). Over recent decades, the incidence of redundancy has become a major factor affecting the operation of the labour market. Redundancies have been closely linked to organisational downsizing during this period. During the late 1990s over half of the redundancies in Britain were due to workforce reductions, with a further quarter due to organisational closures (Terryn, 1999). Britain experienced two major peaks of unemployment during the 1980s and 1990s. Unemployment rose above 1 million in Britain, according to the seasonally adjusted claimant count, at the beginning of 1976. It took 25 years for this figure to drop below 1 million, in March 2001. The claimant count – that is, the number of those claiming unemployment benefit from the state – remained at just over 1 million people (or about 4 per cent of the workforce) until early 1980. Through the early 1980s, unemployment in Britain rose markedly, reaching about 3 million people unemployed and claiming benefit through the mid-1980s. These high levels of unemployment were linked to the economic recession of this period and the organisational downsizing, closures and redundancies associated with it.

Unemployment remained a feature of the British labour market throughout the remainder of the 1980s, with the claimant count never dropping below 1.6 million people, or 5.7 per cent of the workforce. It soon began to rise again in the early 1990s, linked to a further period of economic recession and restructuring. By late 1992 the claimant count again approached nearly 3 million people registered as unemployed. The claimant count remained above 2.5 million people until late 1994 and above 2 million people until late 1996. From this time it fell gradually, until by the end of the 1990s it stood at about 1.1 million people. As in the 1980s, these high and persistent levels of unemployment in Britain in the 1990s were linked to organisational downsizing, closures and redundancies.

According to official estimates from the Labour Force Survey, approximately 709 000 employees were made redundant in Britain in 1995, 651 000 in 1996, 640 000 in 1997, 727 000 in 1998, 719 000 in 1999, 670 000 in 2000 and 758 000 in 2001 (Sly, 2000; Labour Market Trends, 2002). These data are produced by the government's Office for National Statistics, and are a reduction from earlier estimates of the numbers of redundancies believed to have occurred in Britain (Terryn, 1999). An earlier series, based on data collected only for the spring quarters of the years between 1989 and 1994, estimated redundancies in Britain for the three months of spring as follows (Field, 1997):

- 1989, 144 000;
- 1990, 181 000;
- 1991, 391 000;
- 1992, 324 000;
- 1993, 262 000;
- 1994, 205 000.

These data show the impact of the economic recession on the level of redundancies during the earlier 1990s in Britain. On an annualised basis, we may assume that there were about 1 million redundancies per year in Britain during the years 1991–93. These data illustrate that redundancies have been a major factor in the labour market in Britain during the 1980s and 1990s. You are likely to find continuing evidence of the occurrence of redundancies in the labour market in the pages of newspapers and current affairs magazines as we move through the present decade. Various forms of organisational restructuring appear to be an embedded feature of many if not most employing organisations.

12.4 Outlining the stages of and regulatory framework for redundancy

We recognised above that redundancy, as a form of dismissal from an organisation, is subject to legal regulation in many different countries. Planned redundancy will pass through a number of stages, although not necessarily in a standardised order. Many of the stages will be affected by a country's legal regulation. Below we outline a number of these stages and briefly discuss key points that will affect the conduct of the employment relationship during the process of making employees redundant. These stages are:

- identifying the need for and causes of redundancy;
- providing information and conducting consultation;
- using alternatives to redundancy;
- identifying selection criteria and those to be made redundant;
- notifying redundancies and communicating 'bad news' in an organisation;
- compensating those who are to be made redundant;
- supporting those who are to leave the organisation;
- supporting those who are to remain in employment.

Identifying the need for and causes of redundancy

We recognised earlier that employers may declare redundancies for a number of reasons. These may be related to an organisation's full or partial closure, or to the cessation or diminution of work of a particular kind within it. The underpinning reasons for such redundancies may be varied. The closure of a business in a declining industry is likely to be related to structural changes in a country's economy. Examples include the decline of some manufacturing industries and the coal and steel industries in many countries. In other cases, redundancies may result from technological change where demand for a product has not declined but fewer, or different, employees are required to produce it. The increasing use of information technology has resulted in redundancies in many different industries, and from various occupational groups, due to this type of change in recent years. As demand for labour is a derived demand, related to the level of demand for a product, changes in economic activity in general, as well as in a particular product market, will also be likely to affect the level of redundancies in a given period. We saw in the section above how the levels of redundancies reflected, in broad terms, the economic recessions of the 1980s and 1990s in Britain. However, in reality these causes of redundancy are likely to be interrelated and affected by other evident economic and political trends, such as globalisation and deregulation. These have generated further competitive pressures in many industries, leading to attempts to reduce cost and implement organisational restructuring, involving downsizing and the use of redundancy.

At the level of the individual employing organisation, employees' perceptions about the need for and causes of redundancies are likely to influence at least some of their reactions towards this event. These reactions will apply irrespective of whether the redundancies meet the definition of what constitutes a redundancy within the country's legal framework. This will in turn affect the nature of the future of the employment relationship. Employees' perceptions about the need for redundancies are likely to be shaped by a number of factors. These will include:

■ employee assessments about changes in the organisation's external and internal operating environment;
■ whether redundancies are related to a structural downturn in an industry or to firm-specific failures to anticipate market changes that should have been recognised;
■ views about earlier managerial responses to these changes and the extent of their trust in management's decision making;
■ the level of employee feelings about job security;
■ expectations about the likelihood of redundancies occurring.

The history of any previous redundancies is also likely to influence employee perceptions about the need for these to occur. For example, some of the organisations making employees redundant in the 1990s (such as those in water and electricity supply) had previously operated within a culture that had offered long-term employment security within a relational type of psychological contract (e.g. Herriot and Pemberton, 1996). The implications of the resulting changes to the nature of the employment relationship for those who remained in such an organisation may be contrasted with the expectations of those in an organisation where, for example, contract completion frequently leads to redundancies. A previous collective redundancy event in an organisation may also be associated with the belief that this was a unique occurrence; alternatively, it may be seen as part of a recurring pattern of redundancy rounds.

■ Providing information and conducting consultation

Consultation and the provision of information are a critical part of the process of proposing to dismiss employees on the grounds of redundancy. This is a legal obligation in many countries. For member countries of the European Union, this obligation is contained in a series of EU Collective Redundancies Directives issued in 1975 (75/129), 1992 (92/56) and 1998 (98/59). The first of these Directives was transposed into law in Britain in the Employment Protection Act 1975 (IRS, 1992). This required employers to consult about proposed redundancies where independent trade unions were recognised. A succession of legislation and amending regulations has followed since this date. An employer's statutory duty to inform and consult about proposed redundancies is now contained in section 188 of the Trade Union and

Labour Relations (Consolidation) Act 1992. This has been amended, first by the Trade Union Reform and Employment Rights Act 1993 and subsequently by Amendment Regulations of 1995 and 1999.

Following a successful legal challenge by the then EC Commission about the provisions of this legislation, the Collective Redundancies and Transfer of Undertakings (Protection of Employment) (Amendment) Regulations of 1995 introduced a number of significant changes. Notably, the duty to consult about proposed redundancies was broadened to all organisations, not just unionised ones, 'where an employer is proposing to dismiss as redundant 20 or more employees at one establishment within a period of 90 days or less'. The threshold of 20 or more was higher than had previously been the case, although this was now to include proposed redundancies of this scale in non-unionised organisations. The then Conservative government saw the raising of this threshold to 20 or more as a means to remove the need to consult from the 96 per cent of organisations that employed fewer than 20 employees in the UK (IRS, 1995). These regulations also made it possible for employers to choose whether to conduct consultation in unionised organisations with appropriately elected employee representatives where these existed but who were not representatives of the recognised trade union. These changes angered the trade unions, with the General Secretary of the TGWU, Bill Morris, being reported as calling these decisions a 'sacker's charter' (Overell, 1995).

The 1995 Regulations continued to be seen as controversial. The change to a Labour government in 1997 led to further amendments to the regulations governing the duty to provide information and to consult about proposed collective redundancies. These are contained in the Collective Redundancies and Transfer of Undertakings (Protection of Employment) (Amendment) Regulations of 1999. These specified that, where an independent trade union is recognised, employers are now required to conduct consultation through its representatives for affected employees. Where a trade union is not recognised for affected employees, or where these are not within its scope, detailed requirements are now established for the election of appropriate representatives of these employees. The threshold for consultation about proposed redundancies remains at '20 or more employees at one establishment within a period of 90 days or less', but a further group of employees were brought within the scope of the need to consult about this proposal. These regulations require consultation to be conducted with the representatives 'of any of the employees who may be affected by the proposed dismissals or (who) may be affected by measures taken in connection with those dismissals'. This means that consultation will also need to be conducted with representatives of the remaining workforce where these employees will be affected by changes arising from downsizing (IRS, 1999).

The substance of the duty to consult is set out in the 1992 Act (see above), as amended by the Trade Union Reform and Employment Rights Act 1993, which gave effect to the revised EU Collective Redundancies Directive 1992, as well as by the subsequent Amendment Regulations. The initial stage of the consultation process requires employers to provide representatives with the following information:

- reasons for the proposal to declare redundancies;
- numbers and descriptions of employees whom it is proposed to make redundant;
- total numbers of each description of employee at the affected establishment;

- the redundancy selection method(s) that it is proposed to use;
- proposed methods of implementing the dismissals, and the period over which the dismissals are to take place;
- proposed method of calculation of any redundancy payments that will be made other than those required by law.

This information needs to be provided in writing to each of the representatives. The process of consultation needs to be genuine and to avoid the charge of being a 'charade' or a 'sham', where there is little or no intention of considering the views of these representatives. This joint problem-solving approach was established through the EU Collective Redundancies Directives of 1975 and 1992, which required consultation to include consideration about:

- means to avoid the redundancies;
- how the number of redundancies may be reduced;
- ways in which the effects of the redundancies that do take place may be mitigated.

There is also an express requirement that consultation about these and related matters should be undertaken 'with a view to reaching agreement with the appropriate representatives', although agreement does not have to be reached before redundancies start to occur. Consultation is required to begin in 'good time' and must in any case commence at least 90 days before the first dismissal may take effect where the proposal is to dismiss 100 or more employees at one establishment. In other cases, consultation must begin at least 30 days before the first dismissal may take effect.

In addition to collective consultation, employing organisations also need to consider and undertake consultation with affected individuals, linked to requirements about *reasonableness* in carrying out a dismissal situation including a redundancy one. When the House of Lords considered the case of *Polkey* v. *A E Dayton Services Ltd* (1987), Lord Bridge stated:

> ... in the case of redundancy, the employer will normally not act reasonably unless he warns and consults any employees affected or their representative, adopts a fair basis on which to select for redundancy and takes such steps as may be reasonable to avoid or minimise redundancy by redeployment within his organisation.

This statement makes clear what is required in any redundancy situation. Even where consultation occurs within the scope of the Amendment Regulations there is likely to remain a need to consult with individual employees related to the principle of reasonableness (IRS, 1991). There is an exception to this where 'consultation or warning would be utterly useless', based on the facts known to the employer at the time when the dismissal or dismissals occurred. 'Whether, in a particular case, failure to consult renders a dismissal unfair is a matter for the (Employment) Tribunal to consider in the light of the circumstances known to the employer at the time he dismissed the employee' (*Duffy* v. *Yeomans and Partners Ltd*, 1994). There are of course non-legal reasons why consultation with affected individuals occurs, as we recognise later.

Failure to comply fully with requirements to provide information and to consult can lead to a complaint being made to an employment tribunal. We would recommend you to consult an up-to-date edition of an employment law book if you would like to know more about the duty to consult, or about a complaint about consultation, or the possibility of an employer claiming a defence related to 'special reasons' in exceptional circumstances.

■ Using alternatives to redundancy

We recognised earlier that downsizing may be achieved through methods other than redundancy. We also recognised in the previous subsection that the EU Collective Redundancies Directives introduced the requirement in Member States to consider means to avoid redundancies, to seek to reduce the number of any that take place, and to mitigate their effects through measures such as redeployment or retraining (IRS, 1992). A number of alternatives to redundancy may be possible within an organisation that wishes to reduce its headcount. These range from methods that achieve this without any sense of compulsion, and which may therefore be seen as advantageous to those who leave the organisation, through to the possible use of more radical measures to lower headcount, at least in part, related to different means to share work. We now discuss each of these approaches.

The method of downsizing that is likely to create the least hostile response from employees is through *natural wastage*. For management, this has the disadvantage of being slow and untargeted, and is likely to be no more than a supplementary means to achieve headcount reduction. A more commonly used approach is through *voluntary early retirement*. This method presupposes the existence of a sufficiently large pool of employees of an appropriate age whose exit from the organisation would not result in the loss of necessary competence and experience. This approach is colloquially known as *cherry picking*. With appropriate targeting through incentives for those over a certain age, many organisations have been able to use this approach to implement some level of downsizing, at least in its early stages. A further approach to avoid compulsory redundancies may be made through a request for employees to *volunteer for redundancy*. Requesting volunteers to sever their employment should still be seen as redundancy, and requires that this process be treated as such. However, it may be seen to avoid the label of compulsion, even though those who volunteer would often have remained in an organisation's employment had the offer to sever this connection not been made. We discuss the implications of using this approach to achieve downsizing in the next section. A variation of this approach to downsizing, which may help to facilitate a small proportion of voluntary leavers, is known as *transferred redundancies* or 'bumping'. This occurs where an employee in a non-redundant post wishes to volunteer to leave his or her employment, is allowed to do so, and is in turn replaced by an employee whose own job is no longer required.

Each of these methods involves the loss of employees from an organisation. The legal requirements outlined above also require that an attempt is made to mitigate the effects of redundancies occurring through measures such as redeployment or retraining. *Redeployment* may result from an employer taking reasonable measures to find suitable alternative employment for those who would otherwise be dismissed on the grounds of redundancy. Some redeployment may involve attempting to relocate part of the workforce to another place of work in the organisation, possibly in a different part of the country. Identifying suitable alternative employment means taking into account a number of factors in relation to each particular employee. These will include:

- current job, status and conditions of employment;
- place of work and the impact of any change;
- likely prospects of any alternative job;
- aptitude for retraining.

Retraining may help to facilitate redeployment within an organisation, or it may be used to facilitate employment with a different employer, or to facilitate a transition into self-employment. Redundant employees have a statutory right during their notice period to a reasonable amount of time off to arrange retraining or to look for alternative work.

A more radical approach, at least for many economically developed countries, is to consider *worksharing* as a means to allocate diminishing employment opportunities, or a lower demand for employees. This has traditionally happened in many Asian countries. A number of forms of worksharing are being considered by the European Commission and within a number of EU Member States (EIRR, 1999). One approach to worksharing calls for a general reduction in the working time of all employees in order that available employment may be shared. Three countries were cited as leading the way towards the introduction of a 35-hour working week – Germany, France and Italy – with trade unions in particular in other countries attempting to pursue the same outcome. Another approach to worksharing relates to job-sharing. Only Finland explicitly uses *job-sharing* as a means to promote employment, with other countries such as Ireland, Italy and Britain using this measure as a means to promote flexibility (although it may have the same effect). Other approaches to worksharing that may be seen to be related to the voluntary approaches to achieve downsizing that we have discussed include the possibility for part-time early retirement and voluntary part-time working. A number of EU Member States including France, Germany, Sweden, Austria, Belgium and Finland operate schemes to allow employees approaching retirement age to reduce their working hours, with the first three countries explicitly linking this reduction to the recruitment of unemployed people. Voluntarily moving from full-time to part-time working is officially encouraged in some EU Member States including Belgium, France and The Netherlands. Other forms of worksharing include schemes for periods of paid leave and paid and unpaid career breaks (EIRR, 1999).

■ Identifying selection criteria and those to be made redundant

Although redundancy is a potentially fair reason for dismissal, the use of a compulsory approach to determine redundancies is likely to be problematic because of the need to select staff and the subsequent implementation of this selection. This may generate an adverse reaction not only from those directly affected by the advent of redundancies but also from others who are intended to remain within the employment of the organisation. In addition, selection for redundancy may be judged legally unfair where the dismissal is in breach of one of a number of statutory provisions that state that any such dismissal will be automatically unfair. Selection for redundancy will also be legally unfair where it is judged unreasonable. We shall consider each of these legal areas briefly.

In the British context, there are a number of statutory provisions that state that dismissals related to particular reasons will be automatically unfair. These are briefly referred to in Box 12.1. These reasons will operate regardless of an affected person's

> ### Box 12.1 Automatically unfair reasons for dismissal
>
> Dismissals related, or mainly related, to the following reasons will automatically be unfair:
>
> - trade union membership, or non-membership;
> - participation in trade union activities;
> - trade union recognition or derecognition;
> - statutorily protected industrial action;
> - statutorily determined health and safety grounds, for example acting as a health and safety representative, reasonably raising an employer's attention to a health and safety concern, or taking steps to protect him/herself or others;
> - acting as an employee representative in relation to collective redundancies or the transfer of an undertaking;
> - the exercise of rights in relation to the National Minimum Wage Act, Working Time Regulations and Sunday work;
> - pregnancy, maternity and parental leave.

length of service, hours of work or age. However, except in the case of pregnancy, maternity and parental leave, they are applied to selection from an affected group so that where an employee wishes to claim that his or her selection was automatically unfair she or he will need to make a comparison with another person from the same pool of employees who was not dismissed.

An employing organisation must also ensure reasonableness in relation to redundancy selection, in order to avoid the risk of unfair dismissals. Reasonableness in relation to redundancy selection applies to both the choice of criteria and their application. Part of the consultation process may include an attempt to agree the selection criteria to be used with recognised unions or employee representatives. Selection criteria need to display a number of characteristics. Where there is a need to reduce the number of employees in a definable group, or pool, selection criteria need to be objectively and genuinely related to the changing (or diminishing) nature of the work and be able to measure the attributes of those in the pool clearly. Such criteria also need to be clear, non-discriminatory and verifiable. Criteria need to be clear in the sense that they have a reasonably precise meaning to avoid accusations about being vague and permitting subjectivity in the way in which they are applied. They need to avoid the possibility of permitting discrimination to occur, either directly or indirectly, in relation to sex, race or disability. For example, selection should not be related to choosing part-time rather than full-time staff, where this could lead to indirect discrimination. Criteria also need to permit verification to occur by drawing on established evidence that is capable of measurement, comparison and subsequent evaluation.

Actual criteria used by organisations can be categorised under the following headings:

- criteria related to employees' length of service or their age;
- performance-related selection criteria;
- capability-based selection criteria.

In the first category, length of service has been used in the past to select redundancies through the policy of *last in, first out* (or LIFO), although the opposite approach has also been used. Advocates of LIFO claim it has several advantages. These include being objective, being more acceptable to employees, being likely to lessen the likelihood of conflict, retaining experience and being cheap to use. It was generally accepted in the past that trade unions favoured the use of LIFO. However, use of this policy is likely to reduce managerial control over who is retained and to lead to the loss of highly valued employees, and it could well be found to be indirectly discriminatory when applied in particular situations (Lewis, 1993; Croner's, 1993). Our own research found that a small proportion of employers are content to continue to rely on LIFO where the affected workgroup is relatively low-skilled and any costs incurred in making employees redundant need to be minimised (Thornhill *et al.*, 1997). Some organisations have used this criterion as one of a number, and it has been used by others to decide between employees who cannot be separated in relation to other selection criteria. Age provides another possible criterion that has been used in some cases to help to make decisions about whom to select for redundancy. It has been used as an initial means to select those who have reached normal retirement age.

A range of options have been used in relation to performance-related and capability-based selection criteria, including:

- performance and contribution;
- attendance or sickness record and timekeeping;
- disciplinary record;
- skills/competence, qualifications and experience;
- flexibility, adaptability and 'trainability'.

The formulation of selection criteria so that they fulfil the requirement to be objective, clear, non-discriminatory and verifiable is likely to be difficult in practice. There will be a need for accurate and up-to-date information on which to base judgements. A number of different and properly documented records will be needed to verify decisions based on the criteria being used. These are likely to include appraisal, training and competence assessments, and attendance and disciplinary records. Organisations will need to be able to produce these for a reasonable length of time in order for judgements to have some substantive basis rather than simply being based on a series of short-term recollections about those affected. Some criteria, such as absence, are likely to be problematic in practice since those responsible will need to consider not only the total level of absence but also the pattern and reasons for an individual's absence. For example, an individual may have a long period of absence related to one particular condition whereas another person has a number of regular but short periods of absence.

Once selection criteria have been formulated, it has been established through case law that they need to be fairly and consistently applied to all affected employees. This may be particularly problematic in situations where a number of different managers are involved in applying selection criteria. The transparency of selection criteria will be likely to affect the level of consistency achieved in relation to their application. Consistency and fairness have been encouraged through the briefing and training of line managers to understand the nature of selection criteria and how to apply them. A points-scoring approach, with different weightings being given to the categories of selection criteria to reflect their perceived relative importance, using predetermined scales, has been used in many organisations to assess affected individuals in relation to each criterion. This may allow for a better basis for comparison. Monitoring and subsequently evaluating results from the application of selection criteria by different managers has been used to help to encourage consistency across an affected group of employees. Formally recording this process through the use of a specifically designed form allows results and tentative decisions to be moderated and evaluated in order to reveal anomalies that will threaten fairness and consistency in the application of the redundancy selection criteria within each affected employee category. Procedural fairness has also been encouraged through the inclusion of an appeal procedure, to allow claims by aggrieved employees to be considered.

Where selection criteria are used to determine who is to be made redundant, redundancy remains the reason why the dismissal is to occur, rather than the subsidiary reason for choosing who is to lose their jobs. This is important to avoid claims being made that any dismissals are really due to another reason, such as incapability, related to the nature of the selection criteria being used. For example, where absence is used to help to decide who is to be made redundant from a group this will remain a subsidiary reason and cannot be used to justify a dismissal on alternative grounds. Reasonableness in relation to selection for redundancy also extends to other aspects of the process involved, including prior warning and consultation, the consideration of alternatives to redundancy, and the possibility of alternative work.

■ Notifying redundancies and communicating 'bad news' in an organisation

We outlined the requirements regarding consultation earlier. The scope for communication is likely to cover a greater number of stakeholder groups and a wider range of issues than the process of consultation. A number of stakeholder groups may be identified in relation to the need to communicate about redundancies. These include those directly affected by the potential or actual advent of redundancies, whose situation is central to the consultation process. Another affected group are those affected more indirectly by organisational changes arising from downsizing. We recognised earlier that this group has been brought within the scope of the consultation process following the introduction of the 1999 Amendment Regulations (IRS, 1999). However, a number of other stakeholder groups, outside the statutorily defined consultation process, require communication about the events surrounding the advent of redundancies. These include other employee groups and in particular the managers of those who are affected in either a direct or an indirect way. Other employees not closely affected by the advent of downsizing and redundancies will learn about this event and form a view about its justification and the way in which it is managed. These employees will rely on a number of sources of information about organisational events. These range from official organisational sources of information, through organisational actions that provide them with clues, to the generation and dissemination of rumours (Greenhalgh and Rosenblatt, 1984). A fourth source of information may be identified in relation to a downsizing event, which will originate from the public reporting of this event through the local and perhaps even national media. Where official organisational communication does not focus on the specific concerns and interest of those affected, however indirectly, it will not alleviate their inevitable sense of concern, uncertainty and perceived powerlessness (Greenhalgh, 1983; Greenhalgh and Rosenblatt, 1984; Brockner *et al.*, 1990; Shaw and Barrett-Power, 1997). Lack of official organisational communication will undoubtedly increase reliance on unofficial rumours and public reporting.

Following a general announcement of forthcoming redundancies, a number of subcategories of employee will become apparent. We have drawn a distinction between those in threatened areas, those to remain but affected by subsequent changes, and those in areas not affected. It is also important to differentiate between those who may wish to volunteer to be made redundant and those who wish to remain in employment. This highlights a situation of complexity, and the identification of a range of different informational and communication needs that will be challenging for those who manage this scenario, particularly front-line managers. The use of a voluntary redundancy strategy, discussed later, will be likely to reduce any sense of uncertainty, powerlessness and stress, whereas the announcement of forthcoming compulsory redundancy selection is likely to increase the incidence and strength of these reactions. The nature of a general announcement is also likely to shape subsequent reactions to downsizing and the use of redundancies. These reactions may be related not only to the means to be used to achieve this change but also to employee perceptions about how the message was conveyed and the justification provided for downsizing. The management of the situation following a general announcement of forthcoming redundancies will require managers to be well briefed to respond to questions that arise, to counter unrealistic rumours, and to be able to act as a mechanism to report back issues to permit a higher-level official response. However, where compulsory selection is used, the subsequent specific notification of those to be made redundant will provide a critical incident in the cycle of communication that accompanies downsizing and the use of redundancies.

Line managers have a central role in 'breaking the news' to those being compulsorily made redundant. This places line managers in a demanding and difficult position. This will test the extent to which they have been properly prepared and trained to conduct this role in a sensitive and clear manner so that they can cope with the immediate reactions of those being notified. Affected individuals are likely to be concerned about why they have been selected. This will test an announcing manager's understanding of the criteria being used and his or her ability to present this news in a professional and yet sensitive manner. Individuals being compulsorily made redundant also need to be provided with information about entitlements. This is likely to include:

- redundancy terms and possibly pensions information;
- period of notice;
- remaining work duties;
- place of work;
- assistance in finding alternative employment.

Often notified individuals are unlikely to be receptive to immediate explanations about these rights, and this information is generally given in writing at this stage. A subsequent meeting can be designed to consider these issues, which may occur with a representative from the organisation's personnel department or with an outplacement counsellor, allowing questions to be raised and answered confidentially.

Consideration also needs to be given to when and where the news of redundancy is broken. Logistical difficulties have faced organisations undertaking a significant level of downsizing through this means. An example is where a number of managers may be charged with making this announcement over a short period of time such as a day. This has led some organisations to conduct the process of redundancy notification at offices away from the affected employees' normal place of work and then allowing notified individuals to go home for the rest of the day, perhaps also having had an initial discussion with an outplacement consultant.

Notification of compulsory redundancy to affected individuals and the dissemination of news about this event to those who are intended to remain will not normally be the end of the matter. Although some managers may subsequently attempt to minimise reference to this event, there will be a need to manage the transitional period as those who are being made redundant work their period of notice, and those who are intended to remain adjust to the imminent or recent loss of colleagues. This period of immediate transition, as well as any longer-term adjustment, may require the exercise of a range of change management skills on the part of line managers, underpinned by regular and supportive communication to counteract the often unspoken but adverse impact on the nature of the subsequent employment relationship.

■ Compensating those who are to be made redundant

An important intention of the law relating to the regulation of dismissals on grounds of redundancy is the offer of compensation where an employee has indeed been made redundant. The minimum period of notice and the amount of any redundancy compensation may be specified in an employee's contract of employment. Where this is the case, it will specify terms that match or exceed those established by statute. Redundancy terms may also be offered at the announcement of an organisational downsizing, often with a view to attracting interest among potential volunteers, especially where significantly enhanced terms may be offered only for a specific period. Where no such provision or enhanced offer is made, any statutory minimum conditions that operate will apply. Many European countries have statutory provisions relating to minimum periods of notice and redundancy or severance payments. The nature of these statutory provisions varies between countries. In the British context, the requirement to make a statutory payment is currently contained in section 162 of the Employment Rights Act 1996. This specifies the following means to calculate entitlements:

- one and a half weeks' pay for each year of employment completed after reaching the age of 41, up to normal retiring age, or 65 years old where there isn't one;
- one week's pay for each year of employment completed between the ages of 22 and 40;
- half a week's pay for each year of employment completed between the ages of 18 and 21.

In addition, British law specifies a maximum length of service that can be taken into account – 20 years – and a maximum amount in terms of calculating a week's pay. This is reviewed on an annual basis using the Retail Price Index as a means to calculate the annual increase. From 1 February 2003 the maximum amount of a 'week's pay' for calculating a redundancy payment was set at £260. This provided for a maximum statutory redundancy payment of £7,800 during 2003. This is very much a minimum right, and many redundancy payments in UK organisations are calculated by using a much more generous basis. In these cases, actual pay may be factored by using greater multiples in terms of so many weeks for each year of employment completed, or by offering, for example, the equivalent of, say, 1–2 years' basic salary.

Supporting those who are to leave the organisation

It has become increasingly commonplace to provide those who are to leave an organisation with some transitional help towards re-employment, self-employment or retirement in order to help them overcome the trauma of job loss and change. This help is often targeted at different categories of leavers and is therefore likely to be differentiated in relation to previous grade and status. As a result of this development over recent years, a number of external outplacement consultants have entered the marketplace to fulfil the demand for this particular niche activity, with some concentrating on the 'executive end' of this service and others providing services for a wider range of occupational groups. The impact of this provision may be experienced not only by those directly affected but also by the survivors who remain in employment. This latter group may respond more positively by seeing those who leave being provided with a further type of transitional assistance because it may signal their future redundancy treatment. Outplacement potentially comprises a range of services such as (e.g. Doherty, 1998):

- development of coping strategies through counselling to deal with any emotional trauma associated with this change;
- advice about possible future options, including careers guidance, and assistance in seeking to pursue these;
- practical help in relation to job search activities, composing CVs, letters of application and making applications, networking to potentially find alternative work, preparation for job interviews and other selection activities;
- retraining for alternative employment or self-employment;
- assistance in relation to administrative and secretarial support, temporary office facilities and access to sources of advertised job vacancies;
- retirement advice and financial management.

The exact mix and nature of the services to be provided, and the time over which they will be made available, will need to be decided by the downsizing organisation. This choice is likely to be affected by a range of factors including the status of those being made redundant, costs of provision, the availability of other jobs and the likely length of time to find alternative employment in the prevailing labour market. A choice will also need be made about whether to provide support internally or to contract some or all of the services to be offered to an external provider.

Supporting those who are to remain in employment

In recent years, greater recognition has been placed on those who remain in the employment of an organisation. The emphasis has been on alleviating the indirect effects of downsizing and redundancies. Undoubtedly, much of this interest is related to the very widespread and often repeated incidence of redundancies and related job losses in recent years. The management of the downsizing process and the treatment of those who leave and stay will generate a range of *survivors' reactions* – the term now commonly given to those who remain in the employment of a downsizing organisation. These survivors' reactions may be placed into four broad categories. Survivors' reactions towards those who are to be made redundant are broadly categorised as *sympathetic* or *unsympathetic*. Survivors' reactions towards their downsizing organisation may, in turn, be broadly categorised as *negative* or *positive* (see Figure 12.2). These reactions will be shaped by factors such as the nature of past working relationships and perceptions about the treatment of those who are to be made redundant. These factors and their implications for the future conduct of the employment relationship in downsizing organisations are discussed later in more detail.

There is a business or efficiency case for intervening to manage the survivors of downsizing. In addition, we recognised earlier that there is now a legal imperative requiring consultation to be conducted with the representatives 'of any of the employees who may be affected by the proposed dismissals or (who) may be affected by measures taken in connection with those dismissals'. This has the important legal effect of introducing consultation with representatives of the remaining workforce where these employees will be affected by changes arising from downsizing (IRS, 1999).

self-check question	**12.1** *What are the principal legal requirements associated with proposing to dismiss employees on the grounds of redundancy?*

We now turn in more detail to options in relation to downsizing and redundancy strategies and their implications for the nature of the employment relationship. We then consider further the impact of downsizing on its survivors and on the nature of the employment relationship in a post-downsizing climate.

12.5 Choice of downsizing and redundancy strategies and methods, and their implications

Our discussion so far has indicated a multitude of factors that will affect employee reactions to the advent of downsizing and the use of redundancies. These reactions will in turn affect the conduct of employment relationship. A major determinant of such reactions will be related to the choice of downsizing and redundancy strategies and methods exercised by the organisation. We shall now discuss each of these in turn.

■ Downsizing strategies

Earlier we used the work by Cameron *et al.* (1991, 1993) to identify three possible organisational strategies to achieve downsizing. These strategies may be summarised as the:

- *workforce reduction strategy*, which focuses simply on reducing an organisation's headcount;
- *organisation redesign strategy*, which involves delayering, eliminating areas of work and job redesign, so that the amount of work is reduced as well as the organisation's headcount;

■ *systemic change strategy*, which is a longer-term approach intended to promote more fundamental cultural and structural change incorporating elements of the previous strategies.

All three strategies involve the reduction of an organisation's headcount, although the second and third approaches would also be designed to reduce the amount of work undertaken and to bring about structural and cultural organisational change. The significance of recognising these various approaches to downsizing lies in their potentially different consequences for the organisation and implications for the conduct of the employment relationship. A narrowly focused and short-term cost-reduction strategy is likely to result in a greater range of negative outcomes for an organisation than a more integrative, employee-focused and longer-term strategy to redesign an organisation.

Cameron *et al.* (1993) found that the exclusive use of a workforce reduction strategy was likely to lead to a reduction in organisational performance. Mishra and Mishra (1994) found that organisational performance was adversely affected in relation to both cost and quality where this strategy was used exclusively. The workforce reduction strategy may lead to the loss of valued organisational competence and negative consequences for those who remain – an aspect we discuss below. Its benefits are seen to be short-term, whereas the attendant costs remain into the longer term as the organisation attempts to overcome the loss of required competence and negative survivor reactions (Cameron, 1994b). By comparison, the use of an organisation redesign and/or systemic change strategy has been positively related to organisational performance in terms of both cost reduction and quality improvement (Cameron *et al.*, 1993; Mishra and Mishra, 1994). Moreover, organisations that relied exclusively on the use of a workforce reduction strategy were found to be likely to repeat the use of this approach whenever cost reduction was deemed necessary (Cameron, 1994b). Repeated use of a workforce reduction strategy has also been shown to have further damaging consequences to employee morale as subsequent downsizing programmes are revealed (Thornhill and Gibbons, 1995).

Another approach to differentiate downsizing strategies looks at the extent to which these are *reactive* or *proactive* (Kozlowski *et al.*, 1993). The use of a reactive approach to downsizing has been claimed to be more likely to lead to a failure to achieve intended organisational objectives and to produce other, unintended negative consequences in relation to remaining employees. A reactive approach is likely to constrain the extent to which an organisation's management can engage meaningfully in the stages outlined above to manage the downsizing process, with a view to minimising the adverse effects that are associated with this event (e.g. McCune *et al.*, 1988). By comparison, proactivity, by definition, implies planning to permit an organisation's management to explore alternatives to the use of redundancies, to target organisational areas and competences selectively through voluntary means, and to implement other measures to seek to overcome potentially negative consequences associated with downsizing (Kozlowski *et al.*, 1993).

■ Redundancy strategies and methods

There is a clear distinction between the use of voluntary and compulsory approaches to achieve redundancies. Both should be defined and treated as forms of redundancy, as they arise from a decision taken by management to dismiss employees. But they are likely to lead to different reactions among those who are affected, both directly and indirectly. In practice, the distinction between these two approaches is often blurred because of the tactics that management has used to secure sufficient numbers of volunteers, or to target particular areas within an organisation (e.g. Lewis, 1993; Wass, 1996; Turnbull and Wass, 1997). In this way, a number of intermediate positions may be identified between a purely voluntary and a compulsory approach to achieve redundancies in an organisation. These demonstrate ways in which management may exercise control in relation to organisational downsizing. These are shown in Figure 12.1 and subsequently discussed.

A purely *voluntary* approach to making redundancies will involve an unfocused invitation across an organisation for volunteers to accept published redundancy terms. In this way, in its simplest form, this strategy is essentially employee centred, where it remains up to individuals who may be interested to enquire about redundancy terms without experiencing any pressure to accept or subsequent threat in relation to compulsory selection. This approach may be used in the early phase of downsizing where an organisation is contemplating a very significant workforce reduction, related to a general cost-reduction strategy. A personnel director in one of the former public utilities told us that at the beginning of that organisation's downsizing programme the organisation was 'so over-brained' that it was willing to accept any volunteers. This voluntary approach may also be used in relation to a requirement for each area of an organisation to make a broadly uniform reduction in staffing (Kozlowski *et al.*, 1993). There are potentially a wide range of advantages related to the adoption of a voluntary approach to achieving redundancies. These are outlined in Box 12.2.

For management, a major disadvantage of using a voluntary redundancy strategy is the possible loss of control over the outcomes from this change. This may occur where too many or too few employees volunteer, or where inappropriate numbers

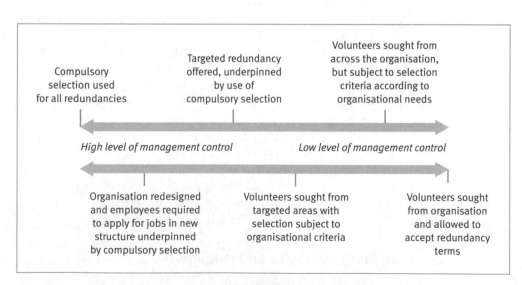

Figure 12.1 **Redundancy strategies and categories of control**

> ### Box 12.2 Likely advantages of a voluntary redundancy strategy
>
> - Should be more effective at facilitating a large-scale reduction in staffing numbers.
> - Redundant staff are more likely to be 'happy leavers'.
> - Less damage to the commitment of the survivors and fewer issues during the transitional period while voluntary leavers remain at work. Feelings of insecurity should be reduced, as should any adverse effects on job performance.
> - Avoids the likely scenario of the 'big issue' which is associated with the trauma of an organisation declaring compulsory redundancies. It should thus reduce stress for employees, and especially for managers who would otherwise be responsible for carrying out compulsory redundancy selection and notification.
> - There is the possibility for greater flexibility in relation to the timing of voluntary leavers, with benefits for the organisation (winding down or handing over particular jobs) and for the individual (matching scheme trigger points for redundancy or other related payments).
> - Should reduce possible public relations and external image issues and reduce the likelihood of adverse media coverage and comment. This may be significant in relation to a number of stakeholders: for example customers, shareholders, future job applicants, elected bodies in relation to public sector organisations.
> - Should reduce potential legal issues associated with the declaration of redundancies, especially in relation to selection.
> - Should reduce the possibility of equal opportunities issues arising in relation to selection for redundancy.
> - Reduces conflict and other issues in a unionised environment, although there will still be a need to meet statutory requirements, for example in relation to collective and individual consultation. This approach may also reduce tensions within a trade union by avoiding the need for it to confront compulsory redundancies.
> - In a strongly unionised environment a voluntary approach will avoid pressures for the use of LIFO and match cultural expectations so that a positive employee relations climate is not unduly damaged during a period of significant organisational change.
> - A voluntary approach should help to avoid the type of disruption that would be damaging where an organisation is reliant on 'quality-based relationships' with key customers. The result of any disruption would threaten the nature and future of such a relationship.
> - In a significant downsizing exercise the use of a voluntary approach is likely to shift the age profile, with the result that the average age of employees is significantly reduced. This may help to facilitate the type of changes that an organisation is likely to be pursuing at the same time that it is significantly reducing its headcount. It will also allow those who do not wish to adapt to such changes to opt out, provided that they can afford to do so.

volunteer in relation to particular categories of staff. This may be related to too many in one category and too few in another. Where management intervenes to decline the interest of some volunteers, the result may be the creation of dissatisfaction. This could lead to some becoming more likely to seek alternative employment than would have been the case before the advent of the redundancy situation. Where volunteers are not accepted, or insufficient numbers of employees express a definite interest to leave, it may be necessary to make compulsory redundancies from among those who did not volunteer, with equally negative consequences for morale. Alternatively, where management allows those who have volunteered to leave, there will be a loss of managerial control with potentially significant repercussions for the organisation in the future in relation to its staffing base, skills mix and the fulfilment of its functions. In relation to this latter scenario, Lewis (1993: 28) states: 'The volunteer population may become an irresistible force and the pattern of volunteers may largely determine the distribution of actual redundancies'.

Another major disadvantage associated with a voluntary redundancy strategy is high cost. Volunteers are likely to be longer-serving employees in many cases. Organisations may actually seek volunteers through the offer of early retirement benefits. However, cherry picking the over-50s has been an expensive option in many organisations. Apart from the relatively higher redundancy costs of longer-serving volunteers, organisations may also suffer the loss of necessary experience. This may even promote further restructuring in order to cope with the loss of a significant number of experienced employees. There are potentially other disadvantages associated with the use of a voluntary redundancy strategy. The use of this strategy may adversely affect the level of natural wastage. Some employees who would have left during the period of the change wait for the opportunity to secure a redundancy payment. Organisations may also find themselves carrying people forward without 'real jobs', where compulsory redundancy is not considered an option. Both of these disadvantages may not be considered significant, especially in the case of large organisations that are more likely to bear any costs associated with these aspects in order to avoid the issue of compulsion.

Some organisations have developed variations to the voluntary approach. They have done this to exercise a greater level of managerial control over the redundancy process and yet avoid the negative connotations associated with a compulsory redundancy strategy. Perhaps the simplest variation is to make clear that all expressions of interest in voluntary redundancy are subject to managerial consideration related to the needs of the business. However, this may lead to dissatisfaction where employees volunteer without knowing the basis on which their application may or may not be accepted. More formally, the use of predetermined selection criteria offers a further means to exercise managerial control in relation to the downsizing process (Turnbull, 1988). Selection criteria may thus be used in relation to an ostensibly voluntary approach. This approach will provide a check in relation to particular individuals whom the organisation wishes to retain.

Through the exercise of more careful planning, management are likely to be able to exercise a greater level of control. This will be achieved by specifically identifying and targeting organisational areas, related either to particular functions, occupational groups, structural layers or by skill level, and inviting expressions of interest only from these. Some organisations achieve this targeting in a very precise way, thereby maintaining considerable managerial control over the process of voluntary redundancy. This approach is also likely to be combined in practice with the formulation and use of selection criteria to choose between volunteers where potential supply exceeds the demand of the organisation. This strategy may fail to secure sufficient interest from among those who are targeted and may be reinforced by the use of compulsory selection to secure the numbers determined by management.

Other approaches to secure volunteers have also been used in conjunction with a voluntary redundancy strategy, in order to secure greater managerial control. The first of these is designed to encourage volunteers, either from targeted groups or from the workforce as a whole, by giving attractive incentives to those who may be interested in volunteering. Such incentives may be offered on a time-specific basis, so that there is a well-publicised date by which the offer of enhanced redundancy terms will close. A second category utilises a structural approach, whereby the structure of an organisation is redesigned, requiring employees to apply for posts within the new structure. Voluntary redundancy would be available for those who failed to secure a post in the new structure. A variant of this structural approach used by some organisations is the re-categorisation of jobs into core and non-core categories. Non-core jobholders would not face compulsory redundancy, but the onus would in effect be placed upon them to apply for jobs that were within the core classification. Where non-core jobholders are unable to achieve this, they may be offered the chance to accept voluntary redundancy. Approaches such as these may be classified as *quasi-voluntary redundancy* strategies.

Compulsory redundancy will be used to select employees for dismissal regardless of their wishes. Managerial decision-making and control will be maximised in relation to this approach. However, the legal requirements outlined earlier to consult collectively and individually, to seek means to avoid, as well as to alleviate the impact of, redundancies including the use of compulsion, will need to be considered.

self-check question	**12.2** Think about the organisation for which you work (or have worked), or one about which you have some knowledge. Which strategy or strategies did it use to downsize? Where it used redundancies, how would you categorise these in relation to what you have just read? Evaluate the implications of this strategy or these strategies for the conduct of the employment relationship in this organisation.

12.6 Evaluating the impact of downsizing and redundancy on survivors and the employment relationship climate

The process of downsizing has been linked to the creation of a range of psychological and behavioural reactions by those who survive this event (e.g. Thornhill *et al.*, 2000). We referred earlier to research that reported organisational deficiencies in relation to the realisation of intended objectives, either in the short term or in the longer term, due in part to the loss of capability, competence and commitment associated with downsizing. In this section we explore the psychological and behavioural aspects of downsizing by looking more closely at the nature of survivors' reactions to this event and the existence of moderating variables that affect the strength of these reactions (e.g. Brockner, 1988). We also explore more generally the effect of the use of downsizing and redundancy on the employment relationship climate.

■ Survivors' reactions and the variables that moderate these

Figure 12.2 illustrates the principal determinants and categories of survivors' reactions to the advent of downsizing. This groups the factors that shape survivors' reactions into three sets of determinants, relating to *organisational actions*, *psychological disposition* and *environmental circumstances*. We shall explore each of these in turn below. Figure 12.2 also presents two sets of categories of reactions that survivors may exhibit, depending upon their perceptions about how leavers are selected and subsequently treated during their period of notice, and their own circumstances.

One set of reactions is labelled *sympathetic* and *unsympathetic*. These refer to survivors' reactions towards those who leave an organisation (e.g. Brockner and Greenberg, 1990). In the context of a downsizing situation, they suggest that an unsympathetic reaction may include the belief that redundancies were justified, particularly in relation to those selected for redundancy, with survivors distancing themselves from the leavers and perhaps even working harder. The other related set of reactions is labelled *positive* and *negative* and these relate to the organisation itself. Reactions that are unsympathetic to redundant colleagues may be associated with those that are positive to the organisation. This may be because survivors feel that such action was necessary in relation to the organisation's future, their own sense of security, and future internal job opportunities.

On the other hand, sympathetic reactions by survivors may include the belief that leavers have been unfairly selected and/or treated, resulting in negative emotions, attitudes and behaviours towards an organisation. In practice, of course, survivors' reactions may be complex, exhibiting a mixture drawn from across these categories.

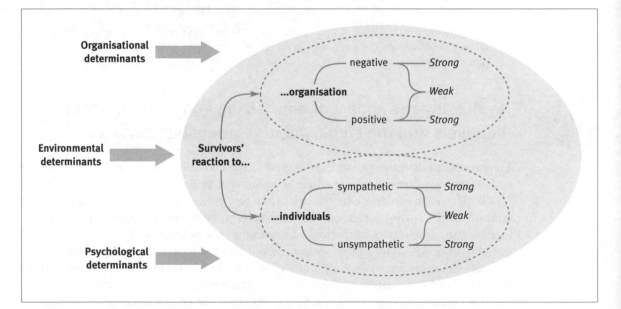

Figure 12.2 **Principal determinants and categories of survivors' reactions to the advent of downsizing**
Source: Thornhill *et al.* (2000: 260). Reproduced with permission

Organisational determinants

We shall use organisational justice theory as an analytical framework to explore the organisational determinants of survivors' reactions to the advent of downsizing and use of redundancies. Organisational justice is a set of related theories about employees' perceptions of the fairness of their treatment in an employing organisation (see Chapter 3). Three types of organisational justice theory have been identified through research into perceptions about organisational treatment: distributive, procedural and interactional (e.g. Folger and Cropanzano, 1998). *Distributive justice* is related to employees' views about the fairness of the decisions that are made – the *outcomes* of the process. Box 12.3 summarises possible elements of distributive justice that will affect employee perceptions about the fairness, or unfairness, of decisions taken in relation to downsizing and the use of redundancies.

Box 12.3 Elements of distributive justice and downsizing

Survivors' reactions to the outcomes of downsizing are likely to be affected by a number of aspects including the following:

- How often has downsizing been used in the organisation, and what was the nature of the experience of its use?
- Is the decision to downsize accepted and seen as legitimate?
- Is the reason to downsize accepted and seen as legitimate?
- Are the scale and nature of the downsizing accepted and seen as legitimate?
- Is the decision to make employees redundant accepted and seen as legitimate?
- Is the need to make employees redundant applied fairly to all affected groups including managers?
- Is there any other course of action as an alternative to making employees redundant?
- Is the level of prior notification provided by management seen as adequate?
- Do the selection criteria that are used produce outcomes that are seen as fair by employees?

The second type of organisational justice theory, called *procedural justice* (Thibaut and Walker, 1975), focuses on employees' perceptions about the fairness of the procedures used to make decisions about downsizing and redundancies. This suggests that not only should the outcomes of downsizing decision-making be seen to be fair but also the procedures and processes used to arrive at such decisions. Negative reactions that arise from outcomes perceived as unfair may also be reduced by the use of procedures that are seen to be fair (Brockner *et al.*, 1990). In this way, an organisational decision to downsize may not be accepted by the workforce, leading to a range of negative reactions, although the impact of these may be reduced by employees' views about the method used to downsize, where this avoids the use of compulsory selection.

Daly and Geyer (1994) report that organisational studies related to procedural justice have focused mainly on two factors that affect perceptions about procedural fairness. These are *voice*, which is linked to the scope for employee involvement in the process, and *justification*, which relates to the nature of explanations and reasons provided for downsizing. Involvement in relation to the use of downsizing and the methods to achieve this is likely to include the:

- use of consultation and communication about the process;
- scope to influence the choice of selection criteria;
- use of a voluntary, as opposed to a compulsory, route to redundancy;
- affected employees being provided with options about redeployment and relocation;
- provision of outplacement support and facilities;
- use of interventions aimed at allowing survivors to adjust to downsizing related changes.

These facets of involvement relate broadly to the stages of downsizing and to the legal requirements of using redundancy that we considered earlier. Guest and Peccei (1992: 55) evaluated the effects of involvement initiatives used during the closure of a British Aerospace site and found that 'employee involvement can work as a strategy for easing the process of plant closure'. However, they also found that certain groups were less involved, with the implication that these employees may have had less favourable perceptions about the fairness of the procedures used.

Involvement or voice in this type of context allows those affected to exercise some degree of *process control*, or personal influence in relation to the process (Thibaut and Walker, 1975; Greenberg and Folger, 1983). Process control has been shown to be linked to a number of attitudinal and behavioural survivor reactions (Davy *et al.*, 1991). Davy *et al.* (1991) found that process control positively affects perceptions about fairness and job satisfaction, which in turn affect level of commitment to the organisation and intention to stay. Organisations may therefore genuinely seek to engender process control through employee involvement to promote perceptions that the process used is just (Davy *et al.*, 1991). Justification may also be promoted through an educative process to explain why downsizing is necessary. A similar finding has been found for this as for process control: justification has been related positively to procedural fairness and, in turn, to intention to stay (Daly and Geyer, 1994). This may be explained through the finding that employees are more likely to accept a decision, even an unfavourable one related to redundancy, when they receive an adequate and genuine reason for it (e.g. Brockner *et al.*, 1990; Brockner and Wiesenfeld, 1993; Daly and Geyer, 1994). An absence of process control may conversely lead to the violation of employees' psychological contracts and adversely affect the nature of their commitment, or attachment, to the organisation (see Chapter 1).

self-check question	**12.3** How does the concept of procedural justice and the elements that comprise this relate to the legal requirements associated with proposing to dismiss employees on the grounds of redundancy?

The third type of organisational justice theory, *interactional justice* (Bies and Moag, 1986), focuses on employee perceptions about the fairness of the interpersonal treatment that they receive during the implementation of downsizing. Line managers have a potentially significant influence over the way their subordinates react to downsizing in terms of their treatment of those who leave and the survivors.

Line managers thus need to be able to demonstrate a range of skills that might be broadly described as change management skills. In addition, line managers need to be able to deal with issues that are specific to a redundancy situation. These will include, as we discussed earlier, communicating notification decisions, providing reasons for these, and the sensitivity with which they treat leavers during their notice period. In Armstrong-Stassen's (1994) study, the survivors who performed better and who were more committed and loyal to their organisation were those who also felt that they had highly supportive line managers.

Psychological determinants

Although organisational justice theory allows us to recognise that outcomes, procedures and interactions will each affect employees' perceptions, it is important to appreciate that these aspects of organisational treatment will not produce a uniform set of reactions from those affected by the advent of downsizing and redundancies. Reactions to downsizing will vary between individuals because of psychological differences. These will include individual differences related to self-esteem, prior organisational commitment, tolerance of insecurity and individual coping resources. For example, Brockner *et al.* (1985) suggest that survivors with low self-esteem may actually improve their work performance because they experience a high level of positive inequity (that is, guilt) about the way in which a downsizing is conducted.

Brockner *et al.* (1992b) found that the survivors who are most likely to suffer from negative reactions are those who were highly committed to the organisation before downsizing, where the management of this process is perceived to be unfair. Greenhalgh and Rosenblatt (1984) report that individuals who have a significant aversion to perceived threats such as job insecurity are also likely to experience the strongest negative reactions. Related to this last aspect, Armstrong-Stassen (1994: 612–13) found that survivors who perceived themselves to be in control of their situation adopted coping strategies that reflected this feeling. Conversely, in this case, those who do not perceive this may be less likely to cope effectively.

Environmental determinants

Environmental conditions are also likely to act as a further determinant of survivors' reactions (Brockner, 1988). We may identify different categories of environmental conditions that are likely to affect survivors' reactions. These will be related to the broader economic environment and to the external labour market within which an organisation functions. They will also relate to the internal operating environment of an organisation, its ownership, recent history and organisational culture. In relation to the broader economic environment and the external labour market, where redundant former colleagues are able to find comparable work elsewhere, survivors' reactions are likely to be less adverse. The occupational and geographical mobility of redundant employees and their economic need to work will also be likely to affect the nature and strength of survivors' reactions (e.g. Greenhalgh and Rosenblatt, 1984).

In relation to the internal operating environment of the organisation, its ownership, recent history and organisational culture, survivors' reactions are likely to be affected by past events and any subsequent changes that have the effect of significantly altering employees' expectations. An organisation operating in the not-for-profit sector of the economy, with no prior history of using redundancies, that announces the need to downsize and shed labour is likely to produce a high level of negative employee reactions to this shift in its employment strategy. Conversely, a holding company operating in the private sector, with a history and culture associated with company takeovers and divestments, is likely to produce a lower level of negative reactions when it announces a downsizing programme. In a similar way, the industrial sector and the history of employee relations to date may also shape expectations about the use of downsizing and redundancies, which will impact on the nature and strength of employees' reactions where these strategies are used.

Moderating variables and the conduct of the employment relationship

The variables that we have discussed in relation to organisational actions, individual differences and environmental conditions suggest that survivors' reactions will vary between downsizing situations and even between individuals in the same change setting. This suggests that organisations need to consider the implications of the actions that they plan to take in relation to the management of downsizing and redundancy. It also suggests that they need to be aware, in general terms, of the nature of differences between individual employees and of prevailing environmental circumstances when they design interventions to alleviate negative survivor reactions to downsizing. This may highlight a need to lay particular emphasis on certain interventions, such as employee communication, and to provide an appropriate focus for others such as outplacement assistance for redundant staff, so that any threats posed by insecurity or lack of coping are alleviated or reduced.

These variables, related to organisational actions, individual differences and environmental factors, are types of *moderator variable*. Such variables affect the incidence and strength of survivors' reactions to downsizing (e.g. Greenhalgh and Rosenblatt, 1984; Brockner, 1988). They help to explain why the incidence and strength of psychological and behavioural reactions may be either more or less pronounced in relation to particular downsizing situations. The identification of moderator variables is therefore a very important step towards any attempt to manage a downsizing programme proactively and effectively. An understanding of possible moderator variables will permit those interested to identify possible effects and to use appropriate procedures to avoid, or at least to seek to alleviate, the potentially negative consequences of downsizing.

Many moderator variables are directly related to events in an organisation. The nature and strength of survivors' reactions may thus be partly explained by prior work interdependence with those who are to leave or who have been made redundant (e.g. Brockner 1988). The strength of sympathetic survivors' responses is likely to be much greater where survivors and leavers have previously been interdependent in terms of carrying out their work. More broadly, these reactions may be partly explained by the existence or absence of shared attitudes, values and experiences (e.g. Brockner and Greenberg, 1990). Where survivors and leavers closely identify with one another there is likely to be a higher level of sympathetic survivor response.

Survivors' beliefs that they may be made redundant themselves may be another source of insecurity affecting the nature and level of their reactions. As we discussed earlier in relation to organisational justice, a major determinant of survivors' reactions will be perceptions about the policies and procedures used by an organisation to decide redundancies. Related to this variable are issues about employee expectations and avoidability, where for example unexpected or avoidable redundancies may result in strong, sympathetic reactions such as anger towards an organisation (e.g. Brockner, 1988).

Our discussion about the nature of survivors' reactions and the existence of moderating variables points to a highly complex scenario within a downsizing organisation. Moreover, these moderating variables will be likely to have a cumulative and compounding effect (Brockner, 1988). Nevertheless, managerial action focused at this level of downsizing should contribute towards the more positive management of the employment relationship. Its intention would be to reduce the incidence or alleviate the consequences of negative survivors' reactions that can arise where downsizing is conceived only as a corporate-level (top-down) strategy without considering the implications for the future conduct of the employment relationship. In this way the strength of negative reactions may be weakened, whereas any sense of legitimacy in the downsizing process combined with procedural fairness may possibly lead to the creation of some positive reactions.

self-check question

12.4 What are the principal adverse survivors' reactions that have been identified and how may these be moderated?

You may care to extend your thoughts about this question and apply it to the organisation for which you work (or have worked), or to one about which you have some knowledge.

12.7 Summary

- Downsizing and redundancy are sometimes used as alternative terms. However, they can be defined as being distinct, and it is useful to treat each separately for analytical purposes. Three principal ways to differentiate between downsizing and redundancy have been identified.
  - The first way is related to the methods used to achieve organisational downsizing. Downsizing uses methods other than just redundancy. In this way, downsizing can be differentiated from the narrower concept of redundancy.
  - The second way relates to organisational strategy. Freeman and Cameron (1993) believe that downsizing should be analysed as an organisational-level concept whereas redundancy is approached at the level of the individual. Downsizing should therefore be seen as a strategic issue whereas redundancy is an operational one.
  - The third way recognises that redundancy is subject to tightly prescribed legal regulation. Downsizing, as a more nebulous concept and one that may use a wider range of methods to reduce organisational headcount, may operate outside the boundaries of some of the laws that regulate dismissal.
- Over recent decades, the incidence of redundancy and downsizing has become a major factor affecting the operation of the labour market. Data illustrate that redundancies have been a major factor in the labour market in Britain during the

1980s and 1990s as well as into the present decade. Organisational downsizing and workforce redundancy appear to be an embedded feature of many if not most employing organisations.

■ Planned redundancy will pass through a number of stages, although not necessarily in a standardised order. Many of the stages will be affected by a country's legal regulation. These stages are:
  - identifying the need for and causes of redundancy;
  - providing information and conducting consultation;
  - using alternatives to redundancy;
  - identifying selection criteria and those to be made redundant;
  - notifying redundancies and communicating 'bad news' in an organisation;
  - compensating those who are to be made redundant;
  - supporting those who are to leave the organisation;
  - supporting those who are to remain in employment.

■ Managerial control will generally be maximised in relation to the use of a compulsory approach to redundancy. Use of a voluntary redundancy strategy may be advantageous in a range of organisational circumstances, but may lead to lower managerial control over the outcomes of this process. However, a number of variations to a voluntary approach to redundancy have been used by management to exercise a higher level of influence and control in relation to its use. A major determinant of employee reactions will be related to the choice of downsizing and redundancy strategy and the level of managerial control over this process. These reactions will in turn affect the conduct of the employment relationship.

■ Survivors' reactions may be placed into four broad categories. Reactions towards those who are to be made redundant may be broadly categorised as *sympathetic* or *unsympathetic*. Survivors' reactions towards their downsizing organisation may, in turn, be broadly categorised as *negative* or *positive*. Three broad categories of determinants of survivors' reactions may be identified. These relate to *organisational*, *psychological* and *environmental* determinants. Organisational justice theory has been used as an analytical framework to explore the organisational determinants of survivors' reactions to the advent of downsizing and use of redundancies. This demonstrates that the outcomes, procedures and interactions associated with downsizing and the use of redundancies will affect levels of perceived employee fairness and survivors' reactions. However, responses to downsizing will also vary between individuals because of a range of psychological differences, as well as because of environmental conditions that help to shape the nature and strength of these reactions. These factors also act as *moderator variables*, with the result that the impact of downsizing on the future conduct of the employment relationship will vary between organisations depending in part on the nature of its management both during and after this event.

References

Armstrong-Stassen, M. (1994) 'Coping with transition: a study of layoff survivors', *Journal of Organizational Behaviour*, 15, 597–621.

Bies, R.J. and Moag, J. (1986) 'Interactional justice: communication criteria of fairness', *in* Lewicki, R., Sheppard, B. and Bazerman, M. (eds), *Research on Negotiation in Organizations*, Vol. 1, Greenwich, CT, JAI Press, pp. 43–55.

Brockner, J. (1988) 'The effects of work layoffs on survivors: research, theory and practice', *in* Staw, B.M. and Cummings, L.L. (eds), *Research in Organizational Behavior*, Vol. 10, Greenwich, CT, JAI Press, pp. 213–55.

Brockner, J. and Greenberg, J. (1990) 'The impact of layoffs on survivors: an organizational justice perspective', *in* Carroll, J.S. (ed.), *Applied Social Psychology and Organizational Settings*, Hillsdale, NJ, Erlbaum, pp. 45–75.

Brockner, J. and Wiesenfeld, B. (1993) 'Living on the edge (of social and organizational psychology): the effects of job layoffs on those who remain', *in* Murnighan, J.K. (ed.), *Social Psychology in Organizations*, Englewood Cliffs, NJ, Prentice Hall, pp. 119–40.

Brockner, J., Davy, J. and Carter, C. (1985) 'Layoffs, self-esteem, and survivor guilt: motivational, affective, and attitudinal consequences', *Organizational Behavior and Human Decision Processes*, 36, 229–44.

Brockner, J., DeWitt, R.L., Grover, S. and Reed, T. (1990) 'When it is especially important to explain why: factors affecting the relationship between managers' explanations of a layoff and survivors' reactions to the layoff', *Journal of Experimental Social Psychology*, 26, 389–407.

Brockner, J., Grover, S., Reed, T.F. and DeWitt, R.L. (1992a) 'Layoffs, job insecurity, and survivors' work effort: evidence on an inverted-U relationship', *Academy of Management Journal*, 32:2, 413–25.

Brockner, J., Tyler, T.R. and Cooper-Schneider, R. (1992b) 'The influence of prior commitment to an institution on reactions to perceived unfairness: the higher they are, the harder they fall', *Administrative Science Quarterly*, 37, 241–61.

Cameron, K.S. (1994a) 'Investigating organizational downsizing: fundamental issues', *Human Resource Management*, 33:2, 183–8.

Cameron, K.S. (1994b) 'Strategies for successful organizational downsizing', *Human Resource Management*, 33:2, 189–211.

Cameron, K.S., Freeman, S.J. and Mishra, A.K. (1991) 'Best practices in white-collar downsizing: managing contradictions', *Academy of Management Executive*, 5:3, 57–73.

Cameron, K.S., Freeman, S.J. and Mishra, A.K. (1993) 'Downsizing and redesigning organizations', *in* Huber, G.P. and Glick, W.H. (eds), *Organizational Change and Redesign*, New York, Oxford University Press, pp. 19–65.

Cascio, W.F. (1993) 'Downsizing: What do we know? What have we learned?', *Academy of Management Executive*, 7:1, 95–104.

Croner's Employment Law Bulletin (1993) *Redundancy rights for individuals*. Issue 18, September, Croner Publications, Kingston-upon-Thames.

Daly, J.P. and Geyer, P.D. (1994) 'The role of fairness in implementing large-scale change: employee evaluations of process and outcome in seven facility relocations', *Journal of Organizational Behaviour*, 15, 623–38.

Davy, J.A., Kinicki, A.J. and Scheck, C.L. (1991) 'Developing and testing a model of survivor responses to layoffs', *Journal of Vocational Behaviour*, 38, 302–17.

Doherty, N. (1998) 'The role of outplacement in redundancy management', *Personnel Review*, 27:4, 343–53.

Duffy v. *Yeomans and Partners Ltd* (1994) Industrial Relations Law Reports, 643.

EIRR (1999) 'Worksharing in Europe – part one', *European Industrial Relations Review*, 300, January, pp. 14–18.

Field, K. (1997) 'Redundancies in Great Britain', *Labour Market Trends*, April, 135–41.

Folger, R. and Cropanzano, R. (1998) *Organizational Justice and Human Resource Management*, London, Sage.

Freeman, S.J. and Cameron, K.S. (1993) 'Organizational downsizing: a convergence and reorientation framework', *Organization Science*, 4:1, 10–29.

Greenberg, J. and Folger, R. (1983) 'Procedural justice, participation, and the fair process effect in groups and organizations', *in* Paulus, P.B. (ed.), *Basic Group Processes*, New York, Springer-Verlag, pp. 235–56.

Greenhalgh, L. (1983) 'Managing the job insecurity crisis', *Human Resource Management*, 22:4, 431–44.

Greenhalgh, L. and Rosenblatt, Z. (1984) 'Job insecurity: toward conceptual clarity', *Academy of Management Review*, 9:3, 438–48.

Guest, D. and Peccei, R. (1992) 'Employee involvement: redundancy as a critical case', *Human Resource Management Journal*, 2:3, 34–59.

Herriot, P. and Pemberton, C. (1996) 'Contracting careers', *Human Relations*, 49:6, 757–90.

IRS (1991) Redundancy 5: Unfair Dismissal, *Industrial Relations Legal Information Bulletin*, 420, London, Industrial Relations Services, 8 March, 2–9.

IRS (1992) Amendment to Collective Redundancies Directive, *Industrial Relations Legal Information Bulletin*, 459, London, Industrial Relations Services, October, 14–15.

IRS (1995) Collective Redundancies and Transfer of Undertakings Regulations 1995, *Industrial Relations Law Bulletin*, 532, London, Industrial Relations Services, November, 14–15.

IRS (1999) Redundancies and Business Transfers Regulations 1999, *Industrial Relations Law Bulletin*, 623, London, Industrial Relations Services, August, 18–19.

Kets de Vries, M.F.R. and Balazs, K. (1997) 'The downside of downsizing', *Human Resources*, 50:1, 11–50.

Kozlowski, S.W., Chao, G.T., Smith, E.M. and Hedlund, J. (1993) 'Organizational downsizing: strategies, interventions, and research implications', *in* Cooper, C.L. and Robertson, I.T. (eds), *International Review of Industrial and Organizational Psychology*, New York, Wiley, pp. 263–332.

Labour Market Trends (2002) 110:5, May, S65.

Lewis, P. (1993) *The Successful Management of Redundancy*, Oxford, Blackwell.

McCune, J.T., Beatty, R.W. and Montagno, R.V. (1988) 'Downsizing: practices in manufacturing firms', *Human Resource Management*, 27:2, 145–61.

Mishra, A.K. and Mishra, K.E. (1994) 'The role of mutual trust in effective downsizing strategies', *Human Resource Management*, 33:2, 261–79.

Overell, S. (1995) 'Non-union firms forced to consult on redundancies', *People Management*, 19 October, 12.

Polkey v. *A E Dayton Services Ltd* (1987) Industrial Relations Law Reports, 503.

Safeway Stores plc v. *Burrell* Employment Appeal Tribunal (1997) Industrial Cases Reports, 523.

Shaw, J.B. and Barrett-Power, E. (1997) 'A conceptual framework for assessing organization, work groups and individual effectiveness during and after downsizing', *Human Relations*, 50:2, 109–27.

Sly, F. (2000) 'Redundancies: enhancing the coherence of Labour Force Survey estimates', *Labour Market Trends*, 108:5, 225–9.

Terryn, B. (1999) 'Redundancies in the United Kingdom', *Labour Market Trends*, 107:5, 251–61.

Thibaut , J. and Walker, L. (1975) *Procedural Justice*, Hillsdale, NJ, Erlbaum.

Thornhill, A. and Gibbons, A. (1995) 'The positive management of redundancy survivors: issues and lessons', *Employee Counselling Today*, 7:3, 5–12.

Thornhill, A., Stead, J. and Gibbons, A. (1997) *Managing Downsizing and Redundancy*, London, Financial Times Pitman Publishing.

Thornhill, A., Lewis, P., Millmore, M. and Saunders, M. (2000) *Managing Change: A human resource strategy*, Harlow, Financial Times Prentice Hall.

Tomasko, R.M. (1992) 'Restructuring: getting it right', *Management Review*, 81:4, 10–15.

Turnbull, P.J. (1988) 'Leaner and possibly fitter: the management of redundancy in Britain', *Industrial Relations Journal*, 19:3, 201–13.

Turnbull, P. and Wass, V. (1997) 'Job insecurity and labour market lemons: the (mis) management of redundancy in steel making, coal mining and port transport', *Journal of Management Studies*, 34:1, 27–51.

Vollmann, T. and Brazas, M. (1993) 'Downsizing', *European Management Journal*, 11:1, 18–29.

Wass, V. (1996) 'Who controls selection under "voluntary" redundancy? The case of the redundant mineworkers payments scheme', *British Journal of Industrial Relations*, 34:2, 249–65.

self-check Answers

12.1 *What are the principal legal requirements associated with proposing to dismiss employees on the grounds of redundancy?*

The principal legal requirements associated with the use of redundancy were summarised as:

- providing information and conducting consultation, with recognised trade unions where these exist, collectively and individually;
- seeking alternatives to redundancy, including redeployment and retraining, as well as permitting time off for those affected to look for alternative work;
- identifying and using fair and lawful selection criteria;
- compensating those who are to be made redundant, through the use of terms that at least match established statutory minima;
- consulting more broadly with the representatives of those affected by the measures taken in connection with the use of redundancies.

12.2 *Think about the organisation for which you work (or have worked), or one about which you have some knowledge. Which strategy or strategies did it use to downsize? Where it used redundancies, how would you categorise these in relation to what you have just read? Evaluate the implications of this strategy or these strategies for the conduct of the employment relationship in this organisation.*

This question asks you to reflect on a downsizing situation of which you have some experience or knowledge in order to analyse the approach used to downsize, to evaluate its impact on the conduct of the employment relationship. In this sense, your response will be specific to the situation that you analyse and evaluate. We hope that in attempting this you will reuse the material in this chapter to deepen your understanding and to reflect further not only on the points that we have included but also on the relationship between theory and practice. Much of the theory in this chapter is empirically based – that is, based on observation and experiment. Because of this, you should be able to 'see' a relationship between the points discussed above and the implications of the strategy or strategies used in the organisation on which you base your analysis and evaluation. This may result in a recognition that the organisation engaged in practices that led to either negative or positive perceptions and outcomes, or perhaps some mixture of the two. Where you are able to identify organisational practices that led to negative outcomes for the conduct of the employment relationship, what would you recommend the organisation to do differently if it were to engage in a further act of organisational downsizing?

The activity associated with this question can usefully be used in a classroom context to provide the basis of a useful discussion.

12.3 *How does the concept of procedural justice and the elements that comprise this relate to the legal requirements associated with proposing to dismiss employees on the grounds of redundancy?*

Hopefully your response will recognise several parallels between elements of procedural justice and the legal requirements related to the use of redundancy. In some ways, this is not surprising, given the way in which law is developed and the fact that organisational justice theory stems from research that had a legal context. Specifically, in the chapter we referred to two factors that have been explored in the context of procedural justice. These relate to the concepts of *voice* and *justification*. Voice has been operationalised through forms of employee involvement or influence in relation to a process, in this case related to the way in which redundancy is applied or used in practice. In the discussion above, we included the following list of points that show how involvement might be achieved in the context of downsizing and redundancy:

- use of consultation and communication about the process;
- scope to influence the choice of selection criteria;
- use of a voluntary, as opposed to a compulsory, route to redundancy;
- affected employees being provided with options about redeployment and relocation;
- provision of outplacement support and facilities;
- use of interventions aimed at allowing survivors to adjust to downsizing related changes.

Several of these points also have a basis in law, as question 12.1 above highlights.

In the chapter, the subsection on the 'provision of information and the conduct of consultation' recognised the legal requirement to provide information that includes the reasons for any proposal to declare redundancies and to engage in meaningful consultation, with a view to reaching agreement. These legal requirements, where applicable, relate to the concept of *justification*, potentially going beyond this where any agreement enjoins the representatives of those affected in the nature of the process to be followed.

12.4 *What are the principal adverse survivors' reactions that have been identified and how may these be moderated?*

Several adverse survivors' reactions have been identified in the literature related to the use of downsizing and redundancy. To help to make sense of these we have categorised them into two broad categories, related to survivors' reactions to an organisation and to those made redundant. Where these reactions are adversely inclined, they will be sympathetic to those made redundant and negative to the organisation (see Figure 12.2). Another way of differentiating between survivors' reactions relates to the distinction between psychological and behavioural reactions, where there is an expectation of a clear relationship between these two types. The determinants of survivors' reactions were related to three further broad categories: the nature of organisational interventions (or the lack of these), psychological or individual differences, and environmental factors. Each of these three may act as a moderating influence on survivors' reactions, with a clear onus on organisations to seek to manage downsizing in ways that alleviate or reduce the incidence of adverse reactions on many of those who remain in employment.

CASE 12   Downsizing at BT[1]

BT has continued to downsize throughout the period from the end of the 1980s, when its workforce stood at nearly a quarter of a million. Through the use of a range of methods, although always avoiding a compulsory approach to redundancy, BT's workforce reduced significantly throughout the 1990s. This change has often been associated with organisational restructuring. For example, the introduction of Project Sovereign in 1990 was designed to promote a more customer-focused culture at BT and involved the use of restructuring, delayering and downsizing. Part of this involved the targeted reduction of 6000 managers and the loss of other posts. From 1992 the *Release Scheme* was used to secure large numbers of voluntary redundancies. By 1991 BT had downsized to about 227 000, including through the use of natural wastage. The Release Scheme, introduced in April 1992 and operated on an annual basis, facilitated large-scale workforce reductions, particularly in its early years of operation. *Release '92* had had a target of 20 000 but, because of concerns that this would not be met, the promotion of this programme combined with the generous terms on offer actually resulted in about 46 000 serious applications, of whom just over 30 000 were accepted (IRS, 1993). Subsequent Release Scheme programmes resulted in further reductions in BT's workforce, so that by 1995 this stood at 135 000 – a reduction of 92 000 in 4 years. Subsequent reductions were more gradual but continuous. At the beginning of 2002, BT's workforce stood at 105 000; in 2003 it is expected to be about 102 000; and it is due to fall below 100 000 in 2004.

This immense reduction has been achieved throughout by the use of enhanced voluntary packages, agreed to by the trade unions that are recognised within BT. Although downsizing has been associated with the generation of some negative survivors' reactions related to loss of colleagues, uncertainty, increased workloads and reduced morale (e.g. IRS, 1993; Doherty *et al.*, 1996), the nature of these events nevertheless led to the creation of a culture of expectation about the right to receive a generous redundancy package. This has been termed an *entitlement culture* within BT. The nature of the voluntary redundancy package remained largely unchanged in BT throughout the 1990s. Its particularly attractive features related to the enhanced severance payments and pensions rights that were offered. For example, staff made redundant aged between 45 and 49 were entitled to an enhanced pension once they reached 50. Those made redundant from 50 years of age were able to receive a pension immediately. Such enhancements resulted in $6\frac{2}{3}$ years of pension entitlement being added at a cost that was borne by the company. Employees responded to the regularity of downsizing and the terms being offered by envisaging a personal date at which they would like to leave the organisation. This would be likely to be between the ages of 45 and 60. It also became common in BT to see copies of the redundancy terms chart pinned up in employees' work areas.

However, the financial cost to BT of securing large-scale downsizing through this means became considerable, and one of a number of strategic issues with which it has had to deal. In relation to its external operating environment, BT has recently undergone several major shifts in its strategy. The cost of acquiring 3G

---

[1] The assistance of Bob Green (BT Group) in the preparation of this case is gratefully acknowledged.

mobile licences and making other investments led to a debt level of £27.9 billion in March 2001 (BT Group, 2002). BT subsequently made a number of major strategic changes, including demerging mmO2; unwinding Concert, its international joint venture with AT&T, which operates in the global communications sector, and reintegrating this provision over which it now has direct control; and disposing of Yell, its international directories and ecommerce business. These changes contributed to the reduction of BT's debt to £13.7 billion by 31 March 2002 (BT Group, 2002). In April 2000 it had also begun a radical restructuring of the organisation, which involved grouping its activities according to the market sectors within which it operated (BT, 2001). In terms of the current BT group, this led to the creation of a number of businesses: BT Retail, BT Wholesale, BT Ignite, BT Openworld and BT exact (BT Group, 2002). These lines of business are seen to be capable of delivering growth and being profitable.

The improved pension longevity combined with a downturn in the investment market has led to many UK pension funds, BT included, having to fund an actuarial deficit. In addition, the cumulative cost to BT's pension schemes from generous voluntary redundancy packages had led to the issue of what is known as *pension strain*. In simple terms, where the amount of money being paid out of a pension scheme exceeds the amount being contributed, this will result in some measure of pension strain. The greater the shortfall, the greater the level of strain. This situation has recently been exacerbated by factors such as changes to the accountancy reporting regulations, which mean that company payments into a pension fund to finance enhanced entitlements have to be disclosed in the year the liability arises. Pension strain was therefore becoming a more significant and visible burden, leading to the need for the company to make annual top-up payments, which required changes to be made to the levels of benefit associated with voluntary severance from BT.

There were, however, other reasons for BT to review its previous approach to offering generously enhanced redundancy terms. The company had identified a number of human resource objectives that it wished to achieve and which included:

- changing the company culture to one of *reskilling*;
- creating a balanced and flexible workforce;
- supporting future human resource requirements;
- supporting BT's diversity strategy through the creation of an age profile that more closely matched that outside the company.

These objectives were in addition to the desire to end the culture that had developed in the company of expecting to leave with an enhanced package; and the need to reduce the cost of financing BT's pension schemes in particular and organisational costs in general. These objectives led to the introduction of a new programme in February 2001, called *NewStart*, which aimed to deal with severance, human resource deployment and retraining in a more integrated way. NewStart was based on six principles:

- that in the first instance BT will redeploy/reskill surplus people;
- that voluntary redundancy terms would only be available where reskilling or reallocation of work were not feasible;

- that new 'leaver payments' would be permitted only where there is mutual agreement between a manager and an employee that he or she may leave;
- that pension packages should become progressively cheaper;
- that line managers should become aware of the implications of the costs of granting an entitlement to leave through devolving costs;
- that the terms and the full business cost of any enhanced leaving package available for the next 2 years should become visible to all employees through the design of the NewStart website that was introduced to support this programme.

The NewStart website was designed to allow managers and other employees to obtain not only an estimate of their leaver terms if they were eligible but also the cost of additional contributions that would have to paid into the pension scheme. This second amount allows managers to understand the costs that would have to be taken out of their operating budgets where they agree to allow an employee, or employees, to leave. Such costs are likely to run into tens of thousands of pounds, or to be in excess of £100 000, per employee. The effect of this change is therefore to make line managers fully responsible for the financial decisions that they take.

NewStart also involved progressively reducing the levels of pension eligibility and enhancement that would be available to those who would still be allowed to leave, while continuing to make these sufficiently attractive. From April 2001, the age at which leavers would be eligible to qualify for a pension was raised from 50 to 52 years old; from October 2001 this was raised again to 55. Levels of pension enhancement were also reduced from the previous maximum of $6\frac{2}{3}$ years, which had operated throughout the 1990s, to a new maximum of 5 added years, from October 2001. From 1 July 2002 pension enhancement, through adding years of entitlement, was abolished altogether.

These changes are designed to eliminate the entitlement culture that had developed whereby employees generally left the organisation with a voluntary redundancy package. The cost saving from this change is projected to run into hundreds of millions of pounds, reducing the level of pension strain considerably. Although the principle of voluntary severance is preserved, with the workforce likely to reduce by about 5000 per annum in 2004 and 2005, the emphasis has shifted to retaining and reskilling employees where possible, and reducing costs associated with downsizing to more manageable levels. Through the 1990s, BT's approach to seeking volunteers for redundancy had become increasingly sophisticated by developing a highly selective and targeted approach, to avoid the issues that it had confronted in 1992 when it had used a general and unfocused trawl among all its employees for volunteers. Its current approach may be seen as a further development of this increasingly selective and targeted approach to secure leavers and retain others. The new approach, associated with NewStart, is focused on retaining 'skilled, experienced and committed people, and maintaining "corporate intelligence" that would otherwise be lost.' Other outcomes from this new approach have included the retention of a more varied and older workforce; in particular, its age profile shows a sharp rise in the proportion of those aged between 50 and 60 years of age. These changes have also been made with the support of the recognised trades unions within BT, who also have a 50 per cent representation on the board that oversees the pension schemes within the company.

Questions

1 Using BT as an example, what linkages are evident between organisational strategy and downsizing strategy?

2 How are the changes outlined in the case study likely to affect the nature of the employment relationship in BT?

3 In particular, how are these changes likely to affect the relationship between line managers and employees who are considering leaving BT?

4 The recognised trade unions in BT have been supportive of the approach taken to downsizing within the company. Why do you think this has been the case?

References

BT (2001) *BT Annual Review 2001: Looking back on last year and forward to the future*, London, British Telecommunications plc.

BT Group (2002) *BT Group Annual Review 2002*, London, BT Group plc.

Doherty, N., Bank, J. and Vinnicombe, S. (1996) 'Managing survivors: The experience of survivors in British Telecom and the British financial services sector', *Journal of Managerial Psychology*, 11:7, 51–60.

IRS (1993) 'Natural selection: BT's programme of voluntary redundancy', *IRS Employment Trends 533*, April, 11–15.

Appendices

Glossary

Advisory, Conciliation and Arbitration Service (ACAS) Independent public body in the UK established in 1974. Its role is to provide advice, prevent and resolve disputes between employees and their employers through conciliation, mediation or arbitration, and seek to build harmonious relationships at work.

appraisal-related pay *See* individual performance-related pay.

arbitration Involves the parties jointly asking a third party to make an award that they undertake to accept in settlement of the dispute.

artefact Manifestation of a culture that is relatively easy to discern but from which the true meaning is difficult to decipher because of its shallow or superficial nature. Material objects, physical arrangements, patterns of behaviour, stories and jokes are often described as artefacts. *See also* symbol.

authority (within an organisation) The exercise of power that is legitimised and defined by a person's formal position within an organisation's hierarchy.

bad and ugly employers Employers who exhibit highly unsophisticated management practices based on the direct coercive control of employees and who are likely to have few procedures to reconcile the worst effects of the antagonism resulting from such practices.

bargained corporatism Situation in which trade union power is strong, based on the ideas of social partnership and maintaining harmony through the trade-offs or 'bargains' that occur between different interest groups while the government has a corporatist ideology. *See also* corporatism.

bargaining agent The organisation appointed to represent the bargaining units; usually a trade union or, possibly, an independent staff association.

bargaining form The form in which the collective agreement is expressed (e.g. in writing).

bargaining level The level at which collective bargaining takes place, e.g. national multi-employer level, national single-employer level, regional level or workplace level.

bargaining scope Defines the subjects to be covered in the collective agreement (e.g. pay, hours, holidays and redundancy) and the way in which they will be covered (e.g. negotiation or consultation).

bargaining unit The group of employees to be covered by a particular collective agreement.

basic underlying assumption An implicit, deep-rooted unconsciously held assumption that people share but which is invisible and, as a consequence, difficult to discover. Such assumptions are so taken for granted that there is little or no variation within a culture. They provide the base upon which the more visible manifestations of a culture are built.

capability procedures The discipline procedure often has a separate aspect dedicated to dealing with poor employee performance as opposed to misconduct. Poor performance may be evident when an employee does not have the ability to achieve the standards set by the manager. The capability procedure is so designed to give that employee every opportunity (usually after remedial training) to reach the required performance standard before any disciplinary action is taken.

Central Arbitration Committee Independent, statutory body in the UK whose functions relate to the statutory recognition and derecognition of trade unions, determining disputes between unions and employers over the disclosure of information for collective bargaining purposes, claims and complaints regarding the establishment and operation of European Works Councils in Great Britain, and voluntary arbitration in industrial disputes.

certification officer Independent, statutory official in the UK whose functions relate to the status and legal responsibilities of trade unions and employers' associations.

code of practice Employment codes of practice relate to issues such as discipline and picketing. Failure to observe any provisions of these codes does not in itself render a person liable to legal proceedings. However, in proceedings before an employment tribunal the content of a code is admissible as evidence, and any provision of a code that appears to the tribunal to be relevant to any question arising in the proceedings is required to be taken into account in determining that question.

co-determination Form of participation where employees or their unions jointly determine organisational decisions. May be used to indicate a situation where employees make up half of the membership of a supervisory board.

collective agreement The outcome of the collective bargaining process; may be defined as an agreement between a trade union(s) and an employer(s) that determines, among other things, the terms and conditions of employment of the employees of the employer who is party to the agreement.

collective bargaining Voluntary, formalised process by which employers and independent trade unions negotiate, for specified groups of employees, terms and conditions of employment and the ways in which certain employment-related issues are to be regulated at national, organisational and workplace levels.

collective conciliation Voluntary process whereby employers, trade unions and worker representatives can be helped to reach mutually acceptable settlements of their disputes by an impartial and independent third party.

collectivism Refers to the employee subordinating her spirit of self-reliance to the collective interests of the workgroup, whether at workplace, company or national level. Such subordination may be by individual choice, the employee deciding that his own interests are best served by banding together with individuals in a similar situation to him. Alternatively, it may be that the individual has little choice as his employer is already part of an arrangement where the employees' interests are progressed through a collective arrangement.

communication *See* disclosure of information, dissemination of information.

competence-related pay Method of rewarding people wholly or partly by reference to the level of competence they demonstrate in carrying out their roles.

constructive dismissal *See* dismissal – constructive.

consultation *See* joint consultation.

contract of employment Formed when an offer of employment is made and is accepted. This may be called a contract *of* service and those who work under it are defined as 'employees'. On the other hand, those workers who work under a contract *for* services are normally thought of as being self-employed.

core worker Employee who has secure employment with an organisation and is likely to have been trained by that organisation to have a variety of specific skills and experience that cannot be bought in easily.

corporatism Ideology based on a belief that social and economic aspects of life are interrelated and that political influence and regulation should be used to manage the employment relationship. In particular the operation of the marketplace must be constrained through interventionist regulation to allow social justice.

culture *See* organisational culture.

custom and practice An established practice at a particular workplace that is so familiar that it may be incorporated into an employee's contract of employment. The introduction of arrangements that are radically different from custom and practice may be seen to be in contravention of the customary terms of employment.

decentralised collective bargaining The process of pushing the responsibility for collective bargaining down from a 'higher' level (e.g. national) to a 'lower' level (e.g. the workplace).

decision-making function This view of collective bargaining conceptualises it as a way in which employees, through their trade unions, participate in the decisions that affect their working lives.

direct control This management strategy of control involves close supervision of employees, a harsher regime of discipline characterised by threats of, say, pay reduction or dismissal. It also entails minimising the individual responsibility given to employees.

direct participation *See* employee involvement.

discipline Action instigated by management against an employee who fails to meet reasonable and legitimate expectations in terms of performance, conduct or adherence to rules.

disclosure of information Requirement, usually statutory, for management to provide a particular type, or types, of information to employees, their representatives or trade unions.

dismissal The terminating of an employee's contract of employment by an employer with or without notice, when a fixed-term contract expires or when the conduct of the employer forces the employee to terminate the contract of employment.

dismissal – constructive The terminating of an employee's contract with or without notice by the employee in circumstances in which she or he is entitled on account of the employer's conduct.

dismissal – potentially fair The terminating of an employee's contract by an employer for one or more of the five potentially fair reasons stated in the Employment Rights Act 1996: (a) misconduct, (b) incapability or lack of qualifications, (c) redundancy, (d) continued employment in breach of statute, (e) some other substantial reason.

dismissal – summary The terminating of an employee's contract by an employer without notice.

dismissal – unfair The terminating of an employee's contract of employment by an employer for a reason other than one or more of the five potentially fair reasons stated in the Employment Rights Act 1996.

dismissal – wrongful The unlawful breaching of an employee's contract of employment by an employer, thereby terminating it outside its terms.

dispute of interest Disagreement over what an agreement between employers and employees (or their representatives) ought to contain.

dispute of right Disagreement over what an agreement between employers and employees (or their representatives) actually means.

dissemination of information Situation where an organisation voluntarily informs its employees about any matter concerning itself. Dissemination of information is linked with employee involvement and aimed at developing employees' identification with, as well as commitment and contribution to, their employing organisation.

distancing flexibility *See* flexibility – distancing.

distributive justice Theory concerned with perceptions about the fairness of organisational allocations and outcomes. *See also* procedural justice, interactional justice.

downsizing *See* organisational downsizing.

employability The ability to gain initial employment, maintain employment and move between jobs and roles within the same organisation, and obtain new employment by moving between organisations and being independent in the labour market. Consequently the skills an individual possesses are likely to be key in both gaining and maintaining employability.

employee communication *See* disclosure of information, dissemination of information.

employee consultation *See* joint consultation.

employee involvement Unitarist and business-centred concept, fostered by employer and managerial interests, designed to generate employee commitment and contribution. Employee involvement encompasses a range of practices that are focused directly on employees, including forms of communicative involvement, task-level involvement and financial involvement, and is affected by managerial actions and styles of leadership.

employee participation Power-centred concept, advanced by trade unions and through legislation in some cases, which takes three principal forms: board-level representation; joint regulation of employment issues; and joint consultation where this allows for the meaningful consideration of employees' views about managerial proposals.

employer regulation Attempt by an employer to regulate the employment relationship unilaterally.

employers' association Collective organisation of employers; defined in UK law as an organisation, whether temporary or permanent, that consists wholly or mainly of employers whose main purpose includes the regulation of relations between these employers and workers or trade unions.

Employment Appeals Tribunal Independent judicial body that hears appeals against the decisions of employment tribunals.

employment relationship Economic, legal, social, psychological and political relationship in which employees devote their time and expertise to the interests of their employer in return for a range of personal financial and non-financial rewards.

employment tribunal Independent judicial body that adjudicates on claims that employees have been unfairly treated by their employers. Employment tribunals were formerly known as industrial tribunals.

espoused value A value of a culture connected with moral and ethical codes that determines what people think ought to be done, rather than what they necessarily will do.

European Trade Union Confederation (ETUC) The major representative body of the trade union movement in Europe. The ETUC is recognised by the European Union, the Council of Europe and the European Free Trade Association as the representative body of the trade union movement at the European level, and as one of the Social Partners at the European social dialogue process.

European Works Council (EWC) Representative body involving employee representatives established in 'Community-scale' companies for the purpose of information sharing and consultation.

express statements of the parties to the contract of employment These may be contained in the written statement of terms and conditions or have been expressed either orally or in writing.

fair dismissal *See* dismissal – potentially fair.

felt-fairness Refers to subjective perceptions that employees have about their pay level or other aspects of their organisational treatment in comparison with other individuals and employee groups.

financial flexibility *See* flexibility – financial.

flexibility – distancing The use of subcontractors to replace employees, thereby distancing workers from the organisation.

flexibility – financial The ability to allow pay to reflect differences in supply and demand for different groups in the labour market. This is commonly termed 'pay flexibility'.

flexibility – functional The redeployment of employees to match tasks required.

flexibility – numerical Changing the number of hours worked by employees in line with fluctuations in organisational demand for their labour.

functional flexibility *See* flexibility – functional.

gainsharing Plans designed so that employees share the employer's financial results of improvements in productivity, cost saving or quality. The resultant payment is paid from cost savings generated as a result of such improvements.

governmental function View of collective bargaining that conceptualises it as a political process in which the collective agreement is the body of law, determined by the management/union negotiators who act as the legislature, with executive authority vested in management, who must exercise it in accordance with the terms of the constitution.

grievances Complaints that are presented formally to management or a union official through the use of a recognised procedure.

gross misconduct Any serious misconduct by the employee that destroys the employment relationship.

harassment Conduct related to age, creed, disability, nationality, race, religion, sex or any other personal characteristics that is unwanted by the individual and that affects the dignity of any individual or group of individuals, at work.

Health and Safety Commission (HSC) Statutory, tripartite body in the UK consisting of ten commissioners whose role is to introduce arrangements for the health, safety and welfare of people at work and for the public from the way in which businesses and organisations operate.

Health and Safety Executive (HSE) Statutory body in the UK responsible for the enforcement of health and safety law.

high-commitment management practices Involves such HRM techniques as employee communication, employee involvement and profit sharing, designed to generate high employee performance and commitment to the job and the organisation.

implied, or common law, duties Apply to both employees and employers and are part of the contract of employment. These duties are derived from the principles developed by the courts over the last 100 years. The cases that have created these duties are ones where the points of law have been complex to interpret. In the event, the judgments made in these cases have led to decisions that clarify the law and act as precedents for later, and more junior, courts to follow.

indirect participation *See* employee participation.

individual performance-related pay Method of payment whereby an individual employee receives increases in pay based wholly or partly on the regular and systematic assessment of job performance.

Individualism Refers to the will of the individual to look after her own interests rather than relying on another person or body to do this for her and the desire of the employer to deal with his employees in the way he thinks fit without outside interference.

industrial action Term that may be applied to a variety of means where individual employees or collective groups of employees express their dissatisfaction with their treatment by their employer.

information disclosure *See* disclosure of information.

information dissemination *See* dissemination of information.

interactional justice Theory concerned with perceptions about the fairness of interpersonal treatment during the implementation of decisions, related to the explanations and justification offered for these decisions and the sensitivity of treatment of those affected. *See also* distributive justice, procedural justice.

interventionism *See* corporatism.

joint consultation Process whereby management and employees or their representatives, who may or may not represent a trade union, meet to consider and discuss employment-related issues. The extent of employee influence in any decision-making process that relates to such consultation is key to understanding its role in the regulation of the employment relationship.

Joint regulation Regulation of the employment relationship (or particular aspects of this) by an employer and a trade union or unions.

Keynesianism Approach concerned with managing the demand side of the economy that aims to promote full employment, price stability, balance of payments equilibrium and economic growth through the use of government fiscal interventions.

laissez-faire Ideology characterised by a free market economy within which competition for goods, services and labour is the basis for regulating society. Consequently, an individual is responsible for her or his well-being rather than this being provided by the state.

liberal collectivism Situation in which employees are organised and have collective economic power through trade unions while the government has a *laissez-faire* ideology. In such a situation, a government may adopt a voluntarist approach or a pluralist approach. *See also laissez-faire*, pluralism, voluntarism.

management style In the context of employee relations, the preferred way of dealing with employees individually or collectively.

managerial regulation Attempt by the management of an organisation to regulate the employment relationship unilaterally.

market function View of collective bargaining that conceptualises it as a market-place where employers and employees meet together to negotiate the price at which labour will be bought and sold.

market individualism Situation in which employees are relatively unorganised and subordinate to a market within which they are little more than a commodity to be bought and sold, while the government has a *laissez-faire* ideology. *See also laissez-faire.*

Marxism View of employee relations that stresses that class conflict is the source of societal change – without such conflict the society would stagnate. Such class conflict arises primarily from the disparity in the distribution of, and access to, economic power within the society – the principal disparity being between those who own capital and those who supply their labour.

mediation Process whereby a third party (e.g. ACAS) works jointly with employers, employees and employee representatives to help to overcome problems that threaten to damage the employment relationship or that constitute a major obstacle to organisational effectiveness.

mobilisation of bias Related to the exercise of power, this arises where the issues and grievances of some groups in an organisation are not considered and thus remain outside its formal decision-making processes.

monetarism Approach concerned with ensuring that the supply side of the economy works efficiently, based upon the argument that if the monetary system is well regulated and inflation is controlled by government, the rest of the economy will be self-regulated by market forces, resulting in economic prosperity.

multi-employer bargaining National multi-employer agreements are negotiated between national trade unions and employers' associations and cover employees of a given description in a specified industry or sub-industry.

multi-unionism (1) Situation where each occupational group in a workplace is organised by a different union. (2) Situation where two or more unions compete for membership within a particular group of workers.

mutuality Situation where employers and employees share goals and agree on the means to achieve these goals.

National Minimum Wage Introduced in the UK in 1999; sets a minimum level below which low-paid workers should not fall. In 2002 this level was £4.10 per hour for those over 21 and £3.50 for those between 18 and 21.

negative deindustrialisation Decline in the number of people in manufacturing employment due to a decline in production capacity.

negotiation Process whereby two or more interested groups seek to reconcile their differences through attempts to persuade the other group to move from their initial position, with the overall aim of reaching an agreement.

non-pay benefits Examples of these are pension schemes, extra-statutory sick pay, other health and medical insurances, extra-statutory redundancy pay, loans, house purchase assistance and recreational facilities.

numerical flexibility *See* flexibility – numerical.

organisational culture 'The patterns of beliefs, values and learned ways of coping with experiences that have developed during the course of an organisation's history, and which tend to be manifested in its material arrangements and in the behaviours of its members' (Brown, 1998: 9).

organisational downsizing Organisational strategy to reduce the size of an organisation's workforce; may use a range of methods including early retirements, natural wastage and voluntary and compulsory redundancy to achieve this outcome.

organisational justice Set of related theories focusing on perceptions about fairness in organisations, which seek to categorise and explain the views and feelings of employees about their own treatment and that of others within an organisation. *See also* distributive justice, procedural justice, interactional justice.

organisational rules Often contained in an employing organisation's personnel handbook or equivalent publication and given to employees upon commencement of their employment.

partnership Approach to trade union recognition and involvement in an employing organisation, where there is a joint commitment by management and union to work for its successful development, implying a model of mutual gain for the employer, employees and union.

payment by results Such schemes are perhaps the simplest form of individual incentive scheme because they relate the pay of individuals to the quantity of their output.

peripheral worker (peripheral group I) Employee who, although employed on a full-time basis by an organisation, has less security than core employees as her or his job is either de-skilled or does not require organisation-specific skills.

peripheral worker (peripheral group II) Employee on temporary and part-time rather than full-time contract.

picketing Process of peacefully obtaining or communicating information or peacefully persuading a person to work or not to work.

piecework schemes Among the most traditional forms of bonus schemes. They pay employees according to the number of 'pieces' of work produced.

pluralism A way of thinking about employee relations that conceptualises the organisation as being a 'miniature democratic state composed of sectional groups with divergent interests over which government tries to maintain some kind of dynamic equilibrium' (Fox, 1966: 2). The most fundamental of these sectional groups is managers and employees. An understanding of the central tenets of pluralism is vital to an understanding of employee relations because many of the institutions, principles, procedures, processes and practices that exist to manage the employment relationship are based on the principle of pluralism.

positive deindustrialisation Decline in the number of people in manufacturing employment due to efficiency gains rather than any decline in production capacity.

power Often defined in terms of one person having 'power over' others, stressing the ability of a person to get others to do what he or she wants, including acting against their will or doing something they wouldn't do otherwise. The concept of power has been analysed further in relation to its different dimensions, types and bases.

procedural justice Theory concerned with perceptions about the fairness of the procedures and processes used to arrive at organisational decisions. *See also* distributive justice, interactional justice.

procedural terms Those terms of the collective agreement that set out the rules and procedures to be used by both sides in regulating the conduct of the employment relationship and bargaining arrangements.

process control The ability to exercise influence during the process of reaching a decision by those who are to be affected by it.

profit-related pay Payment system whereby part of the pay of the employee is linked to the profit of the employing organisation.

psychological contract The expectations of employee and employer, which operate in addition to the formal contract of employment. It therefore is concerned with each party's perceptions of what the other party to the employment relationship owes them. *See also* relational term, transactional term.

redundancy Defined in UK law as a dismissal due, wholly or mainly, to the complete closure of a business; the closure of the employee's workplace; or a diminishing need for employees to do work of a particular kind in the business as a whole, or at the employee's particular workplace.

relational term Aspect of the psychological contract between an employee and an employer that focuses upon mutual trust and commitment.

resignation Termination of the employment contract by an employee, usually prior to taking up other employment.

responsible autonomy Attempt by the employer to mobilise labour power by giving employees the opportunity to have control over their own work situations in a manner that benefits the organisation. In order to achieve this managers give employees status, authority and responsibility. Managers seek to win employee loyalty and attempt to get employees to adopt the goals of the organisation.

retirement Termination of the employment contract and the working career at a certain age by an employee, usually with the expectation that she or he will no longer take paid employment.

Save-As-You-Earn (SAYE) (or savings-related share option schemes) This scheme requires a contribution from the employee. In such schemes, the employee saves for a specified period of 3, 5 or 7 years. The scheme specifies that employees can buy shares at the end of the savings period using the savings fund accumulated. The price of the shares will be the market price at the start of the savings contract or at a discount agreed at the start of the contract. The shares bought at the end of the savings contract attract tax relief.

scientific management Approach to management that sees managers setting clear goals and objectives for employees, organising work duties rationally in order to maximise efficiency, and specifying every detail so that everyone will be sure of the jobs that they have to perform. The founder of scientific management, F.W. Taylor, believed that there was 'one best way' to perform each task.

secondary action Industrial action taken by workers whose employer is not a party to the trade dispute to which the action relates. Usually called sympathy action where workers of one employer take sympathy action in support of a separate dispute between workers and a different employer.

secret ballot In order for a strike to be potentially lawful there must be a secret ballot in which all affected employees have the opportunity of voting by post.

share incentive plans (SIPs) Introduced in the 2000 Finance Bill. Before October 2001 they were known as all-employee share ownership plans (AESOPs). In SIPs the employee may purchase, or is given, shares in the employing organisation. Employees who keep their shares in the scheme for 5 years pay no income tax or National Insurance contributions on the shares.

shop stewards *See* workplace representatives.

single-table bargaining Strategy to cope with the presence of several recognised unions in a workplace by arranging to negotiate jointly with these unions 'around a single table'.

single-union agreement Situation where agreement has been reached between an employing organisation and a trade union for this particular union to represent all relevant employees for collective bargaining and representation purposes.

skill-based pay System of pay whereby employees are rewarded in relation to skills gained as a result of training course completion, satisfactory performance in tests leading to company accreditation, or the attainment of NVQ levels.

SMEs Small and medium-sized enterprises.

sophisticated moderns – constitutionalists (management style) Constitutionalist managers have a similar set of values to the traditionalists. They would prefer to run the organisation without the presence of trade unions. However, these organisations are often large and operate in areas of the economy where there is a tradition of unionisation and where union organisation is strong, so they are obliged to recognise trade unions. This approach develops regulatory mechanisms that are designed to institutionalise conflict.

sophisticated moderns – consultors (management style) The attitude of managers adopting this management style is generally positive to trade unions, founded on the principle that workplace unions can help in the management of the employment relationship. This help may be particularly important when management want to introduce significant change, for example in working patterns. Unions act as a 'voice' of employees, and therefore serve as a convenient channel of communication with the workforce.

sophisticated paternalists (management style) Managers with such a style adopt an essentially unitary stance. They are generally thought to be good employers because they look after their employees in a paternalistic way. This approach seeks to develop employee involvement in and commitment to the organisation, and opposes any suggestion to recognise a trade union.

standard modern (management style) In this management style managing employment relations is likely to be seen as a major issue for consideration only when it is a problem. Trade unions will be recognised, although management's attitude to dealing with unions is likely to be ambivalent. There is not likely to be a clear employment relations strategy, and the approach is more likely to be ad hoc, pragmatic, perhaps incoherent and based on fire-fighting.

state corporatism Situation in which trade unions are politically subordinated or suppressed while the government has maintained long-term dominance and a corporatist ideology.

statism Situation in which trade union power is industrially weak or marginalised while the government has a corporatist ideology. In order to redress the balance of power between employers and employees the government intervenes in the employment relationship, legislating to establish terms and conditions for employees.

statutory regulation Aspects of the employment relationship governed by legislation.

structured antagonism Principle, closely related to pluralism, that assumes that the relationship between employers and employees has the potential for conflict, as the parties seek fundamentally different things from the relationship.

substantive terms Those terms of the collective agreement that concern the content or substantive issues of employment, e.g. pay and hours of work.

summary dismissal *See* dismissal – summary.

symbol Manifestation of a culture that is relatively easy to discern but from which the true meaning is difficult to decipher because of its shallow or superficial nature. Material objects, physical layouts, and events are often described as symbols. *See also* artefact.

team-based pay Here payments, or other forms of non-financial reward, are made to team members on the basis of some predetermined criteria. These criteria may reflect some difference of individual contribution to the team's performance.

termination The ending of an employment contract between an employee and his or her employer.

Third Way The approach adopted by New Labour in 1998 to reconcile a liberalist ideology's emphasis on economic efficiency and dynamism with a more corporatist concern for equality, integration and social inclusion.

trade dispute Legal term. In order for a strike (or similar action) to be potentially lawful it must be wholly or mainly about employment-related matters such as pay and conditions.

trade union Collective organisation of employees that may be defined in relation to its functions to protect its members' interests and to participate in job regulation with employers. Defined in UK law as an organisation, whether temporary or permanent, that consists wholly or mainly of workers and whose main purpose is the regulation of relations between these workers and employers or employers' associations.

trade union recognition The decision by an employer to enter into an agreement whereby a trade union will represent some or all of that employer's employees for a range of purposes. These are likely to include collective bargaining and representation in relation to disciplinary and grievance matters, on consultative bodies and for other employment-related issues.

trade union regulation Attempt by a trade union to determine particular conditions of employment unilaterally and to impose these on an employer.

Trades Union Congress (TUC) Representative body of the trade union movement in the UK, with approximately 70 affiliated unions that collectively represent the considerable majority of union members.

traditionalist (management style) Managers with such a style treat their employees as just another factor of production, much as they would treat plant and machinery. This approach is authoritarian, and the unionisation of the workforce would be strongly opposed.

transactional term Aspect of the psychological contract between an employee and an employer that focuses upon the mutual instrumentality of the work–effort reward bargain.

tribunal *See* employment tribunal.

unemployed Those people in the labour force who are not in work. Unemployment is usually recorded only for those not in work who are claiming unemployment benefit. This figure is often expressed as the percentage of the total labour force.

unfair dismissal *See* dismissal – unfair.

union density The unionised workforce expressed as a percentage of potential membership. Union densities may be calculated in relation to the total in employment, for particular industries, sectors, occupations and workplaces, or in relation to individual and job-related characteristics.

union derecognition 'A decision to withdraw from collective bargaining in favour of other arrangements for regulating employment relations' (Claydon, 1989: 215).

Union of Industrial and Employers' Confederations of Europe (UNICE) The major representative body of employers and business in Europe, recognised by the European Union as one of the Social Partners at the European social dialogue process.

union official (1) Full-time official employed by a trade union at a national or regional level. (2) *See* workplace representatives.

unionateness Concept developed to characterise differences between trade unions. It provides a means to measure the extent to which a trade union uses, or is prepared to use, the full range of potential union methods including collective bargaining and forms of industrial action.

unitarism A way of thinking about employee relations that conceptualises the organisation 'as a team unified by a common purpose', with that common purpose being the success of the organisation. As all employees are assumed to be pursuing the same goal, conflict is seen as irrational: where it occurs it would be seen as the result of poor communication or 'troublemakers' at work who do not share the common purpose as defined by the organisation's management.

unofficial industrial action Situation where workers simply 'walk off the job', irrespective of any role that may be played by trade union officials. In such circumstances the union officials must repudiate the action of the union's members in writing if they do not want to be associated with the action and render the union liable to action taken by the employer.

voice The opportunity for the subjects of organisational decisions to participate in the process of arriving at, including being able to influence, these decisions.

voluntarism Approach adopted by a government in which employees (usually represented by trade unions) and employers are allowed to make decisions regarding matters concerning the management of the employment relationship. Voluntarism is a form of self-determination based on the principle of non-intervention.

voluntary arbitration Scheme drawn up by the Advisory, Conciliation and Arbitration Service to provide an alternative procedure to employment tribunals for straightforward claims that employees have been unfairly treated by their employers. *See also* Advisory, Conciliation and Arbitration Service.

whistle blowing Situation where an employee disapproves of an aspect of the employer's policy or action and reveals this to a party such as a newspaper in order that the employer's policy or action may be exposed to public scrutiny.

work-measured schemes Schemes whereby whole tasks, or parts of tasks, have a 'standard time' defined for their completion. Bonus is related to the difference between the actual time taken to perform the task and the standard time.

workplace representatives Lay officials of a trade union, sometimes referred to as shop stewards or staff representatives.

wrongful dismissal *See* dismissal – wrongful.

References

Brown, A. (1998) *Organisational Culture* (2nd edn), London, Financial Times Pitman Publishing.

Claydon, T. (1989) 'Union derecognition in Britain in the 1980s', *British Journal of Industrial Relations*, 27:2, 214–24.

Fox, A. (1966) *Industrial sociology and industrial relations*, Royal Commission Research Paper No. 3, London, HMSO.

Abbreviations

ACAS	Advisory, Conciliation and Arbitration Service
AEEU	Amalgamated Engineering and Electrical Union
AESOP	all-employee share ownership plan
BIFU	Banking, Insurance and Finance Union
CAC	Central Arbitration Committee
CBI	Confederation of British Industry
CEEP	European Centre for Public Enterprises and Services of General Economic Interest
CGB	Christlicher Gewerkschaftsbund (Christian Federation of Trade Unions, Germany)
CIPD	Chartered Institute of Personnel and Development
COHSE	Confederation of Health Service Employees
CPSA	Civil and Public Services Association
CRE	Commission for Racial Equality
CRM	customer relationship management
DAG	Deutsche Angestelltengewerkschaft (German Salaried Employees' Union)
DBB	Deutscher Beamtenbund (German Civil Servants' Federation)
DfES	Department for Education and Skills
DGB	Deutscher Gewerkschaftsbund (German Trade Union Confederation)
DWP	Department for Work and Pensions
EAT	Employment Appeal Tribunal
EEA	European Economic Area
EEF	Engineering Employers' Federation
EFTPOS	electronic funds transfer at point of sale
EPOS	electronic point of sale
ETUC	European Trade Union Confederation
EU	European Union
EWC	European Works Council
FBU	Fire Brigades Union
FSB	Federation of Small Businesses
GCHQ	Government Communication Headquarters
GPMU	Graphical, Paper and Media Union
HR	human resources
HRM	human resources management
HSC	Health and Safety Commission
HSE	Health and Safety Executive
ICFTU	International Confederation of Free Trade Unions

IPD	Institute of Personnel and Development
IPRP	individual performance-related pay
ITB	Industrial Training Board
JCC	joint consultative committee
LEA	local education authority
LFS	Labour Force Survey
LIFO	last in, first out
LSC	Learning and Skills Council
MSC	Manpower Services Commission
MSF	Manufacturing Science and Finance Union
NALGO	National and Local Government Officers Association
NCU	National Communications Union
NEDC	National Economic Development Council
NGA	National Graphical Association
NMW	National Minimum Wage
NUPE	National Union of Public Employees
OPEC	Organisation of Petroleum Exporting Countries
PBR	payment by results
PFI	Private Finance Initiative
PPP	public–private partnership
PSBR	Public Sector Borrowing Requirement
PTC	Public Services Tax and Commerce Union
RCN	Royal College of Nursing of the United Kingdom
SAYE	save-as-you-earn
SIP	share incentive plan
SMEs	small and medium-sized enterprises
SNB	special negotiating body
SOGAT	Society of Graphical and Allied Trades
TEC	Training and Enterprise Council
TGWU	Transport and General Workers' Union
TUC	Trades Union Congress
TUPE	Transfer of Undertaking of Prior Employment
UAPME	European Association of Craft, Small and Medium-Sized Enterprises
UDEA	Universities and Colleges Employers' Association
UCW	Union of Communication Workers
UNICE	Union of Industrial and Employers' Confederations of Europe
USDAW	Union of Shop, Distributive and Allied Workers
WERS	Workplace Employee Relations Survey

Statutes, regulations and EU directives

■ Statutes

Trades Disputes Act 1906
Redundancy Payments Act 1965
Trades Disputes Act 1965
Equal Pay Act 1970
Industrial Relations Act 1971
Health and Safety at Work etc. Act 1974
Trade Union and Labour Relations Act 1974
Employment Protection Act 1975
Sex Discrimination Act 1975
Trade Union and Labour Relations (Amendment) Act 1976
Race Relations Act 1976
Local Government Planning and Land Act 1980
Employment Act 1980
Employment Act 1982
Trade Union Act 1984
Employment Act 1984
Housing Act 1985
Wages Act 1986
Sex Discrimination Act 1986
Teachers' Pay and Conditions Act 1987
Local Government Act 1988
Employment Act 1988
Employment Act 1990
Trade Union and Labour Relations (Consolidation) Act 1992
Trade Union Reform and Employment Rights Act 1993
Disability and Discrimination Act 1995
Employment Rights Act 1996
Public Interest Disclosure Act 1998
National Minimum Wages Act 1998
Employment Rights (Dispute Resolution) Act 1998
Employment Relations Act 1999
Tax Credits Act 1999
Race Relations (Amendment) Act 2000
Learning and Skills Act 2000
Employment Act 2002

Regulations

Transfer of Undertakings and Protection of Employment (TUPE) Regulations 1991
Collective Redundancies and Transfer of Undertakings (Protection of Employment) (Amendment) Regulations 1995
Health and Safety (Consultation with Employees) Regulations 1996
Working Time Regulations 1998
Transnational Information and Consultation of Employees Regulations 1999
Collective Redundancies and Transfer of Undertakings (Protection of Employment) (Amendment) Regulations 1999
Part-Time Workers (Prevention of Less Favourable Treatment) Regulations 2000
Fixed Term Employees (Prevention of Less Favourable Treatment) Regulations 2002

EU Directives

Collective Redundancies Directive 1975
Equal Treatment Directive 1976
Transfer of Undertakings Directive 1977
Acquired Rights Directive 1977
Health and Safety Framework Directive 1989
Collective Redundancies Directive 1992
Working Time Directive 1993
European Works Councils Directive 1994
Collective Redundancies Directive 1998
Anti Discrimination Framework Directive 2000

Index

Note: page numbers in **bold** indicate glossary
definitions